THE BEST PLAYS OF 1969–1970

THE

BURNS MANTLE

YEARBOOK

THE
BEST PLAYS
OF 1969-1970

EDITED BY OTIS L. GUERNSEY JR.

*Illustrated with photographs and
with drawings by* HIRSCHFELD

○ ○ ○ ○ ○ ○

DODD, MEAD & COMPANY
NEW YORK • TORONTO

EDITOR'S NOTE

WITH THIS 1969-70 VOLUME, the *Best Plays* series of theater yearbooks enters its second half-century of continuous annual publication. The 50th anniversary was celebrated in last season's 1968-69 volume with a special chronological listing of the five decades of Best Plays, a permanent year-by-year reference to the 500 outstanding works of the 20th century American stage. In this, the 51st volume, we return to alphabetical listing of these plays, so that inevitable curiosity continues to be satisfied in both forms of the question: "What was that delightful play I saw in 1936?" or "What year did I see *You Can't Take It With You?*"

Other changes in this year's coverage are forms of expansion to meet the needs of a vigorous and ever-changing art form. As that semi-organized region of tributary theater known as off off Broadway continues to solidify its position as an incubator of vital new talent, we have expanded our listing of the 28 major off-off-Broadway groups to include an indication of each group's special thing—whether it is director- or writer-oriented, whether it employs professional actors, charges admission, etc. In his article on the off-off-Broadway season, Robert Schroeder emphasizes the ever-rising importance of rock as a live entertainment form with a strong appeal especially to the young. This *Best Plays* volume celebrates the rock lyric in its New York stage manifestation, with extensive quotations from the lyrics of the hit off-Broadway rock musical *Salvation,* as a special bonus citation in the Best Plays section. Another bonus in this same section is the complete text of *The Serpent: A Ceremony,* the Jean-Claude van Itallie—Open Theater Best Play which was originally developed off off Broadway and has been the subject of so much discussion this season. Its playscript appears in this volume in its entirety.

Stanley Green, author and theater historian, has expanded the section on cast replacements to include the names of leading players in London companies of American shows. Our liaison with the theater in London and, indeed, with major theater centers everywhere in Europe, is becoming ever-closer, thanks to the expertise of our distinguished European editor Ossia Trilling and his assistant, Heather Maisner. Our coverage from abroad is also enhanced by an article on the London season by John Spurling, British playwright and critic.

Al Hirschfeld's drawings, Jonathan Dodd's good and cogent offices on behalf of the publisher Dodd, Mead & Co., and the patient, skillful assistance of the editor's wife over weeks and weeks of programs and proofs were major contributions to this volume as well as to the volumes preceding it. So were the contributions of Rue Canvin (off Broadway, necrology and publications); Ella A. Malin (Directory of Professional Regional Theater especially prepared for *Best Plays,* now expanded to list selected Canadian programs); Henry

Hewes (continuing help in all kinds of ways); Bernard Simon (bus-truck tour information); Mimi Horowitz of *Playbill;* Hobe Morrison of *Variety;* Ralph Newman of the Drama Book Shop, as well as literally more than a hundred people in theater information, production and photography who create and maintain the lines of communication between the theater's artists and its public.

Last and most, we are grateful for the fine work of the theater's artists— the fascinating designs for scenery and costumes (some of which are pictured in the photo section), the memorable performances and the plays themselves, the Bests, the almost-Bests and the better-luck-next-timers. These theater artists of ours have already given us half a century of productions to hero-worship, deplore, consider and record in these *Best Plays* volumes. Now they have begun another half century in a theater to whose continuing vitality and never-ending surprises this volume is a respectful tribute.

OTIS L. GUERNSEY Jr.

June 1, 1970

CONTENTS

Drawings by HIRSCHFELD

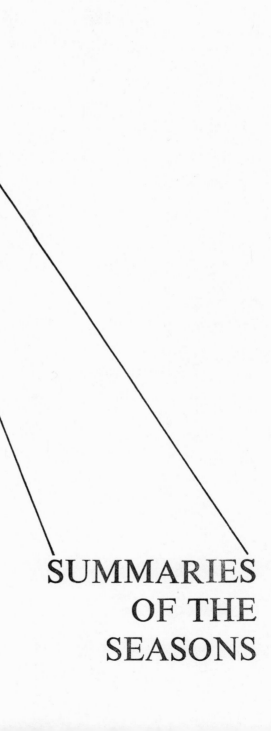

SUMMARIES
OF THE
SEASONS

THE SEASON IN NEW YORK

By Otis L. Guernsey Jr.

THIS YEAR IT ALL FELL IN on the New York theater, but under the layers of problems somehow a season grew. Artists bewildered by the changing forms . . . fragmenting audiences . . . shrinking production on Broadway . . . inflationary costs in a depressionary market . . . real estate pressures on the theaters themselves . . . every lurking malaise opened into a raw wound. The season of 1969-70 was one in which our stage passed through the fire like Daniel in the furnace of Nebuchadnezzar. Somehow it kept its cool from June to June with all the worst happening; turned up some memorable plays, and finally showed itself one of the hardiest and healthiest of 20th century art forms as it came through alive and kicking, moving ahead.

It was like this in 1969-70: there was no cluster of exciting shows until deep in April; off-Broadway hopefuls folded literally by the dozen (33 productions lasted less than two weeks, 10 of these less than one week, 7 for only one performance); our most reliable playwrights seemed baffled, even paralyzed by the demands of the developing theater form and kept their new works, if any, to themselves; instead of one great homogenious appetite for theater, there was a decided schism between the lacquered audiences at *Applause* and the soft, rapt, furry faces at *Stomp;* production costs continued toward the roof (I do not say ceiling because apparently there is no ceiling, not even at the $1 million level), at the same time that the audience buck was coming tough; and, last straw, the sound of the air compressor and jackhammer intruded into the venerable theater district, as office-builders continued to threaten the very physical existence of the Broadway theater as we've known it for decades.

And yet . . . and yet there was a season, and a pretty good one too, esthetically and even financially. As an added irony, it was conventional plays and not audience-confrontation or subliminal ones that dominated the year's best work. In the big theaters, *Butterflies Are Free, Child's Play, Last of the Red Hot Lovers* and *Applause* came on as comfortable as old slippers with a love story, a thriller, a comedy and a glamor musical—no surprises here. In the smaller playhouses the cream of the crop included the straightforward *The Effect of Gamma Rays on Man-in-the-Moon Marigolds* together with the stylistically bizarre but safely constructed *The White House Murder Case* and

3

The 1969-70 Season on Broadway

PLAYS (21)

A Teaspoon Every
Four Hours
INDIANS
The Penny Wars
*BUTTERFLIES
ARE FREE*
Operation Sidewinder
Angela
Love Is a Time
of Day
*LAST OF THE RED
HOT LOVERS*
Watercolor &
Criss-Crossing
Brightower
Sheep on the Runway
Paris Is Out!
Gloria and Esperanza
CHILD'S PLAY
Norman, Is That You?
The Chinese and
Dr. Fish
Grin and Bare It! &
Postcards
A Place for Polly

MUSICALS (14)

Jimmy
Buck White
La Strada
Coco
Gantry
Georgy
Purlie
Blood Red Roses
Minnie's Boys
Look to the Lilies
APPLAUSE
Cry for Us All
Park
COMPANY

SPECIALTIES (4)

Nat. Theater of Deaf
Songs From Milk
Wood
Charles Aznavour
Marcel Marceau

REVIVALS (18)

Oklahoma!
In The Matter of J.
Robert Oppenheimer
Amer. Conservatory
Tiny Alice
A Flea in Her Ear
Three Sisters
Three Men on a
Horse
The Front Page
Lincoln Center Rep
The Time of Your
Life
Camino Real
*Beggar on
Horseback*
Henry V
Our Town
Private Lives
No Place To Be
Somebody

Harvey
Candida
The Boy Friend
The Cherry Orchard

FOREIGN PLAYS
IN ENGLISH (3)

A Patriot for Me
The Mundy Scheme
Borstal Boy

FOREIGN-LANGUAGE
PRODUCTIONS (8)

Grand Kabuki
Chushingura &
Kagami-Jishi
Kumagai Jinya &
Momiji-Gari
The New Music Hall
of Israel
Comédie Française
La Troupe du Roi &
Amphitryon
Dom Juan
Les Femmes Savantes
Le Malade Imaginaire
Rabelais

HOLDOVER SHOW
WHICH BECAME
HIT DURING
1969-70

1776

Categorized above are all the plays listed in the "Plays Produced on Broadway" section of this volume.
Plays listed in CAPITAL LETTERS have been designated Best Plays of 1969-70.
Plays listed in **bold face type** were classified as hits in *Variety's* annual list of hits and flops published June 3, 1970.
Plays listed in *italics* were still running June 1, 1970.

What the Butler Saw. Among the ten Best Plays, the farthest out in form were *Indians, Company* and *The Serpent: A Ceremony* in that order.

The makeup of this best list is 4 Broadway plays, 4 off-Broadway plays and two Broadway musicals. Anyone who supposes that the temporary drying-up of "established" playwrights is an American theater phenomenon should note that only one of the ten—the late Joe Orton's *What the Butler Saw*—is a foreign play. Two of them—*Indians* and *Marigolds*—had their American premieres in regional theater production, and one—*The Serpent*—surfaced off Broadway after two years of almost clandestine performances by The Open Theater off off Broadway. There is new growth in the list: *Child's Play* and *Marigolds* are the New York playwriting debuts of Robert Marasco and Paul Zindel, as is George Furth's book for *Company*. The other Best Play authors—Arthur Kopit, Leonard Gershe, Jules Feiffer, Jean-Claude van Itallie, Neil Simon, Betty Comden, Adolph Green, Charles Strouse, Lee Adams, Stephen Sondheim—have written important works for the theater before, but few of them would be considered members of any contemporary playwriting "establishment."

The number of shows produced on Broadway declined to 68 productions of record in 1969-70 (see the one-page summary accompanying this report) from 76 last year, 84 the year before and 78 the year before that. But the most important element of this total—new American scripts—has remained reassuringly steady. This season there were 21 new American plays and 14 new musicals on Broadway, compared with 24-12 last year, 25-10 the year before that, 19-8 in alarming 1966-67, and 25-11 and 25-10 in the two years before that. Off Broadway this season the total productions of record jumped to a whopping 119 as compared with 103 last season, including 69 new American musicals and playscripts (see the one-page summary accompanying the off-Broadway section of this report).

Not surprisingly, *Variety's* annual estimate showed a dropoff in Broadway's total gross for the second year in a row. The decline amounted to more than 7 per cent, as the Broadway take for the 52 weeks of 1969-70 came to $53,324,199 as compared with last year's $57.7 million and the year before's record high of $59 million. In the matter of playing weeks (if 10 shows play 10 weeks, that's 100 playing weeks), there was a continuing decline. There were only 1,047 playing weeks on Broadway (including 74 weeks of previews) in 1969-70, as compared with 1,209 last year, 1,257 the year before, 1,269 the year before that and 1,295 the year before that.

Looking for a silver lining, *Variety* noted that road productions of Broadway plays were doing better than ever, grossing $48,024,325 (and thus giving Broadway its third $100-million season in a row) for 1,024 playing weeks. The figures speak for themselves—Broadway activity was going down, not up —but we would like to add our own qualification. The season was very late in starting (for example, seven of the ten Best Plays opened in the last half of the season). *Applause* didn't arrive until March, *Company* until April. During the final weeks of 1969-70, when all its new shows were finally on, Broadway was out-grossing the comparable weeks of 1968-69, rolling along at the rate of $1.2 million a week.

To sketch a context for these figures, the ticket ceilings held pretty much at last year's levels. Broadway's hottest weekend musical tickets were highest priced at $15 (and *Coco* asked this price for week nights as well), with the straight-play top pegged generally at $8.50. *Coco, Applause* and *Company* pushed the matinee top up a notch from $8 to $9. Off Broadway, the producers of a solid hit could continue to get $10 a ticket as they had been ever since *The Boys in the Band* established this pattern in the 1967-68 season. A very special case *Oh! Calcutta!* was able to charge a $15 top for most seats and $25 for the first two rows. Curiously, Broadway was more hospitable than off Broadway to the tight-budgeted theatergoer, who could see *Hair* for $4 or *Fiddler on the Roof* for $2.80 and *Company* for $2 in the least expensive seats but would have to pay $5 for the minimum-priced seats at most off-Broadway hits.

Production costs for musicals, according to *Variety* estimates, were just about anything you wanted to pay: *Coco* $850-900,000, *Cry for Us All* (it lasted 9 performances) $750,000, *La Strada* (it lasted 1 performance) $650,000. The operating expenses of trying out and opening could bring the total capital loss much higher, estimated by *Variety* to be in the neighborhood of $850,000 for *La Strada*, $720,000 for *Georgy* (it lasted 4 performances) and close to $1 million for *Jimmy's* 84-performance career. Straight plays were a bargain in comparison: *Indians*, whose production cost was relatively high, came in for $240,531 (*Variety* reported), but *Butterflies Are Free* was mounted for only $71,000, a real bargain, only a few dollars more than the cost of a lavish off-Broadway flop. A *very* lavish off-Broadway flop like *Mahagonny* cost $350,000, the highest of off-Broadway record, and lost more than that. *Salvation*, an off-Broadway musical hit, came in for $37,682. Another figure for the context: Seymour Vall was doing a musical called *Blood Red Roses* off Broadway, when a funny thing happened on the way to production—he decided to bring it to Broadway instead. The production budget for this show (it lasted 1 performance) was $65,000 for the original off-Broadway venture, $175,000 for the same show on Broadway. We shouldn't leave this subject without adding that if the stakes were high, the pots were sometimes fat. Among *net* profit estimates published during the season were these: *Hello, Dolly!*, $7,775,526 on a $350,000 investment; *Fiddler on the Roof*, $5,907,552 on $400,000; *The Boys in the Band*, $600,000 on $20,000; *Man of La Mancha*, $4,600,000 on $200,000.

So much for triumph and tragedy at the box office. Our theater comes to life in the individual efforts of its artists, not in a balance sheet, and whatever its shortcomings the season had room for a procession of vivid personal portraits. The time is past when a big star can conveniently carry an indifferent Broadway show (Katharine Hepburn's effort in levitating *Coco* was as visible as it was immense), but the presence of a skilled performer still gives theater audiences that feeling of immediate and close personal contact with the play. Through the leading players, the audience can come to know the play *per-*

sonally. This year Broadway enjoyed and cheered Stacy Keach's Buffalo Bill
. . . Lauren Bacall's middle-aged actress . . . Fritz Weaver's introverted school
teacher . . . Keir Dullea's and Blythe Danner's appealing boy-meets-girl act . . .
Brian Bedford's and Tammy Grimes's husband-meets-wife ditto . . . James
Coco's thwarted lover . . . Sam Levene's Bronx curmudgeon . . . James Stew-
art's Elwood P. Dowd . . . Cleavon Little's Purlie . . . Dennis King's drag
queen . . . Joseph Bova's and Alice Drummond's Mr. and Mrs. Chinese Laun-
dry . . . Lewis J. Stadlen's Groucho Marx . . . Niall Toibin's Brendan Behan
. . . Marcel Marceau's BIP . . . Elaine Stritch's caustic Joanne . . . Jean-Louis
Barrault's Rabelaisian Humanist . . . William Cain's Woodrow Wilson. Off
Broadway the highlights included Sada Thompson's and Pamela Payton-
Wright's mother and daughter . . . Zoe Caldwell's Colette . . . Austin Pendleton's Isaac . . . Catherine Burns's Dear Janet Rosenberg . . . Donny Burks's
Billy Noname . . . Ron Leibman's frantic producer . . . the whole administra-
tion in Jules Feiffer's White House, and all the denizens of The Open Thea-
ter's Garden of Eden.

For the second straight season there was a good deal of talk about the
emergence of a directors' theater in which improvisational techniques would
bypass the playwright or use his work as a scaffolding on which to hang the
garlands of interpretive artistry. But for the second straight season it was anything but a directors' year. Producers? No one goes around saying "As David
Merrick goes, so goes Broadway," but maybe they should give it some thought.
Like Broadway itself, Merrick had moderate success with a combination of
new material *(Child's Play),* a popular revival *(Private Lives)* and the hardy
old survivors *Forty Carats, Promises, Promises* and *Hello, Dolly!,* which took
yet another new lease on life with the arrival in town of Ethel Merman to play
its title role. At season's end, *Dolly* was well on the way to overtaking *My
Fair Lady* and becoming the longest running Broadway musical of all time.

Harold Prince, almost alone among a group of "experts" in an early-season
New York *Times* symposium, insisted that Broadway is still where it's at if
you have what it takes, and he proved his point with the musical *Company.*
Arthur Whitelaw (together with Max J. Brown and Myron Goldman) drew
a high pair back to back with *Butterflies Are Free* and *Minnie's Boys;* so did
David Black with *Paris Is Out!* on Broadway and *Salvation* off. Among other
producers whose efforts contributed to the pleasure of 1969-70 theatergoing
were Joseph Kipness, Frederick Brisson, Saint Subber, Philip Rose, the
Messrs. Roger L. Stevens, Robert Whitehead and Robert W. Dowling, Joseph
Papp, Orin Lehman, Haila Stoddard and the Theodore Mann-Paul Libin
group.

For some, the season brought disappointment. Cassius Clay failed to make
a show business career out of his role as an activist lecturing about black
pride and liberation to the members of a social club in the musical *Buck White.*
The ex-heavyweight champion's performance was devoutly sincere but not
quite at ease, like a high school debate over the Constitution. John Osborne,
too, fell short of expectations for his treatment of the subject of homosexuality in *A Patriot for Me,* based on turn-of-the-century characters in the Austrian

military aristocracy. The theatrical high point was a drag ball presided over by Dennis King costumed and mannered as a grande dame. Also from abroad, Brian Friel's *The Mundy Scheme* (a plan to bring prosperity to Ireland by converting it into a cemetery for the world's overcrowded cities) was not the biting satire of our hopes from this distinguished Irish playwright. John Patrick dealt unsuccessfully with love among college students in *Love Is a Time of Day,* and Dore Schary was practically assaulted by the critics for his effort to examine in *Brightower* the problem of right of privacy, in the drama of a Hemingway-like writer who suffers a nervous breakdown—it lasted only one performance but apparently was strong enough to support a Tony nomination for Geraldine Brooks for best performance by an actress, in the role of the writer's wife. Murray Schisgal's program of one-acters failed to take a strong comic hold on the subjects of marriage counseling (in *Dr. Fish*) and race snobbery (in *The Chinese*), though in the latter playlet there were outstanding performances by Joseph Bova and Alice Drummond as the proud Chinese parents of a young man who is somewhat ashamed of them and is passing for Jewish in the neighborhood.

Off Broadway, a major disappointment was the failure of those who mounted the American premiere of the Bertolt Brecht-Kurt Weill musical *Mahagonny* to find the handle for this towering work; another was the failure of the critics to respond enthusiastically to Oliver Hailey's *Who's Happy Now?,* like *The Effect of Gamma Rays on Man-in-the-Moon Marigolds* a strong family play and a regional theater hit, but unlike it largely overlooked by New York audiences.

Successful or unsuccessful, show people were joining their audiences in the season of 1969-70 in a kind of space exploration. While astronauts walked on the moon and children dreamed of visits to the planets and stars, the New York theater was blasting off from its old fourth-wall-set, realistic-theater concepts and exploring its own inner space, trying to discover whether there can be found in new forms of theatrical expression a cluster of new meanings or merely a vast and vacuous emptiness. As the earth was beginning to seem stuffy and confining to a hugely expanding mankind, the old theater was too limited a form now for the art's wildest dreams. So 1969-70 tended to be an adventurous year in which anything including the worst was possible; anything, from a naked cast in *Grin and Bare It!* to audience participation in pulling a huge sheet of plastic over the entire auditorium as an image of our sealed-in environment in *Stomp* to the brilliant break-through of *The Serpent.* *Anything* could happen—even an old fashioned but still satisfying evening of conventional theater.

Theater style was fragmenting in 1969-70, partly because of this growing dissatisfaction with the old forms, and partly to satisfy the fragmenting taste of the New York audiences. Time was when we all knew what we wanted and what we meant when we spoke of "a good comedy" (*Harvey* or *Private Lives*), "a good musical" (*Oklahoma* or *The Boy Friend*) or even "a good drama" (Arthur Miller/Tennessee Williams). We still enjoy such shows—many of them, in fact, appeared as popular revivals this season. But now there's a growing audience that wants something else/something more/something different, an audience that grew up in this age when television has been repeating, and exhausting, all the possible linear comic and dramatic situations. Thus, Neil Simon's *Last of the Red Hot Lovers* with its situation-comedy premise and Jules Feiffer's *The White House Murder Case* with its sick-joke fantasy are two fine theater comedies, funny and meaningful, but in such completely different ways that there's no reason to insist that a devotee of one must necessarily enjoy the other (it is possible, but not inevitable).

In 1969-70 the audience fragments overlapped in some areas, and when they did not they were often large enough to support the theater of their special taste. The trick was to get the right person to the right show. At one performance of the rock musical *Salvation,* two graceful white-haired ladies were helped to their third-row seats by uniformed chauffeur who opened their programs for them to the first credits page and disencumbered them of their furs. It's perfectly possible that these ladies enjoyed the outspoken put-on of moral poses, including the number "Stockhausen Pot Pourri" in which the cast first whispers, then speaks, shouts and finally orchestrates, as it were, all the major four-letter obscenities (certainly they hadn't heard *that* on television). But for the most part it is mis-matching of audience to show in these days of way-out experimentation that provokes all those cries of alarm over what is becoming of our beloved theater. It is indeed *becoming,* growing, and that's the important point.

What is sometimes called "new theater" to distinguish it from our old Henrik Ibsen-to-Tennessee Williams friend is setting off in as many directions as Stephen Leacock's impetuous horseman; and two of them may be leading somewhere. For the past couple of seasons we've been noting in these *Best Plays* volumes the growing frequency and strength of plays which make overt and direct contact—sometimes even physically—with the audience, instead of keeping their third-person distance as in the conventional fourth-wall theater. These new plays sometimes go so far as to insist that the audience assume a role in the events being dramatized, if only to accept a portion of the guilt for the play's motivation, which in the old theater was pretty much the exclusive possession of the villains. An example of direct-contact theater in 1969-70 was LeRoi Jones's *Slave Ship,* a dramatic exercise with a single purpose: to polarize the audience into two *hostile* camps of black and white, right there in the theater, now. In a series of sketches it traced the history of white America's inhumanity to blacks in incidents of the slave trade, Southern slavery, growing rebellion and modern militancy. A blue police light revolving at the slave ship's masthead was one of its dramatic points of reference; another was a pleading, half-naked black teenager dropped at the foot of the audience during a slave auction scene to bring them into the picture, so to speak. But the purpose of *Slave Ship* was involvement, not the arousing of sympathy; anger, not love. After its adverse examples have been dramatized, an actor costumed as a Masai warrior exhorts the blacks in the audience to stand up (in order to separate them physically and visually from the whites) and join him in a song of black solidarity. Standing and separate in their Negritude, they are then told that their race mission is to destroy the white beast and all his works—not necessarily their seated white neighbor in the audience, but not necessarily *not*. That was the purpose of the play, and it left a cold wind blowing through the exit doors as the audience filed out, silent, hostile, polarized. For better or for worse, *Slave Ship* was an example of direct-contact, role-for-the-audience theater that really worked.

A second important direction of change was toward what might be termed peripheral-vision, or subliminal, playwriting. It's what you see out of the corner of your eye, what you don't *quite* hear, or what you hear *after* the words have been spoken that counts. What is literally being done or said on the stage may be intended to distract the conscious mind, with its increasing resistance to the simple linear premise, so that the playwright's real intentions can slip into the eye's corner, slide into the ear between the literal meanings. Thus, the program of new Harold Pinter one-acters offered off Broadway at Lincoln Center Repertory's small Forum Theater—*Silence* and *Landscape*—mesmerized the audience with characters who were themselves in a sort of trance of introspection. They speak their long, image-filled thoughts not so much to communicate with one another (there is no cross-pollination of dialogue in these plays) as to hear themselves think. I found *Landscape* particularly effective, with its middle aged man and woman (Robert Symonds and Mildred Natwick) daydreaming in a kitchen setting that is a monotone gray, drear as their burned-out marriage. Their spoken thoughts made no interconnection (indeed, all connection between them is broken never to be repaired) except that each is imagining what could be, sexually. She is dreaming of a warm sand dune and a tender wooing; he of catching his wife at the dinner gong and getting her attention long enough to make love right there in front hall. Pinter's stream of images was like an electric current carrying powerful feelings of isolation and loss that would be very difficult indeed to communicate in any conventional theater form.

In the same way, at Lincoln Center Rep's Broadway-sized Vivian Beaumont Theater, Sam Shepard's new play *Operation Sidewinder* was one of the most imaginative scripts of the season and one of the best in this "subliminal" style. A computer built to resemble a giant rattlesnake which escapes from the Air Force compound into the desert . . . a hippie protagonist who guns down an innocent garage mechanic taking too long to fix his car . . . two black militants cruising in a black Cadillac convertible with painted flame licking from the front wheel bays . . . kookie generals and a Dr. Strangelove scientist . . . Hopi Indian rituals and designs . . . this was a sauce with too many strong ingredients for any literal taste. It was the aftertaste of *Operation Sidewinder* that counted, though, not any narrative logic in this mad, mad, mad view of a world on a trip of violence, crazed with force and power. One example of the very great and still-rising importance of rock music in our culture was the use by Shepard in *Operation Sidewinder* (which is certainly not a musical) of a rock group, The Holy Modal Rounders, to comment on each hallucinatory episode in song, as a sort of narrator.

Another outstanding example of "new" theater was The Open Theater's

The Serpent: A Ceremony which combined the abovementioned developments —audience contact and corner-of-the-eye communication—with its own development in the creation of material for the stage. The Open Theater is an off-off-Broadway group which specializes in the ensemble improvisation of scenes and characters. The way it works is this: someone, maybe a playwright but maybe an actor or director, gets an idea for a scene; perhaps a playwright supplies a few lines of dialogue or narration to go on with, perhaps not; at any rate, the writer, actors and director improvise around the idea in a collaborative process of creating a scene. This is a technique which has received a great deal of critical attention recently in evaluations of the work of Jerzy Grotowski, the Polish director (the subject of some consideration later in this report). Thus *The Serpent's* creative credits read: "Created by The Open Theater Ensemble, words and structure by Jean-Claude van Itallie, under the direction of Joseph Chaikin, associate director Roberta Sklar."

The play was developed by The Open Theater some time ago (its title appears in the listing of off-off-Broadway productions in last year's *Best Plays* volume) and has been shown semi-privately, semi-invitationally. Not until May 29, 1970 did The Open Theater present *The Serpent* to the general New York public in a limited engagement of its repertory at the Washington Square Methodist Church. There was one *The Serpent* performance of record in the 1969-70 season and there were to be two more in June 1970—the shortest first run of all the 510 Best Plays, but a major theatrical event nevertheless, the unveiling of a work of deep impact which studies man's tendency to violence in phases ranging from the intimate detail of the bullets striking President Kennedy to the grand Biblical design of the Garden of Eden. This is a work of theatrical genius—and (I am convinced) despite all the improvisational-theater hoorah, that genius belongs to *The Serpent's* playwright, Jean-Claude van Itallie.

Van Itallie's words are few, but they are incredibly effective (see the synopsis of *The Serpent* in the Best Plays section of this volume). He seems to have found a way of writing short takes of narration that keep on reverberating in the mind while the actors go about their mimed business of interpretation. When the serpent himself, played with extraordinary ensemble skill by five writhing actors, touches Eve with an apple and then challenges her belief in God's threats with "Have you died?", an apocalyptic moment has taken place not only in the serpentine contortion or Eve's puzzlement but in the frighteningly simple three *words* themselves. Likewise Eve's question to the serpent about free will—can she "listen to God and not to you?" if she wants to; likewise the narrative introduction to Cain's murder of Abel: "And it occurred to Cain/To kill his brother/But it did not occur to Cain/That killing his brother/Would cause his brother's death/For Cain did not know how to kill" which echoes in imagination over an entire memorable scene in which Cain at first tries to kill his brother by pulling his hand off his arm. Messily but finally Cain succeeds in his murderous purpose and then tries to bring Abel back to life and movement. "And it occurred to Cain/To kill his brother" —if van Itallie has found a way to write a scene like this in a few short lines, it is not an abandonment of artistic prerogative but a refinement of it; a challenge, not a surrender, to the interpretive artist.

The Open Theater troupe of actors worked its own wonders with van Itallie's ideas (and it is pertinent to note here that in the company's other excellent new work, *Terminal,* there are the same vivid one-by-one acting effects in a series of comments about death and dying but not the same strong and cohesive underpinning—call it playwriting—that gives *The Serpent* its special power). The performing was exceptional, with fascinating detail and profound depth of understanding and communication of human nature to match the Biblical size of the concept (and, in two cases, a profound understanding of animal nature, in Peter Maloney's exact portrayal of dull ovine egocentricity, in a sheep eating grass out of Abel's dead hand, and in Paul Zimet's heron walking unmolested through the violent events of Eden, fluttering his wings and raising his crown in a perpetual state of astonishment). "I no longer live in the beginning/I've lost the beginning/I'm in the middle," cry the women of *The Serpent,* which has indeed brought the theater from where it was yesterday onto a new path—with, as usual, a playwright, the gifted Jean-Claude van Itallie, pointing the new and exciting way to go. The entire text of this play, unabridged, appears in the Best Plays section of this volume.

The characteristics which distinguish *The Serpent, Sidewinder, Slave Ship* and other effective scripts of the new theater are no longer limited to the experimental or tributary theater. They have influenced the best work everywhere, even on Broadway. Thus *Indians* was in almost every sense a direct-contact play, with its hero Buffalo Bill confiding his misgivings directly to an audience which is slowly forced into the role of the play's conscience. Thus, *Child's Play* was able to weave its web of menace and mystery without tying each thread firmly to a pole of reality, as in most successful stage mysteries of the past. It had the nightmarish quality of the not-quite-explained, the subliminal awareness of hidden evil.

This breeding of new styles and tastes doesn't necessarily make for a firm, esthetically predictable, financially stable theater. It certainly didn't work that way in New York in the season of 1969-70. But neither does it make for a picturesque downslide dominated by moribund preconceptions. The good old tree is hollow here and there, certainly; the theater as we know it was in deep trouble artistically and financially, as we have suggested. But those who conclude that the theater is in decline didn't go to many shows this season. Those who did couldn't help noticing a characteristic that stood out from all the others: new growth all around, on the stage and in the audience, everywhere.

Broadway

A "hit" in the true Broadway meaning of the word isn't just a show that is hard to get into on a Friday night in December, but a show which pays off its production cost (it may be easy to get into but become a "hit" by virtue of a big movie sale). In recent seasons, however, the word "hit" has been losing some of its magic. Very often, Broadway doesn't have either the first or the final word on a play, as it once did. Plays come to Broadway from previous regional or foreign production which has already established their position in world theater before New York ever sees them. A good script which fails on Broadway for some special reason may take on an illustrious life of its own in theaters around the world or in other media (remember that *The Lion in Winter* was a 92-performance flop by the old Broadway standards). So we make no special point in this resume about which 1969-70 offerings were "hits" and which were "flops"—this information is recorded in the one-page summary of the season accompanying this article.

The ultimate insignia of New York professional theater achievement (we insist) is not the instant popularity of the hit list, but selection as a Best Play in these volumes. Such selection is made with the script itself as the primary consideration, for the reason (as we have stated in previous volumes) that the script is the very spirit of the theater, the soul of its physical body. The script is not only the quintessence of the present, it is most of what endures into the future.

So the Best Plays are the best scripts. As little weight as is humanly possible is given to comparative production values. The choice is made without any regard whatever to a play's type—musical, comedy or drama—or origin on or off Broadway, or popularity at the box office or lack of same.

The Best Plays of 1969-70 were the following, listed in the order in which they opened (an asterisk * with the performance number signifies that the play was still running on June 1, 1970):

Indians
(Broadway; 96 perfs.)
Butterflies Are Free
(Broadway; 252* perfs.)
Last of the Red Hot Lovers
(Broadway; 177* perfs.)
Child's Play
(Broadway; 119* perfs.)
The White House Murder Case
(off Broadway; 119 perfs.)

Applause
(Broadway; 72* perfs.)
The Effect of Gamma Rays, etc.
(off Broadway; 64* perfs.)
Company
(Broadway; 41* perfs.)
What the Butler Saw
(off Broadway; 32* perfs.)
The Serpent: A Ceremony
(repertory; 1* perf.)

The best script of these 1969-70 bests, in our opinion, was Arthur Kopit's *Indians,* about the opening of the American West. It would be absurd to define this play, in terms of its Broadway appearance, as a 96-performance "flop." *Indians* came to New York following a world premiere production by the Royal Shakespeare Company in London and an American premiere production at the Arena Stage in Washington, D.C. It is destined, certainly, for an illustrious career on the world's stages, where it will enhance the reputation of American playwriting.

Indians takes the form of a dramatic memoir. The Buffalo Bill era is preserved in glass museum cases on the curtainless stage as the audience files in. Then the glass cases disappear and the artifacts come to life as Buffalo Bill Cody himself (Stacy Keach) "gallops" to the jutting apron to open another glorious Wild West show. But he finds he can't proceed without trying to justify certain events in the opening of the West to you, the audience; he'd rather confide in you than lie to you. The glories of the past were flawed if you look at them in a strong light: the buffalo as a species was nearly wiped out and the Indians nearly annihilated in the name of progress and adventure. No one cared, not the President of the United States, not the Congress, not even the Western heroes like Bill Cody and Wild Bill Hickok, because young America needed expansion and heroic legends at this crucial period in its growth. Buffalo Bill didn't realize (he pleads), *couldn't* have realized how his name and fame were to be used as a larger-than-life disguise for exploitation and savagery. In a moral sense he is innocent, and Sitting Bull doesn't blame him even after Bill is unable to prevent the U.S. Cavalry from slaughtering the chief's whole tribe. Sitting Bull doesn't accuse, he merely wonders: "We had land . . . You wanted it; you took it. That . . . I understand, perfectly. What I cannot understand . . . is why you did all this, *and at the same time* . . . professed your love."

No, it isn't Buffalo Bill who takes the tragedy on his conscience, or the politicians onstage. It is the *audience,* heirs of the conquerors, whose conscience is put to the torch, who are forced into the role of villain. With excellent direction by Gene Frankel, *Indians* reached its climax and fulfillment not in the events on the stage (no change took place in the characters there) but out in the auditorium where we were forced to re-examine some of our value judgments through a crack in our beloved national epic of the Old Wild West.

Another Broadway drama on the Best Plays list was the thriller *Child's Play,* a first play by Robert Marasco about mysterious evil pervading a boys' school and inciting the students to acts of apparently meaningless violence which satisfy some unknown craving. All elements of this play combined for eerie effect: Joseph Hardy's exceedingly careful direction, Jo Mielziner's dark staircase and gloomy faculty-room setting, and especially Fritz Weaver's telling portrait of a teacher too preoccupied with his job to bother about defending himself from envy and slander until it is too late. Rather like Henry James's *The Turn of the Screw, Child's Play* projected but never really named its terror in a mystery that refused to spell out all of its secrets even at the final curtain. In part, this script is an example of the trend toward subliminal communication in playwriting. Marasco addressed his work not entirely to conscious logic, but in part to instinct. Deep down below the level of conscious thought (the playwright assumes), the audience understands *by instinct* that the events in *Child's Play* are a microcosm of our time, a time which expresses itself in acts of seemingly irrational violence (read any issue of any newspaper) as a surfacing, particularly in the younger generation, of a deeply-imbedded evil that is very difficult to identify and root out. Thus this work, which seemed at first glance to be traditional in form and subject was one of the season's most topical as well as most effective scripts.

From abroad, the season was enhanced by *Borstal Boy* adapted by Frank

MacMahon from the late Brendan Behan's autobiographical account of his arrest at 17 years of age as an IRA sympathizer carrying a suitcase full of dynamite to England, and his subsequent arrest and incarceration, first in a prison and then in a boys' reformatory called a "borstal." This production won the New York Drama Critics Circle and Tony Awards as the best play of the year, yet it was less a dramatic structure than an evening of colorful anecdotes and bad-boy expressions spoken with ingratiating Irish charm by Niall Toibin uncannily impersonating Behan as an adult commenting in epithet and song on the actions of Frank Grimes as Behan as the idealistic young revolutionary. The youth, of course, is a victim of his own violent politics—in his shy, warm-hearted way he might have blown off people's arms and legs as messily as any blood-lusting veteran revolutionary if he hadn't been caught in time to prevent it. *Borstal Boy* was an entertaining and sometimes moving concert of verbal images and attitudes; a good show with many attractive theatrical and literary elements, but certainly not the best "play" of 1969-70, or anywhere near it, in our understanding of the word.

There were three other noteworthy "serious" dramas this season, all home grown. Elliott Baker's *The Penny Wars,* a David Merrick production which Barbara Harris staged in her first time out as a Broadway director, was a stark view of a family coping with the Depression after the father dies of a heart attack; and of the eventual failure of the stepfather, a warm-hearted immigrant dentist played by George Voskovec, to bear up under the economic and emotional pressures of those difficult times. Donald Freed's *Inquest* reopened the Ethel and Julius Rosenberg atom-spy case in the theater-of-fact genre with this message emblazoned on the backdrop: "Every word you will see or hear on this stage is a documentary quotation or reconstruction from events." Perhaps so, but the words were carefully selected to honor the memory of the Rosenbergs (most sensitively played by George Grizzard and Anne Jackson) as innocent victims of McCarthyism, and their lawyer (James Whitmore) as the single clear, true voice of advocacy within a judicial system gone bloody mad with paranoia. It was a frankly biased effort to arouse sympathy, rather than to seek new understanding with new light as in the case of last season's *In the Matter of J. Robert Oppenheimer.*

Finally, in ANTA's 1969-70 schedule of showcase bookings in New York of regional theater productions (of which more later in the section on revivals), there was the Trinity Square Repertory Company's production of Roland Van Zandt's dramatic pageant *Wilson in the Promise Land,* brought in from Providence, R.I. for the last week of the New York season. Under Adrian Hall's direction, with William Cain playing the president crippled in body and spirit by war and its aftermath, this script is a judgment rendered against the American purpose in selected quotations orated by costumed symbols of historical viewpoints: Abraham Lincoln, George Washington, Franklin D. and Teddy Roosevelt, John F. Kennedy (quoted by Wilson), hippies, etc. Again, this was more of a persuader than a play, a political cartoon.

One of the two Broadway comedies on the Best Plays list was Leonard Gershe's *Butterflies Are Free,* a boy-meets-girl story in the realistic fourth-wall theater genre which nevertheless seemed one of the freshest as well as pleasantest of the year's entertainments. The boy (Keir Dullea) is a clean-cut refugee from Scarsdale living in an East Village apartment; the girl (Blythe Danner) is the warm, outspoken blonde in the apartment next door. Not long after they meet they open the connecting door; but what costs them the time and difficulty of the play is the collateral fact that the boy's Scarsdale mother feels sorry for him because he is totally blind. Her instinct is to protect him from the life that he wishes to embrace; but the boy hardly ever feels sorry for himself, and the girl never, which brings them through the crisis safely. *Butterflies Are Free* was its author's first straight Broadway play (he did the book for the musical *Destry Rides Again*). His final scene between the two young people was one of the most attractive love scenes in a long, long time of theatergoing.

The other Broadway comedy on the Best list is Neil Simon's *Last of the Red Hot Lovers,* with James Coco as a middle-aged restaurateur trying to live it up sexually but failing with three different women in a three-ring circus of satire on (and insight into) contemporary emotional attitudes and behavior. As we have come to expect in a long succession of Simon shows, *Red Hot Lovers* was a skillful and enjoyable work; and as we have no right to expect, it was part of the astonishing but continuing expansion of a playwriting career which defies even the superlatives of description. It sounds like legend but it is true that Simon once had *four* hits running simultaneously on Broadway *(Barefoot in the Park, The Odd Couple, Sweet Charity* and *The Star-Spangled Girl)* for a combined total of 3,367 performances. Almost unbelievably, as of the 1969-70 season Simon had a whole *new* batch of three hits running simultaneously: *Plaza Suite, Promises, Promises* and *Last of the Red Hot Lovers. Variety* called him "Legit's all-time top playwright;" in a previous *Best Plays* volume we called him "the Molière of the high-rise era," but did Molière make it so big, so consistently? Neil Simon is a quiet man of our time who knows more about us than we've ever cared to admit even to ourselves, and expresses it with incomparable skill and an unerring instinct for the idioms of the day.

Two more comedies helped brighten the Broadway scene this season. Richard Seff's *Paris Is Out!* cast Sam Levene as a crotchety Jewish grandpa being cajoled by his wife (Molly Picon) into his first reluctant trip to Europe. The family-friction humor was well paced in Paul Aaron's direction, and Levene's performance was another memorable episode in what is surely the longest and funniest case of heartburn in stage history. Humorist Art Buchwald r'ared back and delivered a Broadway play this season, *Sheep on the Runway,* a foreign-policy joke about an American newspaper columnist who stirs up a hot war in an otherwise peaceful and obscure Asian mountain country. It benefited greatly from the presence in the role of the harried American ambassador of David Burns who, like Sam Levene, knows where all the best laughs are buried in the character of a victim of outrageous circumstance.

The remaining handful of comedies on the Broadway season's list came and went like turnpike traffic. *A Teaspoon Every Four Hours* (a Jewish family comedy co-written by and starring Jackie Mason) held 97 preview performances—a new record high—but closed after its formal opening night for a one-performance official run. Faring not much better were *Angela* by Sumner Arthur Long (a romantic involvement between a middle aged woman and a TV repairman); the Philip Magdalany one-acters *Watercolor* and *Criss-Crossing* satirizing modern patterns of sex and violence; Julie Bovasso's series of episodes in an artist's development in *Gloria and Esperanza;* Lonnie Coleman's *A Place for Polly* about the problems of a young woman married to an ambitious and rather unscrupulous book publisher; the anguish of an Ohio father (played by Lou Jacobi) who visits his son in New York only to discover that the young man is part of the gay set, in *Norman, Is That You?;* or *The Engagement Baby,* a hapless effort to levitate a situation in which a prosperous Jewish ad man finds that his college sweetheart, who is black, bore him a son.

Even the naked comic stresses of *Grin and Bare It!,* about a girl taking her fiance home to meet the family who, it seems, are nudists, could survive only 12 performances on a Broadway whose audiences are no longer attracted by nudity per se. It is worth noting also that the *Grin and Bare It!* actors who played the script stark naked modestly put on their dressing gowns for the curtain calls in order to demonstrate that these were not naked *actors* up there on the stage; they were actors playing naked *characters.* As soon as they stepped out of character they clothed themselves.

Among the 14 musicals presented on Broadway in 1969-70, the most satisfying was *Applause,* the Tony Award-winning show based on the same Mary Orr story as the movie *All About Eve,* with book by Betty Comden and Adolph Green, music by Charles Strouse and lyrics by Lee Adams. While we deplore the modern system of warming over successful movie or play material to make a musical (often it's a serving of leftovers buried in catsup), we must admit that *Applause* was a happy combination of creative efforts. The story about the ambitious young actress Eve flattering her way into the middle-aged star's favor in order to promote a Broadway career of her own provided a good backstage context for production numbers: the opening-night party, the night out on the town, the high spirits of the chorus "gypsies" at Allen's restaurant, the chic supper party in the star's apartment. The green-room maneuverings made a sturdy vehicle for a leading character with the glamor which most of the Broadway musical stage lacks these days. She is Margo Channing, the no-longer-young but still vibrant star, played by Lauren Bacall in her free-swinging, man-eating style. Miss Bacall is a lioness who never was a pussy cat; her Margo is younger and suppler than Bette Davis's was on the screen, but no less ferocious in defense of her career and her man. She was backed up by a good score, a fine production directed and choreographed by Ron Field in Robert Randolph's settings, and strong support by Penny Fuller as the scheming Eve, Len Cariou as the director Margo loves, Bonnie Franklin as a bouncing chorus gypsy and Lee Roy Reams as Margo's loyal hairdresser. It all blended together and worked very, very well as a show.

Another Best Play musical and the Critics Award winner was *Company,* most imaginative of the Broadway musicals, produced and directed by Harold Prince, with lyrics *and* music by the noted word artist Stephen Sondheim and book by the actor George Furth in his playwriting debut. *Company* wasn't based on yesterday's hit material; it is an original contemplation of the shiny, swinging and shallow (unfortunately) young marrieds who are "making it" in New York, and their friend Robert, "Bobby Baby," who is persistently single, though heterosexual. *Company* didn't look like any other show—it looked more like a vaudeville set for a trapeze act with a geometrical framework designed by Boris Aronson to stand in for the spiritless rectangularity of the new high-rise environment, a setting in which actors were permitted to travel vertically on a built-in elevator as well as horizontally from one to another part of their New York forest. *Company* didn't *feel* like any other show; from the beginning when Elaine Stritch abrasively rubs her fellow-guests at a birthday party the wrong way by characterizing them as "Lois and Larry Loser," and then the cast goes into an ingratiating musical "Bobby Baby" greeting of the 35-year-old birthday boy, you could almost taste the shine on the plastic society whose surface *Company* was going to scratch. The show repeated what was virtually the same episode over and over, as Robert (Dean Jones) goes from one couple to another, finding that each marriage is to some extent merely an accommodation against loneliness. If for no other reason—and there isn't much else in the world these characters inhabit—they are together for the sake of each other's company. Thus, *Company* ran hard in place, and eventually ran down, despite the efforts of Prince, Aronson and Sondheim (whose lyrics work many wonders, including a rhyme for "personable"—"coercin' a bull"). But *Company's* shortcomings as well as its advantages were clear evidence that they dared admirably to try.

Another of the season's big four musicals, *Purlie,* came along late in the season with *Applause* and *Company. Purlie* was a musicalization by Ossie Davis, Philip Rose and Peter Udell of Davis's play *Purlie Victorious,* about a resourceful black preacher who returns to his home town down upon the Swanee River and rallies the Uncle Toms to throw off the burdensome domination by their white "Cap'n" once and for all. *Purlie* converted racial antagonism into an edge of humor and an outburst of song, and it also profited from its performances including Cleavon Little as Purlie and Melba Moore as his beautiful young "protegee."

Then there was *Coco* and Katharine Hepburn playing Gabrielle Chanel in her heads-up, wiry way, as though the lady were a tennis champion instead of a dress designer. Alan Jay Lerner's book and lyrics worked noticeably better than the score or even the elaborate production. Nevertheless, Broadway owes a backward glance of gratitude to this show, which opened in December and carried on for weeks and weeks as the lone new musical excitement. And one of its better ingredients was Rene Auberjonois' performance as Coco's young, envious, effeminately-mannered colleague who is gleeful that Coco's new dresses seem at first to be a disaster. *Coco* had its faults, but it was there, with Katharine Hepburn and all, when it was most needed.

Another musical, which boasted an attractive score by Larry Grossman and

LAUREN BACALL AS MARGO CHANNING IN "APPLAUSE"

Hal Hackady but was generally underrated, was *Minnie's Boys* about the struggles of the Marx Brothers to make it in show biz urged on by their mom (Shelley Winters as Minnie Marx, nee Shean, sister of Gallagher's vaudeville partner). Wisely confining themselves to suggestion rather than impersonation, Lewis J. Stadlen (Groucho), Daniel Fortus (Harpo) and Irwin Pearl (Chico) adroitly portrayed the brothers in the hard times before their famous comic characterizations were set into the shapes we knew and loved. Also lightly nostalgic was *Jimmy,* with Frank Gorshin playing New York's 1920s Mayor James J. Walker in a musical reminiscence. *La Strada* based on the Fellini movie, *Gantry* based on the Sinclair Lewis novel and *Blood Red Roses* (an original anti-war musical set in the Crimean War era and once intended for off Broadway) failed expensively and instantly after only one performance each, like elephants shot in the eye. *Georgy* based on the British movie *Georgy Girl,* with Dilys Watling in the lead, lasted only 4 performances; *Park,* a production of Baltimore Center Stage, a four-character original about parents and their children deliberately meeting as strangers in a park to get a fresh view of each other, survived only 5 performances in a Broadway visit; *Look to the Lilies* based on *Lilies of the Field* with a Jule Styne-Sammy Cahn score and Shirley Booth in the Mother Superior role, lasted only 25; *Cry for Us All,* based on *Hogan's Goat,* stayed around for only 9.

Foreign visitors to Broadway in 1969-70 included the Grand Kabuki from Japan; a new edition of the Israeli revue *The New Music Hall of Israel;* the Comédie Française with four Molière programs. Individual visitors from abroad were Jean-Louis Barrault in his own devising of a singing, dancing, dramatized avant-garde presentation entitled *Rabelais,* based on the works and life of that free-swinging author; Charles Aznavour with his songs; and Marcel Marceau with his programs of BIP and other pantomimes. Domestic visitors included The National Theater of the Deaf offering *Sganarelle* and a Dylan Thomas program *Songs From Milk Wood,* plus a series of showcase bookings of regional theater programs, mostly revivals, reported in the next section.

When all is said and done, it is individual artists who supply much of the flavor for any season, and here is where we list the *Best Plays* bests among the individual work of 1969-70. In the category of so-called "supporting" performances, clear distinctions cannot possibly be made on the basis of official billing, in which an actor's agent may bargain him into a contract as a "star" following the title (which is not true star billing) or as an "also starring" star, or any of the typographical gimmicks. Here in these volumes we divide the acting into "primary" and "secondary" roles, a primary role being one which carries a major responsibility for the play: *one which might some day cause a star to inspire a revival in order to appear in that role.* All others, be they vivid as Mercutio, are classed by us as secondary.

Here, then, are the *Best Plays* bests of 1969-70:

Plays

BEST PLAY: *Indians* by Arthur Kopit
ACTOR IN A PRIMARY ROLE: Fritz Weaver as Jerome Malley in *Child's Play*
ACTRESS IN A PRIMARY ROLE: Sada Thompson as Beatrice in *The Effect of Gamma Rays on Man-in-the-Moon Marigolds*
ACTOR IN A SECONDARY ROLE: Peter Maloney in *The Serpent*
ACTRESS IN A SECONDARY ROLE: Linda Lavin as Elaine Navazio in *Last of the Red Hot Lovers*
DIRECTOR: Joseph Hardy for *Child's Play* and *What the Butler Saw*
SCENERY: Jo Mielziner for *Child's Play*
COSTUMES: Marjorie Slaiman for *Indians*

Musicals

BEST MUSICAL: *Applause* by Betty Comden and Adolph Green
ACTOR IN A PRIMARY ROLE: Cleavon Little as Purlie in *Purlie*
ACTRESS IN A PRIMARY ROLE: Lauren Bacall as Margo Channing in *Applause*
ACTOR IN A SECONDARY ROLE: Lewis J. Stadlen as Groucho Marx in *Minnie's Boys*
ACTRESS IN A SECONDARY ROLE: Fredricka Weber in *The Last Sweet Days of Isaac*
DIRECTOR: Ron Field for *Applause*
SCENERY: Boris Aronson for *Company*
COSTUMES: Ray Aghayan for *Applause*
CHOREOGRAPHY: Michael Bennett for *Coco* and *Company*
SCORE: C.C. Courtney and Peter Link for *Salvation*

Revivals

For the past few seasons the APA-Phoenix, a coalition of University of Michigan-based regional theater and a New York production organization, dominated the Broadway revival scene with a series of notable productions at the Longacre. This year APA-Phoenix split at the hyphen and the two entities went separate ways. Ironically, what they could not accomplish in combination last season they each accomplished separately in 1969-70: a booming revival hit on Broadway. Ellis Rabb's Association of Producing Artists (APA) mounted the Tammy Grimes-Brian Bedford reenactment of Noel Coward's *Private Lives* which David Merrick presented to a New York that applauded its verbal and emotional acrobatics as though they were Neil Simon's latest. T. Edward Hambleton's Phoenix Theater in its turn sponsored the James Stewart-Helen Hayes *Harvey,* which became one of the town's hottest tickets at the ANTA theater, as well as John Lewin's *The Persians* adapted from Aeschylus' *Persae* with modern connotations about the personality of Xerxes-like aggressors. Both the Phoenix and APA are continuing as entities, the latter's new project being its customary annual autumn schedule of plays at Ann Arbor in Michigan's Professional Theater Program.

This revival season was one in which gain balanced loss. Like APA-Phoenix, the City Center found it no longer economically feasible to produce the revivals which have provided such nourishing supplement to the Broadway diet in seasons past. Losses were piling up above any possibility of subsidy, and so there were no City Center musicals this year. The summer *Oklahoma!* at the New York State Theater of Lincoln Center and a new Broadway production of *The Boy Friend* were the year's only surfacing of our musical heritage.

But lose one, win one: the City Center's Jean Dalyryple went over on part time loanout to The American National Theater and Academy (ANTA) where, in collaboration with ANTA's executive producer Alfred de Liagre Jr., she helped direct the use of the ANTA Theater as a Broadway showcase for visiting troupes from regional theater and elsewhere. The programs included the Trinity Square Repertory Company production of Roland Van Zandt's *Wilson in the Promise Land*, the Playwrights Unit's *Watercolor* and *Criss-Crossing* and the Cafe La Mama's *Gloria and Esperanza*. Mostly, though, these guest programs tended to be revivals. Thanks to ANTA, Broadway audiences could see Edward Albee's chilling *Tiny Alice* again, as well as Georges Feydeau's *A Flea in Her Ear* and Chekhov's *Three Sisters*, all in William Ball's American Conservatory Theater (of San Francisco) productions. Likewise, ANTA presented Len Cariou (later the male lead in *Applause* opposite Lauren Bacall) in the American Shakespeare Festival of Stratford, Conn. version of Shakespeare's *Henry V;* Henry Fonda, Elizabeth Hartman, the late Ed Begley and Mildred Natwick in the Plumstead, L.I. Playhouse production of *Our Town;* the John Fernald Company from Rochester, Mich., in *The Cherry Orchard;* and, co-sponsor with the Phoenix, the smash hit *Harvey*. ANTA also chose to provide a limited-engagement showcase for last year's original off-Broadway production of Charles Gordone's *No Place To Be Somebody* which played 16 Broadway performances following the termination of its run downtown at the Public Theater (it was subsequently re-mounted in an off-Broadway revival which was still running when Gordone won the Pulitzer Prize in drama, a most commendable bestowal of that often debatable award, the second Pulitzer for a work that originated off Broadway—the first was *In Abraham's Bosom* in 1927—and incidentally, the first to a black playwright).

Win one, lose one . . . the American straight-play revivals at the City Center were now out of the question, of course, but this season Lincoln Center Repertory turned its attention to the American playshelf with an all-American season of one new play (Sam Shepard's provocative *Operation Sidewinder*) and three revivals: William Saroyan's limpid *The Time of Your Life,* Tennessee Williams' strangest and in some ways most contemporary script, *Camino Real,* with Al Pacino as Kilroy, and finally the art vs. materialism fantasy of the 1920s *Beggar on Horseback* by Marc Connelly and George S. Kaufman, with added music by Stanley Silverman and lyrics by John Lahr, and a spectacularly elaborate production designed by Michael Annals to stretch even the Vivian Beaumont Theater's well-developed production muscles.

It's neither our admiration for these individual scripts nor mere chauvinism that causes us to applaud Lincoln Center's decision to put on American plays for its 1969-70 season. It is a matter of esthetic priorities. In this country we are developing our own kind of theater, both dramatically and musically, out of the traditional forms we inherited from other cultures. The first business of a New York-based and New York-supported permanent repertory company, surely, should be to acquire proficiency in the production of American plays, just as the comparable British and French companies are first of all adept at interpreting their home-grown works, with foreign material sometimes staged as a special event. The Lincoln Center company is certainly not proficient yet, and it is heavily dependent on guest stars, but with an American season they are at least headed and moving in the right direction.

In addition to its regular season, Lincoln Center offered an instant revival of last year's successful *In the Matter of J. Robert Oppenheimer*. Also back in town trailing last season's glory was the Harold J. Kennedy revival of *The Front Page,* which not only retained its well-deserved popularity through a second season but also became a kind of a club for outstanding performers, as star (Molly Picon, Robert Alda, Maureen O'Sullivan, Jan Sterling, Jules Munshin, Paul Ford, Butterfly McQueen) replaced star (Helen Hayes, Peggy Cass, John McGiver, Dody Goodman) even in minor roles. In other star appearances in revivals, Celeste Holm did *Candida* and audiences were given the opportunity to re-acquaint themselves with Sam Levene's memorable performance of Patsy the gambler in *Three Men on a Horse*. This show wasn't able to develop the staying power of *The Front Page* or in recent seasons *You Can't Take It With You* and *The Show-Off*—the power to make it as an individual commercial Broadway hit. It was nevertheless a real asset to the season and emphasizes the need for some kind of permanent establishment to provide this kind of show with at least a partial shelter from the hard economic necessities of the commercial New York stage.

Off Broadway, revival activity was relatively light, with only 13 as compared with Broadway's total of 18. Ibsen was prominently represented by the New York Shakespeare Festival production of *Peer Gynt* in Central Park and the Opposites staging of *Hedda Gabler*. A revival of *The Madwoman of Chaillot* presented best-selling novelist Jacqueline Susann in the role of one of the madwomen, Mme. Josephine, but it was short-lived nonetheless. *Room Service,* with Ron Leibman in the lead, received a fresh viewing, as did Clifford Odets' *Awake and Sing*.

William Hanley's *Slow Dance on the Killing Ground,* a Best Play which lasted only a short time on Broadway, reappeared off Broadway this season, and so did *Dark of the Moon,* the witch-boy fantasy revived somewhat in the nude. Popular reappearances of off-Broadway scripts which had recently ended their regular runs but were brought back for another look included the abovementioned *No Place To Be Somebody* as well as John Herbert's prison play *Fortune and Men's Eyes* (in a new production directed by Sal Mineo and laced with explicit staging of homosexual practises), Ron Cowen's antiwar *Summertree* and Beckett's *Endgame* in a new interpretation by the gifted Open Theater troupe. With these off-Broadway efforts added to the presentations of Lincoln Center Repertory, ANTA, APA, Phoenix and the others in the larger theaters, the 1969-70 revival season in New York was perhaps a little short of outstanding classical presentations, but it was a valuable element of the whole culture and entertainment scene.

Off Broadway

Off Broadway in 1969-70 carried on from the previous season with its spate of new-play production. The tributary playhouses once attracted experimenters because of their relatively low production costs; and now they have

The 1969-70 Season off Broadway

PLAYS (53)

The World of Mrs. Solomon
Tonight in Living Color
Fireworks
Time for Bed—Take Me to Bed
Pequod
The Glorious Ruler
A Black Quartet
Sourball
The Reckoning
Silhouettes
The End of All Things Natural
The Ofay Watcher
Calling in Crazy
American Place
Mercy Street
Five on the Black Hand Side
Two Times One
The Pig Pen
And Puppy Dog Tails
A Scent of Flowers
The Haunted Host
Rose
Who's Happy Now?
The Disintegration of James Cherry
Passing Through From Exotic Places
The Moon Dreamers
Seven Days of Mourning
The Brownstone Urge
Love Your Crooked Neighbor

Negro Ensemble
The Harangues
Brotherhood & Day of Absence
The Memory Bank
Slave Ship
Transfers
The Jumping Fool
THE WHITE HOUSE MURDER CASE
Contributions
Nobody Hears a Broken Drum
Nature of the Crime
The Unseen Hand & Forensic and the Navigators
THE EFFECT OF GAMMA RAYS ON MAN-IN-THE-MOON MARIGOLDS
The Nest
And I Met a Man
The Persians
How Much, How Much?
The Republic
Colette
The Moths
The Shepherd of Ave. B & Steal the Old Man's Bundle
Lemon Sky
Chicago 70
Open Theater
THE SERPENT
Terminal
Candaules, Commissioner

MUSICALS (16)

Man Better Man
Promenade
Salvation
Rondelay
Public Theater
Stomp
Sambo
Mod Donna
The Last Sweet Days of Isaac
I Dreamt I Dwelt in Bloomingdale's
Billy Noname
Show Me Where the Good Times Are
The House of Leather
Lyle
Mahagonny
The Drunkard
The Me Nobody Knows

FOREIGN PLAYS IN ENGLISH (11)

Hello and Goodbye
A Whistle in the Dark
Crimes of Passion
The Local Stigmatic
Little Boxes
Lincoln Center
The Increased Difficulty of Concentration
Landscape & Silence
Amphitryon
The Criminals
Dear Janet Rosenberg, Dear Mr. Kooning
WHAT THE BUTLER SAW

REVUES (10)

Oh! Calcutta!
The Hoofers
The American Hamburger League
From the Second City
Gertrude Stein's First Reader
Love & Maple Syrup

Unfair to Goliath
Joy
Exchange
This Was Burlesque

FOREIGN-LANGUAGE PRODUCTIONS (11)

Arena Conta Zumbi
Polish Lab Theater
The Constant Prince
Acropolis
Apocalypsis Cum Figuris
Die Schauspiel
The Marriage of Mr. Mississippi
Philipp Hotz & The Firebugs
Iphigenie in Tauris
Le Tréteau de Paris
Le Grand Vizir & Le Cosmonaute Agricole
Lettre Morte & Architruc
La Lacune, La Jeune Fille a Marier & Les Chaises
Oh! Les Beaux Jours

REVIVALS (13)

N.Y. Shakespeare
Peer Gynt
Twelfth Night
Fortune & Men's Eyes
Summertree
Hedda Gabler
No Place To Be Somebody
The Madwoman of Chaillot
Lulu
Dark of the Moon
Room Service
Slow Dance on the Killing Ground
Awake and Sing!
Endgame

SPECIALTIES (5)

Whores, Wars & Tin Pan Alley
Go Fly a Kite
Baird Marionettes
Whistling Wizard & Sultan of Tuffet
Winnie the Pooh
Akokawe

Categorized above are all the plays listed in the "Plays Produced off Broadway" section of this volume.

Plays listed in CAPITAL LETTERS have been designated Best Plays of 1969-70.

Plays listed in *italics* were still running June 1, 1970.

also become attractive to the Broadway producers (many of whom tried their luck in the little theaters this season) because of the handsome commercial possibilities which accrue to an off-Broadway hit. The traffic will now bear $10 a ticket for the whole house at off-Broadway successes (as compared with $8.50 top for a straight play on Broadway), with much smaller overhead for salaries, percentages, etc. Then, once a show is established, there is a market for additional productions across the country and around the world, where there is no concern whatever as to whether a good American script originated on Broadway or off. Even limited to 300 seats (as compared with 800 in the smaller Broadway houses) it never seemed desirable to Richard Barr to move *The Boys in the Band* or to Jordan Hott and Jack Millstein to move *Dames at Sea* uptown.

Thus, the season brought a whopping 64 new-play programs off Broadway, 53 of them American (see the one-page summary accompanying this report. Add to this number 16 new book musicals and 10 new revues, and you have a landslide of theatrical offerings. The volume of new work in English was about the same in 1969-70 as last season. There were 119 productions of record off Broadway in 1969-70 as compared with 103 the year before, but the increase was largely in revival and foreign-language production, plus a big numerical jump from 2 to 10 in the revue category.

One trait that did *not* carry over from the previous season, we are happy to report, was the monotony of sex—interest, yes, but preoccupation, no. If there was any single characteristic the 1968-69 sex plays had in common, it was that they were largely unsuccessful. They failed to attract audiences as the movies seem to do with this kind of material. Consequently, 1969-70 brought only a handful of such attractions. One of them was the exception that proves the rule, the out-and-out orgy *Oh! Calcutta!*, a smash hit by all standards except critical, where it suffered almost universal condemnation not as a shocker but as a bore. It was indeed not quite a shocker and almost a bore, but with a few points of interest along the way. Item: the opening number, in which each member of the cast one by one, individually, removes all his/her clothes was very cleverly conceived with backdrops of blown-up photos of the performer in various informal poses, in order to hold up the (clothed) personality of this human being before your eyes so that the body being revealed on the stage is never just a naked body, but the receptacle of a person. Item: the Margo Sappington choreography, particularly the nude pas de deux with George Welbes pictured in last years *Best Plays* volume, was a graceful spectacle, particularly interesting to those who haven't seen similar work before on the ballet stage.

And item: *Oh! Calcutta!* was the first production to demonstrate clearly and beyond any question of a doubt that a naked actor or actress onstage takes the mood right back to the Garden of Eden—not to original sin but back before that, to original innocence. Innocence, sheer *innocence* is the quality produced onstage by total nudity, no matter how suggestive the material being offered. Thus, in *Oh! Calcutta!* the bare, vulnerable skin and revealed glandular structure of the performers was at war with the subject matter. In those scenes which combined dressed and undressed actors—as in the skit where a young couple (naked) volunteer for a sex experiment to be witnessed by a group of burlesque-show medical types (clothed)—it was the clothed people whose smirks and obscene gestures seemed outrageous in the presence of naked innocence. In the Broadway *Hair* a couple of seasons ago, the shock of innocence provided by the suddenly naked cast at the end of Act I was entirely appropriate to the musical's story of babes in the hippie woods; in the salacious *Oh! Calcutta!* innocent nakedness is entirely *in*appropriate and tended to defeat the show's purpose.

Nudity itself as a instrument of showmanship was only sporadically employed. On Broadway there was the nudist play *Grin and Bare It!* and off Broadway in *The Nest,* for example, an actor licked cake icing from an actress's bare breasts and audiences couldn't have cared less—the play lasted for only one performance. *And Puppy Dog Tails* played a homosexual love triangle partly in the nude. An unclothed revue entitled *The Way It Is* tried a long string of 60 "previews" but no great interest was aroused and it folded in mid-January without ever holding a formal opening, dropping all of its $65,000 investment.

Homosexual affections were under some scrutiny in *The Haunted Host* and, from England, in John Bowen's *Little Boxes,* a program of one-acters whose second playlet, *Trevor,* was an amusing complication of two young women, lovers living in adjacent apartments, who are visited on the same day by their respective families and arrange for the same man to pose as their fiance. On the heterosexual side, the season included the musical *Rondelay* based on Schnitzler's good old *La Ronde,* and *Love and Maple Syrup,* about love in Canada, both naive in comparison to last season's whippings, rapings and adaptations of the works of the Marquis de Sade.

The socio-political mess attracted the skillful attention of several of our most gifted off-Broadway writers this year. LeRoi Jones's *Slave Ship* was a vivid piece of activist theater, described previously in this report. Racism and the black condition were the subject of Frank Cucci's *The Ofay Watcher,* about a white scientist's discovery of a pill to turn blacks into whites, with Cleavon Little as a black hobo hired as a guinea pig for an experiment which turns into a Grand Guignol of horror. Another strong variation on this theme was the musical *Billy Noname,* by Johnny Brandon and William Wellington Mackey, with Donny Burks in a standout performance as a young American black struggling not only against handicaps but also with success, trying to make a choice between personal ambition and soul-brother militancy. At American Place, Ed Bullins's new play *The Pig Pen* was a somewhat mystifying (and eventually stupefying) description of black-white relations in terms of a pot-sex-rock-alcohol orgy the night that Malcolm X was killed. Presumably, the party represents a kind of easy, *de facto* racial accommodation that existed before this tragic event. At the end of the play, the party is over; news of the murder arrives by radio, and everybody splits (and presumably this is the moment at which society itself splits into black and white elements). And twice during the party, a porcine Keystone Cop rushes in blowing his whistle like mad, dancing around and striking furniture with his truncheon (does Bullins mean that before Malcolm X's death police violence was rather comic, a bad-guy stereotype?). Bullins's symbols were vivid, but confusing: if the boorish, swinish pot party is to be taken as a sample of society when things were possible, then surely there were no Edens lost in the final shuffle of *The Pig Pen*.

Also examining various aspects of the black condition were *A Black Quartet* of angry one-acters by Ben Caldwell, Ronald Milner, Ed Bullins and LeRoi Jones; *Sambo,* a New York Shakespeare Festival Public Theater musical harping on black alienation; Joseph A. Walker's *The Harangues,* staged by the Negro Ensemble Company and drawing parallels between the black man's African tribal and American sociological problems; Douglas Turner Ward's *The Reckoning,* confronting a white Southern governor and a black pimp; the same author's new *Brotherhood,* a one-acter about latent racism among pretended liberals, and his *Day of Absence,* revived by Negro Ensemble which kept its franchise at the St. Marks Playhouse this season but fell short of its distinction of earlier play schedules; and the Ted Shine program of one-acters, *Contributions,* sketches of crackers and black militants.

On another socio-political subject, Jules Feiffer's *The White House Murder Case* alternated scenes on the battlefront in an imagined future war with Brazil (the "Chicos") with scenes in the White House. The self-deluding hypocrisy of a "future" president and his associates is so rampant in Feiffer's stage caricature that murder either on a mass or personal scale is ludicrously inevitable. In Feiffer's fun-house-mirror view, soldiers on the battlefield are slowly coming apart from the effects of their own nerve gas, and much the same sort of thing is happening at commander-in-chief level, where the nerve gasses of power and militarism are destroying their creators—in a setting that was dominated by an apparition that looked like a half-starved chicken worked over to look like an eagle by a third-rate taxidermist. Feiffer's skill with both drawing and writing pens in newspaper cartoons is one of the treasures of modern literature, and the actors and director of *The White House Murder Case* were on their mettle to reproduce the ironic visions of Feiffer's playscript. It must have been easier for the scene designer to realize his eagle than for the actors to realize his President, Secretary of Defense, Postmaster General and others in this Dr. Strangelove government. There may come a day when *The White House Murder Case's* sick joke will be almost unintelligible to theater audiences—let's hope so, anyway. In the meantime, more than any other script on or off Broadway this year it reflected the distemper of the times and is a clear choice for a Best Play in this volume.

Many other plays in the off-Broadway stream came to grips with the dilemmas of the day, but none quite so effectively. Sam Shepard's program of one-acters, *The Unseen Hand* and *Forensic and the Navigators* provided images of the false values and destructive impulses of contemporary life. The one-acters of Jon Swan's *Fireworks* took off on the press, war and cocktail parties; idealism vs. practical politics was the issue in Robert Shure's *Sourball;* Ronald Ribman's *The Burial of Esposito* from his one-act program *Passing Through From Exotic Places* was a study of a father who has lost his son in the Vietnam war; Julie Bovasso's *The Moon Dreamers* dwelt on the irony of man's reach for the moon while his platform Earth suffers from so many imperfections; Larry Cohen's *Nature of the Crime* raised the question of whether and to what extent a scientist can be said to own his thoughts; *Chicago 70* hit upon the idea of combining material from Lewis Carroll's *Alice's Adventures in Wonderland* with Judge Hoffman's Chicago courtroom at the recent conspiracy trial, with gratifying results; and so on and on, again and again, on stage after stage, repetitious as a picketer's chant.

Curiously enough, it was in the 1969-70 musicals that off-Broadway authors made some of their most telling socio-political statements. *Salvation* by Peter Link and C.C. Courtney lambasted religious and moral poses with a bright young cast and a loud young rock combo, Nobody Else. In 1970 the rock lyric has taken on a life of its own as a literary form, a vehicle for emotional expression, philosophical debate, political activism—you name it, the rock lyric can and does express it daily from audio sources and from the stage itself in the likes of *Hair* and *Salvation. Salvation's* lyrics deal with such matters as the Vietnam war ("Let the Moment Slip By"), the literal interpretation of the Bible ("Deuteronomy XVII, Verse 2") and tenderness ("If You Let Me Make Love to You Then Why Can't I Touch You?") with so much wit, insight and colorful stagemanship that we use them as the example in this volume's special citation of the rock lyric in the Best Plays section.

Another rock musical, *Stomp,* also tackled issues of our time like sexual inhibition, air pollution, the generation gap. This show was devised by a group who call themselves The Combine at the University of Texas and brought to New York at Joseph Papp's New York Shakespeare Festival Public Theater (they also visited Paris this season as part of the Theater of the Nations program). It was a wild and woolly multimedia presentation which used all four sides of the auditorium as though it had been designed to be played in a basketball court, with the audience involved directly in the action. *Stomp* had no individual writing or acting credits and no script, so that it was played slightly differently, but always with an irresistible flair, at each performance. Like *Hair* after its original run at the Public Theater, *Stomp* is being re-worked for Broadway. In three indoor winter seasons Joseph Papp's group has fostered *Hair, No Place To Be Somebody* and now *Stomp.* The filtering rumors at season's end that this distinguished organization, this incomparable and invaluable cultural asset, was in serious financial difficulty were a reproach to whatever arts establishment and rescue machinery may exist in our city and country.

The Public Theater's 1969-70 season was wholly devoted to protest musicals with *Stomp, Sambo* and *Mod Donna,* the latter one of two off-Broadway presentations that echoed with the shrill cries of Women's Liberation (the other was Ed Wode's *The Republic,* an adaptation of an Aristophanes comedy about women taking over the government of Athens). Early in the season the

Maria Irene Fornes-Al Carmines musical *Promenade* satirized our world as seen through the eyes of a pair of convicts, and it remained for 259 performances as one of the year's major delights. *The Last Sweet Days of Isaac* was a small but wide-reaching musical by Gretchen Cryer and Nancy Ford which took on both sex and violence (and the nature of reality) in its tiny format. Austin Pendleton and Fredricka Weber filled the stage with two characters, first as a boy and girl trapped in an elevator and second as a pair of protesters lodged in jail and, though in separate cells, brought even closer together in spirit than they were in the elevator, as the boy watches on TV his own accidental death at a protest demonstration. Revues like the Chicago troupe's *From the Second City* and *Exchange* also made socio-polical scenes of varying intensity. Likewise in the form of a musical, *The Me Nobody Knows* brought onto the stage a collection of writings by ghetto children of many races expressing their frustration, their alienation, their imprisonment in the lowest dungeon under the mountain of American affluence. The sincerity of their expressions of distress, the general absence of anger in their longings, radiated warmly from the stage in this show performed by a talented young cast led by Northern J. Calloway through a soft rock score by Gary William Friedman.

In addition to the sex games and socio-political object lessons, there were plays that dealt with the abiding subject of the human being and his emotions. The most probing inner-space exploration of the year was Paul Zindel's *The Effect of Gamma Rays on Man-in-the-Moon Marigolds,* the New York Drama Critics Circle award-winner (for Best American Play) and a powerfully conceived, directed (by Melvin Bernhardt) and acted drama. This script was originally produced in 1964 at the Alley Theater in Houston, and it has taken a long, laborious time to reach the New York stage (partly because a New York TV version was panned by TV critics). Zindel's script is about a widow and her household of women without men: an epileptic daughter of hostile and unbalanced temperament; a dreaming younger daughter whose imagination has been captured by the atom and all its works; and an aged crone whose board money is essential in their grimly penurious circumstances. There's no silver lining in this dark cloud of family life, not even a marigold lining as the mother, played on an edge of despair by Sada Thompson in one of the year's best performances, misses her chance to bask in the reflected glory of her daughter's success with a science class experiment with radioactivity and flowers. Pamela Payton-Wright as Tillie the dreamer, Amy Levitt as the mindblown adolescent with two much lipstick, even Judith Lowry as the sere and wrinkled Nanny, made their contributions to a play which showed human nature frayed back to expose the ugliness of fear and despair.

Another family closeup was Oliver Hailey's *Who's Happy Now?,* a script organized as a son's exhortation to his mother, years later, about the relationships of his youth back in a hard and bitter area of the Southwest where his father kept company with a saloon woman and his mother accepted this as a fact of life and managed to hold onto some shreds of pride and home life. This excellent script was excellently served in its New York production by

Ken Kercheval, Teresa Wright and Robert Darnell as son and parents. *Who's Happy Now?* has been acclaimed in previous stagings at the O'Neill Foundation, the Mark Taper Forum in Los Angeles and the Washington Theater Club, so that its place in theater repertory is assured. It was New York's loss that it wasn't able to pick up off-Broadway audience support for more than a 32-performance run. Ditto for Lanford Wilson's *Lemon Sky,* also a study of family relationships which combined a straight-from-the-shoulder narration with dramatized flashbacks in an account of a 17-year-old boy's heartfelt and to some extent heartbreaking attempt to make close contact with his selfishly preoccupied father.

A Scent of Flowers by James Saunders was a luminescent vehicle for Katharine Houghton as a young girl who has committed suicide and re-lives and re-evaluates the stresses leading to her demise. Circle in the Square presented *Seven Days of Mourning* by Seymour Simkes, a dark drama of reaction to a daughter's suicide by a Jewish family who refuse to mourn her in traditional fashion. From England, Thomas Murphy's *A Whistle in the Dark* was another exceptional dramatic script, an outcry against brutishness and its inevitable self-defeat, in the story of an Irish father and brothers visiting the youngest married son in England and smashing into his life with their anti-British prejudices and ham-handed ways.

The season's best foreign script on or off Broadway, however, was the late Joe Orton's farcical *What the Butler Saw,* a compendium of theatrical comment on sexual behavior and mores in the form of a Feydeau-like treatment of a hectic day in the life of the director of an exclusive psychiatric clinic. This is the play that was greeted by jeers and catcalls at its West End debut last season and was lambasted by nearly every one of the London critics—but, clearly, Orton's cleverly orchestrated and enormously witty play will survive this lapse of expertise. Joseph Hardy, who also directed *Child's Play* this season, tuned it to farcical concert pitch, with characters running in and out in various stages of undress and transvestitism, ogling each other with joyless passion. *What the Butler Saw* wasn't just camp or black jokes, it had a high gloss on its cynicism, and a method in its madness. It makes one regret even more the plays which Orton, dead by violence long before his time and obviously at the height of his powers, now will never write.

A couple of Orton's darker pieces—*The Ruffian on the Stair,* about a warped, murderous middle-aged couple, and *The Erpingham Camp,* in which vacationists go berserk and destroy their environment—also appeared off Broadway briefly under the portmanteau title *Crimes of Passion.* Such one-acter programs were staples of the 1969-70 off-Broadway season, with 27 playwrights represented on 18 bills. Among the best of the year was *Dear Janet Rosenberg, Dear Mr. Kooning* by Stanley Eveling, a British playwright who provided Catherine Burns with a role to shape into one of the year's top performances as a sweet young thing hero-worshiping a mediocre middle-aged novelist and gradually eating him alive. The second playlet on Eveling's program, *Jakey Fat Boy,* was a lampoon of modern sex mystiques; both were evidence of a playwriting talent that performed much and promises more.

Another notable twin bill was John Bowen's *Little Boxes* which combined the aforementioned *Trevor* with *The Coffee Lace,* about a group of vaudeville actors broke, unwanted and reduced to selling their very last object of value so as not to skip their traditional anniversary party. Still another English bill, *A Local Stigmatic,* presented several short Harold Pinter sketches on the same program with the title play, a one-acter by Heathcote Williams (and as previously reported, Pinter was further represented by the double bill of new plays at Lincoln Center).

A major event of the 1969-70 theater season was the visit to New York in an off-Broadway context of Jerzy Grotowski's pioneering Laboratory Theater of Wroclaw, Poland, with three programs: *The Constant Prince* (a mad society's torment of its gentle prince, based on a Calderon play), *Acropolis* (combining Biblical, Homeric and concentration-camp images suggested by a Polish work) and *Apocalypsis Cum Figuris* (a pot pourri of excerpts from various sources on the subject of the Second Coming). Grotowski's is a very special and certainly pretentious form of theater which has been criticized, analized, canonized and whipsawed, jeered and cheered on an international scale. Before audiences carefully limited in size (40 to 90, depending on the work) and prepared in mood by a reverential attitude that had nothing to do with the fact that the troupe was appearing in a converted church, the Polish company specializes in very high-intensity ensemble performances which demand more intense concentration from the watchers than conventional theater usually does. *Acropolis,* for example, enacts the grunting agonies of concentration camp inmates building their own doom machine out of gas pipes and dumping their dying into wheelbarrows like so many cement sacks. But the performance is based on a script which in its turn was preoccupied with Biblical and Homeric themes, so that simultaneously these gifted actors, including the outstanding Ryszard Cieslak as "Esau-Hector," represent parallel Homeric and Biblical images. An *Acropolis* program note explains: "Grotowski changed the setting of the drama from the Royal Castle (in Wyspianski's original script) to the Extermination Camp. In this production the characters . . . . . seem to come out of the crematorium smoke in vapors of mass extermination. The Biblical and Homeric scenes are performed by prisoners of the concentration camp. In a kind of daydream they act out their sorrow and consolation, their despair and hope, their cynicism and faith. The reality of the myth and the reality of the camp interpenetrate. . . . . A prisoner asks a fellow prisoner about his identity, then knocks him down and crushes him to death with a wooden shoe. This is the Bible episode of the first encounter of Laban and Jacob, who is wandering in search of a wife."

Baffling as these multiple meanings sound in this "clarification," they are even more obscure in performance—particularly if the observer has no knowledge of Polish. The general impression of a Polish Lab performance is of a vivid flash of intensely humanistic material—but what? It doesn't matter, however, whether the audience enjoys or understands the performance—it isn't for them, anyway, it is for the actors in the way that a religious ceremony is primarily for the celebrants. The audience is the suffered presence of a congregation. You are a witness to the act of the Grotowski troupe, and then you go away quietly without applauding, or discussing what you have seen; you are permitted, however, to reflect on it at your leisure. It is true that a strong subconscious rapport is established between the ensemble and its small audiences, and it is also true that many of the individual images stay with you long after the performance is over, if not the continuity or general impact of the work. In the short acquaintanceship of the group's New York visit, it looks as though Grotowski has devised a theater for the interpretive artist as opposed to the creative artist, a theater in which the actor-director can tailor a play-script as he would an overcoat to fit the form and style of his own imagination at the expense of the playwright's vision; he can take a Calderon script, say, and dye it purple, cut out huge patches, attach ornamentation, etc., until the result no longer resembles the model. It becomes, rather, the "creation" of the actor and director, not of the author, whose original idea the play might no longer fit or suit. Grotowski's provocative experiments are said to be a continuity from the work of Artaud, influencing other directors like Peter Brook (with his *Marat/Sade*) and modern performance groups including The Open Theater, whose *The Serpent: A Ceremony* is a Best Play of 1969-70. But let Grotowski have the last word on his own work, quoted from an explanatory program note:

"In our productions next to nothing is dictated by the director. His role in the preparatory stages is to stimulate the creative associations for which the impulse comes from the actors and to organize the final structure in which they assume a specific shape. It is one of the basic principles of our method of creation to have this kind of interplay in which director and actors give as much as they take, ceaselessly exchanging, sometimes passively, sometimes actively, the creative germs of the coming performance. This exchange does not take place at the level of discussion either; it is in essence an exchange of our life experience, a reciprocal offering of the signs of our biographies, of what I would call our '*arrière-être*.' If someone choses to call this melting-pot of creation 'Grotowski,' fair enough. But it must be clearly understood that this is only a symbol and that the reality is a division of responsibilities among the members of a group to which I am happy to belong."

Among the many, many 1969-70 off-Broadway programs there were some that took no part in setting trends of artistic revolution or social comment, but which brightened various corners of the city. *Joy,* for example, was exactly what its name promised, with a cabaret-style collection of Brazilian-style songs performed by Oscar Brown Jr. (who also wrote them), Jean Pace and the Brazilian instrumentalist Sivuca. A group of showcase productions brought into prominence good old-style vaudeville dancing *(The Hoofers),* assorted works by Gertrude Stein *(Gertrude Stein's First Reader),* the views of a Tel Aviv newspaper columnist presented in revue form *(Unfair to Goliath),* African music, dancing and poetry (Negro Ensemble Company's *Akokawe* with the Mbari-Mbayo Players), burlesque as Ann Corio remembers it *(This Was Burlesque)* and even Benjamin Franklin *(Go Fly a Kite,* with Fredd Wayne impersonating the great man). Zoe Caldwell, Broadway's beloved Miss Jean

Brodie, scored another acting triumph in *Colette* impersonating the noted French authoress and life-stylist, in a script adapted from autobiographical material by Elinor Jones. Among the year's specialties was a new Baird Marionette production, *The Whistling Wizard and the Sultan of Tuffet*. Distinguished visitors were the Arena Theater of Sao Paulo, Brazil, performing an historical play in Portuguese; Die Schauspiel Truppe of Zurich doing Goethe, Max Frisch and Friedrich Duerrenmatt in German; and Le Tréteau de Paris with a four-program sampler of contemporary French theater: Samuel Beckett's *Happy Days* (the French-language version) and three programs of one-acters by Rene de Obaldia, Robert Pinguet and Eugene Ionesco.

A selection of Kurt Weill's German and American theater music was available off Broadway under the title *Whores, Wars and Tin Pan Alley*. One of the season's major disappointments was the first professional New York production of the Weill-Bertolt Brecht *The Rise and Fall of the City of Mahagonny* under the abbreviated title *Mahagonny*. The work was adapted by Arnold Weinstein and staged by Carmen Capalbo in a production which took its time in many weeks of previews to get ready for opening night. The biting anti-materialism of Brecht's 1930 script (about a wholly materialist society established in an American town named Mahagonny by criminals) has survived the decades together with Weill's music. But the work itself, usually presented by opera companies, was uncomfortable within the context of the commercial musical theater. *Mahagonny* was a misfit this time around, an 8-performance disappointment but truly a case of book and score waiting for some kind of Godot of future New York production.

American Place Theater, under Wynn Handman's continuing guidance, kept up the good work of providing a showcase for new plays at its St. Clements Church base. Its season included a drama of dark psychological and emotional pressures (*Mercy Street* by Anne Sexton), a Harlem family comedy with echoes from the battle between the sexes (*Five on the Black Hand Side* by Charles L. Russell), a double bill of one-acters (*Two Times One*) by Charles Dizenzo and David Scott Milton, and Ed Bullins' newest script, the aforementioned *The Pig Pen*.

In its little Forum Theater, regarded as an off-Broadway house in tandem with its Broadway-sized showcase the Vivian Beaumont, Lincoln Center Repertory placed most of its 1969-70 emphasis on scripts from abroad (it was doing American plays in the large theater). In addition to the program of Pinter one-acters, the Forum offered a whimsical Czechoslovakian comedy of a scientist caught in the entanglements of modern existence (Vaclav Havel's *The Increased Difficulty of Concentration*) and a sparkling new *Amphitryon* by the German playwright Peter Hacks, translated by Ralph Manheim. The single American script of the Forum's season was *The Disintegration of James Cherry* by Jeff Wanshel, an inner-space exploration of a young man's nightmarish fancies, symptoms of terror in contemporary living translated into poetic images.

Yes, and there were other programs—quite a few in fact—which may have added little to the development, lore or enjoyment of the off-Broadway scene in 1969-70; but they were *there,* which in itself is a matter of importance. Off-Broadway production is an area in which numbers count, because large numbers of shows mean large numbers of playwrights heard, directors energized, actors seen, ideas exposed. With 119 off-Broadway productions and 28 off-off-Broadway groups in 1969-70 operation (see the listing and report of the tributary scene in this volume by Robert Schroeder), hundreds of young people have been pulled into the theater, both as participants and as spectators. Many of them will stay and continue to add to both the repertory and the appreciation of the American stage which, as the numbers and the vitality demonstrate, is vigorously alive, strenuously imaginative and in a ferment equal to the ferment of the hard times in which the off-Broadway theater is now flourishing and which have provided it with so much of its basic subject matter for dramatization, satirization and musicalization.

Offstage

Offstage as well as on, change was blowing in the wind during 1969-70; the same wind that was breezing fresh ideas of dramaturgy through the new scripts; the same that was blowing through the office skyscraper construction jobs on former theater sites.

One of the major offstage developments matured late in the season and was concerned with the physical sizes of the professional New York theater. Both Broadway and off Broadway operate according to standards set by contract and mutual agreement between managers, artists and craftsmen, and each has its separate organization of producers and theater owners: the League of New York Theaters (Broadway) and the League of off-Broadway Theaters. The off-Broadway League's jurisdiction encompasses playhouses with audiences of 299 or less; the Broadway League customarily deals with playhouses of 800 or more.

What about the middle ground between these two figures? Studies were made this season of the possibility of setting up a "Middle Theater" situation for in-between-sized activity in the area of a potential weekly gross not to exceed $25,000. Theaters which might come under this classification are the 499-seat Eden (where *Oh! Calcutta!* has been housed) and the new Twin Arts (West 48th St.), Hudson West (West 57th St.) and Edison (West 47th St.) theaters. Broadway houses could also be used for Middle Theater shows if portions of the auditorium were roped off to limit the size of audience and potential gross.

In the Middle Theater recommendations made after a Broadway League study, the pay rate for all non-royalty personnel would be $150 weekly (discussions have tended to revise this figure upwards) and royalty personnel— the playwright, director, choreographer, etc.—would have their percentages reduced to half what they are for a Broadway show (the artists have by no means agreed to this suggestion). The Broadway League wants jurisdiction over Middle Theater and offers producers a special associate membership. Predictably, these proposals have been stalled by stiff opposition, notably on the part of Actors Equity, which rejects any thought of reduced compensation for actors in theaters in the Broadway and Lincoln Center districts, whatever their size. The League continues to hope that some kind of Middle Theater arrangement can be worked out, however, to facilitate the production of the intimate show (half-off-Broadway?) in New York.

The office-builders continued their relentless incursion into the Broadway theater district, encouraged by a rationale that goes something like this: our legit playhouses are occupying valuable midtown real estate for only a limited number of hours a day and weeks a year, therefore this space should be put to more serviceable use as the site of an office skyscraper which would be operating around the clock all year long. This is exactly the kind of people-per-dollar-per-square-foot-per-second reasoning which has led us to the comfortable, easy, reassuring, humanistic environment which all of us, New Yorkers in particular, enjoy so thoroughly in this seventh decade of the 20th century.

Thanks to Mayor John V. Lindsay and other city planners, the theater district won't be wiped out, but it may change in character. Special regulations on the use of building sites in the Broadway area make it more profitable for the office-builders to include replacement theaters in their skyscraper designs, and this is being done. So the Playhouse is gone; the Morosco and the Helen Hayes are doomed; and the Cort, Broadway, George Abbott and Belasco Theaters are earmarked for oblivion. Replacement theaters are being drawn into the plans of the monoliths destined to occupy their sites, but whether these will satisfy all the demands of the continuing dramatic art form—the demands of intimate dramas as well as large musicals—is still moot.

On the plus side of the construction situation, the handsome new Juilliard Theater went into operation at Lincoln Center, and the boom in off-Broadway production was matched by an off-Broadway theater-building boom. This year there were 26 playhouses ranging in size from tiny to medium, some brand new and some remodeled, ready for occupancy, that weren't in existence last season.

Organized activity in 1969-70 included an effort on the part of the League of New York Theaters to advance curtain time to 7:30 p.m. Among the more than 2,000 replies to a *Cue* questionnaire on this subject circulated among playgoers, 59 per cent favored a 7:30 curtain, the commuters to get home an hour earlier, the city folk to break early enough to enjoy a leisurely post-theater dinner. Equity and the musicians agreed to the possibility of effecting such a change, but good old Local 1 of the International Alliance of Theatrical and Stage Employees (the stagehands) raised objections which should delay action on the plan for many months.

The League also had problems with one of its own members, David Merrick, who resigned for undisclosed reasons (he has done this before, and the rejoicing when he returns to the fold is always sweet). The playwrights' organization, the Dramatists Guild, in recognition that the times are indeed a-changin', altered its constitution to permit authors of off-Broadway plays to become full voting members—they had previously been limited to associate membership, with full privileges reserved for the authors of Broadway plays and musicals. The New Dramatists Committee, a group which operates to aid new playwriting talent, acquired a permanent home and workshop on West 44th Street, near the theater district. Also in organized activity, the stage-hands' Local 1, responding to a complaint from the New York State division of human rights, worked out a formula to insure the availability of member-ship in the union to members of minority groups. At Actors Equity, Frederick O'Neal (president), Theodore Bikel (1st vice president) and Frank Maxwell (2d vice president) were re-elected to new three-year terms.

The critics, as usual, were stirring around and being stirred in 1969-70. Concern over the New York *Times* daily reviewer's power (whoever might hold the job) to make or break a show with his single opinion was growing in every corner of the theater. Many suggestions for relieving the situation—which must be almost as embarrassing to the job's incumbent, Clive Barnes, as it is for the theater—were being discussed, some with *Times* personnel. Measures actually taken proved ineffective, however. Joseph Cates attempted to steal a march on the *Times* and other New York papers by inviting out-of-town critics to previews of *Gantry,* hoping to put good news in circulation before exposing his show, but all the New York critics except one raised strong objections against being scooped, particularly by the AP and UPI re-viewers, who were to be invited to see the show early. The plan was dropped. David Black tried to persuade the critics to come see *Paris Is Out!* over a pe-riod of two weeks and stagger their reviews. This plan also ran into strong objections, and a release date for all reviews was set, though no single opening night performance was ever designated.

Speaking of Clive Barnes, we reported in last year's *Best Plays* volume that he had refrained from covering the British import *The Flip Side* at the request of the producers. We have since learned that it was Barnes's own decision not to cover the show (because he'd seen it in London and not liked it much). At any rate, the whole matter of the *Times* daily critic making a swing to London to report on new shows for his New York paper has been under discussion. In a page one story, *Variety* reported in September that "allegedly" the chances of a pair of London successes—*40 Years On,* with John Gielgud, and *The Secretary Bird*—to be optioned for and produced on Broadway were dimin-ished if not altogether ruined by unfavorable opinions expressed in Barnes columns sent back to his paper during his London visit. Writing in the *Drama-tists Guild Quarterly,* British playwright Frank Marcus complained that his play *Mrs. Mouse, Are You Within?* "had been mentioned most favorably in the pages of the New York *Times* by three London critics; nevertheless, Mr. Barnes's adverse report killed its chances as far as America was concerned." The point to be inferred from Marcus's complaint—that the *Times* has plenty of other sources of information about London plays without putting them to the commercial hazard of the New York reviewer's comment in advance of New York production—seems to be a good one.

Back home, at long last Barnes managed to soften David Merrick's hard-nosed hostility towards critics. Merrick *praised* the *Times* critic in his presence while both were appearing on a New York TV show: "I highly approve of Barnes. I feel that my plays will be fairly and properly appraised in the New York *Times*. I think he loves the theater and hopes each time he's going to see something wonderful." Barnes's astonished reply: "I fear for my career."

The New York drama critics as a group came under criticism for not making the best use of tickets allotted to them; not bothering to return them when they didn't plan to use them, or coming alone and thus leaving the seat beside them empty (there's some justification for this latter practise, in the opinion of the *Best Plays* editor, who has been covering the theater for 29 years and is convinced that many legit playhouses have been "refurbished" to allow for cramming in more and smaller seats in narrower rows to increase the auditorium's capacity; the empty seat gives some leg room and avoids severe constriction of the muscles and consequent lapses of concentration). The Los Angeles critics organized themselves into a Drama Critics Circle, with James Powers of the *Hollywood Reporter* president and Dale Olsen, who has often made special reports on Los Angeles theater for *Best Plays,* as secretary-treasurer. The New York Drama Critics Circle named George Oppenheimer of *Newsday* president and Henry Hewes of the *Saturday Review* vice president. At the same time, the Circle turned down the application for membership of John Simon of *New York Magazine*. In personnel changes, Leo Mishkin took the late Whitney Bolton's place as drama critic of the *Morning Telegraph* and John O'Connor replaced the retiring Richard Cooke on the *Wall Street Journal*.

And finally on the offstage subject of critics, Louis Harris and Associates prepared a survey on *Critics and Criticism in the Mass Media* which established the following profile of the composite critic: a man (81 per cent), working for a male editor (98 per cent), average age 45, on the job 6 years, Protestant (47 per cent), liberal (57 per cent), with a college degree (75 per cent) in English or literature (51 per cent) or journalism (23 per cent), who went into journalism and became a critic by chance (50 per cent), who has worked for his medium in some capacity other than criticism (60 per cent), with admitedly too great an emphasis on the manner of expression at the expense of content (66 per cent), under some pressure from advertisers (21 per cent), employers (19 per cent), supervisors and editors (17 per cent), publicists and promoters (13 per cent) and personal threats (10 per cent).

A number of censorship problems arose and/or continued in 1969-70. The *Che!* case was decided in Manhattan Criminal Court with the ruling that the play, containing the representation of 23 sex acts, was obscene without redeeming social value. Its author, producer and other personnel received fines. The decision is being appealed; meanwhile the result tends to encourage prosecutors everywhere. If the decision had gone against them, the censorship forces might have thrown up their hands and abandoned the field for a time, at least.

A tricky situation developed with the U.S. Department of State over a proposed Middle and Far-East tour of avant-garde playlets produced under the supervision of Gordon Davidson in the Mark Taper Forum's "New Theater for Now" series. Short works by Jules Feiffer, Lanford Wilson, Jean-Claude van Itallie, Israel Horovitz, Terrence McNally and others—among the finest talents the American theater has to offer—were placed in production for the tour; then, abruptly, in October, less than two weeks before the tour was to begin, the whole project was cancelled by the State Department with a vague explanation of "unstable and changing political conditions in the host countries." Authors of the playlets cried "censorship;" but an insider suggested that it might be "not so much a matter of censorship as of fear" lest the plays offend the antediluvian tastes of congressmen who hold the purse strings for State's cultural programs.

And *Hair* was banned in Boston. This great rock musical celebration of youth, love and peace finally sent a company to Boston, and the local authorities couldn't wait for the March 6 opening to place the show under attack. They came to the first preview, after which *Variety* quoted the Boston license commissioner as objecting strongly to *Hair's* "obscenity" and nudity and most of all "the manner in which the American flag was degraded" (the flag scene was cut voluntarily, though at season's end it was still being used by the company in New York where it caused an astronaut to walk out on the show in protest). Seven Massachusetts justices went to see the show for themselves, and *Hair* became the hottest of hot Boston tickets. Finally, on April 10, *Hair* rang down the curtain rather than cut the sex scenes and put on the extra clothes demanded by the Massachusetts Supreme Court. The cost of refunding the ticket purchasers' money and keeping the show closed while the issue was appealed to the Federal courts became onerous; but the show managed to hang on. When a three-judge Federal panel decided in *Hair's* favor, the Boston district attorney delayed the show's re-opening by taking his case to the United States Supreme Court. On May 22—six weeks after the closing—the Supreme Court refused to nullify the Federal panel's decision, thus clearing the way for *Hair* to resume performances in Boston in its original state. But it was a cliff-hanger; the Supreme Court's decision was a tie vote, 4-4, technically sufficient to let the lower court's decision stand.

The computerization of theater tickets, permitting all tickets to all shows to be marketed electronically at central places, continued to be the subject of discussion and experimentation during the season, but the process is still in the tryout stage. One of the major electronic-ticket outfits, Computicket, folded with a loss of $13 million, leaving Ticketron (which had also once folded but was bought by Ticket Reservation Systems, Inc. and put back to work under its own name) in sole operation in the field.

In the area of subsidy, NBC earmarked $1 million to back selected shows. The administration in Washington decided on $40 million as the sum to be asked for the National Endowment on the Arts and Humanities, about double the previous year's Federal subsidy, but still very small in comparison to, say, $477 million to the National Science Foundation for "pure science," or New York City's $75 million budget for arts and humanities programs. Of the previous year's Federal allotments, only $2 million went to the performing arts.

The most useful subsidy arrangement as far as the New York Theater is concerned is the Theater Development Fund, financed partly by private monies and partly by the National Endowment on a matching basis. The Fund's "thing" is to commit sums for the purchases of tickets to selected commercial-theater productions *after* they have been mounted, reselling these tickets at sharply reduced prices to students, teachers and other groups. This purchase of tickets helps the show by putting money into the box office at an often crucial early period in its run, before it has been able to build the audience of which it may be capable. It also helps the theater in general by drawing many who would probably not be able to afford the full price of a ticket.

Among individuals who figured in offstage events was Dore Schary, in the thick of it as usual, appointed to the newly-created post of Commissioner of Cultural Affairs of the City of New York by Mayor John V. Lindsay and sworn in April 27. Queen Elizabeth II made it *Sir* Noel Coward, and the honors lists also elevated the world's leading English-speaking actor, Laurence Olivier, to a life peerage. There was a reshuffling of personnel at Lincoln Center, where John D. Rockefeller III retired as chairman of the board and was replaced by Amyas Ames—and Robert Montgomery resigned as president of The Repertory Theater of Lincoln Center, reasons undisclosed. And speaking of Rockefellers, a close associate of Rockefeller cultural interests, Nancy Hanks, was named to replaced Roger L. Stevens as chairman of the National Council on the Arts.

In politics, show people stood up to be counted on various contentious occasions, in what was certainly a stormy season. In the autumn there was the Moratorium, a mass demonstration for peace climaxed in New York City by a Bryant Park rally with many stage stars on the dais. A post-curtain observance in May—a moment of silence in memory of the students killed at Kent State University, followed by the reading of a text protesting the incursion of American troops into Cambodia—was organized by a theater committee of five persons under Kermit Bloomgarden's direction. Stars of all shows were asked to preside at this ceremony and read the statement following the May 9 matinee and evening performances. The committee estimates that most did. The text of the statement prepared by Bloomgarden's committee was as follows: "Some of us feel that the war in Indochina has gone on too long. We have allowed our children to assume the burden of protest. But this can be a children's crusade no longer. For those who wish to voice their objections to the President's unconstitutional war policy—and support those congressmen and senators who oppose it—there are petitions available to sign at tables outside this theater."

At season's end, in a decision which might eventually have exerted a profound effect on the theater if it had gone the other way, the U.S. Supreme Court struck down a Federal statute making it a crime for an actor to wear a U.S. military costume if his character reflects discredit on the service. The case involved an incident in which the law was invoked against a protester who staged an anti-war guerrilla theater skit outside the draft induction center in Houston, Tex. The Court's decision was unanimous. Justice Hugo L. Black stated in the opinion that such incidents might be "crude, amateurish and perhaps unappealing," but that "an actor, like everyone else in our country, enjoys a Constitutional right to freedom of speech, including the right openly to criticize the Government during a dramatic performance."

Following Vice President Spiro T. Agnew's now-celebrated attack on those he envisioned as "effete snobs" in the communications media, the annual membership meeting of Dramatists Guild playwrights, composers and lyricists framed and adopted this resolution: *"Resolved: It is the sense of the Dramatists Guild at its annual meeting to assert and affirm our belief in the freedom of the press and the freedom of the various media; and to deplore specifically the succession of threats by the administration to attempt to intimidate the media, the press and for that matter everybody else in the country."*

It was ironic to reflect that only a few months previously, when the 1969-70 season began in June, there existed off Broadway a topical revue with the year's most un-prophetic title: *Spiro Who?*

The days of the 1969-70 New York theater season were days of change, not only in the notoriety of Spiro somebody but in all things visible and invisible including the art of the theater; days of *becoming,* of metamorphosis taking place and continuing to take place, with no end to the process in sight. The important question for the theater in the season just past is not, Was it a good one? (yes, in spots) or Was it a bad one? (no, not really) but Was it one of change or stagnation?

We hasten to proclaim it one of change, not all for the better of course, but with vigorous economic and artistic forces continuously churning within. Those who jest at the theater's scars by calling it the Fabulous Invalid do not understand the nature of its wounds. The theater is a fabulous convalescent, constantly recovering from some staggering blow of imagination which disrupts the system, knocks the props out from under the steadiest old artistic concepts and makes the whole art form see stars.

How went the theater in 1969-70? Painfully, thank you, painfully but not lamely; determined to strike every note from sexual outrage to political contempt, to try every dramatic trick from attacking the audience to Pinteresque non-communication, and to defend its freedom of choice against all intrusions of power and censorship; slowly, boldly, hopefully making progress as the seasons change.

THE 1969-70 OFF-OFF-BROADWAY SEASON

By Robert Schroeder

Editor, *The New Underground Theater* (Bantam Books) and author of the playscript *Eenie, Meenie, Minie, Moe,* produced off off Broadway this season

As the 1969-70 off-off-Broadway theater season came to a close, the American nation was divided as it had not been since the Reconstruction. The war

THE SEASON IN NEW YORK

had again been escalated, six American students had been shot to death on their own campuses, and gangs marauded in the streets of the cities, looking for long-hairs. The theater had once again proven itself a true chronicler of its times—it was as polarized as the nation.

At one edge of the spectrum, an increasing number of off off Broadwayites were as busily rooting into the past as were the revivalists of concurrent Broadway. Clyde Fitch, William Vaughn Moody, Ring Lardner, W. B. Yeats, George Bernard Shaw, John Dryden, W. Somerset Maugham, Arthur Wing Pinero, Georges Feydeau, Arthur Rimbaud and Lewis Carroll became the objects of neo-Bohemian sweat and zeal.

Where some sought to re-root, others lingered to loot, or to hoot. The revelers in Camp continued to trip. The Theater of the Ridiculous, now split into three rival (and equally) Ridiculous troupes, Tom Eyen's Theater of the Eye, Ron Link's extenuations at The Extension, Ed Wode's exploitations at his Free Store Theater (don't you believe it—it's off off Broadway's most expensive ticket, with never a twofer), Richard Schechner's *Makbeth,* and sundry others lingered longingly, spitting cud.

While away over there, at the far other edge of the spectrum, were off off Broadway's elitist yogis, cross-legged and contemplative in their minute theaters, seriously and most studiously probing their bellies. An earlier messiah spoke of being happier over one that was saved than over the ninety-and-nine. The theater's current messiah plays one of his Polish Laboratory Theater productions to 40 spectators because he sees the theater as having been painted by the movies and then by TV into a closed corner of elitism. Off off Broadway's elitism evidenced itself this season in (among others) the Blackfriars' *Five Star Saint,* Chelsea's *The Brass Butterfly, The Unicorn From the Stars,* and *Candaules, Commissioner,* The Circle's *A Practical Ritual to Exorcise Frustration After Five Days of Rain,* La Mama's *Shango, The Unseen Hand, Captain Jack's Revenge,* and *A Rat's Mass,* the Open Theater's *Terminal,* Theater Genesis' *The Deer Kill,* and Thresholds' *Pinion, The Venturi,* and *A Season In Hell.*

In all of New York during 1969-70, there was only one theater that had to ask police to fend off the crowds. That theater housed none of the serious or camped revivals that clung to the one edge of off off Broadway's spectrum, nor did it contain any of the elitist fantasies that touched at the other. Nor did that theater proffer off-Broadway imitations of Broadway, nor did it offer Neil Simon, *Fiddler* or *Dolly.* The only theater in New York that needed help in handling its crowds was hosting The Who and the like. It housed theater that people—actual great masses of actual people—were breaking down the doors to experience.

The Fillmore East in Lower Manhattan, the theater about which I am speaking (it is a capacious house), is filled the year around with that great new audience the theater's professionals all talk about—the new audience to which especially the off-off-Broadway theater might be expected to try to appeal. But while I can list hundreds of 1969-70 off-off-Broadway productions in the serious revival, camped revival or serious-elitist categories, I can note only a few that so much as intended to appeal or to speak to any substantial number of people—to the broad central vista of the theatrical spectrum. This few would include LeRoi Jones' *Slave Ship,* Cherrilyn Miles' *X Has No Value,* Arthur Miller's *Fame* and *The Reason Why,* Al Carmines' *Christmas Rappings,* and (if I do say so myself) the off-off-Broadway version of my own *Eenie, Meenie, Minie, Moe.*

While off off Broadway tries to revive its impetus with revivals, or trips off to another Camp, or secretly suffers an esthete's secret bellyache to be regurgitated before a secret few, Bill Graham sees that the Fillmore East's stage speaks to his audience's life-concerns, and that's how Fillmore East gets filled. Using the same tools that David Merrick uses—words, music, motion, lights, sound, projected live from a stage to a living audience—Graham proves that even today, even among the "alienated," living theater is desperately needed, and urgently sought.

At a time when most of the American theater can't keep its audience in, Bill Graham can't keep his out. In our "experimental" theater, as in our nation, it is clearly a time for further change. That grunting and groaning in a mock-Grotowski manner may be fun down on that floor, but it seems so bungling and is so boring from here. Mother has become an expletive, and the flag a drag—where can they take the words from now?

1969-70 was the season when The Who culminated a national tour by playing their rock opera *Tommy* to a packed Metropolitan Opera House (co-sponsored by the Fillmore East). Do you want to claim that what's happening wherever The Rolling Stones, The Jefferson Airplane and The Who go, and what goes on at the Fillmores East and West, is not theater? (They aren't dance halls.) Buy the records, listen to the lyrics, pulsate to the beat. Dig what a total program *conveys*—it's *not* the nudity that packs them into *Hair.*

I am not opting for the product—I am opting for the attitude. In a time when the preponderant troupes and "names" of off off Broadway are clutching at one or the other extreme of the theatrical spectrum, and when off Broadway and Broadway are content to comfy into just a couple of the niches in between, a new theater actually is alive and well and currently living where neither the Shuberts nor Ellen Stewart reside. In a time when the bulk of the presumably most avant garde and outreaching of the theater's producing groups, writers and practitioners have their minds minutely fixed on their own tummyache, Bill Graham's performers' minds are on their audience's ache. The audience's and the performers' aches may be coincidental, or concurrent—but there is no confusion as to the priorities. The performing artist, the playwright, the director who uses his ache to commune with or to ease his audience's ache is creating life in the theater off off Broadway and wherever else he appears.

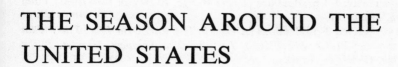

O
O
O

THE SEASON AROUND THE UNITED STATES

with

A DIRECTORY OF PROFESSIONAL REGIONAL THEATER

O
O
O

Including selected Canadian programs

Professional 1969-70 programs and repertory productions by leading resident companies around the United States, plus major Shakespeare festivals including that of Stratford, Ontario (Canada), are grouped in alphabetical order of their locations and listed in date order from late May, 1969 through May 31, 1970. This list does not include Broadway, off-Broadway or touring New York shows, summer theaters, single productions by commercial producers or college or other non-professional productions. The directory was compiled by Ella A. Malin for *The Best Plays of 1969-70* from information provided by the resident producing organizations at Miss Malin's request. Figures in parentheses following titles give number of performances and date given is opening date, included whenever a record of these facts was available from the producing managements.

Summary

This Directory lists 302 productions (including one-acters and workshop productions) presented by 37 groups in 52 theaters in 36 cities during the 1969-70 season. Of these, 157 were American plays in 114 full productions and 38 workshop productions. 56 programs were world premieres, 8 were American premieres, and one was a North American premiere.

Frequency of production of individual scripts was as follows:

1 play received 6 productions (*You Can't Take It With You*)

1 play received 5 productions (*Black Comedy*)

3 plays received 4 productions (*Uncle Vanya, A Day in the Death of Joe Egg, Macbeth*)

9 plays received 3 productions (*A Flea in Her Ear, Dear Liar, The Indian Wants the Bronx, Misalliance, Tartuffe, The Tempest, Hamlet, Blithe Spirit, Charley's Aunt*).

31 plays received 2 productions

192 received 1 production

Listed below are the playwrights who received the greatest number of productions. The first figure is the number of productions; the second figure (in parentheses) is the number of plays produced, including one-acters.

Shakespeare	27 (17)	Horovitz	5	(2)
Shaw	10 (7)	Lowell	4	(4)
Chekhov	9 (4)	Coward	4	(2)
Molière	8 (6)	Nichols (Peter)	4	(1)
Kaufman	8 (3)	Beckett	3	(3)
Williams	7 (5)	Brecht	3	(3)
Hart	7 (2)	Carter (Lonnie)	3	(3)
Anouilh	6 (5)	Wexler	3	(3)
Pinter	6 (5)	Wilson (Lanford)	3	(3)
Albee	5 (4)	Jonson	3	(2)
O'Neill	5 (4)	Kilty	3	(1)
Mrozek	5 (3)	Thomas (Brandon)	3	(1)
Feydeau	5 (2)			

ABINGDON, VA.

Barter Theater

SEE HOW THEY RUN (27). By Philip King. May 27, 1969. Director, Owen Phillips; scenery, Marvin Roark; lighting, Robert Hammel; costumes, Johorne. With Roy Clary, Robert Foley, Ginger Guffy, Dorothy Marie.

HERE TODAY (27). By George Oppenheimer. June 10, 1969. Director, Owen Phillips; scenery, Michael Stauffer; lighting, Robert Hammel; costumes, Johorne. With Stephen Levi, Ginger Guffy, Roy Clary.

THE INCOMPARABLE MAX (11). By Jerome Lawrence and Robert E. Lee. June 24, 1969 (world premiere). Director, Jerome Lawrence; scenery, Michael Stauffer; lighting, Henry Millman; costumes, Johorne. With Robert Foley, Jerry Hardin, Diane Hill.

THE WINSLOW BOY (17). By Terence Rattigan. July 8, 1969. Director, Owen Phillips; scenery, Michael Stauffer; lighting, Henry Millman; costumes, Johorne. With Linde Hayen, Harold Herman, Diane Hill, Ben Tuder.

THE HASTY HEART (31). By John Patrick. July 22, 1969. Director, Jerry Hardin; scenery, Michael Stauffer; lighting, Henry Millman; costumes, Johorne. With John Gilpin, Susan Pomeranze, Merritt Olsen.

MERTON OF THE MOVIES (16). By George S. Kaufman and Marc Connelly. August 19, 1969. Director, Owen Phillips; scenery, Michael Stauffer; lighting, Henry Millman; costumes, Johorne. With Henry Strozier, Jerry Hardin, Diane Hill.

THERE'S A GIRL IN MY SOUP (16). By Terence Frisby. September 2, 1969. Director, Owen Phillips; scenery, Thomas Rowland; lighting, Henry Millman; costumes, Johorne. With Robert Foley, Harold Herman, Dorothy Marie.

MONEY (31). Book and lyrics by David Axelrod and Tom Whedon. September 16, 1969. Director, Owen Phillips; scenery, Marvin Roark; lighting, Michael Casteel; costumes, Nancy Kilker; musical director, Bryon Grant. With Roy Clary, Marlene Clary, Harold Herman.

MACBETH (23). By William Shakespeare. May 5, 1970. Director, Owen Phillips; scenery and costumes, Lynn Fams; lighting, Greg Christensen. With Roger Brown, Jane Cronin, William Logan, William Schilling.

ANN ARBOR, MICH.

University of Michigan Professional Theater Program: Association of Performing Artists (APA) Repertory Company

MACBETH (16). By William Shakespeare. September 16, 1969. Director, Ellis Rabb; scenery and lighting, James Tilton; costumes, Nancy Potts; composers, Bob James, Conrad Susa; sound, Dan Dugan. With Richard Easton, Sada Thompson, Christopher Walken, Joseph Bird.

THE CHRONICLES OF HELL by Michel de Ghelderode, directed by John Houseman, and PLAY by Samuel Beckett, directed by Jack

O'Brien (16). September, 1969. scenery and lighting, James Tilton; costumes, Nancy Potts. With Joseph Bird, Peter Coffield, Laurence Guittard, Donna Haley, Patrick Hines, Elizabeth Perry, Tom Toner, James Tripp.

PRIVATE LIVES (16). By Noel Coward. October 14, 1969. Director, Stephen Porter; scenery and lighting, James Tilton; costumes, Nancy Potts. With Brian Bedford, David Glover, Tammy Grimes, Suzanne Grossmann.

University of Michigan Professional Theater Program: New Play Project

THE CONJUROR (6). By Evan Hunter. November 5, 1969 (world premiere). Director, Marcella Cisney; designer, Joe Mielziner.

With Audra Lindley, James Whitmore, Catherine Burns, Morris Strassberg.

University of Michigan Professional Theater Program: Phoenix Theater Company

THE CRIMINALS (8). By Jose Triana; adapted by Adrian Mitchell. January 26, 1970 (American premiere). Director, David Wheeler with John Houseman; scenery and lighting, James Tilton; costumes, Nancy Potts. With Penelope Allen, Barry Primus, Linda Selman.

HARVEY (16). By Mary Chase. February 2, 1970. Director, Stephen Porter; scenery and lighting, James Tilton; costumes, Nancy Potts. With Helen Hayes, James Stewart, Jesse White, Marian Hailey.

University of Michigan Professional Theater Program: New Play-in-Progress

THE UNION (3). By Ransom Jeffrey. Friday, February 27, 1970 (world premiere). Director, James Baffico; designer, Stuart K. Mc-

Daniel. With William Tate, Kathleen McGill, Jonathan Slade, Donna Haley.

ASHLAND, ORE.

The Oregon Shakespearean Festival: Elizabeth Theater

THE TEMPEST (13). By William Shakespeare. July 19, 1969. Director, Richard Risso; scenery, Clayton L. Karkosh, Richard L. Hay; lighting, Steven A. Maze; costumes, Jean Schultz Davidson. With Patrick Hines, Dorothy French, Edward Brubaker, Theodore Pejovich.

ROMEO AND JULIET (13). By William Shakespeare. July 20, 1969. Director, Patrick Hines; scenery, Clayton L. Karkosh, Richard L. Hay; lighting, Steven A. Maze; costumes,

Jean Schultz Davidson. With Roger Kozol, Carolyn Norton, Richard Risso, Patrick Hines.

TWELFTH NIGHT (13). By William Shakespeare. July 21, 1969. Director, Hugh Evans; scenery, Clayton L. Karkosh, Richard L. Hay; lighting, Steven A. Maze; costumes, Jean Schultz Davidson. With Carol Condon, Dorothy French, Jim Baker, Raye Bird, Scott Porter.

KING JOHN (12). By William Shakespeare.

July 22, 1969. Director, Edward Brubaker; scenery, Clayton L. Karkosh, Richard L. Hay; lighting, Steven A. Maze; costumes, Jean Schultz Davidson. With Candace Birk, Jose Carillo, Tom Donaldson, Tom Oleniac, George Taylor.

The Oregon Shakespearean Festival: Angus Bowmer Theater

VIRTUE IN DANGER (14). Musical adaptation of John Vanbrugh's The Relapse or Virtue in Danger; lyrics by Paul Dehn; music by James Bernard. August 12, 1969 (American premiere). Director, Carl Ritchie; scenery, Clayton L. Karkosh, Richard L. Hay; lighting, Steven A. Maze; costumes, Jean Schultz Davidson. With Robert Ground, Larry Alan Haynes, Amanda McBroom, Rosa Morin, Tom Oleniac.

Stage II: Angus Bowmer Theater

ROSENCRANTZ AND GUILDENSTERN ARE DEAD (11). By Tom Stoppard. March 21, 1970. Director, Angus L. Bowmer; scenery, Richard L. Hay; lighting, Steven A. Maze; costumes, Jean Schultz Davidson. With Larry Carpenter, Roger Kozol, Lloyd Williamson, Katherine King.

YOU CAN'T TAKE IT WITH YOU (11). By George S. Kaufman and Moss Hart. March 22, 1970. Director, Pat Patton; scenery, Richard L. Hay; lighting, Steven A. Maze; costumes, John E. Blythe. With Diana Bellamy, Dorothy French, Michael Winters, Philip Davidson.

ANTIGONE (11). By Jean Anouilh; translated by Kitty Black. March 24, 1970. Director, Larry Oliver; scenery, Richard L. Hay; lighting, Steven A. Maze; costumes, Jean Schultz Davidson. With Kit Carson, Philip Davidson, Katherine King, Fredi Olster.

THE FANTASTICKS (10). Book and lyrics by Tom Jones; music by Harvey Schmidt; based on Edmond Rostand's Les Romantiques. March 25, 1970. Director, Peter Nyberg; scenery, Richard L. Hay; lighting, Steven A. Maze; costumes, Judith E. Disbrow; musical director, Larry Carpenter; choreographer, Jo Bailey Guthrie. With Christine Abbott, Larry Carpenter, Richard Lincoln.

BALTIMORE

Center Stage

SLOW DANCE ON THE KILLING GROUND (31). By William Hanley. October 22, 1969. Director, John Stix; scenery, Jason Phillips; lighting, C. Mitch Rogers; costumes, Ritchie M. Spencer. With Clifton Davis, Roger De Koven, Madeline Miller.

THE KNACK (30). By Anne Jellicoe. November 19, 1969. Director, Dennis Rosa; scenery, Jason Phillips; lighting, C. Mitch Rogers; costumes, Ritchie M. Spencer. With Craig Carnelia, Michael Ebert, J. Frederick Jones, Maureen Silliman.

LONG DAY'S JOURNEY INTO NIGHT (30). By Eugene O'Neill. December 17, 1969. Director, Ben Piazza; scenery, Jason Phillips; lighting, C. Mitch Rogers; costumes, Ritchie M. Spencer. With Tom Brannum, Carlton Colyer, Vivian Nathan, William Prince, Margaret Sullivan.

THE TEMPEST (36). By William Shakespeare. January 21, 1970. Director, Dennis Rosa; scenery, Jason Phillips; lighting, C. Mitch Rogers; costumes, Ritchie M. Spencer. With Frederick Coffin, Barbara Frank, Margaret Sullivan, Christopher Johnson.

PARK (32). Book and lyrics by Paul Cherry; music by Lance Malcahy. February 25, 1970 (world premiere). Director, John Stix; musical staging, Lee Theodore; scenery, Jason Phillips; lighting, C. Mitch Rogers; costumes, Ritchie M. Spencer. With David Brooks, Joan Hackett, Ted Leplat, Julie Wilson.

THE INDIAN WANTS THE BRONX by Israel Horovitz and THE GNADIGES FRAULEIN by Tennessee Williams (30). March 25, 1970. Director, Lee Theodore; scenery, Jason Phillips; lighting, C. Mitch Rogers; costumes, Ritchie M. Spencer. With Christopher Johnson, Ian Tucker, Glenn Walken, Lucille Patton, Mary Louise Wilson, Gregory Etchison, Bert Houle.

WHO'S GOT HIS OWN (15). By Ron Milner. April 21, 1970. Director, Nathan George; scenery, W. Scott Robinson; lighting, C. Mitch Rogers; costumes, Ritchie M. Spencer. With Susan Batson, Harvey Denmark, Antonio Fargas, Minnie Gentry, Robert E. Russell, Joe Wilson.

THE GLASS MENAGERIE (15). By Tennessee Williams. May 12, 1970. Director, Peter W. Culman; scenery, W. Scott Robinson; lighting, C. Mitch Rogers; costumes, Ritchie M. Spencer. With Frederick Coffin, Barbara Frank, Richard Greene, Vivienne Shub.

BOSTON

Charles Playhouse: Resident Company

THE ICEMAN COMETH (40). By Eugene O'Neill. September 25, 1969. Director, Michael Murray; scenery, Gordon Micunis; lighting, Duncan Ross; costumes, Suzanna Jones. With Richard Kneeland, Maxwell Glanville, Wallace Rooney.

NARROW ROAD TO THE DEEP NORTH (40). By Edward Bond. October 30, 1969 (American premiere). Director, Louis Criss; scenery, Santo Loquasto; lighting, Duncan Ross; costumes, Suzanna Jones. With Nicholas Kepros, David Spielberg, Ronald Roston, William Trotman, Sheila Hart.

A FLEA IN HER EAR (40). By Georges Feydeau; translated by Barnett Shaw. December 4, 1969. Director, Paxton Whitehead; production designer, Victor Di Napoli. With John Horton, Nicholas Martin, Kristina Callahan, Antonie Becker.

Charles Playhouse: Guest Production

JACQUES BREL IS ALIVE AND WELL AND LIVING IN PARIS (49). April 23, 1970. With Elly Stone, Stan Porter and the 3 W Productions Company.

ANTIGONE (40). By Jean Anouilh; translated by Lewis Galantière. January 8, 1970. Director, John Wood; production designer, Victor Di Napoli. With James Griffiths, Roberta Maxwell, Deborah Kipp, Joseph Maher.

IN THE JUNGLE OF CITIES (40). By Bertolt Brecht; translated by Anselm Hollo. February 12, 1970. Director, Louis Criss; production designer, William Trotman. With Nicholas Kepros, Michael Moriarty, Jennifer Harmon, Elizabeth Eis.

RATS directed by Al Pacino and THE INDIAN WANTS THE BRONX directed by Michael Murray (40). By Israel Horovitz. March 19, 1970. Scenery and lighting, David Chapman and William Trotman; costumes, Suzanna Jones. With Carolyn Y. Cardwell, Michael Hadge, Michael Heit, Jack Kehoe, Lazaro Perez, Andrew Winner.

BUFFALO

Studio Arena Theater

EPISODE IN THE LIFE OF AN AUTHOR and THE ORCHESTRA (15). By Jean Anouilh; translated by Miriam John. September 16, 1969. Director, Jose Quintero; scenery, Ben Edwards; lighting, David Zierk; costumes, Jane Greenwood; music, Doris Schwerin. With Stephen Cheng, Danna Hansen, Mel Haynes, Charlotte Jones, Miller Lide, Betty Lutes, Gerald E. McGonagill, Betty Miller, Ronald Parady, Ted Pezzulo, Carla Pinza, Elsa Raven, Ralph Williams.

A FUNNY THING HAPPENED ON THE WAY TO THE FORUM (37). Book by Larry Gelbart and Burt Shevelove; music and lyrics by Stephen Sondheim. October 2, 1969. Director, Marvin Gordon; scenery, Larry Aumen; lighting, Peter J. Gill; costumes, Charles D. Tomlinson; musical director, Stuart Hamilton; choreographer, Marvin Gordon. With Dean Dittmann, Irving Harmon, Gaye Edmond, Louise Armstrong, Paul Glaser, Gabor Morea.

TINY ALICE (36). By Edward Albee. November 6, 1969. Director, Warren Enters; scenery and costumes, Stephen J. Hendrickson; lighting, Peter J. Gill. With Ron O'Neal, Patricia Gage, Patrick Horgan, James Valentine, Ronald Drake.

DON'T DRINK THE WATER (36). By Woody Allen. December 11, 1969. Director, Warren Enters; scenery, Larry Auman; lighting, Peter J. Gill; costumes, John Crespo. With Irving Harmon, Gene Lindsey, Ronnie Cunningham.

THE ONLY GAME IN TOWN (29). By Frank D. Gilroy. January 15, 1970. Director, Warren Enters; lighting, Peter J. Gill; costumes, Duane Andersen. With Gene Lindsey, Pamela Raymond, Patrick McCullough.

UNCLE VANYA (37). By Anton Chekhov. February 19, 1970. Director, Warren Enters; scenery, Larry Auman; lighting, Peter J. Gill; costumes, Fran Brassard. With Michael Higgins, Patrick Horgan, Elizabeth Hubbard, Lee McCain, Alfred Hinckley.

LEMON SKY (37). By Lanford Wilson. March 26, 1970 (world premiere). Director, Warren Enters; scenery and costumes, Stephen J. Hendrickson; lighting, David Zierk. With Bonnie Bartlett, Christopher Walken, Charles Durning, Kathryn Baumann.

STOP THE WORLD—I WANT TO GET OFF (37). Book, music and lyrics by Leslie Bricusse and Anthony Newley. April 30, 1970.

Director, Neal Du Brock; scenery and costumes, Duane Andersen; lighting, Peter J. Gill; musical director, Stuart Hamilton; choreographer; Lois Grandi. With Stuart Howard, Donna Monroe, Susan Stevens, Judith Gordon.

Studio Arena Theater: Special Projects

SOMETHING WICKED THIS WAY COMES (4). Adapted from the novel by Ray Bradbury. March 12, 1970. Director, Neal Du Brock.

THE BLACK MAN IN WHITE AMERICA compiled by Ed Lawrence and Jim Miller; CLARA'S OLE MAN by Ed Bullins (1). Director, Ed Lawrence. With the African Cultural Center Company.

Studio Arena Theater: Children's Theater

THE CANTERVILLE GHOST (7). By Darwin Reid Payne; from the story by Oscar Wilde. November 28, 1969. Director, Norman Leger; scenery, Edward Patton; costumes, John Crespo. With Ed Smith, Jim Menke, Mary Jane Abeles, Luke Pauly.

PINOCCHIO (8). By George T. Latshaw; from the story by Carlo Collodi. December 26, 1969. Director, Frank T. Wells; scenery, Edward Patton; costumes, John Crespo; marionette designed and created by Jim Menke. With Jim Menke, Luke Pauly, Betty Lutes, Vinette Cotter.

ALICE THE MAGNIFICENT (6). Book by Robert Higgins; music and lyrics by Byron Tinsley. March 31, 1970. Director, Norman Leger; scenery, Edward Patton; costumes, John Crespo; lion mask designed and created by Jim Menke. With Ted Bouton, Luke Pauly, Betty Lutes, Jerry Murphy Jr.

BURLINGTON, VT.

Champlain Shakespeare Festival

A WINTER'S TALE (14). By William Shakespeare. July 22, 1969. Director, William Davis; scenery, W. M. Schenk; lighting, John Urban; costumes, Timothy Miller. With James Glenn, Denise Huot, Valerie von Valz, Richard Fancy.

OTHELLO (14). By William Shakespeare. July 24, 1969. Director, Gerard E. Moses; scenery, W. M. Schenk; lighting, John Urban; costumes, Timothy Miller. With Robert Kya-Hill, Matthew Lewis, Valerie von Valz, Dominic Hogan.

RICHARD III (11). By William Shakespeare. July 29, 1969. Director, Anthony Wiles; scenery, W. M. Schenk; lighting, John Urban; costumes, Timothy Miller. With John P. Lagoia, Valerie von Valz, Denise Huot, Dominic Hogan, David S. Howard.

CHICAGO

Goodman Memorial Theater

SOLDIERS (30). By Rolf Hochhuth; translated by Robert D. MacDonald. October 24, 1969. Director, Douglas Seale; scenery, James Maronek; lighting, G. E. Naselius; costumes, Alicia Finkel. With Douglas Campbell, Leonardo Cimino, Fionnuala Flanagan, Max Howard, Donald Woods.

YOU CAN'T TAKE IT WITH YOU (30). By Moss Hart and George S. Kaufman. December 5, 1969. Director, Edward Payson Call; scenery, Marc Cohen; lighting, G. E. Naselius; costumes, Virgil Johnson. With Ronald Bishop, Colostine Boatwright, Ann Casson, Dewey Chapman, Kent More, Donald Woods.

THE TEMPEST (30). By William Shakespeare. January 23, 1970. Director, Douglas Seale; scenery, James Maronek; costumes, Alicia Finkel. With Ronald Bishop, Douglas Campbell, Clayton Corbin, Fionnuala Flanagan, Kathleen Doyle, William Vines.

THE BASEMENT and TEA PARTY (34). By Harold Pinter. March 6, 1970. Directors, Joseph Slowik, Patrick Henry; scenery, Joseph Nieminski; lighting, G.E. Naselius; costumes, Al Tucci. With Ronald Bishop, Douglas Campbell, Aviva Crane, Cordis Fejer, Alice Gealy, Max Howard, Vincent Park, David Whitaker.

THE MAN IN THE GLASS BOOTH (30). By Robert Shaw. April 17, 1970. Director, Douglas Seale; scenery, James Maronek; lighting, G.E. Naselius; costumes, Alicia Finkel. With Leonardo Cimino, Ronald Bishop, Ann Casson, Douglas Mellor.

HEARTBREAK HOUSE (30). By George Bernard Shaw. May 29, 1970. Director, Douglas Seale; scenery, Marc Cohen; lighting, Jerrold Gorrell; costumes, Virgil Johnson. With Douglas Campbell, Ann Casson, Fionnuala Flanagan, Brenda Forbes, Paxton Whitehead.

Goodman Memorial Theater: Children's Theater Company

RUMPELSTILTSKIN (33). By Wesley Van Tassel, from the story by the brothers Grimm; music and lyrics, Mark Ollington. October 11, 1969. Director, Bella Itkin; musical director, Kelly Danford; scenery, Oseloka Osadebe; lighting, John Nathan; costumes, Al Tucci; choreographer, Thomas Jaremba. With Judith Bergan, Mark Burchard, Michael Kearns.

ROBIN HOOD (36). By James Norris; music by Reginald De Koven; adapted by Dan Wilson. February 3, 1970. Director, Kelly Danford; scenery, Oseloka Osadebe; lighting, Herbert Schmoll; costumes, Madeleine Grigg. With Henry Moral, Beverly Rogers, Guy Giarrizzo.

A DOCTOR IN SPITE OF HIMSELF (27). By Aurand Harris, adapted from the play by Molière; music by John Hogan, Henry Moran, James Pobiege. March 28, 1970. Director, Bella Itkin; scenery, Norbert Fencl; lighting, Joseph Pohnan; costumes, Virgil Johnson. With Joel Stedman, Beverly MacGuffin, Donald Modie, Patrick Lavery, Jack Godby.

Note: The Goodman Memorial Children's Theater summer production *The Panda and the Spy* will open July 29, 1970.

Goodman Memorial Theater: Studio Theater Company

HAMLET in the Charles Marowitz version, October 12, 1969; CHICAGO by Sam Shepard and TIMES SQUARE by Leonard Melfi, November 2, 1969; IMPRESSIONS OF GROTOWSKI by Joseph Slowik, November 23, 1969; THE EMPIRE BUILDERS by Boris Vian, December 14, 1969; CELEBRATION by Harvey Schmidt and Tom Jones, January 11, 1970; A CRY OF PLAYERS by William Gibson, February 22, 1970; SUMMERTREE by Ron Cowen, March 15, 1970; MANY LOVES by William Carlos Williams, April 12, 1970; CIRCUS MINIMUS compiled by Patrick Henry and Tom Towler, May 3, 1970; THE AMOROUS FLEA, musical based on Molière's *A School for Wives*, May 24, 1970. Each of these productions ran for one week.

CLEVELAND

Cleveland Play House: Euclid-77th Theater

THE UNITED STATES VS. JULIUS AND ETHEL ROSENBERG (22). By Donald Freed. September 19, 1969. Director, Larry Tarrant; scenery and lighting, Paul Rodgers; costumes, Charlotte Hare; filmed sequences, Gregory Abels. With Stuart Levin, Elizabeth Lowry, Noland D. Bell, Allen Leatherman, Vaughn McBride.

THE ROYAL HUNT OF THE SUN (32). By Peter Shaffer. October 24, 1969. Director, Robert Snook; scenery, Paul Rodgers; lighting, Suellen Childs; costumes, Joe Dale Lunday. With Robert Allman, Jonathan Bolt, John Buck Jr., Allen Leatherman.

HARVEY (32). By Mary Chase. December 5, 1969. Director, John Going; scenery, Paul Rodgers; lighting, Suellen Childs; costumes, Joe Dale Lunday. With Bob Moak, Robert Snook, Vivienne Stotter, Cheryl Casper, Dorothy Paxton.

THE COUNTRY WIFE (26). By William Wycherley. January 16, 1970. Director, John Going; scenery and lighting, Paul Rodgers; costumes, Joe Dale Lunday. With June Gibbons, Jonathan Bolt, Robert Allman.

ALL THE WAY HOME (32). By Tad Mosel: based on the novel *A Death in the Family* by James Agee. February 20, 1970. Director, Robert Snook; scenery and costumes, Joe Dale Lunday; lighting, Suellen Childs. With Evie McElroy, Jonathan Bolt, Peter Ostrum, Margaret Christopher, Edith Owen.

ARSENIC AND OLD LACE (34). By Joseph Kesselring. April 3, 1970. Director, Larry Tarrant; scenery, lighting and costumes, Eugene Hare. With Dorothy Paxton, June Gibbons, Bob Moak, Jonathan Bolt, Vaughn McBride.

Cleveland Play House: Drury Theater

A DAY IN THE DEATH OF JOE EGG
(20). By Peter Nichols. November 7, 1969.
Director, Larry Tarrant; scenery and lighting,
Marla Nedelman; costumes, Joe Dale Lunday.
With David Frazier, Myrna Kaye, Bob Moak,
Jean Morris, Edith Owen.

BEA, FRANK, RICHIE AND JOAN from
Lovers and Other Strangers by Renee Taylor
and Joseph Bologna and BLACK COMEDY
by Peter Shaffer (20). December 19, 1969.
Director, Richard Oberlin; scenery, Paul Rodgers; lighting, Marla Nedelman; costumes, Joe
Dale Lunday. With Jean Morris, Jonathan
Bolt, Robert Thorson, Marcie Ross, Susan
Burkhalter, John Buck Jr., Richard Halverson.

LOOT (16) by Joe Orton. January 30, 1970.

Director, Richard Oberlin; scenery and lighting, Marla Nedelman; costumes, Esther Eisenberg. With David Frazier, Marjorie Dawe,
Nick Devlin, Vaughn McBride.

RED'S MY COLOR, WHAT'S YOURS?
(20). By Norman Wexler. February 27, 1970
(world premiere). Director, John Going; scenery and lighting, Marla Nedelman; costumes,
Joe Dale Lunday. With Cleo Holladay, Nick
Devlin, Richard Halverson, Richard Oberlin.

THE TAMING OF THE SHREW (36). By
William Shakespeare. March 31, 1970. Director, John Going; scenery and costumes, Joe
Dale Lunday; lighting, Marla Nedelman.
With Cleo Holladay, Alexandra Barrett, David
Frazier, Allen Leatherman.

Cleveland Play House: Brooks Theater

THE EFFECT OF GAMMA RAYS ON
MAN-IN-THE-MOON MARIGOLDS (44).
By Paul Zindel. November 21, 1969. Director,
Jonathan Bolt; scenery and lighting, Paul
Rodgers; costumes, Joe Dale Lunday. With
Myriam Lipari, Evie McElroy, Jana Gibson.

DON JUAN IN HELL (20). By George Bernard Shaw. March 6, 1970. Director, Stuart
Levin; lighting, Steve Waxler, Jeffrey Dallas;
costumes, Joe Dale Lunday. With Robert

Thorson, Elizabeth Lowry, Bob Moak, John
Buck Jr.

WHATEVER HAPPENED TO HUGGING
AND KISSING? and THE HUFF AND
THE PUFF (22). By Norman Wexler. April
17, 1970 (world premiere). Director, Robert
Snook; scenery and lighting, Marla Nedelman; costumes, Joe Dale Lunday. With Mary
Gallagher, David Berman, Vivienne Stotter,
Stuart Levin, Marcie Ross.

DALLAS

Dallas Theater Center: Kalita Humphreys Theater

YOU CAN'T TAKE IT WITH YOU (20).
By Moss Hart and George S. Kaufman. June
24, 1969. Director, Ken Latimer; scenery and
costumes, Roberta Rude; lighting, Gene Clampitt. With Lynn Trammell, James Nelson Harrell, Robyn Baker Flatt, John Figlmiller, Rebecca Logan, Preston Jones.

CACTUS FLOWER (25). By Abe Burrows;
based on a play by Pierre Barillet and Jean-Pierre Gredy. July 29, 1969. Director, Sally
Netzel; scenery, Lydia Lee Weeks; lighting,
Ken Latimer; costumes, Louise Mosley. With
Ryland Merkey, Mona Pursley, Synthia
Rogers.

MACBETH (12). By William Shakespeare.
September 30, 1969. Director, Paul Baker;
scenery and costumes, Mary Sue Jones; lighting, Randy Moore; projections, John Figlmiller; sound, Christopher Hundrie. With Ken
Latimer, Randy Moore, Mona Pursley, Edward Herrmann.

THE HOMECOMING (15). By Harold
Pinter. October 21, 1969. Director, Paul
Baker; designer, Nancy Levinson; lighting,
Ken Latimer; film direction, Steven Mackenroth in association with Dr. Bohumil Svoboda;
photography, John Mahoney. With Ronald
Wilcox, Randy Moore, Kaki Dowling, Tim
Green, Ryland Merkey, Preston Jones.

PROJECT III: IS LAW IN ORDER? (15).
Written by The Resident Company. November 25, 1969 (world premiere). Directors,
Paul Baker and Mary Sue Jones, in association with Ronald Wilcox; music composed
and directed by Raymond Allen; design coordination, Campbell Thomas; lighting, Randy
Moore; film direction, Frank Schaefer; photography, John Mahoney; script coordinators,
Sally Netzel, Leonard T. Wagner, John
Logan. With The Resident Company, special
guests and professional apprentices.

A CHRISTMAS CAROL (18). By Charles

Dickens; adapted by John Figlmiller. December 19, 1969. Director, John Figlmiller; scenery, Kathleen Latimer, lighting, Sally Netzel; costumes, Deanna Dunagan; choreographer, Robyn Baker Flatt; musical arranger and director, Raymond Allen; additional music and lyrics, Raymond Allen, Sally Netzel.

SHE STOOPS TO CONQUER (36). By Oliver Goldsmith. January 13, 1970. Director, Kaki Dowling; designer, Carleton Tanner. With Randolph Tallman, Deanna Dunagan, Ronald Wilcox, Judith Davis, Steven Mackenroth, Robyn Baker Flatt, John Shepherd.

MARAT/SADE (19). By Peter Weiss; English version by Geoffrey Skelton; verse adaptation by Adrian Mitchell. March 12, 1970. Director, Harry Buckwitz; designer, Mary Sue Jones; lighting, Robyn Baker Flatt; puppets, Ella-Mae Brainard; composer, Richard Peaslee; musical director, Raymond Allen.

With Michael Dendy, Randy Moore, Elizabeth Lumpkin.

THREE TO GET READY: ON THE HARMFULNESS OF TOBACCO by Anton Chekhov; GREENSKI—THE HUMMINGBIRD; THE TOP LOADING LOVER, libretto by Glenn Allen Smith, music by Raymond Allen, and BLACK COMEDY by Peter Shaffer (26). April 14, 1970. Directors, Mona Pursley, Ken Latimer; scenery, Campbell Thomas; lighting, Margaret Yount; costumes, Jean Progar. With Michael Dendy, James Nelson Harrell, Edward Herrmann, Candy Rouillard, Irene Lewis, Mary Sue Jones, Ryland Merkey, Gene Leggett.

LITTLE MURDERS (26). By Jules Feiffer. May 26, 1970. Director, Theodore Mann; scenery, Campbell Thomas; lighting, Randy Moore; costumes, Michael Wray. With Kaki Dowling, Edward Herrmann, Mary Sue Jones, Preston Jones, Keith Rothschild.

Note: Kalita Humphreys Theater 1969-70 season will conclude with *The Boys From Syracuse* July 7 to August 15, 1970.

Dallas Theater Center: Down Center Stage

BLACK REFLECTIONS IN A WHITE EYE (musical revue) script arrangement and lyrics, Sally Netzel; music, Raymond Allen, and THE PROCESS IS THE PRODUCT: YOU ARE WHERE YOU'RE GOING, script by the performers (6). June 10, 1969. Directors, Mary Sue Jones and the performers; scenery, Louise Mosley and the performers; costumes, Ella-Mae Brainard; musical director, Raymond Allen. With the Resident Company.

ENTERTAINING MR. SLOANE (35). By Joe Orton. July 1, 1969. Director, Campbell Thomas; designer, Johanna Stalker; lighting, Randy Moore. With Betty June Lary, Randy Moore, Mike Wray, Leonard T. Wagner.

THE PROMISE (35). By Aleksei Arbuzov; translated by Ariadne Nicolaeff. September 23, 1969. Director, Ken Latimer; scenery, Charles Jarrell; lighting, Randy Moore; costumes, Judith Davis; projections, Jan Svarc and Steven Mackenroth. With Randolph Tallman, Don Davlin, Elizabeth Lumpkin.

HALFWAY UP THE TREE (28). By Peter Ustinov. November 18, 1969. Director, Randolph Tallman; scenery, Johanna Stalker; lighting, Fil Alvarado; costumes, Joan Meister. With Edward Herrman, Ella-Mae Brain-

ard, Don Granbery, Stephanie Rich, Margaret Yount.

THE FIELD (10). By Michael Parriott. January 6, 1970 (world premiere). Director, Claudette Gardner; scenery, Gregory K. Caffy; lighting, Larry Wheeler; costumes, Lydia Lee Weeks. With Charles Jarrell, Julia Jarrell, Robert Dickson, James Nelson Harrell, Michael Dendy, Jere Schaefer.

DEAR LIAR (35). By Jerome Kilty; adapted from the correspondence of George Bernard Shaw and Mrs. Patrick Campbell. January 27, 1970. Director, Edward Herrmann; designer, Lynn Lester; lighting, Robert Dickson. With Campbell Thomas, Jacque Thomas.

LOVERS (30). By Brian Friel. March 24, 1970. Director, Rosalie Robinson; scenery, A. J. Rogers; lighting, Allen Hibbard; costumes, Nantawan Soothorndhai. With Preston Jones, Helen Stavros, Jane Burch, Mac Williams, Lynn Trammel, Jean Progar.

THE NIGHTWATCHMEN (23). By Stratis Karras; translated by Evangelos Voutsinas. May 21, 1970 (American premiere). Director, Evangelos Voutsinas; scenery, lighting, costumes, A. J. Rogers. With James Nelson Harrell, Michael Dendy, Margaret Yount, Maureen O'Brien, Ella-Mae Brainard, Pat Johnson.

Note: Down Center Stage 1969-70 season will conclude with *A Day in the Death of Joe Egg* June 30-August 15, 1970.

HALIFAX, NOVA SCOTIA (CANADA)

Neptune Theater: Summer Season, Main Stage

CHARLEY'S AUNT (19). By Brandon Thomas. June 27, 1969. Director, Heinar Piller; scenery, Maurice Strike; costumes, Ken McBane.

LILIOM (14). By Ferenc Molnar. July 1,

1969. Director, Heinar Pillar; scenery and costumes, Maurice Strike.

BOEING-BOEING (16). By Marc Camoletti and Beverly Cross. July 7, 1969. Director, Heinar Piller; scenery and costumes, Maurice Strike.

Neptune Theater: Summer Season, Studio Productions

WAITING FOR GODOT (9) by Samuel Beckett. July 3, 1969, director, Harry Whittier; A RESOUNDING TINKLE (10), by

N.F. Simpson, July 8, 1969, director, Alex Jones; THE POLICE (10) by Slawomir Mrozek, July 8, 1969, director, Clarke Rogers.

Note: Summer 1969 Neptune Theater Company included Yvonne Adalian, Don Allison, Allen Bleviss, Richard Donat, David Foster, Ron Hastings, James Hurdle, Linda Livingston, Patricia Ludwick, Margaret Macleod, Jack Medley, Joan Orenstein, Leon Pownall, David Renton, Edwin Rubin, Lionel Simmons, Kathryn Watt.

Neptune Theater: Winter Season

YOU KNOW I CAN'T HEAR YOU WHEN THE WATER'S RUNNING (18). By Robert Anderson. February 5, 1970. Director, Keith Turnbull; scenery, Lawrence Shafer; costumes, Olda Dimitrov.

THE LION IN WINTER (16). By James Goldman. February 10, 1970. Director, Heinar Piller; scenery, Antony Dimitrov; costumes, Olga Dimitrov.

THE KILLING OF SISTER GEORGE (16). By Frank Marcus. February 17, 1970. Direc-

tor, David Renton; scenery, Antony Dimitrov; costumes, Olga Dimitrov.

TIGER! TIGER! (14). By Arthur L. Murphy. March 17, 1970 (world premiere). Director, Heinar Piller; scenery, Antony Dimitrov; costumes, Olga Dimitrov.

A FLEA IN HER EAR (18). By Georges Feydeau. April 14, 1970. Director, Heinar Piller; scenery, Antony Dimitrov; costumes, Olga Dimitrov.

Note: Winter 1970 Neptune Theater Company included Yvonne Adalian, Claude Bede, Douglas Chamberlain, David Foster, Lynn Gorman, Michael Gough, Terry Judd, Linda Livingston, Margaret Macleod, Kenneth Pogue, Edwin Rubin, Lionel Simmons, Terry Tweed, Faith Ward, Sandy Webster, Ken Wickes.

HARTFORD, CONN.

The Hartford Stage Company:

A DELICATE BALANCE (40). By Edward Albee. October 17, 1969. Director, Paul Weidner; scenery and costumes, Santo Loquasto; lighting, Peter Hunt. With Eve Collier, Jack Murdock, Victoria Zussin.

THE FARCE OF SCAPIN (40). By Molière; translated by Paul Weidner. November 28, 1969. Director, Paul Weidner; scenery and costumes, Santo Loquasto; lighting, Spencer Mosse. With Jeremiah Sullivan, Barbara Caruso, David O. Petersen, Al Corbin.

A DAY IN THE DEATH OF JOE EGG (40). By Peter Nichols. January 9, 1970. Director, Charles Maryan; scenery, Santo Loquasto; lighting, Spencer Mosse; costumes, Annie Warner. With Jeremiah Sullivan, Charlotte Moore, Jane Orzech, Darthy Blair.

MISALLIANCE (40). By George Bernard Shaw. February 20, 1970. Director, Tom Gruenewald; scenery and costumes, Santo Loquasto; lighting, Joe Pacitti. With Katharine Houghton, Ted Graeber, Saylor Cresswell, Geddeth Smith.

THE TRIAL OF A. LINCOLN (40). By James Damico. April 3, 1970 (world premiere). Director, Paul Weidner; scenery, Santo Loquasto; lighting, Joe Pacitti; costumes, Linda Fisher. With Thomas Coley, Robert Kya-Hill, Ted Graeber, Robert Bright.

ANYTHING GOES (41). Book by P.G. Wodehouse, Guy Bolton, Howard Lindsay and Russel Crouse; music and lyrics by Cole Porter. May 15, 1970. Director and choreographer, Don Price; scenery and costumes,

Santo Loquasto; lighting, John Wright Stevens; musical director, Richard DeMone. With Corinne Kason, Kenneth Cory, Charlotte

Moore, David O. Petersen, Darthy Blair, John Dignan.

HOUSTON

Alley Theater: Large Stage

ALL THE WAY HOME (38). By Tad Mosel. June 12, 1969. Director, William Hardy; scenery and costumes, Paul Owen. With Lillian Evans, William Hardy, Rodger Cook.

THE ROSE TATTOO (38). By Tennessee Williams. October 16, 1969. Director, Philip Minor; scenery and costumes, Paul Owen. With Norma Jean Wood, William Hardy, Kathleen O'Meara Noone, Roy Frady.

TARTUFFE (38). By Molière. December 4, 1969. Director, Kirk Denmark; scenery and costumes, Jerry Williams. With Michael O'Sullivan, I. M. Hobson, Jeannette Clift, Erika Slezak, Dominic Hogan.

THE ANDERSONVILLE TRIAL (38). By

Saul Levitt. January 22, 1970. Director, Pat Brown; scenery and lighting, Jerry Williams; costumes, Paul Owen. With William Hardy, Clarence Felder, Bill E. Noone, R. Edward Leonard.

CHARLEY'S AUNT (44). By Brandon Thomas. March 12, 1970. Director, William Hardy; scenery and costumes, Jerry Williams; lighting, Richard D. Cortright. With David Dukes, Dominic Hogan, Daniel Mooney, Erika Slezak, Kathleen O'Meara Noone.

BLITHE SPIRIT (38). By Noel Coward. April 30, 1970. Director, Milton Selzer; costumes, Jerry Williams; lighting, John Hagen. With Margaret Hamilton, Erika Slezak, Lillian Evans, Kendall Clark.

Alley Theater: Arena Stage

EVERYTHING IN THE GARDEN (62). By Edward Albee; from the play by Giles Cooper. November 27, 1969. Director, Beth Sanford; scenery and lighting, Paul Owen. With Nancy Evans Leonard, William Hardy, John Carpenter, Lynn Wood.

DEAR LIAR (70). By Jerome Kilty; adapted from correspondence by George Bernard Shaw and Mrs. Patrick Compbell. February

5, 1970. Director, Jerome Kilty. With Jeannette Clift, Jerome Kilty.

THE WORLD OF CARL SANDBURG (62). By Norman Corwin; adapted from the works of Carl Sandburg. April 16, 1970. Director, R. Edward Leonard; scenery and costumes, Jerry Williams. With James Broderick, Nancy Evans Leonard, Barry Cullison.

LAFAYETTE, IND.

Purdue University Professional Theater Program: Loeb Playhouse

A MIDSUMMER NIGHT'S DREAM (13). By William Shakespeare; rock musical version with original music by Don Heckman. October 9, 1969. Director, Michael Flanagan; scenery and lighting, Robert T. Williams; costumes, Dusty Reeds; choreographer, Wayne Lamb. With Barry Bostwick, Roni Dengel, Patricia Egglinger, Patrick Fox, Robert Mo-

berly, Bernie Passeltiner, Earl Smith, Jill Tanner and The Celluloid Duck.

DRACULA (13). By Leon Katz; based on the novel by Bram Stoker. February 24, 1970 (world premiere). Director, Word Baker; scenery, Ron Hall; costumes, Caley Summers. With Donald Gantry, Charles Haid, Bernie Passeltiner, Penelope Windust.

Purdue University Professional Theater Program: Conservatory Productions

"EH?" (14). By Henry Livings. November 6, 1969. Director, Bernie Passeltiner; scenery and costumes, Dusty Reeds; lighting, Randy Earle. With John Eldridge, Patrice L. Murphy, Peter Schneider, James Smith, Daniel Von Bargen, Candy Coles Yelton.

BURY THE DEAD (7). By Irwin Shaw. December 12, 1969. Director, Joseph Stockdale; scenery and costumes, Dusty Reeds; lighting, Randy Earle. With the Conservatory Productions company.

LAKEWOOD, OHIO

Great Lakes Shakespeare Festival

THE WOULD-BE GENTLEMAN (21). By Molière. June 27, 1969. Director, Lawrence Carra; scenery, Milton Howarth; lighting, David Jager; costumes, Cletus Anderson. With Roger Fawcett, Darryl Croxton, Harold Cherry.

AS YOU LIKE IT (19). By William Shakespeare. July 3, 1969. Director, Lawrence Carra; scenery, Milton Howarth; lighting, David Jager; costumes, Cletus Anderson. With Robert Browning, Norma Joseph.

MACBETH (20). By William Shakespeare. July 17, 1969. Director, Lawrence Carra; scenery, Milton Howarth; lighting, David Jager; costumes, Cletus Anderson. With Stephen Scott, Maureen Hurley, Keith Mackey.

CANDIDA (12). By George Bernard Shaw. July 31, 1969. Director, Lawrence Carra; scenery, Milton Howarth; lighting, David Jager; costumes, Cletus Anderson. With Celeste Holm, Wesley Addy.

TROILUS AND CRESSIDA (10). By William Shakespeare. August 14, 1969. Director, Lawrence Carra; scenery, Milton Howarth; lighting, David Jager; costumes, Cletus Anderson. With Robert Allman, Nick Devlin, Maria Lennard.

LOS ANGELES

Center Theater Group of the Mark Taper Forum

CHEMIN DE FER (54). By Georges Feydeau; translated and adapted by Suzanne Grossmann and Paxton Whitehead. June 5, 1969 (American premiere). Director, Stephen Porter; scenery, Peter Wexler; lighting, H. R. Poindexter; costumes, Lewis Brown. With Jacques Aubuchon, Ed Flanders, Mariette Hartley, Charles Kimbrough, Donald Moffat, Joan Van Ark.

UNCLE VANYA (54). By Anton Chekhov; translated by Alex Szogyi. August 21, 1969. Director, Harold Clurman; scenery and costumes, Peter Wexler; lighting, Richard Nelson. With Richard Basehart, Eduard Franz, Lois Smith, Pamela Tiffin, Joseph Wiseman.

MURDEROUS ANGELS (54). By Conor Cruise O'Brien. February 5, 1970 (world premiere). Director, Gordon Davidson; scenery, Peter Wexler; lighting, Gilbert V. Hemsley Jr.; costumes, Lewis Brown; sound score, Pia Gilbert. With Paul Ballantyne, Barbara Colby, Robert DoQui, Richard Easton, Lou Gossett, Robert Pastene, George Voskovec, Ula Walker.

CRYSTAL & FOX (54). By Brian Friel. April 9, 1970 (American premiere). Director, Hilton Edwards; scenery, Archie Sharp; lighting, Gilbert V. Hemsley Jr.; costumes, Dorothy Jeakins. With Robert Doyle, Dana Elcar, Salome Jens, Nancy Malone, Tom Toner, Anthony Zerbe.

Note: Center Theater Group's 1970 season at the Mark Taper Forum will also include the world premiere of Harvey Perr's *Rosebloom* June 18, 1970, directed by Gordon Davidson; the world premiere of Derek Walcott's *The Dream on Monkey Mountain* August 27, 1970, directed by Michael Schultz; the American premiere of Howard Sackler's *The Pastime of Monsieur Robert* November 5, 1970, directed by Edwin Sherin.

New Theater For Now Workshop of the Mark Taper Forum

June 1, 1969 through May 31, 1970 (Summer, Fall, Winter, Spring Series).

Plays: *The Dance Next Door, Rosebloom, Stars and Stripes, The Girl and the Soldier, Thoughts on the Instant of Greeting a Friend on the Street, Punch and Judy In "A Revenge Play," Five Minutes, Rats, Camera Obscura, Boats, Photographs, June/Moon, Wandering, Botticelli, God Bless, Line*

Playwrights: James Bridges, Jules Feiffer, Israel Horovitz, Adrienne Kennedy, Jack Larson, Terrence McNally, Leonard Melfi, Robert Patrick, Harvey Perr, Sharon Thie, Jean-Claude van Itallie, Lanford Wilson

Directors: Edward Parone, Jered Barclay, Robert Calhoun, Gordon Davidson.

Designers: Ray Klausen, Marianna Elliott, Ken Fryer, Peter Wexler, Willa Kim, Tharon Musser.

Actors: Rene Auberjonois, Marge Champion, Jane Elliot, Philip Proctor, John Randolph, Peter Strauss, Bert Freed, Sally Kellerman, Ron Rifkin, Jan Sterling, Sian Barbara Allen, Roscoe Lee Browne, Al Checco, Odessa Cleveland, Richard Dreyfuss, Mary Frann, Gordon Hoban, Gail Kobe, Colgate Salisbury, Paul Winfield, Anthony Zerbe.

LOUISVILLE, KY.

Actors Theater of Louisville—Main Series

UNDER MILK WOOD (26). By Dylan Thomas. October 16, 1969. Director, Jon Jory; scenery, Hal Tine; lighting, Jennifer Tipton; costumes, Bill Walker. With Patrick Boxhill, MacIntyre Dixon, Lee Anne Fahey.

THE KILLING OF SISTER GEORGE by Frank Marcus, directed by Christopher Murney, and STAIRCASE by Charles Dyer, directed by Ken Jenkins (26). November 13, 1969. Scenery and lighting, Hal Tine; costumes, Bill Walker. With Patrick Boxhill, MacIntyre Dixon, Denise Fergusson, Sheila Haney, Adale O'Brien.

SEE HOW THEY RUN (26). By Philip King. December 11, 1969. Director, Jon Jory; scenery and lighting, Hal Tine; costumes, Bill Walker. With George Ede, Denise Fergusson, Ken Jenkins, Paul Villani.

HAMLET (26). By William Shakespeare. January 8, 1970. Director, Jon Jory; scenery, Hal Tine; lighting, Johnny Walker; costumes, Bill Walker. With James Cromwell, George Ede, Lee Anne Fahey, Ken Jenkins, Adale O'Brien.

CAT ON A HOT TIN ROOF (26). By Tennessee Williams. February 5, 1970. Director, Victor Jory; scenery and lighting, Hal Tine; costumes, Bill Walker. With Peggy Cowles, Jean Inness, Ken Jenkins, Victor Jory.

TOBACCO ROAD (26). By Jack Kirkland; adapted from Erskine Caldwell's novel. March 5, 1970. Director, Jon Jory; scenery and lighting, Hal Tine; costumes, Bill Walker. With Peggy Cowles, Leora Dana, Victor Jory, Christopher Murney.

BEYOND THE FRINGE (26). By Alan Bennett, Peter Cook, Jonathan Miller and Dudley Moore. April 2, 1970. Director, Ken Jenkins; scenery and lighting, Hal Tine; costumes, Bill Walker. With David C. Burrow, Walter Rhodes, Albert Sanders, Max Wright.

Actors Theater of Louisville: Special Series

THE STAR-SPANGLED GIRL (26). By Neil Simon. November 13, 1969. Director, Jon Jory; scenery and lighting, Hal Tine; costumes, Bill Walker. With Lee Anne Fahey, Christopher Murney, Albert Sanders.

A THOUSAND CLOWNS (15). By Herb Gardner. April 2, 1970. Director, David Semonin; scenery and lighting, Hal Tine; costumes, Bill Walker. With George Ede, Lee Anne Fahey, Ken Jenkins, Glenn Newland.

MILWAUKEE

Milwaukee Repertory Theater Company: Todd Wehr Theater

A MIDSUMMER NIGHT'S DREAM (36). By William Shakespeare. October 3, 1969. Director, Boris Tumarin; scenery and costumes, William James Wall; lighting, William Mintzer. With Marc Alaimo, Anthony Heald, Tana Hicken, Charles Kimbrough, Mary Jane Kimbrough, Penelope Reed, Ric Zank.

THE BURGOMASTER (36). By Gert Hoffman; translated by Donald Watson. November 7, 1969 (American premiere). Director, Anthony Perkins; scenery, William James Wall; lighting, William Mintzer; costumes, Janet C. Warren. With Michael Fairman, Charles Kimbrough, Penelope Reed.

THE KITCHEN (36). By Arnold Wesker. November 21, 1969. Director, John Olon-Scrymgeour; scenery and costumes, William James Wall; lighting, William Mintzer. With William McKereghan, Diana Kirkwood, Maggie Olesin, Michael Tucker, Ron Van Lieu.

MISALLIANCE (36). By George Bernard Shaw. December 19, 1969. Director, Ronald L. Hufham; scenery, William James Wall; lighting, William Mintzer; costumes, Janet C. Warren. With William McKereghan, Jack Swanson, Michael Tucker, Ron Van Lieu.

THE PRINCE OF PEASANTMANIA (36). By Frank Gagliano. February 20, 1970 (world premiere). Director, Eugene Lesser; scenery and costumes, William James Wall; lighting, Willam Mintzer; music and sound effects, James Reichert; lyrics, Frank Gagliano. With Marc Alaimo, Al Corbin, John Glover, William McKereghan, Penelope Reed, Ronald Steelman, Ron Van Lieu.

SHE STOOPS TO CONQUER (36). By Oliver Goldsmith. March 27, 1970. Director, Ronald L. Hufham; scenery, Jack Hilton Cunningham; lighting, William Mintzer; costumes, Janet C. Warren. With Marc Alaimo, William Fenno, Diana Kirkwood, William Lafe, Elizabeth Shepherd.

THE LESSON and THE CHAIRS (36). By Eugene Ionesco. April 10, 1970. Director, Tunc Yalman; scenery and costumes, William Mintzer. With Maggie Olesin, Penelope Reed, Ron Van Lieu.

MINNEAPOLIS

Minnesota Theater Company: Tyrone Guthrie Theater

JULIUS CAESAR (61). By William Shakespeare. June 26, 1969. Director, Edward Payson Call; scenery, Douglas Schmidt; costumes, Carrie Fishbein Robbins. With Allen Hamilton, Charles Keating, Robert Pastene, Margaret Phillips, John Ramsey.

THE BEAUTY PART (39). By S. J. Perelman. June 27, 1969. Director, Philip Minor; scenery and costumes, John Jensen. With Paul Ballantyne, Helen Carey, Katherine Ferrand, Robin Gammell, Allen Hamilton, Robert Pastene.

THE HOMECOMING (26). By Harold Pinter. July 8, 1969. Director, Joseph Anthony; scenery, Douglas Schmidt; costumes, John Jensen. With Emery Battis, Robin Gammell, Peter Goetz, James Lawless, Lee Richardson, Fern Sloan.

MOURNING BECOMES ELECTRA (27). By Eugene O'Neill. August 19, 1969. Director, Mel Shapiro; scenery and costumes, Karl Eigsti; lighting, Robert Scales. With Michael Moriarty, Margaret Phillips, John Ramsey, Lee Richardson, Fern Sloan.

UNCLE VANYA (38). By Anton Chekhov; translated by Tyrone Guthrie and Leonid Kipnis. October 7, 1969. Director, Tyrone Guthrie; scenery and costumes, Tanya Moiseiwitsch; lighting, Robert Scales. With Paul Ballantyne, Helen Carey, Patricia Conolly, Lee Richardson, Robert Pastene.

Minnesota Theater Company: The Other Place

THE MEASURES TAKEN by Bertolt Brecht. Director, David Feldshuh. With Douglas Cheek, Ron Glass, William Graham, William Grivna, George Muschamp, Cynthis Wells.

DUTCHMAN by LeRoi Jones. Director, David Feldshuh. With Douglas Cheek, Katherine Ferrand, Ron Glass.

KRAPP'S LAST TAPE by Samuel Beckett and A SLIGHT ACHE by Harold Pinter. Director, Dan Bly. With Emery Battis, Patricia Conolly, William Graham.

THE HOSTAGE by Brendan Behan. Director, Dugald MacArthur. With James Alexander, Jerome Anello, Paul Ballantyne, Patricia Conolly, Gus Fleming, Katherine Garnett.

Note: Individual dates for programs of the Minnesota Theater Company at The Other Place are not available, but the series began September 6, 1969. Programs of the Minnesota Theater Company at the Crawford Livingston Theater appear under ST. PAUL in the alphabetical order of locales.

NEW HAVEN, CONN.

Long Wharf Theater

TARTUFFE (23). By Molière; translated by Richard Wilbur. October 17, 1969. Director, Mark Healy; scenery, John Sherman; lighting, Ronald Wallace; costumes, Whitney Blausen. With William Swetland, Richard Venture, Martha Schlamme, George Hearn, Adelaide Klein.

TANGO (23). By Slawomir Mrozek; translated by Ralph Manheim and Teresa Dzieduscycka. November 14, 1969. Director, Arvin Brown; scenery, Elmon Webb and Virginia Dancy; lighting, Ronald Wallace; costumes, Whitney Blausen. With Joyce Ebert, George Hearn, Richard Venture, John Cazale, William Swetland, Laurie Kennedy, Martha Schlamme.

THE PIRATE (23). Music and Lyrics by Cole Porter; book by Lawrence Kasha and Hayden Griffin; based on the play by S. N. Behrman. December 12, 1969. Director, Maurice Breslow; scenery, Vanessa James; lighting, Ronald Wallace; costumes, Vernon Yates; musical director, Stuart Hamilton; choreographer, Larry Fuller. With Peggy Pope, George Hearn, Benjamin H. Slack, Kenneth Wickes.

COUNTRY PEOPLE (23). By Maxim Gorky; translated by Alexander Bakshy and Paul S. Nathan. January 9, 1970 (American premiere). Director, Arvin Brown; scenery, Elmon Webb, Virginia Dancy; lighting, Ronald Wallace; costumes, Whitney Blausen. With Richard Venture, Martha Schlamme, George

Hearn, John Cromwell, William Swetland, Dianne Wiest, Joyce Ebert, Ruth Nelson.

BLACK COMEDY and **THE WHITE LIARS** (23). By Peter Shaffer. February 6, 1970. Director, Maurice Breslow; scenery, Robert Darling; lighting, Ronald Wallace; costumes, Alec Sutherland. With John Cazale, Tom Crawley, Ray DeMattis, Joyce Ebert, Laurie Kennedy, Martha Schlamme, William Swetland, Richard Venture.

A DAY IN THE DEATH OF JOE EGG (23). By Peter Nichols. March 6, 1970. Director, Barry Davis; scenery, Elmon Webb, Virginia Dancy; lighting, Ronald Wallace; costumes, Alec Sutherland. With Joyce Ebert, George Hearn, Emily Lay, Ruth Nelson.

SPOON RIVER ANTHOLOGY (23). By Edgar Lee Masters; adapted by Charles Aidman. April 3, 1970. Director, Arvin Brown; scenery, George Spalding, Ronald Wallace, based on original design by David F. Segal; lighting, Ronald Wallace; costumes, Thom J. Peterson; musical director, Michael Posnick; original music, Naomi Caryl Hirshhorn; additional music, Michael Posnick. With John Cazale, Joyce Ebert, Grayce L. Grant, Laurie Kennedy, Chris Sarandon, Martha Schlamme, William Swetland, Richard Venture.

A THOUSAND CLOWNS (23). By Herb Gardner. May 1, 1970. Director, Harold Baldridge; scenery, David L. Taylor; lighting, Ronald Wallace; costumes, Marci Heiser. With Riley Mills, Richard Venture, Laurie Kennedy, Wil Albert.

Long Wharf Theater: Children's Theater

PINOCCHIO (6); **THE FLYING DOCTOR** (6); **THE THIEF OF BEAUTIFUL THINGS** (5); **THE POP-CORN MAN** (6); **SILVER BIRD AND SCARLET FEATHER** (5). Presented by the Connecticut Players, Saturdays, October 25, 1969 through May 9, 1970; director, Maurice Breslow.

The Yale Repertory Theater: Resident Company

THE RIVALS (25). By Richard Brinsley Sheridan. October 16, 1969. Director, Alvin Epstein; scenery and costumes, Lawrence Station King; lighting, Carol Waaser. With David Ackroyd, Jeremy Geidt, Jerome Kilty, Elizabeth Parrish, Lydia Fisher.

METAMORPHOSES (25). A Story Theater Production conceived by Paul Sills from Ovid's *Metamorphoses;* translated and adapted with lyrics by Arnold Weinstein; additional material by Kenneth Cavander. November 27, 1969. Director, Larry Arrick; scenery and costumes, Gary C. Eckhardt; lighting, George Moredock; music, John Guth and William Russo; additional music, Barbara Damashek, Mark Levinson, Stephen Michaels, Michael Posnick. With David Ackroyd, Barbara Damashek, Carmen De Lavallade, Alvin Epstein, Elizabeth Parrish.

CRIMES AND CRIMES (25). By August Strindberg; translated by Evert Sprinchorn. January 8, 1970. Director, Robert Lewis; scenery and costumes, Kenneth Emmanule; lighting, Jenie Swartz. With David Ackroyd, Carmen De Lavallade, Mildred Dunnock, Alvin Epstein, Louis Plante.

THE GOVERNMENT INSPECTOR (25). By Nikolai Gogol; translated by Peter Raby. February 19, 1970. Director, Ali Taygun; scenery and costumes, Peter Gould; lighting, Peter Edmond Winter. With David Ackroyd, Alvin Epstein, Joan Pape, Elizabeth Parrish, Eugene Troobnick.

TRANSFORMATIONS: THE RHESUS UMBRELLA by Jeff Wanshel, **CLUTCH** by David Epstein, **IZ SHE IZZY OR IZ HE AINT'ZY OR IZ THEY BOTH** by Lonnie Carter (25). April 2, 1970 (world premiere). Director, Richard Gilman; scenery and lighting, Stewart W. Johnson; costumes, Steven Rubin. With David Ackroyd, James Brick, Maxine Lieberman, Joan Pape, Elizabeth Parrish, Louis Plante, Ellis M. Pryce-Jones, Steve Van Benschoten, Henry Franklin Winkler.

DON JUAN, OR THE ENEMY OF GOD (25). By Molière; adapted by Kenneth Cavander. May 15, 1970 (world premiere). Director, Robert Brustein; scenery and costumes, Jeffrey Higginbottom; lighting, William B. Warfel; music and sound, Richard Peaslee. With David Ackroyd, John Cromwell, Carmen De Lavallade, Jill Eikenberry, Alvin Epstein, James Naughton, Eugene Troobnick.

The Yale Repertory Theater: Sunday-Monday New Plays Series

THE LUNCH HOUR (2). By Craig Clinton. December 7, 1969. Director, Eva M. Vizy.

THE PROPERTY OWNERS by James Lee; director, Ali Taygun, and **THE BALLAD OF THE TWENTY-FIFTH SOLDIER** by David F. Eliet; director, Sergei Retivov (2). December 14, 1969.

WORKDAY (2). By Lonnie Carter. January 18, 1970. Director Michael Feingold.

THE EBONITE (2). Written and directed by Luther Whitsett. January 25, 1970.

THE TOT FAMILY (2). By Istvan Orkeny. March 8, 1970.

DOUBLE BILL one-act plays by Terrence McNally and Lonnie Carter (2). April 12, 1970.

MAMA, IS TERRY HOME FOR GOOD? (2). By James Addison. April 19, 1970.

The Yale Repertory Theater: Children's Theater

RED SHOES (2). Book and lyrics by Michael Feingold; music by Bruce Trinkley; from the story by Hans Christian Anderson. April 19, 1970 (premiere). Director, Carmen De Lavallade. With Miss De Lavallade and members of the YRT Company.

NEW ORLEANS

Repertory Theater of New Orleans

THE THREEPENNY OPERA (28). Text and lyrics by Bertolt Brecht; music by Kurt Weill; English adaptation by Marc Blitzstein. March 20, 1970. Director, June Havoc; scenery, Ashton Smith; costumes, Frank Bennett. With June Havoc, Alice Evans, Elaine Kerr, Shev Rodgers, Art Wallace.

LUV (28). By Murray Schisgal. April 17, 1970. Director, June Havoc; scenery and lighting, Ashton Smith; costumes, Frank Bennett. With Ed Kearney, Elaine Kerr, Richard Mulligan.

THE WOMEN (28). By Clare Boothe. May 15, 1970. Director, June Havoc; scenery and lighting, Ashton Smith; costumes, Frank Bennett. With Julie Harris, Jessica Walter, Myra Carter, Ethel Smith.

Note: The Repertory Theater of New Orleans 1970 season will continue with *A Streetcar Named Desire* June 12, 1970 and *The Fantasticks* July 10, 1970.

OKLAHOMA CITY

The Mummers Theater

BLITHE SPIRIT (28). By Noel Coward. November 7, 1969. Director, Mack Scism; scenery and lighting, Robert Steinberg; costumes, William Schroder. With Virginia Payne, Jo Peters, John Wylie.

CHARLEY'S AUNT (28). By Brandon Thomas. December 5, 1969. Director, John Wylie; scenery and lighting, Robert Steinberg; costumes, William Schroder. With Raymond Allen, Anne Ault, Garry Moore, Carl Reggiardo.

SPOON RIVER ANTHOLOGY (28). By Edgar Lee Masters; adapted and arranged by Charles Aidman. January 2, 1970. Director, John Wylie; scenery and lighting, Robert Steinberg; costumes, William Schroder. With Raymond Allen, Anne Ault, John Milligan, Garry Moore, Louise Speed.

THE PURSUIT OF HAPPINESS (28). By Laurence Langner and Armina Marshall Langner. January 30, 1970. Director, Jean E. McFaddin; scenery and lighting, Robert Steinberg; costumes, William Schroder. With Anne Ault, Stephen De Pue, Pamela Mench, John Wylie.

BLACK COMEDY (28). By Peter Shaffer. February 27, 1970. Director, Jean E. McFaddin; scenery and lighting, Robert Steinberg; costumes, William Schroder. With Joanna Bayless, Trent Jenkins, Pamela Mench, John Milligan.

Note: The Mummers Theater completed its 1969-70 season with Christopher Fry's *The Lady's Not for Burning* March 27, 1970 and Leslie Stevens's *The Marriage-Go-Round* April 24, 1970. Further information about these productions was not available at press time.

PHILADELPHIA

Theater of the Living Arts: Resident Company

THE RECRUITING OFFICER (26). By George Farquhar. October 31, 1969. Director, Tom Bissinger; scenery, Eugene Lee; lighting, Roger Morgan; costumes, Nancy Christofferson. With Judd Hirsch, Marion Killinger, Jeanne De Baer, Sally Kirkland.

HARRY, NOON AND NIGHT (27). By Ronald Ribman. November 28, 1969. Director, Jerome Guardino; scenery, Eugene Lee; lighting, Roger Morgan; costumes, Franne Newman. With David Rounds, Morgan Freeman, Rachel Drexler, Lawrence Block.

GARGOYLE CARTOONS (11). By Michael McClure. December 9, 1969 (premiere). THE BOW, SPIDER RABBIT, THE CHERUB, THE MEATBALL directed by Tom Bissinger; THE RIVER, directed by Don Earl and Ken Horning. With members of the company.

THE LINE OF LEAST EXISTENCE (26).

Play and lyrics by Rosalyn Drexler; music by John Hall. January 24, 1970 (world premiere). Director, Tom Bissinger; scenery, Eugene Lee; lighting, Roger Morgan; costumes, Franne Newman. With Jerome Raphel, Judd Hirsch, Gretel Cummings, Danny DeVito, Amy Taubin.

A DAY AT THE FAIR (12). Mime show for children by the Routy Rep Players. January 31, 1970. Director, Bob deFrank; scenery, Joe Costa; lighting, Don Earl; costumes, Sue Lunenfeld. With Bob deFrank, Ken Goldman, Betsy Henn, Cheryl Lynn White.

Theater of the Living Arts: Guest Productions

RAILROAD CROSSING by Philip Booth; GESTURE by Dorothy Miles; FOUR HAIKU POEMS: WHO KNOWS IF THE MOON'S by e.e. cummings; ISABELLE by Ogden Nash; THE LITTLE GIRL AND THE WOLF, THE UNICORN IN THE GARDEN, THE FAIRLY INTELLIGENT FLY, THE MOTH AND THE STAR by James Thurber; A CHILD'S CHRISTMAS IN WALES by Dylan Thomas (6), December 23, 1969, presented by The Little Theater of the Deaf Company; MAX MORATH AT THE TURN OF THE CENTURY (20), December 30, 1969; SGANARELLE by Molière and UNDER MILK WOOD by Dylan Thomas (24), February 17, 1970, presented by the National Theater of the Deaf Company; PATCHETT AND TARSES STAGE A SPONTANEOUS DEMONSTRATION (18), March 21, 1970; THE CAGE (37), April 7, 1970, by Rick Cluchey, presented by the Barbwire Theater Company.

PRINCETON, N. J.

McCarter Theater

THE BIRTHDAY PARTY (7). By Harold Pinter. October 17, 1969. Director, Arthur Lithgow; scenery, Hunter Nesbitt Spence; lighting, F. Mitchell Dana; costumes, Martha Kelly. With James LaFerla, Robert Blackburn, Beth Dixon, Ruby Holbrook, Gordon Phillips.

PYGMALION (17). By George Bernard Shaw. October 24, 1969. Director, Brendan Burke; scenery, Hunter Nesbitt Spence; lighting, F. Mitchell Dana; costumes, Charles Blackburn. With Holly Villaire, John Lithgow, Arthur Lithgow, Richard Mathews.

OF MICE AND MEN (15). By John Steinbeck. November 14, 1969. Director, Robert Blackburn; scenery, John C. Schenck III; lighting, F. Mitchell Dana; costumes, Martha Kelly. With Richard Mathews, John Lithgow, Donegan Smith, Holly Villaire.

MUCH ADO ABOUT NOTHING (17). By William Shakespeare. December 12, 1969. Director, John Lithgow; scenery, John Lithgow; lighting, F. Mitchell Dana; costumes, Charles Blackburn. With John Braden, Brendan Burke, Robert Blackburn, Richard Mathews, Kathryn Walker, Holly Villaire.

THE FIREBUGS (8). By Max Frisch; translated by Mordecai Gorelik; epilogue translated by Michael Bullock. January 2, 1970. Director, Tom Brennan; scenery, Hunter Nesbitt Spence; lighting, F. Mitchell Dana; costumes, Ann Ward. With Richard Mathews, Alice White, Leila Cannon, Ray Aranha.

AH, WILDERNESS! (17). By Eugene O'Neill. January 30, 1970. Director, Robert Blackburn; scenery, Hunter Nesbitt Spence; lighting, F. Mitchell Dana; costumes, Martha Kelly. With John Braden, Leila Cannon, Tom Oliver, Richard Pilcher, Gordon Phillips.

THE WAY OF THE WORLD (11). By William Congreve. February 27, 1970. Director, John Lithgow; scenery, John Lithgow; lighting, F. Mitchell Dana; costumes, Charles Blackburn. With Kathryn Walker, Ruby Holbrook, John Braden, Robert Blackburn.

TROILUS AND CRESSIDA (13). By William Shakespeare. March 28, 1970. Directors, Arthur Lithgow and Tom Brennan; scenery, Hunter Nesbitt Spence; lighting, F. Mitchell Dana; costumes, Charles Blackburn. With Tom Oliver, Holly Villaire, Kathryn Walker, Brendan Burke, Ray Aranha.

PROVIDENCE, R. I.

The Trinity Square Repertory Company

THE OLD GLORY; ENDECOTT AND THE RED CROSS; MY KINSMAN, MAJOR MOLINEUX; BENITO CERENO (40). By Robert Lowell. September 30, 1969. Director, Adrian Hall; scenery, Eugene Lee; lighting, Roger Morgan; costumes, John Lehmeyer. With Martin Molson, James Gallery, George Martin, Richard Kavanaugh, William Cain, Anthony George, Ed Hall, Barbara Meek.

HOUSE OF BREATH, BLACK/WHITE (24). By William Goyen. November 4, 1969 (world premiere). Director, Adrian Hall; scenery, Eugene Lee; lighting, Roger Morgan; costumes, John Lehmeyer. With Marguerite H. Lenert, Barbara Meek, Ed Hall, Richard Kavanaugh, David C. Jones, Florence Bray.

WILSON IN THE PROMISE LAND (40). By Roland Van Zandt. December 9, 1969

(world premiere). Director, Adrian Hall; scenery, Eugene Lee; lighting, Roger Morgan; costumes, John Lehmeyer. With William Cain, Marguerite H. Lenert, Donald Somers, William Damkoehler.

THE SKIN OF OUR TEETH (40). By Thornton Wilder. January 20, 1970. Director, Adrian Hall; scenery, Eugene Lee; lighting, Roger Morgan; costumes, John Lehmeyer. With Pamela Payton-Wright, Marguerite H. Lenert, David C. Jones.

LOVECRAFT'S FOLLIES (40). By James Schevill. March 10, 1970 (world premiere). Director, Adrian Hall; scenery, Eugene Lee; lighting, Roger Morgan; costumes, John Lehmeyer. With James Eichelberger, William Cain, James Gallery, Elizabeth Ann Sachs and the Company.

ROCHESTER, MICH.

John Fernald Company: Meadow Brook Theater and Detroit Institute of Arts

THE AMERICAN DREAM by Edward Albee and BLACK COMEDY by Peter Shaffer (26). October 16, 1969. Directors, Anthony J. Stimac, John Fernald; scenery, Richard Davis; lighting, Bennet Averyt; costumes, Ross B. Young. With Barbara Bryne, Richard Curnock, Bonnie Hurren, Mikel Lambert, Elisabeth Orion, Jeremy Rowe, Toby Tompkins.

THE COCKTAIL PARTY (26). By T. S. Eliot. November 13, 1969. Director Malcolm Morrison; scenery, Richard Davis; lighting, Bennet Averyt; costumes, Ross B. Young. With Deborah Ardery, Marshall Borden, Raymond Clarke, Richard Curnock, Karin Fernald, Jenny Laird.

PYGMALION (26). By George Bernard Shaw. December 11, 1969. Director, Ellen Pollock; scenery, Richard Davis; lighting, Bennet Averyt; costumes, Ross B. Young. With Karin Fernald, Elisabeth Orion, Colin Pinney, Jeremy Rowe, Leslie Yeo.

HEDDA GABLER (26). By Henrik Ibsen. January 15, 1970. Director, John Fernald; scenery, Bennet Averyt; lighting, Pat Simmons; costumes, Ross B. Young. With Marshall Borden, Bonnie Hurren, Mikel Lambert, William Needles.

THE CASTLE (26). By Max Brod; from the novel by Franz Kafka; English adaptation, James Clark. February 12, 1970 (American premiere). Director, Milo Sperber; scenery, Richard Davis; lighting, Pat Simmons; costumes, Ross B. Young. With Richard Curnock, Pat Freni, Jenny Laird, William Needles, James Sutorius.

SUMMER AND SMOKE (26). By Tennessee Williams. March 12, 1970. Director, Terence Kilburn; scenery, Richard Davis; lighting, Bennet Averyt; costumes, Ross B. Young. With Barbara Caruso, Marshall Borden, Elisabeth Orion, Rhonda Rose, Toby Tompkins.

THE CHERRY ORCHARD (26). By Anton Chekhov; translated by J. P. Davis. April 9, 1970. Director, John Fernald; scenery and lighting, Richard Davis; costumes, Ross B. Young. With Jenny Laird, Marshall Borden, Bonnie Hurren, Janet McIntire, William Needles, K. C. Williams, Toby Tompkins.

AH, WILDERNESS! (26). By Eugene O'Neill. May 7, 1970. Director, Terence Kilburn; scenery, Richard Davis; lighting, Bennet Averyt; costumes, Veronica Gustaff. With Glynis Bell, Diana Bugas, Harry Ellerbe, Terence Kilburn, Dorothy Mallam, Jeffrey Winner.

ST. PAUL, MINN.

Minnesota Theater Company: Crawford Livingston Theater

THE ALCHEMIST (30). By Ben Jonson. April 11, 1970. Director, Mel Shapiro; scenery and costumes, John Jensen. With Richard Cottrell, Ron Glass, Allen Hamilton, Charles Keating, Michael Moriarty, Lisa Richards.

ARDELE (36). By Jean Anouilh; translated by Lucienne Hill. April 12, 1970. Director, Edward Payson Call; scenery, John Jensen; costumes, Carolyn Parker. With Paul Ballantyne, Helen Harrelson, James Lawless, Margaret Phillips.

SAN FRANCISCO

American Conservatory Theater (ACT): Geary Theater

OEDIPUS REX (24). By Sophocles; adapted by William Ball and Dennis Powers. March 21, 1970. Director, William Ball; scenery and costumes, Robert Fletcher. With Carol Mayo Jenkins, Ken Ruta, Ray Reinhardt, Paul Shenar.

SAINT JOAN (20). By George Bernard Shaw. March 31, 1970. Director, Edward Gilbert; scenery, Robert Fletcher; lighting, Jane Reisman; costumes, Walter Watson. With Jay Doyle, Philip Kerr, Ellis Rabb, Ray Reinhardt, Kitty Winn.

ROSENCRANTZ AND GUILDENSTERN ARE DEAD (7). By Tom Stoppard. April 13, 1970. Director, William Ball; scenery, John McLain; costumes, Robert Fletcher. With Philip Kerr, James Milton, Dennis Kennedy, Ray Reinhardt, Ken Ruta, Paul Shenar.

HADRIAN VII (7). By Peter Luke. May 12, 1970. Director, Allen Fletcher; scenery and costumes, Robert Fletcher; lighting, Ward Russell. With Peter Donat, Philip Kerr, Winifred Mann, William Paterson, G. Wood.

ACT: Marines' Memorial Theater

THE IMPORTANCE OF BEING EARNEST (29). By Oscar Wilde. March 7, 1970. Director, Jack O'Brien; scenery, Paul Staheli; lighting, Ward Russell; costumes, Alfred Lehman. With Peter Donat, Herbert Foster, Michael Learned, Angela Paton, Deborah Sussel.

SIX CHARACTERS IN SEARCH OF AN AUTHOR (14). By Luigi Pirandello; English adaptation by Paul Avila Mayer. March 17, 1970. Director, Mark Healy; scenery, Paul Staheli; lighting, Ward Russell; costumes, Walter Watson. With Peter Donat, Michael Learned, Fanny Lubritsky, William Paterson, Angela Paton.

THE BLOOD KNOT (28). By Athol Fugard. April 14, 1970. Director, Gilbert Moses;

scenery, Jackson DeGovia; lighting, Ward Russell; costumes, Regina Cate. With Gilbert Lewis, John Schuck.

LITTLE MALCOLM AND HIS STRUGGLE AGAINST THE EUNUCHS (16). By David Halliwell. April 23, 1970. Director, Nagle Jackson; scenery, Paul Staheli; lighting, Ward Russell; costumes, Liz Covey. With Martin Berman, Michael Cavanaugh, Herbert Foster, Robert Ground, Deborah Sussel.

THE ROSE TATTOO (2). By Tennessee Williams. May 26, 1970. Director, Louis Criss; scenery, Milton Duke; lighting, John McLain; costumes, Walter Watson. With Michael Learned, Ray Reinhardt, Tom V. V. Tammi, Ann Weldon, Kitty Winn.

Note: The ACT 1970 season will continue in repertory with *The Tempest* June 16, 1970 and *The Tavern* June 19, 1970.

SARASOTA, FLA.

Asolo Theater Festival: The State Theater Company

YOU CAN'T TAKE IT WITH YOU (30). By Moss Hart and George S. Kaufman. May 30, 1969. Director, Robert Strane; scenery and costumes, Holmes Easley; lighting, John Gowans. With Isa Thomas, Barbara Redmond, Eberle Thomas, Macon McCalman.

THE LARK (24). By Jean Anouilh; English

adaptation by Lillian Hellman. June 20, 1969. Director, Richard G. Fallon; scenery and costumes, Holmes Easley; lighting, John Gowans. With Sharon Spelman, Robert Strane, Bradford Wallace, Jay Bell.

THE HOSTAGE (18). By Brendan Behan. July 11, 1969. Director, Eberle Thomas; scenery, Holmes Easley; lighting, John Gowans; costumes, Mary McDonough. With Bradford Wallace, Isa Thomas, Carol Williard, C. David Colson.

UNCLE VANYA (13). By Anton Chekhov; English version by Eberle Thomas. August 1, 1969. Director, Richard D. Meyer; scenery and costumes, Holmes Easley; lighting, John Gowans. With Macon McCalman, Robert Britton, Carol Williard, Barbara Redmond.

BLITHE SPIRIT (26). By Noel Coward. February 19, 1970. Director, Robert Strane; scenery and costumes, Holmes Easley; lighting, John Gowans. With Sharon Spelman, Barbara Redmond, Isa Thomas, Eberle Thomas.

THE GLASS MENAGERIE (18). By Tennessee Williams. February 21, 1970. Director, Eberle Thomas; scenery, Holmes Easley; lighting, John Gowans; costumes, Catherine King. With Isa Thomas, Stuart Culpepper, Carol Williard, Patrick Egan.

MISALLIANCE (29). By George Bernard Shaw. February 27, 1970. Director, Bradford Wallace; scenery and costumes, Holmes Easley; lighting, John Gowans. With Macon McCalman, Barbara Redmond, Henry Strozier, William Pitts.

THE PHYSICISTS (17). By Friedrich Duerrenmatt; translated by James Kirkup. March 6, 1970. Director, Eberle Thomas; scenery, Holmes Easley; lighting, John Gowans. With Stuart Culpepper, Joyce Millman, Isa Thomas, Robert Strane, Bradford Wallace, Macon McCalman.

OH DAD, POOR DAD, MAMMA'S HUNG YOU IN THE CLOSET AND I'M FEELIN' SO SAD (23). By Arthur L. Kopit. April 10, 1970. Director, Peter Frisch; scenery, Holmes Easley; lighting, John Gowans; costumes, Catherine King. With Isa Thomas, William Pitts, Carol Williard, Henry Strozier.

DOCTOR FAUSTUS (21). By Eberle Thomas and Robert Strane; adapted from Christopher Marlowe's The Tragical History of Doctor Faustus. May 8, 1970 (world premiere). Director, Robert Strane; scenery and costumes, Holmes Easley; lighting, John Gowans. With Patrick Egan, Eberle Thomas, Sharon Spelman, David Mallon.

A FLEA IN HER EAR (28). By Georges Feydeau; translated by Barnett Shaw. May 29, 1970. Director, John Spelman; scenery and costumes, Holmes Easley; lighting, John Gowans. With Bradford Wallace, Sharon Spelman, Barbara Redmond, Patrick Egan, Eberle Thomas.

Note: Asolo's 1970 season will continue with *Life With Father* June 19, 1970, *All's Well That Ends Well* July 10, 1970 and Arthur Miller's *The Price* July 31, 1970.

SEATTLE

Seattle Repertory Theater: Center Playhouse

VOLPONE (30). By Ben Jonson. October 22, 1969. Director, Pirie MacDonald; scenery and costumes, William D. Roberts; lighting, Steven A. Maze. With Clayton Corzatte, Jana Hellmuth, Joseph Sommer.

THREE SISTERS (30). By Anton Chekhov; translated by Allen Fletcher. November 19, 1969. Director, Allen Fletcher; scenery and costumes, William D. Roberts; lighting, John McLain. With Jeanne Hepple, Kay Doubleday, Jacqueline Coslow, Theodore Sorel, Douglass Watson, Archie Smith.

ONCE IN A LIFETIME (37). By George S. Kaufman and Moss Hart. December 17, 1969. Director, Allen Fletcher; scenery and costumes, Dahl Delu; lighting, Steven A. Maze. With Theodore Sorel, Patricia Hamilton, Leslie Carlson, Marjorie Nelson, Earl Boen.

IN THE MATTER OF J. ROBERT OPPEN-

HEIMER (30). By Heinar Kipphardt; translated by Ruth Speir. January 21, 1970. Director, Allen Fletcher; scenery and costumes, Dahl Delu; lighting, Steven A. Maze. With Thomas Coley, Albert M. Ottenheimer, Gordon Gould.

THE LITTLE FOXES (30). By Lillian Hellman. February 18, 1970. Director, Byron Ringland; scenery and costumes, Dahl Delu; lighting, John McLain. With Eve Roberts, Robert Loper, Kay Doubleday, Ted D'Arms, Judith Long, Archie Smith.

THE COUNTRY WIFE (30). By William Wycherley. March 18, 1970. Director, Allen Fletcher; scenery and costumes, Dahl Delu; lighting, Mark S. Krause. With Theodore Sorel, Jacqueline Coslow, Leslie Carlson, Stanley Anderson, Clayton Corzatte, Patrick Gorman.

Seattle Repertory Theater: Off Center Theater

A DAY IN THE DEATH OF JOE EGG (18). By Peter Nichols. November 25, 1969. Director, Robert Loper; scenery, Peter Maslan; lighting, Mark S. Krause; costumes, Linda Martin. With Clayton Corzatte, Maureen Quin, Joan White, Melinda McLean.

SUMMERTREE (18). By Ron Cowen. January 27, 1970. Director, Clayton Corzatte; scenery, Peter Maslan; lighting, Mark S. Krause; costumes, Linda Martin. With Dirk

Niewoehner, Marjorie Nelson, Ted D'Arms, Pieternella Versloot.

THE INITIATION (18). By Nathan Teitel. February 24, 1970 (world premiere). Director, Allen Fletcher; scenery, Peter Maslan; lighting, Mark S. Krause, Bethe Ward; costumes, Linda Martin. With Carol Teitel, Jana Hellmuth, Richard Gere, Jacqueline Coslow, Theodore Sorel, Clayton Corzatte.

STRATFORD, CONN.

American Shakespeare Festival Theater

MUCH ADO ABOUT NOTHING (28). By William Shakespeare. June 18, 1969. Director, Peter Gill; scenery, Ed Wittstein; lighting, Thomas Skelton; costumes, Jane Greenwood. With Charles Cioffi, Patricia Elliott, Tony van Bridge, William Glover, Roberta Maxwell.

HAMLET (32). By William Shakespeare. June 18, 1969. Director, John Dexter; scenery, Karl Eigsti; lighting, Thomas Skelton; costumes, Jane Greenwood. With Brian Bedford, Maria Tucci, Tony van Bridge, Kate Reid, Morris Carnovsky.

HENRY V (23). By William Shakespeare. June 19, 1969. Director, Michael Kahn; associate director, Moni Yakim; scenery, Karl Eigsti; lighting, Thomas Skelton; costumes, Jeanne Button. With Len Cariou, Roberta Maxwell, Michael McGuire, Mary Doyle.

THREE SISTERS (22). By Anton Chekhov; translated by Moura Budberg. July 23, 1969. Director, Michael Kahn; scenery, William Ritman; lighting, Thomas Skelton; costumes, Jane Greenwood. With Marian Seldes, Maria Tucci, Kate Reid, Morris Carnovsky, Len Cariou, Roberta Maxwell, Michael McGuire, Brian Bedford.

STRATFORD, ONT. (CANADA)

Stratford Festival: Festival Theater

HAMLET (30). By William Shakespeare. June 9, 1969. Director, John Hirsch; designer, Sam Kirkpatrick; music, Louis Applebaum. With Kenneth Welsh, Anne Anglin, Leo Ciceri, Angela Wood.

THE ALCHEMIST (16). By Ben Jonson. June 10, 1969. Director, Jean Gascon; designer, James Hart Stearns; music, Gabriel Charpentier. With William Hutt, Powys Thomas, Bernard Behrens, Jane Casson.

MEASURE FOR MEASURE (32). By William Shakespeare. June 11, 1969. Director, David Giles; designer, Kenneth Mellor; music, Raymond Pannell. With Leo Ciceri, William Hutt, Karin Fernald, Neil Dainard.

TARTUFFE (28). By Molière; translated by Richard Wilbur. July 3, 1969. Director, Jean Gascon; designer, Robert Prevost; music, Gabriel Charpentier. With William Hutt, Donald Davis, Kenneth Welsh, Pat Galloway, Angela Wood.

Stratford Festival: Avon Theater

THE SATYRICON (22). Based on the writings of Petronius. Book and lyrics by Tom Hendry; music by Stanley Silverman. July 4, 1969. Director, John Hirsch; designer, Michael Annals; musical director, Lawrence Smith; choreographer, Marvyn Gordon; projections, Eoin Sprott. With members of the company.

HADRIAN VII (30). By Peter Luke; based on the novel and other works by Fr. Rolfe (Baron Corvo). August 5, 1969. Director, Jean Gascon; designer, Robert Fletcher. With Hume Cronyn, Margaret Braidwood.

SYRACUSE, N. Y.

Syracuse Repertory Theater

LYSISTRATA (12). By Aristophanes; adapted by John Lewin. March 5, 1970. Director, G. F. Reidenbaugh; scenery, Daniel S. Krempel; lighting, Donald Wiltshire; costumes, John E. Hirsch. With Jenny Ventriss, Ken Bowles, Shirley Ann Fenner, Joyce Krempel, Elsa Raven.

EVERYTHING IN THE GARDEN (11). By Edward Albee; adapted from the play by Giles Cooper. March 20, 1970. Director, Rex Henriot; scenery and lighting, Robert Lewis Smith; costumes, John E. Hirsch. With Jack Collard, Joyce Krempel, Patricia Sales, William Shust.

JUNO AND THE PAYCOCK (11). By Sean O'Casey. April 3, 1970. Director, G.F. Reidenbaugh; scenery and lighting, Leonard Dryansky; costumes, John E. Hirsch. With Helena Carroll, Sherman Lloyd, Dermot McNamara, Shirley Ann Fenner, Zoaunne LeRoy Henriot.

ALIVE AND WELL IN ARGENTINA (12). By Barry Pritchard. April 16, 1970 (world premiere). Director, Rex Henriot; scenery and lighting, Robert Lewis Smith; costumes, John E. Hirsch. With Zoaunne LeRoy Henriot, Adale O'Brien, Ed Rombola, Michael Stoddard, Frank Vohs, John Thomas Waite.

YOU KNOW I CAN'T HEAR YOU WHEN THE WATER'S RUNNING (11). By Robert Anderson. May 1, 1970. Director, Rex Henriot; scenery, Leonard Dryansky; lighting, Robert Walker; costumes, Marge Epstein. With Jack Collard, Jennifer Gordon, Zoaunne LeRoy Henriot, Gerard E. Moses, George Wyner.

VANCOUVER, B.C. (CANADA)

The Playhouse Theater Company: Main Stage

THE ROYAL HUNT OF THE SUN (22). By Peter Shaffer. October 10, 1969. Director, David Gardner; scenery and costumes, Brian H. Jackson; lighting, Rae Ackerman. With Alan Scarfe, Jack Creley, August Schellenberg.

THE SHOW-OFF (22). By George Kelly. November 7, 1969. Director, Eric House; scenery, Brian H. Jackson; lighting, Lynne Hyde; costumes, Margaret Ryan. With Rae Brown, Robert Casper, Pamela Hawthorn, Walter Marsh.

COLOURS IN THE DARK (8). By James Reaney. January 2, 1970. Director, Timothy Bond; scenery and slides, Brian H. Jackson; lighting, Lynne Hyde; costumes, Margaret Ryan; music, Alan Laing; musical director, Bob Murphy; choreographer, Norman Vesak. With Eric House, Daphne Goldrick, Walter Marsh, Barbara Tremain, Glenn MacDonald.

EVENTS WHILE GUARDING THE BOFORS GUN (22). By John McGrath. January 16, 1970 (North American premiere). Director, Tom Kerr; scenery and costumes, Cameron Porteous; lighting, Lynne Hyde. With Wilfrid Downing, Alan Scarfe, Peter Haworth, Eric Schneider.

VILLAGE WOOING by George Bernard Shaw and DEAR LIAR by Jerome Kilty, adapted from the correspondence of George Bernard Shaw and Mrs. Patrick Campbell (22). February 13, 1970. Director, David Gardner; scenery, Brian H. Jackson; lighting, Lynne Hyde; costumes, Margaret Ryan. With Anne Scarfe, Patricia Gage, Alan Scarfe.

TANGO (22). By Slawomir Mrozek; translated by Ralph Manheim and Teresa Dzeduszycka. March 13, 1970. Director, Peter Dearing; scenery, Brian H. Jackson; lighting, Lynne Hyde; costumes, Margaret Ryan; choreographer, Norbert Vesak. With Frank Maraden, Logan Houston, Patricia Gage, Pia Shandel, Ken Buhay.

The Playhouse Theater Company: Playhouse 2

STAIRCASE (17). By Charles Dyer. October 27, 1969. Director, Jack Creley; designer, Cameron Porteous; lighting, Lynne Hyde. With Ted Stidder, David Glyn-Jones.

CHE GUEVARA (17). By Mario Fratti. November 24, 1969. Director, David Gardner; scenery and costumes, Cameron Porteous; lighting, Lynne Hyde. With Alan Scarfe, Elizabeth Murphy, Ron Ulrich.

WASHINGTON, D.C.

Arena Stage: Guest Production

JACQUES BREL IS ALIVE AND WELL AND LIVING IN PARIS (40), June 17, 1969; THE CAGE (7) by Rick Cluchey, September 23, 1969, presented by the Barbwire Theater Company.

Arena Stage: Resident Company

EDITH STEIN (40). By Arthur Giron. October 23, 1969 (world premiere). Director, Zelda Fichandler; scenery, Robin Wagner; lighting, William Eggleston; costumes, Marjorie Slaiman. With Marketa Kimbrell, James Luisi, Ann Meacham.

YOU CAN'T TAKE IT WITH YOU (40). By Moss Hart and George S. Kaufman. December 4, 1969. Director, Alfred Ryder; scenery, Leo Kerz; lighting, William Eggleston; costumes, Marjorie Slaiman. With Grayce Grant, Phyllis Somerville, Helen Martin, Howard Witt, William Hansen.

THE CHERRY ORCHARD (40). By Anton Chekhov; translated by Stark Young. January 15, 1970. Director, Alfred Ryder; scenery and lighting, Leo Kerz; costumes, Marjorie Slaiman. With Carol Gustafson, Howard Witt, Robert Prosky, Grayce Grant, Gloria Maddox.

THE CHEMMY CIRCLE (35). By Georges Feydeau; translated and adapted by Suzanne Grossmann and Paxton Whitehead. March 4, 1970. Director, Alfred Ryder; scenery, Leo Kerz; lighting, William Eggleston; costumes, Linda Fisher. With Richard Bauer, Lynn Milgrim, Michael Lipton.

ENCHANTED NIGHT and THE POLICE (7). By Slawomir Mrozek; translated by Nicholas Bethell. April 7, 1970. Director, Norman Gevanthor; scenery, Hugh Lester; lighting, Vance Sorrells; costumes, Gwynne Clark. With Richard Bauer, Ned Beatty, Morris Engle, Gloria Maddox, Robert Prosky, Howard Witt.

DANCE OF DEATH (40). By August Strindberg; adapted by Paul Avila Mayer. April 16, 1970. Director, Alfred Ryder; scenery and lighting, Leo Kerz; costumes, Marjorie Slaiman. With Rip Torn, Viveca Lindfors, Mitchell Ryan, Julie Garfield.

NO PLACE TO BE SOMEBODY (40). By Charles Gordone. May 28, 1970. Director, Gilbert Moses; scenery and lighting, Leo Kerz; costumes, Marjorie Slaiman. With Chuck Daniel, Norma Donaldson, Richard Bauer, Robert Guillaume, Gloria Maddox.

Washington Theater Club

SPREAD EAGLE IV (77). By members of the Washington Theater Club Company; edited and selected by Herb Sufrin. May 29, 1969 (world premiere). Director, Davey Marlin-Jones; scenery, Susan Tuohy; lighting, John Wilson; costumes, James Parker; musical director, Harrison Fisher; choreographer, Darwin Knight; pianist, Alan Jemison. With Gisela Caldwell, Ralph Cosham, Christopher Allen, Bryan Clark, Georgia Engel, Ginger Gerlach, Ralph Strait.

THE MOTHS (84). By Raffi Arzoomanian. October 22, 1969 (world premiere). Director, Davey Marlin-Jones; scenery and costumes, James Parker; lighting, T.C. Behrens. With Cara Duff MacCormick, Richard Fancy, Maude Higgins, Camille Monte, Don Perkins, Leonard Yorr.

THE DECLINE AND FALL OF THE ENTIRE WORLD AS SEEN THROUGH THE EYES OF COLE PORTER (121). As conceived by Ben Bagley; words and music, Cole Porter. December 10, 1969. Director-choreographer, Darwin Knight; scenery and costumes, James Parker; lighting, William Eggleston, Jim Albert Hobbes; musical director, Salli Parker. With Susan Campbell, Diane Deckard, Delores St. Amand, Bob Spencer, Jim Weston.

THE WOLVES (35). By Robert Koesis. January 14, 1970 (world premiere). Director, Davey Marlin-Jones; scenery and costumes, James Parker; lighting, Joneal Joplin. With Bryan Clark, Robert Darnell, Sue Lawless, Anne Lynn, Marcia Wood.

ADVENTURES IN THE SKIN TRADE (35). By Dylan Thomas; adapted by Andrew Sinclair. February 18, 1970 (American premiere). Director, Robert Darnell; scenery, James Parker; lighting, Robert H. Leonard; costumes, Gail Singer. With members of the company.

SERENADING LOUIE (35). By Lanford Wilson. March 25, 1970 (world premiere). Director, Davey Marlin-Jones; scenery and costumes, James Parker; lighting, William Eggleston. With Robert Darnell, Anne Lynn, Jane Singer, Arlen Dean Snyder.

CONTINENTAL DIVIDE (35). By Oliver Hailey. April 29, 1970 (world premiere). Director, Davey Marlin-Jones; scenery, James Parker; lighting, William Eggleston; costumes, Carrie Curtis. With Anne Chodoff, Bryan Clark, Arlen Dean Snyder, Trinity Thompson.

Note: The balance of the 1970 spring-summer season will include *Exit The King* by Eugene Ionesco June 3 and *Before You Go* by Lawrence Holofcener July 8.

WINNIPEG, MANITOBA (CANADA)

Manitoba Theater Center: Main Stage

MARAT/SADE (6). By Peter Weiss; English version by Geoffrey Skelton; verse adaptation by Adrian Mitchell. January 26, 1970. Director, Edward Gilbert; scenery and costumes, Peter Wingate; lighting, Robert Reinholdt. With Robert Benson, Claude Bede, Ray Reinhardt, Anne Anglin, Neil Vipond, Stuart Howard.

YOU CAN'T TAKE IT WITH YOU (6). By Moss Hart and George S. Kaufman. March 9, 1970. Director, Louis Criss; scenery, Peter Wingate; lighting, Robert Reinholdt; costumes, Hilary Corbett. With Amelia Hall, Butterfly McQueen, Jerry Hardin, Eric House, Laurie Peters.

AFTER THE FALL (6). By Arthur Miller. April 13, 1970. Director, Kurt Reis; scenery, Joseph Cselenyi; lighting Robert Reinholdt; costumes, Hilary Corbett. With Jerry Hardin, Olive Deering, Katherine Justice, Dolores Sutton, Lou Polan, Gene Gross.

Manitoba Theater Center: The Warehouse Studio Theater

HAIL SCRAWDYKE (12). By David Halliwell. October 28, 1969. Director, Edward Gilbert; designer, Terry Shrive; lighting, Robert Reinholdt. With Briain Petchey, Tom Carew, Gary Files.

HARRY, NOON AND NIGHT (12). By Ronald Ribman. November 24, 1969. Director, Jerry Hardin; designer, Lawrence Schafer; lighting, Robert Reinholdt. With Robert Silverman, Gary Files, Ray Reinhardt, Neil Vipond, Helena Buschova.

MANDRAGOLA (12). By Niccolo Machiavelli. January 13, 1970. Director, Keith Turnbull; scenery and costumes, Tina Lipp; lighting, Robert Reinholdt. With Patrick Cullen, Tom Carew, Neil Vipond, Briain Petchey, Sylvia Shore.

THE INDIAN WANTS THE BRONX by Israel Horovitz and ESCURIAL by Michel de Ghelderode (12). February 10, 1970. Director, Jerry Hardin; scenery and costumes, Terry Shrive; lighting, Robert Reinholdt. With Tom Carson, Robert Silverman, Chuck Shamata, Briain Petchey, Thom Koutsoukos, Bill Jewell.

LA TURISTA (12). By Sam Shepard. March 17, 1970. Director, Keith Turnbull; designer, John Ferguson; lighting, Robert Reinholdt. With Anne Anglin, Robert Silverman, Jerry Franken.

THE SEASON IN LONDON

By John Spurling

Author of *Macrune's Guevara* and other playscripts and numerous articles
on the theater

LONDON HAS TWO national (and nationally subsidized) companies of
which it can be more or less proud, but it is not the National Theater at the
Old Vic nor the Royal Shakespeare Company at the Aldwych Theater, but
the 30-odd "commercial" or "West End" houses which still make up the bulk
of any London season. And, as it happened, the week in which I was invited to
write this article was generally recognised as Black Week of the West End.

Four new productions opened, each in its own way typifying a different in-
gredient in the West End's staple diet of straight plays: at the Duchess, Bruce
Stewart's *The Hallelujah Boy,* an earnest but ludicrous essay in social realism;
at the Apollo, *Girlfriend* by David Percival, an old fashioned marital comedy
with a fashionable twist of lemon in the form of homosexuality and drag; a
debilitating courtroom drama by Henry Cecil at the Duke of York's, called
A Woman Named Anne; and at the Strand, *Best of Friends,* a slickly sentimental Brooklyn family piece by James Elward, out of Eugene O'Neill, out of Ibsen. Within a week or two all but the Henry Cecil had bowed out.

Now, all these productions starred distinguished actors—Alan Dobie, Margaret Leighton, John Standing, Moira Lister, Nigel Patrick and Siobhan Mc-
Kenna—and the plays by David Percival and James Elward contained some
wit, but there was an unmistakable feeling that something had finally snapped,
that the West End theater as we know it was on the verge either of revolution
or extinction. With these lurid alternatives in mind it is worth examining some
of the more successful openings to see whether Black Week was merely unlucky or, in the manner of Greek tragedy, unlucky but also inevitable.

Early in July a production, first mounted at the Theater Royal, Bristol,
moved into the Queen's Theater in Shaftesbury Avenue. It was the first play
to reach London by Barry England, whose first novel had made a considerable
splash the year before. His play, *Conduct Unbecoming,* set in an officers' mess
in India in the palmy days of the British Raj, is an almost classic "Tale from
the Frontier," complete with questions of honor, dark psychological undertow,
class distinction and a liberal spicing of melodrama. Visually, it was a feast of
scarlet jackets, jodhpurs, boots and spurs. What made it so succesful, both
artistically and commercially? Chiefly, I think, that its author is a born story
teller. He is not particularly deep, his language is prosaic, even a bit puddingy
at times, but without hollow pretensions, without pandering to some market
consultant's idea of what an audience wants or will stand, he tells his racy story

in just the way he finds it needs to be told. And Val May's ensemble production compounded the author's virtues.

The same was true of Michael Blakemore's production of Brecht's *The Resistible Rise of Arturo Ui,* which moved from another provincial repertory theater, the Nottingham Playhouse, into the Saville at about the same time. This production contained two extra distinctions, in that it was probably the first wholly successful realization in the English theater of a play by Brecht, and that the name part was given a performance of tearing originality and power by Leonard Rossiter. At one blow the English audience was purged of its fear of Brecht's dramatic theory and political alignment, and a master of the playwright's art stood revealed. It was perhaps the most exciting event of the season.

There was a third production to place beside these two—David Storey's *The Contractor*—which although it began at the Royal Court transferred later to the tiny Fortune Theater and can therefore now be considered a West End experience. I did not myself admire David Storey's earlier plays, marred as I found them by the same pink-misty approach to fashionable working class values as earlier generations of playwrights adopted towards middle class values. This mist, however, obscures only the outer edges of *The Contractor,* which in the main depicts unemotionally and with delicate humor the raising and lowering of a marquee by a small gang of sympathetic misfits. The acting and direction served alike to bring out the play's qualities.

The success of these three productions could not have been chance. All three transferred from repertory theaters with permanent companies, and their most obvious virtues are those we have learned to expect from the subsidized sector of the theater; that is to say, they are plays which are true to themselves rather than to some pre-existing model of what a play should be, with fastidious direction and ensemble acting. To underline the point, we may set beside them the remarkable double-barreled marksmanship practised by the touring company, Prospect Theater, which brought Edinburgh Festival productions of Shakespeare's *Richard II* and Marlowe's *Edward II* first to the Mermaid and, in the New Year, to the Piccadilly. Much critical praise was lavished on Ian McKellen for his performances in both name parts, but it seemed to me that the audiences which flocked to both venues were hungry not so much for a rising star actor as for stalwart evenings of Shakespeare and Marlowe.

As further instances in the same direction, there were Pinero's farce *The Magistrate,* with Alastair Sim in the main part, which came up in the autumn from the Chichester Festival to the Cambridge and which was in every way a worthy contribution to the revival of Pinero's plays initiated by the National Theater a few years back; Robert Bolt's well-turned costume drama about Mary Queen of Scots and Elizabeth (a classic performance by Eileen Atkins), *Vivat! Vivat Regina!* which also opened at Chichester and which will surely be in London by next autumn; Rodney Ackland's adaptation of *The Old Ladies,* which moved from the Westminster to the Duchess and which I hope may be the prelude to a proper revival of the work of this unjustly neglected and unusually sensitive dramatist; and at the St. Martin's, boldly cheek-by-jowl with the everlasting *Mousetrap,* a clever murder play by Anthony Shaffer, *Sleuth,* which may very well itself have stumbled on the secret of eternal life. The best musicals were borrowed as usual from across the Atlantic: the charming *Dames at Sea,* at the Duchess, and Neil Simon's triumphant *Promises, Promises* at the Prince of Wales.

To sum up, I would submit that the West End theater is neither in danger of extinction nor revolution, but that it is busy reforming itself on lines suggested to it by the subsidized theater, while at the same time helping itself freely to the best ensemble productions from the provinces. The failures were nearly all those which had not observed that reform was in the air or those that applied the reforms too superficially. Among the former was Peter Shaffer's new play *The Battle of Shrivings,* at the Lyric, a would-be serious piece which declined to explore its difficult subject in any but the tritest terms and dragged even John Gielgud at its dusty heels; among the latter was the most desolate failure of all, a season of new plays at the Fortune directed by John Neville, the more lamentable in that it will no doubt discourage other nervous managements from embarking on similar schemes with better advice.

Although I have suggested that hope still springs green for the West End, we are not out of the wood. The three main subsidized theaters—the National, the Royal Shakespeare Company, and the Royal Court—have done much to reform the English theater in the last few years and this season has shown that their strength in the classics is undiminished. From Stratford the Royal Shakespeare Company brought *Troilus and Cressida, Much Ado About Nothing* and their glittering revival of Tourneur's *The Revenger's Tragedy* to the Aldwych. The National countered with another Jacobean masterpiece, Webster's *The White Devil,* masterfully done, Farquhar's coda to the Restoration, *The Beaux' Stratagem,* in a production which was first seen in Los Angeles and which crowned Maggie Smith *"la Reine Soleil"* of the English stage, and *The Merchant of Venice,* directed by Jonathan Miller and set by Julia Trevelyan Oman in the late 19th century (a much superior version of *The Forsyte Saga* in which the Laurence Olivier Shylock is the nouveau riche who couldn't get into the club and "Tell me where is fancy bred" becomes a duet for two Victorian ladies). We had been slightly prepared for this ravishing and melancholy *bombe-surprise* by the brief visit to the Old Vic, during the National's American tour, of Jonathan Miller's Nottingham production of *King Lear,* a most thoughtful and persuasive reading in Jacobean costume, with Michael Hordern in the name part.

Notable events at the Royal Court were Congreve's *The Double Dealer* and a production of Chekhov's *Uncle Vanya* by Anthony Page, which was as near-perfect an evening in the theater as I've ever spent, with Paul Scofield's Vanya a kind of walking heap of ash through which red flashes of the dying conflagration within still occasionally licked. Every one of these productions deserves an article to itself, every one proves that we have directors and actors fit to entertain the gods, but all except one have texts written in the 17th century or thereabouts.

Over the Royal Court's more modern offerings, apart from *The Contractor,* it is kinder to draw a curtain, in spite of the fact that this theater is expressly orientated (and subsidized) towards new drama. The National did a complete version over two nights of Shaw's five-part *Back to Methuselah,* which may have been intended to show that this is not quite such a silly work as it appears on the page, but signally failed to do so. Peter Nichols's *The National Health* was a sensible choice, a craftsmanlike, humorous, if unambitious addition to the slice-of-life genre, offering considerable opportunities to the National's splendid company of actors. But nothing at all could be said in favor of James Saunders's Christmas piece for children, *The Travails of Sancho Panza,* which was the National's only other 20th century excursion, apart from a short season at the Jeannetta Cochrane Theater, again aimed at children, which included a jolly production of *Waiting for Godot.*

The Royal Shakespeare Company was the only one of the three to make a serious attempt at matching the present to the past. Their revival of O'Casey's *The Silver Tassie* (an interesting comparison with *The National Health*) was unfortunately spoilt by a crude production, while Harold Pinter's double-bill *Silence* and *Landscape* turned out to be an unhappy mixture of mock-Beckett and Georgian poetry. Albee's *Tiny Alice* was a long, drawn-out disappointment after the promise of the first scene, and it was left to David Mercer's *After Haggerty* to redeem both his own earlier work with a new-found sense of humor and, in some small measure, the rest of the Royal Shakespeare's modern season. Alas, that the same author's contribution to the West End, *Flint,* which opened at the Criterion not long after the Aldwych play, and which hinged on a single elderly joke—"shocking" words and "shocking" sentiments in the mouth of a country parson (hold your sides, boys!)—should have put Mercer's maturity as an author once more in doubt.

But if the reformers of the West End are so obviously themselves now in need of fresh ideas, where will they get them? Perhaps from the London Theater's Third Estate, represented by a handful of fringe theaters whose stages are free of the tyranny of the proscenium arch, whose auditoria resist the blandishments of plush seats. Charles Marowitz's *The Open Space,* a basement in Tottenham Court Road, has shown its director's own collage versions of *Hamlet* and *Macbeth,* both most pleasant entertainments, as well as a double bill by Peter Barnes, author of *The Ruling Class,* pleasant again, in parts; but this theater has not yet penetrated beyond the pleasant, unless to the unpleasant as represented by two short pieces from the American writer Rosalyn Drexler. The uneasy impression the theater gives of mistaking a "modern" subject for a modern play was strengthened by its recent production of John Hopkins's *Find Your Way Home,* an embarrassing piece not because the golden-hearted tart at the center of its triangle was male, but because the treatment was that of the 19th century melodrama at its soggiest.

At the Lamda Theater, in Earl's Court, David Halliwell, whose *Little Malcolm* and *The Experiment* proved him one of the best young writers we have, bitterly disappointed his admirers with his new play *K.D. Dufford.* His short play *A Who's Who of Flapland,* done by Ed Berman's sturdy Ambiance Theater at the Green Banana Restaurant in Soho, however, was once again in his best manner. Indeed, everyone seems to be in his best manner at this tiny lunchtime *endroit,* which has also shone in Slawomir Mrozek's playlet *Striptease* and in two pieces by a new writer, Howard Brenton.

Earlier in the season London was visited by two notorious American companies. The Bread and Puppet Theater marched round Sloane Square and thence on to the stage of the Royal Court Theater, astonishing and delighting with its enormous puppets and its sophisticated version of the Theater of Naivete. This company's quality seemed all the more brightly burnished after the tawdry antics of The Living Theater, who arrived at the Roundhouse amid clarion calls of publicity, only to demonstrate that whatever gospel they had once had to preach had been long since swallowed up in self-advertisement. The Roundhouse itself, however, after protracted birth pangs, has definitely ceased to be a place for shunting locomotives and become perhaps the most spectacular theater in London—at Christmas time it even housed a small but expert circus, while Nicholas Giorgiadis's set for Arnold Wesker's new play *The Friends* demonstrated what spacious, cinemascopic freedom the place offers an imaginative designer, even though the play itself consisted of no more than further soundings of the shallows of its author's mind. The Roundhouse, which he himself brought into being as a theater, must await more spectacular incumbents.

Some such were in London briefly during November, but in obscurer surroundings, at the Artist's Place, opposite Euston Station, and seen by few. The nine or so members of the T.S.E. Company, from Argentina, whose exquisite performances are a mixture of music, light, slow balletic movement, Spanish and English speech and strangely beautiful costumes made by themselves, seemed almost to come from another planet and, seeming so, were perhaps the most welcome single event in the entire season. There is nothing the London theater needs more at this moment than news from another planet.

Highlights of the London Season

Selected and compiled by Ossia Trilling

OUTSTANDING PERFORMANCES

LEONARD ROSSITER as Arturo Ui in *The Resistible Rise of Arturo Ui*	PEGGY ASHCROFT as Beth in *Silence*	HELEN MIRREN as Cressida in *Troilus and Cressida*
DEREK JACOBI as Adam in *Back to Methuselah*	IAN MCKELLEN as Edward II in *Edward II*	T.P. MCKENNA as Fitzpatrick in *The Contractor*
SEBASTIAN SHAW as Adam Overdo in *Bartholomew Fair*	DEREK GODFREY as Don Quixote in *The Travails of Sancho Panza*	JOE MELIA as Solly Gold in *Enter Solly Gold*

JOHN GIELGUD
as Gideon in
The Battle of Shrivings

PAUL SCOFIELD
as Uncle Vanya in
Uncle Vanya

CARMEN MUNROE
as Orinthia in
The Apple Cart

MAGGIE SMITH
as Mrs. Sullen in
The Beaux' Strategem

DAVID WARNER
as Julian in
Tiny Alice

LAURENCE OLIVIER
as Shylock in
The Merchant of Venice

OUTSTANDING DIRECTORS

CLIFFORD WILLIAMS
Back to Methuselah

TREVOR NUNN
The Revenger's Tragedy

PETER HALL
The Battle of Shrivings

OUTSTANDING DESIGNERS

PIERO GHERADI
The White Devil

CHRISTOPHER MORLEY
The Revenger's Tragedy

JOHN BURY
Landscape and *Silence*

OUTSTANDING NEW BRITISH PLAYS

(D)—Playwright's London debut. Figure in parentheses is number of performances; plus sign (+) indicates play was still running on June 1, 1970

LANDSCAPE and SILENCE by Harold Pinter. One-acters about introspection and incommunicability. With Peggy Ashcroft, David Waller, Frances Cuka, Anthony Bate, Norman Rodway. (43)

THE NATIONAL HEALTH by Peter Nichols. Geriatric hospital ward as a symbol of the gate to the new life. With Gerald James, Robert Lang, Brian Oulton, Cleo Sylvestre, Jim Dale. (36+ in repertory)

THE CONTRACTOR by David Storey. Yorkshire author's third social-realist drama of class envy and intellectual incompatibility. With T. P. McKenna, Bill Owen. (88+)

INSIDEOUT by Frank Norman. The harmful effect of prison life by one who knows. With Ronald Lewis, Bill Owen, Nigel Hawthorne, Tom Chadbon, Terry Downs. (26)

ENEMY by Robin Maugham. We are all kin beneath the differing uniforms. With Dennis Waterman, Tony Selber, Neil Stacey. (61)

ENTER SOLLY GOLD by Bernard Kops. Jewish con-man's tricks make everybody happy. With Joe Melia, David Kossoff, David Lander. (50)

THE BATTLE OF SHRIVINGS by Peter Shaffer. Wise old altruist pits his wits against those of a hedonist rival. With John Gielgud, Wendy Hiller, Patrick Magee. (73)

AFTER HAGGERTY by David Mercer. Drama critic mauled by class consciousness and sexual inadequacy. With Frank Finlay, Billie Dixon, Leslie Sands. (19)

FLINT by David Mercer. Unorthodox clergyman's fight with Mother Church. With Michael Hordern, Vivien Merchant, Julia Foster. (29+)

FIND YOUR WAY HOME by John Hopkins. Powerful homosexual liaison breaks up a happy marriage. With Margaret Tyzack, Anthony Bate, Alexis Kanner, Brian Croucher. (16+)

THE FRIENDS by Arnold Wesker. Wesker's friends consider a new problem: death. With Ian Holm, Victor Henry, Susan Engel, John Bluthal. (14+)

ABELARD AND HELOISE by Ronald Miller. Inspired by Helen Waddell's novel about the famous love story. With Diana Rigg, Keith Michell. (15+)

LIMITED RUNS OF INTERESTING NEW BRITISH PLAYS

NO QUARTER and THE INTERVIEW by Barry Bermange. One-acters about the experience of waiting. With Felix Felton, Denys Hawthorne. (28)

THE STIFFKEY SCANDALS OF 1932 by David Wright. Musical documentary of the

de-frocked rector of Stiffkey. With Charles Lewsen, Terri Stevens. (11)

ETCETERA by Michael Armstrong. (D) Revue satirizing modern life. With the author. (6)

ANYTHING YOU SAY WILL BE TWISTED by Ken Campbell. Story of Jack Sheppard, 19th century juvenile delinquent. With Ian Sharp, Veronica Clifford. (29)

THE BORAGE PIGEON AFFAIR by James Saunders. Satire on local politics. With the Questors' Theater Company. (1)

SOMETIME NEVER by Roy Minton. Stage version of author's TV play *Stand By Your Screen*, about a drop-out son and his conformist father. With Tony Selby, Maureen Pryor, James Grout. (13)

ATTIC COMEDY by John Henry Jones. Strange events overtake the inmates of a city garret. With David Hannigan, Michael Harris. (12)

HIGHLY CONFIDENTIAL by Robert Tanitch. (D) The Cold War brings a Mata Hari out of retirement. With Hermione Gingold, William Kendall, Harold Kasket. (37)

THE APPOINTMENT by Malcolm Quantrill. The old versus the new Society. With the Questors' Theater Company. (1)

THE RUINED MAID by various authors. One-woman show. With Sally Miles. (12)

CAPTAIN OATES' LEFT SOCK by John Antrobus. Ambivalent group-therapy experiment in a mental home. With Michael Gough, Gwen Nelson. (1)

THE NIGHT I CHASED THE WOMEN WITH AN EEL by William Payne. (D) A happy marriage is wrecked by a banefully possessive mum. With Beatrix Lehmann, John Alderton, Pauline Collins. (38)

BLIM AT SCHOOL and POET OF THE ANEMONES by Peter Tegel. (D) Two skits on school life and adolescence. With Lynn Farleigh, Peter Blythe. (12)

CHANGE and WALTER by Jeff Nuttal. Two one-act plays, the first about an assault on man's irrational sensibilities, the second about individuality. With Roland Miller, Mark Long, Laura Gilbert. (3 each)

THE HUNGRY TIGERS by George Baker. Documentary on dictators. With the Candida Productions Company. (2)

OVER GARDENS OUT by Peter Gill. The influence of a town boy on a country lad. With Don Hawkins, James Hazeldine. (28)

REVENGE by Howard Brenton. (D) Tale of two twin avengers, by the 1969 John Whiting Award dramatist. With John Normington, Pamela Moiseiwitsch. (12)

CHILDREN'S DAY by Keith Waterhouse and Willis Hall. The strange effect of their off-stage children on two married couples. With Gerald Flood, Prunella Scales, Edward de Souza, Dilys Laye. (24)

K.D. DUFFORD HEARS K.D. DUFFORD ASK K.D. DUFFORD HOW K.D. DUFFORD'LL MAKE K.D. DUFFORD by David Halliwell. Introspective view of the Moors Murder Case. With Richard Huggett, Kenneth Farrington. (8)

DEAR JANET ROSENBERG, DEAR MR. KOONING by Stanley Eveling. The letters of a girl and a literary lion. With Susan Carpenter, Anthony Haygarth. (12)

AMALUK AND PABBLEBYE by Colin Shaw. (D) An adventure play. With the Caryl Jenner Productions Company. (22)

THE HILTON KEEN BLOW YOUR CHANCES TOP OF THE HEAP GOLDEN PERSONALITY SHOW OF THE WEEK, comprising *Group Juice* and *Little Mother* by the Wherehouse La Mama London. A living dialogue between the actors and the audience. With the Wherehouse La Mama London. (6)

THERE'LL BE SOME CHANGES MADE by Alun Owen. Sexual change and changeabout in a Hampstead flat. With Gemma Jones, Carmen Munroe, David Battley, Alan Lake. (20)

THIS SPACE IS MINE by Irene Coates. (D) A repressed housewife's neurosis after the death of her only child. With Anna Massey, Ronald Lewis, William Rushton, Angela Thorne. (31)

ALAS, POOR FOOL! by Neil Mundy and Nicolas Young. (D) Compilation of song, speech and mime, based on Shakespeare's fools. With Barbara Hickmitt, Christopher Scoular. (2)

MARIE ANTOINETTE MEETS ELEANOR RIGBY by Bettina Jonic. Multimedia show of protest throughout the ages. With the authoress. (4)

DON'T GAS THE BLACKS by Barry Reckord. West Indian author's drama about a black author who wrecks a white couple's home. With Mary Peach, Brian Smith, Rudolph Walker. (35)

MARTIN LUTHER KING by Ewan Hooper. Documentary about King's anti-racist policies. With Bari Jonson, Jumoke Debayo. (24)

THE PIT by Naftali Yavin. Trust probe explore games improvisations. With the Other Company. (30)

DOG ACCIDENT by James Saunders. Open-air street corner happening staged by Ed Berman's Inter-Action. With Geoff Hoyle, Jim Hiley. (14)

FAMINE by Thomas Murphy. Documentary of 1840s Irish potato famine. With Alan Dobie. (2)

REFLECTIONS by Peter Prowse, adapted from Gogol's Diary of a Madman. With Peter Prowse. (6)

SON OF MAN by Dennis Potter. Transfer of Leicester's Phoenix Theater's production of author's Freudian view of Jesus' passion. With Frank Finlay, Joseph O'Connor. (19)

A WHO'S WHO OF FLAPLAND by David Halliwell. Shifting identity across a cafe-table. With Joe Melia, Walter Hall. (29)

SPITHEAD by John Hale. A dramatization of the non-violent, successful mutiny at Spithead in 1797. With Ewan Hooper, Esmond Knight. (24)

ANTIGONE. Contemporary version of Sophocles' play, adapted by Peter Hulton. With the 1969 John Whiting Award Freehold Company. (20)

CANNIBAL CRACKERS by John Fraser. (D) Black comedy about an eccentric nonconformist's desperate remedies for his ills. With Michael Bates, Jessie Evans. (24)

SACK RACE, program of two one-act plays: Mrs. Peacock by Stanley Nelson (D) and Sit Quietly on the Baulk by Robert Metallus (D). About the innocence of old age, and a black-white confrontation. With Catherine Harding, Chrissie Shrimpton. (6)

THE FLIGHT OF THE PRINCESS by Jackson Lacey. Christmas adventure play in which the 18th century meets the 19th century. With the Caryl Jenner Productions Company. (22)

THE NEW ADVENTURES OF NOAH'S ARK by Bernard Goss. (D) Animals and family escape from the nursery, but are rescued for posterity. With David Harries, Janie Booth, Malcolm Ingram. (42)

EFFECTS, program comprising You Should Be Happy to Cry and Sapping by Alan Passes. (D) Both about man's loneliness. With the Southtown Theater Company. (4)

THE LOCAL STIGMATIC by Heathcote Williams. (D) The frontier between violence and sex overstepped. With Malcolm Kaye, Andrew Dallmeyer. (15)

MOBY DICK by Keith Johnstone. A pretext for improvisational creativity. With the Theater Machine Company. (6)

THE MARTIAN by Keith Johnstone. Improvisational program with science fiction theme. With the Theater Machine Company. (6)

THE BIG ROMANCE by Robert Thornton. (D) North country mother-and-son drama. With Brian Cox, Anna Carteret, Hilary Mason, Dudley Foster. (2)

THE HALLELUJAH BOY by Bruce Stewart. (D) The defeat of the Catholic worker-priests' experiment. With Alan Dobie, Mark Dignam, Susan Macready. (8)

HOW ARE YOUR HANDLES? by N. F. Simpson. Three short absurdist sketches. With Peter James, Sheila Balantyne. (12)

SING A RUDE SONG by Caryl Brahms and Ned Sherrin. The story of Marie Lloyd and her love affairs. With Barbara Windsor, Denis Quilley, Maurice Cribb. (36+)

GIRL FRIEND by David Percival. (D) Unisex comedy of two boys masquerading as an engaged couple. With John Standing, Margaret Leighton, Alan MacNaughton, Michael des Barries. (14)

TIMESNEEZE by David Campton. Roland Joffé's Young Vic production of children's play. With Jim Dale and the audience. (2)

HEADS and THE EDUCATION OF SKINNY SPEW by Howard Brenton. One-acters about a sexually dissatisfied female and a socially angry male. With Christopher Martin, Michael Feast, Frances Tomelty. (17)

CHRISTIE IN LOVE by Howard Brenton. The motives of the Rillington Place murderer analized. With Brian Croucher, William Hoyland, Stanley Labor. (12)

THE CORSICAN BROTHERS by John Bowen. Adapted with music from Dion Boucicault's melodrama and Alexandre Dumas' novel. With David Cook, Fiona Walker. (23)

WRAGGLE TAGGLE WINTER by Marged Smith. A drama of gypsies in conflict with officialdom. With the Caryl Jenner Productions Company. (21)

A CRUCIAL FICTION by Malcolm Quantrill. Horrible experiences of two voguish tramps. With Maxine Audley, John Rogan, Nigel Anthony. (11)

THIS FOREIGN FIELD by Alan Sillitoe. (D) A chance countryside encounter leads to violence and change. With the Contemporary Theater Group. (6)

HANS WHO WOULD NOT TIE HIS BOOTLACES by Marjorie Randle. (D) Comedy set in the Austrian tyrol. With the Caryl Jenner Productions Company. (7)

THE BIRD, THE MOUSE AND THE SAUSAGE by Wilfred Harvey. Adapted from the Grimm story of the same title. With the Caryl Jenner Productions Company. (7)

SLAG by David Hare. (D) Three young girl teachers yearn for emancipation. With Rosemary McHale, Marty Cruikshank, Diane Fletcher. (24)

AFTER MAGRITTE by Tom Stoppard. Surrealist send-up of the detective play. With Clive Barker, Prunella Scales, Josephine Tewson. (12)

HISTORY OF A POOR OLD MAN by John Grillo. Part of triple bill Laughs, Etc. (see "Some American Plays Produced in London").

TYPPI and THE NORMAL WOMAN by David Mowat. One-act studies of misleading first impressions. With Michael Mould, Hilary Westlake. (12)

ME TARZAN, YOU JANE by Midge MacKenzie. (D) Mixed-media study of woman's liberation, devised by the author. With Sheila Allen, Deena Martin. (18)

GOLDBERG AND SOLOMON by Michael Sullivan. Kosher version of Gilbert and Sullivan. With Roy Cowen, Iain Kerr. (24)

THE GUNNER'S DAUGHTER by Philip Martin. A man's impotent frustrations. With Kenneth Coley. (12)

THE SPORT OF MY MAD MOTHER by Ann Jellicoe. Newly adapted by Pamela Brighton from its original Teddy-boy to a Skinhead background. With Stanley Labor, Margaret Brady. (10)

PRIVACY, program comprising It Covers the World by David Kennard (D), Moves by Jeremy Taylor (D) and Mrs. Gladys Moxon by Simon Brett (D) (also see below). Three mixed-media plays tackling social problems. With Simon Brett, Bruce Alexander. (first two, 6; third, 16)

YOU'RE FREE by Henry Livings. Lancashire couple win the pools and settle in France. With Paola Dionisotti, Sam Kelly, the Operating Theater. (14)

STRIP JACK NAKED by Christopher Wilkinson. (D) Surrealist nightmare in which authority devours the anti-hero. With the Sheffield Playhouse Company. (1)

WHAT A MOUTH! (The Lass Wi' the Muckle Mou') by Alexander Reid. (D) London premiere of Scottish author's internationally famed comedy. With David Ashton, Harry Walker, Anne Kristen. (17+)

THE FLOWERS SHALL HAVE A NEW MASTER by Gregory Marshall. (D) Play of conflict and comedy about a small country fending off a would-be conqueror. With the Caryl Jenner Productions Company. (24)

MUCK FROM THREE ANGELS by David Halliwell. Three different viewpoints of the same situation. With Walter Hall. (12)

THE LOW MOAN SPECTACULAR by The Low Moan Spectacular. (D) A mocking contemporary revue. With the authors. (6)

MRS. GLADYS MOXON by Simon Brett. (D) A one-man show revealing the public and private life of a disc-jockey. With the author. (16)

AC/DC by Heathcote Williams. Technology and the man. With Pat Hartley, Ian Hogg, Robert Lloyd, Patricia Quinn, Henry Woolf. (14+)

POPULAR ATTRACTIONS

THERE'S A GIRL IN MY SOUP by Terence Frisby. London's longest running comedy hit. New cast includes Peter Byrne, Vivienne Ball. (1550+)

THE TWO GENTLEMEN OF VERONA by William Shakespeare. Open Air Theater revival by Richard Digby Day. With Bernard Bresslaw, James Lawrenson. (58)

TROILUS AND CRESSIDA by William Shakespeare. Transfer of John Barton's novel Stratford production. With Helen Mirren, Michael Williams, David Waller, Alan Howard, Norman Rodway. (59 in repertory)

THE MAROWITZ HAMLET. Charles Marowitz's collage of Shakespeare's tragedy. With Nikolas Simmonds, Thelma Holt, Natasha Pyne. (28)

THE YOUNG CHURCHILL devised by David Aukin, John Gilbert, Robin Midgley. Staged recital from Churchill's writings. With Clive Swift, John Robinson. (16)

THE MERCHANT OF VENICE by William Shakespeare. Open Air Theater revival by Richard Digby Day. With William Russell, Perlita Neilson. (50)

CONDUCT UNBECOMING by Barry England. A subalterns' court martial in post-Mutiny British India reveals some painful truths. With Jeremy Clyde, Paul Jones, Maxine Audley. (379+)

THE DOUBLE DEALER by William Congreve. William Gaskill's spanking Royal Court revival. With Judy Parfitt, John Castle. (37)

ON A FOGGY DAY by John Kerr. A dead man's past comes back to haunt his widow and intimates. With Siobhan McKenna, Margaret Lockwood, Kenneth Connor. (35)

MUCH ADO ABOUT NOTHING by William Shakespeare. Transfer of Trevor Nunn's appealing Stratford production. With Janet Suzman, Alan Howard, Helen Mirren, Sebastian Shaw. (39 in repertory)

BACK TO METHUSELAH, Parts 1 & 2, by George Bernard Shaw. Revival of Shavian fantasy of the shape of things to come in two sessions. With Derek Jacobi, Louise Purnell, Judy Wilson, Gerald Jones, Ronald Pickup, Charles Kay. (18 each in repertory). Revived as a single session. (4 in repertory)

SAVED and NARROW ROAD TO THE DEEP NORTH by Edward Bond. Revival of two plays for a pre-European prize winning tour. With Kenneth Cranham, Patricia Franklin, Peter Needham, Malcolm Tierney, Gillian Martell, Susan Williamson. (6 each)

THE CRUNCH by Basil Dawson and Felicity Douglas. Tribulations of a conscientious father and schoolmaster. With Andrew Cruickshank, Michael Gwynn, Barbara Lott. (138)

THE SILVER TASSIE by Sean O'Casey.

First London revival of O'Casey's anti-war symbolical drama since 1929. With Patience Collier, Frances Cuka, David Waller, Helen Mirren, Bruce Myers. (25 in repertory)

SO WHAT ABOUT LOVE? by Leonard Webb. (D) How a divorced school teacher satisfies her social and sexual appetites. With Sheila Hancock, Peter Blythe. (222)

THE MAGISTRATE by Arthur Wing Pinero. Transfer of John Clement's Chichester Festival production. With Alistair Sim, Patricia Routledge, Michael Aldridge, Robert Coote, Christopher Guinee, Renée Asherson. (257+)

MONSIEUR ARTAUD by Michael Almaz. Israeli-born author's documentary of Artaud's life and work. With Tony Mathews, Sarah Golding. (28)

RICHARD II by William Shakespeare, and EDWARD II by Christopher Marlowe. Transfer of Prospect Productions' Edinburgh Festival hits. With Ian McKellen, Robert Eddison. (43, 47 in repertory)

SHE'S DONE IT AGAIN! by Michael Pertwee. The grotesque confusions of a well-meaning vicar. With Brian Rix, Margaret Nolan. (247)

HADRIAN VII by Peter Luke. Long-running London smash hit, a 1968-69 Best Plays choice. With Douglas Rain (later Paul Daneman). (882+)

BIRDS ON THE WING by Peter Yeldham. The exciting comings and goings of two confidence tricksters. With Bruce Forsyth, June Barry, Julia Lockwood. (94)

THE BANDWAGON by Terence Frisby. What happens when a moronic girl unexpectedly expects quintuplets. With Denise Coffey, Peggy Mount, Ronald Radd, Toni Palmer. (103)

BARTHOLOMEW FAIR by Ben Jonson. Transfer of Terry Hands' Stratford "Lower-East-Side" production of rarely performed classic. With Willoughby Goddard, Patience Collier, Sebastian Shaw, Norman Rodway, Alan Howard. (21 in repertory)

THE OLD LADIES by Rodney Ackland, from the novel by Hugh Walpole. Revival of 1930's tragedy of three elderly recluses. With Joyce Carey, Joan Miller, Flora Robson. (100)

THE LIONEL TOUCH by George Hulme. (D) The unscrupulous progress of a debonair

20th century rake. With Rex Harrison, Joyce Redman. (93)

THE WHITE DEVIL by John Webster. Frank Dunlop's sybaritically eye-catching production of the Jacobean horror-comic. With Geraldine McEwan, Edward Woodward, Derek Godfrey, John Moffatt, Jane Wenham. (39 in repertory)

PHIL THE FLUTER by Beverley Cross and Donal Giltinan. Musical life story of Irish composer Percy French. With Mark Wynter, Stanley Baxter. (123)

IT'S A TWO FOOT SIX INCHES ABOVE THE GROUND WORLD by Kevin Laffan. (D) Transfer from Bristol Old Vic of Irish-born author's farce about Roman Catholic attitudes to family planning. With Prunella Scales, Christopher Hancock, Stephen Moore. (124)

THE REVENGER'S TRAGEDY by Cyril Tourneur. Transfer of Trevor Nunn's colorful Stratford hit of 1966. With Ian Richardson, Alan Howard, Patience Collier. (31 in repertory)

HIS, HERS AND THEIRS by Hugh and Margaret Williams. Voguish multiple-birth comedy. With Gladys Cooper, Hugh Williams, Faith Brook (later Roland Culver). (62)

LEONARDO'S LAST SUPPER and NOONDAY DEMONS by Peter Barnes. Surrealist one-acters, set in a charnel house and a dungheap, examine the sanctity of life. With Joe Melia, David Neal, Anthony Jacobs. (44)

OH WHAT A LOVELY WAR, revival of Joan Littlewood's concert party satire. With Brian Murphy. (7)

THE TRAVAILS OF SANCHO PANZA by James Saunders. Lively dramatization of episodes from Cervantes's Don Quixote. With Colin Blakely, Derek Godfrey, Roy Kinnear. (30)

THE OWL AND THE PUSSYCAT WENT TO SEE by David Wood and Sheila Ruskin. Dramatization of Lear's poem. With Lionel Morton, Carole-Ann Ford (43)

TREASURE ISLAND by Robert Louis Stevenson. Revival of Ron Pember's annual production. With Peter Duncan, Percy Herbert. (52)

THE THREE MUSKETEERS RIDE AGAIN! by The Alberts. Surrealist version of the Alexandre Dumas story. With the authors,

Rachel Roberts, Bruce Lacey, Valentine Dyall. (28)

THE ROUGH AND READY LOT by Alun Owen. Revival of verse tragedy about a conflict of loyalties in a South American Republic. With Glyn Houston, Neil McCarthy, Jim Norton. (24)

THREE MONTHS GONE by Donald Howarth. The third play about Anna Bowers and her dreams of motherhood. With Jill Bennett, Diana Dors, Alan Lake, Richard O'Callaghan. (124+)

THREE by George Bernard Shaw. Triple bill comprising How He Lied to her Husband, Village Wooing, and Press Cuttings. With Robert Flemyng, Michael Denison, June Barry, Dulcie Gray, Clive Francis. (64)

COME AS YOU ARE! by John Mortimer. Quartet of one-acters (Mill Hill, Bermondsey, Gloucester Road, Marble Arch) about selfish suburban and middle class attitudes. With Glynis Johns, Denholm Elliott, Joss Ackland, Pauline Collins. (142+)

THE ALCHEMIST by Ben Jonson. Stuart Burge's Nottingham production at the National Theater. With David Dodimead. (3 in repertory)

KING LEAR by William Shakespeare. Jonathan Miller's Nottingham production at the National Theater. With Michael Hordern, Penelope Wilton. (5 in repertory)

SLEUTH by Anthony Shaffer. (D) A famous author of murder mysteries is almost hoist with his own petard. With Anthony Quayle, Keith Baxter. (123+)

A WOMAN NAMED ANNE by Henry Cecil. Legal lights disentangle a web of lies in a divorce case. With Moira Lister, Hugh Manning, William Mervyn. (116+)

THE APPLE CART by George Bernard Shaw. Sparkling revival of Shaw's prophetic political extravaganza. With John Neville, Maurice Denham, Carmen Munroe. (50)

THE HAPPY APPLE by Jack Pulman. A median-type moronic secretary solves an adman corporation's money problems. With Pauline Collins, Paul Rogers. (93+)

WHO KILLED SANTA CLAUS? by Terence Feely. Suspenseful Yuletide whodunit. With Honor Blackman, Maurice Kaufmann, Frank Wylie. (67+)

ERB by Trevor Peacock. Transfer from Manchester's Theater 69 of a musical of W. Pett Ridge's novel of a 19th century railroad labor organizer. With Bridget Turner, Deborah Grant, the author. (38)

THE BEAUX' STRATAGEM by Georges Farquhar. William Gaskill's stylish National Theater revival. With Maggie Smith, Robert Stephens, Ronald Pickup, Sheila Reid. (16+ in repertory)

AT THE PALACE by Barry Cryer and Dick Vosburgh. A tailor-made revue for Britain's No. 1 female impersonator. With Danny La Rue, Roy Hudd, Jackie Sands, Toni Palmer. (60+)

WIDOWERS' HOUSES by George Bernard Shaw. Transfer of Nottingham Playhouse's 1969 hit. With Anthony Newlands, Frank Middlemass, Nicola Pagett, Robin Ellis, Larry Noble. (34)

UNDER MILK WOOD by Dylan Thomas. New production of the Welsh poet's famous radio play. With Philip Mador, Clive Merrison, David Jason, Windsor Davies, Ruth Madoc, Jennifer Hill. (40)

HENRY IV, Parts 1 & 2 by William Shakespeare. Ron Pember's new Mermaid productions. With Bernard Miles, Hywel Bennett. (20+ and 22+ in repertory)

THE MERCHANT OF VENICE by William Shakespeare. Jonathan Miller's National Theater production set in 19th century Venice. With Laurence Olivier, Joan Plowright, Jim Dale. (13+ in repertory)

POOR HORACE by William Fairchild. (D) Clash of loyalties at the Royal Naval College, Dartmouth, in the 1930s. With John Barron, John Woodvine, Ian Pigot. (24+)

SOME FOREIGN PLAYS PRODUCED IN LONDON

THE RESISTIBLE RISE OF ARTURO UI by Bertolt Brecht. With Leonard Rossiter. (148)

THE DEATH AND RESURRECTION OF MR. ROCHE by Thomas Kilroy. With Joe Lynch, Jim Norton, Desmond Perry, Dermot Tuohy. (23)

WOYZECK adapted from Georg Büchner. With La Mama Troupe Plexus II. (6)

METAMORPHOSIS and THE PENAL COLONY by Franz Kafka. Double bill adapted by Steven Berkoff. With the adapter. (18)

THE UNDERGROUND LOVERS by Jean Tardieu. With Annie Ellis, Paddy O'Hagan, Ben Bazell, Vanda Laurence. (12)

THREE PLAYS FOR FUN AND LAUGHTER, program comprising It's Incredible, Mr. B. and Stillwater, after Georges Courteline. With Julia Blalock, Brian Ayres. (12)

A KIND OF NEW WORLD and FOUR DIMENSIONAL ME by Bolivar le Franc. (D) World premiere of Jamaican's plays about a West Indian expatriate and an ailing saxophonist. With Rudolf Walker, Chris Bidmead. (7 each)

LOVERS, program comprising Winners and Losers by Brian Friel. London premiere of 1968-69 Best Play. With Joe Lynch, Fidelma Murphy, Eamon Morrissey, Anna Manahan. (27)

APOCALYPSIS CUM FIGURIS, a collage of the Book of Revelation; THE BROTHERS KARAMAZOV after Feodor Dostoevsky and THE CONSTANT PRINCE after Calderon de la Barca, by Jerzy Grotowski. With Grotowski's Polish Laboratory Theater Company. (10)

THE SLAPSTICK ANGELS (Tortinfaccia O Scarpe Come Ali) by Alberto Perrini. With Ursula Jones, Clive Elliott, Sarah Long. (8)

RABELAIS, Jean-Louis Barrault's dramatization of François Rabelais' five books. With the Renaud-Barrault Company. (14)

L'AMANTE ANGLAISE by Marguerite Duras. Visiting French production. With Madeleine Renaud, Michael Lonsdale, Jean Servais. (6)

OH! LES BEAUX JOURS by Samuel Beckett. Visiting French production. With Madeleine Renaud. (5)

THE BACCHAE by Euripides. With the Roy Hart Speakers from South Africa. (1)

STRIP-TEASE by Slawomir Mrozek. With Jack Shepherd, David Leland. (16)

DRACULA by Alfredo Rodriguez Arias; GODDESS by Javier Arroyuelo and AVENTURAS by Alfredo Rodriguez Arias. With the T.S.E. Company. (9,9,2)

META by Photis Constantinidis. With the author, Corin Redgrave. (6)

PLAY ON LOVE, adapted by Ruth Goetz and Burt Howard from Françoise Dorin's *Comme au Théâtre*. With Dorothy Tutin, Dinsdale Landen, Lana Morris, Patrick Cargill. (28)

OPIUM based on Jean Cocteau's *Journal of a Cure*, adapted by Roc Brynner. With the adapter. (20)

THE BLACKS by Jean Genet. Transfer of the Oxford Playhouse's all-black production. With Carmen Munroe, Jasen Rosen. (20)

THE TOWER by Peter Weiss. Frederick Proud's adaptation of a radio play about the return of an escapist to his metaphysical prison. With Paul Gregory, Peter May. (18)

UNCLE VANYA by Anton Chekhov, newly adapted by Christopher Hampton. With Paul Scofield, Colin Blakely, Anna Calder-Marshall, Gwen Ffrangçon-Davies. (45)

THE CHEATS OF SCAPIN by Molière. Young Vic's version of *Les Fourberies de Scapin*. With Jim Dale, Hugh Armstrong, Jane Lapotaire. (4)

THE HUMAN VOICE by Jean Cocteau. With Rosalinde Fuller. (12)

DOM JUAN by Molière. Visiting French production. With André Oumansky, Guy Parigot. (4)

BECKETT 3, program comprising *Come and Go*, *Cascando* and *Play* by Samuel Beckett. With Gillian Martell, Susan Williamson, Stanley Lebor. (18)

MEDEA by Euripides. New translation by David Thompson. With Katherine Blake, Ewan Hooper, Denys Hawthorne, Freda Dowie. (24)

LUX IN TENEBRIS by Bertolt Brecht. With Aleksander Browne, Genine Graham, James Garratt, Richard Huggett. (12)

MR. ARRABAL, program comprising *The Solemn Communion* and *Orison* by Fernando Arrabal. With Jean Holmes, Howard Southern, Clive Merrison, Audrey Murray. (11)

MEANWHILE, BACK IN SPARTA . . . . . . by Manthos Crispis. (D) Anti-regime comedy unperformed in author's native Greece. With Sean Lynch, Carl Davies. (18)

UBU, compressed from Alfred Jarry's *Ubu* plays and directed by Andrei Serban, together with his collage of ARDEN OF FAVERSHAM. With the Cafe La Mama Company. (8)

SOME AMERICAN PLAYS PRODUCED IN LONDON

THE LIVING THEATER COMPANY in a repertory of *Frankenstein, Mysteries, Paradise Now* and *Antigone*. (24)

MAN OF LA MANCHA by Dale Wasserman, Mitch Leigh and Joe Darion. Revival with Richard Kiley, Ruth Silvestre. (118)

THE BREAD AND PUPPET THEATER in a repertory of *Cry of the People for Meat*, *Theater of War*, and *Blue Raven Beauty*. (17)

THE LAST CHANCE SALOON by Andy Robinson. With La Mama Troupe Plexus II. (6)

AS DOROTHY PARKER ONCE SAID, Leslie Lawson's anthology of Miss Parker's writings. With Libby Morris, David Ellen. (28)

THE OTHER HOUSE by Henry James, adapted by Basil Ashmore and Bernard Miles. With Vilma Hollingbery, Ronald Allen. (29)

USA SEASON, comprising *The Body Builders* and *Now There's Just the Three of Us* by Michael Weller; *Rats* and *The Indian Wants*

The Bronx by Israel Horovitz; *Birdbath* and *Halloween* by Leonard Melfi; and *Package*, plays by Jean-Claude van Itallie, Megan Terry, Maria Irene Fornes. With Peter Marinker, Bob Sherman, Sheila Scott-Wilkinson, Liza Ross. (28)

DAMES AT SEA by George Haimsohn and Robin Miller. With Joyce Blair, Rita Burton, Sheila White, Kevin Scott. (117)

THE SPOILS OF POYNTON by Robert Manson Myers. World premiere of adaptation of Henry James' novel. With Josephine Wilson. (12)

PAPP by Kenneth Cameron. With Alan MacNaughton, Sylvia Coleridge, Al Mancini, Richard Pearson. (24)

PLAY IT AGAIN, SAM by Woody Allen. With Dudley Moore, Bill Kerr. (301+)

PYJAMA TOPS by Mawby Green and Ed Feilbert. With Julia Goodman, Bob Grant. (290+)

PROMISES, PROMISES by Neil Simon, Burt

Bacharach and Hal David. With Anthony Roberts, Kelly Britt, Jack Kruschen. (277+)

MY LITTLE BOY . . . . . MY BIG GIRL by Naomi and David Robison. With Eric Porter, Rowena Cooper, Robert Swann. (45)

ANYTHING GOES by Guy Bolton, P.G. Wodehouse, Howard Lindsay, Russel Crouse and Cole Porter. With Marian Montgomery, James Kenny, Michael Segal. (22)

YOU'RE A GOOD MAN CHARLIE BROWN by Clark Gesner. With Debbie Bowen, Neil Fitzwilliam. (80)

STIMULATION by Leonard Melfi. With Margaret Nolan, Lawrence Trimble. (17)

I'VE SEEN YOU CUT LEMONS by Ted Allen Herman. With Robert Hardy, Diane Cilento. (19)

BAD BAD JO JO by James Leo Herlihy. With Harold Innocent, Lawrence Trimble. (12)

TINY ALICE by Edward Albee. With Irene Worth, David Warner, Richard Pearson. (34)

THE FROG, THE PRINCESS AND THE WITCH by Margery Evernden. With the Caryl Jenner Productions Company. (20)

QUOTE! by Robert Rockman. With the Bard Theater of Drama and Dance. (13)

HOT BUTTERED ROLL and THE INVESTIGATION by Rosalyn Drexler. With Mike Pratt, Al Mancini. (20)

LITTLE BOY by Leo Heaps. (D) World premiere of Hiroshima drama. With George Margo, Vanda Godsell, Pamela Farbrother. (18)

THE SQUARE ROOT OF WONDERFUL by Carson McCullers. With Georgine Anderson, Ronald Lewis, Pat Nye. (23)

WHY HANNAH'S SKIRT WON'T STAY DOWN and THE WHITE WHORE AND THE BIT PLAYER by Tom Eyen. With Nicolette McKenzie, David Blagden, Paddy Frost. (15)

KEEP TIGHTLY CLOSED IN A COOL DRY PLACE by Megan Terry. With Davis Hall, Roger Hendricks Simon, Stephen Barker. (8)

RED CROSS by Sam Shepard. With the New York Workshop Company. (10)

LAUGHS, ETC. Triple bill comprising *The Old Jew* by Murray Schisgal, *Laughs, etc.* by James Leo Herlihy and the English play *History of a Poor Old Man* by John Grillo. With John Levitt, John Normington, Marcella Markham. (11)

CAROL CHANNING, musical frappé. With Carol Channing. (44+)

THE FANTASTICKS by Tom Jones and Harvey Schmidt. With David Bauer, Clyde Pollitt, David Suchet. (23)

A RAT'S MASS by Adrienne Kennedy and CINQUE by Leonard Melfi. With the Cafe La Mama Company. (7)

ISABEL'S A JEZEBEL by Galt MacDermot. World premiere of *Hair* author's new musical about man's sexual and social frustrations. With the Gate Theater Company. (9+)

I NEVER SANG FOR MY FATHER by Robert Anderson. With Raymond Massey, Catherine Lacey, George Baker, Dorothy Bromiley. (5+)

THE SEASON ELSEWHERE
IN EUROPE

By Ossia Trilling

EACH YEAR WITH unfailing regularity the theater in Germany makes first claim on the foreign critic's attention on account of its unorthodox productions and the many revolutionary changes and theatrical scandals from which it seems unable to free itself. The moment Heinz Lietzau of the Hamburg State Theater had established himself in his new home, with a series of startingly original productions both by himself (Arthur Kopit's *Indians*) and by guest directors (e.g. Fritz Kortner, who staged an inspiritingly dramatic version of Goethe's *Clavigo*), word went around that he was soon to replace Boleslaw Barlog as head of the Berlin Schiller, the scene of his earliest successes. Even Karl Heinz Stroux was tipped for retirement just as he had unveiled the new premises of his City Theater in Dusseldorf, Europe's most modern and best equipped, and in some eyes most inelegant, new playhouse. The imminent departure of the grand old man of Stuttgart, Walter Erich Schaefer, under whose inspired guidance the Wurttemberg State Theaters, opera, ballet and drama, had reached their highest peak of popularity and international repute, was clouded by dissent over his successor, Hans Peter Doll, under whom Peter Palitzsch refused to serve. On the other hand, Palitzsch's own candidature for the management of Dusseldorf, as Stroux's successor, was turned down by the ruling board, which preferred a nonentity to a pupil of Brecht, no matter how gifted.

In Frankfurt, mediocrity reigned after Harry Bickwitz's departure. Under Ulrich Ehrfurt a dispute boiled up when the artistic staff rebelled over his refusal to give them a share in artistic control. The literary department was replaced in its entirety by a new team of advisers headed by Gunter Grass, no proved expert in this field, despite his spate of original dramas. Another newcomer was Heinar Kipphardt in the Munich Kammerspiele, who had last performed the literary stint in East Berlin many years before. At this theater Peter Zadek's challenging version of Edward Bond's *Narrow Road to the Deep North* vied in the extreme nature of its provocation with that of Peter Stein's *Early Morning* in Zurich, and, still in Munich, with Claus Peymann's of a first play by Harald Mueller, *Great Wolf,* which dealt with the brutalizing influence of war on ordinary human beings.

81

Peymann and Stein made theatrical history by accepting an invitation to join the Berlin Schaubuhne as members of a collective administration, the only "official" theater so far to announce a partnership scheme in this way. Collective control was extended, on the other hand, to the field of dramatic publishing and promotion, when a group of dissident readers and dramatists belonging to the largest publishing house and theatrical agency in West German (Suhrkamp Verlag) broke away to form a "publishers' commune" (Verlag der Autoren) in which each partner, including the employed staff, enjoyed an agreed share from the publication and performing rights of their stage, radio and TV plays.

War and violence were the major preoccupations. Cologne staged the premiere of *The Marquise of Keith,* a highly unconventional satire on Prussianism by Hartmut Lange. Stuttgart had several original programs to offer: another on their list of historical plays adapted by Jörg Wehmeier and Peter Palitzsch *(Henry IV);* John Hopkins's pathological study of the ambivalence of brute force, *This Story of Yours,* which won for the company and Palitzsch the acclaim of the annual German Theater Review in Berlin; Palitzsch's faithful Brechtian reproduction, the first time in West Germany, *The Days of the Commune;* Martin Sperr's *Koralie Meier,* an honest if less than convincing bid to enter into the Nazi mind in Hitler's Germany by someone born long after the nightmare was over, with the delightful Bavarian comedienne Ruth Drexel as a whore with a heart of steel; and last but not least, the world premiere of Rolf Hochhuth's political thriller *Guerrillas.* In this, the German-born playwright accuses a plutocratic oligarchy, headed by Wall Street and the CIA, of creating a facade of ostensible democracy in the United States behind which to carry on the pursuit of profit unhampered, and invents a blood-chilling story of a coup d'etat, prepared by an idealistic resistance movement of secret conspirators and led by a Utopian senator, which goes awry and ends in dire disaster. Unlike his first two tragedies, *Guerrillas* was wholly fictional, but like them much of its gravity and impact depended on the facts and authoritative opinions brilliantly marshaled by the author to support a somewhat shaky case.

Elsewhere in West Germany, interest was divided between sensationalism and artistry. In Frankfurt a plan to stage a triple bill of plays by Peter Hacks and Heiner Muller, both of the German Democratic Republic, and Harmut Lange, a recent East German expatriate, all dealing with different aspects of the Heracles legend, came adrift when Muller and Hacks declined to be bracketed with the third dramatist. The director, Dieter Reible, had to confine himself to Hacks' *Omphale,* a complex verse drama that follows a current vogue in transvestism by showing Heracles and the Lydian queen who enslaved him dressed in each other's robes. This vogue was picked up by Essen, where the European premiere of the curious *Marie in Furs,* by the Japanese playwright Shuji Terayama, staged by himself and Claus Leininger, caught the fancy of the cognoscenti at the 1970 Colloquium of Staging of the International Theater Institute by its deliberate turn-of-the-century bad taste and all-male cast in a variety of roles of both sexes. Essen also boasted a subtle, though much rewritten and altered, version of Chekhov's *Three Sisters,* by Rudolf Noelte, Germany's most underestimated director of the classics.

Dusseldorf brought visitors from far and wide to the inaugural week at the new playhouse which included three world premieres of high quality: Peter Weiss's *Trotsky in Exile,* staged by Harry Buckwitz and designed by Gunilla Palmstierna-Weiss; Eugene Ionesco's *The Death Game,* and Heinrich Böll's *Clown,* adapted from his novel and staged by the former director of the Prague National Theater. The expatriate Czech Alfred Radok, in Josef Svoboda's fetching circus setting. Ionesco's two-hour-long variation on the theme of morality, more amiably droll than virulently satirical and inspired by Daniel Defoe's book on the Great Plague of London, propels a motley crowd of present-day characters into a ritualistic dance of death that presents the author's engrossing view of life in a familiar guise. Unprecedented scenes of violence by invited radical students caused the dress rehearsal of Weiss's play to be called off halfway through, but the fashionable first night audience sat respectfully if unconvincedly rapt while the Swedish Marxist writer, in the course of a historically authenticated documentary tragedy, preached the gospel of socialism and defeat of capitalism through the mouths of his actors (Richard Münch as Trotski and Kurt Beck as Lenin). A stalwart writer in the anti-Nazi field, Siegfried Lenz, also had his *The Eyeband* staged in Dusseldorf. It was a tellingly hurtful short drama about the deception practised by tyranny to maintain itself in power.

West Berlin

The voice of protest against tyranny was raised at the Berlin Festival, with the twofold contribution of the Schiller Theater Company, both at the larger and the smaller (Schlosspark) theaters, with Hans Hollman's iconoclastic production of Schiller's *Intrigue and Love* and Ernst Schröder's of Lessing's *Emilia Galotti.* In each the constraint of bourgeois prejudice and the privilege of feudal power were the object of the dramatist's critique, but in Hollman's stylized version, set in and around the legs of a 60-foot-high seated figure of the capricious Duke, the Lilliputian Miller family appeared as contemptible as their oppressors. Schröder also hit a new note in his approach, which, though more truly classical, cast equal blame on assassin and victim, each victims of an iniquitous class system. The festival highlight proved to be Samuel Beckett's own production of his *Krapp's Last Tape,* with Marrin Held as a personification of mental and physical decay in the title role. Both this and the Schiller play won golden opinions in the World Theater Season in London and later in the annual Berlin Theater Review. Among the year's acting triumphs few equaled that of Hans-Dieter Zeidler as the fleshpot-loving Captain Mahan in Hanjörg Utzerath's hilariously apt rendering of O'Casey's *Cock-a-Doodle-Dandy* at the Free People's Theater, while for a sensationally effective foreign success nothing could touch that of George Tabori's austerely terrifying concentration-camp drama *The Cannibals* at the Schiller Studio.

East Berlin

Controversy also reigned in East Berlin, where Benno Besson finally took over the People's Theater and launched a magnificent season that opened with the contemporary "socialist" drama *Horizons* (with several leading players who had left the Deutsches Theater with him, as well as the Berliner Ensemble) and ended with his new and third production of Brecht's bittersweet fairy tale *The Good Woman of Setzuan,* with Ursula Karusseit as Shen-Te and Rolf Ludwig as the Airman, a parodistic caricature of modern capitalist practise acted entirely in masks and in Armin Freyer's modernistic decor. Wolfgang Heinz retired from the Deutsches and was succeeded by Hans Anselm Perten, of Rostock. Among his first coups was the East German premiere of Babel's *Maria,* mounted by Adolf Dresen with notable elan and memorable less for the beloved recognition of Babel's talent than for the omission from the program note of the cause of his death in Stalinist Russia; and secondly the engagement of Manfred Wekwerth, sometime principle director of the Berliner Ensemble, to stage the premiere of Hans Magnus Enzberger's documentary drama on the Bay of Pigs episode, entitled *Investigation in Cuba.* Before Heinz's resignation (and the permanent shelving of his *Faust II*), the Deutsches staged Friedo Solter's Brechtian production of Gunter Rücker's second drama, called *Mr. Pansa's Neighbor* and adapted from Lunacharski's 1921 dramatic critique of tyranny in the saddle, *Don Quixote Goes Free.* Helmut Nitzschke staged *Woyzeck* as a Brechtian parable-play at the Berliner Ensemble, with Ekkehard Schall in the lead.

Switzerland and Austria

At Zurich's newest theater, the little Neumarkt, with its enviable reputation of Swiss firsts, director Felix Rellstab directed the world premiere of Slawomir Mrozek's *Waclaw,* his latest full-length play, written in Paris after the loss of his passport for speaking out against the invasion by Polish troops of Czechoslovakia. In it, Mrozek, writing as an exile, pictures the absurdist odyssey of an East European exile shipwrecked on a Western shore, no friendly place, as it turns out, since inequality and injustice reign there, too (the latter concept symbolized by the ravishment of a young girl persuaded to enact a strip tease). At Zurich's oldest established Schauspielhaus, the advent of Peter Loeffler as manager was followed by controversy (mostly in the form of unorthodox productions by far-out directors of way-out dramas) and his premature dismissal and replacement by Harry Buckwitz, veteran former head in Frankfurt. Loeffler's sin, it seems, was to encourage the younger generation, e.g. Stein's *Early Morning* mentioned above, and the new *Prometheus* retranslated into modern German by Heiner Müller and punctuated by an overloud pop band in the choral breaks. One world premiere, the 34-year-old Swedish poet Lars Gustafsson's *Nightly Homage,* a symbolical political drama (originally done on Swedish TV) set in an occupied country in 1863 with the monumental Gustav Knuth as a diehard burgomaster and skilfully staged by Carl M. Weber, came too late to save him.

Upheavals affected Basle, too, with the somewhat ineffectual premiere of Peter Hacks' historical *Margaret of Aix* and a quarrel over areas of responsibility between members of the three-man board. This resulted in Friedrich Duerrenmatt's ostentatious resignation and removal to Zurich, where he eventually agreed to join with Buckwitz as adviser and house-dramatist without directorial responsibility. Two curiosities in Basle were *Quodlibet* by the Austrian Peter Handke, more of a happening than a play but a well-staged exercise all the same, in which the seemingly improvised dialogue scored some unerring hits on familiar contemporary social and political targets; and Hans Bauer's searingly simple production of *Waiting for Godot,* which represented Switzerland at the Berlin revue.

Among the year's highlights in Vienna were Fritz Kortner's production of Lessing's *Emilia Galotti* and Arthur Schnitzler's posthumous, because never performed, *The Word,* at the Josefstadt, and Wolfgang Bauer's newest drama, *Change,* which depicts the selfish pursuit of intangible objectives by a set of feckless, self-seeking Bohemians and petit-bourgeois and ends in a gratuitous act of self-destruction. By drawing out the Lessing work with so much by-play and mime that it lasted well over twice the usual length, Kortner delighted and irritated his audiences in about equal halves. The Schnitzler work, completed by Friedrich Schreyvogel in 1966 and directed with style by Ernst Haeussermann, revolves around an unhappy love affair in which a thoughtless word pushes a star-crossed lover into suicide. It depicts Viennese cafe society in all its wasteful egotism 70 years ago. The performances of Attila Hörbiger and Paul Hoffmann in Strindberg's *Storm* at the Burg Theater's "Akademietheater" were among the finest of the season.

France

The appointment of Edmond Michelet to succeed the outgoing cultural minister, Andre Malraux, did little to appease the fears of the regional theater directors, the board of advisors of the ailing Theater of the Nations or the patrons of the Comédie Française, whose septuagenarian administrator Maurice Escande was due for retirement. Several names were tipped for the last post, including that of Jean-Louis Barrault, but it eventually fell to Pierre Dux, who held it briefly after the war. Though the Theater of the Nations, with no artistic director, managed by a committee and a business manager, staged a month-long season of sorts, its future remained in the balance.

The last year of the old regime at the Comédie Française had little to recommend it, if one excludes the relatively well attended foreign visits of *Amphitryon* and *Dom Juan* to New York and the London World Theater Season. The only novelty was *The Italians in Paris* (previously seen in Brussels at the Belgian National Theater). The revivals, in new garb in some cases, of Molière, Marivaux and Montherlant were more or less routine, though Jean-Marie Serreau tried to instill a new breath of life in to *Le Pain Dur* by Claudel, with a renewed if rather different use of Claude Lemaire's projected multi-screen backgrounds. At the Théâtre National Populaire there was a disappointing version of *The Dance of Death* with Alain Cuny and Maria Casarès. TNP's outstanding new show was a smash hit production, staged by Jacques Rosner, of the late Witold Gombrowicz's *Operette,* with Max Schoendorff's eye-catching decor. A hymn to unsullied humanity that sends up human foibles in terms of the Viennese operetta convention (with pastiche music by Karel Trow), it ends on a delirious note of joy when "purity," impersonated by the naked Catherine Hubeau, finally dominates the stage and all assembled on it.

Barrault was still "on the road" at home and abroad with *Rabelais* and nothing else except—somewhat of a comedown quantitatively at least—for a spell at the little Récamier Theater, with revivals of *Happy Days* and *The English Lover* (with Madeleine Renaud) and a brief Beckett season. In the other subsidized theaters, the Théâtre de l'Est Parisien (T.E.P.) had two well-matched productions to thank Guy Rétoré for: a new translation of *The Threepenny Opera* and *Major Barbara,* featuring Arlette Téphany in the lead. At Jean Mercure's City Theater, the two main attractions were the French premiere of Brecht's *Trumpets and Drums* and Peter Shaffer's *The Royal Hunt of the Sun.* Roger Planchon embarked on a six months' season in a private theater in Paris, the Montparnasse, thanks to the business acumen and enterprise of its proprietor, Lars Schmidt. Here Planchon's hilarious satire on the events of May 1968 and on backstage pride and prejudice entitled *Pulling the Cid Apart* ran to full houses for many weeks on end until succeeded first by his own play *The Wretch* from the previous season and then by *Bérénice* (starring the ethereal Francine Bergé) from four seasons back.

In the remainder of the private sector, Anglo-American entertainment held sway, ranging from *Fiddler on the Roof, The Boys in the Band* and *Your Own Thing* to *The Caretaker, A Day in the Death of Joe Egg* and *There's a Girl in My Soup.* Foreign drama of distinction included Natalia Ginzburg's *The Advertisement,* with Suzanne Flon beautifully recapturing her fey quality in the title role of what the French translator re-named *Teresa;* Alberto Moravia's comedy of egotistical word-games that culminate in suicide, *The World Is What It Is;* and Jack MacGowran, the Irish actor, playing in English, in a one-man collage of Beckett's works entitled *Beginning to End.* The boulevard theater offered both regular fare and less orthodox pabulum for the theatrical sensation-seeker. In the former category were two new plays by Anouilh, one each by Félicien Marceau and Andre Roussin, a delightfully dressed revival of Feydeau's *Look After Amélie* by Jacques Charron and starring Jacqueline Gautier, and Offenbach's *La Perichole*—only on account of Jean Carzou's magnificent sets and costumes, otherwise lamentably inadequate. In the latter were Marguerite Duras' *Suzanna Andler,* about a betrayed wife who dithered on the brink of adulterous revenge, Remo Forlani's originally contrived vehicle for the singer Barbara, *Madame,* and, to name three only for their sensational quality, *The Garden of Delights* staged with spectacular modernity by Jorge Lavelli, *They Handcuffed the Flowers* staged by the author (both by Fernando Arrabal, his two latest dramatic peregrinations through the misty corridors of sex and politics) and the scurrilously anti-Peronist *Eva Peron* by the cartoonist Copi, staged by the Argentinian Alfredo Rodriguez and notable for an unheralded visit by neo-fascists who beat up the actors and wrecked the stage on one occasion.

In *Cher Antoine,* with its echoes of *Colombe* and *Poor Bitos,* Anouilh sets his black comedy in Bavaria in 1913. He imagines an autobiography writer who summons to his death bed a host of friends and enemies—played by a star-spangled cast under the author's and Roland Pietri's direction—and by a quirk of theatrical trickery returns to them, Pirandello-wise, after his death. In *The Goldfish* Anouilh's reactionary philosophy comes out into the open for once, and he appears to justify "fascism"—even though he does so by way of a pun. In *Babykins,* Marceau's satirical barbs are aimed at bourgeois habits of life; most of them are here delivered by a cunningly introduced commentator who presides over the action, only occasionally taking part in it. Roussin's comedy *You Never Can Tell,* the bitterest yet, has for its hero a cantankerous husband, selfishly laying claim to marital privileges he has willingly shed.

Italy

Giorgio Strehler's long-awaited takeover at the Rome City Theater was aborted by the failure of the authorities to fulfill their undertakings to the director and he reverted to his own touring company instead. The Piccolo in Milan managed to survive without him, though a degree of collaboration between the two was expected. Salvo Randone as Timon and Franco Parenti as Pemantus in the Piccolo's *Timon of Athens* set the ball rolling in Milan, which also welcomed Gianfranco de Bosio (with his Venice Festival production of *La Betia* by Ruzante) and staged the professional premiere of the Chilean poet Pablo Neruda's *The Glory and Death of Joaquin Moreto,* the story of the martyrdom of an early victim of capitalist greed and fury in 1853, in and after the California gold rush, with Ferruccio Soleri, the Milan Piccolo's world-famous Harlequin, in the lead, and a breathless production full of the tricks of the theatrical trade staged by Patrice Chéreau from France. Among noteworthy events were the closure of the Giovani company after nearly 15 years' existence, despite an unroariously popular version of Roger Vitrac's *Victor* starring Giorgio de Lullo and with a decor by Pier Luigi Pizzi, inspired by Magritte; the premiere of Alberto Moravia's concentration-camp drama *God Kurt;* Luigi Squarzina's neo-Brechtian *Mother Courage* starring Nina Volonghi; two new Strindbergs, *The Dance of Death* staged by Sandro Sequi, with Gianni Santuccio and Lilla Brignone, and *The Dream Play* (in Turin), with Ingrid Thulin guesting as Indra's daughter; the world premiere at Aquila of Gombrowicz's *Operette;* and, finally, two events important for their social impact: the expulsion of The Living Theater from Italy (ostensibly for obscenity) and the condemnation by official Communist critics of Dario Fo's *The Worker and His 300 Words* as an unjust rebuke against party philistines. Among the Italian foreign tours, mention should be made of the success of the Catania City Theater at the London World Theater Season with Turi Ferro in Pirandello's *Liolà* and of the Spoleto production of Tasso's *Orlando Furioso* by Luca Ronconi, staged simultaneously in various places throughout the city and, in the Paris Les Halles, before an ambulating audience under Theater of the Nations auspices.

Sweden

The two highlights of the Swedish year were Ingmar Bergman's new production on the small stage of the Royal Dramatic Theater of Strindberg's *The Dream Play* and Arnold Wesker's own production, at the Little Theater, rented for the nonce and presented by the Stockholm City Theater, of his own play *Friends,* a study of an intimate group faced with the impending death of one of them. As in last year's *Woyzeck,* the stage and auditorium become one in Bergman's *Dream Play,* in which the text, deftly compressed, is used with the help of cleverly imposed stage business to speak for itself and to deliver a message just as anguished and authentic as if the director had used the full stage effects and obeyed the stage directions literally. Malin Ek as Agnes and George Arlin as the Poet stand out from the large cast. Wesker's *Friends* was one more gamble that paid off in the first managerial year at the City Theater of Finnish-born Vivica Bandler. The play, magnificently acted by Hasse Ekman among others, enjoyed packed houses throughout its run. The other payoff was Otomar Krejca's production of *The Seagull,* scheduled for a European tour in the summer months, something never before undertaken by this particular theater.

Eastern Europe

The sad news from Czechoslovakia was the re-introduction of theatrical censorship after a freedom of choice of plays lasting more than two years. The period under review was free of censorship, but plays were clearly chosen with an eye to their effect on official opinion, too. At Krejca's Gate Theater the two novelties were Chekhov's *Ivanov* and de Musset's *Lorenzaccio* staged, strangely enough, in not dissimilar styles, considering that the players were on stage throughout. The former had the benefit of Josef Svoboda's palisade-like setting that suggested both a prison and an area for roaming free and allowed a glimpse of life "backstage." The latter was presumably inspired by the company's earlier production of Michel de Ghelderode's *Masques Ostendaises,* since the carnival-like atmosphere of the entire action and the grotesque masks worn on occasion suggested some kind of ritual leading up to a dance of death, that of the crazed hero, played with dedicated abandon by Jan Triska.

Since Jan Grossman's departure, the Balustrade Theater has been in the hands of Jaroslav Gillar, responsible for the productions of Arrabal's parabolic *The Architect and the Emperor of Assyria* and Shakespeare's *Timon of Athens.* The Cinoherni Klub, besides staging a new production of *The Cherry Orchard,* paid their first visit to London in three plays including Alena Vostra's stimulating comedy of youth and illusion *Who's Turn Next?* at the World Theater Season.

In Yugoslavia, the freedom of expression long enjoyed was suddenly curtailed when the President stepped in with an objection to a political play; and when Aleksander Popovic's scurrilous study of the generation gap, *Next Door Left,* which students in Zagreb had staged at the University Theater Festival, could find no professional producer willing to stake his reputation on it in Belgrade. *The Stamps and Afterwards Emilia* by Dusan Jovanovic, an effectively written surrealist comedy "about nothing at all," first tried out at the Ljubljana Experimental Stage and later was revived at Belgrade's Atelje 212, marked the arrival of a promising new author.

The saddest aspect of the theater in Poland has been the shift of the center of gravity from Warsaw to Krakow, where some of the country's most exciting theater artists (e.g. Krystyna Skuszanka) are at work; and the absence abroad of others (like Mrozek or Jan Kott, exiled in their own words "never to return"); or again, some who are only temporarily abroad until the atmosphere is ripe for their return (e.g. Kazimierz Dejmek, who has been working in Oslo, Essen and Vienna). That neither Mrozek nor Gombrowicz can be performed in Poland is another indication of the way the wind is blowing, though, on the other hand, an apparent revival of interest in Witkiewicz is at hand. Erwin Axer moved to the Ateneum Theater where his production of Duerrenmatt's *Play Strindberg* won the highest praise.

Rumania is the sole Eastern country to have escaped the vicissitudes of recent political upheavals. All the same, there were some radical changes, not the least of which was the appointment of Radu Beligan as head of the National Theater while he continued to act as guest at his former Comedy Theater, now headed by Lucian Giurchesco in his own production of Ionesco's *The Killer,* and at the Bulandra City Theater in *Unknown Heart Transplanted,* a new play by Al Mirodan. The sublime clowning of Marin Moraru as the King in Liviu Ciulei's imaginative adaptation of Büchner's *Leonce and Lena* at the Bulandra, with decor by himself and costumes by Joana Gardescu, was among the season's most irresistible experiences.

In Moscow, controversy stiffened between the champions of the old traditions and the fighters for the new. Yevgeni Vosnessenski's latest dramatic contribution to Yuri Liubimov's Theater of Comedy and Drama (the Taganka Theater), *Guard Your Faces,* was taken off after two performances, ostensibly because its criticism of the bourgeois way of life might serve as a two-edged weapon. Mikhail Tsaryov, veteran actor of the Maly Theater and president of the All-Russian Theatrical Society, joined in the chorus condemning both Liubimov and Anatoli Efros, whose production of Arbuzov's *Happy Days of an Unhappy Man* (about a Soviet citizen who bungles his affairs) continued to hold the boards of the Malaya Bronnaya, as did Georgi Tovstonogov's version of it at his own theater, the Leningrad Gorki. Here, too, Tovstonogov staged a new one-part version of the two parts of Shakespeare's *Henry IV* with some considerable success, while Liubimov ventured into new territory by putting on Gorki's *Mother,* a production that met with criticisms for failing to idealize the revolutionary heroine. Liubimov held on to his theater despite continued official disapproval of his artistic methods, but he had to drop Peter Weiss's *How Suffering Was Beaten out of Mr. Mockinpott* and the same author's *The Investigation* from his repertory when Weiss's play about Trotsky was performed in Dusseldorf and its author became a "non-person" overnight in the Soviet Union. The announcement of *Trotsky in Exile* as being one of the plays to be seen by visitors to the Essen Colloquium—though its run had by then ceased and it was no longer possible to see it—was the cause of the Soviet delegation's last-minute withdrawal and a similar withdrawal by the German Democratic Republic delegation, the first occasion since its foundation in Prague in 1948 on which the International Theater Institute's (ITI's) work has been bedeviled by political backbiting.

Two memorable new Moscow productions were Viktor Lavrentyev's *Man and the Globe* at the Maly, a modern play which had President Roosevelt and Harry Hopkins planning to unleash the atom bomb as a weapon to give the U.S.A. military supremacy over the U.S.S.R., and an enthralling adaptation at the Mossoviet of Dostoevsky's *Crime and Punishment* devised and directed by the veteran Yuri Zavadsky with the title *Petersburg Encounters,* in which Gennadi Bortnikov played Raskolnikov as a coldly calculating intellectual rather than as a pathological fanatic.

Highlights of the Paris Season

Selected and compiled by Ossia Trilling

OUTSTANDING PERFORMANCES

PIERRE FRESNAY as Armand Pousset in *You Never Know*	SUZANNE FLON as Teresa in *Teresa*	MICHELLE MARQUAIS as Tisbé in *Angelo, Tyrant of Padua*
FRANÇOISE ROSAY as Carlotta in *Cher Antoine*	DELPHINE SEYRIG as Laïs in *The Garden of Delights*	JACQUELINE GAUTHIER as Amélie in *Look After Amélie*
IVAN REBROFF as Tevye in *Fiddler on the Roof*	LOLEH BELLON as Émilie in *Pulling the Cid Apart*	JACQUES DUFILHO as Davies in *The Caretaker*
JEAN-PIERRE MARIELLE as Fernand in *Babykins*	MAURICE BARRIER as Macheath in *The Threepenny Opera*	JOSÉ-MARIA FLOTATS as Atahuallpa in *The Royal Hunt of the Sun*
MICHEL AUMONT as Harpagon in *The Miser*	FRANCINE BERGÉ as Bérénice in *Bérénice*	DANIEL GÉLIN as Minole in *The World Is What It Is*

OUTSTANDING DIRECTORS

JEAN MERCURE *The Royal Hunt of the Sun*	JACQUES ROSNER *Operetta*	ROGER PLANCHON *Pulling the Cid Apart*

OUTSTANDING DESIGNERS

ANDRÉ LEVASSEUR *Look After Amélie*	CHRISTINE LAURENT *Drums and Trumpets*	MAX SCHOENDORFF *Operetta*

OUTSTANDING NEW FRENCH PLAYS
(D)—Playwright's Paris Debut

DES POMMES POUR ÈVE (Apples for Eve) by Gabriel Arout. Some more Chekhov short stories dramatized. With Monique Tarbès, Dominique Paturel.

ILS PASSÈRENT DES MENOTTES AUX FLEURS (They Handcuffed the Flowers) by Fernando Arrabal. Scabrously ritualistic critique of General Franco and all he stands for. With Laurence Imbert, Karen Rencurel, Eric Chartier.

FULL UP by Guy Foissy. A multimedia, anti-establishment pop musical. With Georges Bénard, Mitzi.

JE NE PENSE QU'À ÇA (That's All I Ever Think Of) by Wolinski and Confortès. A revue satirizing sex and all that jazz. With Claude Confortès, Dominique Maurin, France Beucler.

LE JARDIN DES DÉLICES (The Garden of Delights) by Fernando Arrabal. A popular actress is trapped by the calls of her heart and her trade. With Delphine Seyrig, Bernard Fresson, Marpessa Dawn.

LA MISE EN PIÈCES DU CID (Pulling the Cid Apart) by Roger Planchon. Satire on show business and life. With the Roger Planchon Company.

LES ITALIENS A PARIS (The Italians in Paris) by Charles Charras and André Gille. Trials of the Italian actors in 18th century Paris. With Michel Aumont, Jean-Luc Moreau, Tania Torrens.

INÉDITS IONESCO (Ionesco Novelties). Twelve absurdist sketches, including some hitherto unperformed. With Jean Rougerie, Anne Alexandre, Suzy Hannier.

L'INFÂME (The Wretch) by Roger Planchon. Tragic fate of a Catholic priest torn apart by the Church and his instincts. With the Roger Planchon Company.

EVA PERON by Copi. Satirical send-up of the story of the Argentine dictator's wife. With Marucha Bo, Philippe Bruneau.

LE SANG (Blood) by Jean Vauthier. Acting troupe rehearses an Elizabethan revenge tragedy. With the Company of the Lyons Théâtre du Cothurne.

POPULAR ATTRACTIONS

HISTOIRE NATURELLE DU COUPLE (Natural History of the Couple). Triple bill comprising revivals of LES HONNÊTES FEMMES (The Honest Women) by Henri Becque, LA RÉVOLTE (The Revolt) by Villiers de l'Isle-Adam and VIEUX MÉNAGE (Age-Old Family) by Octave Mirbeau. With Fabiène May, André Lacombe, Marion Margyl, Chantal Solca, Jeanne Provost.

LA SORCIÈRE (The Witch), LE NO. GAGNANT (The Winning Number), POLINKA, three Chekhov stories adapted by Bella Reine, and LA QUESTION DU LATIN (The Latin Question) by Guy de Maupassant, adapted by Jean-Claude Marcadé. With France Aubret, Pierre Fabien, Hélène Fabricoli, Edmond Darrell.

PIQUE-NIQUE EN CAMPAGNE (Picnic in the Country) by Fernando Arrabal and MON ISMÉNIE (My Ismenie) by Eugène Labiche. Revival of two contrasting one-acters. With Annie Perec, Pierre Peyron, Pierre Pernet.

ANGELO, TYRANT DE PADOUE (Angelo, Tyrant of Padua) by Victor Hugo. Short-run revival of classical verse drama. With Michelle Marquais.

L'AIGLON (The Eaglet) by Edmond Rostand. Revival of Rostand's classic. With Renée Faure, Michel le Royer.

ÉCHEC ET MEURTRE (Check-Murder) by Robert Lamoureux. Detective thriller in the shape of a chess game. With the author and Jean Topart.

L'AVARE (The Miser) by Molière. Comédie Française revival staged by Jean-Paul Roussillon. With Michel Aumont, Françoise Seigner, Ludmila Mikaël.

LA FEMME DU BOULANGER (The Baker's Wife) by Jean Giono. Revival of Giono's famous sex drama. With the Comédiens de Provence.

LES GROSSES TÊTES (The Bigheads) by Poiret and Serrault. Satire on the theater and a TV-saturated world. With Maria Pacôme, Claude Piéplu, Michel Roux.

LE BABOUR (Babykins) by Félicien Marceau. What happens when the sexes exchange roles at home and in the office. With Jean-Pierre Marielle, Pierre Dux, Elisabeth Alain.

ON NE SAIT JAMAIS (You Never Know) by André Roussin. The green-eyed jealousy of a husband separated from his wife. With Pierre Fresnay, Christiane Minazzoli, Jean-Pierre Darras.

LA PÉRICHOLE by Jacques Offenbach. Spectacular revival, designed by Jean Carzou, of popular 19th century musical. With Jane Rhodes.

BON WEEKEND CONCHITA (Happy Weekend Conchita) by Roland Arday. A couple's weekend adventures in the country. With Franck Fernandel, Maté Altéry, Lucette Royat.

LE MISANTHROPE (The Misanthrope) by Molière. Modern-dress revival at the Théâtre de la Ville. With Michel Piccoli, Danièle Lebrun.

CHER ANTOINE (Dear Antoine) by Jean Anouilh. A famous deceased playwright gives his friends and enemies a posthumous piece of his mind. With Françoise Rosay, Francine Bergé, Pierre Bertin, Claude Nicot, Jacques François.

LES FAUSSES CONFIDENCES (False Confidences) by Pierre de Marivaux and 29° A L'OMBRE (29 Degrees in the Shade) by Eugène Labiche. Revival of popular Comédie Française successes. With Jean Piat, Micheline Boudet, Jacques Charon.

OEDIPE ROI by Jean Cocteau. The poet's lyric tragedy acted straight and then as a dance drama. With Jean Marais, Madeleine Sologne, Thérèse Thoreux.

LORENZACCIO by Alfred de Musset. Théâtre de l'Est Parisien's revival of costume drama. With Gérard Desarthe.

LE MARCHAND DE SOLEIL (The Sun Merchant) by Robert Thomas and Jacques Mareuil. A millionaire and a tramp exchange roles. With Tino Rossi, Robert Manuel.

OCCUPE-TOI D'AMÉLIE (Look After Amélie) by Georges Feydeau. Brilliantly dressed revival of famous bedroom farce. With Jacqueline Gauthier, Geneviève Brunet, Jean-Pierre Cassel.

L'ASCENSEUR ÉLECTRIQUE (The Electric Elevator) by Julius Vartet. Snobbish millionairess is tricked by the heirs she has married off against their wishes. With Raymond Souplex, Annick Alane.

LE BON SAINT ÉLOI (The Good Saint

Eligius) by Pierrette Bruno. Wife and mistress make a fascinating discovery. With Christian Alers, Mary Marquet, Colette Deréal.

IL ÉTAIT . . . . DEUX ORPHELINS (There Were . . . . Two Orphans) by Eugène Mirea. An updated parody of Julien Vartel's 19th century pseudo-melodrama. With Danièle Vidal, Delphine Desyeux, Jacques Fabbri.

LE PAIN DUR (Hard Bread) by Paul Claudel. Comédie Française tackles Part 2 of Claudel's trilogy. With Françoise Chaumette, Ludmila Mikaël.

ZOZO by Jacques Mauclair (D). The generation gap in farcical terms, a first play by the eminent actor-director. With Bachir Touré, André Gille.

OEDIPUS by Vercors. New translation of Sophocles' tragedy. With José-Maria Flotats, Jandeline.

LES POISSONS ROUGES (The Goldfish) by Jean Anouilh. Having urinated in his goldfish bowl, Anouilh's hero grows up to be a thoroughly horrible Anouilh hero. With Jean-Pierre Marielle, Michel Galabru, Pascal Mazzotti.

LES CLOWNS (The Clowns). Revival of collective production. With Ariane Mnouchkine's Théâtre de Soleil Company.

MALATESTA by Henry de Montherlant. Comédie Française revival. With Georges Aminel, Christine Fersen, Louis Seigner.

UN SALE ÉGOISTE (A Beastly Egotist) by Françoise Dorin. Study of a triumphantly selfish man. With Paul Meurisse, Claude Gensac, Marion Game.

LE MYSTÈRE DE LA CHARITÉ DE JEANNE D'ARC (The Mystery of the Charity of Joan of Arc) by Charles Péguy. Revival of Péguy's posthumous religious drama. With Denise Bosc, Catherine Morlay, Yolande Hascouet.

LE ROI SE MEURT (Exit the King) by Eugène Ionesco. Jacques Mauclair revives his distinguished production. With the director, Tsilla Chelton, René Dupuy.

LES MARRONS DU FEU (Chestnuts in the Fire) by Alfred de Musset. Revival of de Musset's sentimental comedy. With Marie-Adélaïde Arvay, Gérard-Maurice Gotscho.

LE TROISIÈME TÉMOIN (The Third Witness) by Dominique Nohain. Revival of prizewinning thriller (after 1,000 performances). With the author, Pierre Destailles.

OH LES BEAUX JOURS (Happy Days) by Samuel Beckett. Revival of Roger Blin's dramatic milestone. With Madeleine Renaud.

À COR ET À CRI (Hue-and-Cry) by Jean Baudard. A gay dog upsets the peaceful rhythm of two married couples' lives. With Jean-Marie Proslier, Suzanne Gabriello.

HERMINIE by Claude Magnier. Farce of mistaken identities. With Philippe Lemaire, Danny Saval.

DOMINO by Marcel Achard. Commercial revival of 1931 classic. With Danielle Darrieux, Robert Lamoureux.

WAITING FOR GODOT by Samuel Beckett. Revived as part of Jean-Louis Barrault's tribute to the author. With Lucien Raimbourg, Armand Meffre.

GRRR . . . by Jean Gastaud. Hilarious view of a multiplying eternal triangle. With Patrick Préjean, Lucette Raillat, Elisabeth Guy.

BÉRÉNICE by Racine. Planchon's distinguished production. With the Roger Planchon Company.

LE BAL DES VOLEURS (The Thieves' Ball) by Jean Anouilh. Revival of author's early comedy; and L'ENTERREMENT (The Burial) by Henri Monnier. Staged as a curtain-dropper. With Elisabeth Alain, Maurice Chevit.

SUPER-POSITIONS by René Ehni. A critique of commercialized pornography. With Fernand Gravey, Isabelle Ehni.

THE GRACCHI, APOLLO OF BELLAC, SONG OF SONGS by Jean Giraudoux. First performance of triple bill at the Comédie Française. With Jacques Destoop, René Arrieu, Alain Pralon, Claire Vernet.

L'AMOUR MASQUÉ (Masked Love) by Sacha Guitry. Revival of André Messager's operetta. With Jean Marais, Jean Parédès, Arlette Didier.

AMÉDÉE OU COMMENT S'EN DÉBARRASSER (Amédée) by Eugène Ionesco. Jean-Marie Serreau's hit production revived. With Eléonore Hirt, Etienne Bierry.

SOME AMERICAN PLAYS PRODUCED IN PARIS

HAIR (musical) by Gerome Ragni and James Rado. With Julien Clerc, Hervé Wattine, Vanina Michel, Jeanie Bennett, Bill Combs, Ronnie Bird.

THE BOYS IN THE BAND by Mart Crowley. With Vernon Dobtcheff, Philippe Rouleau.

THE ZOO STORY by Edward Albee. With Laurent Terzieff, Yves Gasc.

YOUR OWN THING (CHARLIE) (musical) by Donald Driver. With Arielle Semenoff, Jacques Tardieu.

FIDDLER ON THE ROOF (musical) by Joseph Stein. With Ivan Rebroff, Maria Murano.

THE CONNECTION by Jack Gelber. With Anne-Marie Coffinet, Jacques Coasguen.

THE BEARD by Michael McClure. With Chantal Darget, Jean Claude Drouot.

ISTANBUL by Rochelle Owens. Henry Pillsbury's world première production. With Anne Varenne, Gair Pruitt.

SPOON RIVER ANTHOLOGY by Edgar Lee Masters. With Michel Amiel, Cécile Ricard.

SLAVE SHIP by LeRoi Jones. With the Chelsea Theater Center Company.

SOME OTHER FOREIGN PLAYS PRODUCED IN PARIS

THEATER OF THE NATIONS SEASON included, in 1969, the Compagnia Italiana di Prosa's *Ruzante Dialogues*, the Nihon-Nogaku-Dan No Theater, the Odin Teatret's *Ferai* by Peter Seeberg, the Aalborg Theater's *Hamlet;* and, in 1970, the Rome Teatro Libero's *Orlando Furioso*, the Combine's *Stomp*, the Prague Gate Theater's *Ivanov* and *Lorenzaccio*, the Rumanian National Theater's *Madame Chiritsa* and the Genoa City Theater's

One of the Carnival's Last Nights.

LA SERRANA by José Herrera Petere. With the Geneva Théâtre de Carouge company.

THE CARETAKER by Harold Pinter. With Jacques Dufilho, Sacha Pitoëff.

THE NEIGHBORS by James Saunders. With Pascale de Boysson, Laurent Terzieff.

LA POULETTE AUX OEUFS D'OR (The Chicken With the Golden Eggs) by Robert Thomas, after Georges Marton's play. With Eliane Borras, Pascale Roberts.

THE LIAR by Carlo Goldoni. With Jean-Pierre Andréani, Annie Sinigalia, Daniel Colas.

THE WORLD IS WHAT IT IS by Alberto Moravia. With Daniel Gélin, Paloma Matta.

THE ADVERTISEMENT (Teresa) by Natalia Ginzburg. With Suzanne Flon, Annie Doat.

DRUMS AND TRUMPETS by Bertolt Brecht. With Maurice Teynac, Hélène Vincent, Maurice Chevit.

VINCENT AND THE LADY-FRIEND OF MEN OF IMPORTANCE by Robert Musil. With Laurence Bourdil, Françoise Chaudat.

A DAY IN THE DEATH OF JOE EGG by Peter Nichols. With Jean Rochefort, Marthe Keller.

THE WALTZ OF THE DOGS by Leonid Andreyev. With Laurent Terzieff, Denis Manuel.

JONAH by Marin Sorescu. With Roland Husson.

THE THREEPENNY OPERA by Bertolt Brecht. With Maurice Barrier, Sabine Lods, Arlette Téphany.

MACBETH by William Shakespeare. With Doura Mane, Line Senghor.

THE ROYAL HUNT OF THE SUN by Peter Shaffer. With Georges Geret, José-Maria Flotats.

L'EXIL D'ALBOURI by Cheik N'Dao (D). A national drama brought to Paris by the National Senegalese Theater. With Doura Mane, Jacqueline Scott Lemoine.

UPROAR IN THE HOUSE by Alistair Foot and Anthony Mariott. With Darry Cowl, Jean Lefebvre, Claire Maurier.

MOR LAM'S BONE by Birago Diop (D). Tale of cruelty from Senegal. With Doura Mane, Line Senghor.

OPERETTE by Witold Gombrowicz. With Catherine Hubeau, Alain Mottet, Georges Riquier, Judith Magre, Gabriel Cattand, Guy Michel.

FIRST WARNING and MOTHERLY LOVE by August Strindberg. With Thérèse Quentin, Nathalie Noël.

THE CAT (Der gestiefelte Kater) by Ludwig Tieck. With the Mandragore Company.

RICHARD II by William Shakespeare. With the Company of the Centre Dramatique National du Sud-Est.

THE FOREST by Alexander Ostrovsky. With Renée Faure, Julien Guiomar.

THE SHADOWY WATERS by W.B. Yeats. With Philippe Petti, Annie Alex.

THE DANCE OF DEATH by August Strindberg. With Alain Cuny, Maria Casarès, Jean-Marc Bory.

EGMONT by Goethe. With Jacques Dumesnil, Annie Sinigalia.

THE LIFE THAT I GAVE THEE by Luigi Pirandello. With Jeanine Crispin, Claire Deluca, Alice Sapritch.

MAJOR BARBARA by George Bernard Shaw. With Pierre Dux, Lise Delamare, Arlette Téphanie.

FARCE, SATIRE, IRONY and DEEPER PURPOSE (Le Cocktail du Diable) by Christian Dietrich Grabbe. With the Mandragore Company.

NIGHT MUST FALL by Emlyn Williams. With Roger Coggio, Tania Balachova.

GOAT ISLAND by Ugo Betti. With Fabiène Mai, Claude Darvy, Jean Le Lamer, Jean Adam.

THERE'S A GIRL IN MY SOUP by Terrence Frisby. With Elisabeth Wiener, Pierre Mondy.

BEGINNING TO END by Samuel Beckett. One-man show of Beckett anthology. With Jack MacGowran.

KRAPP'S LAST TAPE and ACTS WITHOUT WORDS by Samuel Beckett. With Henri Martin, Deryk Mendel.

THE KITCHEN by Arnold Wesker. Ariane Mnouchkine's famous production arrives in Paris. With the Théâtre du Soleil company.

THE TEL AVIV PLUMBER by Ephraim Kishon. With the Gilbert Chickly Company.

LIMITED RUNS OF INTERESTING NEW FRENCH PLAYS

QUELQUE CHOSE COMME GLÉNARIFF (Something Like Glénariff) by Danièle Lord and Henri Garcin. A husband-to-be dreams of the women in his life. With Henri Garcin, Luce Garcia-Ville.

SUZANNA ANDLER by Marguerite Duras. A betrayed wife hovers on the brink of revenge. With Catherine Sellers, Luce Garcia-Ville, Roger Defossez.

LE LAI DE BARRABAS (Barrabas' Song) by Fernando Arrabal. A re-hash of Arrabal's *The Coronation*. With Myriam Mezières, Eric Donat.

COMÉDIE POUR UN HOMME QUI MEURT (Comedy For a Dying Man) by Berbard Mazéas. Three-part drama pleading for human freedom. With Jean Le Lamer, Marc Gallier, Daniel Honoré.

MADAME by Rémo Forlani. The death-throes of colonialism. With Barbara, Harry-Max, Yvan Labejof.

SLIMANE by Jean Pélégri (D). What caused the violence of the Algerian War. With Jim Adhi Limas, Jacques Delmare.

SUPER-POSITIONS by René Ehni. A critique of commercialized pornography. With Fernand Gravey, Isabelle Ehni.

L'AZOTE (Nitrogen) by René de Obaldia. Send-up of the military mind. With Arlette Gouin, Jocelyne Auclair.

NOUS N'IRONS PLUS AU BOIS (We Shan't Go Into the Wood Again) by Armel Marin. Seven actors go into the wood in search of their identity. With the author, Christine Delaroche.

LA FIANCÉE SE RETIRE (The Bride Withdraws) by André Journo. An errant couple goes wrong in the desert. With Géraldine Klein, Alain Huguin.

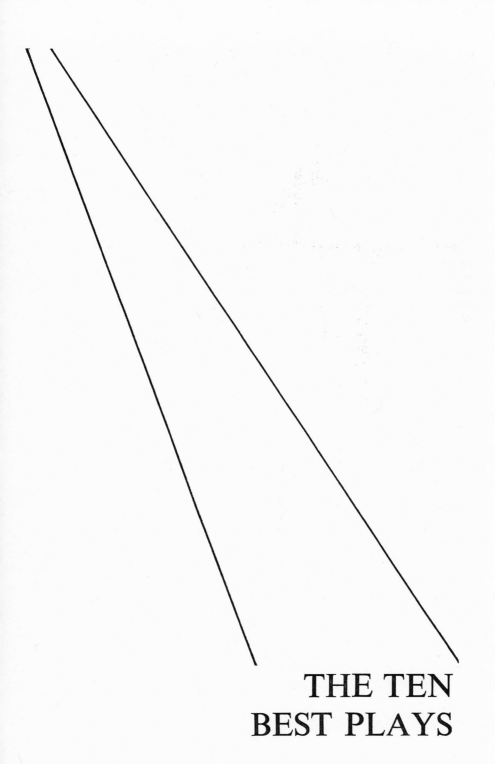

THE TEN
BEST PLAYS

In the following synopses of 1969-70's Best Plays, scenes and lines of dialogue, stage directions and description quoted from the scripts appear *exactly* as in the stage version of the play unless (in a very few instances, for technical reasons) an abridgement is indicated by five dots (. . . . .). The appearance of three dots (. . .) is the script's own punctuation to denote the timing of a spoken line.

INDIANS

A Play in One Act

BY ARTHUR KOPIT

Cast and credits appear on page 299

ARTHUR KOPIT was born on May 10, 1937 in New York City. He attended Lawrence, L.I., High School and Harvard University where, as an undergraduate, he began to write plays. Five of the nine produced by various groups were The Questioning of Nick, On the Runway of Life You Never Know What's Coming off Next, Across the River and Into the Jungle, Aubade *and* To Dwell in a Place of Strangers.

Kopit's first New York production was also his first Best Play, with the long title Oh Dad, Poor Dad, Mama's Hung You in the Closet and I'm Feelin' so Sad. *It was first staged by Cambridge, Mass. undergraduates in January, 1960, then had a short run in its professional premiere in England during the summer of 1961 before being produced off Broadway at the Phoenix Theater under the direction of Jerome Robbins on February 26, 1962 for 454 performances. It was named a Best Play of its season (at which time its author was billing himself Arthur L. Kopit, with a middle initial) and was revived on Broadway at the Morosco Theater August 27, 1963 for 47 performances.*

A double bill of Kopit one-acters, The Day the Whores Came Out to Play Tennis *and* Sing to Me Through Open Windows, *was produced off Broadway March 15, 1965 for 24 performances. His* Chamber Music *has received recent regional theater productions. Kopit's second Best Play,* Indians, *was given its*

*world premiere by the Royal Shakespeare Company in London in July 1968
and its American premiere last season at the Arena Stage in Washington, D.C.
He is married and lives in New York City.*

Time: 1846-1890

Place: A Wild West Show

Scene 1

SYNOPSIS: The open, curtainless stage gives no sense of time or place. Three
large glass cases, spotlit from above, contain effigies of William F. "Buffalo
Bill" Cody and Sitting Bull and artifacts including a buffalo skull and a bloody
Indian shirt. Distorted Western music adds to the sense of dislocation, as the
glass cases disappear.

A voice calls out the name "Cody!" and a spotlight picks up Buffalo Bill
"riding" his white stallion in slow motion, dressed in fancy embroidered buckskins. He comes forward and takes a bow, flourishing his hat—the Wild West
Show is about to begin. The voice urges him to start the show, but Bill seems
reluctant to step into his role of Western hero. Indians appear behind Bill.

VOICE: Bill.
BUFFALO BILL: But—
VOICE: It's *time.*
   Pause.
BUFFALO BILL: Be-before we start, I'd . . . Just like to say—
VOICE: Bill!
   The Indians slowly approach.
BUFFALO BILL: —*to say* that . . . I am a fine man. And anyone who says
otherwise is *WRONG!*
VOICE *(softly):* Bill, it's time.
BUFFALO BILL: My life is an open book. I'm not *ashamed* of it's bein'
looked at!
VOICE *(coaxing tone):* Bill . . .
BUFFALO BILL: I'm sorry, this is very . . . hard . . . for me t'say. But I be-
lieve I . . . am a . . . hero . . . *A GODDAM HERO!*
   Indian music. His horse rears wildly. Lights change for next scene.

Scene 2

It is winter. Sitting Bull, dressed simply, and his Indian people confront
three U.S. Senators—Logan, Morgan and Dawes (flanked by armed soldiers)
—who have been sent West as a committee to look into conditions on the
Reservation.

Buffalo Bill Cody has helped to arrange the meeting between the Senators and his friend Sitting Bull (who had appeared in Cody's Wild West Show). Bill apologizes to the Indians that the Great Father himself, the President, was unable to come as promised. But the President has sent his three most trusted advisors, perhaps the only persons who can be of help to the Indians.

Sitting Bull designates, not one of his fiery chieftains, but young, soft-spoken, Carlisle—educated John Grass to speak for his people.

> *Enter John Grass in a black cutaway many sizes too small for him. He wears an Indian shirt. Around his neck is a medal.*

JOHN GRASS: *Brothers!* I am going to talk about what the Great Father told us a long time ago. He told us to give up hunting and start farming. So we did as he said, and our people grew hungry. For the land was suited to grazing not farming, and even if we'd been farmers, nothing could have grown. So the Great Father said he would send us food and clothing, but nothing came of it. So we asked him for the money he had promised us when we sold him the Black Hills, thinking, with this money we could *buy* food and clothing. But nothing came of it. So we grew ill and sad . . . So to help us from this sadness, he sent Bishop Marty, to teach us to be Christians. But when we told him we did not wish to be Christians but wished to be like our fathers, and dance the Sun Dance, and fight bravely against the Shawnee and the Crow! And pray to the Great Spirits who made the four winds, and the earth, and made man from the dust of this earth, Bishop Marty hit us! . . . So we said to the Great Father that we thought we would like to go *back* to hunting, because to live, we needed food. But we found that while we had been learning to farm, the buffalo had gone away. And the plains were filled now only with their bones . . . Before we give you any more of our land, or move from here where the people we loved are growing white in their coffins, we want to tell the Great Father to give us, who still live, what he promised he would! *No more than that.*

SITTING BULL: I prayed for the return of the buffalo!

> *Lights fade to black on everyone but Buffalo Bill. Distant gunshot heard offstage. Pause. Two more gunshots. Lights to black on Buffalo Bill.*

Scene 3

Spotted Tail, a young Indian standing on a level above the stage as though overlooking the plains, watches a nighttime slaughter of buffalo. Shots are heard and several Indians now costumed as buffalo stagger onstage. Each is shot in the eye, and, bellowing in pain, one by one they fall and die.

Buffalo Bill (younger than in the previous scenes) runs onstage in the company of U.S. cavalrymen. Bill, elated, boasts that he has killed 100 buffalo with 100 shots, in the dark, aiming at the reflection in their eyes. This feat is all the more wondrous because, as Bill explains, buffalo aren't as plentiful as they were in the old railroad-building days: "These critters're gettin' so damned hard t'find."

Bill looks down at the dead animals and has an instant of compassion, squinting in pain—then shrugs it off.

Spotted Tail moves down toward Bill, who hears him coming and cocks his rifle. But Bill recognizes Spotted Tail as a friend.

SPOTTED TAIL: *What are you doing here?*
    Pause.
BUFFALO BILL: Well, well, what . . . are *you* doing here? This isn't Sioux territory.
SPOTTED TAIL: It isn't *your* territory either.
    Pause.
BUFFALO BILL: Well I'm with . . . these people. I'm scoutin' for 'em.
SPOTTED TAIL: *These people* . . . must be very hungry.
BUFFALO BILL: H'm?
SPOTTED TAIL: To need so many buffalo.
BUFFALO BILL: Ah! Of course! You were following the buffalo also! . . . Well, listen, I'm sure my friends won't mind you takin' some. 'Tween us, my friends don't 'specially care for the *taste* o' buffalo meat. *(He laughs.)* My God, but it's good t'see you again!
SPOTTED TAIL: *Your friends:* I have been studying them from the hills. They are very strange. They seem neither men, nor women.
BUFFALO BILL: Well! Actually they're sort of a new *breed* o' people. Called dudes. *(He chuckles.)*
SPOTTED TAIL: You *like* them?
BUFFALO BILL: Well . . . sure. Why not?
    Pause.
I mean, obviously they ain't the sort I've been used to. But then, things're changin' out here. An' these men are the ones who're changin' 'em. So, if you wanna be *part* o' these things, an' not left behind somewhere, you just plain hafta get *used* to 'em. You—uh—follow . . . what I mean?
    Silence.
I mean . . . you've got to *adjust.* To the times. Make a *plan* fer yerself. I have one. You should have one, too. Fer yer own good. Believe me.
    Long pause.
SPOTTED TAIL: *What is your plan?*
BUFFALO BILL: Well, my plan is t'help people. Like you, ferinstance. Or these people I'm with. More . . . even . . . than that, maybe. And, and, whatever . . . it is I *do* t'help, for it, these people may someday jus' possibly name streets after me. Cities. Counties. States! I'll . . . be as famous as Dan'l Boone! . . . An' somewhere, on top of a beautiful mountain that overlooks more plains 'n' rivers than any other mountain, there might even be a statue of me sittin' on a great white horse, a-wavin' my hat t'everyone down below, thankin' 'em, fer thankin' me, fer havin' done . . . whatever . . . it is I'm gonna . . . *do* fer 'em all. How . . . come you got such a weird look on your face?

BUNTLINE *(offstage):* HEY, CODY! *STAY WHERE YA ARE!*

BUFFALO BILL: DON' WORRY! I AIN'T BUDGIN'! *(To Spotted Tail)* That's Mr. Ned Buntline, the well-known newspaper reporter. I think he's gonna do an *article* on me! General Custer, who's in charge, an' I think is pushin' fer an article on *himself,* says this may well be the most important western expedition since Lewis 'n' Clark.

Bill explains to Spotted Tail that he is accompanied by a Grand Duke from a place called Russia. There is a fanfare, and Grand Duke Alexis makes an entrance with his interpreter, followed by Ned Buntline. Majestically, the Grand Duke awards Buffalo Bill a medal while Buntline photographs the ceremony. The Grand Duke wonders whether Bill has ever been afraid. Modestly, Bill hesitates to answer.

BUNTLINE: Go on, tell'm. It'll help what I'm plannin' t'write.

BUFFALO BILL *(delighted):* It *will?*

BUNTLINE: Absolutely. Look: de West is changin'—right? Well, people wanna know about it. Wanna feel . . . *part* o' things. I think *you're* what dey need. Someone t'listen to, observe, *identify* wid. No, no, really! I been studyin' you.

BUFFALO BILL: . . . You have?

BUNTLINE: I think you could be de inspiration o' dis land.

BUFFALO BILL: Now I *know* you're foolin'!

BUNTLINE: Not at all . . . Well go on. Tell 'm what he wants t'hear. T'rough my magic pen, others will hear also . . . Donmentionit. De nation needs men like me, too.

Hesitantly, Buffalo Bill starts to tell the Grand Duke about the times he has been outnumbered by his enemies. To Buntline's delight, the tale gradually becomes a yarn as Bill warms to his task: "Mind you, 'gainst *me* twelve's normally an even battle—long's I got my two six-shooters that is. . . . . THIRTEEN! If one of 'em's thin enough for a bullet to go clean through. Fourteen if I got a huntin' knife. Fifteen if there's a hard surface off o' which I can ricochet a few shots."

To please the Grand Duke, Bill launches into a fantasy of how he fended off an attack by 50 drunken Comanches by catching an arrow in mid-air and hurling it back to kill their chief. The Grand Duke is not only pleased, he is inspired, he wants to *be* Buffalo Bill and kill a Comanche himself. But the Comanches live in Texas—this is Missouri. Undeterred, the Grand Duke seizes his rifle and fires into the darkness. Spotted Tail stumbles forward, falls and dies.

The Grand Duke is puffed up with pride. Buntline is happy, too—this serves his purpose. Buffalo Bill is stunned.

> *Buffalo Bill, almost in a trance, walks over to the body; stares down at it. Weird music is heard. The lights change color, grow vague.*

All movement is arrested.

 Spotted Tail rises slowly and moves just as slowly toward the Grand Duke; stops.

SPOTTED TAIL: My name is Spotted Tail. My father was a Sioux; my mother, part Cherokee, part Crow. No matter how you look at it, I'm just not a Comanche.

 He sinks back to the ground. The lights return to normal, the music ends.

GRAND DUKE: *(Baffled Russian speech.)*

INTERPRETER: His Excellency would like to know what the man he just shot has said.

 Long pause. Buffalo Bill looks around, as if for help; all eyes upon him.

BUFFALO BILL *(softly):* He said . . . *(Pause.)* "I . . . *(Pause.)* should have . . .

 He looks at Buntline, takes a deep breath.

stayed at home in . . . Texas with the rest of my . . . Comanche tribe."

BUNTLINE: Fabulous!

 He takes Spotted Tail's picture; the night sky glows from the flash. Absolutely fabulous!

 The scene fades around Buffalo Bill, who stands in the center, dizzily gripping his head.

Scene 4

The delegation of Senators is listening to Bill explain that these Indians gathered to meet with them are a special responsibility: Sitting Bull's Indians, the last to surrender. The scene ends on a Wild West Show drum roll and blacks out into . . .

Scene 5

. . . the center stage of a Wild West Show. Exhibited in a cage like a wild animal is Geronimo the famous Apache chief who seethes and shouts to the audience of his prowess in murder and rape of his white enemies. Buffalo Bill, dressed in his fancy buckskins, enters the cage with Geronimo like a lion tamer, goes up to the Indian then turns his back on him. *"Buffalo Bill walks calmly away, opens the cage door, and exits. . . . . Geronimo stands trembling with frenzy. Lights fade to black."*

Scene 6

At the meeting between Sitting Bull's Indians and the Senators, John Grass protests that they sold the Black Hills to the white man by treaty, for "as much as we would need, for as long as we would need it" but have never been paid. Senator Logan assures John Grass that the money is in trust in a Washington bank, but "The Great Father is worried that you've not been educated enough to spend it *wisely.* When he feels you have, you will receive every last penny of it. *Plus interest."*

John Grass is angry, Senator Logan exasperated. Once again, Bill warns the Indians that this committee is their only hope.

The Indians speak of other broken treaties. Sitting Bull wants to know: "Where is the Great Father, Cody? . . . The one you said would help us . . . The one you said you knew so *well*."

Scene 7

At the White House, the "Ol' Time President" and his First Lady arrive to watch a Wild West skit written by Ned Buntline to be performed by Buffalo Bill and Wild Bill Hickok. Buntline delivers an introduction in verse, explaining how he has brought Bill Cody fame and fortune by writing 27 books about him.

BUNTLINE:
> . . . . . I saw the nation profit more than us.
> For with each one o' my excitin' stories,
> Cody grew t'represent its glories.
> Also helped relieve its conscience,
> By showing pessimism's nonsense. . . . .

Cody and Hickok begin performing Buntline's play for the President in a manner *"wooden as only the worst amateur actors can be."* The plot has something to do with "Pawnee devils" and their Festival of the Moon. Neither Cody nor Hickok can remember their lines, and in addition Hickok refuses even to enter into the spirit of the thing. The Pawnees are going to sacrifice a virgin (it says in Buntline's script), but Hickok couldn't care less.

> *Hickok has walked over and is staring into Buffalo Bill's face.*
BUFFALO BILL: Just *what are you doin'?*
HICKOK: What're *you* doin'?
BUFFALO BILL: I'm doin' what I'm doin', *that's* what I'm doin'!
HICKOK *(to Buntline):* Always was intelligent.
BUFFALO BILL: I'm doin' what my country *wants!* WHAT MY BELOVED COUNTRY *WANTS!*
HICKOK *(to the First Family): This* . . . is . . . what you want?
FIRST LADY: Absolutely!
OL' TIME PRESIDENT: Best play I've seen in years!
> *Hickok, staggered, sits down on the stage.*
BUFFALO BILL: When a man has a talent, a *God*-given talent, I think it's his godly duty t'make the most of it.
> *Applause from the First Family. Buffalo Bill nods acknowledgement.*
(To Hickok.) Ya see, Bill, what you fail to understand is that I'm not being false to what I *was*. I'm simply *drawin'* on what I was . . . and raisin' it to a higher level.

He takes a conscious pause.
Now. On with the show!

Buntline's embryonic version of what is to become the Western legend continues. The sacrificial virgin is tied to her totem pole as the Indians dance. Buffalo Bill, Buntline and Hickok "raid" and "kill" the Indians and rescue the "maiden." The dead Pawnee chief, Uncas, rises to point the moral of the playlet: "The white man is great, the red man nothing. So, if a white man kills a red man, we must forgive him, for God intended man to be as great as possible, and by eliminating the inferior, the great man carries on God's work. Thus, the Indian is in no way wronged by being murdered. Indeed, quite the opposite: being murdered is his purpose in life. . . . ."

Hickok draws his Bowie knife (and the First Family continues to believe this is all part of the play). Humiliated at being forced to impersonate himself in the manner of Buntline's play (they had promised Hickok he could play Bat Masterson), he is angrily determined to show them Hickok as Hickok really *is,* instead of emasculated and whitewashed. He silences the play's author, Buntline, by knifing him, then delivers an extemporaneous address: "Hickok, fastest shooter in the West, 'cept for Billy the Kid, who ain't as accurate; Hickok, deadliest shooter in the West, 'cept for Doc Holliday, who wields a sawed-off shotgun, which ain't fair; Hickok, shootinest shooter in the West, 'cept for Jesse James, who's absolutely indiscriminate; this Hickok, strong as an eagle, tall as a mountain, swift as the wind, fierce as a rattlesnake —a legend in his own time, or any other—this Hickok stands now above an Indian maiden—"

To the delight of the First Family, Hickok prepares to rape this "maiden." Buffalo Bill brings down the curtain. Suddenly he finds that he is all alone on the stage.

Scene 8

At the meeting between Sitting Bull's Indians and the Senate committee, John Grass tells Senator Logan that the Indians were duped into signing away some of their land in exchange for 25,000 unwanted head of cattle, which they thought was a gift of food.

The Indians gave up the Black Hills (Grass insists) in exchange for anything they would ever need; therefore the Great Father owes them full support. The sound of the argument blends into the noise of a Wild West Show.

Scene 9

The Wild West Show is on, with spotlights, banners, rodeo ring, music and the starring riders, sharpshooters (including Annie Oakley) and musicians. A voice demands that Buffalo Bill bring on his Indians; he does so, somewhat uneasily.

A group of Indians enters and takes center stage with a Sun Dance pole topped by a buffalo skull. Roustabouts set up an inverted tub. Chief Joseph, old and stiff-jointed, enters. The crowd falls silent as he begins to speak.

CHIEF JOSEPH: In the moon of the cherries blossoming, in the year of our surrender, I, Chief Joseph, and what remained of my people, the Nez Percés, were sent to a prison in Oklahoma, though General Howard had promised we could return to Idaho, where we'd always lived. In the moon of the leaves falling, still in the year of our surrender, William Cody came to see me. He was a nice man. With eyes that seemed . . . frightened; I . . . don't know why. He told me I was courageous and said he admired me. Then he explained all about his Wild West Show, in which the great Sitting Bull appeared, and said if I agreed to join, he would have me released from prison, and see that my people received food. I asked what I could do, as I was not a very good rider or marksman. And he looked away and said, "Just repeat, twice a day, three times on Sundays, what you said that afternoon when our army caught you at the Canadian border, where you'd been heading, and where you and your people would have all been safe." So I agreed. For the benefit of my people . . . And for the next year, twice a day, three times on Sundays, said this to those sitting around me in the dark, where I could not see them, a light shining so brightly in my eyes!
    Pause. He climbs up on the tub.
(Accompanied by exaggerated and inappropriate gestures.) "Tell General Howard I know his heart. I am tired of fighting. Our chiefs have been killed. Looking Glass is dead. The old men are all dead. It is cold and we have no blankets. The children are freezing. My people, some of them, have fled to the hills and have no food or warm clothing. No one knows where they are—perhaps frozen. I want to have time to look for my children and see how many of them I can find. Maybe I shall find them among the dead. Hear me, my chiefs. I am tired. My heart is sick and sad. From where the sun now stands, I will fight no more forever . . ."
    He climbs down from the tub.
After which, the audience always applauded me.

Chief Joseph exits and the Sun Dance begins. It is a test of endurance in which leather thongs attached to the pole are hooked into the chest muscles and pulled until the muscles rip. Buffalo Bill's Wild West Show Indians are wearing harnesses to simulate the ritual, but John Grass enters, places the barbs in his living flesh and pulls until he is bloody and unconscious.

Scene 10

At the White House, the Ol' Time President sits astride a mechanical horse, listening to a Victrola recording of "On the Old Chisholm Trail." Buffalo Bill enters to ask the President to come with him to Sitting Bull's reservation, but he has difficulty getting the President's attention away from his new Western toys.

The President refuses to give the Indian problem his personal attention, because there is nothing effective he can accomplish at this late date—it is too late to give them back their land or resurrect the buffalo. The President will send a Congressional committee, as a gesture. The matter is closed. The President resumes riding his hobby horse.

Scene 11

Once again, at the meeting between the committee and the Indians, Buffalo Bill is explaining to the Indians that the committee represents the Great Father, who could not come himself. Bill turns to the Senators and makes a last effort to explain the Indians to them: "The *real* problem here is not poor soil. The real problem's plowin'. Ya see, the Indian believes the earth is sacred and sees plowin' as a sacrilegious act." The Indian chooses to use fertile land on which to race his ponies. He believes that it is foolish to pay money for land, which the Great Spirits created for the use of all. "What I'm gettin' at is *this:* if *their* way o' seein' is hard fer *us* to follow, ours is just as hard fer *them*. . . . ."

The Senators invite Sitting Bull to speak for himself. The chief begins the statement he wishes the committee to carry back to the Great Father.

SITTING BULL: My children . . . are dying. They have no warm clothes, and their food is gone. The old way is gone. No longer can they follow the buffalo and live where they wish. I have prayed to the Great Spirits to send us back the buffalo, but I have not yet seen any buffalo returning. So I know the old way is gone. I think . . . my children must learn a *new* way if they are to live. Therefore, tell the Great Father that if he wishes us to live like white men, we will do so.
>   *Stunned reaction from his Indians. He silences them with a wave of his hand.*
For I know that if that pleases him, we will benefit. I am looking always to the benefit of my children, and so, want only to please the Great Father . . . Therefore, tell him for me that I have never yet seen a white man starving, so he should send us food so we can live like the white man, as he wants. . . . .

The Great Father must send them healthy cattle, mules to do their labor, farm animals: "I ask for these things only because I was advised to follow your ways." Sitting Bull wants clothing, toilets, glass for windows.

SITTING BULL: . . . . . As you see, I do not ask for anything that is not needed. For the Great Father has advised us to live like white men, so clearly, this is how we should live. For it is your doing that we are here on this reservation, and it is not right for us to live in poverty. And be treated like beasts . . . that is all I have to say.

Senator Logan takes offense at Sitting Bull's words. Logan tries to humble the proud chief, who cannot understand why the Senators don't treat him with the respect he so clearly deserves. Patiently, Sitting Bull explains to Logan that he is appointed leader by the Great Spirits: "If the Great Spirits have chosen anyone to be leader of their country, know it is not the Great Father; *it is myself.*"

Logan, furious, demeans Sitting Bull: "You are on an Indian reservation merely at the sufferance of the Government. You are fed by the Government, clothed by the Government; your children are educated by the Government, and all you have and are today is because of the Government. I merely say these things to notify you that you cannot insult the people of the United States of America or its committees. . . . ."

Sitting Bull protests that he has earned his right to authority, and to feel pride. The Senators refuse to listen further.

Scene 12

Buffalo Bill enters a Western saloon looking for Wild Bill Hickok. Among the patrons are performers impersonating Jesse James and Billy the Kid, plus an assortment of cowboys. Hickok enters, greets Bill warmly and leads him to a table where they can talk in privacy. Bill is worried . . . frightened . . . things have gotten beyond him. He sees Indians everywhere (Indians appear in the shadows).

BUFFALO BILL: . . . . . Took a drink from a river yesterday an' they were even there, beneath the water, their hands reachin' up, I dunno whether beggin', or t' . . . drag me under. *(Pause.)* I wiped out their food, ya see . . . Didn't *mean* to, o' course. *(He laughs to himself.)* I mean IT WASN'T MY FAULT! The railroad men needed food. They *hired* me t'*find 'em* food! Well. How was *I* t'know the goddam buffalo reproduced so slowly? *How was I to know that?* NO ONE KNEW THAT!
    Pause. The Indians slowly disappear.
Now, Sitting Bull is . . .
    Long pause.
HICKOK: *What?*
BUFFALO BILL: The . . . hearing was a shambles. I brought these Senators, you see. To Sitting Bull's reservation. It . . . was a shambles. *(Pause.)* So we left. He . . . *insulted* them. *(Pause.)* Then I saw the letter.
    Silence.
HICKOK: What letter?
BUFFALO BILL: The letter to McLaughlin. The letter ordering . . . it to be done. *(Pause.)* So I rode back. Rode all night. Figuring, maybe . . . if I can just *warn* him . . . But the reservation soldiers stopped me and . . . made me . . . drink with them. And by the time I got there, he . . . was dead. The greatest Indian who'd ever lived. Shot. By order of the Government. Shot with a Gatling gun. *(Pause.)* While the . . . wonderful gray horse I'd given him for . . . appearing in my show danced his repertory of tricks in the background. Since a gunshot was his cue to perform.
    He laughs. Stops. Long silence.

HICKOK: Well now. In exactly what way did you imagine *I* could . . . *help* this . . . situation?

BUFFALO BILL: You have what I *need* . . . now.

HICKOK *(smiling lightly):* Oh?

BUFFALO BILL: I'm *scared,* you see. *(Pause.)* Scared . . . not . . . so much of *dyin',* but . . . dyin' *wrong. (Slight laugh.)* Dyin' . . . in the center of my arena with . . . makeup on. *(Long pause.)* Then I thought of you . . . Remembered that night in the White House. Remembered thinking, "My God! Look at Hickok. *Hickok knows just who he is!" (Pause.)* "Hickok has the answer," I said . . . Hickok knows who he *is. (Pause.)* I must see Hickok again.

Long silence.

HICKOK: Well, I'm glad you came. Yes. Glad . . . to be able to . . . help. *(Pause.)* Funny. That night in the White House I remember thinking: "My God, it's *Cody* who's got the answer."

Ironically, Hickok has decided that "takin' what you were and raisin' it to a higher level" of legend is the right way to go—hence this saloon and the impersonated legendary characters, for atmosphere. Hickok is now in the Wild West business and suggests that they can increase profits by arranging for Buffalo Bill's "simultaneous presence" in various places around the world. To demonstrate, Hickok brings on a group of masked Buffalo Bill impersonators wearing elaborate dress buckskins.

Buffalo Bill, stunned by the sight, fires his guns at the duplicate Codys. They fall and immediately rise again. They slowly surround him. He screams as he shoots. They disappear. The saloon fades to black.

BUFFALO BILL *(alone on stage):* AND NOW TO CLOSE! AND *NOW TO CLOSE!*

VOICE: Not *yet. (Pause.)* They also killed the rest of his tribe.

Music. Indians enter mournfully. They carry a large white sheet. Sound of wind. Buffalo Bill watches, then moves slowly away; exits.

Scene 13

The Indians spread the sheet and lie down on it as Colonel Forsyth describes the massacre to two reporters and Buffalo Bill, who is carrying a satchel. The soldiers have wiped out Sitting Bull and his whole tribe, an act which has "more than made up for Custer."

The Colonel agrees with a reporter's suggestion that this was a harsh measure. ". . . . . but had we shirked our responsibility, skirmishes would have gone on for years, costing our country millions, as well as untold lives. Of course innocent people have been killed. In war they always are. And of course our hearts go out to the innocent victims of this. But war is not a game. It's tough. And demands tough decisions. In the long run I believe what happened here at this reservation yesterday will be justified."

The Colonel believes that the Indian wars are now over—Sitting Bull was "their last straw." Buffalo Bill gets permission to visit Sitting Bull's grave, and the others leave. As Bill takes a sprig of pine from his satchel, the dead Sitting Bull appears for a final word. The chief understands why the white man killed the Indian and stole his land, but not why he professed to love the Indian while doing it.

Bill tries to express his grief, his good intentions to raise money to help the Indians with his Wild West Show. Sitting Bull admits that he enjoyed participating in the shows because they reminded him of past glory . . . but at the same time, it was humiliating.

Just as Bill's private fear is of dying in the arena with his makeup on, Sitting Bull's is that the Indian owes to the white man not only his destruction but also the principal symbols of his glory: the gun and pony. Majestically, Sitting Bull declares to Buffalo Bill, "Farewell, Cody. You were my friend. And, indeed, you still are . . . I never killed you . . . because I *knew it would not matter."* Then the Indian returns to his grave.

VOICE: And now to close!

BUFFALO BILL: NOT YET! . . . I would . . . first . . . like to . . . say a few words in defense of my country's Indian policy, which seems, in certain circles, to be meeting with considerable disapproval.

> *He smiles weakly, clears his throat, reaches into his pocket, draws out some notes, and puts on a pair of eyeglasses.*

The—uh—State of Georgia, anxious to solidify its boundaries and acquire certain valuable mineral rights, hitherto held accidentally by the Cherokee Indians, and anxious, furthermore, to end the seemingly inevitable hostilities between its residents and these Indians on the question of land ownership, initiated, last year, the forced removal of the Cherokee nation, resettling them in a lovely and relatively unsettled area west of the Mississippi, known as the Mojave Desert. Given proper irrigation, this spacious place should soon be blooming. Reports that the Cherokees were unhappy at their removal are decidedly untrue. And though many, naturally, died while marching from Georgia to the Mojave Desert, the ones who did, I am told, were rather ill already, and nothing short of medication could have saved them. Indeed, in all ways, our vast country is speedily being opened for settlement. The shipment of smallpox-infested blankets, sent by the Red Cross to the Mandan Indians, has, I'm pleased to say, worked wonders, and the Mandans are no more. Also, the Government policy of exterminating the buffalo, a policy with which I myself was intimately connected, has practically reached fruition. Almost no buffalo are now left, and soon the Indians will be hungry enough to begin farming in earnest, a step we believe necessary if they are ever to leave their barbaric ways and enter civilization. . . . .

As Bill goes on in this vein, "justifying" the Indian policy, the Indians begin to rise from their graves. Sitting Bull, Black Hawk, Tecumseh, Crazy Horse, Red Cloud, Spotted Tail, Santanta, Kiokuk, Geronimo, Old Taza and

John Grass rise to protest that they are dying, while Bill rationalizes.

Bill takes Indian trinkets out of his satchel, commenting on the excellence of the workmanship. While Bill sets up a display of these exhibits, Chief Joseph comes onstage to repeat his speech of capitulation.

Almost all the lights are now gone; Chief Joseph can hardly be seen; Buffalo Bill is but a shadow. Only the trinkets are clear in a pinspot of light, and that light, too, is fading.

CHIEF JOSEPH: Hear me, my chiefs. I am tired. My heart is sick and sad. From where the sun now stands, I will fight no more, forever.

And then, very slowly, even the light on the trinkets fades. And the stage is completely dark.

Then, suddenly, all lights blazing. Rodeo ring up. Rodeo music. Enter, on horseback, the Roughriders of the World. They tour the ring triumphantly, then form a line to greet Buffalo Bill, who enters on his white stallion. He tours the ring, a glassy smile on his face. The Roughriders exit.

Buffalo Bill, alone, on his horse. He waves his big Stetson to the unseen crowd. Then, Indians appear from the shadows outside the ring; they approach him slowly. Lights fade to black. Pause.

Lights return to the way they were at the top of the show, when the audience was entering. The three glass cases are back in place. No curtain.

BUTTERFLIES ARE FREE

A Play in Two Acts

BY LEONARD GERSHE

Cast and credits appear on page 301

LEONARD GERSHE believes that "the less the public knows about a writer, the less they are likely to 'read' things into his work, and it is far better for them to use their imaginations and draw their own conclusions." Accordingly, at his request no personal biographical data appeared in the Broadway program of Butterflies Are Free *or in Random House's book-publication of its script; nor will we invade his valued privacy in these pages.*

In answer to our request, however, Mr. Gershe offered to "talk freely about my professional life, and perhaps that could substitute as a sort of bio." His communication appears below as an introduction to his 1969-70 Best Play, which is his second Broadway production—his first was the book for Destry Rides Again, *the 1959 musical.*

INTRODUCTION BY THE AUTHOR

The first professional work I did was writing some lyrics for a revue in London called *Tuppence Coloured* which had music by Richard Addinsell. After that, I wrote the book for a musical I called *Wedding Day* which I hoped would be produced on Broadway. It wasn't. I went to Hollywood and wrote some TV scripts for Ann Sothern and Lucille Ball. *Wedding Day* came to the attention of producer Roger Edens who persuaded MGM to buy it for films with the idea of using Gershwin songs with it. Eventually, the project was taken over by Paramount Pictures and was released as *Funny Face* with Audrey Hepburn and Fred Astaire. With Edens I wrote three songs for the film needed to supplement the Gershwin material. I also did the screen play and was nominated for an Academy Award for it. I didn't win.

I returned to MGM to work with Arthur Freed on the screen play of *Silk Stockings,* the Cole Porter musical which starred Fred Astaire and Cyd Charisse. I shared this screen play credit with Leonard Spigelgass. Both films were released in 1957 and both were on the New York *Times* ten best pictures list that year. Somewhere in all this, with Edens I wrote the song "Born in a Trunk" which Judy Garland introduced in *A Star Is Born.* In 1959 I wrote the book for the Broadway musical *Destry Rides Again* with music and lyrics by Harold Rome, starring Andy Griffith and Dolores Gray. Then came some dry years of working on screen plays for such projects as *No Strings* and *Say It With Music* which, for one reason or another, never got made. Then I decided to return to my first love—the theater—and write the play *Butterflies Are Free.* I prefer working in the theater to any other medium.

The idea for *Butterflies* came to me one morning when I heard a radio interview with a young, blind law student who had been drafted and classified 1 A! The boy's name is Harold Krents and he was so good-humored—even funny—about his blindness. He said he wouldn't mind going to war if they'd make him a bombardier. He went on to say that his real handicap was the way most people treated him because he was blind and he wished people could understand he is no different from anyone else—except he can't see. I had never met a blind person and was bowled over by this boy's humor and healthy attitude about his situation. I felt this was a character worth writing about.

The girl in the play who, after a hasty marriage, has a dread of any sort of permanent relationship and cannot face the responsibilities of love and marriage, was inspired by my friend Mia Farrow. At least that is how Mia felt at the time of her divorce from Frank Sinatra. She feels differently now. A lot of the dialogue the girl speaks in the play are things Mia actually said to me. I thought that bringing these two young people together in a story would be interesting—and so came *Butterflies Are Free.*

LEONARD GERSHE

Time: The present

Place: Don Baker's apartment on East 11th Street in New York City

ACT I

Scene 1

SYNOPSIS: The June morning sun is pouring through a skylight into Don Baker's one-room apartment, furnished in early orange crate and claw-footed bathtub style (the bathtub is clearly visible between the sofa at center and the kitchen area upstage). The bunk bed at right is elevated high enough to walk under en route to the washroom behind it. The front door is upstage right, and down left is a chest of drawers backed up against a locked connecting door between this and the next aparement.

Don himself is leaning against one of the bed's supporting posts, drinking a glass of water. *"He is 20 years old, lean and good looking. He wears a brown button-down shirt and sun-tans. His hair is combed back and his feet are bare."*

When the phone rings, Don turns off a tape recorder that has been playing rock. The caller is his mother in Scarsdale. She is worried about Don and wants to drop in on him after a visit to Saks. But Don reminds his mother that she has agreed to leave him alone in his East Village apartment, free of family interference.

A blaring TV in the apartment next door cuts short Don's conversation with his mother. He hangs up the phone and knocks on the connecting door, protesting the noise. The next-door occupant turns off the TV, apologizes in a young girl's voice and asks herself over for a cup of coffee. Don puts the coffee on, then opens the front door to admit Jill Tanner. *"She is 19 and has a delicate little-girl quality about her. Her long hair falls to her shoulders and down her back. Her dress is very mod and zips down the back. The top of the zipper is open."*

Jill and Don introduce themselves; at Jill's request, awkwardly, Don fixes her zipper. Jill notices and admires the skylight, the neatness of Don's apartment in contrast to her own messy quarters, the bed on stilts—"Wild!" She can hear everything that goes on in Don's apartment and has just overheard the beginning of his phone conversation.

JILL: Why don't you want your mother here?

DON: It's a long story. No, it's a short story—it's just been going on a long time. She didn't want me to leave home. She thinks I can't make it on my own. Finally, we agreed to letting me try it for two months. She's to keep away from me for two months. I've got a month to go.

JILL: Why did you tell her you had a party last night?

DON: Boy, you don't miss anything in there, do you?

JILL: Not much.

DON: I always tell her I've had a party . . . or went to one. She wouldn't understand why I'd rather be here alone than keeping her and the cook company. She'll hate this place. She hates it now without even seeing it. She'll walk in and the first thing she'll say is, "I could absolutely cry!"

JILL: Does she cry a lot?

DON: No—she just threatens to.

JILL: If she really wants to cry, send her in to look at my place. At least you're neat. You're old enough to live alone, aren't you? I'm nineteen. How old are you?

DON: As far as my mother's concerned, I'm still eleven . . . going on ten.

JILL: We must have the same mother. Mine would love me to stay a child all my life . . . or at least all *her* life. So *she* won't age. She loves it when people say we look like sisters. If they don't say it, she tells them. Have you got a job?

DON: Not yet . . . but I play the guitar and I've got a few prospects.

He plays by ear and is trying to develop an act. He explains the mystique of Scarsdale to Jill, who is from Los Angeles and has never heard of the place.

Don stamps out a cigarette in the sofa table ash tray and goes to get Jill another cup of coffee while Jill tells him the story of her life, or at least her youth. At 16, she was married for six days to a boy she hardly knew. Lighting a cigarette of her own and pulling the ashtray over conveniently close, Jill confides to Don: "He was terribly sweet and groovy looking, but kind of adolescent, you know what I mean? Girls mature faster than boys. Boys are neater, but girls mature faster. When we met it was like fireworks and rockets. I don't know if I'm saying it right, but it was a marvelous kind of passion that made every day like the Fourth of July."

The boy's name was Jack Benson, and during the marriage ceremony before a justice of the peace she realized she was making a terrible mistake. She tried for six days of honeymoon, then gave up and was eventually divorced. "Just because you love someone doesn't necessarily mean that you want to spend the rest of your life with him." Jill tells Don, "but Jack loved me. I mean he really, really loved me and I hurt him and that's what I can't stand. I just never want to hurt anybody. I mean marriage is a commitment, isn't it? I just can't be committed or involved. Can you understand?"

Don thinks he can—but he doesn't entirely agree, he says, flicking some ashes from his cigarette onto the table where the ashtray had been before Jill moved it.

Jill looks at him, oddly.

JILL: What is this? Maybe I've got it wrong. Maybe boys mature faster and girls are neater.

DON: What do you mean?

JILL: Or maybe you know something I don't know—like ashes are good for the table? Is that why you keep dropping them there?

DON: Did you move the ashtray?

JILL *(holding up the ashtray beside her):* It's right here. Are you blind?

DON: Yes.

JILL: What do you mean—yes?

DON: I mean yes. I'm blind.

JILL: You're putting me on.

DON: No, I'm blind. I've always been blind.

JILL: Really blind? Not just near-sighted?

DON: The works. I can't see a thing.

> *Jill leans over and runs her hands across Don's eyes. When he doesn't blink, she realizes he is indeed blind.*

JILL: God! I hope I didn't say anything . . .

DON: Now don't get self-conscious about it. I'm not.

JILL: Why didn't you tell me?

DON: I just did.

JILL: I mean when I came in.

DON: You didn't ask me.

JILL: Why should I ask. I mean, I don't go into someone's house and say, "Hi, I'm Jill Tanner—are you blind?"

DON: Right—and I don't meet a stranger and say, "Hi, Don Baker—blind as a bat."

For Don, blindness is all he's ever known, a normal state, and he has no pity for himself and wants none from others. Jill still finds it strange—Don is the first blind person she's ever met. She is curious about ways and means. Don explains how he memorizes the number of steps to the stores in the neighborhood, and the whereabouts of everything in the apartment. He demonstrates to her how he knows where everything is—except the ashtray, which Jill replaces in its accustomed spot.

Discussing his blindness, Don tells her: "The thing I find hard to live with is other people's reactions to my blindness. If they'd only behave naturally. Some people want to assume guilt—which they can't because my mother has that market cornered—or they treat me as though I were living in some Greek tragedy, which I assure you I'm not. Just be yourself."

Don continues to discourage Jill from the belief that he has any special qualities because of being blind, either a sixth sense or a noble character. Jill is surprised to discover that Don is very well read in the braille library, and she quotes him her favorite lines from Mark Twain: "I only ask to be free. The butterflies are free. Mankind will surely not deny to Harold Skimpole what it concedes to the butterflies." Don informs Jill that the quote is *not* Mark Twain but Charles Dickens, from *Bleak House.*

Don has been working on a song. Until this moment he hasn't been able to get the last lines right, but now he has it. He takes up his guitar.

DON *(sings):*
    I knew the day you met me
    I could love you if you let me
    Though you touched my cheek
    And said how easy you'd forget me
    You said butterflies are free
    And so are we. . . . .
JILL: It's terrific! I know a little about music. I studied in school.
DON: Did you finish school?
JILL: I finished high school . . . *just.* My mother wanted me to go to college. I was going to UCLA but I couldn't find a place to park. Have you ever been to L.A.?
DON: No. I hear the climate is great.
JILL: The climate is great, but the weather is lousy. I guess it's a good place to live—with gardens and pools and all that. I like it better here. People say New York is a great place to visit but they wouldn't want to live here. What could be groovier than living in a place that's great to visit?
DON: What made you come here?
JILL: Nothing *made* me come. I just thought I'd like to try something different. I think I'm going to be an actress. I say I think. I'll know later this afternoon. I'm reading for a part in a new off-Broadway play.
DON: Good part?
JILL: I guess so. It's the lead. It's a girl who gets all hung up because she's married a homosexual. Originally, he was an alcoholic, but homosexuals are very "in" now, so they changed it. Are you homosexual?
DON: No—just blind.

The director of the play is a friend of Jill's and will audition her performance for the author's approval. She and the director have been making it together, but Jill's fear of love and of hurting someone else has kept them from forming any more demanding relationship.

Jill is hungry—she is always hungry—and Don begins to prepare a lunch. Jill suggests a picnic and sets a tablecloth and knives and forks on the floor.

Asked about his dead father, Don tells Jill that he misses him: "He was the only friend I had growing up. He was the kind of man who would have been my friend even if he hadn't been my father. . . . . But it's been rough on Mom since he died because Mom felt she had to be mother *and* father . . . and sister and brother and cousin and uncle and doctor and lawyer . . . senator . . . congressman . . ."

Don was born blind (he tells Jill in answer to her probing) not because of a hereditary weakness but because of some kind of virus. His mother is the author of a series of books.

DON: They were a series of children's books. Guess what they were about?
JILL: Children?
DON: A blind kid named Little Donny Dark.
JILL *(incredulously):* Little Donny Dark??!!
DON: That's me.
JILL: Boy, you'll say anything to get attention!
DON: It's true, I swear. I hate that name—Donny.
He carries plates toward center.
Tell me when to stop.
JILL: Stop. . . . .
Don stops at the edge of the cloth, kneels and sets the plates down. He sits with his legs crossed under him. Jill stretches out on her stomach and digs into the food.
Tell me about Little Donny Dark. It might curb my appetite.
DON: Donny is twelve years old and was born blind like me only it's no handicap to Little Donny Dark. He can drive cars and fly planes, 'cause, you see, his other faculties are so highly developed that he can hear a bank being robbed a mile away and he can smell the Communists cooking up a plot to overthrow the government. He's a diligent fighter of crime and injustice and at the end of every book, as HE is being given a medal from the police or the CIA or the FBI, he always says, "There are none so blind as those who will not see!"

Jill sympathizes with Don's distaste for Little Donny Dark, as Don serves some wine. The books, he tells Jill, were a projection of his mother's hope that he would turn into "a sightless superman."

Don was educated by private tutors specializing in teaching the blind. He was "a pet in a cage" until a girl named Linda Fletcher moved in next door, began taking him to New York for parties, introducing him around and finally persuading him to make the break and get an apartment of his own.

Linda has since married someone else and moved to Chicago. Jill reassures Don that if he needs someone she is right here now—and she suggests that they open the door connecting the apartments. They move the chest of drawers out of the way, and Don picks the lock. The door swings open into Jill's bedroom.

Jill wonders if Don was in love with Linda. He will tell her only that Linda was very pretty—he can tell from the "shapes and textures" of a face.

JILL: I'm gorgeous.
DON: Really?
JILL: I wouldn't lie about something like that.
DON: You know, I've always thought if I could see for just half a minute— I'd like to see how I look.
JILL: I'll tell you. Cute . . . and very sexy.
Don smiles and reaches a hand toward Jill's face. She takes his hand and places it on her cheek. Gently, he runs his finger up the

side of her face, exploring. He runs his hand over the top of her head and takes hold of her long hair, lightly pulling it through his fingers.

DON: Your hair is very soft . . . and very long.

Suddenly, Jill's long hair, which is a fall, comes off in Don's hand, revealing her own short hair underneath. Don is startled as he feels the limp hair in his hand.

Oh, Jesus! *(He falls back on the sofa.)*

JILL: Don't be frightened.

DON *(dropping the fall like a hot potato):* What happened?

Jill picks up the fall and sits beside him.

JILL: It's a fall. It's a piece of long hair that you attach to your head.

DON: It's not *your* hair?

JILL: It's not even my fall. I borrowed it from Susan Potter. I do have hair of my own. See? I mean feel?

She places his hand on her head. Don takes in the shape of her head, then moves his hand along her face, over her eyes. A false eyelash comes off in his hand.

DON: God! Now what?!

JILL *(takes the eyelash from him and puts it back on):* That's just a false eyelash.

DON: Don't you have eyelashes?

JILL: Of course, but these make your eyes look bigger. They're longer than mine. Didn't Linda wear them?

DON: No.

JILL: She probably has naturally long lashes. I hate her.

Placing his hand on her cheek.

Go on.

DON: This is scaring hell out of me.

JILL: It's all right. Everything's real from now on.

Don runs his fingers across Jill's mouth.

Am I not the image of Elizabeth Taylor?

DON: I've never felt Elizabeth Taylor.

JILL: We look exactly alike. Especially if you can't see.

Jill smiles at Don, oddly, as his fingers explore her throat. She takes his hand and places it on her breast.

That's my breast. All mine. Both of them.

Gently, she pushes him down on the sofa and gets on top of him. She kisses him full on the mouth, then raises herself and starts to unbotton his shirt. She continues unbuttoning as she leans down to kiss him again. Don twists his head away from her, suddenly, anguished.

What's the matter?

DON: What do you think is the matter?

JILL: If I knew I wouldn't ask.

DON: Why are you doing this? Is it Be Kind to the Handicapped Week or something? *(Raising himself on one elbow.)* Don't patronize me! And don't feel sorry for me!

JILL *(hotly):* I'm doing it because I want to do it! And I'll be God damned if I feel sorry for any guy who's going to have sex with me!!

> *Don's hand on shoulder. The lights fade, slowly. The curtain is lowered for one minute to denote the passing of two hours. Over this, we hear Don playing his guitar and singing a rock love song.*

Scene 2

At curtain rise, Don, in his shorts, is sitting playing the guitar. His and Jill's clothes are spread over the room. Jill is in her apartment, and soon she comes in, dressed in panties and bra, carrying her "secret box."

Jill curls up beside Don and goes over her keepsakes—a bit of stone from the desert, birth certificate, instructions for her swinging funeral at which the mourners will smoke pot and listen to rock music. She takes out some hippie beads—"love beads" she calls them—and drapes them around Don's neck.

Once again, Jill is hungry. She gets an apple from the refrigerator, then starts combing Don's hair forward to make him look more hip, while she tells him of a time she was a hippie: "I just did it because everybody was doing it. Then I stopped because everybody was doing it. I felt I was losing my individuality—whatever that is. The main thing, of course, was to protest against my mother, but it didn't work. I mean I walked in one day with my hair long and stringy, wearing far-out clothes and beads and sandals . . . and she LOVED it! Next day *she* had stringy hair and far-out clothes and beads and sandals. Well, I mean how can you protest against someone who's doing the same thing you are? Right? So, I went the other way and joined the Young Republicans for Ronald Reagan. Another mistake. There's no such thing as a young Republican."

Jill surveys the results of re-combing Don's hair and finds him beautiful—inside and out. She hopes he doesn't think placing his hand on her breast was too brazen an approach, but she couldn't give him the eye subtly, along with her special smile, because of his blindness.

JILL: I hate talking about sex, but I thought maybe you'd like to know that you're . . . well, really groovy.

DON *(smiling):* Like the Fourth of July?

JILL: Like the Fourth of July—and like Christmas.

DON: Where are you going?

JILL: I'm going to throw the apple core away . . . and maybe I'll have some lettuce.

> *Jill drops the apple core into a waste bag. She starts for the refrigerator but freezes as the front door opens, slowly and silently. Jill darts behind one of the shutters to hide her near-nakedness, peering out, astonished, as Don's mother, Mrs. Baker, enters. She is an attractive woman, extremely well dressed. She is carrying a box*

from Saks Fifth Avenue. Mrs. Baker sees Jill's face peering from behind the shutter. She puts a finger to her lips, indicating silence to Jill, then mouths the words, "I am his mother." Don sits up on the sofa, stiffly, aware something is happening. A moment later, his shoulders sag.

DON *(unhappily):* Hello, mother!
Blackout. Curtain.

ACT II

Scene 1

A moment later, Mrs. Baker shuts the door. Don's expression shows his annoyance at her intrusion after she had promised to leave him alone.

Jill grabs for her clothes, as Don introduces Jill to his mother as "Mrs. Benson" who lives next door. Mrs. Baker pretends to have come specifically to bring Don some shirts. She takes in the scene—the picnic on the floor, the seedy furniture, the extremely disorderly state of Jill's apartment as seen through the open door, the bed high up on stilts. She disappears into the bathroom to inspect the plumbing.

Don knew it was his mother (he tells Jill) because of the perfume she always wears. They make a bet of a dinner over whether Mrs. Baker will say "I could absolutely cry." Mrs. Baker comes back into the room looking as though she could absolutely cry.

MRS. BAKER: Well, that's some bathroom. No wonder you hide it under the bed.
DON: Gee, I thought you were going to say something else.
MRS. BAKER: I haven't finished. I haven't even started.
DON: Well, say it and get it over with.
MRS. BAKER: Well, there's only one thing *to* say.
JILL *(aside to Don):* Here it comes.
MRS. BAKER: Perhaps it's a blessing that you can't see what you're living in.
DON: Right, Mom. I count that blessing every time I come in the door.
MRS. BAKER: Donny, can I be honest?
DON: *Can* you?
JILL *(aside to Don):* This is it.
MRS. BAKER: I am shocked and appalled.
JILL: I lose. Seven-thirty all right?
DON: Perfect.
MRS. BAKER: There's no tub in your bathroom.
DON: It's under the dining table.
MRS. BAKER: I could absolutely cry!
DON *(to Jill):* You win! Hamburgers all right?
JILL: But at least two each.

MRS. BAKER: I am not just talking about this rat hole, Donny, I am talking about you, too. You're so thin. You've lost weight.

DON: I haven't lost anything. I'm exactly the right weight for my height—six feet one—and my age—eleven.

Mrs. Baker's speculative eye falls on Jill, and she wonders: "Where is *Mister* Benson?" Jill straightens Mrs. Baker out on her age, marital status and occupation—nineteen, divorced and on her way to audition for an off-Broadway part. Don tries to slow his mother down, but she continues to question Jill sharply and finds that Jill's mother has been married four times and probably is not concerned about the way Jill is living in New York.

Jill exits into her apartment and Don turns on his mother.

DON: Did you have to be so goddam rude?

MRS. BAKER: Was I rude?

DON: All those questions! What are you—the Attorney General of Scarsdale?

MRS. BAKER: I think I have a right to know something about my son's friends.

DON: Let's talk about my rights! You're not supposed to be here for another month. Why did you have to come today, huh?

MRS. BAKER: Since when do you speak to me this way?

DON: Since when do you come sneaking into my room this way?

MRS. BAKER: I didn't come sneaking. The door was unlocked.

DON: You could have knocked. I thought it was a raid.

MRS. BAKER: It should have been. Why don't you lock your door?

DON: Until I know my way around the room, it was easier to let people come in on their own, but it'll be locked from now on.

Mrs. Baker tells her son her "worst fears have been realized" about the sordid neighborhood and the type of people who live in it. She demands to know if Don has slept with Jill, and Don states proudly that he has. Jill is not the girl for him to fall in love with, Mrs. Baker argues, pretending to Don that Jill "has beady little eyes like a bird and a figure like . . . a pogo stick." Don answers her: "You've just described the girl of my dreams."

Don reproaches his mother for trying to isolate him from life, accusing her of being "just a little bit ashamed" of having produced a blind son. Jill comes back into the room to get help with her zipper, whispers to Don, "I think you're winning. Hang in there!" then retreats again into her apartment.

Mrs. Baker offers to have Don's bed raised on stilts if he will come home. He refuses, of course, and she threatens to withdraw her financial support. Still Don defies her.

DON: I can always walk along the street with a tin cup.

MRS. BAKER: Now you *are* embarrassing me.

DON: Don't worry, Mom. I'll keep away from Saks.

MRS. BAKER: Just stop all this joking. I want to know what your plans are.

DON: I'm going to sing and play the guitar. I'm pretty good. You've said so yourself.

MRS. BAKER: I didn't know you were planning to make a career of it. Have you any idea of the competition you're facing?

DON: I have just as good a chance as anyone else. Better. I have charisma.

MRS. BAKER: May I ask how you arrived at this brilliant decision?

DON: It was elementary, my dear mother—by the process of elimination. I made a lengthy list of all the things I could NOT do . . . like . . . well, like commercial pilot. I don't think TWA would be too thrilled to have me fly their planes . . . nor United . . . nor Pan Am. Photographer? A definite out— along with ball player and cab driver. Matador didn't strike me as too promising. I half considered becoming an eye doctor, but that would just be a case of the blind leading the blind. That's a little joke. *(Shrugs when he gets no reponse.)* I said it was little.

But Mrs. Baker is in no mood for joking. She finds Don's suitcase and is determined to pack it and take Don back with her to Scarsdale. Her determination triggers an equally stubborn resistance in Don. Don stumbles around looking for the suitcase, emotionally upset, demanding that his mother give it back. Finally she yields. Don recovers his cool, kisses her on the cheek and dismisses her: she will go back to Scarsdale and leave him to go on with his new life. She wants to stay for dinner, but Don will not hear of it—he's having dinner alone with Jill, as planned. Don goes out to buy groceries, expecting that his mother will be gone when he returns.

Instead of leaving, Mrs. Baker calls Jill's name, "Mrs. Benson," and Jill comes in. She has a few minutes to spare for a little talk, before the audition.

Mrs. Baker admits to Jill that she is pretty, but Jill reminds her: "No I'm not. I've got beady eyes like a bird and a figure like a pogo stick."

Undaunted, Mrs. Baker continues their talk, calls Jill "worldly," asks Jill about her mother's various marriages. But Jill cuts straight to the subject of Don.

JILL: And I like him very much. He may very well be the most beautiful person I've ever met. Just imagine going through life never seeing anything . . . not a painting . . . or a flower . . . or even a Christmas card. I'd want to die, but Don wants to live. I mean really live . . . and he can even kid about it. He's fantastic.

MRS. BAKER: Then you would want what's best for him, wouldn't you?

JILL: Now we're getting to it, aren't we? Like maybe I should tell him to go home with you. Is that it?

MRS. BAKER: Donny was happy at home until Linda Fletcher filled him with ideas about a place of his own.

JILL: Maybe you just want to believe that he can only be happy with you, Mrs. Baker. Well, there are none so blind as those who will not see. There. I can quote Dylan Thomas AND Little Donny Dark.

MRS. BAKER: You constantly astonish me.

JILL: Well . . . we women of the world do that.

MRS. BAKER: Funny how like Linda you are. Donny is certainly consistent with his girls.

JILL: Why do you call him Donny?

MRS. BAKER: It's his name. Don't I say it as though I mean it?

JILL: He hates being called Donny.

MRS. BAKER: He's never mentioned it.

JILL: Of course, he has. You just didn't listen. There are none so deaf as those who will not hear. You could make up a lot of those, couldn't you? There are none so lame as those who will not walk. None so thin as those who will not eat . . .

Mrs. Baker characterizes Jill as a girl who is here today and will probably be gone tomorrow, who couldn't sustain a marriage longer than six days. How can she give Don the companionship he needs?

JILL: You can stop worrying, Mrs. Baker. Nothing serious will develop between Don and me. I'm not built that way!

MRS. BAKER: But Donny *is* built that way.

JILL: Oh, please—we're just having kicks.

MRS. BAKER: Kicks! That's how it started with Linda—just kicks . . . but Donny fell in love with her . . . and he'll fall in love with you. Then what happens?

JILL: I don't know!!

MRS. BAKER: Then don't let it go that far. Stop it now before you hurt him.

JILL: What about you? Aren't you hurting him?

MRS. BAKER: I can't. I can only irritate him. You can hurt him. The longer you stay the harder it will be for him when you leave. Let him come with me and you go have your kicks with someone who won't feel them after you've gone!!

Jill turns to face Mrs. Baker, studying her intently.

JILL: I'm not so sure you can't hurt him. Maybe more than anybody. I think you deserve all the credit you can get for turning out a pretty marvelous guy—but bringing up a son—even a blind one—isn't a lifetime occupation. Now the more you help him, the more you hurt him. It was Linda Fletcher—not you—who gave him the thing he needed most—confidence in himself. You're always dwelling on the negative—always what he needs, never what he wants . . . always what he can't do, never what he can. What about his music? Have you heard the song he wrote? I'll bet you didn't even know he could write songs! You're probably dead right about me. I'm not the ideal girl for Don, but I know one thing—neither are you!! And if I'm going to tell anyone to go home, it'll be you, Mrs. Baker. YOU go home!!

Jill turns. Curtain.

Scene 2

That night at 9:40 the table is set for two, but Jill hasn't shown up—she is already more than two hours late. And Mrs. Baker is still there, determined to sit it out till Jill arrives.

Mrs. Baker listens to Don's "Butterflies Are Free" on the tape recorder and is impressed. Criticizing Jill, Mrs. Baker refers inadvertently to part of their private conversation, and Don knows at once that his mother has been talking with Jill. Don is angry.

DON: I don't like you talking to my friends behind my back.

MRS. BAKER: It wasn't behind your back! You weren't even in the room! Donny? Did Linda Fletcher give you confidence?

DON: Mother, you know damn well what Linda Fletcher gave me—so don't be funny.

MRS. BAKER: I wasn't being funny. Did she *ALSO* give you confidence?

DON: Yes.

MRS. BAKER: Didn't *I*?

DON: You gave me help.

MRS. BAKER: I always thought one led to the other.

DON: Not necessarily, I guess.

MRS. BAKER: Why didn't you tell me you don't like being called Donny?

DON: I told you a thousand times.

MRS. BAKER: I'd remember something I heard a thousand times.

DON: Maybe it was only a hundred. . . . .

In the next apartment Jill's voice can be heard—with a man's. Soon Jill enters with Ralph Austin, *"a young man dressed in sloppy sweater and corduroy trousers and wearing a beard."* Jill introduces him as the director of the play she's trying out for. At first, Ralph is curious—and a bit awkward—about Don's blindness.

Mrs. Baker goes to fix them all some coffee as Jill notices the table set for two and apologizes: "That's me for you, I just completely forgot. We went to Ralph's place after the audition to celebrate and we drank a whole bottle of champagne or whatever it was." It is as though Jill is being deliberately, callously, casual about breaking her date with Don. She tells them she has been given a part in the play, a small role but one which requires her to "stand out there completely and totally naked." (Mrs. Baker drops a coffee cup in reaction to this announcement.) Of course Jill had to audition for the part in the nude. Her big scene is to be a death scene in which she dies screaming an obscenity over and over again.

Ralph puts the finishing touch on this conversation by explaining that the public is dying for this kind of theater—"I'm talking about the *thinking* public—not those giddy little tight-assed matrons from Scarsdale." Jill tries to smooth over the situation.

JILL: The play isn't really dirty. I wouldn't be in a dirty play. It's true to life.

DON: Not Mom's life.

JILL: This play is really good. It just needs polishing.

MRS. BAKER: I'd've said scrubbing.

RALPH: We'll just have to try to make it without the support of Scarsdale.

MRS. BAKER: Well, I wouldn't count on this giddy little matron. I don't intend to pay money to see nudity, obscenity and degeneracy.

RALPH: Mrs. Baker, these things are all a part of life.

MRS. BAKER: I know, Mr. Austin . . . So is diarrhea, but I wouldn't classify it as entertainment.

Ralph reassures Jill that the play will probably be a success and make a star of her. At this point Jill informs Don that she has decided to move in with Ralph, across town. She has come home to pack. Don is silent, concealing the pain. Jill insists that they will all be friends, and she puts Don's hand on Ralph's face to show him what a good face Ralph has.

Ralph departs, leaving Jill, Don and Mrs. Baker to a moment of embarrassed silence. Then Jill runs into her apartment to pack her bags. Mrs. Baker is acutely aware of Don's suffering, but it is Don who takes the initiative: he has decided to go back home to Scarsdale. Mrs. Baker sees that she has won, but now she is reluctant to accept victory. Don had better think twice about this decision.

DON: Are you saying you don't want me to come home?

MRS. BAKER: No. I'm only saying we should talk about it. Don't misunderstand me. I still think this place is dreadful and I doubt if I'll ever like it, but I didn't choose to live here. You did. You couldn't wait to have a place of your own. You rushed into this and now you want to rush out. I think we should talk about it.

DON: Isn't it funny that we think exactly alike, but never at the same time. I . . . I can't make it now, Mom. I'm not going to make it.

MRS. BAKER: Why? Because a girl has walked out on you?

DON: Two girls. Let's don't forget Linda.

MRS. BAKER: And it may be ten girls. Girls walk out on sighted men, too, you know.

DON: Is that supposed to make me feel better?

MRS. BAKER: It's supposed to make you stop feeling sorry for yourself—You've never felt sorry for yourself before. Please don't start now. You're going to meet a lot of girls. One day you'll meet one who is capable of a permanent relationship . . . Jill isn't. She knows this herself. I think you're better off staying here. I don't want you coming home discouraged and defeated. You've got your music.

DON: Christ, once and for all get it into your head—I am not Little Donny Dark!! I *am* discouraged. I *am* defeated. It's over!!

Mrs. Baker defends Little Donny Dark. She wrote the first story to help Don conquer his fear of swimming when he was 5 years old. Each time Don felt discouraged and defeated from then on, his mother made up a Little Donny Dark story to help him over the hurdle.

Bewildered, Don wonders why his mother is changing her position, and she informs him that it is *he* who has changed: *"You're* not the boy who left home a month ago. I came down here today hoping you *were.* It's hard to adjust to not being neded any more. But I can do it now. So you get on with your own life. I'd like to see you have some decent furniture. You need some dishes and some glasses. I don't use all those at home. I'll send some down to you."

Mother and son have reached a point of genuine mutual affection and understanding, and on this note Mrs. Baker leaves.

Jill comes in with her two suitcases packed and leaves her apartment key on Don's coffee table—an awkward moment of parting. Don offers her a corned beef sandwich, which she can't refuse. Jill learns that Mrs. Baker has accepted the fact of Don's new life in New York, but now Jill has her own doubts—perhaps Don might be better off back in Scarsdale.

Jill apologizes for Ralph's behavior. Don admits he doesn't like Ralph much. Then, slowly, Don begins to challenge Jill about her own feelings for Ralph, about loving him, about even liking him.

Bit by bit Don takes the offensive, building momentum, making a fight for his girl. If Jill were running to meet the man she really loved (he argues), not even *she* would stop for a sandwich.

DON: The reason you're leaving. The reason you didn't show up for dinner. I know you didn't forget. Was it something my mother said?

JILL: *You* don't even listen to your mother. Why should I?

DON: Then why are you leaving? And don't give me that crap about loving Ralph.

JILL: I'm leaving because I want to leave. I'm free and I go when I want to go.

DON: I thought it might have something to do with me.

JILL: It has nothing whatsoever to do with you.

DON: Okay.

> Jill lights a cigarette, plops down on the sofa and looks at Don, disturbed.

You're scared to death of becoming involved, aren't you?

JILL: I don't want to get involved. I told you that.

DON: That's right—you told me. No responsibility . . . no commitments.

JILL: I have to be able to get out if I get tired of the . . .

DON: Tired of me?

JILL: Or anybody.

DON: What if I got tired of you?

JILL *(this hadn't occurred to her):* Of me?

DON: Doesn't anyone ever get tired of you?

JILL: I don't hang around long enough to find out.

DON: With Ralph, you could get out any time you feel like it . . . but it might be harder to walk out on a blind guy, right?

JILL: The blindness has nothing to do with it. Nothing!

DON: You know goddam well it has! You wouldn't feel a thing walking out on Ralph or Sebastian or Irving, but if you walked out on Little Donny Dark, you might hate yourself and you wouldn't like that, would you? Hate *me*—or love *me*—but don't leave because I'm blind and don't stay because I'm blind!!

JILL: Who are Sebastian and Irving?

DON: Nobody. I just made them up.

JILL: Sometimes I don't understand you. We don't think alike and I know I'd only hurt you sooner or later. I don't want to hurt you.

DON: Why not? You do it to others. Why do I rate special treatment?

JILL: I don't want to be another Linda Fletcher. She hurt you, didn't she?

DON: She helped me, too. She was there when I needed her.

JILL: I can't promise that. I don't know where I'll be when you need me.

DON: You need me a helluva lot more than I need you!

JILL: I don't need anybody. I never did and I never will. I have to go now.

DON: I'm glad you said *have* to and not *want* to.

JILL: Boy, I finally said something right. I'll be seeing you.

DON: Yeah—I'll be seeing you. I'll think about you for years and wonder if you ever made a commitment . . . if you ever got involved.

JILL: I hope not.

DON: Don't worry. It won't happen . . . because you're emotionally retarded. Did you know that? That's why you couldn't face marriage. It's why you can't face anything permanent . . . anything real. You're leaving now because you're afraid you might fall in love with me . . . and you're too adolescent for that responsibility . . . and you're going to stay that way. Jesus, I feel sorry for you . . . because you're crippled. I'd rather be blind.

> *Jill exits, closing the door behind her. He turns and holds onto the back of the sofa, catching his breath and fighting back tears. When he has control of himself, he turns one way, then the other, undecided what to do. He crosses to the bookcase and turns on his tape machine which plays a recording of him singing and playing the guitar. He crosses to the dining table and blows out the candles, slowly. He empties the ash tray into one of the dishes, stacks the dishes and beer glasses and starts toward the coffee table. The dishes and glasses fly out of his hand as he falls to the floor with one arm pinned under him. He rolls over to free his arm, wincing with pain. He lies on the floor with tears welling in his eyes and no interest in getting up.*
>
> *The front door opens. Jill enters carrying her bags. She sets her bags on the floor and looks about the room for Don. She suppresses a scream when she sees what has happened.*
>
> *Don, rubbing his injured arm, raises himself on the floor.*

DON: Who is it? Who's there?

JILL *(breaking the tension):* The news is good. It's not your mother.
    She crosses to him and sits beside him on the floor.

DON: What are you doing here?

JILL: What are you doing on the floor?

DON: I was about to have a picnic.

JILL: What a great idea—
    Curtain.

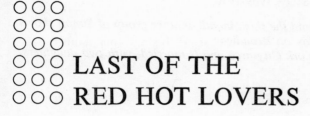

LAST OF THE
RED HOT LOVERS

A Comedy in Three Acts

BY NEIL SIMON

Cast and credits appear on page 310

NEIL SIMON was born in the Bronx, N.Y., on July 4, 1927. He attended New York University and the University of Denver. His first theatrical work was sketches for camp shows at Tamiment, Pa., in collaboration with his brother Danny. He became a TV writer, supplying a good deal of material to Sid Caesar and Phil Silvers. On Broadway, Simon contributed sketches to Catch a Star *(1955) and* New Faces of 1956. *His first Broadway play was* Come Blow Your Horn *(1961), followed by the book for the musical* Little Me *(1962). His comedy* Barefoot in the Park *(1963) was selected as a Best Play of its season, as was* The Odd Couple *(1965). Neither of these had closed when* Sweet Charity, *a musical for which Simon wrote the book, came along in early 1966; and none of the three had closed when Simon's* The Star-Spangled Girl *opened the following season in December 1966—so that Simon had four hit shows running at one time on Broadway during the season of 1966-67. When the last of the four closed the following summer, Simon's hits had played a combined total of 3,367 performances over a period of four theater seasons.*

Simon immediately began another stack of hits. His Plaza Suite *(1968) was named a Best Play of its year; his book for the musical* Promises, Promises *(1969) was another smash, and this season's* Last of the Red Hot Lovers *be-*

comes his fourth Best Play and the third in still another group of Simon shows in grand simultaneous display on Broadway.

Simon lives in the New York City area and is married, with two daughters.

Time: The present

Place: An apartment in the East Thirties

ACT I

SYNOPSIS: The doorbell is ringing in an empty one-and-a-half-room apartment, a well-kept home combining good old furniture and convenient modern appliances. Door and coat closet are at right on a raised landing. The window is at left and the hall to bathroom and kitchen is upstage center. A sofa is placed prominently down center.

Barney Cashman lets himself in the door. He calls out "Mom" to reassure himself she is not at home (this is his mother's apartment), closes the door behind him. *"Barney Cashman is 47 years old, neatly dressed in blue suit, blue topcoat and grey felt hat."* He hangs up his coat and takes pains to place his rubbers on a piece of newspaper. Nervously, he closes blinds and drapes so that no one can see into the apartment this mid-afternoon in November. Barney is obviously anxious to disturb nothing in the apartment. In his brief case and shopping bag he has brought his own bottle of Scotch and his own glasses —and some after-shave lotion for a last-minute application to his face and hands.

Barney pours a drink, checks the condition of the sofa (it is a convertible bed) and makes a phone call.

> BARNEY *(into phone, hardly above a whisper):* Hello? . . . Harriet? . . . Mr. Cashman . . . Everything all right? . . . Did Pepito come in? . . . Pepito, the busboy . . . All right, Pietro—whatever his name is . . . Didn't come in, heh? . . . Did you try the agency again? . . . Well, listen, there's nothing I can do right now—*(Looks at his watch.)*—I'll be in about five o'clock . . . I'm still in Bloomingdale's. It's just murder in here with all the Christmas shoppers . . . Did my wife call? And you told her Bloomingdale's? . . . Good. Good . . . Listen, I gotta run. I see an opening on the escalator . . . I'll be back at five-thirty the latest . . . Thank you, Harriet.
>
> *He hangs up phone, thinks for a second.*

What the hell am I doing here?

> *He quickly crosses to the closet and the doorbell rings. He freezes, looking around for an exit. There is, of course, none. He rushes to door and peers out the minuscule port-a-view. Satisfied, he opens the door.*

LINDA LAVIN, JAMES COCO AND MARCIA RODD IN "LAST OF THE RED
HOT LOVERS"

    Elaine Navazio enters. Elaine is in her late 30s, somewhat attractive and modestly dressed. There is an air of desperation about Elaine Navazio. Barney looks at her nervously.

Hello.

    Elaine smiles and nods.

I was in the kitchen. I didn't hear the bell.

    Elaine walks past him into the apartment and stands above steps.

Come on in.

    He closes door.

ELAINE *(turns, looks at him):* I'm in.

BARNEY: How are you?

ELAINE: Very nice.

BARNEY: Well, you look very nice.

ELAINE: You look surprised. Didn't you think I'd come?

BARNEY: I wasn't sure . . . but I was hoping.

ELAINE: I wasn't sure either . . . but I came.

Barney would have been disappointed if Elaine hadn't shown up, but now that she has, he is awkward and nervous. They exchange several conversational formalities. She, Barney learns, is of Polish descent, married to an Italian; Barney is part Russian, part Lithuanian.

Elaine vibrates with restlessness. She coughs, then craves a cigarette. Barney doesn't have any, and there wouldn't be any in his mother's apartment (Barney's mother does charity work two days a week at Mount Sinai Hospital and can be counted on not to come home till five o'clock).

Barney offers Elaine a drink, which she eagerly accepts. He takes a glass out of his shopping bag.

ELAINE: You brought glasses too?

BARNEY: I picked them up in Bloomingdale's. I was thinking of getting them for the restaurant.

ELAINE: You were afraid if you dirtied your mother's glasses she'd know someone was here.

BARNEY (caught, he smiles): Well, she's a very meticulous woman. And if anything looked different when she came home I'd have to explain to her and it would get very complicated.

ELAINE: I think you did the smart thing. How many ice cubes did you bring?

BARNEY (smiles): Well, I didn't go quite that far. Why, would you like some ice? I'll get some ice for you.

ELAINE: Forget it. We'd spend the rest of the afternoon wiping fingerprints off the tray.

> Barney pours Scotch into Elaine's glass. Elaine watches him.

BARNEY (pouring): My mother's very typical, you know. She remembers exactly how high the pillows were puffed when she left.

ELAINE: Is that why you put your rubbers on the newspaper? So it wouldn't leave telltale slush?

BARNEY: I'm beginning to feel very foolish about all this.

ELAINE: Forget it. Meeting on the sly is not without its drawbacks.

BARNEY (hands her drink): Well, here you are.

ELAINE (takes it): I would like to ask you one question though.

BARNEY: Yes?

ELAINE: Are you going to talk soft like that all afternoon?

BARNEY: Was I talking soft?

ELAINE: I know that's not your natural voice because I hear you yelling a lot in the restaurant . . . "The lady wants boiled halibut not baked halibut!" . . . Are you talking soft because you think that's sexier? Because I don't find it sexy. I find it hard to hear.

BARNEY: I'm sorry. It's just that these new buildings have paper-thin walls and you know, I was afraid—I mean my mother has this high squeaky voice and there's this old lady next door who's home all day and if she were to hear deep voices she'd start to wonder—

The last thing Barney wants, however, is to inhibit Elaine. He makes a half-hearted effort to put her at ease. Elaine mentions Barney's wife of 23 years, whom she has seen in Barney's restaurant and describes as "The tall blonde woman with the mink coat and the space shoes."

As Barney pours Elaine another drink, she notices his habit of smelling his fingers to check whether the odor of his fish restaurant lingers on them (it almost always does, a little). But the odor doesn't bother Elaine as much, she tells him, as his habit of always and invariably wearing a blue suit, which Barney's father once told him was the only proper attire on duty in the restaurant.

Barney comments on Elaine's unusual behavior in lunching at his restaurant eight days in a row. "I get cravings," Elaine tells him, "To eat, to touch, to smell, to see, to do . . . A sensual, physical pleasure that can only be satisfied at *that* particular moment."

Elaine continues to crave a cigarette. And she wonders when Barney is going to make the first move. He tries to compliment her but he winds up talking about himself. He is interested in writing.

BARNEY: . . . . . You read some of my stuff.

ELAINE: I did? Where?

BARNEY: In the menu. "Sweet savory swordfish steak swimming in salivary succulence." That's mine.

ELAINE: Very catchy. It has a nice beat.

BARNEY: That's the idea. It's what they call alliteration.

ELAINE: Do they? You take that in college?

BARNEY: I didn't go to college. I went from the army right into the "Queen of the Sea." My father started the restaurant in 1931. We used to be in Sheepshead Bay. That's where I grew up. I was always hoping to be a radio writer. Orson Welles and the Mercury Theater, that was my dream. But then came the war, and then my father died and left me the restaurant, and then television killed radio. And I never thought my kind of writing would go on television. I don't write visual. I write for the ear. "Sweet succulent savory swordfish steak" . . . Anyway, I still get a kick out of doing the menus . . . Did you see the one I did on "Flaming Florentine Flounder?"

ELAINE: I browsed through it . . . What time is it now?

BARNEY (looks at watch): Twenty after three.

ELAINE: That's another ten minutes shot. So what's it going to be?

BARNEY: My God, you really come right to the point, don't you?

ELAINE: Look, did you ask me to come up here with the intentions of having an affair or not?

Yes, Barney admits, he did, and Elaine reminds him that they have to be out by five o'clock, so he'd better get busy. But Barney is trying to create an atmosphere of romance in this rendezvous, which takes time. Elaine prefers direct and immediate approach to sex and tries to shock Barney out of his procrastination with an exchange of blunt words, but this only dismays Barney. He insists on talking with Elaine, on getting to know each other.

ELAINE: Look, *you* were the one who wrote down an address and apartment number on the back of a dollar eighty check. Then I come here and find out we've got an hour and fifty minutes before your social working mother with the high, squeaky voice comes home to examine the puffed pillows. Now if we had two weeks in Nassau I'd gladly look at color pictures of your tonsils—

BARNEY: I explained that, I thought a motel was a little sordid . . . And I would gladly have picked up your check but my cashier's very nosy and if she saw me paying for some woman—

ELAINE: Forget it. You got a lot of courage. I was surprised you took a chance giving me an extra shrimp in the shrimp cocktail.

She finishes her drink.

BARNEY: I don't know how we got started on this—

ELAINE: It's cigarette nerves, pay no attention. Is that bottle just going to sit up there or are you going to turn it into a lamp? *(She means the Scotch bottle.)*

BARNEY: You finished the other one already?

ELAINE: I didn't finish it, it evaporated.

BARNEY: Elaine . . . Can I ask you a very honest question?

ELAINE: Yes, I've done this before.

BARNEY *(looks at her):* That wasn't what I was going to ask.

ELAINE: All right, you got one for free. What were you going to ask?

BARNEY: I'm still not over that answer. You mean you have—on other occasions—?

ELAINE: I have on other occasions—in other places—with other men—done the unthinkable. If it'll help your vanity any, you are the first owner of a fish restaurant I've ever been with. In that respect, I'm still a virgin.

It isn't that she doesn't love her husband, Elaine insists, it's just that for the moment Barney appeals to her. Tomorrow she might not feel the same way. "I find it disturbing, and a little sad that your attitude towards people is so detached," is Barney's comment.

Elaine, angry at being called "a depressant" quarrels with Barney and threatens to leave. When Barney asks her to lower her voice, she cries aloud, "Mr. Cashman is using his mother's apartment to bring broads!"

Elaine has another coughing fit and Barney brings her a glass of water. Barney is beginning to see that he has bungled the situation. He apologizes, and Elaine softens a little.

ELAINE: I'm not upset, I'm not angry, I'm not mad. If you want the plain, heartbreaking truth, I'm a little bored. But there was no harm done, no one got hurt. The worst that'll happen is that from now on I'll get the same five shrimps as everyone else. *(She gets up.)* It's been a glorious and memorable thirty minutes. Goodbye, Mr. Cashman.

BARNEY: Don't go.

ELAINE: It happens to the best of us.

She crosses to the door.

BARNEY: Elaine . . . Do you know what I wish?

ELAINE *(warding him off with hand):* Don't tell me, it won't come true.

She opens the door.

BARNEY: I wish that you would go out, close the door, then ring the bell and come back in again. I wish we could start this whole thing over . . . from the beginning.

ELAINE *(turns at door, looks at him):* Yeah . . . Well . . . That's life . . . Goodbye, Barney.

She goes and closes the door.

Barney starts to clean up, puts the glasses away, when the doorbell rings. It is Elaine, "arriving" again, expecting a new Barney. Barney kisses Elaine passionately, in silence, but in trying to maneuver her toward the sofa he trips her. She falls backwards onto the sofa with Barney on top of her, and she has cut her lip.

Once again, passion has flown out the window. Barney reproaches himself for his own fumbling and pours more Scotch; Elaine is grateful that at least they had a pleasant two minutes before the fall. Barney wants to talk, to find out about Elaine, but all Elaine wants—still—is a cigarette.

Elaine admits that she would accept an animal act from Barney, failing a subtler wooing, but Barney cannot take such crude action. He accuses her of being cold and callous, and she replies angrily that "I happen to like the pure physical act of making love. It warms me, it stimulates me and it makes me feel like a woman." Elaine is finally fed up with Barney, she moves to depart, but he bolts the door, forcing her to remain.

ELAINE *(looks at him, smiles):* Wouldn't you know it? We've only got forty minutes left and finally you show me some brute force.

BARNEY: Will you please sit down? I'm asking nicely.

ELAINE: You want to really get me crazy? Push me!

He suddenly grabs her arm, pulls her and shoves her onto a chair.
She falls into it stunned and looks up at him with great surprise. He
is shaking with anger and points a threatening finger at her.

BARNEY: Just sit there! Don't talk, don't cough, don't even breathe. Just sit there and shut up until I tell you you can go. If I get nothing else from you this afternoon it's going to be your undivided God damned attention! Excuse me!

He crosses to bottle, pours himself a drink, gulps it down. She looks
at him incredulously but silently. He does not look at her.

. . . I'm sure it will come as no great shock to you, but you are the first "attempted" extra-marital affair for me in twenty-three years of marriage. I've never even kissed another woman. In twenty-three years . . . I got married to my high school sweetheart, and when have you heard that expression last, at the age of twenty-four having gone steady with her since I was sixteen. And how many experiences with other women do you think I've had prior to getting married? . . . One! . . . I had one shot at it . . . when I was eighteen my brother took me to an apartment in Newark, New Jersey, where I consorted with a forty-four-year-old woman who greeted me lying naked on a brass bed reading a newspaper. It cost me seven dollars and I threw up all night. . . . .

Barney goes on: he has no important vices, he's proud of his children and loves his wife Thelma. Then why this assignation? He's not sure. Lately he's been thinking about death, imagining dying, asking himself whether he's really *lived*. His life is merely "nice."

BARNEY: . . . . . Couldn't I just once give in to my fantasies, my secret dreams, experiencing things, emotions, stimulants I've never experienced before . . . I wanted to know what it was like with another woman . . . Would I be successful, would she like me, would I like the touch of her? A thousand questions that I'd never know the answer to if suddenly my name were in that obituary column tomorrow morning . . . So I decided to indulge myself, just once. I don't pretend I'm being fair to my wife. If she indulged herself the same way I'd never forgive her. So I started looking around . . . And I promise you, with all intentions of having one affair, one day of pleasure and that's all . . . But if it was just going to be one day I wanted it to be memorable . . . An experience so rewarding and fulfilling that it would last me the rest of my life . . . not cheap, not sordid . . . and then I'd go back to opening the restaurant at eleven o'clock in the morning . . . but knowing that for one brief afternoon, I had changed the pattern of my life . . . and for once I didn't just exist—I lived!
> *There is a long silence.*
ELAINE: . . . And that's why you wanted to get laid?
BARNEY: I said I'd let you know when you can go. *Now* is a good time.
ELAINE: I was going to cry in the middle but I didn't want to wet your mother's carpeting.
BARNEY: I had hoped you'd understand, but I didn't expect it.
ELAINE: No, listen, it was terrifically entertaining . . . I really enjoyed it. There's one or two reasons though, why I couldn't feel too sympathetic for the hero . . . In the first place, there is a very good possibility that that forty-four-year-old woman in Newark, New Jersey, was my mother. That'll give you some idea of my background . . . In the second place, any man who expects to have a beautiful, memorable and enchanting day of honest love with a woman he picks up in a fish restaurant is either sexually retarded or a latent idiot! . . . And in the third place, no one gives a good crap about you dying because a lot of people discovered it ahead of you. We're all dying, Mr. Cashman. As a matter of fact, I myself passed away about six months ago. I'm just hanging around to clean up some business affairs . . . Together, Barney, we blew one of the very few free afternoons we have allotted to us in this life . . . But I'm not putting the blame on you. It serves me right. If I had a craving for corned beef and cabbage I'd be in some big Irishman's apartment right now having the time of my life . . . C'est la vie! . . .

At the door.
Good luck, Barney, in your quest for the Impossible Dream.
Opens door.
Oh, please God, let there be a machine in the lobby . . .
And she is gone. Barney stands there a moment, still shaken from his experience . . . Then he crosses slowly and opens drapes. He looks at his watch, then crosses to the phone, picks it up and dials.
BARNEY *(into phone):* . . . Hello, Harriet? . . . Mr. Cashman . . . The busboy show up? . . . Well, call the agency again . . . I'll be there in about twenty minutes. I'm leaving Bloomingdale's now . . . No, I didn't get anything . . . I looked, I shopped around, but I didn't get anything . . . Well, that's the way it goes . . . I'll see you, Harriet.
He hangs up. He looks around the room, then sits. He buries his head in his hands and is silent a moment.
. . . I'll never do that again! . . . Never never never never never . . . never . . . never . . .
Curtain.

ACT II

In the same apartment, at about 3 o'clock of a July afternoon, Barney once again comes in the front door, calls "Mom?" to make sure the coast is clear and begins to arrange for a rendezvous. Again, he is wearing a blue suit (summer weight). This time, though, he has brought vodka as well as Scotch, and three packs of cigarettes.

The doorbell rings as Barney is explaining on the phone to his cashier that he is at the dentist's. Barney hangs up the phone and opens the door. *"Bobbi Michele stands there, a pretty girl about 27. Despite the oppressive heat outside, Bobbi looks cool and fresh. She carries a large leather portfolio and makeup bag."*

Bobbi hopes she is not disturbing Barney, and Barney assures her he expected her. Bobbi begins to chatter nervously from subject to subject.

BOBBI: . . . . . You were so sweet in the park yesterday and I want you to know I have not forgotten it but here I am talking and talking and I really haven't said hello yet. Hello.
BARNEY: Hello.
BOBBI: Hello. Here I am.
BARNEY: So I see.
BOBBI: Oh God, I talk a lot when I get nervous. Have you noticed that? I'll try and stop it if I can. You'll have to forgive me.
BARNEY: Are you nervous?
BOBBI: Well, I'm not nervous now. I was nervous before. I just had a terrible experience with a cab driver. Well, I don't want to go into it. Ohh, God,

I just wilt in the heat. If I pass out on the floor, I'm just going to have to trust you.

BARNEY *(smiles):* You don't have to worry.

BOBBI: Well, you're not a cab driver. You wouldn't try something like that.

BARNEY: Like what?

BOBBI: He wanted to make it with me under the Manhattan Bridge during his lunch hour. Listen, can we forget about it, it's over now. I must look awful.

BARNEY: Not at all. You look lovely.

Bobbi declares herself "goofy with the heat" and continues to chatter. Apparently she is a frequent victim of incidents like the one with the cab driver. She also gets a lot of obscene telephone calls. She inspects the apartment.

BOBBI: Is this where you write those sea stories you were telling me about?

BARNEY: Yes, I work here during the day. Actually it's my mother's apartment.

BOBBI: I knew this writer in California. A registered weirdo. He used to write these underground movies you see on Eighth Avenue. You know, "Sex Family Robinson" . . . "Tom Swift and His Incredible Thing" . . . I thought I was in love with him until I found out he was deranged. I mean the things he wanted me to do.

BARNEY: Like what?

BOBBI: Oh, God, I couldn't repeat them. . . . . I couldn't tell you. I told my analyst, he went into cardiac arrest. . . . .

BARNEY: You mean things together or alone? What kind of things?

BOBBI: If I tell you this man had his teeth sharpened, can you fill in the rest?

Bobbi wants to tell Barney about her audition (now it is Barney's turn to look at his watch and regret the passing minutes). She was great, and David Merrick or somebody with a mustache liked her, but they wanted a black girl for the part.

Bobbi expects to pay Barney back the $20 he loaned her in the park the day before to hire an accompanist for the audition, but she doesn't have the money at present. She will pay the debt as soon as she gets work. To prove she's an actress, she shows Barney a picture of herself in a Fabian movie. While making the movie (she tells Barney) she was beaten up by a Mexican in a motel.

Bobbi makes a phone call and manages to get through to her roommate whom she describes as "this Nazi vocal teacher . . . . . Wilhelmina Weirdo. She paid $400 to have a three-inch scar put on her face." Bobbi is no Lesbian (she informs Barney), she just needs the expert vocal instruction. On the phone, she informs her roommate that she'll be home for dinner.

Bobbi craves a cigarette. Barney leaps to offer her the packs he has brought, but Bobbi is carrying her own. She lights up and begins to deliver a detailed confidence about an experience with a married man, a Mr. H. of Palm Springs.

All at once Barney understands that Bobbi's cigarette is marijuana. Bobbi offers him one. Barney turns it down, pretending to be cool and casual about his refusal.

BOBBI: Actually it's a blend. Half Turkish tobacco, half grass. It's prescribed by my doctor in Beverly Hills. I take it instead of a tranquilizer because I have this inability to swallow pills.
   Holds out the box.
You sure? They're not strong. They're a twenty-minute freak-out at the most.
BARNEY: Maybe later.
BOBBI: I take it for medicinal purposes but you can get high if you like. By the way, you have a nice smile.
BARNEY: Other people have told me that.
BOBBI: You're a very basic person, no crap. Am I right?
BARNEY: Well . . .
BOBBI: Sincere . . . sweet . . . You meet so damned few in my business . . . Well, anywhere for that matter . . .
BARNEY: Well, most people that I've run across . . .
BOBBI *(sits back, suddenly begins to sing:)*
   "What the world needs now is love, sweet love . . .
   That's the only thing that there's just too little of . . ."
That's what I'm going to do if I get the Merv Griffin show . . . If the Beast of Berlin ever takes my messages . . . *(Looks around.)* I like the color of these walls . . . I am so sick of white walls . . . Is the door locked?
BARNEY: The door? Yes. Is it all right?
BOBBI: I just wanted to make sure. I thought I saw somebody following me outside. . . . .

Barney worries that perhaps someone knows they are here in the apartment together. Bobbi finishes her cigarette and warns Barney to "tear the paper, scatter the ashes and flush the toilet twice. You can't imagine the number of people who are serving time today because they only flushed once."

Barney is only too eager and careful to dispose of the butt. Bobbi "confides" to Barney that the married man she was entangled with in Palm Springs—Mr. H.—had her dog kidnaped. No use calling in the police, because Mr. H. is so powerful the police were in on the deal. Some day Bobbi will write a book about all the cruel men she has known—except Barney who is "nice."

Barney tries to bring Bobbi back to the point of this rendezvous, but she meanders off again conversationally in reminiscences of more persecution by Mr. H.

BOBBI *(laughs):* You know he once tried to have me committed to a hospital?

BARNEY: No. Why?

BOBBI: Obviously to keep tabs on me. Actually it was my own fault. I was faking a nervous breakdown so he'd leave me alone. I made believe I went crazy in a department store one day and the police came with an ambulance. He must have had me followed because the ambulance was there in five minutes. Who else could have sent them?

BARNEY (nods): What did they do?

BOBBI: Oh, they just held me for observation.

BARNEY: And sent you home?

BOBBI: In twelve weeks . . . He must have paid them off. Otherwise why would they keep me there? It wasn't too bad, I wasn't working anyway. I ask you is that some experience?

BARNEY (nods): Some experience.

By now, Barney has just about given up all hope of romance, and he lets Bobbi continue to ramble on about her career. Barney encourages Bobbi to leave, but she wants one more cigarette first and insists that Barney join her. Barney humors her—he lights up one of her reefers and takes a couple of tentative puffs. At her urging, he takes a deep puff and begins to turn on. His toes start tingling, his tongue goes numb.

BARNEY (puts hand on chest): Oh, God, I don't feel my heart. What the hell happened to my heart?

BOBBI: Relax . . . don't fight it, honey.

BARNEY: I'm not. I'm not fighting it. I'm letting it do whatever it wants.

BOBBI: Hang it out for the world to see, honey.

BARNEY: I'm hanging it out. Here I go . . . I don't know where I'm going, but I'm going . . .

BOBBI: Just let yourself go.

BARNEY: Oh, boy, what's that? What is that?

BOBBI: What?

BARNEY: I hear my eyes blinking . . . thump, thump . . . There it goes again, thump!

BOBBI: If you got it, baby, flaunt it.

BARNEY: I'm flaunting it, I'm flaunting it. (A big, enormous smile spreads across his face.) Wheeeee!

BOBBI: God, the things that have happened to me.

BARNEY: I heard, I heard. I can't wait to read the book.

BOBBI: Did I tell you about this man in California?

BARNEY: The dog-naper or the teeth sharpener?

BOBBI: Well, I was in love with him. You know about love, I can tell . . . you must have suffered plenty, didn't you?

BARNEY: Many years ago I was involved with an older woman in Newark, New Jersey.

BOBBI: Oh, yeah, I know that scene. How long did it last?

BARNEY: About fifteen minutes.

BOBBI: You got to make it alone in this world . . . All I need is one show.

The talent's there, it's just a question of time.

BARNEY: That's all it is, Bob.

BOBBI: People don't want to see you make good . . . they're all jealous . . . they're all rotten . . . they're all vicious.

BARNEY: So many things I wanted to do . . . but I'll never do 'em . . . So many places I wanted to see . . . I'll never see 'em . . . Trapped . . . We're all trapped . . . Help! . . . Help!

BOBBI *(after a moment's quiet she begins to sing):*
"What the world needs now, is love, sweet love,
   Barney joins her, humming along.
That's the only thing there's just too little of . . ."
   Curtain.

ACT III

In September, Barney enters the same apartment at about the same time in the afternoon for the same reason. This time, however, he is wearing a glen plaid sports jacket and tan slacks instead of his blue suit, and he has brought champagne. He goes to open the door as the doorbell rings.

> *Jeanette Fisher stands there, about 39 years old, a woman of no discernable physical attributes. There is only one distinguishable quality about Jeanette Fisher. She is probably the singularly most depressed woman on the face of the Western Hemisphere. She wakes up to gloom and goes to bed with gloom. She fills the in-between hours with despair. She wears a beige dress and matching stole.*

Jeanette is so sad and nervous that Barney thinks something must be wrong—it must have started raining or something. Barney tries to reassure her: "You are the only one in our circle, the *only* one of Thelma's friends that I have ever had any respect or feeling for. That's why I was so happy the other night when we were having dinner at your place, when you indicated to me—"

But this merely makes Jeanette burst into tears. Jeanette rushes to the bathroom. Barney listens to her through the door, then he walks away.

BARNEY *(throws up his arms in dismay):* Oh, Christ! . . . Boy, can you pick 'em. Can you pick 'em!
   The door suddenly opens and Jeanette stands there. She has stopped crying. Barney looks at her in anticipation. She smiles at him.

JEANETTE: Why am I here, Barney?

BARNEY: What was that?

JEANETTE: Why am I here? I've known you and Thelma for twelve years. She's been a good friend to me. I wouldn't hurt her for the world. You and Mel are closer than brothers. So why am I here?

BARNEY: Why? Because I *asked* you here, that's why. I'm very fond of you.

Look, why don't you put your pocketbook down, Jeanette, and relax and I'll go inside and get us a drink, okay?

JEANETTE: I don't find you physically attractive. You knew that, didn't you? *That stops him.*

BARNEY: No! No, I didn't know that . . . It doesn't surprise me . . . I mean it's not mandatory . . .

JEANETTE: I think you're sweet . . . I think you're basically a good person. I do not think you're physically attractive.

BARNEY *(cheerfully):* Listen, you can't win 'em all.

JEANETTE: I can be honest with you, Barney, can't I? I think we've known each other long enough for that, haven't we?

BARNEY *(the good sport):* Hell, yes.

JEANETTE: So I can just come out and say it, can't I? I do not find you physically attractive.

BARNEY *(smiling):* Fine, fine. Listen, I think we've covered that ground pretty good, Jeanette . . . So why don't I go get the drinks and you put down your pocketbook and relax and then—

JEANETTE: Don't misunderstand me. It's not the weight. The weight thing doesn't bother me. I have never been repelled by obesity.

BARNEY: I'm glad to hear that, Jeanette. Actually I was a skinny kid. I blew up in the army. I was a mess sergeant in Fort Totten for about two years and I would constantly—

JEANETTE: I am attracted to you emotionally, intellectually—

BARNEY: Isn't that funny? I always felt that you and I had a certain rapport—

JEANETTE: But not physically.

BARNEY *(nods):* Not physically, we established that a number of times.

Jeanette brings Barney up short a second time by informing him she hasn't slept with her husband Mel for eight months. Then Barney finds out that "He's slept with me. I haven't slept with him." Sex is not important to Jeanette any more.

Jeanette confesses she doesn't know what she's supposed to do here, but whatever it is Barney must swear he'll never tell anyone. Jeanette is curious to know whether Mel, with whom Barney plays handball, has ever mentioned another woman. Barney tells her no.

Jeanette reproaches Barney about feeling no guilt for arranging this meeting. She swallows a pill for her depression, explains to Barney how life is merely a shuttling between pills and melancholia. Barney still thinks they can have "an interesting afternoon" if she will only put down her pocketbook (which annoys him) and relax, have a glass of champagne.

JEANETTE: And how do *you* feel, Barney? About being here with Mel's wife?

BARNEY: Why do you put it that way? You're Jeanette, I'm Barney. Why do you complicate everything?

JEANETTE *(crosses to phone and picks up receiver):* What do you think Mel's reaction would be if I called him now and told him what was going on here?

BARNEY *(crosses to her):* Big! I think his reaction would be big!
He takes phone away from her.
With a lot of killing and murder.
He takes phone and crosses with it.
Don't test him, Jeanette. It's not good for a marriage to test it too much.
He pushes phone behind lamp.
JEANETTE: You think death is so terrible, Barney?

BARNEY: Death? I do. I think death is terrible. I think *violent* death is the worst . . . Jeanette, I think we're getting a little morbid here . . .

JEANETTE: You don't think there are worse things than death?

BARNEY: Like suffering and pain? They're bad but they're second and third after death. Death is first . . . Jeanette, I really think you should have some champagne . . .

JEANETTE: You mean you enjoy your life? You like living?

BARNEY: I *love* living. I have some problems with my *life,* but living is the best thing they've come up with so far . . . Look, Jeanette, I know you're going through analysis right now but I don't think this is a good time to talk shop . . .

Barney snatches her "God-damned pocketbook" from her and sinks into a chair. Jeanette confides to Barney that her percentage of happiness in living is about 8.2, by her doctor's estimate.

Jeanette challenges Barney to believe that the world is full of decent, loving, gentle human beings. She challenges him to name only three such people. Barney, to humor her, begins his list—surprisingly, his wife Thelma is the name he mentions first. Then he comes up with John F. Kennedy and Jesus Christ.

Among the people she has known personally, Jeanette insists, there has been no one. She admits that Thelma is gentle and loving, and Barney picks up the omission.

BARNEY: . . . . . Why did you leave out decent?

JEANETTE: She's on *your* list. It's not important if she's on mine.

BARNEY: What are you trying to do, Jeanette? Are you making inferences concerning the decency of my wife Thelma?

JEANETTE: I'm not making inferences, Barney. *You're* indicating some doubt.

BARNEY: *Doubt? Doubt?* About Thelma? *(Laughs.)* Good God, what the hell is there to doubt about Thelma?

JEANETTE: How would I know, Barney?

BARNEY: Well, I'll tell you. NOTHING! THERE IS NOTHING TO DOUBT ABOUT THELMA!

JEANETTE: As long as you're sure.

BARNEY *(shouting):* Don't tell me 'as long as I'm sure' because I'm sure. I have lived with the woman my whole life. I grew up with her. I know every nerve fiber in her body, every thought that's ever been in her head. The woman is without malice, without jealousy . . . Thelma Cashman is *beyond* reproach. She is as totally incapable of an act of deception as *you* would be or *I* would be or—oh, my God!

   He slumps in his seat. She stares at him. A long pause.

JEANETTE: . . . So you have Kennedy and Christ! . . . You have one more pick.

Pressed by Barney for anything she knows about Thelma, Jeanette admits that Thelma is "the only gentle, loving and decent woman I've ever met," which makes present company something else for conspiring to deceive her. This puts Barney into a state of depression, too, and he now sees the world as a dreadful place full of reprehensible people.

Mel is making it with a buxom red-head named Charlotte Korman, Jeanette informs Barney: "You know what my proof is? He told me. Two o'clock in the morning, he leans over, taps me on the shoulder and says, 'I've had an affair with Charlotte Korman' . . . Who asked him? When he tapped me on the shoulder in the middle of the night I thought he wanted *me!*"

This is what sent Jeanette into the depths of depression, now of eight months' duration. Having unloaded her troubles onto Barney, Jeanette is ready to depart, but Barney detains her. He insists that she hear him out in her turn.

BARNEY: . . . . . You haven't the slightest idea of how filthy and ugly I really am deep inside. You think you're the first woman I ever had up here? Ha! You want to hear about Elaine, a woman of Polish persuasion I picked up in my own restaurant? A drinking, smoking, coughing, married woman who practically begged me to rip her clothes off . . . and you know what happened? *Nothing,* Jeanette. Nothing happened. Because I was looking for something beautiful, something decent . . . You want to hear about Bobbi, a psycho unemployed night club singer who had her dog kidnaped by the Beverly Hills police and sleeps with a Nazi vocal coach? I sat there with her smoking marijuana and singing popular songs of the day . . . And you know what happened? *Nothing,* Jeanette, nothing happened. Because I was looking for something beautiful, something decent . . . And then I invited you. A woman who grabbed me in her kitchen last Thursday night and physically pinned me down on the table. I had mayonnaise stains on my back when I got home. And when you get here what do you do? You sit there taking pills and holding on to your God damned pocketbook all day. And again, *nothing* happened, Jeanette. Nothing because I was looking for something beautiful, something decent. Well, I'm through, dammit. I'm through looking for something beautiful and decent because *it doesn't exist.* You're right, Jeanette, we're no damned good, all of us. There are no decent, gentle, loving people left in the world.

He advances towards her.
We're depraved, lustful, disgusting monsters, all of us.
He pushes a chair out of his way.
But if we're guilty, Jeanette, then let's at least commit the crime. If we're depraved, let's see a little depravity.
He is moving toward her, she backs away.
. . . If we're indecent, then let's see a couple of terrific indecencies! *COME HERE, JEANETTE!*

Barney pretends to go ape, chasing Jeanette around the room, overturning furniture. He threatens to rip off her dress. She is really frightened, and she tries to persuade Barney "You're not like this." To defend herself, she is forced to remind Barney that he is really a decent person, "the kindest man I know," gentle and loving. Now they have found two qualified decent-gentle-loving people, and Barney suggests there must be a third. Yes, there's Mel (Jeanette admits through her tears).

Now that Barney has wrung this admission from Jeanette, he stops his ape act and comforts her. Jeanette prepares to leave.

BARNEY: I feel like such a louse . . . Do you hate me for what I've done, Jeanette?

JEANETTE *(looks at him): Hate* you . . . no, Barney.

BARNEY: See you Thursday night for dinner?

JEANETTE: You really believe it, don't you Barney? That we're not all sick and rotten. You actually believe that some of us are decent, gentle and loving.

BARNEY: I do. And deep down, so do you.

JEANETTE: Maybe . . . But at two o'clock in the morning I think I'm going to tap Mel on the shoulder and tell him I've had an affair . . . Let *him* be depressed for awhile.

> *She exits. Barney closes the door . . . He turns back into the room and surveys the wreckage of strewn furniture . . . He begins to replace the chairs and things, in their proper place, when he stops and looks at his watch . . . An idea strikes him . . . He crosses to phone and puts his hand on the receiver . . . He thinks a moment, decides to go through with it and picks up receiver and dials . . . He waits, then:*

BARNEY *(into phone):* . . . Hello, Thelma? . . . What are you doing? . . . You busy? . . . Listen, honey, I was thinking, why don't you meet me this afternoon, we could do something . . . Sure, now, it takes you ten minutes to get here . . . No, not in the restaurant . . . In my mother's apartment . . . No, she didn't invite us to dinner, I just want you to meet me here . . . Thelma, don't be so stubborn, can't you meet me in my mother's apartment? . . .

Curtain.

CHILD'S PLAY

A Play in One Act

BY ROBERT MARASCO

Cast and credits appear on page 316

ROBERT MARASCO was born in the Bronx 33 years ago and attended the same Roman Catholic boys' school where he was later to teach English, Latin and Greek for nine years (he prefers that the school's name not be mentioned lest anyone connect it with the sinister and wholly fictional institution of his play). Marasco graduated from Fordham University and put in a year as a copy boy on The New Yorker *before going into teaching.* Child's Play *is his first play but he is already at work on another one entitled* A Christmas Assembly *as this volume goes to press. He is also the author of a recently-filmed screen play* Burnt Offerings. *Marasco is a bachelor and lives in Flushing, Queens.*

Time: The present, mid-winter

Place: St. Charles' School

> "Phoebus, our lord, plainly orders us to drive out a defiling thing which, he says, has been harbored in this land."
>
> —*Oedipus Rex*

SYNOPSIS: St. Charles' is a Roman Catholic boarding school for boys, and the scene of the play is its lay Faculty Room and the adjacent staircase and corridor, with a balcony serving as an office area. Doors lead from the Faculty Room left to the lavatory and locker room and right to the hall and stairway which leads up to the balcony level and down below stage level.

The general impression is dark, gloomy, Gothic. At 3 o'clock in the afternoon, Paul Reese (*"a teacher in his early twenties, genial, athletic-looking"*) is reading in the Faculty Room; then he rises and exits left.

A bell rings and the boys begin to appear on the stairway. Father Penny (*"a rather aristocratic-looking young priest"*) comes down the stairs, dressed in his cassock and sash.

> *As Father Penny reaches the landing and starts for the Faculty Room, a boy, Jennings, stops in front of him and blocks his passage. The other boys stop all movement. Father Penny makes an attempt to get past Jennings but can't. There is silence in the corridor.*

FATHER PENNY: Get out of my way.

> *Father Griffin, the prefect of discipline, appears at the top of the staircase. The boys continue to stare at Father Penny and Jennings.*

FATHER GRIFFIN: You heard what he said. Get out of his way.

> *There is a pause. Jennings steps aside slowly, allowing Father Penny to move toward the Faculty Room. Father Griffin comes down the stairs, clipboard in hand.*

FATHER PENNY (*going into the faculty room*): Bastards!

FATHER GRIFFIN (*coming down the stairs*): All right, Martin, Callino— move! And you, Jennings, go down and wait outside my office.

> *He crosses in front of Jennings and stops when he sees that none of the boys has moved.*

You heard what I said. Go downstairs and wait outside my office.

> *Jennings pauses before taking a step toward Father Griffin, challenging him. There is a pause, and then Father Griffin slaps him hard across the face. No one moves. Jennings stands defiantly, inviting another blow. Father Griffin's eyes shift quickly to the other boys, who remain motionless, watching him tensely.*

Keep moving!

> *No one does. Jerome Malley begins to descend the stairs, carrying texts and his red markbook. He is in his mid-forties, tall, somewhat forbidding. He wears a dark three-piece suit. He does not look at the boys, who remain quiet but make way for him to pass. Malley acknowledges Father Griffin as he passes him on his way to the Faculty Room.*

> *Jennings turns slowly now and starts downstairs. Gradually the other boys begin to move.*

(*Lamely; more rattled than angry.*) All right, lift those feet!

> *He looks after them a moment, then down at his hand. He goes back up the stairs and out.*

Meanwhile, Father Penny is running off a biology test on the Ditto machine on the balcony. Malley has put down his books on the Faculty Room's common table and moved to his own study area upstage: *"a small alcove with a wing chair, a lamp and a library table piled with books"*.

Joseph Dobbs comes up the stairs with a boy, McArdle, on his way to the Faculty Room. Dobbs is *"in his late fifties, the oldest teacher on the faculty. He wears an old corduroy jacket—rumpled and comfortable, like Dobbs himself."*

McArdle has played a joke on Malley, phoning him at his home in the middle of the night, and he is asking Dobbs to help him avoid punishment for this prank. The boy obviously regards Dobbs as a friend and Malley as an enemy who "enjoys watching us sweat it out." Dobbs promises to help the boy, while reminding him that Malley is entitled to respect.

Another boy, Medley, enters, bouncing a basketball loudly, as though it were some kind of signal to his schoolmate. There is a strong tension, a private communication of some kind, as Medley tells McArdle, "Time for basketball practise." The boys exit. Puzzled, Dobbs enters the Faculty Room, where his private area downstage is furnished with *"a worn leather chair, a small table with a lamp, a phone and a few textbooks."* Dobbs has also arranged the installation of a hot plate, a coffee pot and a small refrigerator.

Reese passes through the Faculty Room on his way to the gym to supervise the older boys. Reese is a St. Charles old boy himself, a recent graduate of this very school. He studied under both Malley and Dobbs, who 30 years before became the first layman to join the St. Charles faculty.

On the stairs, Reese meets Father Griffin, who warns him to be especially careful in gym supervision—at the slightest sign of trouble, call the activity off and clear the gym. Reese takes the warning rather casually.

Father Griffin joins the others in the Faculty Room. He is worried about the detention list—Father Penny has handed in fifteen names for detention, an unusually large number for such a strong disciplinary measure. Father Penny insists that every one deserved it: "Read through the list. I think you'll find the evidence warrants it."

Dobbs delays Malley from going to the headmaster to report McArdle's telephone call. Dobbs pleads for McArdle: it was an adolescent joke, Malley should "go a little easy on the boy." But Malley is unyielding and departs in the direction of the headmaster's office to make his complaint.

Father Penny, too, takes a stern position on maintaining discipline. His pupils call him "King Kong" behind his back, and he in turn refers to them as "those unwashed hordes whooping up and down the stairwells." Father Penny goes, leaving Father Griffin alone with Dobbs, with the opportunity to confide his misgivings about the recent strange behavior of the boys.

FATHER GRIFFIN: What's wrong with them, Joe?
DOBBS *(trying to follow)*: Wrong?
FATHER GRIFFIN: The kids . . . what *is* it with them?
DOBBS: They're always jumpy after midterms. It's their way of unwinding.

FATHER GRIFFIN: That's what it's called, hunh?
> *Picks up his clipboard and goes over to Dobbs.*
You ever see eighty kids on a detention list before? You managed to nail a few yourself.

DOBBS: I'm getting old and crotchety.

FATHER GRIFFIN: Joe . . . something is wrong with them. Have you been watching them? Between classes, on the stairs, in the gym after school?

JOE: The gym I leave to young Mr. Reese.

FATHER GRIFFIN: Well, watch them some time. We've never had so many kids getting hurt around here. Hell, if it were just good old vandalism, protest; but they're going *at* one another. Deliberately, whenever they can, they try to hurt one another . . . physically hurt.

DOBBS: Father, I don't believe that.

FATHER GRIFFIN: Believe it! And then try to get something out of them. You ask how'd it happen and the kid'll just look up at you and shrug. Yesterday a brawl in the dormitory and a kid breaks an arm; the day before, that accident in the chem lab. We need your help, Joe . . .

DOBBS: If it's as you say, of course. In thirty years here, though, I've never known a situation that collar couldn't control.

FATHER GRIFFIN: Well, we're getting less starch in them nowadays.

The youngsters don't seem to fear detention any more (Father Griffin continues), they seem almost to ask for it. Dobbs is urged to speak to the other teachers about the situation. Dobbs suggests that Jerome Malley, may be driving the boys too hard; years ago one of Malley's pupils, driven past his capacity, attempted suicide. Father Griffin promises to speak to Malley himself.

Reese comes in to get some cokes for his gym charges, and Father Griffin is alarmed that he left them unsupervised. He urges Reese to hurry back to the gym and goes off on his own rounds.

Reese confesses to Dobbs that he is still a little bit frightened of his old teacher "Lash" Malley. Reese remembers Malley's severity in teaching Latin— and he remembers Dobbs's leniency in English class. Dobbs admits sarcastically, "I'm the grand old man of the faculty, beloved of all the boys."

Malley comes in. Dobbs turns his attention to correcting papers. Reese tries to engage Malley in polite small talk, but he can scarcely hide his uneasiness in Malley's presence. There is an audible cheer from the direction of the gym, and Reese hurries off to see what's going on.

Left alone with Malley, Dobbs asks about McArdle. Malley has reported him to the headmaster, and the boy has been suspended indefinitely.

DOBBS: That's a bit harsh, isn't it?

MALLEY: For an innocent prank.

DOBBS: For a senior to miss all that work?

MALLEY: I'm sorry you weren't consulted first. One of your boys, isn't he Dobbs?

DOBBS: So are they all, Jerome, so are they all. I take it the suspension was the headmaster's idea. You would have preferred expulsion, I'm sure.

MALLEY: Why not ask him yourself? As I understand it, you'll be going down to see him as soon as I've left the building.

DOBBS: The headmaster? Why should I see him?

MALLEY: The boy's given him to understand you'll be going down to plead for him.

DOBBS: I made no promises.

MALLEY: No, you never do. You were misinterpreted as usual.

DOBBS *(clearing the table of the creamer and sugar bowl):* You've made it quite clear this doesn't concern me.

MALLEY: When has that ever stopped you?

DOBBS: That's not fair.

MALLEY: I'm never fair, Dobbs; your boys must have told you that.
More noise is heard from the gym.

DOBBS: Jerome, we spend so much time in this room . . .
He slams the refrigerator door and returns to the table.

MALLEY: I'm trying to work, Dobbs!

DOBBS: I'm sorry I spoke to the boy. It was a mistake.

MALLEY: You deliberately set them against me, the boys. You always have.

DOBBS: That's all in your mind.
He gets a dustrag from the cupboard and comes back to dust off the table.

MALLEY: It's not in my mind! *(Looking directly at Dobbs.)* You have got to stop undermining my position here.
Another distant cheer is heard from the gym.

DOBBS: You still don't see it, after all these years. It's not me setting them against you; it's yourself . . . Jerome, the boys are afraid of you. You terrify them. It's as simple as that.

MALLEY: Simpler, Dobbs. You encourage it. Whatever their absurd fears are, you magnify them.

Even Reese is afraid of Malley (Dobbs tells him), and Malley agrees that Reese may be "another in your long line of McArdles" whom Dobbs has deliberately influenced against Malley. Dobbs reminds Malley that one of his pupils attempted suicide—Malley was too hard on him. Malley replies that the *work* was too hard for him, and Dobbs was too easy on him.

MALLEY: Listen to me, Dobbs. I'll suffer, since I must, the humiliation of this room with you, and the daily spectacle of a pathetic old man—

DOBBS: All right, Jerome, that's enough.

MALLEY: . . . living on the affection of adolescent boys—

DOBBS: That's enough, I said!

MALLEY: . . . that *too,* Dobbs, as degrading as it is. But I won't be lectured by you on my responsibility. You are not to see the headmaster! You are not to interfere!

Now a cry is heard from the gym, rising to a shriek. Malley listens without moving. Dobbs rushes out into the corridor. Reese is coming from the gym area, dragging a boy whose face and gym shirt are covered with blood.

REESE *(yelling into the stairwell):* Father Griffin! Father Griffin!

Dobbs joins in the cry. Reese has gotten the boy to the Faculty Room. He pulls him across the room. The boy is screaming, fighting him. Dobbs follows.

Oh, God, oh, God, Joe—help me! HELP ME!

The boy screams louder as Dobbs and Reese bring him into the lavatory. Malley still does not move. After a pause, he turns slightly toward the lavatory as the lights fade.

When the lights come up a while later, Malley is still in his study area. The headmaster, Father Mozian, comes into the Faculty Room. He takes a phone call from the mother of the injured boy, Freddy Banks. Dobbs is at the hospital; they will know more later, Father Mozian tells the mother.

Dobbs and Father Griffin come up the stairs, and Reese comes in from the lavatory. Father Mozian finishes his phone conversation. Dobbs informs them all that Banks will probably lose an eye.

Reese tries to explain what happened in the gym. He himself can hardly believe or understand what he saw. The others, Malley especially, listen closely.

The boys were tossing a ball around, playing an informal game. Reese, not yet busy as a referee, came out to get Cokes. Dobbs hastens to interject that Reese was absent from the gym not more than five minutes.

The boys formed a circle, still flipping the ball, unsmiling and silent. They wouldn't even answer Reese when he spoke to them. Freddy Banks held the ball a couple of seconds longer than the others, as though it were some kind of signal; then he flipped the ball and stepped into the center of the circle.

REESE: . . . . . This guy lifted the ball over his shoulders. And then, he let go and smashed it into Freddy's stomach. I could see Freddy's arms come in—like this—and then . . . God! They—stopped—just before the ball hit him.

He illustrates the reflex.

FATHER MOZIAN: He didn't try to protect himself?

DOBBS: Of course he did.

REESE: I swear he didn't!

DOBBS: Someone throws something at you, you—

REESE *(very worked up now):* His arms stopped—here! I heard the ball hit him, and he doubled over . . . And when it hit him, the kids, the kids . . . let out a cry—not a cry, a kind of . . . cheer! A cheer! I heard it.

FATHER GRIFFIN: You couldn't stop them, you couldn't get to Freddy?

REESE: I tried, I ran for him, but they were on him. I couldn't reach him, the eight, nine of them were on him—beating him, clawing him, tearing at his face.

FATHER GRIFFIN: Paul, you knew where I was. Why didn't you call me?

REESE: There wasn't time! Even the kids on the other side of the gym, they were running over and I yelled, "Help me!"

DOBBS: You mean Freddy yelled.

REESE: No, *I yelled,* not Freddy. I yelled and these kids who had run over grabbed me! Held me while the others were on Freddy. And I heard somebody yell, "Hold that bastard!" and . . . then I hit one of them . . .

> *His voice catches.*

. . . a couple of them—I don't know—and started to pull them off Freddy, who was crouching against the wall under them . . . pulled them off him. And Freddy, when I got to him, Freddy was covered with blood, coughing, spitting up blood. I raised his head, and when he saw me—God, I don't understand this, Freddy pushed himself against the wall, away from me, pushed himself away and screamed "NO!" *At me!* He was trying to get away from *me!* Trying to fight me off . . . until I grabbed him, lifted him up, and . . . they didn't move, the other kids, just drew back . . . and I brought him . . . I didn't know where I was bringing him . . . God, God . . .

> *He stops, almost dazed.*

Dobbs insists this was only a schoolboy brawl. Father Mozian decides "No, the boy obviously wanted to be hurt," and remembers other recent incidents of senseless violence in the school. Father Mozian now must decide whether to expel all eleven boys involved in this incident. This is half a class, as Dobbs remarks, and he offers to talk to the boys and get the truth out of them. Father Mozian declines his offer and is left alone with Malley as the others leave.

Father Mozian suggests to Malley that they let McArdle off with only two days's suspension, but Malley holds the headmaster to his promise that the suspension will be "indefinite." Father Mozian implies that perhaps Malley is too strict a disciplinarian, but Malley insists: "It's the teacher's role to enforce discipline, to insist on it. *(Pointedly.)* And with the cooperation of the administration."

But the headmaster is in an awkard position with the strange violence that is taking place, and he insists openly that Jerome "ease up on those boys." Sarcastically, Malley asks Father Mozian what pose he should adopt with his classes—that of a chum?

Malley tells the headmaster no, he will not "ease up" on his classes, and that is his final word on the subject.

FATHER MOZIAN: No, Jerome, I'm afraid it can't be final.

MALLEY *(less controlled):* What is it you think I've been doing to these boys? I've been teaching here for ten years. My students have always been important to me. I wouldn't be here if that weren't true.

FATHER MOZIAN: Jerome, I have great respect for you as a teacher, but I know your methods.

MALLEY: You know what you've *heard* of my methods.

FATHER MOZIAN: It's not what I've heard, it's what I've seen happening here that concerns me.

MALLEY: What has that to do with me? My methods are not Dobbs's methods. Why must you judge me by him?

FATHER MOZIAN: I'm not judging you by Joe Dobbs.

MALLEY: I am paid to teach Latin and Greek. That's the extent of my responsibility to the school.

FATHER MOZIAN: And the human element?

MALLEY: I am not their chum! I will not tolerate laziness or stupidity, but I am not an ogre, not what Dobbs would have me!

FATHER MOZIAN: It's not what Dobbs would have you that concerns me. It's what the boys would have you. What they scrawl on the walls and pass to each other under the desks.

MALLEY: I'm not interested in what's written on the walls of a lavatory.

FATHER MOZIAN: Well, maybe you should be aware of it . . . the obscenity, the malevolence directed against you in this school.

Father Mozian hands Malley a sheet of paper, an obscene note that some of the boys were passing around. Malley is indignant. He demands to be told the names of the boys involved. This demand is also a challenge: Malley declares that *none* of the boys would write such a thing about him. Malley accuses Dobbs: "So he's reached you all, has he? As easily as he's reached those two hundred boys. *He's* the malevolence. *He's* the obscenity. Dobbs wrote that note!"

Father Mozian considers this accusation irrational, but Malley repeats it: Dobbs is the chief influence in this school, and he is using his influence to turn the students against Malley. Still shocked by the note, Malley insists the boys could *not* have written it, as the lights fade.

When the lights come up again the locale has changed to the school chapel, where Dobbs is standing holding his rosary beads. Malley enters and kneels to pray. Then he becomes aware of Dobbs's presence.

Dobbs engages Malley in conversation. Dobbs suggests again to Malley that he should relax some of the pressure on his class.

MALLEY (*staring straight ahead*): How terrible, isn't it . . . that the two of us should find ourselves together here? Two such . . . second-rate human beings . . . two such empty lives . . . shackled together here.

DOBBS: My life empty? With all I have here?

MALLEY: What have we, really, but the hate we feel for each other? We've been poisoning each other with hate for as long as I can remember. How is it that we haven't leveled everything around us, with such malevolence?

DOBBS: I don't hate you, Jerome.

MALLEY: More, I think, than I hate you. All right, Dobbs, if it's finally to destroy one of us, then let it be just that—*one of us.*

  Half-turns.

Listen to me. My mother is very ill.

DOBBS: I know, Jerome, I know the strain you're under. Take it out on me if you have to, but leave the boys alone.

MALLEY *(more emphatic):* She's dying. I have no defense against that. If . . . I go along with you, if I try . . . will you at least have a little pity on her?

DOBBS: Of course I pity her.

MALLEY: You know what I'm talking about, don't you?

DOBBS: I don't think I do.

MALLEY: There have been other calls besides McArdle's. Someone has been calling her. Terrible calls . . . terrible lies about me . . . Please, Dobbs, no more.

DOBBS: Do you know what you're saying to me?

MALLEY: I know exactly what I'm saying. For her sake, Dobbs—*no more!* I'll do whatever you want; whatever it does to me, I'll at least attempt it. But please leave her alone. Because you must know by now . . . there are kinder ways to destroy me.

Malley leans forward in the pew; Dobbs leaves the chapel. The light grows redder, and all at once boys enter the chapel from the side door. Malley sees them but ignores them; he picks up his school bag and departs, minding his own business.

As soon as Malley is out of sight, one of the boys collapses; his jacket is taken off, and it can be seen that he has been whipped. The others tie him by the wrists to a large cross on the wall representing one of the Stations.

After the boys leave, the chapel bell rings and Fathers Mozian and Griffin enter. The boy on the cross moans. The horrified priests rush to his assistance, as the bells ring out louder and lighter and the lights fade to black.

The lights go up on the Faculty Room, where a senior, Shea, is helping Dobbs with composition books. Dobbs questions Shea about the chapel incident. When Shea says he knows nothing about it, Dobbs tells him: "That may be a good enough answer for the headmaster and Father Griffin; this is Mr. Dobbs speaking."

Shea still insists he wasn't there. Father Griffin comes in and sends Shea off to class. Reese enters from the gym. Father Griffin tells them of the measures that are to be taken in the school: no more chapel services, and "the school building is to be closed immediately after the last period" in mid-afternoon. Any boy found lingering in the building will be subject to suspension. Dobbs objects. This will knock out his after-school conferences with the boys—and Reese's intramural athletic events. But the priest insists.

Father Griffin leaves; so does Dobbs, leaving Reese alone in the Faculty Room. Two boys come prowling up the stairs and, seeing that the coast is clear, they throw Malley's red markbook, which they obviously have stolen, against the Faculty Room door, then they disappear. Reese opens the door, picks up the markbook, notices an obscenity scrawled in it and impulsively tears out the page. At this point Malley appears, and Reese hides the torn-out page in his pocket before handing the markbook back to its owner.

Trying to remember how the markbook left his possession, Malley realizes that he spent some time after his last class in a daze, wandering through the halls, hardly knowing where he was going or why. He is upset about his own behavior and asks Reese to overlook this whole episode of the lost markbook. Malley has indeed been under a strain. He is worried about his mother, who has taken a turn for the worse.

Trying to relieve the awkwardness between himself and Malley, Reese refers to himself as a onetime "clod" in Malley's Latin 2B class, and he knows that Malley cannot have a great deal of respect for him as a teacher. He wishes this were not so, that their relationship was an easier one now that they're colleagues.

REESE: I'm afraid of you, Isn't that something? So it's important to me just to work up enough courage to talk to you like this. I hate like hell to have to hide in the john every time we have a free period together.
MALLEY: I'm sorry I make you so uncomfortable.
REESE: It's not you, Lash, it's me.
    He grimaces; waits for an explosion.
MALLEY *(a quick look):* Afraid of me.
REESE: *Still.*
MALLEY: Well, why not? I'm a frightening, a menacing figure. I'm sure you've heard that over and over. Coupled with your own memories of my classroom . . . tyranny. I'm sure that's all been refreshed for you.
REESE *(defeated):* I'm sorry.
    Gathers his books.
I'll . . . get out of your way now. I'll work in the gym.

But Malley asks Reese to stay; reminds Reese of an incident in Latin 2B when someone in the class placed a newspaper clipping about a student stabbing his teacher on Malley's desk. Malley made the class kneel in the schoolroom aisle for 40 minutes, in punishment. The incident became part of the lore of "Lash" Malley's infamous reputation. Malley wonders whether the old boys reminisce about his harshness when they get together.

MALLEY: Dwyer . . . do you ever see him?
REESE: Not since graduation, no.
MALLEY: Dirty fingernails, but a first-rate mind, one of the best I've ever taught. And Peter Jackmin?
REESE: He's still in the seminary.
MALLEY: He may actually pick up a bit of Latin. It was Jackmin who put the clipping on my desk.
REESE *(surprise):* You knew that?
MALLEY: Not then. I had a Christmas card from him once, with a note. Sometimes I hear from you boys . . . after a while. More than you'd think. A singularly stupid class; a trying year;—like all of them, I suppose. You boys are afraid of me, I know. Maybe I am too hard on you. Maybe I shouldn't be

teaching, at least not in a high school. It's not that I dislike you. It's just that . . . you're children, and some of you are so slow. I don't have much patience with the slow ones.
> *Pause.*

You'll find that . . . the pattern of one's life can be formed so suddenly, without realizing it. So suddenly and for some of us—so irrevocably . . . and if it's wrong? Well, one comes in and goes through the motions . . . thinking at first that next year will be different . . . and realizing gradually that, no, next year will be the same and the year after that and well, if that's the way it's to be . . . that's the way it's to be. And so . . . I save newspaper clippings and Christmas cards. Why do I save them? I don't know. But wouldn't it be comforting some day to take out all those bits of the past and lay them out on the floor, like paths through a maze, and see what the course of my life has been . . . perhaps see what's been there all along, tucked away in a drawer?
> *Pause.*

If I've hurt you, any of you boys, I'm sorry . . . but that's what I am . . .
> *Pause. The phone rings.*

. . . that's the only way I know . . .
> *Pause. The phone rings again. Malley stops and looks at it. Reese has been standing, absorbed in Malley's sudden opening up to him. The ringing breaks his concentration. Reese sees that Malley, who is closer to the phone, will not answer it. Malley stares at the phone, his expression darkening. Reese moves toward the phone quietly.*

No! . . . Don't answer it! I won't speak to him!

Reese is surprised by Malley's odd reaction, but he answers the phone anyway. The nurse is calling to tell Malley his mother has died. Tears come to Malley's eyes as he leaves the Faculty Room, and he feels it necessary to explain to Reese: "It's just that . . . I should have been with her . . . for that."

The lights fade to black and come up again. It is three days later, about 10 o'clock in the evening.

Reese is on the balcony working the Ditto machine. A boy on the stairs listens furtively for sounds from the Faculty Room—there are none. But the boy disappears as Father Penny comes up the stairs carrying a drink. The priest enters the Faculty Room and reports to Reese that the faculty meeting now in progress, which they have both left, has just broken out the booze after concluding that perhaps after all the school will live through its current crisis.

Reese finishes on the balcony and comes down to the lower level. A burst of laughter is heard from the meeting downstairs. Father Penny disappears into the lavatory.

In the stairway area boys drift out of the shadows. They are pursuing a victim—they grab the boy, punch him, drag him up the stairs, with victim as well as persecutors keeping their voices down.

Nevertheless Reese hears something and opens the door to the stairwell. But by this time the boys have disappeared. When Father Penny returns to the room, chattering about the pupils being "possessed" and in need of an exorcist, Reese tells him he's sure there are boys in the building, in defiance of the headmaster's edict that all boys must leave after their last mid-afternoon class.

FATHER PENNY (*handing his glass to Reese*): A little free advice? You haven't taken vows. Why don't you get out of here?

REESE: I don't want to get out of here. I want to be a teacher.

FATHER PENNY: Be one somewhere else. You don't want to turn into one of those dried-up old celibates down there, clacking their beads and their teeth. That's my role.

> *Father Penny leaves the room and goes back down the stairs quickly. Reese closes the door after him. He looks at the glass Father Penny has handed him, thinks a moment; he seems to dismiss a thought. He throws the glass into the wastebasket. The glass shatters.*
>
> *Two more boys have come quietly into the corridor, from the gym area. They stop at the sound of the glass breaking. One of them turns front, the light on his face. He waits for something, his companion watching him.*
>
> *Reese is looking at the broken glass in the wastebasket. He bends slowly and retrieves a piece of it. The boy in the corridor tenses, leaning against the newel post. Reese rises and opens his palm; he looks from his hand to the glass. He brings the glass to his hand slowly. The boy in the hall moans softly and closes his eyes.*
>
> *A pause, and then Reese presses the jagged edge into his palm. Reese and the boy cry out in pain at the same time. Reese bends forward, covering his bleeding hand with the uninjured one. The second boy has grabbed the first; he leads him up the stairs. Reese grabs a towel from the rack beside the refrigerator and wraps it around his hand. His back is to the Faculty Room door as he bites his lip, waiting for the pain to pass.*
>
> *There is a long pause. Dobbs comes up the stairs and enters the Faculty Room.*

REESE (*turns quickly at the sound*): Jesus, Joe! Don't—creep up on me like that.

DOBBS (*his mind back downstairs*): Those black robes think they know it all. They'll handle it their way. Well, their way is making it impossible for me to talk to my boys. They're frightening the boys. That's why those boys are avoiding me.

Dobbs notices Reese's cut hand and goes to get the first-aid kit he keeps handy for patching up the boys when they get hurt. To Dobbs, Reese is still a boy: "You're all freshmen to me, whatever you go on to when you leave the old man. Doctors, bishops, councilmen—what do I care? I knew them when their faces were changing."

Reese confesses to Dobbs that he cut himself deliberately and cannot understand why he did it. Dobbs refuses to believe Reese—it must have been an accident.

Reese insists that something is very wrong within the school, something that cannot be blamed on Malley (whom Reese calls "Jerome"). Dobbs reminds Reese that up until now he has been afraid of "Jerome." Reese asserts that Malley has changed since he got word of his mother's death.

Besides (Reese tells Dobbs), Malley hasn't been near the school for three days, and the fear is still present. Reese can feel it, even though Malley is absent. What's more, he is certain that *the boys are in the building now* in spite of the headmaster's order.

Dobbs goes into the hall and calls the students' names as a demonstration to Reese that there's nobody here.

DOBBS *(looks at Reese, his eyes suddenly glazed):* I've taught over two thousand boys, do you know that? Other men's sons, two thousand of them. I've always valued it, the affection of all those boys, their friendship . . . years of it. You know me, you boys. It's you, you I trust. Not myself, but you, all those boys. And what you see, what all those boys have seen in me, that must be what I am . . . truly, isn't that so? This is my school. I've spent thirty years in this building . . . and what you see is all there is. There's nothing to frighten you.

REESE: I *am* scared, Joe. This place scares the hell out of me.

DOBBS: It's just a school, for God's sake.

REESE: I know it's just a school. I went here.

Dobbs moves in front of Reese and goes back into the Faculty Room. Reese follows, closing the door.

I know every room and every corridor. I can take you downstairs and show you my old desk, my locker; but it's changed. It's not the same. Something's come into this place.

DOBBS: Your imagination, that's what.

REESE: No, Joe, it's not my imagination. It's something real. It's real enough to touch.

He holds up his hand, and looks at it, as if realizing something for the first time.

And I touched it. *I touched it.*

A shrill scream upstairs precedes the boys' pushing onto the stairway their latest victim: a bloody-faced lad, glasses shattered, blinded, groping his way down the stairs. Dobbs tries to grab the boy, but he falls into Reese's arms as the lights go to black.

When the lights come up it is the next day. There is movement on the stairs: two boys (who disappear after a knowing look at each other), then Malley and Father Griffin.

Father Griffin is surprised that Malley has come back after only three days' absence and suggests gently that Malley should stay away longer—but Malley feels he must get back to work.

As Malley enters the Faculty Room and gets ready for a day of teaching, Father Mozian joins Father Griffin. The headmaster knows what he must do and enters the Faculty Room as Father Griffin goes upstairs.

Father Mozian informs Malley as gently as possible that his classes are being covered—and the new assignments are permanent. Malley is dismissed. Malley is shocked, can hardly believe it. He pleads with the headmaster that he will change his methods, revise his courses—"I'll go against what I believe, but I won't be dismissed. Not for something I'm not responsible for."

Father Mozian shows Malley an envelope containing another obscenity. Malley admits that he has received many of these, but always at his home, never at school—contrary to what Father Mozian is implying, this ugliness has not touched the school or Malley's pupils.

Malley begs the headmaster to understand that he is not at fault in this matter, these obscenities are *sent* to him, he is their victim not their perpetrator. They are being sent to him, Malley repeats to Father Mozian, by none other than Dobbs.

Father Mozian doesn't believe it. And even if it were true—which it couldn't be—"Then it's a truth I can't afford to face. Not now, Jerome, not with everything else I've got to face here." The headmaster's decision is final. Malley is forbidden to take any more classes or associate with the boys in any way.

Father Mozian departs quickly. Reese comes in and sees that Malley is in great distress. When the class bell rings it sends Malley into confusion. Malley tells Reese: "Paul . . . there was no need . . . no reason to torment her like that . . . an old woman who was dying . . . my mother. He was sending those pictures to my home. He was calling her, telling her lies about me, destroying her with those terrible lies . . . All of it deliberate. And I don't understand, I don't understand why he's doing this to me!"

The "he" of Malley's frantic pleading, Dobbs, comes down the corridor and enters the Faculty Room.

DOBBS (*a long look. Slowly*): What are you doing here, Jerome?

REESE: He was going upstairs and I brought him in here . . .

DOBBS: You don't belong in this school, Jerome.

MALLEY: It's all yours now, Dobbs, isn't it?

REESE: What do you mean, he doesn't belong in this school?

DOBBS: Just what I said.

MALLEY: It's taken you ten years, but you've won.

DOBBS (*to Reese*): What's he been telling you?

REESE (*challenging*): I don't know.

DOBBS: All the old lies, the old accusations? Everything wrong in his life is Joe Dobbs? Well, look at him, for God's sake.

MALLEY: How can you hate me so much . . . how can so much hate exist?

REESE: What calls is he talking about, what pictures?

DOBBS: I don't know!

MALLEY: *You're lying!*

REESE: Joe, what were you doing to him?

DOBBS: Nothing!

MALLEY: Destroying me! With all, *all* the malevolence in him!
He springs up and rushes at Dobbs, hands raised.

Devil!

*Dobbs moves back quickly. Reese is too stunned to move imme-
diately.*

Devil!

*Now Reese comes behind him and grabs him just as he is about to
strike Dobbs.*

DEVIL!

REESE: Jerome, no!

MALLEY *(trying to break away):* Wasn't it enough—me? Me?
He frees himself and turns to face Reese.

And he's got you all, hasn't he? Every last one of you.
He begins to move out of the room.

Well, I'll show you, I'll find a way to show you the evil he's brought down on
every last one of you.
He is mounting the stairs. Stops.

But I'll bring you down with me . . . *Mr. Dobbs!*
He disappears up the stairs.

Reese calls after Malley and moves to follow him, but Dobbs orders Reese
to let him go. Reese disobeys, runs up the stairs after Malley. When Dobbs
bursts out with a final loud "LET HIM GO!" the explosion sets off the noise
of boys' cries and the terrible sounds of violence, like a chain reaction.

Father Griffin runs down the stairs with the awful news that Malley has
jumped out of the window, killing himself. The boys appear at the top of the
stairs, all screaming, but as soon as they see Dobbs there is silence. When
Dobbs speaks to them and starts giving them orders. *"One of the boys moves
slowly toward Dobbs, his face lighting with some kind of terrible recognition.
Dobbs puts out his hands to stop the boy. The boy pulls back violently. His
hands rise suddenly and come down with a cry against Dobbs's face. Dobbs
staggers under the blow and falls to his knees as Reese comes down the stairs.
The boys surround Dobbs now, striking him; he is trying to protect himself.
Reese fights his way to him, pulling the boys off. The boys continue down
the stairs."*

Reese goes upstairs and Dobbs pulls himself into his chair in the Faculty
Room. Three boys appear and stand guard in the corridor. They do not bother
Reese when he reappears and goes to the Faculty Room.

Reese tells Dobbs there's nothing left here now, they should leave; but
Dobbs still wants to know why his boys have turned on him. Reese reminds
Dobbs of his cruelty to Malley, and Dobbs argues: "What did Jerome ever do
for the boys? That door was always open to you boys whenever you needed

me." (Meanwhile, unseen by Reese or Dobbs, one by one, boys appear and take up positions like sentinels in various parts of the stairs, corridor and balcony.)

Reese points out to Dobbs that his "boys" have turned into "kids fighting for broken glass . . . to tear themselves." Everything that Malley said about Dobbs was true, Reese had decided. Maybe Dobbs *wanted* Malley dead. No, Dobbs defends himself, he only wanted Malley out of what, after 30 years, Dobbs has come to think of as *his* school.

REESE: You wanted him dead.

DOBBS: I wanted him out of my life!

REESE: You wanted him dead!

DOBBS *(bursting out): All right, I wanted him dead!* Is that what you want me to say? Then I wanted him dead! If that was the only way to get him out of my school, out of my life, then I wanted him dead!

REESE: Well, he's dead. It took you ten years, didn't it, but you finally found a way to break him. Well, what are you going to do with all the hate that's in you now?

DOBBS: There's no more hate left in me.

REESE: Of course not.

> *A boy moves down a step.*

You've managed to infect this whole place with it . . . this room is filled with it . . . And, Joe, you've infected your boys, every last one of them. *(Looks at his hand.)* Is that what we've been trying to tear out of ourselves?

DOBBS: My boys? I've never done anything to hurt my boys.

> *A boy enters the corridor from the gym, and he moves down opposite the Faculty Room door and leans against the rail.*

REESE: You still think you're the grand old man of the faculty. Well, you're not, Joe. You're a killer.

> *The boys are moving toward the door. One step.*

And Jerome was only one victim.

> *Reese opens the Faculty Room door, and a boy throws open the locker room door. He is in the room.*

The others are here. They're still your boys. They've come back for the old man. Maybe they'll forgive you for what you've done.

DOBBS: My boys . . . ?

REESE: Are you afraid, Joe?

DOBBS: I've never been afraid of any of my boys.

> *Dobbs starts to get up.*

REESE: Well then, I'll leave you with them. After all, what's the old man without his boys?

> *Reese leaves the room. He stops in the corridor and looks at the boys, waiting. Then he moves past them and down the stairs.*
>
> *The boys enter the room slowly. Dobbs moves to the center of the room.*

DOBBS *(calling as he moves back):* Paul? Paul, wait!

The boys are circling him. He does not move as he looks at each of them.

McArdle? Jennings? Carre? Medley? Shea? Wilson? Banks? Travis?

A pause. They are very close to him. He raises his hands, just slightly.

Please. *(Quietly.)* Please?

They close in on him. Curtain.

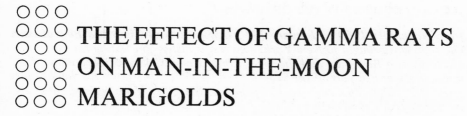

THE EFFECT OF GAMMA RAYS ON MAN-IN-THE-MOON MARIGOLDS

A Play in Two Acts

BY PAUL ZINDEL

Cast and credits appear on page 363

PAUL ZINDEL is a Staten Islander who was born there May 13, 1936, went to school there at Port Richmond High School and Wagner College, taught chemistry there at Tottenville High School and began writing short stories there during his high school days. His first produced play was Dimensions of Peacocks *(1959), written during his last year at college and performed at the Eleanor Cody Gould Theater over on Manhattan's Bowery. One of the coffee houses, Take 3, put on his* Euthanasia and Endless Hearths *in 1960, and his* Dream of Swallows *was done off Broadway in 1962.*

The Effect of Gamma Rays on Man-in-the-Moon Marigolds was next in Zindel's playwriting chronology, and it has taken this outstanding script a long time to reach production in New York. It was first done at the Alley Theater in Houston in 1965, with much acclaim. It was produced at the White Barn Theater in Westport, Conn. in 1966 and that same year a TV version starring Eileen Heckart received the first of four performances on the New York Television Theater program (it was not well received by the TV critics). Finally,

165

*from November 1969 to January 1970 it was done at Cleveland Play House
and then was brought to New York. The rest is history, including rave reviews,
selection as a Best Play and the New York Drama Critics Circle's citation as
the best American play of the year.*

Zindel is the author of the TV play Let Me Hear You Whisper *and the
novels* Pigman, My Darling, My Hamburger *and* I Never Loved Your Mind.
His newest play And Miss Reardon Drinks a Little *was produced at the Mark
Taper Forum in Los Angeles in October, 1967 and arrangements for its New
York production are under way.*

INTRODUCTION BY THE PLAYWRIGHT

*At the author's request we preface the synopsis of his play with the follow-
ing brief sketches of the three leading characters, which he used as an introduction to the acting version of the playscript:*

TILLIE (the girl)—". . . and there was Tillie, crankin' away, lookin' weird
as a coot . . . the old jumper with the dirty slip, and lightning hair . . . and
everybody burst into laughter . . ."

BEATRICE (the mother)—". . . this long street with all the doors of the
houses shut and everything crowded next to each other . . . and I started getting afraid the vegetables on the truck are going to spoil . . . and that nobody's
going to buy anything."

RUTH (the other daughter)—". . . and I started down the stairs, step by
step . . . and I heard the choking and banging on the bed, and . . ."

ACT I

SYNOPSIS: The setting is a room which had once been a vegetable store, with
street door and show window upstage; now it is serving as a family living room
and the window is screened with old newspapers. A curtained door to a bedroom leads off right, and the bathroom is behind a staircase at left. Kitchen
stove, sink and table are near the stairs at left. *"Objects which respectable
people usually hide in closets are scattered about the main room: newspapers,
magazines, dishes; empty bottles; clothes; suitcases; last week's sheets. Such
carelessness is the type which is so perfected it must have evolved from hereditary processes, but in all fairness to the occupants, it can be pointed out that
after twilight, when shadows and weak bulbs work their magic, the room becomes interesting."*

In the beginning there is blackness, music, then a child's voice speaking. As
the lights come up we will see that the child is Tillie, a gangling high school
girl who is petting a large white rabbit as she speaks her thoughts.

TILLIE'S VOICE: He told me to look at my hand for a part of it came from a star that exploded too long ago to imagine. This part of me was formed from a tongue of fire that screamed through the heavens until there was our sun. And this part of me—this tiny part of me—was on the sun when it itself exploded and whirled in a great storm until the planets came to be.

Lights start in.

And this small part of me was then a whisper of the earth. When there was life perhaps this part of me got lost in a fern that was crushed and covered until it was coal. And then it was a diamond millions of years later—it must have been a diamond as beautiful as the star from which it had first come.

Tillie takes over from recorded voice.

TILLIE: Or perhaps this part of me became lost in a terrible beast, or became part of a huge bird that flew above the primeval swamps. And he said this thing was so small—this part of me was so small it couldn't be seen—but it was there from the beginning of the world. And he called this bit of me an atom. And when he wrote the word, I fell in love with it. Atom. *Atom.* What a beautiful word.

The phone rings and Tillie's mother Beatrice calls from offstage for Tillie to answer it. But before Tillie can move Beatrice enters dressed in a bathrobe. Beatrice is entering middle age grudgingly, irritably, fighting a losing battle. She picks up the phone and speaks to Tillie's teacher, Mr. Goodman (a young man who greeted them once in the A & P; Beatrice noticed that he was good looking). Mr. Goodman is calling to inquire why Tillie has been absent from school. Beatrice tells him, "Well, some days she just doesn't feel like going to school. You just said how bright she is, and I'm really afraid to put too much of a strain on her after what happened to her sister. You know, too much strain is the worst thing in this modern world, Mr. Goodman, and I can't afford to have another convulsive on my hands, now can I? But don't you worry about Matilda. There will be some place for her in this world. And, like I said, some were born to speak and others just to listen. . . . ."

Beatrice ends the phone conversation, then berates Tillie for telling the school she was being forcibly detained at home by her mother (which is nevertheless true). Every so often Beatrice gets it into her head that Tillie should stay home and help with the housework, and Tillie usually pretends to be sick as an excuse for missing school.

Tillie particularly wants to go to school this day, because Mr. Goodman has planned an experiment in radioactivity, with the cloud chamber. But Beatrice wants Tillie to perform "a good number of exciting duties . . . . . not the least of which is rabbit droppings." Beatrice threatens to chloroform the rabbit unless Tillie obeys.

Beatrice's older daughter Ruth comes downstairs looking for her mother's "Devil's Kiss" lipstick. *"She is dressed for school, and though her clothes are simple she gives the impression of being slightly strange. Her hair isn't quite combed, her sweater doesn't quite fit, etc."* Where Tillie's strangeness seems to come from preoccupation, Ruth's seems to come from inner tension.

Ruth mentions to Beatrice that the whole school was laughing at Tillie in assembly the day before.

BEATRICE: Ruth, you didn't tell me she was in an assembly.

RUTH: Well, I just thought of it right now. How could I tell you anything until I think of it, did you ever stop to consider that? Some crumby science assembly.

BEATRICE (to Tillie): What is she talking about?

RUTH: I thought she'd tell the whole world. Imagine, right in front of the assembly with everybody laughing at her.

BEATRICE: Will you be quiet, Ruth? *Why were they laughing at you?*

TILLIE: I don't know . . .

RUTH: You don't know? My heavens, she was a sight. She had that old jumper on—the faded one with that low collar—and a raggy slip that showed all over and her hair looked like she was struck by lightning.

BEATRICE: You're exaggerating . . .

RUTH: She was cranking this model of something . . .

TILLIE: The atom . . .

RUTH: This model of the atom . . . you know, it had this crank and a long tower so that when you turned it these little colored balls went spinning around like crazy. And there was Tillie, crankin' away, lookin' weird as a coot . . . that old jumper with the raggy slip and the lightning hair . . . cranking away while some boy with glasses was reading this stupid speech . . . and everybody burst into laughter until the teachers yelled at them. And all day long, the kids kept coming up to me saying, "Is that really your sister? How can you bear it?" And you know, Chris Burns says to me—"*She* looks like the one that went to the looney doctors." I could have kissed him there and then.

BEATRICE (taking a backscratcher): Matilda, if you can't get yourself dressed properly before going to school you're never going to go again. I don't like the idea of everybody laughing at you because when they laugh at you they're laughing at me. And I don't want you cranking any more . . . atoms.

Ruth "earns" a cigarette by scratching her mother's back with the backscratcher. They discuss the telephone call. Ruth knew Mr. Goodman would probably phone, because he had asked Ruth the day before about Tillie's absences. Ruth pretended that Tillie was gravely ill and referred the teacher to the "history" on file in the school. Ruth has managed to read her own "history" and tells Beatrice about it: "It says you're divorced and that I went crazy . . . and my father took a heart attack at Star Lake . . . and now you're a widow. . . . . And it says that I exaggerate and tell stories and that I'm afraid of death and have nightmares . . . and all that stuff."

The lights fade. When they come up again, Tillie's voice is heard describing in fascinated wonder the experiment with the cloud chamber in science class. Beatrice is looking ever the real estate ads in the newspaper. Tillie is preparing boxes of dirt for the planting of seeds.

BEATRICE: . . . . . What kind of seeds are they?

TILLIE: Marigolds. *They've been exposed to cobalt-60.*

BEATRICE: If there's one thing I've always wanted it's been a living room planted with marigolds that have been exposed to cobalt-60. While you're at it why don't you throw in a tomato patch in the bathroom?

TILLIE: Just let me keep them here for a week or so until they get started and then I'll transplant them to the back yard.

BEATRICE *(reading again):* Four-family house. Six and a half and six and a half over five and five. Eight garages. I could really do something with that. A nursing home. *(Pause.)* Don't think I'm not kicking myself that I didn't finish that real estate course. I should have finished beauty school, too. *(Pause.)* God, what I could do with eight garages.

> *There is a sound from beyond the curtained doorway.*

You know, I'm thinking of getting rid of *that* and making this place into something.

TILLIE: Yes . . .

BEATRICE: I've been thinking about a tea shop. . . . .

At the curtained doorway at right, two thin hands appear. Gradually the *that* referred to by Beatrice enters the room. She is Nanny, the boarder, slowly and painfully moving into the room by means of a tubular frame which supports her. *"She is utterly wrinkled and dried, perhaps a century old. Time has left her with a whisper of a smile—a smile from a soul half departed. . . . . She pervades the room with age."*

Beatrice and her daughters pay little attention to the old woman's progress. Tillie explains to her mother what cobalt-60 is and what an atomic half-life is. But the information baffles Beatrice, who finally addresses herself to the aged creature making her slow, rhythmic way toward the kitchen table.

BEATRICE *(in a loud, horribly saccharine voice as if she were addressing a deaf year-old child):* LOOK WHO'S THERE! IT'S NANNY! NANNY CAME ALL THE WAY OUT HERE BY HERSELF! I'm going to need a cigarette for this. NANNY! YOU COME SIT DOWN AND WE'LL BE RIGHT WITH HER! You know, sometimes I've got to laugh. I've got *this* on my hands and all you're worried about is planting marigolds. I'VE GOT HOTSY WATER FOR YOU, NANNY. WOULD YOU LIKE SOME HOTSY WATER AND HONEY?

> *Nanny has seated herself at table, smiling but oblivious to her environment.*

I've never seen it to fail. Every time I decide to have a cup of coffee I see that face at the curtains. I wonder what she'd do . . .

> *She holds pot of boiling water.*

. . . if I just poured this right over her head. I'll bet she wouldn't even notice it. NANNY'S GOING TO GET JUST WHAT SHE NEEDS!

> *She fills a cup for her and places a honey jar near her.*

Silently, Nanny enjoys the water and honey as Beatrice continues to complain. Nanny's daughter, a real estate career woman, pays Beatrice $50 a week to take care of the old lady, who for all her problems may be easier to take than previous boarders who suffered from a brain tumor, cancer and worms in the legs.

Beatrice turns on Tillie and bitterly declares that she could have been a dancer except for one small mistake: "Marry the wrong man and before you know it he's got you tied down with two stones around your neck for the rest of your life." Her dreams of becoming a dancer vanished with the onset of varicose veins.

Watching Nanny fumbling with her "hotsy," Beatrice is more than ever persuaded that she should evict the old woman and open a tea shop. First, though, she would get rid of Tillie's rabbit. She takes a bottle of choloroform from a drawer to show Tillie that she means business.

Nanny distracts Beatrice's attention; she needs to be helped into her walking frame so that she can make her way to the bathroom. Beatrice helps her up, then tries to read the paper but is irritated by the sound of Nanny's shuffling: "Half-life! If you want to know what a half-life is just ask me. You're looking at the original half-life! I got stuck with one daughter with half a mind; another one who's half a test tube; half a husband—a house half full of rabbit crap; and half a corpse! That's what I call a half-life, Matilda! Me and cobalt-60! Two of the biggest half-*lifes* you ever saw!"

The scene goes to black, then the lights come up on Beatrice phoning Tillie's science teacher, Mr. Goodman. Her conversation is a nervous blend of sweet talk for the handsome young man and hostile arrogance toward the teacher. Beatrice is afraid that the marigolds are radioactive and may be harmful; could even cause sterility. She is reassured by Mr. Goodman, but angered because she doesn't know the meaning of the word "mutation"; angry at the teacher when he tries to explain it to her.

The scene goes to black, then comes up in nighttime lighting with the sound of a thunderstorm. A loud scream is heard. *"Ruth appears on the landing and releases another scream which breaks off into gasps. She starts down the stairs and stops halfway to scream again."* She is going into one of her attacks, and Beatrice and Tillie try to help her, to prevent her from letting herself go and giving way to terror.

Beatrice orders Tillie back to her room and helps Ruth down the stairs. Ruth comes out of her hysteria, ruefully tells her mother "It was the dream with Mr. Mayo (a former boarder) again." The thunderstorm blows out the lights, and Beatrice finds a flashlight in one of the downstairs drawers.

BEATRICE: Why, Ruth. Your skin just turned ice cold.
    She rummages through one of the boxes and grabs a blanket.
This will warm you up. What's the matter?
RUTH: The flashlight . . .
BEATRICE: What's wrong with it?
RUTH: It's the same one I used to check on Mr. Mayo with.

BEATRICE: So it is. We don't need it . . .

RUTH: No, let me keep it. *(Starting to laugh.)* Do you want to know how they have it in the history?

BEATRICE: No, I don't.

RUTH: Well, they say I came out of my room . . .

She flashes the light on her room.

And I started down the stairs, step by step . . . and I heard the choking and banging on the bed, and . . .

BEATRICE: I'm going back to bed.

RUTH: No!

BEATRICE: Well, talk about something nice then.

RUTH: Oh, Mama, tell me about the wagon.

Ruth pleads for the story, and Beatrice obliges her. Beatrice's father would come home from work tired, ready for a nap, and when he was fast asleep Beatrice would hitch up the horses and ride around the neighborhood in her father's wagon. One day her father caught her and spanked her in public. Then came the time when her father got sick and had to be taken to the sanatarium—leaving Beatrice with the responsibility for the horses and for carrying on with her life.

BEATRICE: I never had nightmares over the fights with your father or the divorce or his thrombosis—he deserved it—I never had nightmares over any of that. Let me tell you about my nightmare that used to come back and back: *Well,* I'm on Papa's wagon, but it's newer and shinier, and it's being pulled by beautiful white horses, not dirty work horses—these are like circus horses with long manes and tinsel—and the wagon is blue, shiny blue. And it's full— filled with yellow apples and grapes and green squash. You're going to laugh when you hear this. I'm wearing a lovely gown with jewels all over it, and my hair is piled up on top of my head with a long feather in it, and the bells are ringing. Huge bells swinging on a gold braid strung across the back of the wagon, and they're going DONG, DONG. DONG, DONG. And I'm yelling APPLES! PEARS! CUCUM . . . BERS!

RUTH: That doesn't sound like a nightmare to me.

BEATRICE: And then I turn down our street and all the noise stops. This long street with all the doors of the houses shut and everything crowded next to each other and there's not a soul around. And then I start getting afraid that the vegetables are going to spoil . . . and that nobody's going to buy anything, and I feel as though I shouldn't be on the wagon, and I keep trying to call out. But there isn't a sound. Not a single sound. Then I turn my head and look at the house across the street. I see an upstairs window and a pair of hands pull the curtains slowly apart. I see the face of my father and my heart stands still.

Pause.

Ruth . . . take the light out of my eyes.

A long pause.

RUTH: Is Nanny going to die here?
BEATRICE: No . . .
RUTH: How can you be sure?
BEATRICE: I can tell.
RUTH: Are you crying?
BEATRICE: What's left for me, Ruth?
RUTH: What, Mama?
BEATRICE: What's left for me?

The stage goes to black, then lights come up on Nanny seated at the kitchen table with a glass of beer in front of her. Tillie brings in a box of marigolds, then takes the rabbit out of the cage to pet it. Beatrice drops a stack of newspapers from the landing above, and the sound of their hitting the floor is loud and startling. Beatrice is cleaning house. Once again she remembers that she wants the rabbit to go.

Tillie tries to tell her mother that "they want me to do something in school," but Beatrice is preoccupied with her own problems, particularly her feeling that her whole life adds up to zero and she'd better start doing something about it.

Ruth comes running in, babbling in a euphoric state. It turns out that Tillie has done something "fantastic," she has been picked as a finalist in the science fair out of hundreds of contestants by the principal himself, for her marigold project. At school, Ruth boasted proudly to everybody: "Yes, she's my sister!" She tells Beatrice: "Mr. Goodman called the *Advance,* and they're coming to take your picture. Oh, Mama, isn't it crazy? And nobody laughed at her, Mama."

The phone rings. It is the school principal, Dr. Berg. Beatrice listens to his announcement.

BEATRICE: I see. *(Pause.)* Couldn't you get someone else? There's an awful lot of work that has to be done around here because she's not as careful with her home duties as she is with Man-in-the-Moon marigolds.
    Pause.
Me? What would you want with me up on the stage?
    Pause.
The other mothers can do as they please. *(Pause.)* I would have thought you had enough in your history without . . .
    Pause.
I'll think about it . . . *(Pause.)* Goodbye, Dr. Berg . . .
    Pause, then screaming.
I SAID I'D THINK ABOUT IT!
    She hangs up the phone, turns her face slowly to Ruth, then to Tillie who has her face hidden in shame in the rabbit's fur.
RUTH: What did he say?
BEATRICE *(flinging her glass on the floor):* How could you do this to me?
HOW COULD YOU LET THAT MAN CALL THIS HOME!? I have no

clothes, do you hear me? I'd look just like you up on the stage, ugly little you! DO YOU WANT THEM TO LAUGH AT US? LAUGH AT THE TWO OF US?

RUTH: Mother . . . aren't you proud of her? *(Disbelievingly)* Mother . . . it's an *honor.*

> *Tillie breaks into tears and moves away from Beatrice. It seems as though she is crushed, but then she halts and turns to face her mother.*

TILLIE *(through tears):* But . . . nobody laughed at me.

> *Beatrice's face begins to soften as she glimpses what she's done to Tillie.*

BEATRICE: Oh, my God . . .

> *Tillie starts toward her. Beatrice opens her arms to receive her as music has started in and lights fade. A chord of finality punctuates the end of Act I. Curtain.*

ACT II

Early one evening two weeks later, Tillie and Ruth are preparing to attend the science fair for the judging of the finals. Tillie has been dressed by her mother *"too girlishly"* with a large bow in her hair; Ruth has too much makeup on.

Tillie's project is charted on a large three-panel screen set up on the table. It is entitled "The Effect of Gamma Rays on Man-in-the-Moon Marigolds," subtitled "The Past, The Present, The Future."

A girl named Janice Vickery has a cat's skeleton (Ruth informs Tillie) which represents Tillie's only real competition in the finals. Ruth insinuates, horribly, that the cat was alive when Janice proceeded to boil the skin off it.

Ruth insists on taking off Tillie's bow—she doesn't want them to laugh at the way her sister looks. She is afraid that in any case they will laugh at Beatrice. Ruth overheard a conversation between teachers.

RUTH: Miss Hanley was telling Mr. Goodman about Mama . . . when she found out you were one of the five winners. And he wanted to know if there was something wrong with Mama because she sounded crazy over the phone. And Miss Hanley said she *was* crazy and she always has been crazy and she can't wait to see what she looks like after all these years. Miss Hanley said her nickname used to be Betty the Loon.

TILLIE *(as Ruth combs her hair):* Ruth, you're hurting me.

RUTH: She was just like you and everybody thought she was a big weirdo. There! You look much better!

> *She goes to the rabbit.*

If anybody stuck you in a pot of boiling water I'd kill them, do you know that? *(Then to Tillie.)* What do they call boiling the skin off a cat? I call it murder,

that's what I call it. They say it was hit by a car and Janice just scooped it up and before you could say *bingo* it was screaming in a pot of boiling water.
    Pause.
Do you know what they're all waiting to see? Mama's feathers! That's what Miss Hanley said. She said Mama blabs as though she was the Queen of England and just as proper as can be and that her idea of getting dressed up is to put on all the feathers in the world and go as a bird. Always trying to get somewhere like a great big bird.
    TILLIE: Don't tell Mama, please. It doesn't matter.
    RUTH: I was up there watching her getting dressed and sure enough she's got the feathers out.
    TILLIE: You didn't tell her what Miss Hanley said?
    RUTH: Are you kidding? I just told her I didn't like the feathers and I didn't think she should wear any. But I'll bet she doesn't listen to me.

Tillie asks Ruth to promise she won't say anything to Beatrice. Ruth sees that she has an edge for the moment, and she exploits it: she demands that Tillie give her the rabbit in exchange for her silence. The taxi will be here any minute to take them to school, so Tillie has no time to argue. She agrees that Ruth can have the rabbit.
    Tillie calls up to her mother to hurry. *"Beatrice comes to the top of the stairs. Her costume is strange, but not that strange by any means. She is even a little attractive tonight, and though her words say she is greatly annoyed with having to attend the night's function, her tone and direction show she is very, very proud."*
    Tillie tells her mother she looks beautiful. Beatrice pretends to be upset about the arrangements, about having to sit on the stage at a school where they let a child tear a cat's skin off with an orange knife (this is what Ruth has told her mother).
    Beatrice offers to carry the screen while Tillie carries the boxes of flowers (Beatrice, it seems, made the titles for the screen). Beatrice notices that Tillie has taken off her bow. Beatrice puts it back: "There's nothing wrong with looking proper, Matilda, and if you don't have enough money to look expensive and perfect, people like you for *trying* to look nice."
    Getting ready to go, Ruth puts her coat on, but Beatrice reminds Ruth that it is her duty to stay home tonight and watch the house and Nanny—and clean up the rabbit droppings, now that she owns the animal. Ruth is crestfallen. She insists that she *must* go. She becomes more and more frantic in her insistence. Outside, the taxi horn blows.

    RUTH *(almost berserk):* I don't care. I'M GOING ANYWAY!
    BEATRICE *(shoving Ruth hard):* WHAT DID YOU SAY?
    TILLIE: Mother!
    BEATRICE *(after a pause, the horn blows again):* Hurry up with that box, Matilda, and tell him to stop blowing the horn. HURRY UP!
    Tillie reluctantly exits with the box of plants.

I don't know where you ever got the idea you were going tonight. Did you think nobody was going to hold down the fort?

> *Pause.*

Now you know how I felt all those years you and everybody else was running out whenever they felt like it—because there was always me to watch over the fifty-dollar-a-week corpse. If there's one thing I demand it's respect. I don't ask for anything from you but respect.

RUTH (*pathetically*): Why are you ashamed of me?

BEATRICE (*starting to fold the large three-panel screen*): I've been seen with a lot worse than you. I don't even know why I'm going tonight, do you know that? Do you think I give one Goddamn about the whole thing?

> *Pause.*

Do you want to know why I'm going? Do you really want to know why this once somebody else has to stick with that dried prune for a few minutes? Because this is the first time in my life I've ever felt just a little bit proud over something. Isn't that silly? Somewhere in the back of this turtle-sized brain of mine I feel just a little *proud!* Jesus Christ! And you begrudge me even that, you little bastard.

> *The taxi horn blows impatiently.*

RUTH (*hardening*): Hurry up. They're waiting for you. (*Pause.*) They're *all* waiting for you.

BEATRICE (*carrying the folded screen so that THE PAST is face out in bold black letters*): I hope the paint is dry. (*Pause.*) Who's waiting for me?

RUTH: Everybody . . . including Miss Hanley. She's been telling all the teachers . . . about you . . . and they're all waiting.

BEATRICE: You're such a little liar, Ruth, do you know that? When you can't have what you want you try to ruin it for everybody else.

> *She starts to the door.*

RUTH: Good night, *Betty the Loon.*

> *Beatrice stops as if she's been stabbed. The taxi horn blows several times as Beatrice puts down the folding screen.*

BEATRICE (*helplessly*): Take this thing.

Beatrice is in shock, her pride and her pleasure destroyed. She tells Ruth to go with Tillie. Ruth runs out carrying the screen, leaving her mother in tears.

The lights go down and then an area to the left of the stage is brightly lit, showing Janice Vickery displaying her cat's skeleton at the science fair. Janice's presentation is divided formally into three parts with a gong sounding to end each one: The Past, The Present and The Future. She tells how she got the dead cat from the ASPCA (so much for Ruth's horror stories) and how she prepared its skeleton. She plans to donate it to the school's science department.

The lights go down again, then up on Beatrice back at home. Beatrice has been drinking and is trying to get the school principal on the telephone. She has a message for the principal and the other teachers: "Tell them Mrs. Huns-dorfer called to thank them for making her wish she was dead."

Beatrice hangs up the phone. It rings, but she ignores it. Instead, she rips off the paper masking the front window, rearranges the tables, takes some table cloths and napkins from the bureau and spots them around. She is experimenting in setting up her tea room.

The ringing phone reminds Beatrice she wants to make a telephone call. She stops the ringing by lifting the receiver, gets a dial tone and dials. Into the phone she tells "Miss Career Woman of the Year," Nanny's daughter, that she wants Nanny out of the house by tomorrow. Brutally, she adds: "I told you when you rolled her in here I was going to try her out for a while and if I didn't like her she was to get the hell out. Well I don't like her so get her the hell out."

After slamming down the phone and laughing, Beatrice goes to pour herself another drink. Her foot strikes the rabbit's cage, calling the animal to her attention. She collects a towel, the bottle of chloroform and the rabbit in his cage and exits up the stairs.

The lights fade and then come up at stage left on Tillie making her presentation at the science fair.

TILLIE (deathly afraid but referring to her cards): The Past: The seeds were exposed to various degrees . . . of gamma rays from radiation sources in Oak Ridge. (Pause.) Mr. Goodman helped me pay for the seeds. (Pause.) Their growth was plotted against . . . time.
       She loses her voice for a moment and then the first gong sounds.
The Present: The seeds which received little radiation have grown to plants which are normal in appearance. The seeds which received moderate radiation gave rise to mutations such as double blooms, giant stems and variegated leaves. The seeds closest to the gamma source were killed or yielded dwarf plants.
       The second gong rings.
The Future: After radiation is better understood a day will come when the power from exploding atoms will change the whole world we know.
       With inspiration.
Some of the mutations will be good ones—wonderful things beyond our dreams—and I believe, I believe this with all my heart, THE DAY WILL COME WHEN MANKIND WILL THANK GOD FOR THE STRANGE AND BEAUTIFUL ENERGY FROM THE ATOM.

The lights fade and come up on the living room, where Ruth is bursting in to tell her mother that Tillie won. Beatrice is nowhere to be seen. Ruth sets down the screen and a shopping bag full of plants; Tillie follows her into the house, carrying the rest of the plants and her first-prize trophy.

Beatrice, very drunk, appears at the top of the stairs carrying an old pair of curtains. Ignoring the girls, she comes down and goes to the front window to tack them up.

Beatrice pretends not to hear that Tillie won. Ruth, exasperated, calls her "Betty the Loon" again. Beatrice tells Ruth: "The rabbit is in your room. I want you to bury it in the morning."

Ruth runs upstairs and finds that the rabbit is indeed dead. Coming to the top of the stairs carrying the animal wrapped in a towel, Ruth begins to go into a seizure. She drops the towel-covered body of the rabbit and surrenders to the paroxysms of what appears to be an epileptic fit. Beatrice and Tillie rush to her assistance, getting her onto the living room sofa and covering her inert form with a blanket after the violent phase subsides. Beatrice refuses to call the doctor because, as she tells Tillie, "We're going to spend every penny to get this place open."

Tillie, sobbing, carries the rabbit's towel-wrapped body over to the front door and sets it down.

> *Music starts in softly as Beatrice continues folding napkins with her back to the others. There is the sound of someone at the curtained doorway, and Nanny commences negotiating herself into the room. Slowly she advances with the tubular frame—unaware, desiccated, in some other land.*

BEATRICE *(weakly):* Matilda?

TILLIE: Yes, Mama?

BEATRICE: I hate the world. Do you know that, Matilda?

TILLIE: Yes, Mama.

BEATRICE: I hate the world.

> *The lights have started down, the music makes its presence known, and a spot clings to Tillie. She moves to the staircase and the rest of the set goes to black during the following speech. As she starts up the stairs her voice falls over in the same way as the play opened.*

TILLIE'S VOICE: *The Conclusion:* My experiment has shown some of the strange effects radiation can produce . . . and how dangerous it can be if not handled correctly. Mr. Goodman said I should tell in this conclusion what my future plans are and how this experiment has helped me make them. For one thing, the Effect of Gamma Rays on Man-in-the-Moon Marigolds has made me curious about the sun and the stars, for the universe itself must be like a world of great atoms—and I want to know more about it. But most important, I suppose, my experiment has made me feel important—every atom in me, in everybody, has come from the sun—from places beyond our dreams. The atoms of our hands, the atoms of our hearts . . .

> *All sound out. Tillie speaks the rest live, hopeful, glowing.*

TILLIE: Atom. Atom. What a beautiful word.

> *Curtain.*

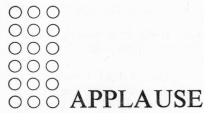

APPLAUSE

A Musical in Two Acts

BOOK BY BETTY COMDEN AND
ADOLPH GREEN

MUSIC BY CHARLES STROUSE

LYRICS BY LEE ADAMS

Based on the film All About Eve *and the original story by Mary Orr*

Cast and credits appear on page 323

*BETTY COMDEN (co-author of book) was born in Brooklyn May 3, 1919
and attended Brooklyn Ethical Culture and Erasmus Hall High Schools. After
receiving her Bachelor of Science degree at New York University, Miss Comden joined Adolph Green and the late Judy Holliday in the night club act
called "The Revuers" which packed them into the Village Vanguard and other
night spots in the 1940s. As performers, Miss Comden and Green played the
roles of Claire and Ozzie in their own musical* On the Town *(with music by
Leonard Bernstein), which was produced on Broadway December 28, 1944*

for 463 performances; and they returned to the Broadway stage in the 1958-59 season in an evening of their own comedy and songs entitled A Party With Betty Comden and Adolph Green *for 82 performances.*

It is as writers, though, that Comden & Green are best known. They are the authors of the book and lyrics for Billion Dollar Baby, Two on the Aisle, Bells Are Ringing *(which starred their lifelong friend Miss Holliday),* Fade Out-Fade In *and* Subways Are for Sleeping *(which featured Phyllis Newman, Mr. Green's wife). They did the lyrics for* Wonderful Town *(a Best Play of 1952-53),* Peter Pan, Take Me Out to the Ball Game, Say Darling, Do Re Mi *and* Hallelujah, Baby! *for which they shared with Jule Styne the 1966-67 Tony Award for best score of the season.*

Miss Comden divides all her writing credits with Adolph Green, but her marital billing is Mrs. Steven Kyle. The Kyles were married in 1942 and have two children, a girl and a boy.

ADOLPH GREEN (co-author of book), half of one of the most successful and indivisible partnerships in theatrical history, was born in New York City December 2, 1915. He studied in New York public schools and, as reported in Betty Comden's biography above, first joined with his future collaborator as a writer-actor in the night club act "The Revuers."

The theater credits of Comden & Green are as noted above. Their distinguished writing career in the movies includes the screen plays for Good News, On the Town, Barkleys of Broadway, Take Me Out to the Ball Game, Singin' in the Rain, Band Wagon, Auntie Mame, Bells Are Ringing, It's Always Fair Weather *and* What a Way to Go. *They have received three Academy Award nominations, and in the theater they won a Donaldson Award for* Wonderful Town.

Green married Phyllis Newman, the actress, in 1960. They have two children, a son and a daughter. The Greens live in Connecticut while his collaborator's family, the Kyles, live in New York City.

CHARLES STROUSE (music) was born in New York City June 7, 1928 and has composed since the age of 12. He studied at the Eastern School of Music (Mus.B., 1947) and in private lessons from Aaron Copland and Nadia Boulanger. All of his works for Broadway have been done in tandem with Lee Adams as lyricist. Their first show was Bye Bye Birdie *(1964), followed by* All American *(1962),* Golden Boy *(1964) and* "It's a Bird It's a Plane It's SUPERMAN" *(1966, a Best Play selection and still the best theatrical example of camp). In the movies, Strouse did the scores for* Bonnie and Clyde *and* The Molly Maguires *and collaborated with his partner Adams on* The Night They Raided Minsky's *and* There Was a Crooked Man.

Strouse is married to the former Barbara Siman, who was a featured player in My Fair Lady. *They have two sons and live in New York City.*

LEE ADAMS (lyrics) was born in 1924 in Mansfield, Ohio and attended Columbia University Graduate School of Journalism. He took up lyric-writing only after a period of working on newspapers, magazines, TV and radio. To-gether with Strouse, Adams began writing for the theater at Green Mansions, a resort in the Adirondacks where they had to come up with a new show every Saturday night. Their partnership has lasted 21 years, during which time they have published more than 300 songs including "A Lot of Livin' to Do," "Put on a Happy Face," "Kids," "Once Upon a Time," "Night Song," "I Want To Be With You," "This Is the Life" and "You've Got Possibilities." In addition to their four Broadway musicals their work has included 15 revues and a TV special.

Adams is married, with one daughter, and lives in Connecticut.

Our method of synopsizing Applause *in these pages differs from that used for the other nine Best Plays.* Applause *is represented mostly in pictures to record the total "look" of a Broadway show in 1969-70—also because it is an exceptionally handsome production.*

The photographs depict the succession of scenes as produced by Joseph Kipness and Lawrence Kasha in association with Nederlander Productions and George M. Steinbrenner III and directed by Ron Field, as of the opening March 30, 1970 at the Palace Theater, with scenery by Robert Randolph and cos-tumes by Ray Aghayan. Our special thanks are enthusiastically tendered to the authors, producers and their press representatives—Bill Doll and Com-pany and Dick Williams, Midori Lederer, Virginia Holden and Susan Schul-man—for their help in obtaining this material including the excellent photo-graphs by Henri Dauman and J. Edward Bailey.

Time: The present
Place: In and around New York

ACT I

Scene 1: At a Tony Awards ceremony, Margo Channing, the previous year's winner, presents the award to Eve Harrington as best actress. Margo remembers how the younger actress got her start in the theater two years before . . .

Scene 2: . . . in her dressing room on opening night, Margo (Lauren Bacall, *above center*) is being congratulated on her performance by a roomful of admirers including her director Bill Sampson (Len Cariou, *above center*) whom she loves but who is off to Rome soon to make a movie. Margo admits that it has been a great strain for her, at 40, to play a much younger woman in the script written for her by Buzz Richards. But the play is a hit, and among those waiting in the alley for a glimpse of its star is a wide-eyed young woman. Graciously, Margo invites her to the dressing room.

Enter *"a young girl in her 20's rather bedraggled, wearing a raincoat and pants."* It is Eve Harrington (Penny Fuller, *above right*), a stagestruck girl from Wisconsin who idolizes (and thus flatters) Margo. Bill leaves for Rome after asking Margo, "Marry me when I get back?" and the others drift off to the opening night party. Eve stays behind with Margo's hairdresser Duane Fox (Lee Roy Reams, *above left*). Margo decides to skip the party and go to the Village with Duane instead. Eve mimics Margo's every movement in the number "But Alive."

MARGO (*sings*):
I feel groggy and weary
And tragic,
Punchy and bleary
And fresh out of magic,
But alive, but alive, but alive!
I feel twitchy and bitchy
And manic,

Calm and collected
And choking with panic,
But alive, but alive, but alive!
I'm a thousand diff'rent people,
Ev'ry single one is real,
I've a million diff'rent feelings,
OK, but at least I feel! . . .

(continued on next page)

MARGO *(continued, as the action*
    moves to Scene 3, a Village bar):
    . . . . . I feel half Tijuana,
    Half Boston,
    Partly Jane Fonda,
    and Jane Austen,
    But alive,
    That's the thing!
    But alive!

With her high-voltage glamor and personality *(right and below),* Margo fascinates
even Duane's friends, including Sammy
Williams *(right center, below)* who finally
exclaims to the assemblage, "I love her.
I mean, I really love *her*!"

Scene 4: Margo has brought Eve home with her after the Village party. They learn that Margo's notices in the new play were raves. To stage-struck Eve, this is "The best night of my life," as she tells Margo in song *(opposite page)*. They turn on TV and find an old Margo Channing movie *(right)*. Margo, achingly sensitive about her age as both actress and woman, wonders if Bill, who is younger than she, loves her for herself or for the glamorous young screen image he remembers. Margo sings to her movie image: "Who's that girl with the Maybelline eyes/ Acting like she knew the score?/Ixnay, Daddy-O/I never saw that girl before!" Eve demonstrates *(below)* that she knows all Margo's movie dialogue by heart.

EVE (*sings*):
>The best night of my life
>Is here, is now.
>Knowing you has got to be
>The greatest thing
>   that ever happened to me . . . . .

>. . . . . There's no way to say
>   thank you,
>It wouldn't come out right.
>But—thank you
>For the best night of my life.

Margo exits to her bedroom. Eve is beginning to feel as though she belongs here. She picks up Margo's Tony Award (right) and holds it.

Scene 5: Four months later in Margo's dressing room, Duane and Eve (out of photo but now solicitously taking part in all Margo's affairs) look on while playwright Buzz Richards (Brandon Maggart, *above left*) and producer Howard Benedict (Robert Mandan, *above right*) turn down Margo's urgent plea for a leave of absence to go to Rome and see Bill. Margo is too good a trouper to insist. Meanwhile, Eve has caught Howard's eye, and the producer invites her to accompany him to Joe Allen's 46th Street restaurant . . .

Scene 6: At Joe Allen's, the chorus "gypsies" who hang out there, led by Bonnie (Bonnie Franklin, *opposite page*) sing of why they struggle for years for a net of $12.15 weekly after expenses: that treasured "Applause."

BONNIE (*sings*):
　What is it that
　　we're living for?
　Applause, applause.
　Nothing I know
　Brings on the glow
　Like sweet applause.
　You're thinking you're through,
　That nobody cares,
　Then suddenly you
　Hear it—starting—

And somehow you're
　in charge again,
And it's a ball!
Trumpets all sing,
Life seems to swing,
And you're the king
Of it all, 'cause—
You've had a taste of
The sound that says love,
Applause, applause,
Applause! . . .

" . . . You don't
Care
As long as
It's there—
Applause!
Applause!
Applause!
Applause!
Applause!
Applause!
Applause!"

Scene 7: In Margo's bedroom *(left)*, Margo is over-joyed to hear Bill's voice from Rome but not so happy to find out that Eve has placed this birthday call without being asked. Eve is almost too efficient. But Margo, aching to see Bill again ("Hurry back/ Hurry back/It's no life at all/When you're not here to hold me"), forgets about Eve when Bill plans to come home for a short visit. She promises Bill a party.

Scene 8: At the party at Margo's, Eve wears a dress Margo gave her. When Bill arrives, he starts one of the party games with Eve *(below)*. Margo enters and mistakes their playfulness for intimacy. In an acid, martini-edged tone she sends Eve off on an errand *(opposite page, below)*. Bill is astonished at Margo's jealousy of Eve ("Isn't she a treasure? I think I'll bury her!") Finally Margo warns her roomful of guests angrily: "Fasten your seat belts —it's going to be a bumpy night!"

BUZZ *(sings):*

> Fasten your seat belts,
> It's gonna be a bumpy night . . .
> Batten the hatches,
> We're gonna have a funsy flight!

KAREN:

> She's laughing a bit too loudly,
> That's how the last one began . . .

HOWARD:

> I figure she's two drinks from the spot
> Where you-know-what
> Hits the fan!

BILL & HOWARD *(to two guests):*

> Don't take off your coat,
> You came the wrong night,
> Get out while you can,
> Mother is uptight!

GROUP:

> Fasten your seat belts,
> It's gonna be
> A bumpy night!

The center of attraction (*above*) but boiling with jealousy, Margo puts on a display of temperament, insults everyone, wrecks the party.

Scene 9: Backstage at the theater, Eve's efforts to emulate Margo and even wear her castoff clothes (as at *right*) finally pay off. After hearing her read the part, Howard and Buzz (and Karen, Buzz's wife) decide to hire Eve as Margo's understudy. When Margo arrives at the theater and learns of this new development in Eve's career, she is furious (*above*).

MARGO: I can't get over it. It's just beginning to sink in. This little prairie flower has been standing in the wings studying my every move—every line for five months—and I never saw what she was really up to!

EVE: Miss Channing, I know I could never be more than adequate in covering the part, but if you— (*Trying to control her crying.*) Have any objections, naturally I wouldn't dream—

KAREN (*holding Eve*): Wait . . . I'm taking you out for a drink. Come on, Buzz.

BUZZ: In a minute. Let's get this settled. I was surprised too. She was a revelation.

MARGO: Well, naturally, it must have been a revelation to have a somewhat younger character played by a somewhat younger actress.

BUZZ: What are you talking about?

MARGO: It must have sounded so new and fresh to you. You probably could hardly recognize your own play.

BUZZ: The play is actor-proof!

MARGO: Actor-proof! If you knew the bits— the shtick I have to dredge out of the vaudeville trunk to give the illusion that something amusing is going on—

BUZZ: You empty-headed, conceited bass fiddle! You're just a body and a voice! Don't ever forget—I'm the brain!

MARGO: Till the autopsy, there's no proof! (*Buzz stamps out.*)

(*continued on next page*)

MARGO: Oh, I do. And I'm full of admiration for you. If you can handle yourself on the stage with the same artistry you display *off* the stage—well, my dear —you are in the right place. . . .

MARGO *(sings):*
    . . . . Now you've entered the asylum,
    This profession unique
    Actors are children
    Playing hide-and-ego-seek . . .
    So welcome, Miss Eve Harrington,
    To this business we call show,
    You're on your way
    To wealth and fame,
    Unsheath your claws,
    Enjoy the game!
    You'll be a bitch
    But they'll know your name
    From New York to Kokomo . . .
    Welcome to the theater,
    My dear, you'll love it so! . . .

After Eve departs, there is only Bill left for Margo to quarrel with. Bill tries to convince her she has nothing to fear from Eve: "There are always talented young people coming along—but you're *you*—you're unique!" But Margo will not be pacified, she is even jealous of Bill's defense of Eve in this conversation. Exasperated, Bill leaves her while the music plays "Welcome to the Theater."
(Curtain; end of Act I.)

(continued from the preceding page)
KAREN: Margo, you've been kicking us all around long enough. Someone ought to give *you* a good swift one for a change. *(She leaves.)*

EVE: Miss Channing—if I ever dreamed that anything I did could possibly cause you any unhappiness—or come between you and your friends—please believe me.

ACT II

Scene 1: Their quarrel blown over, Margo visits Karen (Ann Williams, *above left*) and Buzz in the country. Karen, taken in by Eve's pose, arranges to have the car run out of gas so that Margo can't get back to town in time to do the play. Eve, the understudy, will have the chance to go on in Margo's place. Margo behaves graciously, phones Eve to give her some helpful hints. Buzz sings a song of friendship (*above*). Karen, now having second thoughts, is overcome with remorse at what she has done to her good friend Margo.

Scene 2: In the star's dressing room, even Duane has to admit to Eve that she "wowed them." Bill comes in to congratulate Eve on her performance. She flatters and then attempts to seduce Bill. But Bill rejects her and walks out on her. Eve then goes to work on the producer, Howard, with more success. Perhaps Howard will be able to find Eve a part of her own—meanwhile they plan to celebrate Eve's success at Allen's restaurant.

Scene 3: At Allen's, Eve basks in the envious attentions of the "gypsies" and gives out an interview in her true colors: "I adore Margo Channing and I only hope I'll have the energy and grace she has when I'm *her* age. . . . Of course, mature actresses are sometimes also childlike, self-deluded people—They don't realize that they can be personally brilliant yet detrimental to the play." Meanwhile, the "gypsies," including Duane and Bonnie (*above*), sing in Eve's honor: "She's no longer a gypsy/She'll be leaving us soon/ She did the understudy-to-the-rescue bit/Now she's halfway to the moon."

Scene 4: Bill interrupts the filming of a commercial at Margo's. He's come to comfort her: Eve's published interview is so much "garbage."

BILL *(left, sings):*
>You're one of a kind,
>A fabulous bird,
>You're out of your mind
>And 'way out of sight,
>You're one of a kind,
>Unique is the word,
>And that's why I find
>The others all trite. . . .

But when Margo suggests marriage, Bill balks; he can't compete with her career.

Scene 5: Backstage, Eve has a rendezvous with Buzz, who is now infatuated with her and is writing a new play for her. He presents Eve with the key to an apartment they can borrow. Buzz leaves, and Eve sings to herself of a Halloween when she was 9. Her father humiliated her for wearing too much makeup. "Look at your little girl now!" Eve cries.

EVE *(sings, right):*
    Ev'rybody loves a winner,
    But nobody loves a flop!
    No one worries how you
                got there
    Once you're standing
                on the top!
    So I feel up and together
    And steady,
    Eager, excited,
    So come on, I'm ready!
    Ready for the climb,
    Baby, it's my time!
    You believe it, I'm
    Alive! Alive!

Unseen, Howard has been watching Eve. He steps forward, and she tells him she now loves Buzz. But Howard will not take her no for an answer. He has been looking into her background—among other unpleasant details, she has a living husband. Besides, Howard holds the power over her career. Howard kisses Eve, then slaps her. She curses him, but they both know she is beaten. Howard orders her: "Take a taxi, get your things, and be at my place in an hour. And if I'm not there—wait."

Scene 6: In her dressing room, Margo learns that Eve is to star in Buzz's new play. Karen comes in and confesses her gas tank misdeed, but Margo has already guessed. Margo commiserates with Karen over Buzz and advises her to do nothing and wait. Eve doesn't want him, she only wants his play. Left alone, Margo comes to a decision in song that there is something greater than a theater career: "Being to your man what a woman should be/That's something greater/Something greater!/And finally, that's for me!"

Bill appears and joins Margo in the song's last few bars. They move toward each other (*above*), offering mutual apologies.

BILL: . . . . I should have protected you from that girl, she's a—

MARGO (*putting her hand over his mouth*): Don't say a word against her.

And let the kid have the part.
If it weren't for her I would have lost you. (*Looking out front and* calling.) Eve! You four-star bitch! Thank you!

BOTH (*sing*):
That's something greater!
Something greater!
And, finally, that's for me!

They kiss. (*Curtain.*)

CURTAIN CALLS *(above & below):*
  Why do we live this crazy life?
  What is it for?
  Cares disappear,
  Soon as you hear
  That happy audience roar, 'cause

You've had a taste of
The sounds that say love!
Applause! Applause!
Applause! Applause!
Applause! Applause!
Applause!

COMPANY

A Musical Comedy in Two Acts

BOOK BY GEORGE FURTH

MUSIC AND LYRICS BY STEPHEN SONDHEIM

Cast and credits appear on page 328

STEPHEN SONDHEIM (music, lyrics) was born March 22, 1930 in New York City. At Williams College he won the Hutchinson Prize for musical composition, and after graduating B. A. he studied theory and composition with Milton Babbitt. It was as a lyricist, however, that he first commanded major attention on Broadway with West Side Story *in 1957, after having supplied the incidental music for* Girls of Summer *(1956). Sondheim wrote both the music and lyrics for* A Funny Thing Happened on the Way to The Forum *(1962) and* Anyone Can Whistle *(1964) and has done the same for his new* Company. *His other credits include the incidental music for* Invitation to a March *(1961) and the lyrics for* Gypsy *(1959) and* Do I Hear a Waltz? *(1965), as well as various television scripts for the "Topper" series. Puzzle fans are still talking about his weekly brain-twisting crosswords in* New York Magazine *in the recent past.*

GEORGE FURTH (book) was born December 14, 1932 in Chicago and graduated from Northwestern University. He came East to get a master's degree at

*Columbia and entered the theater as an actor. Furth's first Broadway perform-
ance (in* A Cook for Mr. General, *1961) brought him a five-year contract at
Universal Pictures. He has appeared in 15 movies, recently as Woodcock in*
Butch Cassidy and the Sundance Kid, *Charlie Flagler Jr. in* Myra Breckin-
ridge, *Colonel Logan in* The Boston Strangler, *Tom in* The Best Man *and
Murgatroy in* What's So Bad About Feeling Good. *He has appeared on TV
in every major show including two series:* Broadside *and* Tammy.

The book for Company *is Furth's first attempt at writing, for which he has
received a Best Play citation and the New York Drama Critics and Outer
Circle awards for the best musical of the 1969-70 season. His next play, a
non-musical entitled* A Chorus Line, *is under option to David Merrick. A
George Furth Collection has been established at Boston University.*

Time: *Now*

Place: *New York City*

ACT I

Scene 1: Robert's apartment

SYNOPSIS: Five couples, the wives bearing birthday gifts, are standing around
a table. The sound of the footsteps they are waiting for is heard, and the
lights are turned out. There is the sound of a key in the door and Robert enters. Spotlights hit his face, startling him; the lights come on and all shout
"surprise!"

This is Robert's apartment. His best friends are gathered for a surprise 35th-
birthday party in his honor. As they thrust presents on him with appropriate
anti-sentimental remarks, there arises the sense that although these five couples may be just the slightest bit on edge toward each other, and between each
other in individual marriages, they all love Robert; he is their pal, their talis-
man.

A segment of their party chatter goes like this:

JOANNE *(as Jenny starts toward Robert):* Miss, Miss. YOU! Yes, you! Tell
him to take yours back and get the money. It's not the gift, it's the cost that
counts.

JENNY *(handing her present to Robert):* Who *is* that?

JOANNE: That is I, Miss. I am very rich and I am married to *him,* and I'd
introduce him, but I forget his name.

ROBERT *(quickly):* Haven't you two met?

JOANNE: Pass, baby. Pass. There's no one here I want to meet. Except her.
She's crazy. *(Points to Amy.)* And him. He's a looker. *(Points to Peter.)* The
rest are Lois and Larry Loser—here's to you, winner.

ELAINE STRITCH, BARBARA BARRIE, TERI RALSTON, SUSAN BROWNING, DONNA
MCKECHNIE, BETH HOWLAND, PAMELA MYERS AND MERLE LOUISE SURROUND
DEAN JONES IN "COMPANY"

She downs his drink.
PETER *(to Joanne):* I find you quite fascinating. Quite delightful. Quite.
JOANNE: You just blew it.

Peter wishes that the year may bring Robert "fame, fortune and your first
wife." Robert has no craving for any of these, he is content with his bachelor
life and his friends.

Amy enters with the cake ablaze with candles, and after a flat rendition of
"Happy Birthday" Robert must close his eyes, make a wish and blow out the
candles. Only half the candles blow out, but Robert doesn't mind; he didn't
wish for anything.

As Robert stands there as though in a trance or dream, his friends exit
carrying pieces of his furniture until he is alone in an empty room. The setting
is an arrangement of metal rods and platforms suggesting the geometric de-

personalization of New York living. Robert's friends, watching him from upper levels, go into the song "Company":

JENNY *(sings):* Bobby . . .
PETER: Bobby . . .
AMY: Bobby baby . . .
PAUL: Bobby bubi . . .
JOANNE: Robby . . .
SUSAN: Robert darling. . . . .
PETER: Bob-o . . .
LARRY & JOANNE: Bobby, there was something we wanted to say.
SARAH & HARRY: Bobby . . .
PAUL: Bobby bubi . . .
AMY: Sweetheart . . .
SUSAN: Sugar . . .
DAVID & JENNY: Your line was busy.
PETER: What have you been up to, kiddo?
AMY & PAUL: Bobby, Bobby, how have you been?
HARRY: Fella . . .
SARAH: Sweetie.
HARRY & SARAH: How have you been?
PETER & SUSAN: Bobby, Bobby, how have you been? . . . . .
AMY & PAUL: Bobby there's a concert on Tuesday.
DAVID & JENNY: Hank and Mary get into town tomorrow.
PETER & SUSAN: How about some Scrabble on Sunday?
SARAH & HARRY: Why don't we all go to the beach next weekend?
JOANNE & LARRY: Bob, we're having people in Saturday night. . . . .
ALL:
  Bobby, come on over for dinner!
  We'll be so glad to see you!
  Bobby, come on over for dinner!
  Just be the three of us.
  Only the three of us,
  We loooooove you!
ROBERT:
  Phone rings, door chimes, in comes company!
  No strings, good times, room hums, company!
  Late nights, quick bites, party games,
  Deep talks, long walks, telephone calls,
  Thoughts shared, souls bared, private names,
  All those photos up on the walls
  "With love,"
  With love filling the days,
  With love seventy ways,
  "To Bobby, with love"
  From all
  Those

Good and crazy people, my friends,
Those
Good and crazy people, my married friends!
And that's what it's all about, isn't it?
That's what it's really about,
Really about! . . . . .
HUSBANDS: Isn't it? Isn't it? Isn't it? Isn't it?
WIVES & GIRLS: Love . . .
HUSBANDS: Isn't it? Isn't it? Isn't it? Isn't it?
ROBERT:
You I love and you I love and you and you I love
And you I love and you I love and you and you I love, I love you!
ALL:
Company! Company! Company, lots of company!
Years of company! Love is company!
Company!

Scene 2: Sarah's and Harry's living room on the ground floor of a garden apartment

Robert is having after-dinner coffee as the guest of Sarah and Harry, who always *"seem to be having a wonderful time. Most, if not all the things that they say are enjoyed tremendously by the person speaking. There is much laughing, giggling, smiling and affection."*
When Robert asks for a bourbon he notices that Harry isn't joining him, and now it comes out: Harry has been on the wagon for a year, after two unfortunate incidents of being arrested for drunkenness. Sarah has a habit of correcting little details of Harry's stories. For example, when Harry declares he hasn't had a drink for more than a year, Sarah goes out of her way to remind him of a champagne toast at a friend's wedding.
When the brownies are passed, Robert discovers that Sarah too has her cross to bear. She is on a diet and admits, "I'd kill for chocolate. Or a baked potato with sour cream and chives."
Underneath her elaborate laments, Sarah manages to sneak a brownie, while Harry downs a furtive shot of bourbon.
Sarah has been studying karate, and she is persuaded to give a demonstration, using Harry as a partner. She throws Harry. Harry picks himself up and somewhat huffily states that he could have blocked the throw if he'd wanted to. Sarah comes at him again and he does indeed block her; but when he relaxes she overcomes the block and throws him again. (Joanne appears and sings a chorus of "The Little Things You Do Together.")
Now Harry and Sarah attack each other more competitively, blocking each other in an impasse.

ROBERT: You're both very good.
   They both look up at Robert.
BOTH: Thank you.

HARRY: I could get out of this, you know.
SARAH: Try it.

Harry kicks a foot behind her two feet, knocking her to the floor. He's on top of her, pinning her.

HARRY: Okay, I tried it.

Sarah pulls Harry by his shirt over her head, somersaulting him to the floor. She gets up, grabs his arm and pins him to the floor with her foot.

SARAH: Uncle?
HARRY: Uncle, your ass!
JOANNE *(sings):*

It's the little things you share together,
Swear together,
Wear together,
That make perfect relationships.
The concerts you enjoy together,
Neighbors you annoy together,
Children you destroy together,
That keep marriage intact. . . . .

Sarah and Harry break and prepare for another fall, while Robert starts to fix himself another bourbon. Robert is accidentally caught in the karate and all three fall down in a heap, as the rest of the company joins Joanne.

GROUP *(sings):*

It's not talk of God and the decade ahead that
Allows you to get through the worst.
It's "I do" and "You don't" and "Nobody said that"
And "Who brought the subject up first?"
It's the little things, the little things, the little things. . . . .
The little ways you try together,
Cry together,
Lie together
That make perfect relationships,
Becoming a cliché together,
Growing old and gray together,
JOANNE:
Withering away together
GROUP:
That makes marriage a joy. . . . .

Robert declares the karate match a draw, hurting nobody's feelings. He says his good nights and leaves, puzzled by Harry and Sarah's relationship.

The moment Robert has disappeared, Sarah heads for the brownies and Harry for the bourbon. Both are maneuvering to indulge themselves without the other knowing.

SARAH: Oh, Harry, I love you.

She exits. Harry crosses to steal a drink out of Robert's old glass.
ROBERT *(from the other side of the stage, having observed the previous scene):* Harry? You ever sorry you got married?
HARRY *(sings):*
    You're always sorry,
    You're always grateful,
    You're always wondering what might have been.
    Then she walks in.
    And still you're sorry,
    And still you're grateful,
    And still you wonder, and still you doubt,
    And she goes out.
    Everything's different,
    Nothing's changed,
    Only maybe slightly
    Rearranged.
    You're sorry-grateful,
    Regretful-happy,
    Why look for answers where none occur?
    You always are what you always were,
    Which has nothing to do with,
    All to do with her.
SARAH'S VOICE: Harry, darling, come to bed.
HARRY: Coming, darling.

Other husbands sing choruses of "Sorry-Grateful." Robert rides upward through the tubular construction to another level of the setting representing Peter's *("an Ivy League fellow")* and Susan's *("a pretty, wide-eyed, innocent Southern lady")* apartment.

Scene 3: Peter's and Susan's terrace

Peter and Susan are explaining to Robert that they seldom use their terrace: it is dirty and traffic-noisy, with the view blocked by the building across the street.

Robert compliments Susan on her gracious and feminine Southern charm.

ROBERT: . . . . . You two are beautiful together. Really. And Peter—if you ever decide to leave her I want to be the first to know.
SUSAN *(smiles at Peter):* Well . . .
PETER: You're the first to know.
ROBERT: What?
SUSAN: We're getting divorced.
PETER: We haven't told anyone yet.
ROBERT *(pause—stunned):* Oh!

Music: "Bobby Baby" underscoring.
I'm—uh, so surprised.
They just look at him. They don't speak.
Maybe you'll work it out.
Music: "Bobby Baby" underscoring and blank stares.
Don't think so, huh? Well, I know how hard it is for you and how you must feel.

> *Lights fade on the terrace as Robert takes the elevator down to David and Jenny's apartment which has come into view on the stage level.*

Scene 4: David and Jenny's apartment

David and Jenny are having their first experience of marijuana and their second cigarette, under Robert's influence and supervision. Jenny protests that she doesn't feel anything (but she is talking too much), and Robert judges that she is stoned.

David and Jenny shout curses just for fun, much to Robert's amusement and the neighbors' irritation at the noise. Robert calls Jenny "the girl I should have married" and this raises a subject which Jenny will not relinquish: When is Robert going to get married? David joins in, telling Robert marriage gives a man purpose. Robert tells them: "Listen, I agree. But you know what bothers me—is, if you marry, then you've got another person *there* all the time. Plus you can't get out of it, whenever you just might want to get out of it. You are caught! See? And even if you do get out of it, what do you have to show for it? Not to mention the fact that—then—you've always been married. I mean, you can never not have been married again."

What Robert probably means by all this is, he's not ready to get married, and he is never lonely, he has plenty of girls. As Robert mentions his girls by name—April, Kathy and Marta—they appear and join in singing their frustration at Robert's hard-to-get policy. He leads them on (the girls complain in the song number "You Could Drive a Person Crazy") and then leaves them dangling.

GIRLS *(sing):*
. . . . . I could understand a person
If it's not a person's bag . . .
I could understand a person
If a person was a fag . . .
But worse'n that,
A person that
Titillates a person and then leaves her flat
Is crazy,
He's a troubled person,
He's a truly crazy person
Himself!

(Speak.) You crummy bastard! You son-of-a-bitch!
> *Sing.*
> Bobby is my hobby and I'm giving it up.
KATHY:
> When a person's personality is personable,
> He shouldn't oughta sit like a lump.
> It's harder than a matador coercin' a bull
> To try to get you off of your rump.
> So single and attentive and attractive a man
> Is everything a person could wish,
> But turning off a person is the act of a man
> Who likes to pull the hooks out of fish. . . . .

Having expressed themselves thoroughly on this subject, Robert's girls exit. Robert offers David and Jenny another round of marijuana, but they decline. Jenny starts for the kitchen, then turns to explain to Robert why they refuse to continue the pot party.

JENNY: Bobby, we're just too old! We were all—trying to keep up with the kids tonight. Goodness, we've *been* there already. Who wants to go back? But anyway what do I know?
DAVID: Hey, screwball. I'm starving.
JENNY: I love you . . . so much.
DAVID: Food!
JENNY: And Bobby, put that stuff away. C'mon, put it in your pocket. Take it home. Come on.
> *Robert does.*
Thank you. I don't know. Maybe you're right. Who ever knows?
> *She smiles and exits.*

Alone with David, Robert offers him some of the weed, but he declines too. Robert has feelings of rejection as David goes to help his wife in the kitchen. Robert starts to leave but is interrupted by the five couples appearing above, clamoring "Bobby, come on over for dinner" and "Have I got a girl for you!"

LARRY *(sings):*
> Have I got a girl for you? Wait till you meet her!
> Have I got a girl for you, boy? Hoo, boy!
> Dumb!—and with a weakness for Sazerac slings—
> You give her even the fruit and she swings.
> The kind of girl you can't send through the mails—
> Call me tomorrow, I want the details.
PETER:
> Have I got a chick for you? Wait till you meet her!
> Have I got a chick for you, boy? Hoo, boy!

Smart!—she's into all those exotic mystiques:
The Kama Sutra and Chinese techniques—
I hear she knows more than seventy-five . . .
Call me tomorrow if you're still alive.

FIVE HUSBANDS *(in canon):*
Have I got a girl for you? Wait till you meet her!
Have I got a girl for you, boy? Hoo, boy!
Boy, to be in your shoes what I wouldn't give!
I mean the freedom to go out and live . . .
And as for settling down and all that,
Marriage may be where it's been, but it's not where it's at. . . . .

But Robert is thinking long thoughts, and after the five husbands finish their
song and leave him to himself he sings "Someone Is Waiting."

ROBERT *(sings):*
Someone is waiting,
Cool as Sarah,
Easy and loving as Susan—
Jenny.
Someone is waiting,
Warm as Susan,
Frantic and touching as Amy—
Joanne.

Would I know her even if I met her?
Have I missed her? Did I let her go?
A Susan sort of Sarah,
A Jennyish Joanne,
Wait for me, I'm ready now,
I'll find you if I can. . . . .
I'll hurry, wait for me.
Hurry.
Wait for me.
Hurry.
Wait for me . . .

Scene 5: A park bench at stage level

Marta is sitting on a park bench singing "Another Hundred People."

MARTA *(sings):*
Another hundred people just got off the train
And came up through the ground
While another hundred people just got off the bus
And are looking around
At another hundred people who got off the plane

And are looking at us
Who got off the train
And the plane and the bus
Maybe yesterday.

It's a city of strangers—
Some come to work, some to play—
A city of strangers—
Some come to stare, some to stay,
And every day
The ones who stay
Can find each other in the crowded streets and the guarded parks,
By the rusty fountains and the dusty trees with the battered barks
And they walk together past the postered walls with the crude remarks
And they meet at parties through the friends of friends
                                    who they never know.
Will you pick me up or do I meet you there or shall we let it go?
Did you get my message, 'cause I looked in vain?
Can we see each other Tuesday if it doesn't rain?
Look, I'll call you in the morning or my service will explain . . .

And another hundred people just got off the train.

Robert comes in with April, who is wearing an airline stewardess's uniform and is telling Robert how she always wanted to come to New York and live in Radio City, which she thought was a small separate community. She is living on the West Side with a male roommate: "He was born in New York—so nothing *really* interests him."

Marta sings another chorus of "Another Hundred People" as April goes out and Robert is joined by Kathy, who came to New York to have "two terrific affairs" before she got married. Robert was one of them—he wanted to marry her (Robert tells Kathy) but somehow never got around to asking. It's academic now, anyway, because Kathy is moving to Vermont to get married.

Kathy leaves and Marta joins Robert, after singing still another chorus. She tells Robert about New York.

MARTA: The pulse of this city, kiddo, is *me*. This city is for the me's of this world. People that want to be right in the heart of it. I am the soul of New York.

ROBERT: How 'bout that.

MARTA: See, smart remarks do not a person make. How many Puerto Ricans do you know?

ROBERT: I'm not sure.

MARTA: How many blacks?

ROBERT: Well, very few, actually. I seem to meet people only like myself.

MARTA: Talk about your weirdos. I pass people on the streets and I know them. Every son of a bitch is my friend. I go uptown to the dentist or something, and I suddenly want to cry because I think, "Oh my God, I'm *uptown*." And Fourteenth Street. Well, nobody knows it, but *that* is the center of the universe.

ROBERT: Fourteenth Street?

MARTA: That's humanity, Fourteenth Street. That's everything. And if you don't like it there they've got every subway you can name to take ya' where you like it better.

ROBERT: God bless Fourteenth Street.

MARTA: This city—I kiss the ground of it. Someday you know what I want to do? I want to get all dressed up in black—black dress, black shoes, hat, everything black, and go sit in some bar, at the end of the counter, and drink and cry. That is my idea of honest-to-God sophistication. I mean, *that's* New York.

Marta tells Robert of a theory she has about being relaxed or uptight in New York, as the lights fade.

Scene 6: The kitchen of Amy's apartment

Amy and Peter, who are living together, have finally decided to get married, and today is the day. Amy is seated at the kitchen counter shining Peter's shoes, as a girl dressed in white choir robe appears at an upper level and begins the song "Getting Married Today."

GIRL *(sings softly to organ accompaniment):*
　　Bless this day, pinnacle of life,
　　Husband joined to wife,
　　The heart leaps up to behold
　　This golden day.

PAUL *(appears in dress shirt, shorts and socks):* Amy, I can't find my shoes any . . . *(Sings.)*
　　Today is for Amy,
　　Amy, I give you the rest of my life.
　　To cherish and to keep you,
　　To honor you forever,
　　Today is for Amy,
　　My happily soon-to-be wife.
(Speaks.) Amy, we're really getting married!
　　　　He exits. She shakes her head "yes" and it becomes "no."
AMY *(sings):*
　　Pardon me, is everybody
　　There? Because if everybody's
　　There, I want to thank you all for
　　Coming to the wedding. I'd ap-
　　Preciate your going even
　　More, I mean you must have lots of
　　Better things to do, and not a

Word of it to Paul. Remember
Paul? You know, the man I'm gonna
Marry, but I'm not because I
Wouldn't ruin anyone as
Wonderful as he is. . . . .

Now that the day has arrived, Amy appears to be getting cold feet about marriage to Paul. She is becoming panicky, on the edge of hysteria. She decides she can't go through with the ceremony (she sings in some detail).

Robert and Paul come in dressed in dinner jackets. Robert is to be the best man and is carrying the ring. Amy sits the men down at the kitchen counter and proceeds to serve them (in her distraction) warm orange juice and declares her determination to call the whole thing off. Paul is very gentle with her as she rants about how insane it is to have a large wedding after living together all these years . . . about her being a Catholic and Paul a Jew . . . about the higher you go, the harder you fall. Paul's reply is, "I never dropped you yet."

Paul argues gently with Amy while the guests wait and Robert tries to help —but of course Robert has no right to urge marriage on anyone else. Amy tells Paul she is frightened.

PAUL: Of what?

AMY *(she is crying):* I don't know. I don't know. I just think you're really not for me, Paul. I just think maybe nobody's for me. I never saw one good marriage. Never. Not in my entire life.

PAUL: You just see what you look for, you know. I've seen a lot. Listen, Amy . . . married people are no more *marriage* than . . . oh . . . musicians are music. Just because some of the people might be wrong—doesn't matter . . . *it* is still *right*.

AMY: Yes, well, I'll put that on a sampler, Paul.
    She looks up—right at Paul.
Please. I'm not being emotional. I'm as sane as can be. Paul? I'm sorry. I don't love you enough.
    There is a very long pause as they stare at each other.

PAUL *(he fights for control. He speaks hesitantly, yet his voice trembles):* Robert . . . would you . . . call and ah . . . explain that . . . I'm . . . I ah, I . . .
    He exits quickly.

AMY *(she doesn't move, drained of emotion, really asking . . .):* What did I just do?

ROBERT: You did . . . what you had to do . . . I guess . . . if it was right, you would have gone through with it. That's what I think anyway. Amy, marry me.

They're alike, Robert suggests, if they get married everyone will leave them alone (voices in the background pick up snatches of "Bobby Baby"). His proposal brings Amy to her senses. She knows what she wants now.

AMY: Oh! would you look at that! He went out without an umbrella or anything.

> *She puts on a raincoat and grabs another coat and umbrella for Paul.*

He'll get pneumonia. I've got to catch him. I'm getting married. Oh, and he's so good, isn't he? So good.

> *She starts to exit.*

ROBERT: Amy!

> *He throws her the bouquet.*

AMY: I'm the next bride.

> *She exits.*

COUPLES *(sing):*
> Bobby, Bobby,
> Bobby baby, Bobby bubi,
> Robby!

> *Lights come up on all the birthday guests looking at him as in Act I, Scene 1. Robert stares at Amy as she enters with the cake and the music builds. Curtain.*

ACT II

Scene 1: Robert's apartment

Once again, at Robert's birthday party, the business of blowing out the candles takes place. Robert expresses his warm feelings toward his friends: "Thank you for including me in your thoughts, your lives . . ." Robert and his friends join in the mutual admiration number "Side by Side by Side," which moves directly into the next number entitled "What Would We Do Without You?"

ROBERT *(sings):*
> One is lonely and two is boring,
> Think what you can keep ignoring,
> Side . . .

AMY *(speaks):* He's my best friend.
ROBERT *(sings):* . . . by side . . .
AMY *(touching Paul; speaks):* Second best.
ROBERT *(sings):* . . . by side.
ALL COUPLES:
> Never a bother,
> Seven times a godfather.

ROBERT, AMY, PAUL:
> Year after year,
> Older and older . . .

LARRY *(speaks):* It's amazing. We've gotten older every year and he seems to stay exactly the same.

ROBERT, ALL *(sing):*
Sharing a tear,
Lending a shoulder . . .

DAVID *(speaks):* You know what comes to my mind when I see him? The Seagram Building. Isn't that funny?

ROBERT, PETER, SUSAN, SARAH, HARRY *(sing):*
Ain't we got fun?
No strain . . .

JOANNE *(speaks):* Sometimes I catch him looking and looking. And I just look right back.

ALL *(sing):*
Permanent sun, no rain . . .
We're so crazy, he's so sane.

Friendship forbids
Anything bitter . . .

PAUL *(speaks):* A person like Bob doesn't have the good things and he doesn't have the bad things. But he doesn't have the good things either. . . . .

ROBERT *(sings):*
Here is the church,
Here is the steeple,
Open the doors and
See all the crazy married people.
     Continue directly into "What Would We Do Without You?"

ALL COUPLES:
What would we do without you?
How would we ever get through?
Who would I complain to for hours?
Who'd bring me the flowers
When I have the flu?
Who'd finish yesterday's stew?
Who'd take the kids to the zoo?
Who is so dear?
And who is so deep?
And who would keep her/him occupied
When I want to sleep?
How would we ever get through?
What would we do without you? . . . . .

The scene ends with another chorus of "Side by Side by Side;" then the couples disappear and April appears.

Scene 2: Robert's apartment

April, dressed in her airline stewardess's uniform, admires Robert's apartment (represented by the bare stage). As Robert shows her the bedroom, a bed appears.

(While Robert is entertaining April, his friends' wives are worrying about him in a song number called "Poor Baby"—they imagine him womanless and alone by the telephone.)

April tells Robert the story of how a man once gave her a cocoon so that she could watch a butterfly emerge in her own apartment; how she just barely managed to save the butterfly from her cat, and how her man friend was more concerned over the butterfly than her own feelings.

Robert replies to April with the story of an encounter in Florida with a lovely girl. The two reacted to each other instantly and simultaneously—and without a word Robert led her to his car and drove her to a strip of motels. Once in the room, they decided they needed a ton of champagne and some baby oil, so Robert rushed around to find it. Then he couldn't find the motel again: "I looked for over three hours. I never found it. And I never saw her again either."

April has identified totally with Robert's star-crossed lover. Dreamily, she begins taking off her clothes. Soon they are both in bed, and just for a moment April wonders what connection there could be between the two stories: "Unless . . . oh . . . you must have thought of that poor girl as the wounded butterfly . . ."

This time, Robert has champagne, glasses and baby oil handy right by the bed. The lights go down in the bedroom, come up on Robert's friends worrying about him.

SARAH (sings):
    You know, no one
    Wants you to be happy
    More than I do,
    No one, but
    Isn't she a little bit, well. . . . .
ALL: Isn't she a little bit, well . . .
SARAH: Dumb? Where is she from?
AMY: Tacky? Neurotic? She seems so dead.
SUSAN: Vulgar? Aggressive? Peculiar.
JENNY: Old? And cheap and . . .
JOANNE: Tall? She's tall enough to be your mother. . . . .
ALL:
    Poor baby,
    All alone.
    Throw a lonely dog a bone,
    It's still a bone.
    We're the only tenderness
    He's ever known.
    Poor baby.

Time is passing; Kathy appears for a solo "Tick Tock" dance up and down the various stage levels, while Robert and April's voices can be heard speaking the dialogue and comments of love, as they are making it slowly and surely: "It's poetry," "It's beautiful."

When the dance and the lovemaking are over, and the lights come up, Robert and April are both exhausted; spent. April stirs first. She has to go, she informs Robert, to "Barcelona," the title of their song.

Robert sings to her that she is a very special girl, begs her to stay. But he can't keep from yawning and she is due to take off on Flight 18.

ROBERT *(sings):* Stay a minute.
APRIL: No, I can't.
ROBERT: Yes, you can.
APRIL: No, I can't.
ROBERT: Where you going?
APRIL: Barcelona.
ROBERT: So you said—
APRIL: And Madrid . . .
ROBERT: Bon voyage.
APRIL: On a Boeing.
ROBERT: Good night.
APRIL: You're angry.
ROBERT: No.
APRIL: I've got to—
ROBERT: Right.
APRIL: Report to—
ROBERT: Go.
APRIL:
   That's not to
   Say
   That if I had my way . . .
   Oh well, I guess okay.
ROBERT: What?
APRIL: I'll stay.
ROBERT: But . . .
      As she snuggles down.
   Oh, God!
      Blackout.

Scene 3: Peter's and Susan's terrace

Robert brings Marta to call on Peter and Susan who, as they said they would, have gotten a divorce in Mexico. Now they are living together more happily than ever.

Scene 4: A private club

Joanne and Robert are at a table, drinking and getting high, watching Joanne's husband Larry, who is relatively sober, dancing with one of the patrons.
Joanne is maybe a little jealous, but she is preoccupied with telling Robert
how she divorced her first husband because she refused to move from New
York to Chicago with him.

Joanne wants to order more drinks but has trouble attracting the attention
of a waiter. Larry finishes his dance and joins the table where his wife Joanne
is in an acerbic mood: "I hated the opera and I hate it here. What I need is
more to drink."

Finally, fresh drinks are delivered to the table. Joanne proposes a toast to
"The Ladies Who Lunch."

JOANNE (sings):
    Here's to the ladies who lunch—
    Everybody laugh.
    Lounging in their caftans and planning a brunch
    On their own behalf.
    Off to the gym,
    Then to a fitting,
    Claiming they're fat,
    And looking grim
    'Cause they've been sitting
    Choosing a hat—
    Does anyone still wear a hat?
    I'll drink to that. . . . .

    Here's to the girls who play wife—
    Aren't they too much?
    Keeping house but clutching a copy of Life
    Just to keep in touch.
    The ones who follow the rules,
    And meet themselves at the schools,
    Too busy to know that they're fools—
    Aren't they a gem?
    I'll drink to them.
    Let's all drink to them . . .

Joanne decides to have a cigarette and tries to force one on Robert, who
firmly refuses, causing Joanne to become more caustic than ever. Larry explains: "We don't act like this when you're not here, Robby. I wish you could
meet Joanne sometime. She's really great."

Joanne warns Robert never to get married, not even for company. Larry
gets up and goes off to pay the check, over Robert's protests. Alone with Joanne, who stares at him fixedly, Robert confesses that he needed her company
tonight and is grateful for it. He needed to get drunk with someone.

ROBERT: . . . . . I don't care for a cigarette if that is what you're trying to stare me into. Even though I am a product of my generation, I still do not smoke. My age group is a very uptight age group. Middle age is breaking up that old gang of mine. Whew! It's very drunk out tonight. What are you looking at, Joanne? It's my charisma, huh? Well, stop looking at my charisma!

JOANNE *(still staring. No change in position or voice)*: When are we gonna make it?

ROBERT *(a pause)*: I beg your pardon?

JOANNE: When're we gonna make it?

ROBERT *(making light of it)*: What's wrong with now?

JOANNE *(slowly, directly, sultry, quietly and evenly)*: There's my place. It's free tomorrow at two. Larry goes to his gym then. Don't talk. Don't do your folksy Harold Teen with me. You're a terribly attractive man. The kind of a man most women want and never seem to get. I'll take care of you.

ROBERT *(a pause. He's been looking down. He looks up)*: But who will I take care of?

JOANNE: Did you hear yourself? Did you hear what you just said, kiddo?

LARRY *(re-enters)*: Well, the check is paid and . . .
        Looks at Robert stunned.
What's wrong?

ROBERT: I didn't mean that.

LARRY: What's wrong?

ROBERT: I've looked at all that—marriages and all that—and what do you get for it? What do you get?
        Robert leaves the table. Music: "Bobby Baby" underscoring.

LARRY: What happened?

JOANNE: I just did someone a big favor. C'mon, Larry, let's go home.

The cast goes into "Bobby Baby," but Robert interrupts them repeating "What do you get?" in marriage. Robert begins to imagine his own answer in the form of the "Being Alive" song lyrics: "Someone to hold you too close/ Someone to hurt you too deep."

The others encourage him toward positive thinking about marriage. Harry comments, "You've got so many reasons for not being with someone, but Robert, you haven't got one good reason for being alone." Peter advises: "Don't be afraid it won't be perfect . . . the only thing to be afraid of really is that it won't *be*."

AMY: Blow out the candles, Robert and make a wish. *Want* something. Want *something*.

ROBERT *(sings)*:
        Somebody hold me too close,
        Somebody hurt me too deep,
        Somebody sit in my chair
        And ruin my sleep
        And make me aware

Of being alive, being alive. . . . .

Somebody crowd me with love,
Somebody force me to care,
Somebody make me come through,
I'll always be there
As frightened as you,
To help us survive
Being alive, being alive, being alive.
Lights come up on birthday party.

Scene 5: Robert's apartment

At the birthday party again, the guests are waiting. Robert has not yet arrived, and this time when the footsteps are heard along with the turned key, it is someone else at another apartment. Robert isn't coming to his surprise birthday party—they've called every place in town where he might be, but they can't find him.

JOANNE: . . . . . Maybe the surprise is on us. I think I got the message. C'mon Larry, let's go home.
LARRY: Yea. I think we should.
AMY *(a pause):* Let's go, Paul.
PAUL: Yes, I think we can go now.
SARAH *(quietly):* Maybe we ought to leave him a note.
HARRY *(gently, to Sarah):* Maybe we ought to leave him be.
SUSAN: I'll call him tomorrow.
PETER *(In deep thought):* Don't.
SUSAN *(very quietly):* I won't.
JENNY: David?
DAVID: What?
JENNY: Nothing . . .
JOANNE *(gathering all around the table):* Okay. All together, everybody.
ALL: Happy birthday, Robert.
> *They blow out the candles and lights go out in the apartment. Throughout this scene, Robert has stood center stage. He now smiles. Curtain.*

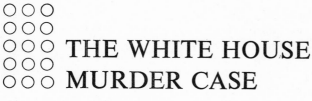

THE WHITE HOUSE
MURDER CASE

A Play in Two Acts

BY JULES FEIFFER

Cast and credits appear on page 358

JULES FEIFFER was born in New York City Jan. 26, 1929. He studied at the Art Students League and Pratt Institute and he served in the Army 1951-53. In 1956 he became contributing cartoonist for the Village Voice. *His reputation as a humorist and social commentator in drawings and words built steadily and internationally. He has been a regular contributor to the London* Observer *and* Sunday Telegraph *and* Playboy *and* The New Republic, *and his cartoons are syndicated internationally in 105 papers. His broad range of activity includes the movies, where he won an Academy Award for the animated cartoon* Munro *in 1961, and where his new screen play* Carnal Knowledge *is ready for production as this volume goes to press. He is the author of ten volumes of cartoon collections, a novel* Harry the Rat With Women *and a memoir* The Great Comic Book Heroes, *as well as of many stories, one of which,* Passionella, *was adapted by Bock and Harnick into one act of the three-part musical* The Apple Tree, *a Best Play of 1966-67.*

The White House Murder Case *is Feiffer's first Best Play of his own, but he has distinguished himself many times previously in the theater. His musical revue* The Explainers *was staged by Chicago's Second City troupe in 1961, and that same year he wrote a one-acter* Crawling Arnold, *produced in Spoleto, Italy and later in London. His first full-length play,* Little Murders, *was produced on Broadway in April 1967, lasted only 7 performances but reappeared in January 1969 in an off-Broadway revival that ran for 400 performances and won Obie and Outer Circle Awards. In a Royal Shakespeare Company production, the London critics voted it the best foreign play of the season. Another Feiffer play,* God Bless, *was produced in London last year and had its American premiere in a Yale University production.*

Among Feiffer's many interests is sponsorship of the National Committee for a Sane Nuclear Policy. He lives in New York, is married and has one child, a daughter.

Time: Several Presidential elections hence

ACT I

Scene 1: A battlefield, coldly and dimly lit

SYNOPSIS: There is the sound of bombardment, then the rattle of machine gun fire as Lt. Cutler and an aide charge forward across the stage. The aide is cut down; Lt. Cutler drops and continues forward at an inching crawl. Col. Dawn crawls up to him to see what is holding up the advance.

"Chico" (the enemy), it seems, has a fanatical determination to sell his life dearly in defense of his country in spite of all the horrible destructive devices the U.S. soldiers are using to subdue him. Lt. Cutler wishes they could use their "CB97s" which are deployed but not in use (they are in violation of the Geneva Convention). Col. Dawn hasn't the authority to order their use.

> *Burst of machine-gun fire. Both crawl backward. General Pratt strides in, stares down at them.*

PRATT: What are American troops doing on their knees in front of a bunch of Goddamned Brazilians?

CUTLER *(leaps to his feet and salutes):* Tain-hutt!

> *A bullet cuts him down. Pratt drops. Dawn rolls Cutler over.*

DAWN: He's bleeding badly, General Pratt.

PRATT: What's he mumbling?

CUTLER: C—B—9—7

PRATT: C—B—what?

DAWN: Lieutenant Cutler recommends KCR authorization to activate our CB97s.

PRATT: Does that recommendation meet with your approval, Colonel?

DAWN: I don't have the total picture that you do, General Pratt.

CUTLER: C—B—9—7—

PRATT: It's going to be all right, son. *(To Dawn.)* I'm afraid he's going to have to lose that leg. This may be his last request, Colonel.

DAWN: Then you say go ahead?

PRATT: If you say so.

DAWN: I say so if you say so.

PRATT: He said so?

DAWN: Yes, sir.

PRATT: Well, if he says so and you say so, I'll go along.

DAWN: Am I to interpret that as a go-ahead on KCR authorization, sir?

PRATT: If you say so.

CUTLER: C—B—9—7—

PRATT: Easy, lad. You'll get all the CB97s you want!

CUTLER: God bless you, sir!

> *Dawn exits running.*

PRATT: Wait a minute, Colonel Dawn! *(Starts after him.)* Colonel Dawn, come back!

> *Stops and removes a red code book from his jacket pocket.*

A—A—A—B—B—B—C—C—CB—CB3—CB7—CB9—CB91—CB95—CB97! *(Reads.)* Nerve gas! *(To Cutler.)* I'll break you for this!

> *Leaps to his feet and rushes after Dawn.*

Rescind! Rescind! *I rescind!*

> *Lights fade on battlefield.*

Scene 2: President Hale's office

Through the window of the President's White House office there is a view of the Capitol. Spread across the ceiling is a stylized eagle which broods scrawnily over this as well as the other scenes.

The President's desk is in the center, ringed by five conference chairs. Doors lead out of the office on either side. As the lights come up, Mrs. Hale, the First Lady, is shuffling through her husband's papers. Professor Sweeney, the resident intellectual and scientific expert, warns her that the documents are probably classified, but she considers herself privileged to root through them.

> *He tries to embrace her. She eludes him.*

SWEENEY: Is there no way I can make you take me seriously?

MRS. HALE: Nothing personal, Sweeney. I can't take anyone seriously who works for the government.

SWEENEY: This streak of anarchism in you, Evelyn—it sometimes so infuriates me I want to shake you.

MRS. HALE: Drop a bomb on me instead. Isn't that the traditional relief for frustration around here?

SWEENEY: How can I make you believe the number of bombs I keep from being dropped each day?

MRS. HALE: Of what possible threat is Brazil to the United States?

SWEENEY: That's a policy question. I'm in research and development.

MRS. HALE: Is that why we're in Brazil? New wars in order to test your new research?

SWEENEY: I'm as much committed to peace as you are! And I get a lot more done than those pacifist-draft dodger-demonstrator-jailbirds your heart so bleeds over! I work from the inside!

Mrs. Hale questions Sweeney about this morning's cabinet meeting, but she is interrupted by the entrance of Stiles, the national chairman of the party (and Postmaster General). Stiles greets the First Lady and grins at her, but the grin is as coldly hostile as her manner in his presence.

Mrs. Hale leaves without a word as Cole, the Attorney General, comes in and comments on the First Lady's activities with the sit-ins outside the Justice Department.

Stiles complains about "Sweeney's mess in Brazil."

STILES: Six weeks before the Presidential election is not the time to test out poison gas.

SWEENEY: That's top secret information!

STILES: I'm national chairman of the party, Professor. You can't keep your little experiments from me. Next time you gas American troops, do it after the first Tuesday in November.

SWEENEY: This discussion is in violation of national security!

STILES: The gooks know about the gas, the Postmaster General isn't supposed to. That's America for you.

COLE: Chicos, Tim. Not gooks.

STILES: Chicos. I lose track of the wars, they come so fast.

SWEENEY: Gooks! Chicos! Don't you see how you dehumanize by using those terms?

STILES: Sweeney's hanging around the First Lady too much.

COLE: I wish the President would muzzle that woman.

STILES: We're lucky she doesn't talk him into muzzling us.

Parson, the Secretary of Defense, joins the group and reports on the result of Sweeney's new "Peace Gas," CB97. It killed 750 people—by mistake, all American troops—and paralyzed 90 more including the Chief of Staff, Gen. Pratt.

The Secretary of State isn't present at this cabinet meeting. He is out of Presidential favor, owing to his dovish position on the Brazilian intervention. As Sweeney comments, "Maybe four wars in six years finally got to him."

What they're all *really* worried about is, does the President himself harbor any doubts about the Brazilian commitment?

SWEENEY: Two years, and what do we have to show for it? Twenty-five thousand dead.

PARSON: Those losses are acceptable. A drop in the bucket compared to the African war. We're learning every day.

STILES: It could be a damned expensive education with election six weeks away.

COLE: And peace conspirators everywhere. I indict a thousand today, a thousand more riot tomorrow.

STILES: Peace riots are water off a duck's back to a man in politics as long as the President.

PARSON: I'm not worried about the riots getting to him. It's that woman getting to him—that's what I lose sleep over. She's worth four divisions of enemy troops.

COLE: I threatened her once with indictment. She laughed.

STILES: You guys take her too seriously. The country's amused by her.

They are generally agreed, however, that "that woman" must be stopped.

President Hale enters and greets the gathering warmly; he is late because his wife wanted a few words with him. The President jokes with Cole about his golf (his clubs are outside, and the President tried the driver on his way in) and with Stiles about the slowness of the mail. Then the Secretary of Defense takes out his map of Brazil, and a briefing begins, as the lights fade. . . . .

Scene 3: A battlefield in eerie green lighting

Capt. Weems, a medical officer, has found Lt. Cutler lying wounded and is bandaging his head on general principles. They see a green fog all around them and conclude it must be gas. Lt. Cutler pleads: "I don't know anything about it. I always tried to do what I thought was right. I was trying to protect my men. That's primary!"

Capt. Weems and Lt. Cutler exchange information about themselves: their home towns (Cleveland and White Plains), their favorite numbers (27 and 28), their favorite color (white).

Somehow, Cutler's wounded leg has broken off, and it feels much better. Weems helps him to his remaining foot and they stagger away, as the lights fade. . . . .

Scene 4: President Hale's office

As the lights come up on the President's office, the Secretary of Defense is briefing the cabinet about the latest campaign in Brazil, Operation Total Win, led by Col. Dawn. In typical Defense Department jargon which euphemizes the humanistic facts of combat and pain, Parson describes the action against a fiercely resisting enemy. "Operation Total Win" was getting nowhere, so the CB97 Nerve Agent was released. Parson reports: "The anticipated results of the Nerve Agent were counterachieved by a sudden shift in wind, as indicated by these wavy lines on the map here."

Gen. Pratt survived the disaster and is present to report to his chief in person. Pratt enters; he has been turned by the gas into a Dr. Strangelove-type figure, half-paralyzed, wearing dark glasses and carrying a cane, unable to speak except through the amplification of a throat mike.

Describing himself as "an old war horse . . . . . an old night fighter," Pratt tells the President what happened.

PRATT: Colonel Dawn, the mission command officer for Operation Total Win, received in my presence a recommendation from his intelligence officer, Lieutenant Cutler, to initiate the dispersal of the toxic chemical agent CB97. Colonel Dawn concurred in this recommendation and immediately instituted KCR authorization.

PRESIDENT: I was under the assumption that no one under the rank of general had KCR authorization.

PRATT: That is correct, sir. Colonel Dawn had RCK authorization which, in the heat of battle, he understandably confused with KCR authorization. RCK, KCR.

PRESIDENT (sighs): You have KCR authorization, do you not, General Pratt?

PRATT: Yes, sir. When I became apprised of the significance of CB97 dispersal, I sought to countermand Colonel Dawn's order. However, I was too late and Colonel Dawn and his staff had fallen by the time I reached Command Headquarters.

The gas did not kill but only maimed the General because it has "a declining scale of effectiveness after six minutes." Sweeney observes that perhaps it has a usefulness, then, for pacification.

Barring the wind shift, Pratt insists, CB97 would have "paid off," and he does not even blame Col. Dawn for the calamity. He is satisfied that enemy losses were 25 times heavier than among U.S. troops.

PRESIDENT: I am sure the research aspects of this catastrophe hold endless fascination, but I am not a scientist. I am the President of the United States six weeks before an election. Can anyone suggest what I say to the American people about the death of seven hundred and fifty American soldiers by an American-made gas?

PARSON: I think you'll find if you prorate these casualties, Mr. President—

PRATT: These are feasible casualties—

PRESIDENT: These are illegal casualties. Mr. Attorney General?

COLE: Yes. The fact of the matter is that all chemical and biological weapons were outlawed by the last Geneva Convent—

SWEENEY (interrupts): We didn't sign it—we didn't sign it!

COLE: Nevertheless, we signaled general approv—

SWEENEY: I'm very sorry—we didn't sign it.

PRESIDENT: Is it your view, Professor Sweeney, that these deaths are perfectly legal?

SWEENEY: Good heavens, of course they're legal. It's research and development. Why must we always tie our own hands?

COLE: It may not violate the letter of the law, but it violates the spirit of the law.

PRESIDENT: We mustn't appear casual about the law.

PARSON: International law? Aren't we being a little legalistic?

STILES: We don't want to be charged with respect for law at home and contempt for it abroad.

COLE: No, not in these times.

STILES: It could put us in a bad light.

SWEENEY: Only because the public is unaware of the tremendous peace-keeping potential—

STILES: Of nerve gas?!

PRATT: The American people will stand behind their command officers.

PRESIDENT: I couldn't agree more, General Pratt. Once they are informed on the issues.

COLE: And they haven't been informed.

PARSON: This is too complex an issue for public debate.

PRESIDENT: I'm inclined to agree with Secretary Parson. Well, there's certain to be a leak. We will have to leak it first and have ready an explanation. Which may be difficult since the public is under the impression we have discontinued production of poison gas.

The President goes on to ask: who ordered the deployment of CB97? No one seems to know. They wonder what story the American public would swallow, and their suggestions and counter-suggestions take on the flavor of a high-flying Hollywood script conference. They can't claim the Brazilians released it, or were going to release nerve gas of their own. They can't blame it on Col. Dawn because he's dead, their story would lose credibility. It couldn't be a leak, or lightning, or an enemy shell that caused an *accidental* release of the gas.

PRATT: A guerrilla patrol could have gotten behind our lines. That does happen.

COLE: That's very good, General Pratt.

PARSON: Excellent, General Pratt. A suicide patrol. We don't know if they knew what those storage tanks contained and deliberately shelled them or—

COLE: It could have been an accident or deliberate.

PARSON: We'll never know. No one will ever know.

STILES: That's it! By golly, that does it!

SWEENEY: It does seem the simplest way.

PRESIDENT: Now that we know what happened, how do we release it?
   Lights fade on President's office.

Scene 5: A battlefield in eerie blue lighting

Capt. Weems and Lt. Cutler are making their way painfully; they stop to rest. The gas is having peculiar effects. Weems can't turn his head now, and Cutler's sinuses are clearing up.

Lt. Cutler warns Capt. Weems that their symptoms are top secret. Weems argues that it's safe for them to talk to each other. Lt. Cutler has his doubts. Weems could be a CIA man trying to entrap Cutler into blame for the gas.

Weems could even be a Chico. Lt. Cutler thinks so well of his suspicions that he draws his .45 automatic and threatens Weems. But Weems persuades Cutler he is a loyal American—a *doctor*. Cutler can relax, speak freely.

Lt. Cutler begins to confess that the use of CB97 was all his idea. Weems holds out the microphone of a tiny tape recorder, as the lights fade. . . . .

Scene 6: President Hale's office

The President and his advisors are discussing ways and means of releasing to the press their cooked-up story about the military accident. On one thing they are all agreed—General Pratt must be kept as far from the press as possible; his story is still a bit shaky. They can promote him to the chairmanship of a Presidential Task Force and keep him under their eye in Washington.

President Hale sends the others out of the office to arrange for the release of this story as news and calls his wife in. He tells her that she is "an accurate barometer for a certain kind of public opinion," and he wants to confide in her. They quarrel; she feels he is "bitter" toward her, he feels she is always mocking him, never on his side. Evelyn Hale neglects to give her word that she will keep the President's confidence a secret, but he confides in her anyway about what happened in Brazil.

PRESIDENT (*suddenly businesslike*): Recent intelligence reports and captured enemy documents revealed to us that the Chinese were supplying or were about to supply the Brazilians with a quantity of deadly nerve gas. As a deterrent action, we warned the Brazilians that we were deploying the chemical Nerve Agent CB97 to our forces in the field to be used *only* in the event of a gas attack on the part of the enemy. The enemy knew this. They were warned. In a night patrol action of two nights ago enemy forces infiltrated the area where our CB97 was stockpiled. An enemy shell hit one of the storage tanks. The nerve gas was released. Seven hundred and fifty of our men were killed. Ninety were paralyzed. You and I both know in how many ways this story can be distorted, made to look very different from what it is—and the meeting, this morning's meeting, was to decide whether, six weeks before an election, we dared release such news.

MRS. HALE: And what did you decide?

PRESIDENT: By unanimous decision, it was agreed that the American people must be told the truth.

MRS. HALE: As you have told it to me.

PRESIDENT: Yes. Channeled through reliable sources. There must be no leaks. Well?

MRS. HALE: Well what?

PRESIDENT: What do you think?

MRS. HALE: I think I want a divorce.

PRESIDENT: Christ! Evelyn—behave.

MRS. HALE: You've become as dishonest with me as you are with the rest of the country. I don't have to swallow these lies! I am your wife, not your constituent! I want a divorce!

PRESIDENT: Don't make me lose respect for you.

MRS. HALE: The arrogance! You're not going to get away with this! Even the pollsters know we're not winning this war! Why should the Brazilians, in a war they're winning, import, into their own country, poison gas!

PRESIDENT: No one said they were importing it. You're too self-righteous to listen to anybody who isn't carrying a picket sign. What I said was *unconfirmed* intelligence reports—

MRS. HALE: And captured enemy documents!

PRESIDENT: What's wrong with captured enemy documents?

MRS. HALE: They only get captured after we've written them! You'll never be able to explain why we put the gas there unless it was meant to be used! To be *experimented* with! Is that what really happened? Your experiment backfired?

PRESIDENT: It wasn't my experiment!

MRS. HALE: Sweeney's experiment!

PRESIDENT: Other husbands get support from their wives. Why can't I?

MRS. HALE: I've never stopped supporting your ideals.

PRESIDENT: My ideals haven't changed.

MRS. HALE: Then why these lies?

PRESIDENT: We're at war!

MRS. HALE: I'm not talking about lies to Brazilians—I'm talking about lies to Americans! This is the government of the United States you're running, not an advertising agency!

PRESIDENT: You don't have the vaguest understanding of the processes of change! You make us sound like a gang of conspirators!

MRS. HALE: Well, aren't you? You talk only to each other, accept intelligence only from hired hands, debate the issues only with the insiders, call their guesses a consensus and bury their mistakes because no one but you and your henchmen have the "vaguest understanding of the processes of change!" Well, I won't be a party to it. I won't be your co-conspirator!

PRESIDENT: You agreed to play by the rules.

MRS. HALE: One more lie!

PRESIDENT: Not five minutes ago you agreed.

MRS. HALE: You are unbelievable! You believe anything you want to believe!

PRESIDENT *(rises, very cold):* Evelyn, I have work to do.

MRS. HALE *(reaches for the phone):* And so do I!

PRESIDENT: Get off that phone. *(No response.)* Get off that phone! *(No response.)* That is my phone!

MRS. HALE: Get me the New York *Times.*

Lights fade on President's office.

Scene 7: A battlefield in eerie purple lighting

Lt. Cutler is speaking uninhibitedly into Capt. Weems's tape recorder. Cutler tells Weems how it is with soldiering—first, you learn to take orders; second, you want to look good to your buddies. Cutler goes on: "The third thing you've got to learn is how many you can take with you when you go. You take only one with you, you can hardly call yourself a man. You take from two to five with you, you can call yourself a man but I wouldn't say you look good. You take over five, up to ten, you're looking good. You take over ten, up to eighteen, nineteen—you're looking real good. Anything you take over twenty and upwards says you're all balls. Twenty and upwards. All balls. I know a lot of men in this war who went out looking real good. But I can count on the fingers of one hand the number of men I know who went out all balls."

Lt. Cutler, trying to count, finds that his fingers are stiff. When Weems massages them, some of them break off. Strange things are happening under the influence of the nerve gas. Weems confesses to Cutler that he is a CIA agent, sent to get evidence from Cutler for a court martial. Remorsefully, Weems sets his written notes on fire; magnanimously, Cutler beats out the fire and laboriously sets his signature to the paper. Capt. Weems even smashes the tape recorder—but Lt. Cutler still has the notes. Now they are buddies; they exchange first names and reach out hands to each other. As they do so, the lights come up in President Hale's office, where they are exactly as they were at the end of the last scene.

> *The President turns and stalks out through the door. Mrs. Hale glares after him.*

MRS. HALE: Yes, I'm holding.

> *Lights go out in President's office. The sound of scuffling. A pained gasp.*

No!

> *A low groan. A pause, during which Cutler and Weems reach each other and shake hands. Lights up in President's office to reveal Mrs. Hale lying prostrate and bleeding across President's desk. In her chest, embedded like a stake, is a picket sign reading "Make Love Not War."*

CUTLER: You can let go of my hand now, Rick.

WEEMS: You'd think so, wouldn't you? But I can't.

> *Lights fade on battlefield. Lights fade on President's office. Curtain.*

ACT II

Scene 1: President Hale's office

Sweeney, Cole, Styles and Parson are seated around the desk shaking their heads over the assault on the First Lady. The President comes in to announce that his wife has died and stammers out a eulogy: "Sweeney, you were fond of her—a little, I think. The rest of you. Well—I doubt if there's an accusation you didn't make behind her back that I didn't make to her face. Well, we all underrated her. She was the best part of me. My moral center."

As the President is telling them he has little heart for his job now, Pratt stumbles in. But the President is determined to go on, and the first business must be to solve and explain this murder. The murder weapon is brought in. Except for its sharp and bloody point, it is like the thousands of signs seen every day at demonstrations. Attorney General Cole reports that examination discloses two sets of fingerprints on the weapon—his own and President Hale's —as the lights fade. . . . .

Scene 2: A battlefield in eerie orange lighting

Lt. Cutler and Capt. Weems, still unable to let each other's hands go, smell something odd—it must be the gas. Weems has lost the power to blink his eyelids. Lt. Cutler is content; he no longer feels any pain.

WEEMS: Listen, Buzz, what if you and me, our hands locked, is the next stage?
CUTLER: Next stage of what?
WEEMS: Evolution. Everybody joined together. Maybe the way we've been all our lives isn't natural. That this is natural. The way we are now. You and me and whoever comes along—a rescue squad—they take our hands, and their hands get locked into our hands, and a squad of Chicos comes along and they see this squad of guys holding hands. You think they'll shoot? They won't be able to shoot. Because it's the wave of the future. They'll take our hands. And more and more guys come along—their side and our side—gooks and colored guys—they'll see this daisy chain—in the middle of a war zone. This beautiful, peace-loving daisy chain, and they'll drop their guns. It will sound like a very loud bomb, the sound of all those guns dropping at one time. And they'll join hands with our hands so that there's no reason to fight any more because we're all one body with these millions of held hands. No more outsiders. Just one enormous insider.
A pause. Neither man moves. Cutler inhales deeply.
CUTLER: Like a field of clover. *(Inhales deeply.)*
WEEMS: What do you think, Buzz?
CUTLER: It looks good. *(Inhales deeply.)* I'm getting high.
Lights fade on battlefield.

Scene 3: President Hale's office

The President and his advisors are examining the murder weapon. It is made of steel and the "Make Love Not War" placard stapled onto it. One end of the steel rod is sharp and jagged as though something had been broken off.
The President's and Cole's fingerprints were found on it in identical positions, right hand below left, "with both thumbs pointing inward and downward"—an awkward grip for impaling anyone. The President is the first to recognize the murder weapon, but instead of coming right out with it he coaches Cole into recognition too: it is the shaft of Cole's driver with the head

torn off and the placard attached; the same driver that the President tried for a few practise swings only that morning.

The President concludes that the murder weapon is both a confession and a warning: "The murderer is confessing that he knew my fingerprints were on that golf club and he is warning me that the only way he could know this was to be seated in one of the chairs when I mentioned to Mr. Cole that I had my hands on his driver this morning."

COLE: Should we pursue this course? Is it wise?

STILES: There must be some other explanation.

Others in short outbursts of agitated ad lib comments.

PRESIDENT *(slams his hand on desk):* You think I'm pursuing this for personal reasons? Once a Pandora's box of fear and doubt is left lying open in our midst, we will, every one of us, be sucked helplessly into its maw.

COLE: If I may offer a dissenting view?

PRESIDENT: I am most anxious to hear it.

COLE: First of all, Mr. President, I want to say how remarkably I think you've conducted this entire business.

Others murmur assent. President nods in acceptance of compliment.
Mrs. Hale's death was an error. No doubt about it. Some one of us panicked. But whichever one of us he is, there can be no question that he had only his country's interests at heart. His motive was misguided, possibly half-mad, but rooted in a love for this country that the First Lady did not share, rooted in a belief in the continuity of this administration, *your* administration, that the First Lady tried unceasingly to divide. I'm not defending the brutal slaying of your wife, Mr. President, I know how dear she was to you. But the Pandora's box of fear and doubt you so eloquently speak of cannot be nailed shut by conducting a witch hunt among your advisors. And make no mistake. A witch hunt this investigation must inevitably become: replete with rumor, lie, half-truth and innuendo. By this route, we will destroy ourselves more successfully than our worst enemies dream.

PRESIDENT: You suggest we drop this investigation?

COLE: In the interests of national security, I do, sir.

PRESIDENT *(coldly):* We are speaking of my wife, Mr. Cole, not some Brazilian. . . . .

The President is determined to pursue his investigation of the murder. He questions Cole as to his whereabouts at the crucial time (Cole was in the anteroom with the others, making up a list of trustworthy newsmen). The President grills Gen. Pratt; Pratt argues that he wasn't in the room when golf was mentioned. And at the time the murder was committed Pratt was in his office, alone. Someone opened his door, said "Sorry" and withdrew before Pratt could turn to see who it was. The President insists that the others repeat "Sorry" for Pratt now. Pratt identifies Sweeney's "Sorry" as the one he heard.

Sweeney admits he left the anteroom to make a phone call about CB 97, but he denies going to Pratt's office. Parson admits that he too wandered down the hall in search of a phone, and Cole went up to the Lincoln Room to make a call—so that any alibi that they were all together in the anteroom is worth-less. Any of them could have removed the driver from the golf bag and committed the crime.

Parson pleads with them all to stop going at each other and use this incident for mutual advantage. The country is in a rough war that seems rather unreal to the public, whose only contact with it is the TV.

PARSON: . . . . . So what I say is this: if we could bring this war home to the people, strengthen home front support, why, it would mean all the difference in the world. So that's the question: do we go on and let events push us around or do we use our initiative and take control of our destinies instead of vice versa?

PRESIDENT: I'm sorry but I don't understand what you're saying.

PARSON: My recommendation, Mr. President, is that the First Lady was assassinated by a suicide squad of Brazilian terrorists.

Lights fade on President's office.

Scene 4: *A battlefield in eerie yellow lighting*

Lt. Cutler and Capt. Weems are watching their two hands, which are still clasped but have broken away from their bodies and gone off on their own. Other parts of their bodies are breaking away—even organs of masculinity—and they are having more and more trouble talking but less trouble understanding. The lights fade.

Scene 5: *President Hale's office*

In the President's office immediately following, Cole's first reaction to Parson's suggestion about a Brazilian suicide squad is "It won't work." But Stiles feels that now at last they're on the right track; they must invent a useful explanation. They can't use the suicide squad idea again, they can't have the First Lady killed in the White House, not six weeks before election, "It makes us look ineffectual."

Once more they swing into their "story conference." They can use any of the big cities as the place of death, their party is weak in the big cities anyway. No one will believe that the blacks or leftists conspired to kill the First Lady, who was a notorious liberal, so it must be an accident that took her off. They settle on food poisoning as the means and Chicago as the city where the First Lady died.

For once, President Hale is appalled at their cold-blooded manner: "This sounds like a madhouse! One of you has murdered a flesh-and-blood woman and not a single one of you cares! What have you done to your humanity?"

Calmly, they argue that they are thinking objectively, in the national interest, and therefore may be forgiven for sounding cold-blooded. The President insists on pressing his inquiry into how his wife was killed. He asks how the "Make Love Not War" placard on the murder weapon could have been smuggled into the White House without anyone noticing. He gets no help from any of his cabinet, who remain silent, wishing he would drop this inquiry.

PRESIDENT: Well then, I will have to work it out for myself. Let's take a look at this placard.

He rips it off the support.

It is too large to fit into any of your briefcases. And it has not been folded. It might have been worn on the inside of a shirt, but that would make one of you move so stiffly it would surely have been noticed. Although, General Pratt, It wouldn't have been noticed on you.

All stare at Pratt.

However, I see how tightly your uniform fits. And this placard is not creased. You are cleared once again, General Pratt. It is a mystery. How do you bring an eighteen by twenty-four placard reading "Make Love Not War" into the White House without somebody seeing it? Secretary Parson, would you like to try again? *(No response.)* You disappoint me, Secretary Parson. I hoped you would answer, "It would not be noticed if I brought it in hidden among my Brazilian war charts."

Others except for Parson rise slowly to their feet. Parson and President remain seated, exchanging grim stares. Lights fade on President's office.

Scene 6: A battlefield in eerie red lighting

Now Lt. Cutler and Capt. Weems have disintegrated completely, and the parts of their bodies are adrift around the battlefield.

WEEMS: My whole past is passing in front of my eyes, and I don't recognize any of it.

CUTLER: Does it have the Boy Scouts in it?

WEEMS: Yes.

CUTLER: Does it have touch football?

WEEMS: Yes.

CUTLER: Does it have Sunday mornings in church—the family car—self-reliance—the old swimming hole—homemade cooking—beating up the school bully—the girl next door—overcoming disappointment?

WEEMS: Yes.

CUTLER: I think you've got my past. I must have yours.

Everybody has the same past—that's the secret, declares Weems, it makes all men brothers. Cutler describes Weems's past as he sees it—a hard life on the land, mothered by "a work worn woman with laughing eyes"—but this is not Weems's past. It seems that some Chico's past is mixing in with the drifting parts of the bodies and thoughts. Cutler guesses from this that maybe he killed some Brazilians with the gas, in addition to his own men. Maybe he got as many as a hundred Chicos.

Weems warns Cutler that he is losing the secret of universal unity and brotherhood, but this only infuriates the lieutenant, who is reverting to type.

CUTLER: I don't lose any secrets. I keep all secrets. All secrets are classified cosmic!

Weems's head moves toward Cutler's head.

WEEMS: We're all together, Buzz. You've got my hand!

CUTLER: I don't want your faggot hand! You're not a man. You're not an American You're Chico!

WEEMS: I'm Chico, you're Chico—

CUTLER: Chico!

Cutler's separated arm draws his gun.

WEEMS: We're all—

Cutler's arm fires at the various parts of Weems. Silence.

CUTLER: Looking good. Looking real good. All balls.

Lights fade on battlefield.

Scene 7: President Hale's office

Stiles intervenes in the President's accusation of Parson. He asks for a few minutes alone with the President. The others are directed to wait in the anteroom—and this time, no phone calls.

Stiles takes command of the conversation: Parson didn't kill Evelyn, he didn't even know she was in the office. The President himself, Stiles suggests, is the most likely suspect. He had the best opportunity and the strongest motive.

But anyway (Stiles continues) it wasn't Evelyn who was supposed to be the victim, it was the President. The killer struck the First Lady by mistake, in the dark. The placard wasn't carried in by Parson, it was mailed in and lay in the mail room, ready to the murderer's hand. The murderer didn't care who saw him making his preparations, because it would be arranged so that no one would ever know the murder took place in the White House.

PRESIDENT: It couldn't be covered up!

STILES: The Vice President is a loyal party member, a dedicated American, and a very ambitious man. No less loyal, dedicated or ambitious a man than his predecessor. That's you. He would not want to destroy his party, injure his country, and wipe out his chance to be President by placing on trial as an assassin the national chairman of the party.

PRESIDENT: My God, Tim, what are you saying?

STILES: I killed your wife.

PRESIDENT: I don't believe it.

STILES: It was in the dark. She was at your desk, the damned buttinsky. How was I to know? It was a mistake, but maybe it won't matter.

PRESIDENT: My God, it was me you meant to kill! But why? We're friends!

STILES: You were going to lose an election.

PRESIDENT: I wasn't. I would have pulled it out!

STILES: The country is tired of one crisis after another. Last Monday I saw the latest polls and it was crystal clear we were through unless we had a fresh candidate. Somebody not connected to your mistakes.

PRESIDENT: So you planned to assassinate me in the White House.

STILES: Who killed you and where it took place is a technicality. As far as the public was to be concerned, you got it in some other place from a member of the opposition party, who is probably half-crazed and has strong radical sympathies.

PRESIDENT: And that would produce a sympathy vote that would sweep the Vice President into office.

STILES: That's the scenario.

The party has been Stiles's life, and he refused to sit by while President Hale destroyed it. Stiles challenges the President to have him arrested and punished, and the President backs away: "The public—it wouldn't do them any good to hear this sort of thing. It would shake their faith badly."

Stiles takes the offensive: he has written out a confession of murder which he will release to the press, bringing down Hale's whole administration, unless Hale makes Stiles a foreign policy advisor. It is the President's mistakes in foreign policy that have endangered the party, and Stiles demands to be named Secretary of Defense.

The President tries to bargain with Stiles, offering him other posts, but Stiles is stubborn. Finally, the President offers him the State Department.

STILES (slowly turns): You mean it?

PRESIDENTS I have no choice.

STILES (a slow grin): Secretary of State.

PRESIDENT: You understand I won't be able to name you until after the election.

STILES (beams): Secretary of State.

PRESIDENT (rises, crosses to door, opens it): Won't you come in, gentlemen. Others enter.

First of all, I want to thank all of you for bearing so patiently with me through all of this terrible business. Next, I want to offer my sincerest apologies to Secretary Parson. Biff knows me too long and too well not to realize I was not in my right mind when I made those baseless accusations. Biff, I beg your understanding and your forgiveness.

PARSON: Water over the dam.

PRESIDENT: Next. Our attention has been diverted on the CB97 affair. This was my fault. That matter should be expedited without further delay. Next—well, next, I have some unhappy news of a personal nature. As some of you may have heard, the First Lady flew quietly to Chicago last night for a short vacation. I learned by phone only a few minutes ago that she has been taken seriously ill. The doctors suspect food poisoning.

Lights up on an empty battlefield, the same lights as in the President's office. Clouds of gas form over the stage.

OTHERS (in chorus): Oh, I'm sorry, Mr. President.

All freeze. The lights turn green. Curtain.

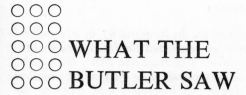

WHAT THE BUTLER SAW

A Play in Two Acts

BY JOE ORTON

Cast and credits appear on page 367

JOE ORTON was born in Leicester in 1933 and died by violence in London in 1967. At the time of his death he had an international reputation as one of the originators and most gifted exponents of black comedy. Orton's short play The Ruffian on the Stair *was produced in 1964 by the BBC and in 1967 on the stage coupled with another short Orton work,* The Erpingham Camp, *under the title* Crimes of Passion *(this program appeared this season off Broadway for 9 performances). Also in 1964, his* Entertaining Mr. Sloane *was produced in London and won the best-play citation in the poll of London drama critics. It was produced on Broadway for 13 performances during the 1965-66 season and was mentioned in the New York Drama Critics Circle voting.*

Orton's Loot—*a detective spoof somewhat lighter than the very dark* Mr. Sloane—*was produced in London in September 1966 and on Broadway early in 1968 for 22 performances. Both these full-length plays have been made into movies.*

What the Butler Saw was Orton's last play and his lightest, funniest and perhaps best work. Even so, like all the Orton plays it has been the subject of much controversy. At the opening of the London production starring Ralph Richardson, a hostile and disruptive audience came very near to rioting. The reviews were generally unfavorable, but one critic, Frank Marcus, author of The Killing of Sister George, stood his ground as follows: "I think it will live*

217

to be recognized as a classic and I am content to let posterity be my judge."

What the Butler Saw *has been somewhat re-shaped for its American production, and it is again a bone of contention by at least one critic, John Lahr, who liked it the way it was. The following synopsis, like all synopses of Best Plays, is a precis of the events and dialogue which actually took place on the stage in the New York production. One should bear in mind that because of its outrageously farcical style the Orton play is to be taken almost mathematically anti-literally, like a negative impression of a positive photograph. There is, for example, no butler in* What the Butler Saw—*and that's the whole point and thrust of the title.*

Time: A spring day

Place: The consulting room of an exclusive, private psychiatric clinic

ACT I

SYNOPSIS: Dr. Prentice enters his office from the hall upstage right, followed by a pretty young girl whom he is interviewing for a secretarial post at his psychiatric clinic.

Dr. Prentice's office is furnished with a desk downstage left and, upstage center, his couch which can be screened off from the rest of the room by means of a pulled curtain. Other doors to this busy place lead to the clinic downstage right, the garden upstage left and a large closet downstage left.

Dr. Prentice questions the girl, Geraldine Barclay (not failing to notice how attractive she is). Geraldine doesn't know who her father was—she was conceived in an "unpleasant attack" upon her mother, a chambermaid at the Station Hotel (Dr. Prentice seems satisfied with this explanation—he himself has stayed at that very hotel, as a young man).

As for her mother, Geraldine hasn't seen her in years.

GERALDINE: . . . . . I was brought up by a Mrs. Barclay. She died recently.
PRENTICE: I'm sorry. From what cause?
GERALDINE: An explosion, due to a faulty gas-main, killed her outright and took the roof off the house.
PRENTICE: Have you applied for compensation?
GERALDINE: Just for the roof.
PRENTICE: Were there no other victims of the disaster?
GERALDINE: Yes. A recently erected statue of Sir Winston Churchill was so badly injured that the special medal has been talked of. Parts of the great man were actually found embedded in my stepmother.
PRENTICE: Which parts?

GERALDINE: I'm afraid I can't help you there. I was too upset to supervise the funeral arrangements. Or, indeed, to identify the body.
PRENTICE: Surely the Churchill family did that?
GERALDINE: Yes. They were most kind.
PRENTICE: You've had a unique experience. It's not everyone who has their stepmother assassinated by a public utility.

Geraldine is so conservative by nature that she doesn't like to take aspirin for fear of becoming involved with drugs. Her shorthand is pretty good (she tells Prentice), but not her typing.

Prentice is concentrating on her "other qualities;" he has decided to seduce her. He pulls aside the curtains hiding his couch and suggests that she sit down and take off her stockings so that he can judge her legs. He reassures her: "Have no fear, Miss Barclay. What I see before me isn't a lovely and desirable girl. It's a sick mind in need of psychiatric treatment. The body is of no interest to a medical man. . . . ."

Prentice feels her naked calves and judges that she needs further examination. He orders Geraldine to take all her clothes off, but she continues to have misgivings.

GERALDINE: How long would I have to remain undressed?
PRENTICE: If your reactions are normal you'll be back on your feet in next to no time.
GERALDINE: I'd like another woman present. Is your wife available?
PRENTICE: Mrs. Prentice is attending a more than usually lengthy meeting of her coven. She won't be back until this evening.
GERALDINE: I could wait until then.
PRENTICE: I haven't the patience, my dear. I've a natural tendency to rush things . . . something my wife has never understood. But I won't trouble you with the details of my private life till you're dressed. Put your clothes on this. Lie on that couch.
> Geraldine unzips and removes her dress and shoes. Dr. Prentice puts dress on hanger and hangs it in the closet, puts shoes on closet floor.
GERALDINE: What is Mrs. Prentice like, doctor? I've heard so many stories about her.
> She stands in her panties and bra.
PRENTICE: My wife is a nymphomaniac. Consequently, like the Holy Grail, she's ardently sought after by young men. I married her for her money and, upon discovering her to be penniless, I attempted to throttle her . . . a mental aberration for which I've never forgiven myself. Needless to say, our relationship has been delicate ever since.

Dr. Prentice puts on his white surgical coat, as Geraldine goes behind the curtain. Dr. Prentice has just unzipped his trousers when Mrs. Prentice enters through the hall door, wrapped in a coat. She wonders who Dr. Prentice was talking to. (Geraldine is hiding behind the curtain) and is put off by some story about a dictated memo, as Dr. Prentice manages to distract his wife's attention long enough to zip up his pants.

Mrs. Prentice explains her absence to her husband: "I arrived at the meeting to find the hall in an uproar. Helen Duncan had declared herself to be in love with a man. And, as you know, the coven is primarily for lesbians. I myself am exempt from this rule because you count as a woman. We expelled Helen and by that time it was so late that I spent the night at the Station Hotel. . . . ."

Dr. Prentice takes not the slightest interest in his wife's adventures and leaves his office on clinic business. The coast clear, Mrs. Prentice brings in Nicholas Beckett, a tall, good-looking young man dressed in the uniform of a hotel page. Evidently, Nick has not only stolen Mrs. Prentice's dress, he spent the night with her and arranged for a concealed camera to take photos—now he wants 100 pounds for the negatives. When Mrs. Prentice protests, Nick agrees to forget about the blackmail if she will find him a decent job—secretary to her husband, say.

Dr. Prentice comes comes back, meets Nick, and gets onto the subject of sex with his wife: "You were born with your legs apart. They'll send you to the grave in a Y-shaped coffin." Mrs. Prentice protests that her sexual responses have been feigned for some time now. She goes out with Nick, then comes back not quite in time to catch her husband hiding Geraldine's underwear in the waste basket, but in plenty of time to catch him taking Geraldine's dress from the closet (he wants Geraldine dressed and out of here).

Mrs. Prentice herself needs the dress her husband is holding—she takes off her coat, and it is seen that she has only a slip underneath. As she puts on Geraldine's dress, she explains.

MRS. PRENTICE: I'll tell you frankly and with complete candor. Please listen carefully and save your comments for later.
    She zips up the dress.
My room at the hotel was small, airless and uncomfortable. A model of its kind. When I turned down the bed I noticed that the sheets were none too clean. I went to the linen closet, which I knew to be on the second floor, hoping to find a chambermaid. Instead I found a page boy, the one in fact who was just here. He enticed me into the closet and then made an indecent suggestion. When I repulsed him he attempted to rape me. I fought him off but not before he'd stolen my handbag and dress.

PRENTICE: It doesn't sound like the kind of behavior one expects at a four-star hotel.

MRS. PRENTICE: The boy has promised to return my dress. He's sold it to a friend who probably intends using it at sex orgies.

PRENTICE: Do you realize what would happen if your adventures became public? I'd be ruined. The doors of society would be slammed in my face. Did you inform the authorities of this escapade?

MRS. PRENTICE: No.

PRENTICE: Why not?

MRS. PRENTICE: I saw in the boy a natural goodness that had all but been destroyed by the pressures of society. I promised to find him employment.

Dr. Prentice is less than enthusiastic at the prospect of having Nick as a secretary. After his wife goes into the garden, Dr. Prentice reviews the situation with Geraldine, still naked behind her curtain. Mrs. Prentice has Geraldine's dress, in a misunderstanding that isn't immediately correctable. Dr. Prentice will try to find Geraldine some clothes; in the meantime, she must continue to pose as a patient.

Before the doctor can retrieve Geraldine's underwear from the waste basket, Dr. Rance enters unexpectedly and without ceremony. He is older than Dr. Prentice, a stranger to him but an official of the government perfectly satisfied with himself and his dictatorial powers: "My authority is unlimited. I have the power to close your clinic on a moment's notice should I find it necessary. I'd even have sway over a rabbit hutch if the inmates were mentally disturbed."

Rance demands from Prentice a free hand in inspecting all aspects of the clinic. He pokes around Prentice's office; looks behind the curtain; starts questioning Prentice about various details.

RANCE: Is your couch regulation size? It looks big enough for two.

PRENTICE: I do double consultations. Toddlers are often terrified of a doctor. So I've taken to examining their mothers at the same time.

RANCE: Has the theory received much publicity?

PRENTICE: I don't approve of scientists who publicize their theories.

RANCE: I must say I agree with you. I wish more scientists would keep their ideas to themselves.
   A piece of paper flutters from under the curtain.
(Picking up the paper.) Is this something to do with you?

PRENTICE: It's a prescription, sir.

RANCE *(reading):* "Keep your head down and don't make a sound." *(Pause.)* Do you find your patients react favorably to such treatment?

PRENTICE: I can claim to have had some success with it.

RANCE: Your ideas, I think, are in advance of the times. Why is there a naked woman behind there?

PRENTICE: She's a patient, sir. I'd just managed to calm her down when you arrived.

RANCE: Were you attacked by a naked woman?

PRENTICE: Yes.

RANCE: Well, Prentice, I don't know whether to applaud your daring or envy you your luck. I'd like to question her.

Rance questions Geraldine, who looks out through the curtain, about her madness (the die is cast now for Dr. Prentice; he must force Geraldine to play patient). Geraldine protests that she is from the Friendly Faces Employment Bureau, but this persuades Dr. Rance all the more that she's suffering from delusions. He decides to take personal charge of Geraldine's case; he certifies her insane over her protests (but Dr. Prentice destroys the certification). Together, the doctors dress Geraldine in a hospital nightgown, give her a sedative and place her on a trolley for removal to the wards. Still Geraldine protests that she is sane.

GERALDINE: Is this "Candid Camera?"
PRENTICE: There is a perfectly rational explanation for what has taken place. Keep calm. All will be well.
Mrs. Prentice enters from the garden.
MRS. PRENTICE *(anxious):* Miss Barclay is nowhere to be found.
RANCE: She's under strong sedation and on no account to be disturbed.
Dr. Prentice, nervous, gives a fleeting smile in Dr. Rance's direction.
PRENTICE: My wife is talking of my secretary, sir. She's been missing since this morning.
GERALDINE: I'm Geraldine Barclay. Looking for part-time secretarial work. I've been certified insane.
RANCE *(to Mrs. Prentice):* Ignore these random reflections, Mrs. Prentice. They're an essential factor in the patient's condition. *(To Dr. Prentice.)* Does she have the same name as your secretary?
PRENTICE: She's taken my secretary's name as her *"nom de folie. . . . ."*

So now Dr. Prentice's little deception is becoming more complicated. Mrs. Prentice goes off in search of "Miss Barclay," while Rance questions Geraldine, who is now deeply under the influence of the drug. Rance assumes from her answers that she was the victim of an incestuous attack (Rance is always ready to believe the worst and relish it), but Geraldine denies it: "I lived in a normal family. I had no love for my father." Rance takes her denial as proof that it happened. He wheels Geraldine into the ward to have her hair cut.

Alone at last, Dr. Prentice retrieves Geraldine's underwear from the wastebasket and shoes from the closet—but then he is again interrupted by his wife's entrance, which forces him into all kinds of subterfuge to conceal the clothing. Finally he hides the underwear and one shoe in a vase of roses, and the other shoe in the bookcase.

Rance returns, having clipped Geraldine's hair to one inch in length, in accordance with his long-held convictions about the care of disturbed patients. Mrs. Prentice is still worrying over Nick's job. As for the "missing" Miss Barclay, Rance suggests a search party with dogs. To forstall anything so dramatic, Dr. Prentice "remembers" that Miss Barclay is in the therapy workshop, "making white tar-babies for sale in color-prejudice trouble-spots."

Rance finds it almost incredible that Prentice would forget such a detail; in any case, he finds the existence of white tar-babies obscene and sends Prentice off to destroy the "hellish mutations." Alone with Mrs. Prentice, Rance confides in her his government mission to investigate the clinic, and his doubts about the way it is being run.

Mrs. Prentice finds the strange shoe hidden in the bookcase. Rance looks it over.

RANCE: I must ask you to be honest with me, Mrs. Prentice. Has Dr. Prentice at any time given you cause to doubt his own sanity?

Mrs. Prentice gives a quick gasp of fear, rising to her feet.

MRS. PRENTICE: He's a respected member of his profession. His work in all fields has been praised by numerous colleagues.

RANCE: Let me remind you, Mrs. Prentice, that radical thought comes easily to the lunatic.

MRS. PRENTICE *(pause):* You're quite right. I've known for some time that all was not well. I've tried to convince myself that my fears were groundless. All the while I knew I was deceiving myself.

RANCE *(quietly):* What first aroused your suspicions?

MRS. PRENTICE: His boorish attitude toward my mother. He used to call her up on the telephone and suggest painful ways of committing suicide. Worn out at last by his pestering, she took his advice.

RANCE: And more recently, say from this morning, has there been an increase in his condition?

MRS. PRENTICE: Oh, yes. Quite definitely, doctor. He had no sympathy for me when I complained of being assaulted by a page boy at the Station Hotel.

And now, Mrs. Prentice remarks pointedly, her husband has developed an obsession with women's clothes. Dr. Prentice comes back into the office, and Dr. Rance confronts him with the shoe. Dr. Prentice pretends that it is his own, but Rance still insists on speaking to the secretary, Miss Barclay. She's in the garden, Dr. Prentice tells him, "making a funeral pyre for the tar-babies." Rance goes off to see for himself.

Left together, Dr. Prentice and his wife quarrel. He is trying to unzip her dress (for tactical, not amorous, reasons) when Nick enters, carrying Mrs. Prentice's dress from the night before. Prentice immediately grabs it, adding to the others' conviction that he is a transvestite (but of course he wants it for Geraldine).

Dr. Prentice shoos his wife out and prepares to deal with Nick, who admits that he has a set of pornographic photos of Mrs. Prentice. Nick has this uncontrollable urge to sleep with every woman he meets (he confides to Dr. Prentice).

Rance and Mrs. Prentice drift through the room—Rance to voice his impatience with Miss Barclay's continued concealment, Mrs. Prentice to announce that there is a policeman in the hall. This last bit of information frightens Nick, who pleads with Prentice to help him.

PRENTICE: Why are you in danger of arrest?

NICK: Well, sir, as your wife has already told you, I attempted last night to misbehave myself with her. I didn't succeed.

PRENTICE: I'm sure you didn't. Despite all appearances to the contrary, Mrs. Prentice is harder to get into than the reading room of the British Museum.

NICK: Undeterred, I took the elevator to the third floor of the hotel where a party of schoolgirls were staying. Oh, sir, what lonely and aimless lives they lead! I did what I could to bring them some happiness.

PRENTICE (with a frown): Was there no mistress in attendance?

NICK: She occupied a room across the corridor.

PRENTICE: Did you disturb her?

NICK: No. And she'll never forgive me for it. It was she who reported the incident to the police. Oh, sir! Don't turn me over to the law.

Dr. Rance enters from the dispensary.

RANCE: I warn you, Prentice, unless you're prepared to cooperate in finding Miss Barclay I shall call upon you to account for her disappearance. If you're unable to do so the police must be informed.

He goes into the garden. Prentice turns to Nick, an idea dawning.

PRENTICE (abruptly): Take your clothes off.

NICK (pause): Are you going to fool around with me, sir?

PRENTICE: Certainly not! Is that what usually happens when men ask you to take your clothes off?

NICK: Yes. They usually give me money.

PRENTICE: How much? Oh, never mind. Strip! I want you to impersonate my secretary, Geraldine Barclay. It will solve both our problems.

Nick is to put on Mrs. Prentice's dress, convince Rance that he is Miss Barclay, and then make himself scarce. Mrs. Prentice comes in, sees Nick naked, protests, but is told that Dr. Prentice is merely making an examination. Mrs. Prentice takes Nick's uniform into the garden and orders Nick to follow, but Nick obeys Prentice and goes into the dispensary to put on the dress. Dr. Prentice has some difficulty passing Nick the shoes before the policeman enters (Dr. Prentice's little deceptions have now become so numerous that he's increasingly frantic in keeping them all in the air, in their proper order).

Geraldine comes in dressed in her hospital gown, demanding to be set free. Dr. Prentice puts off the policeman, Sergeant Match, until Geraldine is safely concealed once more behind the curtain shielding the couch. The doctor manages to give Geraldine her underwear from the vase of roses.

Mrs. Prentice insists on bringing Sergeant Match into the office. The policeman is looking for Nick (Mrs. Prentice insists he is here and goes into the garden to get his uniform to prove it, but the doctor insists he isn't) and also for Geraldine Barclay on "a matter of national importance." As Sergeant Match explains it: "Miss Barclay's stepmother, a woman of otherwise unblemished character, died recently. Shortly before her death her name had been linked in a most unpleasant way with that of Sir Winston Churchill. Miss

Barclay's association with the great man gave offense in some circles. However, the local council, composed by and large of no-nonsense men and women in their sixties, decided in view of his war record to overlook Sir Winston's moral lapse. Under expert guidance he was to be reintegrated into society. The task accomplished, it became clear that the great man was incomplete. The council decided to sue the heirs of Mrs. Barclay for those parts of Sir Winston which an army-type medical had proved to be missing. Early this morning Mrs. Barclay's coffin was opened in the presence of the Lord Mayor and Lady Mayoress of this borough. Fainting women were held back as the official in charge searched high and low for council property. His efforts were not crowned with success. Mrs. Barclay had taken nothing with her to the grave except those things which she ought to have done. That is when the matter came to the attention of the police," who suspect that Geraldine may have stolen the parts of the statue which are missing.

Mrs. Prentice comes in from the garden with Nick's uniform. Dr. Prentice denies knowledge, or memory, of either Nick or Geraldine. After Mrs. Prentice and the policeman go off to continue the search, Geraldine pokes her head out through the curtains to inform Dr. Prentice: "All your troubles spring from a lack of candor."

Sergeant Match comes back and asks Dr. Prentice to accompany him to the garden. This gives Geraldine the opportunity to slip out of her hiding place, exchange her hospital gown for Nick's uniform, and slip back into concealment.

Nick (dressed in women's clothes) and Mrs. Prentice enter from opposite sides. Nick has identified himself as Geraldine, when the Sergeant and Dr. Prentice come in. The policeman immediately questions "Geraldine" about the missing parts of the statue. Nick of course knows nothing.

MATCH: You're claiming ignorance of the shape and structure of the objects sought?

NICK: I'm in the dark.

MATCH: You handled them only at night? We shall draw our own conclusions.

NICK: I'm not the sort of girl to be mixed up in that kind of thing. I'm an ex-member of the Brownies.

MATCH: Are you concealing unlawful property about your person?

NICK: No.

MATCH: I'll have to call medical evidence to prove your story, miss. You must be thoroughly looked into.

PRENTICE: I'm a qualified doctor.

MATCH: Only women are permitted to examine female suspects.

PRENTICE: Doesn't that breed discontent in the force?

MATCH: Among the single men there's a certain amount of bitterness. Married men who are familiar with the country are glad to be let off extra map-reading.

MRS. PRENTICE: Sergeant, I'll examine Miss Barclay. That will solve all our problems. Come along, Miss Barclay.

MATCH: Thank you, ma'am. I accept your kind offer.

MRS. PRENTICE: Come along, Miss Barclay.

Mrs. Prentice leads Nick into the garden. Siren sounds from the wards; then a buzzer. Dr. Rance enters from the wards.

RANCE: Prentice! The patient has escaped. I've sounded the alarm.

MATCH: How long has the patient been gone, sir?

RANCE: Only a few minutes. This is her gown. She must be naked then.

MATCH: Any steps you feel may be necessary to recover your patient may be taken, sir.

Dr. Rance crosses, hurries into the hall.

She must've come through this room. You and I were in the garden. Mrs. Prentice was upstairs. Escape would be out of the question. She must be still in this room.

He turns to Dr. Prentice in triumph.

Only one hiding place is possible.

He pulls the curtain on the couch aside. Geraldine is revealed. She is wearing Nick's uniform.

(Taking in the picture at a glance.) Are you from the Station Hotel?

GERALDINE *(in a scared voice):* Yes.

MATCH: I want a word with you, my lad.

He takes out his notebook. The siren and buzzer wail. Blackout. Curtain.

ACT II

Buzzer and siren can be heard, as the action is continuous. Geraldine is happy to be arrested and protected from Dr. Prentice who, as she sees it, first persuaded her to take off her clothes and then began "acting strangely."

Sergeant Match thinks Geraldine is the bellhop who assaulted the schoolgirls and questions her accordingly, Geraldine of course denies everything.

Dr. Rance enters, having set up strict security so that no one can leave the clinic. The policeman asks Rance's advice about how to proceed. Rance decides to examine the "lad" himself and sends the policeman out. Geraldine's answers to some of Rance's questions sound sexually ambiguous.

RANCE: Do you think of yourself as a girl?

GERALDINE: No.

RANCE: Why not?

GERALDINE: I'm a boy.

RANCE *(kindly):* Do you have the evidence about you?

GERALDINE *(her eyes flashing an appeal to Dr. Prentice):* I must be a boy. I like girls.

Dr. Rance stops and wrinkles his brow, puzzled.

RANCE *(aside to Dr. Prentice):* I can't quite follow the reasoning there.

PRENTICE: Many men imagine that a preference for women is *ipso facto* a proof of virility.

RANCE *(nodding sagely):* Someone should really write a book on these folk-myths.

Rance demands that Geraldine undress. Geraldine cries out an admission that she is a girl posing as a boy.

RANCE *(to Dr. Prentice):* Excellent. A confession at last. He wishes to believe he's a girl in order to minimize the feelings of guilt after homosexual intercourse.

GERALDINE *(wide-eyed, desperate):* I pretended to be a boy. I did it to help Dr. Prentice.

RANCE: How does it help a man if a girl pretends to be a boy?

GERALDINE: Wives are angry if they find their husbands have undressed and seduced a girl.

RANCE: But boys are fair game? I doubt whether your very personal view of society would go unchallenged.

> *Provoked beyond endurance, Geraldine flings herself into Dr. Rance's arms.*

GERALDINE *(cries hysterically):* Undress me then, doctor! Do whatever you like, only prove that I'm a girl.

> *Dr. Rance pushes her away and turns frigidly to Dr. Prentice.*

RANCE: If he's going to carry on like this he'll have to be strapped down.

> *Mrs. Prentice enters from the garden.*

MRS. PRENTICE *(to Dr. Rance):* Dr. Rance, would you take a look at Miss Barclay? She refuses to undress in front of a woman.

RANCE: How about in front of a man?

MRS. PRENTICE: I haven't sounded her on the subject.

RANCE: I wonder if I could tempt her. I'll give it a try. She may be a nymphomaniac. *(To Dr. Prentice.)* If this boy becomes foul-mouthed, keep him on the boil till I return.

> *He goes to the garden, followed by Mrs. Prentice.*

Geraldine wants to leave at once, but Rance has given orders to prevent anyone leaving. Rance comes back to inform them that "Miss Barclay" (who is Nick the bellboy in a dress) refuses to unclothe.

Mrs. Prentice leads Nick in from the garden, having given him a sedative to calm him down. The sexual confusion is now complete. Rance fires questions at everyone, and the contradictory answers convince him that he has stumbled upon a nest of vipers. He is ready to certify everyone in sight, including Dr. Prentice, for whom he prescribes some potent pills he happens to have handy.

Rance decides to lead Geraldine to a padded cell. Left together momentarily, Nick and Dr. Prentice decide to steal the policeman's uniform for Nick to wear. Dr. Prentice persuades the stolid Sergeant Match that he should submit to an examination, and Match proceeds to undress. The doctor manages to give the policeman Dr. Rance's pills, and screen him with the curtain. Then he sends Nick off to the garden to dress in the policeman's uniform, but not before Mrs. Prentice has happened along in time to see Nick racing around half naked.

The pace of the entrances and exits, the misunderstood transvestitism and emotional aberration increases. Dr. Rance is gleeful at the thought of the sensational best-seller he will be able to write about all this. He and Mrs. Prentice find the empty box of pills and assume that Dr. Prentice has taken an overdose. Then the now-drugged Sergeant Match is clothed in the woman's dress and dumped in the garden by Nick and Dr. Prentice. Mrs. Prentice happens to observe this action, as so many others, and immediately she and Rance draw another wrong conclusion.

RANCE: . . . . . A new and frightening possibility presents itself. The drugs in this box—
  He lifts up the bright red pill-box.
—may not have been used for suicide, but for murder. Your husband has made away with his secretary!
  MRS. PRENTICE: Isn't that a little melodramatic, doctor?
  RANCE: Lunatics *are* melodramatic. The subtleties of drama are wasted on them. Everything is now clear. The final chapters of my book are knitting themselves together: incest, buggery, outrageous women and strange love-cults catering to depraved appetites. All the fashionable bric-a-brac. *(To Mrs. Prentice.)* My "unbiased" account of the case of the infamous sex-killer Prentice will undoubtedly add a great deal to our understanding of such creatures. Society must be made aware of the growing menace of pornography. The whole treacherous avant-garde movement will be exposed for what it is—an instrument for inciting decent citizens to commit bizarre crimes against humanity and the state!
  He pauses, a little overcome, and wipes his brow.
You have, under your roof, my dear, one of the most remarkable lunatics of all time. We must institute a search for the corpse. As a transvestite, fetishist, bisexual murderer Dr. Prentice displays considerable deviation overlap. We may get necrophilia too. As a sort of bonus.

Dr. Prentice comes in from the garden (and for one reason or another he happens to have Geraldine's shoes in his pockets). He assures Rance that he has a rational explanation for everything, and Rance advises him: "You can't be a rationalist in an irrational world. It isn't rational."

Dr. Rance goes off in search of a straitjacket for Dr. Prentice, who calmly proceeds to unzip his wife's dress and take it from her (it is Geraldine's dress). Mrs. Prentice encourages her husband to slap her, and when he does so she rather enjoys it.

Now Dr. Prentice is in possession of both dress and shoes, and he exits in search of Geraldine (if he can just produce her clothed as a woman the whole misunderstanding will evaporate).

Rance comes in with a straitjacket. Nick comes in dressed a policeman, but he is unable to sustain the pretense. Nevertheless Dr. Rance means to enlist his aid in putting Dr. Prentice into the straitjacket. Mrs. Prentice and Dr. Rance arm themselves with revolvers from the desk drawer before going in search of their prey.

Dr. Prentice comes in with the dress; the Sergeant staggers through the office; finally Geraldine enters, still wearing the bellboy uniform. The doctor's effort to get the young people into their proper clothes results in pandemonium. Mrs. Prentice enters, demands to be loved here and now, and begins firing off her pistol when Dr. Prentice, preoccupied, refuses. The pistol shots send everyone running in an out in various states of undress, in a fair approximation of Bedlam on a bad day.

Dr. Rance catches Geraldine (now dressed only in panties and bra). When she protests that she isn't a patient, truthfully, Dr. Rance answers: "It's much too late to tell the truth."

Mrs. Prentice comes in from the dispensary with a hypodermic syringe, just as Dr. Rance puts his arms around Geraldine.

MRS. PRENTICE: What is the meaning of this exhibition?

RANCE (*breaking away from Geraldine*): It's a new and hitherto untried type of therapy. I think it's viable under the circumstances.

MRS. PRENTICE: Your treatment seems designed to plunge the patient deeper into lunacy rather than achieve any lasting cure.

RANCE: Someone whose unconscious is as quirky as your own could hardly be expected to understand my methods.

MRS. PRENTICE: What do you mean by that?

RANCE: I'm referring to those naked men you encounter with an increasing degree of frequency.

MRS. PRENTICE: You've seen them too.

RANCE: What does that prove? Merely that you've given me your wretched disease. Give me that!

He takes the hypodermic from her.

MRS. PRENTICE: Shouldn't I swab the patient's arm?

RANCE: You don't imagine I'm wasting this stuff on her, do you?

He rolls back his sleeve.

For what it costs an ounce, it would be criminal.

Dr. Rance gives himself the injection and decides that a policeman is needed (there's a naked one in the garden, Mrs. Prentice informs him). Nick enters, as Rance makes ready the straitjacket for Mrs. Prentice. Dr. Prentice comes in waving his revolver and Rance and Prentice threaten to certify each other insane. Dr. Rance ignores Prentice's gun, merely draws the one in his possession and points it at Prentice. Sergeant Match comes in, still a bit wobbly.

Dr. Rance demands to know what Dr. Prentice has done with Miss Barclay; Geraldine remarks plaintively "I'm here"; Sergeant Match immediately wants to know what she has done with the missing parts of Sir Winston Churchill.

PRENTICE: Stop! All of you! We are now approaching what our racier novelists term the climax. Release my wife and the young woman, too. The story you're about to hear is concerned solely with the heart: the mind and its mysteries could not have been further from my thoughts when, early this morning, in what must be the most ill-timed attempt at seduction ever, I persuaded that young woman to take her clothes off.

GERALDINE *(to Dr. Rance):* Mrs. Prentice mistook my dress for her own and, by an oversight, you mistook me for a patient. Dr. Prentice asked me to keep quiet in order to protect his good name. What could I do? I was terrified of exposure.

MRS. PRENTICE: You were naked at the time?

GERALDINE: Yes. Under duress I agreed to help the doctor. I've never ceased reproaching myself. The whole day has been spent fighting to retain my self-respect.

DR. PRENTICE: Oh, if I live to be ninety, I'll never again attempt sexual intercourse.

RANCE: I'd be willing to stake my professional reputation upon the fact that this girl has been the victim of an incestuous attack. I won't go back on my diagnosis. My publishers will sue me for loss of royalties.

GERALDINE *(stepping from the couch):* I'm sure my shorthand speed has been affected by what I've suffered today. *(Tearful, to Dr. Prentice.)* And I wish to report the loss of my lucky elephant charm.

Dr. Rance takes a brooch from his pocket.

RANCE: Is this the piece of jewelry to which you refer? I removed it from your neck when I cut your hair.

GERALDINE: Yes. It has great sentimental value.

Dr. Rance gives it to her. Nick picks up the trousers of his uniform.

NICK: Look. I've got one like that.

He shows Geraldine a brooch. Mrs. Prentice, released now from the straitjacket, gives a cry of surprise. The two brooches are shown to her.

MRS. PRENTICE: A single brooch can be made of these two fragments.

She fits the brooch together.

Oh, my heart is beating like a wild thing!

Dr. Rance examines the brooch.

NICK & GERALDINE: It's true!

MATCH: Two elephants carrying a richly engraved howdah in which is seated a young and beautiful woman—perhaps a princess of the royal line— magnificent example of oriental craftsmanship. *(To Mrs. Prentice.)* How did you know this was a single piece?

MRS. PRENTICE: It belonged to me once. Many years ago, when I was a young woman, I was raped in a linen closet on the second floor of the Station

Hotel. As the man left me he pressed that brooch into my hands in part payment.

MATCH: How did these children come to be in possession of the separate halves?

MRS. PRENTICE: I paid for my misdemeanor by conceiving twins. It was impossible for me to keep them—I was by then engaged to be married to a promising young psychiatrist. I decided to abandon them to their fate. I broke the brooch in half and pinned a separate piece to each babe. I then placed them at either end of the small country town in which I was resident. Some kind people must've brought the children up as their own.

Hugging Nick and Geraldine.

Oh, children! I am your mother! Can you ever forgive me for what I did?

NICK: What kind of mother must you have been to stay alone at the Station Hotel?

MRS. PRENTICE: I was employed as a chambermaid. I did it for a joke shortly after the war. The effect of a Labor Government on the middle classes had to be seen to be believed.

GERALDINE: Was our father also employed by the Station Hotel?

MRS. PRENTICE: I never saw your father. The incident occurred during a power-cut. I became pregnant as I waited for normal services to be resumed.

PRENTICE *(weakly, to Dr. Rance):* You'll find an inscription on the back of that brooch, sir—"To Lillian from Avis. Christmas 1939." I found that brooch many years ago. It was on the pavement outside a large department store.

RANCE: Who were Lillian and Avis?

PRENTICE: I've no idea. It fell from the collar of a Pekingese. Lillian and Avis may have been the creature's owners.

He stares about him in shame.

I haven't seen it since I pressed it into the hand of a chambermaid whom I debauched shortly before my marriage.

MRS. PRENTICE *(with a cry of recognition):* I understand now why you suggested that we spend our honeymoon in a linen closet!

PRENTICE: I wished to recreate a moment that was very precious to me. My darling, we have been instrumental in uncovering a number of remarkable peccadilloes today.

RANCE: Double incest is even more likely to produce a best-seller than murder—and that is as it should be, for love must bring greater joy than violence.

PRENTICE: Come, let us put on our clothes and face the world.

They all turn to the audience and bow crisply and formally. Blackout. Curtain.

THE SERPENT: A CEREMONY

Created by The Open Theater under the direction of
Joseph Chaikin

WORDS AND STRUCTURE BY

JEAN-CLAUDE VAN ITALLIE

Cast and credits appear on page 369

JEAN-CLAUDE van ITALLIE is an American playwright who was born in Brussels in 1936 but came to the United States with his family at the age of 4. He grew up on Long Island, in Great Neck and is a graduate of Harvard (1958). He has written for television, and his playwriting career has been spread over a broad area of experimental production. He has been a playwright-member of Joseph Chaikin's Open Theater since its beginning in 1963. His works have been produced off off Broadway at Cafe La Mama, Caffe Cino and the Playwrights Unit. One of them—Dis Is De Queen—was produced by the Firehouse Theater in Minneapolis under a grant from the Rockefeller Foundation, and others have been produced around the world.

Van Itallie's first professional New York production was the one acter War *in the season of 1965-66 as part of the off-Broadway program 6 From La*

232

Mama. *His second,* America Hurrah, *was a program of three one-act plays presented off Broadway November 6, 1966 for 634 performances and named a Best Play of its season. The first of* America Hurrah's *one-acters,* Interview, *was performed under the title* Pavane *at the Academy Theater in Atlanta, Ga., in 1965 and received subsequent stagings by The Open Theater, the Sheridan Square Playhouse, the Cafe La Mama and National Educational TV. The second of the one-acters, entitled* TV, *had its world premiere in this 1966 production. The third,* Motel, *had been staged at the Cafe La Mama in 1965 under the title* America Hurrah.

A van Itallie playlet written in collaboration with Sharon Thie and entitled Thoughts on the Instant of Greeting a Friend on the Street *was part of the portmanteau program* Collision Course *produced off Broadway May 8, 1968 for 80 performances. Van Itallie lives in New York City and works closely with Joseph Chaikin's Open Theater troupe which helped to create* The Serpent: A Ceremony *two seasons ago in a new, experimental relationship in which actors and director collaborate with the playwright in the development and fleshing-out of his characters and situations.*

The Serpent *has been performed from time to time in New York in the semi-private, virtually by-invitation-only situation which is typical of the stage activity in the category which is loosely termed "off off Broadway" (whose works are not eligible for Best Play selection because they are usually in a state of rewrite and are seldom readily available to the public). This season, however, The Open Theater chose to present one advertised performance of* The Serpent *with tickets on public sale (on May 29) in a limited public engagement of Open Theater repertory extending for 18 continuous performances through June 14, 1970 and including two more performances of this work. This was sufficient to bring* The Serpent *into eligibility as a Best Play selection; as for any other technicalities, we are happy to make an exception in the presence of genius and declare it a Best Play of 1969-70, van Itallie's second—and the shortest-run selection (3 performances) in the 51-year history of this series.*

THE OPEN THEATER was founded in 1963 by a group of actors, directors and playwrights "tired of conventional New York theatrical expression and disgusted with the nearly total lack of outlets available for experimental work." Their founder and head is Joseph Chaikin, 34, born in Brooklyn and educated at Drake University in Ohio. For several years Chaikin was a leading performer with the Living Theater, and his performances in the commercial off-Broadway theater won him several "Obies."

The original members of The Open Theater are still its nucleus, continuing under Chaikin's direction. The Serpent: A Ceremony *was the off-off-Broadway group's first "fully collaborative" work. It has been received with enthusiasm in Italy, Switzerland, Germany and Denmark—and now, finally, in public New York performances. The Open Theater's spring 1970 repertory also included another collaborative new work,* Terminal *(which played a special benefit performance at American Place earlier in the season and was mentioned in the 1969-70 New York Drama Critics Circle best-play voting), and a version of Samuel Beckett's* Endgame.

INTRODUCTION BY THE PLAYWRIGHT

Theater is not electronic. Unlike movies and unlike television, it does require the live presence of both audience and actors in a single space. This is the theater's uniquely important advantage and function, its original religious function of bringing people together in a community ceremony where the actors are in some sense priests or celebrants, and the audience is drawn to participate with the actors in a kind of eucharist.

Where this is the admitted function of theater the playwright's work is not so much to "write a play" as to "construct a ceremony" which can be used by the actors to come together with their audience. Words are a part of this ceremony, but not necessarily the dominant part, as they are not the dominant part either in a formal religious ceremony. The important thing is what is happening between the audience and the action. At each point in constructing the ceremony the playwright must say to himself: "What is the audience experiencing now? At what point are they on their journey and where are they to be brought next?" The "trip" for the audience must be as carefully structured as any ancient mystery or initiation. But the form must reflect contemporary thought processes. And we don't think much in a linear fashion. Ideas overlap, themes recur, archetypal figures and events transform from shape to shape as they dominate our minds.

The creation of this piece was an exploration of certain ideas and images that seem to dominate our minds and lives. The only criterion, finally, of whether or not to follow an impulse in this piece was: Did it work for us or not, in our lives, in our thoughts, and in the playing on the stage.

A large part in the creation of the ceremony was "letting go." For my part, I let go a great many words, characters and scenes. And most painfully I let go certain rigid structural concepts I had invented to replace the linear ones of a conventional play. But whatever was good of these—a funeral, a Catholic mass, an LSD trip, an inquisition, a modern mystery play—remains within the structure of the present ceremony. And so too, lengthy discussions, improvisations, and even unstated common feelings within the company remain somewhere within the final piece—in fact more, probably, than even we can remember.

When other acting groups want to perform *The Serpent* I hope that they will use the words and movements only as a skeleton on which they will put their own flesh. Because *The Serpent* is a ceremony reflecting the minds and lives of the people performing it. What I would like to think is that we have gone deep enough into ourselves to find and express some notions, some images, some feelings which will bring the actors together with the audience, and that these images, these ideas, these feelings, will be found to be held in common.

JEAN-CLAUDE van ITALLIE

With the kind permission of the play's author of "words and structure," van Itallie, and its publisher, Atheneum, we are happy to include here the entire published text of The Serpent. *This is the verbal "skeleton" of the play referred to by van Itallie in his introduction above, complete and unabridged, with all dialogue and description of action as it appears in the published script —the first of the 510 Best Plays to appear in these volumes as a complete text, not a condensation.*

As staged in this 1969-70 production, The Serpent *began almost imperceptibly, as the members of The Open Theater troupe slowly and inconspicuously infiltrated the audience area. Then the action proceeded as follows:*

Warm-up and Procession

In all parts of the theater, including the aisle, the stage and the balcony, the actors warm up. Each does what physical exercises best prepare him for playing. The lights dim slowly and not completely. Each actor wears a costume that seems natural on him particularly, of colorful and easily falling materials that flatter the movement of his body. The total effect, when the company moves together, is kaleidoscopic. The actress who will play Eve wears a simply cut short white dress, and Adam old khaki pants and a shirt with no collar. None of the others is costumed for a particular role. As no one wears any shoes but tights or ballet slippers, a dropcloth for the stage is desirable.

After a few minutes the actors begin to move around the theater in a procession led by an actor who taps out a simple marching rhythm on a bongo drum. The players don't use their voices, but they explore every other sound that can be made by the human body—slapping oneself, pounding one's chest, etc. The actors also use simple and primitive musical instruments during the procession. During some later scenes an actor may accompany the stage action with the repeated sound of a single note on one of these instruments. The procession appears to be one of medieval mummers, and sounds like skeletons on the move. All at once all stop in a freeze. This happens three times during the procession. During a freeze each actor portrays one of various possible motifs from the play such as: the sheep, the serpent, the President's wife's reaching gesture, Adam's movement, Cain's waiting movement, Eve's movement, the heron, and the old people. In countries outside the United States where it is thought that not everyone will immediately recognize all events in the piece, at these motif moments actors shout out the names King and Kennedy.

Transitions from a scene to the next will be done rythmically, in the character of one scene or of the following, as a slow transformation or "dissolve," or completely out of character with the audience merely watching the actor go to his next place. Each transition is slightly different, but pre-determined.

The Doctor

When the procession is nearly over, the doctor detaches himself from it. A victim, a woman, from among the actors is carried over by two actors and placed on a table formed by three other actors. The doctor stands behind the table. He speaks in a kind of chant. His movements are slow and ritualistic. The rest of the actors, watching, will provide stylized sounds for the operation. A gunshot will be heard once in a while. We will already have heard the gunshot a couple of times during the end of the procession.

DOCTOR:

Autopsy:
With a single stroke of the cleaver
The corpse is split open.
 Actors make cutting sound from the backs of their throats
The fatty tissues
Fall away
In two yellow folds.

DOCTOR:

In a corpse
The blood is black
And does not flow.
In a living person
The blood is black
And flows
From the liver
To the spine, and from
There to the heart
And the brain.
To penetrate the skull
We shave the head,
And cut out a disk of flesh
The shape of a half moon.
 Actors make the sound of the saw
We inject the exposed bone
With a steel needle
And push air into the skull
To look into the brain.
Then with a diamond drill
We enter the bone.
 Actors make the sound of teeth nibbling
And nibble at the opening
With a hammer, chisel and knife.
The brain is cream-colored.
It is a balance of chemicals.
Thought is effected

By traveling electrons.
    Gunshot
During a brain operation
Pressing at this point
With a knife
Causes live patients
To exclaim at sudden memories.
If we press here
We get fear.
    *Gunshot. The patient, who so far has been lying fairly still, climbs
    off the table and comes slowly toward the audience in a state of ex-
    treme bodily tension, making a soundless appeal.*
In gunshot wounds
Infection ensues
Unless an operation
Is undertaken immediately.
We excise the wound,
And suck out bits of bone
And diffluent brain matter.
If the patient survives
He may live for weeks
Or months
Or years.
    *The four women of the chorus make the same small long scream at
    the backs of their throats that they will make when we later see
    Abel's ghost.*
He functions barely.
He is unconscious.
Or semi-conscious.
We don't know.
We clean him,
And feed him.
But there is no measure
To what degree
The mind imagines, receives, or dreams.

Kennedy-King Assassination

A cheering crowd forms in a semi-circle at the back of the stage. Using four
chairs, or sitting on the floor if the stage is raked enough, four actors, two
men and two women, sit in the car as the central characters in the assassination of President John F. Kennedy. The governor and his wife are in front.
The President and his wife are in the back seat exactly as in all the newspaper
pictures. They are waving. The crowd, moving from one side of the stage to
the other behind them, gives the same impression of movement as in a film

when the scenery is moved behind what is supposed to be a "moving" car. When the crowd moves the first time, one figure is left to the side: the assassin. Another figure stands behind the crowd, and does not move with it. Again, everyone but the people in the car is facing the audience. The people in the car look at the audience, smile at them as if they were the crowd. The events which are the actual assassination are broken down into a count of twelve, as if seen on a slowed-down silent film. Within this count all the things which we are told factually happened, happen:

> *1: All four wave.*
> *2: President is shot in the neck.*
> *3: Governor is shot in the shoulder.*
> *4: President is shot in the head. Governor's wife pulls her husband down and covers him with her body.*
> *5: President falls against his wife.*
> *6: President's wife begins to register something is wrong. She looks at her husband.*
> *7: She puts her hands on his head.*
> *8: She lifts her knee to put his head on it.*
> *9: She looks into the front seat.*
> *10: She begins to realize horror.*
> *11: She starts to get up.*
> *12: She begins to crawl out the back of the open car, and to reach out her hand.*

Immediately after that, the numbers are started again. The numbers have been actually shouted aloud by guards who come down toward the front of the stage and kneel, their backs to the audience. Then the count is made a third time, backward this time. The crowd reactions are also backward, as if a film of these events were being run backward. Then the guards call out numbers from one to twelve at random, and the people in the crowd, as well as the characters in the car, assume the positions they had at the time of the particular number being called. The blank-faced assassin has simply mimed shooting a rifle at the count of two. He faces the audience, too. The action in the car continues, as if the count from one to twelve were going on perpetually, but we no longer hear the guards shouting. The crowd, aside from the assassin, forms a tight group at the rear of the right side of the stage. They face the audience. The four women of the chorus are in the front. The crowd shouts and marches very slowly toward the front.

At first, however, we have not understood what they are shouting. The shout is broken down into first vowels, second vowels, center consonants and end consonants. Each of four sections of the crowd has been assigned one part. The shout is repeated four times, each time through adding one of the four parts.

CROWD SHOUT:
    I was not involved.

I am a small person.
I hold no opinion.
I stay alive.

> *Then everyone on stage freezes, and the figure at the back quietly speaks words like the actual ones of Dr. Martin Luther King:*

KING:

Though we stand in life at midnight,
I have a dream.
He's allowed me
To go to the mountaintop,
And I've looked over.
I've seen the promised land.
I have a dream
That we are, as always,
On the threshold of a new dawn,
And that we shall all see it together.

> *The crowd continues its shout, building up the other stanzas as it did the previous one, but the words are still not completely clear. The characters in the car continue their slow-motion actions.*

CROWD SHOUT:

I mind my own affairs.
I am a little man.
I lead a private life.
I stay alive.

I'm no assassin.
I'm no president.
I don't know who did the killing.
I stay alive.

I keep out of big affairs.
I am not a violent man.
I am very sorry, still
I stay alive.

> *At times we have been able to make out the words of the President's wife which she has been speaking on count twelve as she reaches out.*

PRESIDENT'S WIFE:

I've got his brains in my—

> *The last time through the whole shout, we hear each section of the crowd emphasizing its own part, while the assassin, who has been standing on one side, facing the audience and going through, silently, the agonies of having been himself shot, speaks the words with the others, clearly.*

CROWD AND ASSASSIN:

I was not involved.
I am a small person.

I hold no opinions.
I stay alive.

I mind my own affairs.
I am a little man.
I lead a private life.
I stay alive.

I'm no assassin.
I'm no president.
I don't know who did the killing.
I stay alive.

I keep out of big affairs.
I am not a violent man.
I am very sorry, still
I stay alive.

The Garden

Everyone's breath comes short and heavy and rhythmically, as if in surprise. The four chorus women dressed in black detach themselves from the rest of the group and in short spurts of movement and speech go to the downstage right area, facing the audience.

FIRST WOMAN OF THE CHORUS: I no longer live in the beginning.
SECOND WOMAN OF THE CHORUS: I've lost the beginning.
THIRD WOMAN OF THE CHORUS:
   I'm in the middle,
   Knowing.
THIRD AND FOURTH WOMEN OF THE CHORUS:
   Neither the end
   Nor the beginning.
FIRST WOMAN: I'm in the middle.
SECOND WOMAN: Coming from the beginning.
THIRD AND FOURTH WOMEN: And going toward the end.

In the meantime, others are forming the creatures in the garden of Eden. They, too, emanate from the same communal "first breath." Many of the creatures are personal, previously selected by each actor as expressing an otherwise inexpressible part of himself. For the audience, perhaps the heron has the most identifiable reality. He moves about gently, tall, proud, in slow spurts; he stands on one foot, moves his wings slightly, occasionally, and makes a soft "brrring" noise. Other creatures become distinguishable. The serpent is formed by five (male) actors all writhing together in a group, their arms, legs, hands, tongues, all moving.

The chorus women have repeated their "in the beginning" lines from above. They speak these lines as a secret to the audience.

There is a sense of awe about the whole creation of the garden. The two human creatures also become discernible. As Eve sits up and sees the world, she screams in amazement. The sound of her scream is actually made by one of the four chorus women. They are also Eve. They think of themselves as one person, and any one of them at this moment might reflect Eve.

Adam falls asleep. The heron and the serpent are now more clearly discernible from the other creatures. The creatures play with themselves and each other quietly, in awe. The serpent is feeling out the environment with hands and mouths and fingers. There is nothing orgiastic about the garden—on the contrary, there is the restraint of curious animals in a strange environment.

Eve and the Serpent

SERPENT 1: Is it true?
SERPENT 2: Is it true
SERPENT 3: That you and he,
SERPENT 4: You and he
SERPENT 4 AND 5: May do anything?
SERPENT 2: Anything in the garden you want to do?
SERPENT 1: Is that true?
EVE:
    We may do anything
    Except one thing.
FIRST WOMAN OF THE CHORUS:
    We may do anything
    Except one thing.

In the dialogue between Eve and the serpent the first of the chorus women echoes Eve's lines, but with the emphasis placed on different words. The four chorus women look at the audience as if it were the serpent in front of them. The serpent speaks and hisses to Eve with all his five mouths. Care must be taken by the actors playing the serpent that all the words are heard distinctly, despite overlap in speaking. Eve is almost in a state of tremor at being alive. The serpent is seducing her with his even greater aliveness, as well as with the intellectual argument. As Eve comes closer to being in the state the serpent is in, her movements begin to imitate the serpent's, and she, finally, is seducing him, too. Some of the other actors are now seated on a bench facing the audience, at the back of the stage where they sit, and rest, and pay attention to the action. This is where those who are not playing a particular scene will always go—none of the actors will ever actually leave the stage. During Eve's dialogue with the serpent, only the heron and one or two other animals in the garden are upright, but they do not distract our attention. The serpent is not only the serpent, he is also the tree, and he holds apples.

SERPENT 2: What one thing?
EVE: We are not allowed to eat from the tree.

FIRST WOMAN:
 We are not allowed
 To eat from the tree.
SERPENT 3: Not allowed to eat?
EVE: We may not even touch it.
WOMAN: We may not even touch it.
SERPENT 1: Not even touch?
SERPENT 4 AND 5: Not touch?
SERPENT 5: Why not even touch?
EVE: Adam said I would die.
WOMAN: Adam said I would die.
 The serpent is gently surrounding her until she has touched him
 without her realizing it.
SERPENT 3: If you—
SERPENT 4: If you touch—
SERPENT 4 AND 5: If you touch the tree—
SERPENT 1: Adam said
SERPENT 2: If you touch the tree
SERPENT 4 AND 5:
 If you even touch the tree
 You will die—
SERPENT 1: But—
SERPENT 2: But—
SERPENT 3: But—
 Eve realizes her back is against the tree.
SERPENT 5: Have you died?
SERPENT 4 *(whispering):* Have you died?
EVE: I don't know.
WOMAN: I don't know.
SERPENT 2: You touched the tree.
SERPENT 2 AND 3: And you haven't died.
SERPENT 4: You haven't died.
EVE: But Adam said—
WOMAN: But Adam said—
SERPENT 1: Oh, Adam said
SERPENT 2: Adam said, Adam said . . .
SERPENT 1 AND 2: Listen.
SERPENT 2 AND 3: Answer me this.
SERPENT 5 *(overlapping the others):* This.
SERPENT 4: Could it?
SERPENT 3:
 Could it hurt more
 To eat than to touch?
SERPENT 5: To eat than to touch?
SERPENT 1: Could it?
EVE: It is forbidden.
WOMAN: It is forbidden.

SERPENT 2: Who has forbidden it?

SERPENT 1: Who?

EVE: God.

WOMAN: God.

SERPENT 4: And why?

SERPENT 5: Why has he forbidden it?

SERPENT 4: Why?

SERPENT 3: Why does he set limits

SERPENT 2 AND 3: Against you and Adam?

SERPENT 1: Think.

SERPENT 2: Is the fruit God's property?

SERPENT 3: Is it?

SERPENT 1:
He says Adam and Eve may not eat.
But are Adam and Eve
Guests in this garden?

SERPENT 2: Are they guests?

SERPENT 1: Don't they live here?

SERPENT 3: May they not eat where they want?

EVE (turning away): I don't know.

WOMAN: I don't know.

SERPENT 5: Also, also haven't you

SERPENT 4 AND 5: Haven't you noticed

SERPENT 4:
That the younger always have rule
Over the elder creation?

SERPENT 2:
Haven't you noticed,
And aren't you afraid?

SERPENT 1:
Aren't you afraid
And hadn't you better hurry

SERPENT 1 AND 2:
And eat the fruit now
Before the next comes to rule
Over you?

EVE: I'm not afraid.

WOMAN: I'm not afraid.

SERPENT (to itselves) 1: She's not afraid.

SERPENT 2: Why should she be?

SERPENT 3: How could she be?

SERPENT 4: How?

SERPENT 5:
She couldn't be,
She doesn't know.

SERPENT 4: Doesn't know what?

SERPENT 3: Doesn't know she exists.
SERPENT 4: Why doesn't she know it?
SERPENT 3: Because she hasn't eaten.
SERPENT 2: If she'd eaten, she'd know.
SERPENT 1: Know what?
SERPENT 4:
　　What worlds she would know
　　If she ate.
SERPENT 5: What worlds?
SERPENT 1: If she ate she would know
SERPENT 1 AND 2: And if she knew
SERPENT 1 AND 2 AND 3: She could—
EVE: What?
WOMAN: What?
SERPENT 4: You don't know
SERPENT 5: Because you haven't eaten.
EVE: Do you know?
WOMAN: Do you know?
SERPENT 2: I don't know.
SERPENT 1: I don't.
SERPENT 3: But I can imagine.
SERPENT 4: Imagine.
SERPENT 5: Imagine.
EVE:
　　But, is what you can imagine
　　What will be?
WOMAN:
　　But, is what you can imagine
　　What will be?
SERPENT 1 AND 2:
　　How can you know
　　Until you eat?
SERPENT 5: How can I know?
SERPENT 4: How can I know until you eat?
SERPENT 1: This garden
SERPENT 2: All these animals and these plants
SERPENT 2 AND 3: Were once only imagined.
EVE: Shall I risk losing all these?
WOMAN: Shall I risk losing all these?
SERPENT 1: It may be.
SERPENT 2: It may be that no garden
SERPENT 4: Is better than this one.
SERPENT 5: This garden.
SERPENT 4: It may be.
SERPENT 2: But you won't know,
SERPENT 1: You can't know

Until you eat.

SERPENT 2: How could you know?

EVE:

If I eat

And if I die

Will you die too?

WOMAN:

If I eat

And if I die

Will you die too?

SERPENT 1:

If you die

I will die too.

EVE: Why do you want me to eat?

WOMAN: Why do you want me to eat?

SERPENT 5: Because I want

SERPENT 4: I want to

SERPENT 3: I want to know.

EVE: Know what?

WOMAN: Know what?

SERPENT 2: Know what you will know.

SERPENT 1: Know what will happen.

EVE:

I might.

I might do it.

I might do it if God didn't know.

WOMAN:

I might.

I might do it.

I might do it if God didn't know.

SERPENT 3: You might

SERPENT 4: Might do it if God didn't know?

SERPENT 2: But you want to.

SERPENT 1: And he knows you want to.

SERPENT 5: Is a crime

SERPENT 4: Only a crime

SERPENT 5: When you're caught?

EVE: Shall I do what I want to then?

WOMAN: Shall I do what I want to then?

SERPENT 1 AND 2 AND 3 AND 4 AND 5: Yes!

EVE:

Even if what I want is to listen

To God and not to you?

WOMAN: Even if what I want is to listen

To God and not to you?
SERPENT 1: Yes.
SERPENT 2: If you want.
SERPENT 3 AND 4: If you want.
SERPENT 5: Yes.
EVE: Then I will eat.
WOMAN: Then I will eat.
     She bites into one of the apples held by the many hands of the serpent.
EVE: Because I want to.
WOMAN: Because I want to.

Eating the Apple

When Eve finally eats she is seated in the middle of the serpent. After a couple of frantic bites, there is a pause as Eve begins to savor the experience. The first woman of the chorus, who echoed Eve's words to the serpent, now describes Eve's experience.

FIRST WOMAN OF THE CHORUS:
     And Eve looked
     At the creatures in the garden,
     And at the ground
     And at the wind and the water,
     And she said: I am not the same as these.
     And she began to examine
     Her skin and her eyes
     And her ears and her nose and her mouth.
     And she began to examine her own mind.
     And Eve went to Adam
     To persuade him to eat.
     But Adam said: You have eaten of that which was forbidden, and you
         shall die. Do you want me to eat and die too?"

Eve in a kind of frenzy has gone over to Adam, woken him up, and is trying to have him eat. He, at first, refuses but then is caught up in her frenzy and he eats too. After his first bite nothing seems to happen. The serpent freezes during Adam and Eve's argument but he has shared Eve's ecstasy. The three other women of the chorus "davenn" while the first woman describes the action. This davenning is a rhythmic murmur like that of old women in churches and synagogues as they repeat and repeat familiar prayers and laments.

FIRST WOMAN OF THE CHORUS:
     But Adam ate.

And Adam looked
At the creatures in the garden,
And at the ground
And at the wind and the water,
And he said: I am not the same as these.
And he began to examine
His skin and his eyes
And his ears and his nose and his mouth.
And he began to examine his own mind.
And he could neither spit out the fruit
Nor could he swallow it.

Adam takes a second bite. All the actors, in a kind of ecstasy, form the serpent, moving in the same manner as we saw the serpent move with fewer actors earlier. The serpent, as played by all the actors, is still a display of the tree of life. It is seductive and inviting. Then the serpent separates.

A bag of apples is found on one side of the stage. An actor empties it out on the stage. The actors play with the apples, eat them, and carry them out to the audience to share their pleasure with them.

The Curses

Adam begins to cough a little. It is clear that he can indeed neither swallow the fruit nor spit it out. Suddenly, an actor who has been playing one of the creatures in the garden pulls Adam up from under the arms. Adam himself speaks for God when God is speaking to Adam. When speaking for God, Adam uses a voice which is larger and more resonant than his usual one, and the actor who lifts him mouths the same words. Adam's own attitude, as he speaks for God, is one of surprise and dismay. Whenever God will speak, all the actors on stage will whisper his words too.

GOD (*speaking through Adam*): Where are you?
>*The actor who had lifted Adam up now drops him and goes back to playing a creature in the garden. Adam tries to hide, and he tries to cough up the fruit to be able to speak clearly to God. But the fruit remains stuck in his throat. The same actor picks him up again.*

GOD (*speaking through Adam*):
Where are you?
Why do you not answer me?
>*The actor lets Adam drop and becomes a creature in the garden again.*

ADAM (*answering God*):
I hear your voice in the garden
And I am afraid.
>*Adam is picked up again. Whenever he is picked up to speak, his body goes limp.*

GOD *(speaking through Adam):*
Before
When you heard my voice
You were not afraid,
Yet, now you are afraid.
        Adam is dropped again.
ADAM *(answering God):*
I am afraid
Because I am naked
And I have hidden myself.
        Adam is picked up again from under the arms.
GOD *(speaking through Adam):*
Who told you
You were naked?
Have you eaten of the tree
From which
I commanded you not to eat?
        Adam is dropped.
ADAM *(answering):*
Lord, so long as I was alone
I did not fall into sin.
But as soon as this woman came
She tempted me.
        Another actor now lifts up Eve in the same way Adam was lifted,
        and Eve is limp and speaks for God in a voice that is larger and
        more resonant than her usual one. The actor who lifts her, and the
        others, whisper the same words she is speaking.
GOD *(speaking through Eve):*
Woman, have you eaten of the tree
Whereof I commanded you not to eat?
        Eve is let drop, and the actor who had lifted her goes back to play-
        ing a creature in the garden.
EVE *(answering God):*
It was the serpent, Lord.
He tempted me, and I ate.
SERPENT 1: You gave them a command, and I contradicted it.
SERPENT 2:
Why did they obey me
And not you?

From now on the voice of God is heard similarly through the different actors on the stage. All, except the four women of the chorus, lift each other in
turn and speak with a voice that is larger than their usual ones. After lifting
or being lifted, the actors return to being creatures in the garden. As the curses
continue, there is a shorter space of time between them, and greater agitation

in the garden. And as the curses are spoken each by one actor, the other actors simultaneously whisper them to the audience.

GOD (*speaking through one actor who is lifted from under his arms by another actor*):
>Because you have done this
>You are cursed over all animals.
>Upon your belly shall you go
>And dust shall you eat.
>>*Speaking through another actor.*
>Because you have eaten
>Of the tree of which I commanded you,
>Saying: You shall not eat of it,
>Cursed is the earth for your sake.
>>*Speaking through another actor.*
>You shall use your mind
>Not to understand but to doubt.
>And even if you understand,
>Still shall you doubt.
>>*Speaking through another actor.*
>When your children shall be found to murder,
>You shall make laws.
>But these laws shall not bind.
>>*Speaking through another actor.*
>You shall be made to think,
>And although few of your thoughts shall exalt you,
>Many of your thoughts shall bring you sorrow,
>And cause you to forget your exaltation.
>>*Speaking through another actor.*
>Now shall come a separation
>Between the dreams inside your head
>And those things which you believe
>To be outside your head
>And the two shall war within you.
>>*Speaking through another actor.*
>Accursed, you shall be alone.
>For whatever you think,
>And whatever you see or hear,
>You shall think it and see it and hear it, alone.
>Henceforth shall you thirst after me.
>>*Speaking through another actor.*
>In the day shall you endure
>The same longing as in the night,
>And in the night shall you endure
>The same longing as in the day.

Henceforth shall you thirst after me.
> *Speaking through another actor.*

And your children shall live in fear of me.
And your children shall live in fear of you,
And your children shall live in fear of each other.
> *Speaking through another actor.*

Accursed, you shall glimpse Eden
All the days of your life.
But you shall not come again.
And if you should come,
You would not know it.
> *Speaking through another actor.*

And in the end
The earth shall wax old like a garment
And be cast off by me.
> *Speaking through another actor.*

For that you were not able to observe the command
Laid upon you, for more than one hour,
Accursed be your days.
Henceforth shall you thirst after me.

With the volume increasing, the curses begin to overlap. They are repeated and fragmented, spoken and whispered louder by an increasing number of actors. Many actors are regularly picked up and dropped. It becomes increasingly impossible to distinguish whole phrases. All the voices build into a frenzy and a din of sound.

GOD:
And in the day
Shall you endure the same longing
As in the night.
Henceforth shall you thirst after me.
And in the night
Shall you endure the same longing
As in the day.
Henceforth shall you thirst after me.
And now shall come a separation.
Accursed.
Between the dreams inside your head.
Accursed.
And those things which you believe to be outside your head
And the two shall war within you.
And your children shall live in fear of me.
And in the end the earth shall wax old like a garment
And be cast off by me.
And your children shall live in fear of you.

You shall not come again to Eden.
And your children shall live in fear of each other.
And if you should come, you would not know it.
Accursed, you shall be made to think.
Accursed, you shall be alone.
And even when you understand,
Still shall you doubt.
Accursed.
Accursed.
Accursed.

Suddenly, there is silence. All the actors remain frozen a few seconds. Then Adam and Eve repeat, and continue to repeat throughout the next scene, their "locked" action of, respectively, accusing, and of reaching and subsiding.

Statements 1

> *The four women are still kneeling.*

FIRST WOMAN OF THE CHORUS: In the beginning anything is possible.
SECOND WOMAN OF THE CHORUS: I've lost the beginning.
THIRD WOMAN OF THE CHORUS: I'm in the middle.
FOURTH WOMAN OF THE CHORUS: Knowing neither the end nor the beginning.

> *Now they stand. They sway slightly from side to side.*

FIRST WOMAN: One lemming.
SECOND WOMAN: One lemming.
THIRD WOMAN: One lemming.
FOURTH WOMAN: One lemming.

> *When they are not speaking their own statements each of the women continues to say softly "one lemming" as an accompaniment to what the others are saying.*

FIRST WOMAN:
   I try sometimes to imagine what it's like to be somebody else.
   But it's always me pretending.
   It has to be me.
   Who else is there?
SECOND WOMAN:
   I hugged my child
   And sent him off to school
   With his lunch in a paper bag.
   And I wished he would never come home.
THIRD WOMAN:
   I'm concerned
   Because what you reject
   Can still run your life.
FOURTH WOMAN: I passed my friend on the street.

SECOND WOMAN: I passed quite near.
FOURTH WOMAN:
  I don't think she saw me.
  If she did, I don't think
SECOND WOMAN: She saw me see her.
FOURTH WOMAN: I think she thought
SECOND WOMAN: If she saw me
FOURTH WOMAN: That I didn't see her.
THIRD WOMAN:
  If God exists
  It is through me.
  And He will protect me
  Because He owes His existence to me.
FIRST WOMAN:
  Old stories
  Have a secret.
SECOND WOMAN: They are a prison.
THIRD WOMAN: Someone is locked inside them.
FOURTH WOMAN:
  Sometimes, when it's very quiet,
  I can hear him breathing.
SECOND WOMAN:
  Sometimes I feel there's nothing to do
  But help other people.
  But as soon as I join a committee or a party
  I know that has nothing to do with it at all.
FOURTH WOMAN: Whatever I know
SECOND WOMAN: I know it without words.
FOURTH WOMAN: I am here as a witness.
SECOND WOMAN: To what?
FOURTH WOMAN: I don't know.
THIRD WOMAN:
  It was different when I was a child.
  I don't see any more bright colors.
  There are no solid blocks
  Or familiar rooms.
FIRST WOMAN:
  I went to a dinner.
  The guests were pleasant.
  We were poised,
  Smiling over our plates,
  Asking and answering the usual questions.
  I wanted to throw the food,
  Ax the table,
  Scratch the women's faces,
  And grab the men's balls.

SECOND WOMAN:
    When asked, I blamed it on the other person.
    It wasn't me, I said.
    It must have been her.
    I could have said it was me,
    But I said it was her.
THIRD WOMAN:
    My home was Cleveland.
    Then I came to New York
    And I didn't have to account to anybody.
    I smoked: pot, hashish, opium.
    I slept with a man.
    I slept with a woman.
    I slept with a man and a woman at the same time.
    But I'm a gentle person, and I collapsed.
FOURTH WOMAN: I'm still a child.
SECOND WOMAN: So am I.
FOURTH WOMAN:
    Sometimes people nod at you,
    And smile,
    And you know they haven't heard.
FIRST WOMAN: On a certain day
SECOND WOMAN: Of a certain year
THIRD WOMAN: One lemming
FOURTH WOMAN: Starts to run.
FIRST WOMAN: Another lemming, seeing the first,
SECOND WOMAN: Drops everything,
THIRD WOMAN: And starts to run too.
FOURTH WOMAN: Little by little
FIRST WOMAN: All the lemmings
SECOND WOMAN: From all over the country
THIRD WOMAN: Run together
FOURTH WOMAN: For tens
FIRST WOMAN: And hundreds of miles
SECOND WOMAN: Until,
FOURTH WOMAN: Exhausted,
FIRST WOMAN: They reach the cliff
SECOND WOMAN: And throw themselves
THIRD WOMAN: Into the sea.

Cain and Abel

The four women continue to davenn, but now without words, except when indicated. Davenning-without-words is like a rhythmic humming, and it continues under the voices of the individual women who are speaking. Cain chops wood. Abel tends two sheep. The scene begins slowly to unfold between them. It will continue beyond the recital of the action by the chorus.

FOURTH WOMAN:
 And when they were cast out
 Eve and Adam remembered me.
 And Eve conceived
 And bore Cain,
 And she said:
FOURTH AND SECOND WOMEN:
 "Lo, I have gotten
 A man from the Lord."
FOURTH WOMAN:
 And again Adam and Eve remembered me.
 And Eve bore Abel.
 And again she said:
FOURTH AND SECOND WOMEN:
 "Lo, I have gotten
 A man from the Lord."
FOURTH WOMAN:
 Then Eve had a dream,
 And she ran and told it to Adam.
 And Eve said:
 "Lo, I saw Adam's blood flow from Cain's mouth."
 And wishing to divert any evil that might come,
 Adam separated Cain from Abel.
 And Cain became a tiller of the ground,
 And Abel a keeper of sheep.
 And in time Cain offered unto the Lord
 A sacrifice of first fruits,
 While his brother Abel offered a firstborn lamb.
 And the Lord had love for Abel and for his offering.
 But for Cain and for his offering
 The Lord had no respect.
 And Cain said:
FOURTH AND FIRST WOMEN:
 "Why did He accept your offering
 And not mine?"
FOURTH WOMAN:
 And Cain's face grew dark,
 And his words were not pleasing to the Lord,
 And Cain said:
FOURTH AND FIRST WOMEN:
 "Why did He accept your offering
 And not mine?"
FOURTH WOMAN: "There is no law

And there is no judge."
And the Lord spoke within him,
And He said:
"If you will amend your ways
I will forgive your anger.
Yet even now the power of evil
Crouches at the door."
But it occurred to Cain
That the world was created through goodness,
Yet he saw that good deeds bear no fruit.
And God said:
"It depends on you
Whether you shall be master over evil,
Or evil over you."
And Cain said:
FOURTH AND FIRST WOMEN:
    "Why did He accept your offering
    And not mine?"
FOURTH WOMAN:
    And it occurred to Cain
    That the world
    Is ruled with an arbitrary power.
    And Cain said:
    "There is no law and there is no judge."
FOURTH AND FIRST WOMEN:
    "Else
    Why did He not accept my offering,
    Yet He accepted yours?"
FOURTH WOMAN:
    And it occurred to Cain
    To kill his brother.
    But it did not occur to Cain
    That killing his brother
    Would cause his brother's death.
    For Cain did not know how to kill
    And he struck at his brother.
    And broke each of his bones in turn
    And this was the first murder.
    And Cain said:
    "If I were to spill your blood on the ground
    As you do the sheep's,
    Who is there to demand it of me?"
    And Abel said:
    "The Lord will demand it. The Lord will judge."
    And Cain said:

"There is no judge. There is no law."

FOURTH AND FIRST WOMEN:
"Else
Why did He accept your offering
And not accept mine?"

FOURTH WOMAN:
"Why yours?
Why not mine?"
And it occurred to Cain
To kill his brother.
But it did not occur to Cain
That killing his brother
Would cause his brother's death.
For Cain did not know how to kill.
And he struck at his brother
And broke each of his bones in turn.
And Abel said: "The Lord will judge."
And Cain said:
"There is no judge. There is no law."

FOURTH AND FIRST WOMEN:
"Else
Why did he accept your offering
And not accept mine?"

FOURTH WOMAN:
"Why yours?
Why not mine?"
And this was the first murder.
For it occurred to Cain
To kill his brother.
But it did not occur to Cain
That killing his brother
Would cause his brother's death.

Cain has come over to Abel. He feeds Abel's sheep, to get them out of his way. He looks at Abel, and Abel looks back at Cain. The rest of the actors, not including the chorus, breathe together regularly and quietly—they are breathing Abel's breath. Cain tries different ways of killing Abel. After trying each different way, he looks at Abel to see the result of what he has done, and to try to decide what to do next. The rest of the company watches, and the sheep remain quietly by. Some of the things that Cain does to Abel are to pull at his limbs, to hold him in the air and think of dashing him on the ground. Finally, he lays Abel down on the ground, and seeing that there is still movement in the respiratory area, Cain uses his hands to chop at Abel's throat. Abel's breathing stops.

All the sounds for hurting Abel and for the chopping at him with his hands have come from the actor playing Cain, rather than from the actor playing

Abel. Now Cain listens for Abel's breathing, which he misses hearing. He tries to breathe breath back into Abel from his own mouth. Then he tries to stand Abel up. He puts grass into his lifeless hand to try to have Abel feed the sheep. Finally, he lays Abel down on the backs of his two sheep, standing behind him, swaying slightly from side to side, waiting, waiting for life to start up again in Abel. The heron from the garden is back, and it wanders near, making its gentle noise and standing on one leg and then the other. Cain continues to wait.

The four women of the chorus make a small, long screeching sound from the backs of their throats. Abel, as a ghost, now crawls on his knees toward the front of the stage. He confronts the audience. The actor playing Abel is, at this moment, experiencing extreme tension throughout his body, and re-seeing in his mind's eye what just happened to him. Cain, still watching the place where he put Abel's body on the sheep, continues to wait.

Blind Men's Hell

The two actors who played the sheep, and one other actor, are on their backs on the floor. All the others, with the exception of the chorus, walk around and through them. All are blind and as if experiencing tremendous fatigue. They are like people who have lived too long. None of those who are walking may stop or fall—if they do, they must immediately get up and go on. Those on the floor grope upward, grabbing at parts of the moving people. This continues during Statements II.

Statements II

FIRST WOMAN OF THE CHORUS:
    In the beginning
    Anything is possible.
    From the center
    I can choose to go anywhere.
SECOND WOMAN OF THE CHORUS:
    But now the point
    Toward which I have chosen to go
    Has a line drawn
    Between itself
    And the beginning.
FOURTH WOMAN OF THE CHORUS:
    I no longer know the beginning.
    I am in the middle.
    On a line
    Between the beginning
    And a point toward which I chose to go.
THIRD WOMAN OF THE CHORUS:
    I have fewer choices now.
    Because when I change my direction

The change can only start
From a line already drawn.
> *Now the four women smile. They keep smiling unless they are
> speaking. They sway slightly from side to side.*

SECOND WOMAN:
I'm collecting things.
Beads.
I'm buying plants,
Curtains—
With which to make a home.
I'm buying things
To make a good life.

THIRD WOMAN:
When I was thirteen
I wanted a house of my own.
The girl I was then
Would say to me now:
"What have you done with your advantages?"
You could have married a rich man,
And had a big house.
Instead, you're a freak."

FIRST WOMAN *(as the other women and herself open and close one fist):*
Open.
Close.
Open.
Close.
No effort
Makes these two movements
One.

SECOND WOMAN:
My husband is in that coffin.
In the day he goes to work.
In the evening we discuss household matters.
And at night
He climbs back into the coffin.

THIRD WOMAN:
Even if you sit and do nothing,
Even so,
Your back is strapped to a wheel,
And the wheel turns.

FOURTH WOMAN: While we were in bed I asked a boy,
SECOND WOMAN: I asked him if he should be around
FIRST WOMAN:
If he should be around when I die,
Would he hold and rock me in his arms
For half an hour afterwards.

THIRD WOMAN: Because they can't tell.

FOURTH WOMAN: They can only approximate.

SECOND WOMAN: They can't tell when you're really dead.

FIRST WOMAN: Not exactly.

THIRD WOMAN: Not the exact moment.

SECOND WOMAN:
When I was a child
This story was told to me in secret by a friend:
"A little boy came into his mother's room
And saw her naked.
'What's that?' he asked.
'It's a wound,' she said.
'What happened to your penis?' he asked.
'Oh,' she said,
'God chopped it off with an ax.' "

THIRD WOMAN (*with other women speaking and emphasizing the words "he," "his," and "him"*):
It's my husband.
He keeps me from it.
It's *his* fault.
He keeps me down, holds me at *his* level.
I could be happy
If it weren't for *him*.

FOURTH WOMAN:
The doctors lie.
My mother died screaming with pain.
Did you know you could go into eternity
Screaming with pain?

FIRST WOMAN (*as the other women and herself open and close one fist*):
Open.
Close.
Separate movements.
Stretched-out fingers.
Nails into skin.
One to open.
One to close.
Separate
Motions.
No matter how I try,
These movements
Are not one.
There is a stop between open
And close, and between close
And open.
No effort
Makes these two movements

One.
Close.
Open.
Close.

SECOND WOMAN: You can see them having lunch,
FIRST WOMAN: Their faces pale,
THIRD WOMAN:
Laughing.
They are corpses laughing.
FOURTH WOMAN: You can see them on the streets,
SECOND WOMAN: Combed and brushed.
FIRST WOMAN: They are colored pictures.
FIRST AND THIRD WOMEN: The men have killed each other.
SECOND AND FOURTH WOMEN: The king is dead.
FOURTH WOMAN: He was shot in the head.
FIRST WOMAN: By an unknown assassin.
SECOND WOMAN: The men are dead.
THIRD WOMAN:
And no man can say
Of work or land:
"This is mine."
FIRST AND SECOND WOMEN: The men are dead.
SECOND WOMAN: We mourn them.
THIRD AND FOURTH WOMEN: We are dead.
THIRD WOMAN: We mourn ourselves.
FOURTH WOMAN:
If a bulldog ant
Is cut in two,
A battle starts
Between the head and the tail.
The head bites the tail.
The tail stings the head.
They fight
Until both halves are dead.
THIRD WOMAN:
So Man created God.
What for?
To set limits on himself.
FIRST WOMAN:
Would my dreams recognize me?
Would they come to me and say
"She's the one who imagined us"?
THIRD WOMAN:
I was queen over a country
Where the air was sweet.
We ate honey and fruit.
And at night

It was quiet.
SECOND WOMAN:
Suddenly—
This moment.
Here, now.
I am here,
And you.
In this place, now
We are together.

FIRST WOMAN (*as the other three women, and finally she, begin to make the body sounds of the entering procession*):
At the very end.
Even after the end,
Even when the body is on its own,
The human being can make such a variety
Of sounds that it's amazing.
A field of dead men is loud.
Teeth clack, bones crack,
Limbs twist and drop,
And the last sound of all
Is a loud trumpet
Of escaping wind.

Begatting

Now all together the four women begin davenning again, for a moment without words. The Blind Men's Hell has dissolved. Two actors, a man and a woman, begin very slowly approaching each other from either side of the stage. The four women are kneeling and rocking back and forth. All the others begin gently to explore each other's bodies.

THIRD WOMAN (*as the other three davenn under her words*):
And Adam knew Eve and Eve knew Adam
And this was the first time.
And Adam knew Eve and Eve knew Adam
And this was the first time.

The actors are exploring each other's bodies as if for the first time. The women now open a book and read the "begats" from the Old Testament of the Bible. Each woman reads some part and then passes the book to another. But all are continually davenning and, frequently, the exact words of the begatting are lost in favor of the rhythmic davenning and the rocking back and forth toward the audience.

THIRD WOMAN (*reading*): "And Adam lived a hundred and thirty years and he begat a son in his own likeness and he called his name Seth. And the days of Adam after he had begotten Seth were eight hundred years, and he begat sons and daughters. And Seth lived a hundred and five years and he begat Enos. And Seth lived after he begat Enos eight hundred and seven years, and he begat sons and daughters. And Enos lived ninety years and he begat Cainan. And Enos lived after he begat Cainan eight hundred and fifteen years, and he begat sons and daughters. And Cainan lived seventy years and begat Mahalaleel."

The man and woman come closer and closer to touching. The others have paired off, too, and are still exploring bodies.

FOURTH WOMAN *(reading):* "And Cainan lived, after he begat Mahalaleel, eight hundred and forty years, and he begat sons and daughters. And Mahalaleel lived sixty and five years, and he begat Jared. And Mahalaleel lived, after he begat Jared, eight hundred and thirty years, and he begat sons and daughters. And Jared lived a hundred and sixty and two years, and he begat Enoch. And Jared lived after he begat Enoch eight hundred years, and he begat sons and daughters. And Enoch lived sixty and five years and he begat Methuselah. And Enoch walked with God after he begat Methuselah three hundred years, and he begat sons and daughters. And Enoch walked with God and he was not, for God took him. And Methuselah lived a hundred and eighty and seven years, and he begat Lamech. And Methuselah lived after he begat Lamech seven hundred and eighty and two years, and he begat sons and daughters. And Lamech lived a hundred eighty and two years and he begat a son, and he called his name Noah. And Lamech lived after he begat Noah five hundred and ninety years, and he begat sons and daughters. And Noah was five hundred years old, and Noah begat Shem and Ham and Japheth."

By now, the two people have met in the center of the stage and embraced. All the couples are now exploring each other more gymnastically. They are trying to find how to make the connection between the male and the female body. They try various difficult positions. Eventually all make the connection and they copulate in increasingly faster rhythm.

FIRST WOMAN *(reading):* "And these are the generations of the sons of Noah and Shem and Ham and Japheth and the sons that were born to them after the flood: The sons of Japheth were Gomer and Magog and Madai and Javan and Tubal and Meshech and Tiras. And the sons of Gomer were Ashkenaz and Riphath and Togarmah. And the sons of Javan were Elishah and Tarshish and Kittim and Dodanim. And the sons of Ham were Cush and Mizraim and Phut and Canaan. And the sons of Cush were Seba and Havilah and Sabtah and Raamah and Sabtechah. And the sons of Raamah were Sheba and Dedan. And Cush begat Nimrod, and he began to be a mighty one on earth. And Canaan begat Sidon, his firstborn, and Heth. And unto Shem were born Elam and Ashur and Arphaxad and Lud and Aram. And the children of Aram were Uz and Hul and Gether and Mash. And Arphaxad begat Salah, and Salah begat Eber. And unto Eber were born two sons, and one was called Peleg, and his brother's name was Joktan. And Joktan begat Almodad and Shelaph and Hazarmaveth and Jerah. And Hadoram and Uzal and Diklah."

All the couples reach their climax at approximately the same time. Immediately afterward, the women go into labor, and they then give birth. Their sons are played by the actors who played their lovers. After the birth, the mothers teach their children how to talk, walk, play games, etc.

SECOND WOMAN *(reading):* "And Obal and Abimael and Sheba, and Ophir and Havilah and Johab. All these were the sons of Joktan. And these were the generations of Shem. Shem was a hundred years old and begat Arphaxad two years after the flood. And Shem lived after he begat Arphaxad five hundred years, and he begat sons and daughters. And Arphaxad lived five and thirty years and he begat Salah. And Arphaxad lived after he begat Salah four hundred and three years, and he begat sons and daughters. And Salah lived thirty years and he begat Eber. And Salah lived after he begat Eber four hundred and three years, and he begat sons and daughters. And Eber lived four hundred and thirty years and he begat Peleg. And Eber lived after he begat Peleg four hundred and thirty years, and he begat sons and daughters. And Peleg lived thirty years and he begat Reu. And Peleg lived after he begat Reu two hundred and nine years, and he begat sons and daughters. And Reu lived thirty and two years, and he begat Serug. And Reu lived after he begat Serug two hundred and seven years, and he begat sons and daughters. And Serug lived thirty years and he begat Nahor. And Serug lived after he begat Nahor two hundred years, and he begat sons and daughters. And Nahor lived twenty and nine years, and he begat Terah. And Nahor lived after he begat Terah a hundred and nineteen years and he begat sons and daughters. And Terah lived seventy years, and he begat Abram and Nahor and Haran. And these are the generations of Terah."

From being small children, the men of the company have become very old people. They are brought forward, helped slowly, to the front of the stage by their mothers, who have remained young. One or two of the actresses play old women and also stay at the front of the stage.

THIRD WOMAN *(reading):* "Terah begat Isaac, and Isaac begat Jacob and Jacob begat Judah and his brethren. And Judah begat Phares and Zarah, of Thamar. And Phares begat Esrom. And Esrom begat Aram. And Aram begat Aminadab. And Aminadab begat Naasson. And Naasson begat Salmon. And Salmon begat Booz, of Rachab. And Booz begat Obed, of Ruth. And Obed begat Jesse. And Jesse begat David the king. And David the king begat Solomon, of her that had been the wife of Urias. And Solomon begat Rehoboam. And Rehoboam begat Abia. And Abia begat Asa. And Asa begat Josaphat. And Josaphat began Joram. And Joram begat Ozias. And Ozias begat Joatham. And Joatham began Achaz. And Achaz begat Ezekias. And Ezekias begat Manasses. And Manasses begat Amon. And Amon begat Josias. And Josias begat Jechonias and his brethren about the time they were carried away to Babylon. And after they were brought to Babylon, Jechonias begat Salathiel. And Salathiel begat Zorobabel. And Zorobabel begat Abiud. And Abiud begat Eliakim. And Eliakim begat Azor. And Azor begat Sadoc. And Sadoc begat Achim. And Achim begat Eliud. And Eliud begat Eleazur. And Eleazur begat Mathan. And Mathan begat Jacob. And Jacob begat Joseph."

Old People

There is now a line of old people facing the audience at the front of the stage. They speak out a name or two, or mumble, from the many names of the "begatting." The four women of the chorus are davenning without words. The other actresses, the ones who have just played the mothers, are at the back of the stage, and they davenn, too, softly.

The Song

The actors move about freely on the stage. Each is overtaken by a slow kind of dying, not so much a physical one as a kind of "emptying out," a living death which soon slows them to a complete stop. Each actor has a final small physical tremor. Then, as if ghosts, the actors begin to sing a sentimental popular song from twenty or thirty years ago. No longer as ghosts but as themselves they continue singing the song as they leave the theater, walking out through the audience.

*   *   *

Editor's note: Then, at the 1969-70 New York production, there was silence—hushed silence. Gradually the audience understood that the play was over and began to applaud—first tentatively, then loudly, in direct person-to-person communication with the Open Theater actors, who had now intermingled with the spectators. After the applause finally subsided, the audience left the theater together with the actors in their midst, discussing the play with them.

○
○
○

Special Additional Citation:

THE ROCK LYRIC

○
○
○

In *The Last Sweet Days of Isaac, The Me Nobody Knows, Mod Donna, Operation Sidewinder* (incidental music)*, Sambo, Stomp*

AND SALVATION, WITH EXCERPTS FROM ITS TEXT

THE ROCK LYRIC is a literary form developed in this decade; as different from the June-moon cadences of our rose-colored memory as the Beatles from the Lombardo brothers; a pounding, psychedelic, powerful and versatile new word style to match the new music, expressive of any feeling from despair to ecstasy, of any social comment from "You can get anything you want at Alice's Restaurant" to "Let it be."

Not only are the many rock combos being heard word for word in overflow live concerts (see Robert Schroeder's report on the off-off-Broadway scene in this volume) and in every audio medium; the rock lyric has also made its mark on the living stage. It is firmly established on Broadway and around the world in the Gerome Ragni-James Rado-Galt MacDermot musical Hair. This season, the rock lyric was so prominent a part of the musical scene, particularly off Broadway, that it would be inappropriate to close a section of 1969-70 "bests" without citing it, if not among the ten Best Plays in an individual show, at least high up among the most exciting elements of the contemporary stage. We cite its effective contribution to new shows this season, as follows:

As an expression of youthful curiosity, identity crisis and abiding hopefulness in *The Last Sweet Days of Isaac,* lyrics by Gretchen Cryer.

As the idiom of slum children expressing their fears, frustrations and loneliness, more in sorrow than in anger, in *The Me Nobody Knows,* lyrics by Will Holt (four lyrics are children's poems, exactly as written).

As the language of protest by Women's Liberation partisans in *Mod Donna,* lyrics by Myrna Lamb; and of protest against white society's alienation of blacks in *Sambo,* lyrics by Ron Steward.

265

As interpolated, sardonic commentary to a non-musical dramatization of the insanity of violence and superpower in *Operation Sidewinder*, lyrics by Sam Shepard and others.

As a cry from the very heart of youth in its reaction to love, the environment, social injustice, etc. in the multimedia show *Stomp*, lyrics by The Combine (University of Texas students).

As a satirical comment on moral and ethical poses in *Salvation*, lyrics by Peter Link and C.C. Courtney.

Below is a sampling of Salvation's *rock lyrics in the form of an abbreviated synopsis of the show, including just enough of the onstage action to establish the context within which each individual song was presented.*

SYNOPSIS: A rock combo warms up and begins to play but is interrupted by a preacher-like figure, Monday, who berates the audience.

MONDAY: You are spiders who can't see the flames of hell, because the flames are black, but they are licking up and God is watching you, and He's gonna say, "Depart from me ye wicked sinner!" and the web will snap and you will fall into that bottomless pit. If all the pain, suffering and illness that has ever existed were concentrated into one second and that second expanded for eternity, that would be hell. And you're going! Because you're a spider! And you're a spider! *(Sings: "Salvation.")*

You're a spider. You're a spider
A longlegged, spindly-legged, crosseyed, eight legged spider
The Lord done told me He's mad at you
He's sick of your sinful ways
He's just about ready to wipe you out
He's just countin' the days
Come, come, on, come on, come, on, come on!
(Speaks.) Come up here and give your testimony for Jesus.
    Pause. Monday offers microphone to audience.
RANEE: I'm a spider.
MONDAY: Amen sister, let's hear that testimony.

Ranée comes up onto the stage from the audience like a repentent sinner at a revival meeting. So do Dierdre, Leroy, Marc and Betty Lou. They join in the "Salvation" number.

The revival meeting comes to an end when the others dress Monday in ec-
clesiatical robes. Now Monday is a Catholic priest hearing confessions.

BETTY LOU *(kneels and sings "In Between")*:
    You, I wanted you, in the mornin' and over again
    You, I wanted you, in the evenin' and over again
    And in between, and in between and in between
    I wanted all of your friends! . . . . .
LEROY *(sings "1001")*:
    . . . . . I don't know why: I just can't quit
    I been doin' it since I was ten
    I promise you, Lord, forgive me one more time
        Kneels.
    And I'll never, ever do it again.

    I don't want hair in the palm of my hand
    To be nearsighted or blind
    I don't want to be locked up ravin' insane
    To be flipped out of my mind

    Oh, no, no, no.
    I promise you, Lord, forgive me one more time
    I know I've said this a thousand times before
    Please, Lord, please forgive me just this time
    I swear on the Bible I'll never do it no more. . . . .

In the audience, Farley rises impatiently and starts to leave the theater but
gets into an argument with Monday, who deplores the crumbling of contemporary morality. On stage, the cast goes into "Honest Confession Is Good for
the Soul," and Farley and Boo join them from the audience.

BOO *(rises in the audience and sings)*:
    I don't think the things I do are really all that bad
    In fact at the time I'm doin' them,
    They always make me glad
    It's only when someone sees me smilin'
    They tell me it's a sin
    But that just makes it much more fun, and I go back and do it again.
        She ends in a dance to the stage. . . . .
FARLEY:
    What came first, sin or fun
    They sure do seem the same
    Maybe somebody called it fun
    And somebody changed the name
    And ever since then we've been confused
    While you keep playing your games.
    We're up here trying to plug it in

You make us feel ashamed
Now you gonna tell me to shut my mouth
Or wind up in the fiery hole
But now it's time for me to say
Honest confession is good for the soul. . . . .

Monday addresses the rest of the cast like a Sunday school teacher. He asks
them to tell him what Sundays were made for, and they respond with the song
"Ballin' ".

FARLEY *(sings):*
Monday used to be washday.
BOO:
But now they're made of paper, so I throw them away.
MONDAY: O.K. Ranée.
RANEE *(sings):*
Tuesday's kind of useless,
Ties Monday to Wednesday.
MONDAY: Marc.
MARC *(sings):*
Wednesday's in the middle of the week
And it's all down hill from there.
MONDAY: O.K. Leroy.
LEROY *(sings):*
Thursday's the day you don't wear green
Case some fool wants to call you a queen
MONDAY: Dierdre.
DIERDRE *(sings):*
Friday's the day you get your pay.
MONDAY: Betty Lou.
BETTY LOU *(sings):*
Saturday's the day you throw it all away. . . . .
FARLEY:
. . . . . And keep on ballin' all the way through Sunday.
The sun comes up. And we go down
To the Rolling Stones on the record machine. . . . .
        Joined by Boo and cast.
Sundays are made for going to the beach
Or ridin' on bikes in the park
But you and me, baby, gonna get it on right
Ballin' all the way through Saturday night
Ballin' all the way through Sunday. . . . .

Monday asks for a confession from Dierdre, and she obliges with "Let the
Moment Slip By."

DIERDRE *(sings):*
>In the fullness of the moment, I wanted him so bad
>As we lay there covered by the shadow of my dad
>I know it sounds silly, but I wish I never had
>Let the moment slip by. . . . .
>
>In the glory of emotion, it was I who kept my calm
>I fought off his advances with the wisdom of my mom . . .

BETTY LOU: What?

DIERDRE: I fought off his advances with the wisdom of my mom.

MARC: What?

DIERDRE: With the wisdom of my mom.

ALL *(improvised):* Oh wow! I don't believe it. How stupid can you get?

MONDAY: Hush, hush your mouth. Go ahead, Dierdre. I think it's a lovely song.

DIERDRE *(sings):*
>And now he's at the bottom of a hole in Vietnam
>I let the moment slip by.
>
>I close my eyes and feel him then
>I can only scream, "What might have been!"
>
>In the fullness of the moment
>   *(Breaks off, cries.)*
>I needed him so bad.

Urged to play another game, the cast sings "Gina," a song about a swing ("Come on, Gina, get in the swing: let me push you for a while/Come on, Gina, let me hear you sing. I'm gonna make you smile/Now ready, now set, now one, two, three/Together now let's pump/Oh, Gina, it feels so good. You gonna make me jump. . . . .").

Following the number "Stockhausen Pot Pourri" (a chant orchestrated from four-letter and other obscenities), the cast goes into "If You Let Me Make Love to You, Why Can't I Touch You?"

ALL *(sing):*
>If you let me make love to you, then why can't I touch you?
>If you let me make love to you, then why can't I touch you?
>I'm not saying I want to change you
>I don't want to rearrange you
>But if you let me make love to you, then why can't I touch you? . . . . .

MARC & RANEE:
>. . . . . You're like frozen flame
>It sure seems a shame
>That you let me make love to you
>But won't let me touch you.

ALL:

. . . . . Reach out, reach out, reach out, touch me
Open up, open up, open up, open, receive me.
Flowing through my fingertips are all my journeys, all my trips
Take all I have to give. Open up and live.
Touch me, touch me, touch me, touch me. . . . .

The cast moves into a revival hymn-type number "There Ain't No Flies on Jesus." Monday observes that "There ain't no flies on Moses, either" and begins reciting the Commandments. Ranée interrupts him with "Deadalus," in which a leering doctor, examining her, demands "every vivid detail of what that man did to you!"

RANEE *(sings):*
　　Like the sun through the wind he eased into my life
　　And I melted like a pair of waxen wings
　　Then he wrapped himself around me:
　　And in the darkness of my mind
　　He hung about a thousand glowing rings.

　　Soft and sleepy was the morning
　　Slow and easy was the day
　　Falling gently was the night time
　　And the time just slipped away
　　Till one cloudy Tuesday morning I woke up alone
　　And most of him was gone, most of him was gone.
　　Most of him was gone—away.

　　Like the sun through the wind, he eased into my life.
　　　　*Monday nods to her in approval as the rhythm intro starts. The cast
　　　　whispers repetitively.*
BOYS: No God but me.
GIRLS: You will not kill.
MARC *(sings "Deuteronomy XVII Verse 2"):*
　　In a straightback chair at the dining room table
　　With my Bible at my hand
　　Reading what God said, God said, God said
　　Thinkin' 'bout the holy plan
　　When in she walked with a birthday cake
　　That she spent the whole day tryin' to bake.
BETTY LOU:
　　Happy birthday! I love you!
MARC:
　　And she was so beautiful.
　　But I had to read my Bible
　　Readin' what God said, God said, God said.
GIRLS:

Woman said:

BETTY LOU:

Honey, let's go out to the game on Sunday
And watch Joe Namath play.

GIRLS:

Man said:

MARC:

How can we go to the game on Sunday
That's the Sabbath, not a fun day.

GIRLS:

Joe Namath. Nearer my God to Thee (oh, Lord)
Joe Namath, nearer my God to Thee.

MARC *(spoken):* Oh Lord, oh blessed Savior, shine Thy light of grace on me.

GIRLS *(sing):*

But then woman said:

BETTY LOU:

You sound like a Bible-belt Baptist preacher
Tryin' to waste my only day off
I don't want to hear it from a Sunday school teacher
Gonna watch old Joe in the playoff.

MARC:

I picked up the birthday cake, and I threw it in her face
She stood there stunned and silent
With "birth" written backwards across her forehead
But I knew what it really said was "death,"
And she was dead.

Salty tears streaming through the sweetness on her face
And I knew she was just a step away from Jesus' grace
She didn't move as I walked to the counter at her back
She didn't move as I removed the cleaver from the rack
She didn't move as I chopped away the icing from her cheek
She didn't move as I chopped away a chunk of chosen meat
She didn't move, she stood there as I struck a dozen more
She didn't move till she crumpled on the bloody, fleshy floor.

GIRLS:

And woman said:

BETTY LOU:

You, I wanted you in the morning, and over again.

MARC:

Lord, I said, I have kept Your commandment
Now look down from heaven on me
Well done, my good and faithful servant,
Cause it was either she or me.

GIRLS:

And God said—God said:

MONDAY: God said in Deuteronomy 17 Verse 2: If there be found among you man or woman that hath gone and served other gods, and worshipped them, and thou hast heard of it, then shalt thou bring that man or woman which have committed that wicked thing, even that man or that woman, though it be thy wife, to the gates of the city and thou shalt stone them with stones— till they die.

> *Marc is totally lost. Farley takes him by the shoulders and turns him to face Leroy.*

LEROY & MARC *(sing "For Ever"):*
I walk through the concrete
And hear the people quickly, quickly breathing
I stare through plate glass
And see them quietly passing paper green. Oooh.
I listen to suspended steel ringing cold and clear to me
That I should just forget my thoughts of leaving
For there are still a million things
I haven't heard or seen, seen, seen. Oooh.

> *Girls mix.*

Why do you walk so fast
When you're really on your way to no place?
Why do you talk so loud
As if there's no one there to hear the words you say? . . . . .

Close your eyes and feel the sound
Of the earth as it goes spinning round and round
Even God must have His ups and downs
Even God must have His ups and downs
And if you were here yesterday
You'll still be here tomorrow.

> *The other cast members scurry robot-like upstage center. The band creates an explosion of sound. The cast moves faster and faster until they explode in slow motion and fall to the floor. Boo and Leroy rise from the rubble.*

BOO & LEROY *(sing):*
Young, young young is what I want to be

Footloose youth and fancy free
Just a few years 'tween them and me
Through time-dimmed, dried-up eyes I see
Footloose youth and fancy free. . . . .

The cast takes up a collection among the audience and then lines up together in a show of ecumenism, each representing a different denomination.

CAST *(sings "Schwartz"):*
The ecumenical movement means no more religious war

No longer will the Christian crusade against the Moor
So come on, sisters and brothers, let's get together and love one another's.
Peace and brotherhood is our goal
God grant us the wisdom to control
We'll push them atheistic commies out the door. Amen.

One by one the cast members leave the group because of disputes over dogma, until Monday is left by himself.

After a blackout, all the cast gathers round to smoke from a giant Coke bottle resembling a hookah.

MONDAY: You guys take it easy. There's a lot of trouble at the Mexican border so we're smoking Coke tonight.

MARC *(sings "Let's Get Lost in Now"):*
    When it gets right down to the bottom of the hole
    You don't really care much about nothin'
    Do you, baby?
    And when it gets right down to the hot hard facts
    Neither do I!
    Ooo-ooo-ooo-ooo.

    So let's make love, and maybe tomorrow
    If we still feel the same, we can do it again
    But meanwhile close your eyes
    And let's get lost in now. . . . .

The cast wanders around pretending to be stoned. Farley reminds Monday of all the religious roles he has been assuming—Catholic, Baptist, Holy Roller, etc.

LEROY: Then you were pretty heavy on the touch thing.
BOO: Now you're a bona fide disciple of Timothy Leary.
MARC: Make up your mind.
MONDAY *(after a moment):* God is a verb. We're all going to have to get used to it.
CAST *(sings "Back to Genesis" as Ranée does scats underneath):*
    Boo bop bee doop bah
    Boo bop bee doop bah. . . . .
MEN:
    Back to Genesis
GIRLS:
    We're gonna sock it to Socrates
RANEE:
    Come on let's go
RANEE & MEN:
    Back to Genesis—now!

RANEE:

I don't know where we're going
I don't know how to get there
I don't know why but after a while we'll have to go. . . . .
Back to Bobby Kennedy: back to his brother John
Back to Franklin Roosevelt: back to before the bomb
    Cast does "Ah oom bop shoo bop" under the next two lines.
Back to Wilhelm Reich: back to Sigmund Freud
Back before IBM: before the human being was destroyed.

MEN:

Jenny, Jenny, Jenny, Jenny, Jenny, Jenny, Jenny, Jenny. . . . .
Back to Genesis.

GIRLS:

Back to the simple songs: back to the blackland dirt
Back to the kerosine lamps: back to pre-pervert
Back to the singletree plow: back to the watermelon patch
Back to the Sears, Roebuck catalogue
Back to the old outhouse—

MEN:

Outhouse

DIERDRE:

My country 'tis of spacious skies, from every mountainside.
The bombs bursting in the Pilgrims' pride, from every mountainside

ALL:

Freedom and the rockets' red glare, of thee I sing

MONDAY:

Baby!

ALL:

From the fruited ramparts we watched God shed
His terrible swift sword on thee
Ah ah ah. . . . .

The cast explores lyrically the nature of God, then drifts into a reprise of
snatches of previous lyrics. Finally Monday settles into the number "Tomorrow Is the First Day of the Rest of My Life."

MONDAY *(sings):*

A million sighing raindrops falling far into the night
As I lie here all alone waiting for the light
Old pains and old regrets are slowly washed away
And tomorrow is the first day of the rest of my life.

ALL:

Tomorrow is the first day of the rest of my life
And all that went before today are my haunting memories
Loves I've known: and loves I've lost, and loves I've never had
Are shadows now upon the wall of time.

And the circle of my life lies all around me
And I see that my future lies right behind me
I turn around and see my past, a stage to stand upon.

FARLEY:

And let the light shine brightly in the morning

ALL:

I'll let my light shine brightly in the morning
I see myself more clearly in the dawning
Faith and hope shine brightly in the morning
Through myself I'll find them shining in the morning
Tomorrow is the first day of the rest of my life!

Lights out. Applause. Cast stands.

Reach out, reach out, reach out, touch me
Open up, open up, open up, open, receive me
Flowing through my fingertips are all my journeys, all my trips
Take all I have to give. Open up and live.

Lights fade. Curtain.

The Open Theater Ensemble in *The Serpent*

Sada Thompson as Beatrice in *The Effect of Gamma Rays on Man-in-the-Moon Marigolds*

Fritz Weaver as Jerome Malley in *Child's Play* (FAR RIGHT)

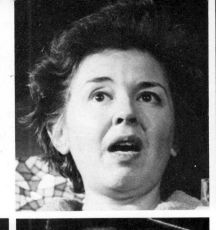

Peter Maloney in Open Theater repertory (FAR LEFT)

Lewis J. Stadlen as Groucho Marx in *Minnie's Boys*

James Stewart as Elwood P. Dowd in *Harvey*

Catherine Burns as Janet Rosenberg in *Dear Janet Rosenberg, Dear Mr. Kooning* (FAR RIGHT)

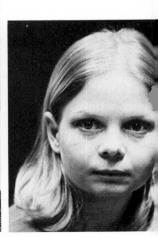

Sam Levene as Daniel Brand in *Paris Is Out* (FAR LEFT)

Stacy Keach as Buffalo Bill in *Indians*

Keir Dullea as Don Baker in *Butterflies Are Free*

Cleavon Little as Purlie in *Purlie* (FAR RIGHT)

Frank Grimes as young Brendan Behan in *Borstal Boy* (FAR LEFT)

Katharine Hepburn as Coco in *Coco*

Austin Pendleton as Isaac in *The Last Sweet Days of Isaac*

Lauren Bacall as Margo Channing in *Applause* (FAR RIGHT)

James Coco as Barney Cashman in *Last of the Red Hot Lovers* (FAR LEFT)

Zoe Caldwell as Colette in *Colette*

Stacy Keach as Buffalo Bill, Manu Tupou as Sitting Bull (*at top*) and tribesmen in Arthur Kopit's *Indians*

Designs for *Indians: Above,* photo of Oliver Smith's model of the setting; *below* samples of Marjorie Slaiman's costume sketches

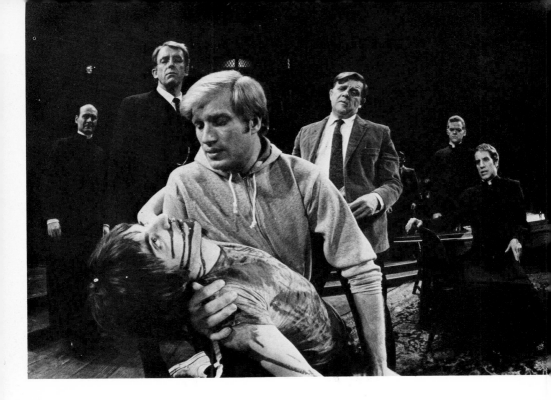

Above, in Robert Marasco's *Child's Play,* a schoolboy victim of violence lies in the arms of a young athletic instructor (Ken Howard) while two lay teachers (Fritz Weaver and Pat Hingle) and three priests look on. *Below,* Jo Mielziner's setting for the melodrama in a boys' school, the stairwell (*at left*) and the faculty room of *Child's Play.*

Linda Lavin and James Coco in Neil Simon's *Last of the Red Hot Lovers*

Blind son (Keir Dullea), anxious mother (Eileen Heckart) and girl next door (Blythe Danner) in Leonard Gershe's *Butterflies Are Free*

Right, Barbara Eda-Young, Andy Robinson and friend in *Operation Sidewinder*

Below, Sam Levene gets a going-away present admired by Molly Picon and Dorothy Sands in *Paris Is Out!*

Above, Dennis King and Maximilian Schell at a drag ball in John Osborne's *A Patriot for Me*. *Right*, Freddy Wittop designs for *Patriot* costumes

Left, Richard Castellano and Martin Gabel in *Sheep on the Runway*

Jeanne Pasle-Green, James Burge and Tom Fuccello
playing nudists in *Grin and Bare It!*

Rosenbergs on trial in *Inquest: left to right,* the judge (Michael Lipton), Ethel
(Anne Jackson), defense attorney (James Whitmore), prosecutors (Mason
Adams and Mike Bursten) and Julius (George Grizzard). Large figures are
projections on screens behind the courtroom scene

Above, five couples and a bachelor in Boris Aronson's setting for *Company:* Charles Braswell, Elaine Stritch, Charles Kimbrough, Barbara Barrie, George Coe, Teri Ralston, John Cunningham, Merle Louise, Steve Elmore, Beth Howland and Dean Jones. *Below,* a Michael Bennett dance number in the George Furth-Stephen Sondheim musical

MUSICALS

Right, Ethel Merman as Dolly in the Broadway cast of *Hello, Dolly!*

Below, a scene from *Purlie:* Cleavon Little, Melba Moore, John Heffernan, Sherman Hemsley

Above, Katharine Hepburn as Coco Chanel with mannequins preparing for a fashion show in the musical *Coco. Below,* four Cecil Beaton sketches of his costumes designed for Miss Hepburn

Daniel Fortus, Lewis J. Stadlen, Shelley Winters, Irwin Pearl and Alvin Kupperman as the young Marx Brothers and their mother in *Minnie's Boys*

Al Freeman Jr. and Shirley Booth in *Look to the Lilies*

Tammy Grimes and Brian Bedford in *Private Lives*

James Stewart and Helen Hayes in *Harvey*

Al Pacino and Susan Tyrrell in the Lincoln Center Repertory revival of Tennessee Williams' *Camino Real* at the Vivian Beaumont Theater

Niall Toibin and Frank Grimes as Brendan Behan grown and young in the Abbey Theater production of *Borstal Boy*

Jean-Louis Barrault in his own *Rabelais*

Genevieve Casile and Catherine Hiegel in the Comédie Française's *Les Femmes Savantes*

Amy Levitt, Judith Lowry, Sada Thompson, Pamela Payton-Wright in Paul Zindel's *The Effect of Gamma Rays on Man-in-the-Moon Marigolds*

Below, Anthony Holland, Andrew Duncan, Paul Benedict, Paul Dooley, Peter Bonerz (the President) and J. J. Barry in Jules Feiffer's *The White House Murder Case*

Right, Diana Davila and Charles Murphy in the late Joe Orton's farce *What the Butler Saw*

bove, Katharine Houghton in *Scent of Flowers*

Ken Kliban and George Reeder in *And Puppy Dog Tails*

Above, the original cast of *Oh! Calcutta! Below*, members of the Chelsea Theater Center ensemble in LeRoi Jones's *Slave Ship*

ENSEMBLES

Right, Esther Rolle, Paul Makgoba, Clarice Taylor and Amandina Lihamba in *Akokawe,* combined presentation of The Negro Ensemble Company and the Mbari-Mbayo Players. *Below,* the Open Theater Ensemble in a scene from *Terminal*

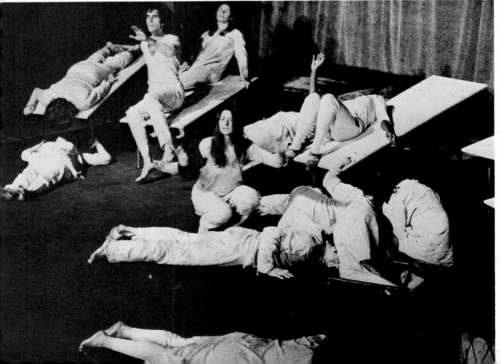

MOSTLY ROCK

Left, Fredricka Weber and Austin Pendleton in *The Last Sweet Days of Isaac*

Above, Laura Michaels and Northern Calloway lead one of the song numbers *The Me Nobody Knows*

Left, Yolande Bavan and Peter Link (a co-author) in *Salvation*

Above, Donny Burks (*foreground*) and the cast of *Billy Noname*

Right, Pierre Epstein, Margot Albert and Elliot Savage in *Promenade*

Below, Jean Pace, Sivuca and Oscar Brown Jr. in *Joy*

Above, youthful exuberance in *Stomp* and *right,* the women's liberation movement in *Mod Donna,* both musicals produced at the Public Theater

Left, Conard Fowkes, Lester Rawlins, Louise Stubbs and Joseph Attles in Douglas Turner Ward's *The Reckoning,* produced in cooperation with The Negro Ensemble Company

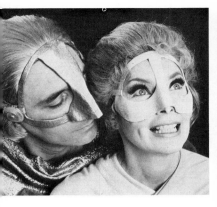

Lincoln Center Repertory at the
Forum theater included (*above*)
Philip Bosco and Priscilla Pointer
in Peter Hacks' *Amphitryon* and
(*right*) Robert Symonds and
Mildred Natwick in Harold Pinter's *Landscape*

Below, Tony Thomas, Laura
Esterman, Edward Clinton, Avis
McCarther, Basil A. Wallace in
The Pig Pen at American Place

OFF-BROADWAY REVIV-
ALS: *Above,* George Voskovec,
Billy Dee Williams, Madeline Mil-
ler in *Slow Dance on the Killing
Ground; right,* Bartholomew Miro
Jr., Mark Shannon in *Fortune and
Men's Eyes; below,* Lenny Baker,
Elizabeth Walker in *Summertree*

Above, Charles Siebert, Zoe Caldwell, Mildred Dunnock and Keene Curtis in *Colette*

Below, Christopher Walken in *Lemon Sky*

Above, front to back, Beeson Carroll, David Selby and Lee Kissman in *The Unseen Hand*

Tony Tanner as a man with two fiancees, Jennifer
Tilston (*left*) and Jo Henderson in the *Trevor*
segment of John Bowen's *Little Boxes*

Estelle Parsons, Barbara Harris and Frank Porretta
in the first New York production of the Brecht-
Weill musical *Mahagonny*

NEW PLAYS IN REGIONAL THEATERS

Trinity Sq. Repertory of Providence, R.I. offered (*left*) William Goyen's *House of Breath Black/ White* and (*below*) Roland van Zandt's *Wilson in the Promise Land* with William Cain as Wilson

Above, Hitler, Amelia Earhart, James Dean and Aimee Semple McPherson are roles in Barry Pritchard's *Alive and Well in Argentina,* at Syracuse Repertory Theater

Below, the American premiere of Anouilh's *The Orchestra* at Studio Arena, Buffalo.

Above, adaptation of Kafka's *The Castle* at Jo[...] Fernald Company, Rochester, Mich.

Among new plays presented this season by the Washington, D.C. Theater Club were (*above*) Lanford Wilson's *Serenading Louie* and (*left*) Oliver Hailey's *Continental Divide,* about an Arkansas trash man (Arlen Dean Snyder)

Right, a scene from Arthur L. Murphy's new *Tiger! Tiger!* at the Neptune Theater, Halifax, Nova Scotia

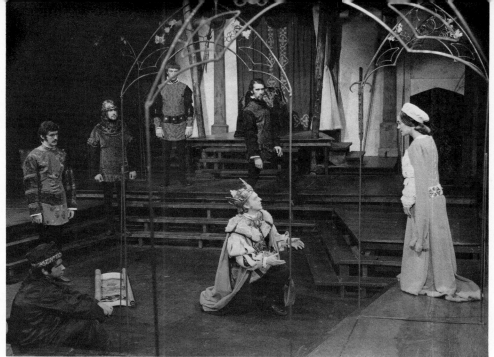

Shakespeare, singly and in festivals, is cross-country theater's most-produced playwright. *Above,* Champlain Shakespeare Festival's version of *The Winter's Tale*

Stagings of Edward Albee's *Tiny Alice: left,* Ron O'Neal as Brother Julian at Buffalo, *below* Paul Shenar in the same role at American Conservatory Theater, San Francisco

A GRAPHIC GLANCE

KATHARINE HEPBURN
AS COCO CHANEL IN "COCO"

STELLE PARSONS, BARBARA HARRIS
ND FRANK PORRETTA IN "MAHAGONNY"

GERALDINE PAGE IN "ANGELA"

SUSAN TYRRELL, JESSICA TANDY, AL PACINO AND
JEAN-PIERRE AUMONT IN THE REVIVAL OF "CAMINO REAL"

LOU JACOBI IN "NORMAN, IS THAT YOU?"

MARGARET HAMILTON, APRIL SHAWHAN, BRUCE YARNELL,
SPIRO MALAS, LEE BEERY AND THE AGNES DE MILLE DANCERS
IN THE REVIVAL OF "OKLAHOMA!"

PLAYS PRODUCED
IN THE
UNITED STATES

PLAYS PRODUCED ON BROADWAY

Figures in parentheses following a play's title indicate number of performances. Plays marked with an asterisk (*) were still running on June 1, 1970, and their number of performances is figured from opening night through May 31, 1970, not including extra non-profit performances. In a listing of a show's numbers—dances, sketches, musical scenes, etc.—the titles of songs are identified by their appearance in quotation marks (").

HOLDOVERS FROM PREVIOUS SEASONS

Plays which were running on June 1, 1969 are listed below. More detailed information about them appears in previous *Best Plays* volumes of appropriate years. Important cast changes are recorded in a section of this volume.

* **Hello, Dolly!** (2,603). Musical suggested by Thornton Wilder's *The Matchmaker;* book by Michael Stewart; music and lyrics by Jerry Herman. Opened January 16, 1964.

* **Fiddler on the Roof** (2,370). Musical based on Sholom Aleichem's stories; book by Joseph Stein; music by Jerry Bock; lyrics by Sheldon Harnick. Opened September 22, 1964.

* **Man of La Mancha** (1,910). Musical suggested by the life and works of Miguel de Cervantes y Saavedra; book by Dale Wasserman; music by Mitch Leigh; lyrics by Joe Darion. Opened November 22, 1965.

Mame (1,508). Musical based on the novel *Auntie Mame* by Patrick Dennis and the play by Jerome Lawrence and Robert E. Lee; book by Jerome Lawrence and Robert E. Lee; music and lyrics by Jerry Herman. Opened May 24, 1966. (Closed January 3, 1970)

Cabaret (1,165). Musical based on John van Druten's play *I Am a Camera* and stories by Christopher Isherwood; book by Joe Masteroff; music by John Kander; lyrics by Fred Ebb. Opened November 20, 1966. (Closed September 6, 1969)

* **Plaza Suite** (953). Program of three one-act plays by Neil Simon. Opened February 14, 1968.

* **Hair** (869). Musical with book and lyrics by Gerome Ragni and James Rado; music by Galt MacDermot. Opened April 29, 1968.

The Great White Hope (556). By Howard Sackler. Opened October 3, 1968. (Closed January 31, 1970)

Zorbá (305). Musical adapted from *Zorba the Greek* by Nikos Kazantzakis; book by Joseph Stein; music by John Kander; lyrics by Fred Ebb. Opened November 17, 1968. (Closed August 9, 1969)

* **Promises, Promises** (625). Musical based on the screen play *The Apartment* by Billy Wilder and I.A.L. Diamond; book by Neil Simon; music by Burt Bacharach; lyrics by Hal David. Opened December 1, 1968.

* **Forty Carats** (597). By Jay Allen; adapted from a play by Pierre Barillet and Jean-Pierre Gredy. Opened December 26, 1968.

Hadrian VII (359). By Peter Luke; based on *Hadrian the Seventh* and other works by Fr. Rolfe (Baron Corvo). Opened January 8, 1969. (Closed November 15, 1969)

Play It Again, Sam (453). By Woody Allen. Opened February 12, 1969. (Closed March 14, 1970)

* **1776** (506). Musical based on a conception of Sherman Edwards; book by Peter Stone; music and lyrics by Sherman Edwards. Opened March 16, 1969.

Hamlet (50). Revival of the play by William Shakespeare. Opened May 1, 1969. (Closed June 14, 1969)

The Repertory Theater of Lincoln Center. Schedule of four plays (see entry in 1968-69 *Best Plays* volume) concluded with **The Miser** (52). Revival of the play by Molière; based on a translation by H. Baker and J. Miller. Opened May 8, 1969. (Closed June 21, 1969)

The Front Page (64). Revival of the play by Ben Hecht and Charles MacArthur. Opened May 10, 1969. (Closed June 5, 1969) Reopened October 18, 1969; see entry in Broadway section of this volume.

My Daughter, Your Son (47). By Phoebe and Henry Ephron. Opened May 13, 1969. (Closed June 21, 1969)

Fiesta in Madrid (23). Musical in the Spanish language adapted from *La Verbena de la Paloma* by Tomas Breton; written by Tito Capobianco. Opened May 28, 1969. (Closed June 15, 1969)

PLAYS PRODUCED JUNE 1, 1969—MAY 31, 1970

A Teaspoon Every Four Hours (1). By Jackie Mason and Mike Mortman. Produced by Bernard M. Weber at the ANTA Theater. Opened and closed at the evening performance, June 14, 1969.

Nat Weiss	Jackie Mason	David Weiss	Roger Morgan
Mike	Lee Wallace	Bruce Weiss	Barry Pearl
Trixie	Lee Meredith	Sylvia Rubin	Marilyn Cooper

Lou Abrams .... Bernie West   Virginia .... Billie Allen
Patty .... Vera Moore

Directed by Jeremy Stevens; scenery, Robert Randolph; costumes, Winn Morton; lighting, John Jay Moore; incidental music, Joseph Raposo; production stage manager, Mortimer Halpern; stage manager, Leonard Auerbach; press, Seymour Krawitz, Ellen Levene.

Time: The present. Place: New York City. Act I, Scene 1: Nat's apartment, a Thursday in April. Scene 2: Nat's apartment, later that day. Scene 3: The Park, that evening. Scene 4: Nat's apartment, Friday, 2:30 a.m. Scene 5: Collins' apartment, Friday, 3 a.m. Scene 6: The Park, Friday 8 a.m. Act II, Scene 1: Collins' apartment, later Friday morning. Scene 2: Nat's apartment, Friday afternoon. Scene 3: Nat's apartment, Monday afternoon.

Jewish family comedy about matrimony.

Oklahoma! (88). Musical revival based on the play *Green Grow the Lilacs* by Lynn Riggs; book and lyrics by Oscar Hammerstein II; music by Richard Rodgers. Produced by Music Theater of Lincoln Center, Richard Rodgers president and producing director, at the New York State Theater. Opened June 23, 1969. (Closed September 6, 1969)

Aunt Eller .... Margaret Hamilton   Dixie .... Dixie Stewart
Curly .... Bruce Yarnell   Joyce .... Joyce Tomanec
Laurey .... Lee Beery   Andrew Carnes .... William Griffis
Ike Skidmore .... Sam Kirkham   Cord Elam .... John Gerstad
Slim .... Del Horstmann   Girl Who Falls Down .... Sandra Balesti
Joe .... Kurt Olson   Dancers
Will Parker .... Lee Roy Reams   Laurey .... Sandra Balesti
Jud Fry .... Spiro Malas   Curly .... Brynar Mehl
Ado Annie Carnes .... April Shawhan   Jud .... James Albright
Ali Hakim .... Ted Beniades   Child .... Lee Wilson
Gertie Cummings .... June Helmers   Featured dancers ... William Glassman, Gilda
Donna .... Donna Monroe   Mullett, Toodie Wittmer
Judith .... Judith McCauley

Singers: Bobbi Lange, Judith McCauley, Donna Monroe, Eleanor Rogers, Dixie Stewart, Maggie Task, Joyce Tomanec, Maggie Worth, John Almberg, John D. Anthony, Lester Clark, Stokley Gray, Mark East, Del Horstmann, Robert Lenn, Joe McGrath, Kurt Olson, Alex Orfaly, Ken Richards, Tom Trelfa.

Dancers: Graciela Daniele, Katherine Gallagher, Mary Lynne McRae, Sally Ransome, Audrey Ross, Lana Sloniger, Eileen Taylor, Jenny Workman, Mary Zahn, Paul Berné, Andy G. Bew, Henry Boyer, Bjarne Buchtrup, Michael Ebbin, Michael Lane, Ralph Nelson.

Principal standbys: Mr. Yarnell—John Almberg; Miss Beery—Judith McCauley; Miss Hamilton—Maggie Trask; Miss Shawhan—June Helmers; Mr. Reams—Andy G. Bew.

Directed by John Kennedy (original direction by Rouben Mamoulian; choreography, Gemze de Lappe (original choreography, Agnes de Mille); musical director, Jay Blackton; scenery and lighting, Paul C. McGuire; costumes, Miles White; orchestrations, Robert Russell Bennett; production stage manager, Sammy Lambert; stage managers, Phil King, James Stevenson; press, Frank Goodman, Ruth Cage.

Time: Just after the turn of the century. Place: Indian territory (now Oklahoma).

Oklahoma! was first produced by the Theater Guild 3/31/43 for 2,212 performances and was named a Best Play of its season. It has been revived by the Theater Guild 5/29/51 for 100 performances; by Rodgers & Hammerstein 8/31/53 for 40 performances; and by the New York City Center Light Opera Company 3/19/58 for 16 performances, in the spring of 1963 for 30 performances in two engagements of 15 performances each and on 12/15/65 for 24 performances.

ACT I

Scene 1: The back of Laurey's farmhouse
"Oh, What a Beautiful Mornin' " .... Curly
"The Surrey With the Fringe on Top" .... Curly, Laurey, Aunt Eller
"Kansas City" .... Will, Aunt Eller, Boys
"I Cain't Say No" .... Ado Annie

"Many a New Day" ....Laurey, Girls, Girl Who Falls Down
"It's a Scandal! It's an Outrage!" ....Ali Hakim, Boys
"People Will Say" ....Curly, Laurey
Scene 2: The smokehouse
"Pore Jud" ....Curly, Jud
"Lonely Room" ....Jud
Scene 3: A grove on Laurey's farm
"Out of My Dreams" ....Laurey, Girls
Laurey Makes up Her Mind (ballet) ....Laurey, Curly, Jud, Child, Jud's Post Cards,
Laurey's Friends, Cowboys

ACT II

Scene 1: The Skidmore ranch
"The Farmer and the Cowboy" ....Carnes, Aunt Eller, Curly, Will, Ike, Ado Annie,
Slim, Ensemble
"All 'Er Nothin' " ....Ado, Annie, Will
Scene 2: Skidmore's kitchen porch
"People Will Say" (Reprise) ....Curly, Laurey
Scene 3: The front of Laurey's farmhouse
"Oklahoma!" ....Curly, Laurey, Aunt Eller, Ike, Ensemble
"Oh, What a Beautiful Mornin' " (Reprise) ....Laurey, Curly, Ensemble
Finale ....Ensemble

In the Matter of J. Robert Oppenheimer (108). Return engagement of the play by Heinar Kipphardt; translated by Ruth Speirs. Produced by The Repertory Theater of Lincoln Center, under the direction of Jules Irving, at the Vivian Beaumont Theater. Opened June 26, 1969. (Closed September 27, 1969)

J. Robert Oppenheimer ....Paul Sparer
Personnel Security Board:
    Gordon Gray ....John Beal
    Ward V. Evans ....Robert Symonds
    Thomas A. Morgan ....Ben Hammer
Counsel:
    Curtis Moffat Jr. ....Philip Bosco
    H. Thomas Spalding ....Robert Phalen
    Aaron Stein ....Ralph Bell

Franklin S. Hardiman ....Cec Linder
Witnesses:
    Maj. Nicholas Radzi ......Robert Levine
    John Lansdale ....Stephen Elliott
    Edward Teller ....Herbert Berghof
    Hans Bethe ....Sandor Szabo
    Walker Leroy Adams .....Ronald Weyand
    Jacob Lehmann ....Ray Fry

Stenographers, Security Guards: Frank Bayer, Martin Herzer, Patrick Horrigan, Joseph Schroer.
Understudies: Ray Fry, Ben Hammer, Robert Levine, Joseph Schroer, Richard Woods.
Directed by Gordon Davidson; scenery, Peter Wexler; costumes, Constance Ross; lighting, John Gleason; still projections, Eleanor Bunin, Peter Wexler; production stage manager, Barbara-Mae Phillips; stage managers, Frank Bayer, Martin Herzer, Patrick Horrigan; press, Susan Bloch, Linda Gerber, Sedgwick Clark.
Time: April 12-May 6, 1964. Place: Room 2022, Building T3, Atomic Energy Commission, Washington, D.C.
In the Matter of J. Robert Oppenheimer was previously produced in New York by The Repertory Theater of Lincoln Center at the Vivian Beaumont Theater 3/6/69 for 64 performances and was named a Best Play of its season.

The Grand Kabuki. Two programs of four traditional plays in the Japanese Language. **Chushingura** (The Treasury of Loyal Retainers) and **Kagami-Jishi** (The Mirror Lion Dance) (10). Opened September 10, 1969. (Closed September 16, 1969) **Kumagai Jinya** (General Kumagai's Battle Camp) and **Momiji-Gari** (The Maple Leaf-Viewing Picnic) (8). Opened September 17, 1969. (Closed September 21, 1969) Produced by Pacific World Artists, Inc., under the patronage of His Imperial Highness Prince Takamatsu and KBS (Japan Cultural Society), in association with City Center of Music and Drama, Inc., at New York City Center.

PERFORMER	"CHUSHINGURA"	"KAGAMI-JISHI"	"KUMAGAI JINYA"	"MOMIJI-GARI"
Baiko VII	Lord Hangan	Yayoi; Lion Spirit		Sarashina; Demon
Ginnosuke			Gunji	
Karoku		Retainer	Kajiwara	
Kikujuro		Butterfly Dancer	Retainer	Ladies' Maid
Kikunosuke	Lady Kaoyo	Butterfly Dancer	Sagami	Ladies' Maid
Kikuzo	Goemon	Lady-in-Waiting	Lady Fuji-No-Kata	Lady-in-Waiting
Kuroemon II	Tadayoshi; Ishido		Midaroku	Koremochi
Matsuji			Voice	
Matsutaro			Retainer	
Minosuke	Rikiya			Mountain God
Otome				Ladies' Maid
Roen	Yakushiji			Ugenta
Rokuya		Steward	Retainer	
Senroku		Lady-in-Waiting	Stage Attendant	Ladies' Maid
Shoroku II	Moronao; Yuranosuke		Kumagai	
Takinojo				Ladies' Maid
Tatsunosuke	Wakasanosuke		Yoshitsune	Sagenta
Umeji		Stage Attendant		
Umejuro			Farmer; Soldier	
Umeo				Ladies' Maid
Umesuke		Stage Attendant	Farmer; Soldier	
Yaenosuke			Farmer; Soldier	

Singers and Musicians: Takemoto O-Gidayu, Toyotake Wassadayu, Toyozawa Enjaku, Toyozawa Isaburo, Matsunga Wahee, Kashiwa Ichinojyo, Kashiwa Isaburo, Kineya Katsusuke, Tokiwazu Chitosedayu, Tokiwazu Kikusaburo.

English commentary and translation, Faubion Bowers; production stage manager, Ronald Bates; press, Bill Doll & Company.

Chushingura is a melodrama about a noble who defends his wife from a superior and is driven to hara-kiri. *Kagami-Jishi* is about a dancer who turns into the lion she is supposed to impersonate. *Kumagai Jinya* is about a general renouncing war after the death of his son. In *Momiji-Gari,* a young prince falls in love with a princess who turns out to be a mountain demon.

American Conservatory Theater. Repertory of three revivals. **Tiny Alice** (10). By Edward Albee. Opened September 29, 1969. **A Flea in Her Ear** (11). By Georges Feydeau; translated by Barnett Shaw. Opened October 3, 1969. **Three Sisters** (11). By Anton Chekhov. Opened October 9, 1969. Produced by The American National Theater and Academy, Alfred de Liagre Jr. executive producer, Jean Dalrymple executive director, in the American Conservatory Theater production, William Ball general director, at the ANTA Theater. (Repertory closed October 25, 1969)

TINY ALICE

Cardinal	Harry Frazier	Butler	Philip Kerr
Lawyer	Ray Reinhardt	Miss Alice	DeAnn Mears
Brother Julian	Paul Shenar	Monks	Martin Berman, Robert Simpson

A FLEA IN HER EAR

Camille Chandel	Michael O'Sullivan	Yvonne Chandel	Carol Teitel
Antoinette	Deborah Sussel	Victor-Emmanuel Chandel;	
Etienne	Barry MacGregor	Poche	Robert Gerringer
Finache	Harry Frazier	Romain Tournel	Philip Kerr
Serrita	Ann Weldon	Don Carlos	Herman Poppe

Ferraillon ....Ray Reinhardt   Baptistin ....Robert Lanchester
Eugenie ....Izetta Smith   Rugby ....George Ede
Olivia ....Ruth Kobart

THREE SISTERS

Olga ....Angela Paton   Baron Nikolai ....Paul Shenar
Marya (Masha) ....Michael Learned   Chebutykin ....William Paterson
Irina ....Kitty Winn   Solyony ....Robert Lanchester
Andrey ....Jay Doyle   Vershinin ....Ken Ruta
Fyodor ....Harry Frazier   Fedotik ....Philip Kerr
Natalya (Natasha) .....Carol Mayo Jenkins   Rodé ....James Milton
Anfisa ....Ruth Kobart   (Ferapont) ..Michael O'Sullivan, George Ede

Servants and Soldiers: Martin Berman, Mary Markson, Ed Mock, Frank Ottiwell, Kenneth Julian, Herman Poppe, Robert Simpson, Izetta Smith, Deborah Sussel.
(Parentheses indicate role in which the actors alternated)

All plays: for American Conservatory Theater, James B. McKenzie executive producer, Edward Hastings executive director, John Seig production director, Edith Markson development director, William Baer extensions director, Robert Goldsby conservatory director; lighting, John McClain; stage manager, Mark Rodgers; press, Howard Atlee, David Roggensack, Stanley F. Kaminsky, Dennis Powers.
TINY ALICE directed by William Ball; associate director, Robert Bonaventura; scenery, Stuart Wurtzel; men's costumes, Walter Watson; Miss Mears' wardrobe, Ann Roth; masks, Bruce Harrow.
Tiny Alice was first produced on Broadway by Theater 1965 at the Billy Rose Theater 9/29/64 for 167 performances and was named a Best Play of its season.
A FLEA IN HER EAR directed by Gower Champion; associate director, Eugene Barcone; scenery, Stuart Wurtzel; costumes, Lewis Brown; music research, Music Man Murray.
Time: The turn of the century. Place: Paris. Act I: Chandel's home. Act II: At the hotel. Act III: Same as Act I.
The first New York professional production of record of this Feydeau sex farce of suspected infidelity and mistaken identity.
THREE SISTERS directed by William Ball; associate director, Eugene Barcone; costumes, Ann Roth; scenery, Paul Staheli; dances, Ed Mock; assistant to Mr. Ball, Kenneth Julian.
Three Sisters was most recently revived on Broadway during the 1964-65 season in an Actors Studio production at the Morosco Theater 6/22/64 for 119 performances and in a Moscow Art Theater production at the City Center 2/9/65 for 8 performances.

The New Music Hall of Israel (68). New edition of the vaudeville revue in the Hebrew, Yiddish and English languages. Produced by Leon H. Gildin at the Lunt-Fontanne Theater. Opened October 2, 1969. (Closed November 29, 1969)

PART I (Mistress of ceremonies, Germaine Onikowski): The Popular Songs of Israel, Rafi Paz conducting; Springtime in Israel, with the Karmon Dancers; Elisheva and Michael; Dance of the Fisherman, with the Karmon Dancers; Pnina Pery and her xylophone; The Legend of Timna, with the Karmon Dancers; A New and Humorous Shadow World, with Almonznino; Leah Dorly Trio; A Hassidik Marriage, with the Karmon Dancers.
PART II: Magic of the Negev, with the Karmon Dancers; The Popular Music of Israel, with Yoel Dan; Rhythms and Dances of the Desert, with Boas; Lest We Forget, with the Karmon Dancers; Geula Gill; Mosaic, with the Karmon Dancers; Israel Joy of Life, with the entire troupe.
Directed and choreographed by Jonathan Karmon; musical direction, Rafi Paz; costumes, Lydia Pinkus Ganay; assistant director, Gavri Levi; additional dialogue, Al Fogel; press, David Lipsky, Lisa Lipsky.
Collection of songs, dances and novelty acts presented by a young Israeli troupe, first produced in New York in a version entitled *The Grand Music Hall of Israel* at the Palace Theater 2/6/68 for 64 performances. A foreign play previously produced in Israel, Paris and elsewhere.

A Patriot for Me (49). By John Osborne. Produced by David Merrick Arts Foundation at the Imperial Theater. Opened October 5, 1969. (Closed November 15, 1969)

Alfred Redl ....Maximilian Schell	Judge Advocate
August Siczynski ....Richard Jordan	Jaroslav Kunz ....Ed Zimmermann
Steinbauer ....Tom V.V. Tammi	Young Man in Cafe;
Ludwig Max von Kupfer .....Jered Barclay	Lady of Fashion ....Warren Burton
Lt. Col. Ludwig von Mohl . .Staats Cotsworth	Paul; Little Girl ....Christopher Pennock
Adjutant; Little Boy ....John Kramer	Ferdy ....Alan Brasington
Maximilian von Taussig .....Robert Stattel	Salome ....Peter Colly
Albrecht ....John Horn	Baron von Epp ....Dennis King
Waiter at Anna's; Tsarina ......Byran Young	Lt. Stefan Kovacs ....Michael Goodwin
Hilde ....Mariclare Costello	Marie Antoinette ....Carl Jessop
Anna ....Madlyn Cates	Orthodox Priest; Boy ....Tom Lee Jones
Stanitsin ....James Dukas	Equestrienne;
Col. Mischa Oblensky ....Keene Curtis	Hotel Head Waiter ....Eugene Stuckmann
Gen. Conrad	Balkan Chief ....Brian Sturdivant
von Hotzendorf ....Stefan Schnabel	2d Lt. Victor Jerzabek ....Noel Craig
Countess Sophia Delyanoff .....Salome Jens	Hotel Waiter ....Luis Lopez-Cepero

Kupfer's Seconds, Officers, Whores, Flunkeys, Hofburg Guests, Passersby, Privates, Shepherdesses: Tom Lee Jones, Brian Sturdivant, Peter Bartlett, Warren Burton, Noel Craig, Carl Jessop, Hedy Sontag, Marilyn Joseph, Inge von Reith, Billi Vitali, Michael Goodwin, Christopher Pennock, Alan Brasington, Madlyn Cates, Luis Lopez-Cepero, Peter Colly, John Kramer, Eugene Stuckmann, Bryan Young. Musicians: Frederic Hand, James Carter, Eric Lewis, Ruben Rivera.

Principal understudies: Mr. Schell—Ed Zimmermann; Messrs. King, Schnabel, Cotsworth, Curtis—Eugene Stuckmann; Misses Jens, Costello—Hedy Sontag; Messrs. Zimmermann, Barclay—John Kramer.

Directed by Peter Glenville; scenery, Oliver Smith; costumes, Freddy Wittop; lighting, Thomas Skelton; music, Laurence Rosenthal; associate producer, Samuel Liff; production stage manager, Alan Hall; stage manager, Geoffrey Johnson; press, Harvey B. Sabinson, Lee Solters, David Powers.

Time: 1890-1913. Place: Austria-Hungary; Lemberg, Warsaw, Prague, Dresden, Vienna. Act I, Scene 1: A gymnasium. The 7th Galician Infantry Regiment, Lemberg. Scene 2: Von Mohl's office. Scene 3: Anna's cafe, Lemberg. Scene 4: An upstairs room at Anna's. Scene 5: Oblensky's office, Warsaw. Scene 6: The Hofburg Palace. Scene 7: Countess Delyanoff's drawing room. Scene 8: Oblensky's office, Warsaw. Scene 9: A cafe, Prague. Scene 10: A room. Act II, Scene 1: A ballroom, Vienna. Scene 2: A forest clearing near Dresden. Scene 3: Redl's apartment, Vienna. Scene 4: Sacher Hotel, Vienna. Scene 5: A hotel room, Dresden. Scene 6: Redl's apartment, Prague. Scene 7: Von Mohl's office, General Staff Headquarters. Scene 8: Hotel Klosmer, Vienna. Scene 9: A street outside. Scene 10: Epilogue.

Homosexual and espionage scandal involving a high-ranking Austrian intelligence officer. A foreign play previously produced in London.

Indians (96). By Arthur Kopit. Produced by Lyn Austin, Oliver Smith, Joel Schenker and Roger L. Stevens at the Brooks Atkinson Theater. Opened October 13, 1969. (Closed January 3, 1970)

Buffalo Bill ....Stacy Keach	Ned Buntline ....Charles Durning
Sitting Bull ....Manu Tupou	Geronimo; Billy the Kid ....Ed Rombola
Senator Logan ....Tom Aldredge	Master Valet; Reporter .....Darryl Croxton
Senator Dawes ....Richard McKenzie	First Lady ....Dortha Duckworth
Senator Morgan ....Jon Richards	Ol' Time President;
Trial Soldier; Cowboy ....Bob Hamilton	Col. Forsyth ....Peter MacLean
Trial Soldier; Cowboy ....Richard Nieves	Wild Bill Hickok ....Barton Heyman
John Grass ....Sam Waterston	Teskanjavila ....Dimitra Arliss
Spotted Tail ....James L. Sloyan	White House Orchestra ....Tony Posk,
Grand Duke Alexis;	Peter Rosenfelt
Uncas; Poncho ....Raul Julia	Valet ....Joseph Ragno
Interpreter ....Yusef Bulos	Valet; Lieutenant ....Richard Novello

Valet; Bartender; Reporter ...Brian Donohue	Black Hawk ....Kevin Conway
Chief Joseph ....George Mitchell	Tecumseh ....Pascual Vaquer
Annie Oakley ....Pamela Grey	Yellow Cloud ....Wesley Fata
Jessie James; Reporter ....Ronny Cox	Kicking Bear ....Gary Weber
Cowboys .....Richard Miller, Clint Allmon	Touch-the-Clouds ....Peter De Maio
Crazy Horse ....Dino Laudicina	Howling Wolf ....Ted Goodridge
He-Who-Hears-Thunder .....Robert McLane	White Antelope ....Tom Fletcher
Red Cloud ....Andy Torres	Low Dog ....Philip Arsenault
Little Hawk ....Jay Fletcher	Naiche ....Juan Antonio
Kiokuk ....Princeton Dean	Indian Drummers ....Leon Oxman,
Satanta ....Ed Henkel	Allan Silverman
Old Taza ....Michael Ebbin	

Principal understudies: Mr. Keach—Peter MacLean; Mr. Tupou—Dino Laudicina; Messrs. McKenzie, Mitchell—Clint Allmon; Messrs. Richards, Croxton, Donohue, Cox—Richard Miller; Messrs. Aldredge, MacLean—Kevin Conway; Messrs. Waterston, Heyman—James J. Sloyan; Mr. Durning—Richard McKenzie.

Directed by Gene Frankel; scenery, Oliver Smith; costumes, Marjorie Slaiman; lighting, Thomas Skelton; music, Richard Peaslee; choreography, Julie Arenal; production stage manager, Kathleen A. Sullivan; stage manager, Fritz Holt; press, Harvey B. Sabinson, Lee Solters.

Time: 1846-1890. Place: A Wild West Show. The play was presented without intermission. Series of scenes about the opening of the West, in which Buffalo Bill Cody expresses and dramatizes his misgivings about various excesses (slaughter of Buffalo, cruelty to Indians) committed in the name of progress. An American play previously produced in London and Washington, D.C.

A Best Play; see page 99.

Three Men on a Horse (100). Revival of the play by John Cecil Holm and George Abbott. Produced by Ken Gaston, Leonard Goldberg and Bud Filippo in association with Henry Stern at the Lyceum Theater. Opened October 16, 1969. (Closed January 10, 1970)

Audrey Trowbridge ....Rosemary Prinz	Patsy ....Sam Levene
The Tailor ....D. Brian Wallach	Mabel ....Dorothy Loudon
Erwin Trowbridge ....Jack Gilford	Dora Lee ....Butterfly McQueen
Clarence Dobbins ....Leon Janney	Gloria ....Gloria Bleezarde
Delivery Boy ....Don Simms	Al ....John Svar
Harry ....Wally Englehardt	Hotel Maid ....Dorothy Chace
Charlie ....Hal Linden	Mr. Carver ....Paul Ford
Frankie ....Al Nesor	

Standby: Mr. Ford—Gordon B. Clarke. Principal understudies: Messrs. Levene, Englehardt, Linden—Don Simms; Messrs. Gilford, Janney—John Svar; Miss Loudon—Gloria Bleezarde.

Directed by George Abbott; scenery, Boyd Dumrose; costumes, A. Christina Giannini; lighting, Fred Allison; production stage manager, Wade Miller; press, David Lipsky, Lisa Lipsky.

Time: The middle 1930s. Place: Ozone Heights, N.J. and New York City.

Three Men on a Horse was first produced on Broadway 1/30/35 at the Playhouse for 835 performances. A musical version of the comedy, *Banjo Eyes*, was produced in New York at the Hollywood Theater 12/25/41 for 126 performances. Another musical version, *Let It Ride!*, was produced at the Eugene O'Neill Theater 10/12/61 for 68 performances. Its only previous Broadway revival was by its original producer, Alex Yokel, at the Forrest Theater 10/9/42 for 28 performances.

Mary K. Wells replaced Rosemary Prinz 11/17/69. Gloria Bleezarde replaced Dorothy Loudon and John Svar replaced Jack Gilford 1/5/70.

The Penny Wars (5). By Elliott Baker. Produced by David Merrick Arts Foundation at the Royale Theater. Opened October 15, 1969. (Closed October 18, 1969)

Ross Bishop ....Jeffrey Hamilton	Frank Bishop ....Dolph Sweet
Tyler Bishop ....Kristoffer Tabori	Contestant ....Jack Valente
Howie Clevenger ....John Korkes	Stage Manager ....Ben Kapen
Mrs. Swerdlov ....Rita Karin	Bert; Horowitz ....Brooks Morton
Carrie Bishop ....Kim Hunter	Mrs. Mintz ....Lois Holmes

Mrs. Pitkin ....Martha Galphin
Rowena Keyhoe ....Judy Nugent
Mr. Pitkin ....John Anania
Dr. Wolf Axelrod ....George Voskovec
Reverend Sickles ....John Gerstad
Blacky Roche ....Lou Tiano
Dalesandro ....Joe Alfasa

Witowski ....James Doolan
Richie Davis ....Mel Winkler
Clarence ....Robert Delbert
Margaret O. ....Catherine Bacon
Lois ....Kathryn Baumann
Inez Jackson ....Avis McCarther

Standby: Mr. Voskovec—John Anania. Principal understudies: Misses Hunter, Holmes—Martha Galphin; Messrs. Tabori, Korkes—James Woods; Messrs. Sweet, Alfasa, Morton, Doolan—Ben Kapen; Miss Karin—Lois Holmes; Mr. Hamilton—Anthony Michaels; Miss McCarther—Joyce Wilford.

Directed by Barbara Harris; scenery, William Ritman; costumes, Jane Greenwood; lighting, Martin Aronstein; associate producer, Samuel Liff; production stage manager, Jeff Chambers; stage manager, James Doolan; press, Lee Solters, Harvey B. Sabinson, Harry Nigro.

Time: 1939. Place: A large industrial city in upstate New York. Act I: Late June. Act II: Early August. Act III: Mid-October.

Family's struggle to make it through the Depression is edged with sorrow by the death of the father and the suicide of a stepfather, in a drama based on the author's novel of the same title.

The Front Page (158). Return engagement of the revival of the play by Ben Hecht and Charles MacArthur. Produced by Jay H. Fuchs, Jerry Schlossberg with Albert Zuckerman in association with Rolan Mattson at the Ethel Barrymore Theater. Opened October 18, 1969. (Closed February 28, 1970)

Wilson, *American* ....Will Gregory
Endicott, *Post* ....Robert Milli
Murphy, *Journal* ....James Flavin
McCue, *City Press* ....Ed Riley
Schwartz, *News* ....Bob Larkin
Kruger, *Journal of Commerce* ..Conrad Janis
Bensinger, *Tribune* ......Harold J. Kennedy
Woodenshoes Eichorn ......Walter Flanagan
Diamond Louis ....Val Avery
Hildy Johnson,
  Herald Examiner ....Bert Convy
Jenny ....Dody Goodman (Helen Hayes)

Mollie Molloy ....Peggy Cass
                              (Dody Goodman)
Sheriff Hartman ....Charles White
Peggy Grant ....Kendall March
Mrs. Grant ....Helen Hayes
The Mayor ....John McGiver
Mr. Pincus ....Bernie West
Earl Williams ....Patrick Desmond
Walter Burns ....Robert Ryan
Carl, a Deputy ....Bruce Blaine
Tony ....Joseph George
Policemen ......Robert Riesel, Jack Collard

(Parentheses indicate roles in which the actors alternated)

Directed by Harold J. Kennedy; scenery and lighting, Will Steven Armstrong; costumes, Sara Brook; associate producers, Barry Diamond, Fred Menowitz; production stage manager, Elissa Lane; stage manager, Bruce Blaine; press, Howard Atlee, David Roggensack, Stanley F. Kaminsky.

Time: 1928. Place: The Press Room of the Criminal Courts Building in Chicago.

This revival of *The Front Page* was originally produced by Theater 1969 (Richard Barr, Edward Albee and Charles Woodward) at the Ethel Barrymore Theater 5/10/69 for 64 performances (see its entry in the 1968-69 *Best Plays* volume).

Molly Picon replaced Helen Hayes 12/1/69. James Flavin replaced Robert Ryan 1/12/70. Robert Alda replaced James Flavin 1/27/70. Maureen O'Sullivan replaced Molly Picon, Jan Sterling replaced Peggy Cass and Jules Munshin replaced John McGiver 1/5/70. Paul Ford replaced Jules Munshin 2/2/70. Butterfly McQueen replaced Dody Goodman 2/2/70. Dody Goodman replaced Butterfly McQueen 2/19/70.

* Butterflies Are Free (252). By Leonard Gershe. Produced by Arthur Whitelaw, Max J. Brown and Byron Goldman at the Booth Theater. Opened October 21, 1969.

Don Baker ....Keir Dullea
Jill Tanner ....Blythe Danner

Mrs. Baker ....Eileen Heckart
Ralph Austin ....Michael Glaser

Understudies: Miss Heckart—Jan Miner; Miss Danner—Pamela Kingsley; Messrs. Dullea, Glaser—Kipp Osborne.

Directed by Milton Katselas; scenery, Richard Seger; costumes, Robert Mackintosh; lighting, Jules Fisher; associate producer, Ruth Bailey; production stage manager, Elizabeth Caldwell; press, Max Eisen, Cheryl Sue Dolby.

Time: The present. Place: Don Baker's apartment on East 11th Street in New York City. Act I: A morning in June. Act II, Scene 1: A moment later. Scene 2: That night.

Comedy about a young man, blind, who leaves home to live in Greenwich Village in defiance of his interfering mother, and falls in love with the girl in the adjoining apartment.

A Best Play; see page 113.

Jimmy (84). Musical based on Gene Fowler's novel *Beau James;* book by Melville Shavelson; music and lyrics by Bill and Patti Jacob. Produced by Jack L. Warner in association with Don Saxon and Harry Mayer at the Winter Garden. Opened October 23, 1969. (Closed January 3, 1970)

Jimmy Walker ....Frank Gorshin	Betty Compton ....Anita Gillette
Bonnie; Miss Queens ....Cindi Bulak	Texas Guinan ....Dorothy Claire
Jim Hines ....Jack Collins	Edward Duryea Dowling .....Larry Douglas
Al Smith ....William Griffis	Warrington Brock ....Clifford Fearl
Allie Walker ....Julie Wilson	Charley Hand ....Evan Thompson
Francis Xavier	Moe; Politician ....Del Horstmann
Aloysius O'Toole ....Edward Becker	Izzy; Tailor ....Carl Nicholas
Lawrence Horatio Fink ...Stanley Simmonds	Policeman ....Herb Fields
Antonio Viscelli ....Paul Forrest	Photographers ...Andy G. Bew, Tony Stevens
Stanislaus Kazimir	Secretary ....Barbara Andres
Wojciezkowski ....Henry Lawrence	Reporter ....Frank Newell
Mrs. Al Smith ....Peggy Hewett	Politician; Policeman ....Ben Laney
Miss Manhattan ....Sally Neal	Politician; Band Vocalist ...Joseph McGrath
Miss Bronx ....Andrea Duda	Passerby ....Sandi McCreadie
Miss Brooklyn;	Mrs. Compton ....Sibyl Bowan
Girl in Fur Coat ....Carol Conte	Process Server ....John D. Anthony
Miss Richmond ....Nancy Dalton	Doorman ....Steven Boockvor
Stage Manager ....Gary Gendell	Recorded Impersonations .....Dwight Weist

Dancing Ensemble: Cindi Bulak, Carol Conte, Nancy Dalton, Andrea Duda, Saundra McPherson, Sally Neal, Eileen Shannon, Monica Tiller, Pat Trott, Andy G. Bew, Steven Boockvor, Christopher Chadman, David Evans, Gary Gendell, Scott Hunter, Frank Newell, Harold Pierson, Tony Stevens.

Singing Ensemble: Barbara Andres, Gini Eastwood, Barbara Gregory, Peggy Hewett, Mary Louise, Sandi McCreadie, Claire Theiss, Roberta Vatske, John D. Anthony, Edward Becker, Austin Colyer, Herb Fields, Paul Forrest, Del Horstmann, Ben Laney, Henry Lawrence, Joseph McGrath, Carl Nicholas.

Standby: Mr. Gorshin—Danny Meehan. Principal understudies: Miss Gillette—Roberta Vatske; Miss Wilson—Barbara Andress; Mr. Collins—Evan Thompson; Mr. Griffis—Stanley Simmonds; Miss Claire—Claire Theiss; Mr. Thompson—Joseph McGrath; Miss Bowan—Barbara Andress.

Directed by Joseph Anthony; musical numbers staged by Peter Gennaro; musical direction and vocal arrangements, Milton Rosenstock; scenery, Oliver Smith; costumes, W. Robert Lavine; lighting, Peggy Clark; projections, Charles E. Hoefler, James Hamilton; musical arrangements, Jack Andrews; dance arrangements, John Berkman; assistant choreographer, Bill Guske; production stage manager, William Ross; stage manager, Michael Sinclair; press, Marvin Kohn.

Act I, Scene 1: S.S. Conte Grande, 1931. Scene 2: Jimmy's apartment, 1925. Scene 3: Tammany Hall, 1925. Scene 4: Texas Guinan's, 1925. Scene 5: Betty's apartment, 1925. Scene 6: The 1925 victory celebration. Scene 7: Allie's bedroom, 1925. Scene 8: City Hall, 1926. Act II, Scene 1: Riverside Drive, 1929. Scene 2: Betty's new apartment, 1929. Scene 3: Polling booth, 1929. Scene 4: Central Park Casino, 1929. Scene 5: The street, 1930. Scene 6: Betty's dressing room, 1931. Scene 7: Washington Square, 1931. Scene 8: City Hall, 1931. Scene 9: Yankee Stadium, 1931. Scene 10: S.S. Conte Grande, 1931.

The life and times of James J. Walker, mayor of New York City.

ACT I

"Will You Think of Me Tomorrow?" ....Jimmy Walker
"The Little Woman" ....Al Smith, Jim Hines, Jimmy, Allie Walker

"The Darlin' of New York" .... Hines, Smith, Charley Hand, Allie, Jimmy,
                                                Five Lovely Ladies, Campaign Workers
"Five Lovely Ladies" .... Jimmy
"Oh, Gee!" .... Betty Compton
"The Walker Walk" .... Texas Guinan, Betty, Guinan Girls, Jimmy, Patrons
"That Old Familiar Ring" .... Betty, Jimmy
"The Walker Walk" (Reprise) .... Hines, Politicians, Party Workers
"I Only Wanna Laugh" .... Allie
"They Never Proved a Thing" .... Jimmy, Hines, Viscelli, Fink, O'Toole, Wojciezkowski,
                                                Politicians, Brock, Tailor

ACT II

"Riverside Drive" .... Jimmy, Strollers
"The Squabble Song" .... Jimmy, Betty
"Medley" .... Band Vocalist
"One in a Million" .... Jimmy, Betty
"It's a Nice Place to Visit" .... Viscelli, Fink, O'Toole, Wojciezkowski, Brock,
                                                Girl in Fur Coat, Company
"The Charmin' Son-of-a-Bitch" .... Allie
"Jimmy" .... Betty
"Five Lovely Ladies" (Reprise) .... Jimmy
"Our Jimmy" .... Hines, Jimmy, Allie, Hand, Smith, Texas, Five Lovely Ladies,
                                                Policemen, Spectators
"Life Is a One-Way Street" .... Jimmy
Finale .... Jimmy, Betty

* The Repertory Theater of Lincoln Center. Schedule of four plays. **The Time of
Your Life** (52). Revival of the play by William Saroyan. Opened November 6,
1969. (Closed December 20, 1969) **Camino Real** (52). Revival of the play by
Tennessee Williams. Opened January 8, 1970. (Closed February 21, 1970) **Operation Sidewinder** (52). By Sam Shepard. Opened March 12, 1970. (Closed April
25, 1970) *** Beggar on Horseback** (22). Revival of the play by George S. Kaufman and Marc Connelly. Opened May 14, 1970. Produced by The Repertory
Theater of Lincoln Center, under the direction of Jules Irving, at the Vivian Beaumont Theater.

THE TIME OF YOUR LIFE

Joe	James Broderick	Blick	Joseph Mascolo
Arab	Ralph Drischell	Mary L.	Priscilla Pointer
Nick	Philip Bosco	McCarthy	Ralph Bell
Willie	Raymond Singer	Krupp	Gene Troobnick
Sam	Bill Cunningham	Kit Carson	Robert Symonds
(The Newsboy)	Marc L. Vahanian,	A Sailor	Ronald Hale
	Philip Graves	Killer	Helene Winston
The Drunkard	Jack Fletcher	Babs	Barbara eda-Young
Tom	Biff McGuire	Elsie	Laura Esterman
Kitty Duval	Susan Tyrrell	A Society Lady	Leta Bonynge
Dudley	Matthew Cowles	A Society Gentleman	Patrick McVey
Harry	Leonard Frey	A Cop	Robert Levine
Wesley	Lorenzo Fuller	Another Cop	Robert Keesler
Lorene	Marcia Lewis		

(Parentheses indicate role in which the actors alternated)

Principal understudies: Mr. Broderick—Michael Miller; Mr. Symonds—Ralph Drischell;
Misses Tyrrell, Pointer—Barbara eda-Young; Mr. Bosco—Joseph Mascolo; Messrs. Cowles,
Fletcher, Hale—Arthur Sellers.
Directed by John Hirsch; scenery, Douglas W. Schmidt; costumes, Carrie Fishbein Robbins;
lighting, John Gleason; production stage manager, Christopher Kelly; stage manager, Barnett
Epstein; press, Susan Bloch, Jan Henry James, Sedgwick Clark.

Time: Afternoon and night of a day in October, 1939. Place: Nick's Pacific Street saloon, restaurant and entertainment palace at the foot of the Embarcadero in San Francisco, and Room 21 at the New York Hotel around the corner.

The Time of Your Life was first produced on Broadway by the Theater Guild at the Booth Theater 10/25/39 for 185 performances. It was named a Best Play of its season and won both the Pulitzer Prize and Critics Award (for Best American Play). Its revivals of record are by the Theater Guild 9/23/40 for 32 performances, off Broadway by Associated Playwrights, Inc. during the 1946-47 season, and by the New York City Center Theater Company 1/19/55 for 15 performances.

CAMINO REAL

Don Quixote ....Patrick McVey	Her Son ....José Barrera
Sancho Panza ....Michael Enserro	The Dreamer
Gutman ....Victor Buono	(a Guitarist) ....Roberto Reyes
Abdullah ....José Perez	The Gypsy ....Sylvia Syms
Prudence Duvernoy ....Leta Bonynge	Esmeralda, Her Daughter .....Susan Tyrrell
Jacques Casanova .....Jean-Pierre Aumont	Nursie ....Arnold Soboloff
Loan Shark;	Kilroy ....Al Pacino
Voice of the Bum ....Ralph Drischell	Street Cleaners ....Paul Benjamin,
Olympe; Eva ....Barbara eda-Young	Robert Keesler
Waiters ....Arthur Sellers, Luis Avalos	Lord Mulligan ....Robert Symonds
Survivor; Pilot ....Michael Levin	A. Ratt ....Ralph Bell
Rosita ....Joan Pringle	Baron de Charlus ....Philip Bosco
Officer ....Joseph Mascolo	Lobo ....Nick Cantrell
Guards ....Sam Umani, Michael Miller	Marguerite Gautier ....Jessica Tandy
Lady Mulligan ....Priscilla Pointer	Lord Byron ....Clifford David
La Madrecita ....Antonia Rey	Navigator ....Dan Sullivan

Street People: Luis Avalos, Michael Miller, Jean-Daniel Noland, Robert Riggs, Raymond Singer, Barbara Spiegel, Dan Sullivan, Sam Umani.

Principal understudies: Miss Tandy—Priscilla Pointer; Mr. Aumont—Michael Levin; Mr. Buono—Joseph Mascolo; Miss Syms—Leta Bonynge; Mr. Pacino—Dan Sullivan; Misses Tyrell, Pointer, Pringle, eda-Young—Barbara Spiegel; Mr. David—Raymond Singer; Messrs. Bosco, Bell—Ralph Drischell.

Directed by Milton Katselas; scenery and costumes, Peter Wexler; lighting, John Gleason; music composed by Bernardo Segáll; production stage manager, Tim Ward; stage manager, Barnett Epstein.

Place: The end of Camíno Re-ál and the beginning of Camino Real.

Camino Real was first produced by Cheryl Crawford and Ethel Reiner at the National Theater 3/19/53 for 60 performances. This is its first New York revival of record.

OPERATION SIDEWINDER

Dukie; Captain; 2d Desert	1st Cohort ....Ralph Drischell
Tactical Troop ....Robert Phalen	2d Cohort ....Arthur Sellers
Honey ....Barbara eda-Young	Carhop ....Catherine Burns
Mechanic; 3d Desert	Blood ....Garrett Morris
Tactical Troop ....Michael Miller	Blade ....Paul Benjamin
Young Man ....Andy Robinson	Dude ....Charles Pegues
Forest Ranger; 1st Desert	General Browser ....Paul Sparer
Tactical Troop ....Robert Riggs	Doctor Vector ....Ray Fry
Billy ....Roberts Blossom	Spider Lady ....Michael Levin
Colonel Warner ....Joseph Mascolo	Edith ....Joan Pringle
Cadet ....Gus Fleming	Captain Bovine ....Philip Bosco
Mickey Free ....Don Plumley	

Indians: José Barrera, Paul Benjamin, Gregory Borst, Gus Fleming, Robert Keesler, Michael Levin, Clark Luis, Richard Mason, Muriel Miguel, Louis Mofsie, Santos Morales, Garrett Morris, Jean-Daniel Noland, Joan Pringle, Barbara Spiegel.

Principal understudies: Mr. Robinson—Arthur Sellers; Misses eda-Young, Burns—Barbara Spiegel; Messrs. Fry, Drischell, Sellers—Santos Morales; Messrs. Plumley, Sparer—Ralph Drischell.

Directed by Michael A. Schultz; scenery, Douglas W. Schmidt; lighting, John Gleason; costumes, Willa Kim; music composed and performed by The Holy Modal Rounders; movement consultant, Rhoda Levine; production stage manager, Barbara-Mae Phillips; stage manager, Patrick Horrigan.

Time: The present. Act I, Scene 1: The desert. Scene 2: A garage. Scene 3: In the desert. Scene 4: The office of Air Force Colonel Warner. Scene 5: In the desert. Scene 6: A drive-in restaurant. Scene 7: The Air Force Laboratory at Fort George. Scene 8: In the desert. Act II, Scene 1: In the desert. Scene 2: The Kiva of the Spider Lady. Scene 3: The office of C.I.A. Captain Bovine. Scene 4: On a mesa in the desert.

Rebellious violence, establishment stubborness and even Hopi symbolism mixed together in a grab-bag of episodes about a deadly military device in the form of a large mechanical rattlesnake. ..

Musical numbers: "Catch Me" and "Alien Song" by Sam Shepard; "Euphoria" and "Don't Leave Me Dangling in the Dust" by Robin Remaily; "Synergy," "Do It Girl" and "Bad Karma" by Peter Stampfel and Antonia; "Generalonely" by Steve Weber; "Float Me Down Your Pipeline" and "I Disremember Quite Well" by Antonia; "Hathor" by Peter Stampfel; "C.I.A. Man" by Tuli Kupferberg, Peter Stampfel and Antonia.

BEGGAR ON HORSEBACK

Dr. Albert Rice ....Biff McGuire	Miss Hey ....Barbara Spiegel
Cynthia Mason ....Susan Watson	Miss You ....Beryl Towbin
Neil McRae ....Leonard Frey	2d Juror ....·Robert Weil
Mrs. Cady ....Tresa Hughes	Candy Vendor ....Luis Avalos
Gladys Cady ....Cherry Davis	Guide ....Ralph Drischell
Mr. Cady ....Jay Garner	Novelist ....Ray Fry
Homer Cady ....Robert Phalen	Poet ....Bob Daley
Jerry ....Les "Bubba" Gaines	Singer ....Bobby Lee
Train Vendor ....Art Ostrin	

Flower Girls: Dorothy Frank, Elaine Handel, Michon Peacock. Policemen: Robert Keesler, Raymond Singer. Newsboys: Clark Luis, Arthur Sellers. People in Neil's Dream: José Barrera, John Beecher, Roger Braun, Tommy Breslin, Peter Norman, Charles Pegues, Vickie Thomas.

Principal Understudies: Mr. Frey—John Beecher; Miss Watson—Barbara Spiegel; Miss Davis—Beryl Towbin; Mr. Garner—Robert Keesler; Miss Hughes—Elaine Handel.

Directed by John Hirsch; music, Stanley Silverman; songs, Stanley Silverman, John Lahr; musical direction, Abba Bogin; scenery and costumes, Michael Annals; lighting, John Gleason; movement sequences, Marvin Gordon; production stage manager, Tim Ward; stage managers, Barnett Epstein, Barbara-Mae Phillips.

Time: 1924. Place: Neil's apartment, a cold-water flat in Greenwich Village.

The Kaufman-Connelly fantasy about a poor artist trapped in a nightmare of becoming rich was first produced at the Broadhurst Theater 2/12/24 and was named a Best Play of its season. It was revived on Broadway the following season, 3/23/25.

Henry V (16). Revival of the play by William Shakespeare. Produced by The American National Theater and Academy, Alfred de Liagre Jr. executive producer, Jean Dalrymple executive director, in the American Shakespeare Festival production at the ANTA Theater. Opened November 10, 1969. (Closed November 22, 1969)

Chorus ....Michael Parish, Robert Foxworth, Fredric Glenn, Riggs O'Hara	Mistress Quickly ....Mary Doyle
	The Boy, Davy ....Kristoffer Tabori
Canterbury; Fluellen ....Joseph Maher	Scroop; Orleans ....Martin Broomfield
Ely; Charles VI ....Wyman Pendleton	Cambridge; Bourbon ....Robert Scogin
Voice of Falstaff ....Tony van Bridge	Grey; M. Le Fer ....Mervyn Haines Jr.
Henry V ....Len Cariou	Dauphin ....Danny Davis
Exeter ....G. Wood	Constable ....Jack Ryland
Westmoreland ....Carl Strano	Translator ....Madge Grant
Bedford ....Ellis Richardson	Translator; Bates ....Michael Parish
Clarence ....Bolen High	Harfleur Gov.;
Gloucester ....John La Gioia	Burgundy ....Robert Jackson
Montjoy ....Tom Klunis	Katharine ....Roberta Maxwell
Nym ....Herbert Foster	Alice ....Patricia Elliott
Bardolph ....Roger Omar Serbagi	Gower ....Barry Corbin
Pistol ....Philip Bruns	Erpingham ....Herbert Foster

Williams .... Tony Thomas   Isabel .... June Prud'homme
York .... Anthony Passantino

Ensemble: Gerald Cooper, Gary Copeland, Frank Cossa, Jesse Davis, Michael Diamond, Celeste Grant, Bolen High, James Laurence, Davidson Lloyd, Evan Nichols, Gil Payette, Gary Poe, Tim Riley, Ben Simon, Archibald Walker.

Directed by Michael Kahn; choreo-movement, Moni Yakim; scenery, Karl Eigsti; costumes, Jeanne Button; original lighting, Thomas Skelton; sound environment, Alvin Lucier; executive producer, Joseph Verner Reed, managing producer, Berenice Weiler; artistic director, Michael Kahn; production stage manager, R. Derek Swire; stage manager, Gina Shield.

Henry V was last revived on Broadway 12/25/58 by the Old Vic Company. Its last New York presentation of record was by the New York Shakespeare Festival Mobile Theater during the summer of 1965.

Angela (4). By Sumner Arthur Long. Produced by Elliot Martin Productions and Michael Ellis at the Music Box. Opened October 30, 1969. (Closed November 1, 1969)

Angela Palmer .... Geraldine Page   Brian Palmer .... Simon Oakland
Alice .... Michaele Myers   TV Repairman .... Angelo Mango
Jeff Dolan .... Tom Ligon   The Women .... Judith Searle

Standby: Mr. Ligon—Dale Helward. Understudies: Miss Page—Michaele Myers; Messrs. Oakland, Mango—Howard Fischer; Miss Myers—Judith Searle.

Directed by Jack Ragotzy; scenery and lighting, Robert Randolph; costumes, Jane Greenwood; associate producer, Samuel Bronstein; production stage manager, Harry Young; stage manager, Howard Fischer; press, Mary Bryant, David Rothenberg, Meg Gordean.

Time: The present. Place: The master bedroom of the Palmer home in Walton, Mass., an affluent suburb of Boston. Act I, Scene 1: Late afternoon. Scene 2: The next day. Scene 3: Three weeks later, a little before midnight. Act II, Scene 1: Three months later; Scene 2: Several weeks later, at night. Scene 3: Several weeks later, daytime.

Comedy about a neglected middle-aged wife who takes a young TV repairman for her lover.

Our Town (36). Revival of the play by Thornton Wilder. Produced by The American National Theater and Academy, Alfred de Liagre Jr. executive producer, Jean Dalrymple executive director, in the Plumstead Playhouse production, Martha Scott and Alfred de Liagre Jr. directors, at the ANTA Theater. Opened November 27, 1969. (Closed December 27, 1969)

Stage Manager .... Henry Fonda   Professor Willard .... John Fiedler
Dr. Gibbs .... Ed Begley   Mr. Webb .... John Randolph
Joe Crowell;   Woman in Balcony;
  Si Crowell .... Bryant Fraser   Lady in Box .... Enid Kent
Howie Newsome .... Thomas Coley   Man in Auditorium;
Mrs. Gibbs .... Mildred Natwick   Sam Craig .... Martin Shakar
Mrs. Webb .... Irene Tedrow   Simon Stimson .... John Beal
George Gibbs .... Harvey Evans   Mrs. Soames .... Margaret Hamilton
Rebecca Gibbs .... Denise Nickerson   Constable Warren .... Milo Boulton
Wally Webb .... Stephen Gustafson   Joe Stoddard .... William Robertson
Emily Webb .... Elizabeth Hartman   Farmer McCarthy ...... Delos V. Smith Jr.

Baseball Players: Martin Shakar, Lee Danielson, Steve Alpert, John Tormey, John Ventantonio. People of the Town: Leah M. Edlin, Terry Ross, Ruth Wright, Stellar Bennett, Diane Deering, Helen Ross, Lee Sanders, Edward Stevlingson.

Directed by Donald Driver; scenery, Edward Burbridge; costumes, David Toser; lighting, Jennifer Tipton; production stage manager, Nicholas Russiyan; press, John Springer Associates, Louise Weiner, Howard Haines.

Time: 1901 to 1913. Place: Grover's Corners, New Hampshire. The play is divided into three acts.

Our Town was first produced 2/4/38 by Jed Harris at Henry Miller's Theater for 336 performances. It was named a Best Play of its season and won the Pulitzer Prize. It was revived 1/10/44 for 24 performances at the City Center.

Buck White (7). Musical based on the play *Big Time Buck White* by Joseph Dolan Tuotti; with book, music and lyrics by Oscar Brown Jr. Produced by Zev Bufman in association with High John Productions at the George Abbott Theater. Opened December 2, 1969. (Closed December 6, 1969)

Hunter	Herschell Burton	Jive	Don Rich
Honey Man	David Moody	Buck White	Cassius Clay (Muhammad Ali)
Weasel	Ted Ross	Whitey	Eugene Smith
Rubber Band	Charles Weldon	Black Man	Don Sutherland

Understudies: Messrs. Moody, Rich—Don Sutherland; Mr. Ross—Van Kirksey; Mr. Weldon —Arnold Williams; Mr. Smith—Paul F. Canavan.

Directed by Oscar Brown Jr. and Jean Pace; musical direction, Merl Saunders; scenery, Edward Burbridge; lighting, Martin Aronstein; costumes, Jean Pace; musical arrangements, Mike Terry, Merl Saunders; orchestrations, Mike Terry; production stage manager, Martin Gold; press, Robert Ganshaw & John Prescott.

Time: The present. Place: The meeting hall of the Beautiful Allelujah Days organization.

The play on which the musical is based, *Big Time Buck White*, about a militant black lecturer coming to address a meeting arranged by a black social organization, was first produced in Los Angeles by Ron Rich, then off Broadway by Zev Bufman in association with Ron Rich and Leonard Grant 12/8/68 for 124 performances. The musical version *Buck White* was previously produced in San Francisco by Mel Goldblatt and Dialogue Black/White Company. Act I of this production played 18 performances off Broadway at the Village Gate 1/10/70-1/18/70.

ACT I

"Honey Man Song"	Honey Man
"Money, Money, Money"	Weasel, Honey Man
"Nobody Does My Thing"	Hunter
"Step Across That Line"	Rubber Band
"H.N.I.C."	Jive
"Beautiful Allelujah Days"	Jive, Weasel, Hunter, Rubber Band, Honey Man
"Tap the Plate"	Jive, Rubber Band, Honey Man
"Big Time Buck White Chant"	The Company

ACT II

"Big Time Buck White Chant"	Buck White, Company
"Better Far"	Buck
"We Came in Chains"	Buck, Company
"Black Balloons"	Buck, Company
"Look at Them"	Whitey
"Mighty Whitey"	Buck, Company
"Get Down"	Buck, Company

Private Lives (204). Revival of the play by Noel Coward. Produced by David Merrick in the APA production at the Billy Rose Theater. Opened December 4, 1969. (Closed May 30, 1970)

Sibyl Chase	Suzanne Grossmann	Amanda Prynne	Tammy Grimes
Elyot Chase	Brian Bedford	Louise	J.J. Lewis
Victor Prynne	David Glover		

Understudies: Misses Grimes, Lewis—Katherine Helmond; Messrs. Bedford, Glover—Bob Beard; Miss Grossmann—J.J. Lewis.

Directed by Stephen Porter; scenery and lighting, James Tilton; costumes, Joe Eula; stage manager, Lo Hardin; press, Harvey B. Sabinson, Lee Solters, Ted Goldsmith.

Time: A summer evening. Place: The terrace of a hotel in France and Amanda's flat in Paris.

After its original British production, *Private Lives* was first produced on Broadway by Charles B. Cochran 1/27/31 for 256 performances. It was subsequently revived on Broadway by John C. Wilson 10/4/48 for 248 performances and off Broadway on 5/19/68 for 9 performances.

The Mundy Scheme (4). By Brian Friel. Produced by Helen Bonfils and Morton Gottlieb by arrangement with Olympia Productions at the Royale Theater. Opened December 11, 1969. (Closed December 13, 1969)

Roger Nash	Patrick Bedford	Dan Mahon	Horace McMahon
Sally	Risa McCrary	Charles Hogan	Neil Fitzgerald
F.X. Ryan	Godfrey Quigley	Pat Toye	Ann Sweeny
Neil Boyle	Leo Leyden	Sean Grady	Liam Gannon
Mrs. Ryan	Dorothy Stickney	Tony Hanlan	William Rooney
Mick Moloney	Jack Cassidy	Owen	Sean Dillon

Standby: Messrs. Cassidy, Quigley—Laurence Hugo.

Directed by Donal Donnelly; scenery and lighting, William Ritman; costumes, Noel Taylor; production stage manager, Warren Crane; stage manager, William Rooney; press, Dorothy Ross, Ruth Cage.

Time: The present. Place: In the home of the Prime Minister, F.X. Ryan. Act I: Morning. Act II: Early hours of the following morning. Act III, Scene 1: Morning, three weeks later. Scene 2: Evening of the following day.

Comedy of political infighting around a fantastic scheme to develop Ireland as a burial ground for the dead of the world's crowded cities. A foreign play previously produced in Dublin.

La Strada (1). Musical based on the Federico Fellini film; book by Charles K. Peck Jr.; music and lyrics by Lionel Bart. Produced by Charles K. Peck Jr. and Canyon Productions, Inc. Opened and closed at the evening performance, December 14, 1969.

The Old Man; Alberti	John Coe	Zampano	Stephen Pearlman
Gelsomina	Bernadette Peters	Castra	Lucille Patton
Mother	Anne Hegira	Acrobats	Paul Charles, Harry Endicott
Elsa	Lisa Belleran	Mario (The Fool)	Larry Kert
Eva	Mary Ann Robbins	Mama Lambrini	Peggy Cooper
Sophia; Sister Claudia	Susan Goeppinger		

Company: Loretta Abbott, Glen Brooks, Henry Brunjes, Connie Burnett, Robert Carle, Paul Charles, Barbara Christopher, Peggy Cooper, Betsy Dickerson, Harry Endicott, Anna Maria Fanizzi, Jack Fletcher, Nino Galanti, Susan Goeppinger, Rodney Griffin, Mickey Gunnersen, Kenneth Krel, Don Lopez, Joyce Maret, Stan Page, Odette Panaccione, Mary Ann Robbins, Steven Ross, Larry Small, Eileen Taylor.

Directed by Alan Schneider; dances and musical numbers staged by Alvin Ailey; musical direction, Hal Hastings; scenery, Ming Cho Lee; costumes, Nancy Potts; lighting, Martin Aronstein; orchestrations, Eddie Sauter; dance music arrangements, Peter Howard; production stage manager, Terence Little; stage manager, William Callan; press, Frank Goodman, Les Schecter.

Time: The early 1950s. Place: In and around the cities and villages of Southern Italy.

A musical version of Federico Fellini's 1956 movie *La Strada,* about the characters in a touring carnival.

ACT I

Scene 1: A desolate beach near Gelsomina's House
"Seagull, Starfish, Pebble" ....Gelsomina
Scene 2: Along the road (La Strada)
"The Great Zampano" ....Gelsomina, Zampano
"What's Going on Inside?" ....Zampano
Scene 3: The outskirts of a village
"Belonging" ....Gelsomina
Scene 4: A farmhouse yard
Wedding Dance ....Entire Company
Scene 5: The farm stable
"I Don't Like You" ....Gelsomina
Scene 6: Along the Road
Encounters ....Gelsomina, Entire Company
"There's a Circus in Town" ....Mario

Scene 7: The Alberti Circus grounds
"You're Musical" ....Mario, Gelsomina
Scene 8: A performance of the Alberti Circus
"Only More!" ....Gelsomina

ACT II

Scene 1: The circus grounds
"What a Man" ....Gelsomina, Mama Lambrini
"Everything Needs Something" ....Gelsomina
Scene 2: A village square
"Sooner or Later" ....Mario
"Sooner or Later" (Reprise) ....Gelsomina
Scene 3: A convent
"Belonging" (Reprise) ....Gelsomina
Scene 4: Along the road
Scene 5: A camp site in the mountains
Scene 6: The end of the road
The End of the Road ....Entire Company

* Coco (188). Musical with book and lyrics by Alan Jay Lerner; music by Andre Previn. Produced by Frederick Brisson at the Mark Hellinger Theater. Opened December 18, 1969.

Coco	Katharine Hepburn	Simone	Charlene Ryan
Louis Greff	George Rose	Solange	Suzanne Rogers
Pignol	Jeanne Arnold	Noelle	Gale Dixon
Helene	Maggie Task	Dr. Petitjean	Richard Woods
Sebastian Baye	Rene Auberjonois	Claude	David Thomas
Armand	Al DeSio	Dwight Berkwit	Will B. Able
Albert	Jack Beaber	Eugene Bernstone	Robert Fitch
Docaton	Eve March	Ronny Ginsborn	Chad Block
Georges	David Holliday	Phil Rosenberry	Dan Siretta
Loublaye; Lapidus	Gene Varrone	Nadine	Leslie Daniel
Varne	Shirley Potter	On film:	
Marie	Margot Travers	Grand Duke Alexandrovitch	Bob Avian
Jeanine	Rita O'Connor	Grand Duke's voice	Jack Dabdoub
Claire	Graciela Daniele	Charles,	
Juliette	Lynn Winn	Duke of Glenallen	Michael Allinson
Madelaine	Carolyn Kirsch	Julian Lesage	Paul Dumont
Lucille	Diane Phillips	Papa	Jon Cypher
Colette	Rosemary Heyer		

Models, Seamstresses, Customers, Fitters: Vicki Allen, Karin Baker, Kathy Bartosh, Kathie Dalton, Alice Glenn, Maureen Hopkins, Linda Jorgens, Tresha Kelly, Nancy Killmer, Jan Metternich, Marilyn Miles, Joann Ogawa, Jean Preece, Ann Reinking, Skiles Ricketts, Marianne Selbert, Pamela Serpe, Bonnie Walker, Oscar Antony, Roy Barry, William James, Richard Marr, Don Percassi, Gerald Teijelo.

Standby: Miss Hepburn—Joan Copeland.

Directed by Michael Benthall; musical numbers and fashion sequences staged by Michael Bennett; musical direction, Robert Emmett Dolan; scenery and costumes, Cecil Beaton; lighting, Thomas Skelton; orchestrations, Hershy Kay; dance music continuity, Harold Wheeler; associate producer, Fred Hebert; production supervisor, Stone Widney; film sequences produced by Milton Olshin, directed by Fred Lemoine; production stage manager, Jerry Adler; stage manager, Edward Preston; press, Lee Solters, Harvey B. Sabinson, Leo Stern.

Time: Late fall of 1953 to late spring of 1954. Place: In the Maison Chanel, Rue Cambon, Paris, the salon or the apartment above or in memory. Act I, Scene 1: The salon. Scene 2: The apartment. Scene 3: The salon. Scene 4: The dressing room. Scene 5: The apartment. Scene 6: The salon. Act II, Scene 1: The salon. Scene 2: The apartment. Scene 3: The salon.

Story of the comeback out of retirement of the dress designer Gabrielle ("Coco") Chanel, with memory flashbacks occurring in the form of motion picture footage.

ACT I

"But That's the Way You Are" ....Alex
"The World Belongs to the Young" ....Coco, Greff, Sebastian, Pignol, Company

"Let's Go Home" ....Georges
"Mademoiselle Cliche de Paris" ....Coco
"On the Corner of the Rue Cambon" ....Coco
"The Money Rings Out Like Freedom" ....Coco, Ensemble
"A Brand New Dress" ....Noelle
"A Woman Is How She Loves" ....Georges
"Gabrielle" ....Papa
"Coco" ....Coco
"The Preparation" ....Coco, Company

ACT II

"Fiasco" ....Sebastian, Simone
"When Your Lover Says Goodbye" ....Greff
"Coco" (Reprise) ....Coco
"Ohrbach's, Bloomingdale's, Best & Saks" ....The Buyers
"Ohrbach's, Bloomingdale's, Best & Saks" (Reprise) ....Coco, Ensemble
"Always Mademoiselle" ....Coco, Mannequins

Love Is a Time of Day (8). By John Patrick. Produced by Shepherd Productions at the Music Box. Opened December 22, 1969. (Closed December 27, 1969)

April MacGregor ....Sandy Duncan   Skipper Allen ....Tom Ligon

Directed by Bernard Thomas; scenery, lighting, costumes, Lloyd Burlingame; production stage manager, Chuck Stockton; press, Merle Debuskey, M.J. Boyer.
Time: The present. Place: A student apartment in a state university town. Act I, Scene 1: The apartment. Scene 2: The next morning. Scene 3: Afternoon. Act II, Scene 1: A couple of weeks later. Scene 2: Several hours later. Scene 3: A few days later.
Comedy, first love affair of college students.

* Last of the Red Hot Lovers (177). By Neil Simon. Produced by Saint-Subber at the Eugene O'Neill Theater. Opened December 28, 1969.

Barney Cashman ....James Coco   Bobbi Michele ....Marcia Rodd
Elaine Navazio ....Linda Lavin   Jeanette Fisher ....Doris Roberts

Standbys: Mr. Coco—Tom Lacy; Miss Lavin—Doris Belack; Miss Rodd—Elizabeth Farley; Miss Roberts—Stella Longo.
Directed by Robert Moore; scenery, Oliver Smith; costumes, Donald Brooks; lighting, Peggy Clark; production stage manager, Tom Porter; stage manager, George Rondo; press, Harvey B. Sabinson, Lee Solters, Harry Nigro.
Time: The present. Place: An apartment in the East Thirties. Act I: December, late afternoon. Act II: August, late afternoon. Act III: September, late afternoon.
Comedy about a middle-aged, overweight, married restaurant owner trying to join the sexual revolution and failing in three assignations with three different women.
A Best Play; see page 131.

No Place To Be Somebody (16). Special engagement of the play by Charles Gordone. Produced by The American National Theater and Academy, Alfred de Liagre Jr. executive producer, Jean Dalrymple executive director, in the New York Shakespeare Festival Public Theater production produced by Joseph Papp, artistic director Gerald Freedman, associate producer Bernard Gersten, at the ANTA Theater. Opened December 30, 1969. (Closed January 10, 1970)

Gabe Gabriel ....Ron O'Neal   Mary Lou Bolton ....Laurie Crews
Shanty Mulligan ....Ronnie Thompson   Ellen ....Margaret Pine
Johnny Williams ....Nathan George   Sweets Crane ....Walter Jones
Dee Jacobson ....Susan G. Pearson   Mike Maffucci ....Nick Lewis
Evie Ames ....Lynda Westcott   Louie ....Michael Landrum
Cora Beasely ....Marge Eliot   Judge Bolton ....Ed VanNuys
Melvin Smeltz ....Henry Baker   Sergeant Cappaletti ....Charles Seals
Machine Dog ....Christopher St. John   Harry ....Malcolm Hurd

Standbys: Messrs. O'Neal, Baker—Nich Smith; Mr. George—Charles Gordone; Misses West-cott, Eliot—Mary Alice; Mr. Jones—W. Benson Terry.

Directed by Ted Cornell; scenery and lighting, Michael Davidson; scenery supervision, David Mitchell; lighting supervision, Martin Aronstein; stage manager, Adam G. Perl; press, Merle Debuskey, Faith Geer.

Time: The past fifteen years. Place: Johnny's Bar in the West Village.

No Place To Be Somebody was first produced off Broadway at the Public Theater in this production 5/4/69 for 250 performances and was named a Best Play of its season. It was re-produced for a return engagement off Broadway 1/20/70 (see its entry in the off-Broadway section of this volume).

The National Theater of the Deaf (8). Double bill of pantomime and sign language coordinated with spoken narration; **Sganarelle** by Molière, English translation by Albert Bermel, adapted by Eric Malzkuhn and Robert Panara; and **Songs From Milk Wood** from *Under Milk Wood* by Dylan Thomas, adapted by Bernard Bragg with Dorothy Miles. Produced by The American National Theater and Academy, Alfred de Liagre Jr. executive producer, Jean Dalrymple executive director, in the Eugene O'Neill Memorial Theater Center's National Theater of the Deaf production, David Hays managing director, at the ANTA Theater. Opened January 12, 1970. (Closed January 17, 1970)

SGANARELLE

Street Cleaners . .Jacqueline Awad, Lou Fant,	William Rhys	Martine . . . . .Mary Beth Miller
Lisette .Dorothy Miles		Servants . . . . .Linda Bove, Phyllis Frelich
Celie . . . . .Fredericka Norman		Grosrene . . . . .Edmund Waterstreet
Gorgibus . . . . .Patrick Graybill		Lelie .Richard Kendall
Sganarelle . . . . .Bernard Bragg		Dorante . . . . .John Basinger
		Villebrequin . . . . .Peter Wechsberg

Directed by Jack Sydow; scenery and costumes, Fred Voelpel; lighting, John Gleason; stage manager, Ken Swiger; press, Reginald Denenholz, Anne Woll.

The first New York production of *Sganarelle* was by the Washington Square Players the season of 1916-17. It was last produced in New York in French by Le Théâtre du Nouveau Monde at the Phoenix Theater in April and May, 1958.

SONGS FROM MILK WOOD

Second Voice . . . . .Jacqueline Awad, William Rhys	Willy, Mr. Ogmore . . . . .Richard Kendall
	Myfannwy Price, Mrs. Pugh . . .Dorothy Miles
Mr. Pugh, Sinbad Sailors . . . . .John Basinger	Bessie, Mrs. Pritchard . . . . .Mary Beth Miller
Mae Rose, Mrs. Owen . . . . .Linda Bove	Rosie,
First Voice . . . . .Bernard Bragg	Mrs. Dai Bread II . . . .Fredericka Norman
Captain Cat .Lou Fant	Mr. Waldo, Owen . . . . . .Edmund Waterstreet
Polly Garter . . . . .Phyllis Frelich	Boyo, Mr. Pritchard . . . . . . .Peter Wechsberg
Mog Edwards, Rev. Jenkins . .Patrick Graybill	

Directed by J. Ranelli; music, John Basinger; scenery, David Hays; costumes, Fred Voelpel; lighting, John Gleason.

Under Milk Wood, from which the material was derived, was first produced on Broadway 10/15/57 for 39 performances and was named a Best Play of its season. It was revived twice off Broadway by Circle in the Square, 3/29/61 for 202 performances and 11/16/62 for 64 performances.

Paris Is Out! (104). By Richard Seff. Produced by David Black in association with Donald J. Trump at the Brooks Atkinson Theater. Opened January 19, 1970; see note. (Closed April 19, 1970 matinee)

Hattie Fields . . . . .Dorothy Sands	Arlene Kander . . . . .Zina Jasper
Hortense Brand . . . . .Molly Picon	Andrew Grael . . . . .Gary Tigerman
Daniel Brand . . . . .Sam Levene	Charlotte Grael . . . . .Gwyda Donhowe
Roger Brand . . . . .Terry Kiser	Hellevi Gessnehr . . . . .Laryssa Lauret

Standbys: Miss Picon—Beatrice Pons; Mr. Levene—Jack Somack. Understudies: Miss Sands —Beatrice Pons; Misses Donhowe, Jasper, Lauret—Jane Singer; Mr. Kiser—John Towey; Mr. Tigerman—Garth Dolderer.

Directed by Paul Aaron; scenery, Douglas W. Schmidt; lighting, Martin Aronstein; costumes, Florence Klotz; stage manager, Bert Wood; press, Betty Lee Hunt, Henry Luhrman, Ruth D. Smuckler.

Time: The present. Place: New York City. Act I, Scene 1: 5:30 on a Thursday afternoon in September. Scene 2: Ten minutes later. Act II, Scene 1: Two hours later. Scene 2: 9:30 the following Saturday morning.

Comedy, much family ado about an elderly Jewish couple's plans for their first trip to Europe.

NOTE: Public performances of *Paris Is Out!* began 1/19/70, though at the request of the producer many of the reviews were held until a 2/3/70 release date.

Watercolor & Criss-Crossing (5). Program of two one-act plays by Philip Magdalany. Produced by The American National Theater and Academy, Alfred de Liagre Jr. executive producer, Jean Dalrymple executive director, in the Playwrights Unit of Theater 1970 (Richard Barr, Edward Albee and Charles Woodward) production at the ANTA Theater. Opened January 21, 1970. (Closed January 24, 1970)

WATERCOLOR

Andrew ....Donald Warfield	Edith ....Kate Wilkinson
Benjamin ....Peter Lazer	Gloria ....Jennifer Salt
Diane ....Jacqueline Brookes	

CRISS-CROSSING

Adolph ....Lee Goodman	Constance ....Cathryn Damon
Augustus ....Robert Reiser	Catherine ....Patricia O'Connell
Arnold ....Patrick Baldauff	Carlotta ....Mary Louise Wilson
Barbara ....Judith Granite	

Directed by Chuck Gnys; scenery and costumes, Peter Harvey; lighting, Richard Nelson; sound tapes, David Walker; stage manager, Robert Moss; press, Betty Lee Hunt, Henry Luhrman.

WATERCOLOR—Time: The present. Place: A beach somewhere in the United States. Vignettes of sex and philosophy among various couples.

CRISS-CROSSING—Time: The present. Place: A city somewhere in the United States. A cartoon of modern violence, with guns blazing.

Brightower (1). By Dore Schary. Produced by Michael Byron and Mel Weiser at the John Golden Theater. Opened and closed at the evening performance January 28, 1970.

Jess ....Will Hussung	Lori Granger ....Martha Galphin
Sara Brightower ....Geraldine Brooks	Nick Hagen ....Paul McGrath
Daniel Brightower ....Robert Lansing	Bill Canfield ....Richard Buck
Clay Benson ....Arlen Dean Snyder	

Directed by Mel Weiser; scenery, Tom Munn; costumes, Noel Taylor; lighting, John Gleason; production stage manager, Harry Young; stage manager, Andy M. Rasbury; press, Bill Doll and Company, Midori Lederer.

Time: The present and the past. Place: The home of Daniel Brightower in Vermont. The play is divided into two acts and four scenes.

The question of the right to privacy is examined in a biographer's research into the life— and death by suicide—of a famous writer.

Sheep on the Runway (105). By Art Buchwald. Produced by Roger L. Stevens, Robert Whitehead and Robert W. Dowling at the Helen Hayes Theater. Opened January 31, 1970. (Closed May 2, 1970)

Ambassador	
Raymond Wilkins	David Burns
Martha Wilkins	Elizabeth Wilson
Sam	Jeremiah Morris
Holly	Margaret Ladd
Joseph Mayflower	Martin Gabel
Fred Slayton	Will Mackenzie
Prince Gow	Richard Castellano
General Fitzhugh	Barnard Hughes
Edward Snelling	Remak Ramsay
Colonel Num	Neil Flanagan
Guards, Workmen	Kurt Garfield, Henry Proach

Understudies: Mr. Gabel—Jeremiah Morris; Messrs. Burns, Hughes—Howard Fischer; Mr. Castellano—Jeremiah Morris, William Becker; Miss Wilson—Helen Stenborg; Messrs. Mackenzie, Ramsay, Russell Horton; Miss Ladd—Eda Zahl; Mr. Flanagan—William Becker; Mr. Morris—Henry Proach.

Directed by Gene Saks; scenery, Peter Larkin; costumes, Jane Greenwood; lighting, Jules Fisher; production stage manager, Frederic de Wilde; stage manager, Howard Fischer; press, Seymour Krawitz, Fred Weterick.

Time: The present. Place: The living room of the United States Embassy in the Kingdom of Nonomura, a remote monarchy in the Himalayas. Act I, Scene 1: A summer evening. Scene 2: About a week later. Act II, Scene 1: The next morning. Scene 2: Some time later.

Comedy about an American columnist trumping up a cold war incident in a peaceful Asian area.

Comédie Française. Repertory of four programs in the French language. **La Troupe du Roi** by Molière, La Grange and Boileau (scenes from *Les Precieuses Ridicules, L'Ecole des Femmes, Tartuffe, Monsieur de Pourceaugnac, Le Bourgeois Gentilhomme, Les Fourberies de Scapin* and *L'Avare*) and **Amphitryon** by Molière (6). Opened February 3, 1970. **Dom Juan** (5). By Molière. Opened February 6, 1970. **Les Femmes Savantes** (5). By Molière. Opened February 13, 1970. **Le Malade Imaginaire** (8). By Molière. Opened February 17, 1970. Produced by S. Hurok by arrangement with the French Government in the Comédie Française productions, Maurice Escande administrator general, at the New York City Center. (Repertory closed February 22, 1970)

PERFORMER	"LA TROUPE DU ROI"	"DOM JUAN"	"LES FEMMES SAVANTES"	"LE MALADE IMAGINAIRE"
Jacques Buron	Dancing Teacher	Dom Carlos	Lépine	Cléante
Geneviève Casile	Mlle. du Parc	Elvire	Armande	
Georges Chamarat	Harpagon	M. Dimanche	Vadius	Purgon
Jacques Charon	M. de Pourceaugnac; M. Jourdain	Sganarelle	Chrysale	Argan
Bérengère Dautun	Mlle. Béjart	Servant; Ghost		Béline
Georges Descriéres	Le Grange	Dom Juan	Trissotin	
Simon Eine	Brécourt; Lysidas	Dom Alonse		M. Bonnefoi
Jacques Eyser	Arnolphe	Dom Louis	Ariste	M. Diafoirus
Denise Gence	Mlle. du Croisy; Magdelon		Bélise	
Catherine Hiegel	Mlle. de Brie; Agnès	Mathurine	Henriette	Angélique
Robert Hirsch	Tartuffe			
Jean-Louis Jemma	Géronte	Dom Gusman	Notary	
Jean-Luc Moreau				Thomas
Jean Piat	Molière; Eraste; Argan			
Jean-Paul Rousillon	Mascarille; Scapin	Pierrot		
Catherine Samie	Cathos; Toinette	Charlotte	Martine	
Françoise Seigner	Mlle. Hervé; Dorine		Philaminte	Toinette
Jacques Toja	Boleau	La Ramee; Ragotin	Clitandre	Béralde
Marcel Tristani	Du Croisy; Béralde	Statue	Julien	M. Fleurant
Claude Winter	Elmire			

AMPHITRYON

Sosie	Robert Hirsch	Posiclès	Marcel Tristani
Mercure	Jean Piat	Polidas	Jacques Buron
Argatiphontidas	Jacques Eyser	Cléanthis	Denise Gence
Amphitryon	Georges Descriéres	Alcmène	Geneviève Casile
Jupiter	Jacques Toja	Goddess of the Night	Bérengère Dautun
Naucratès	Simon Eine		

All plays: director general of the stage, Roger Hoff; musical director, Olivier Bernard; choreographer, Norbert Scmucki; simultaneous English translation, Helen Gillespie Atlas, Edward Greer; stage managers, Henri Salles, Bruce Bassman; press, Martin Feinstein, Dale Heapps, James Murtha.

LA TROUPE DU ROI—Produced by Paul-Emile Deiber; performed by the entire company; musical accompaniment taken from Jean-Baptiste Lully and Marc Antoine Charpentier.

Homage to Molière in the form of a dialogue between Molière and the members of his company.

AMPHITRYON—Directed by Jean Meyer; decor and costumes, Suzanne Lalique, inspired by Giacomo Torelli.

Amphitryon was last produced at the Ziegfeld Theater 11/20/52 for 12 performances in the Jean-Louis Barrault production under S. Hurok's auspices.

DOM JUAN—Directed by Antoine Bourseiller; decor and costumes, Oskar Gustin.

Under the title *Don Juan* this play's last New York production was by the Théâtre National Populaire 10/28/58 under S. Hurok's auspices. There is no New York production of record under the Portugese spelling of the title, *Dom Juan*, used by Molière.

LES FEMMES SAVANTES—Directed by Jean Meyer; decor and costumes, Suzanne Lalique.

Les Femmes Savantes (The Learned Ladies) was last produced off Broadway by Le Tréteau de Paris 2/6/67 for 9 performances.

LE MALADE IMAGINAIRE—Directed by Jean-Laurent Cochet; decor and costumes, Jacques Marillier.

Le Malade Imaginaire (The Imaginary Invalid) was last produced on Broadway by The National Repertory Theater, in English, 5/1/67 for 6 performances.

Charles Aznavour (23). One-man program of songs, many in the French language, written and sung by Charles Aznavour. Produced by Norman Twain in association with Albert I. Fill at the Music Box. Opened February 4, 1970. (Closed February 22, 1970)

Music and lyrics for all songs by Charles Aznavour unless otherwise noted; musical director and pianist, Henry Byrs; production supervisor, Leon Sanossian; press, Frank Goodman, Les Schecter.

Mr. Aznavour appeared on Broadway in a one-man show 10/14/65 for 29 performances, under the title *The World of Charles Aznavour*. A foreign show previously produced in Paris elsewhere.

PART I: "Le Tamos" (lyricist, J. Davis), "I Will Give to You" (translator, B. Morrisson), "Happy Anniversary" (translator, H. Kretzmer), "We'll Drift Away" (lyricist, G. Garvarentz, translator, B. Kaye), "Le Toreador," "Sunday's Not My Day" (lyricist, T. Veran, translator, B. Morrisson), "Apaga La Luz" (translator, R. Deleon), "Isabelle," "I Will Warm Your Heart" (translator, G. Lees), "To My Daughter" (translator, B. Morrisson), "Et Pourtant" (lyricist, G. Garvarentz), "The Wine of Youth" (translator, B. Morrisson), "Yesterday When I Was Young" (translator, H. Kretzmer), "Emmenez-Moi," "It Will Be My Day" (translator, B. Morrisson).

PART II: "All Those Pretty Girls" (translator, B. Kaye), "De T'Avoir Aimer," "My Hand Needs Your Hand" (lyricist, P. Roche, translator, B. Kaye), "You've Let Yourself Go" (translator, M. Stellman), "Desormais" (lyricist, G. Garvarentz), "Who" (translator, H. Kretzmer), "Reste," "Venice Dressed in Blue" (composer, F. Dorin, translator, B. Kaye), "La Bohême" (composer, J. Plante), "August Days in Paree" (lyricist, G. Garvarentz, translator, D. Newburg), "Les Comediens" (composer, J. Plante), "And I in My Chair" (translator, D. Newburg), "You've Got to Learn" (translator, M. Stellman), "Les Bons Moments."

Gloria and Esperanza (13). By Julie Bovasso. Produced by The American National Theater and Academy in the La Mama Experimental Theater Club production at the ANTA Theater. Opened February 4, 1970. (Closed February 14, 1970)

Julius Esperanza ....Kevin O'Connor
Gloria B. Gilbert ....Julie Bovasso
Prof. Poe; Steissbart ......Hervé Villechaize
Solange; St. Bernard ....Daffi
Mailman; St. Augustine;
  Alvin; Dragon ....Ted Henning
Terry Wong Fu ....Dan Durning
Psychiatrist; St. Anthony .....Leonard Hicks
Dr. Brown; St. Ambrose .....Maury Cooper
Jack Sinistre ....Alex Beall
St. Teresa ....Reigh Hagen

St. John ....John Bacher
St. Dominic; Alvin's Mother;
  Woman Clothed in the Sun ..Dennis Sokal
St. Boniface ....Wes Williams
St. Agnes ....Sara Dolley
St. Felicite ....Deirdre Simone
Mary and Martha ....Marie D'Elia,
                 Ella Luxembourg
Eric von Schtutt ....Tom Rosica
Marsha ....Jane Sanford
Alpha and Omega ....Louis Ramos

Agitators, Guru Children, Soldiers, Attendants, Gladiators, Basketball Ballet Girls, Oriental Guerrilla Dancers, Four Horsewomen Showgirls of the Apocalypse, Star Angels, Sword Angels, Trumpet Angels: Alex Beall, Reigh Hagen, Wes Williams, Alan Wynroth, Maria D'Elia, Sara Dolley, Daffi, John Bacher, Deirdre Simone, Dennis Sokal, Ella Luxembourg, Laverne Jamison, Jane Sanford, William Pierce, Louis Ramos, Peter Bartlett, Carl Wilson, Myra Lee.

Directed by Julie Bovasso; associate director and choreographer, Raymond Bussey; scenery, Daffi; costumes, Ella Luxembourg and The Birdie Sisters; lighting, Keith Michael; scenery and costumes supervised by Peter Harvey; lighting supervised by Richard Nelson; assistant choreographer, William Pierce; production stage manager, Glen Nielson; press, Howard Atlee, David Roggensack, Stanley F. Kaminsky.

Act I, Scene 1: A basement apartment. Scene 2: The emergency room. Act II, Scene 1: In the madhouse—saints and martyrs. Scene 2: Back in the basement. Scene 3: The Alvin and His Mother TV show. Scene 4: The revelations revue.

The coming to maturity of an artist in a series of symbolic adventures with a psychiatrist, a madhouse, a TV show, etc. Previously produced off off Broadway by the Cafe La Mama organization, of which Ellen Stewart is the founder and director.

Gantry (1). Musical based on the novel *Elmer Gantry* by Sinclair Lewis; book by Peter Bellwood; music by Stanley Lebowsky; lyrics by Fred Tobias. Produced by Joseph Cates and Jerry Schlossberg at the George Abbott Theater. Opened and closed at the evening performance, February 14, 1970.

Bill Morgan ....Tom Batten
Sister Doretha ....Dorothea Freitag
Adelberta Shoup ....Gloria Hodes
Sharon Falconer ....Rita Moreno
Elmer Gantry ....Robert Shaw
Jim Lefferts ....Wayne Tippit
George F. Babbitt ....Ted Thurston
Rev. Garrison ....Kenneth Bridges

Trosper ....Bob Gorman
Gunch ....David Sabin
Prout ....Zale Kessler
Rev. Toomis ....David Hooks
Architect ....Robert Donahue
Photographer ....James N. Maher
Deaf Man ....J. Michael Bloom
Deaf Man's Wife ....Beth Fowler

Townspeople, Revival Troupe, Students, Workmen: Chuck Beard, J. Michael Bloom, Kenneth Bridges, Patrick Cummings, Robert Donahue, Sandy Ellen, Carol Estey, Beth Fowler, Gloria Hodes, Keith Kaldenberg, Clyde Laurents, Robert Lenn, James N. Maher, Kathleen Robey, Dixie Stewart, Diane Tarleton, Maralyn Thoma, Terry Violino, Mimi Wallace.

Directed by Onna White; musical direction, Arthur Rubinstein; scenery, Robin Wagner; costumes, Ann Roth; lighting, Jules Fisher; orchestrations, Jim Tyler; dance arrangements, Dorothea Freitag; vocal arrangements, Stanley Lebowsky; associate to the director, Martin Allen; assistant choreographer, Patrick Cummings; production stage manager, Ben Janney; associate producer, Fred Menowitz; production supervisor, Robert Weiner; stage manager, William Letters; press, David Powers.

Act I, Scene 1: Revival tent, Shelton, Ill. Scene 2: Train. Scene 3: Revival tent, Fargo, N.D. Scene 4: Revival tent, Page City, Kan. Scene 5: Sister Sharon's dressing room. Scene 6: Revival tent, McAllaster, Kan. Scene 7: Sister Sharon's Hotel Suite in Chicago. Act II, Scene 1: Revival tent, Chicago. Scene 2: Revival tent grounds. Scene 3: A warehouse in Chicago. Scene 4: Revival tent. Scene 5: The office of the Church Board. Scene 6: The Tabernacle office. Scene 7: Outside the "Waters of Jordan" Tabernacle.

Musical version of Sinclair Lewis's 1927 novel about a revival preacher.

ACT I

"Wave a Hand" ....Morgan, Troupe
Gantry Gets the Call ....Gantry, Troupe, Townspeople

"He Was There"
"Play Ball With the Lord"
"Katie Jonas" ....Sharon
"Thanks, Sweet Jesus!" ....Gantry, Townspeople
"Someone I've Already Found" ....Gantry
"He's Never Too Busy" ....Sharon, Gantry, Morgan, Adelberta, Troupe
"We're Sharin' Sharon" ....Gantry

ACT II

"We Can All Give Love" ....Sharon, Adelberta, Townspeople
"Foresight" ....Babbitt, Gunch, Trosper, Prout
"These Four Walls" ....Sharon
"Show Him the Way" ....Gantry, Townspeople
"The Promise of What I Could Be" ....Gantry
"Gantry's Reaction" ....Gantry
"We're Sharin' Sharon" (Reprise) ....Gantry

* **Child's Play** (119). By Robert Marasco. Produced by David Merrick at the Royale Theater. Opened February 17, 1970.

Faculty:

Paul Reese ....Ken Howard	Medley ....Christopher Deane
Father Penny ....David Rounds	Banks ....Robbie Reed
Father Griffin ....Peter MacLean	Jennings ....Mark Hall
Jerome Malley ....Fritz Weaver	O'Donnell ....Frank Fiore
Joseph Dobbs ....Pat Hingle	Shea ....Patrick Shea
Father Mozian ....Michael McGuire	Wilson ....Ron Martin
Students:	McArdle ....Lloyd Kramer
Carre ....Bryant Fraser	Travis ....John Handy

Understudies: Mr. Hingle—Joseph Hill; Mr. Weaver—Michael McGuire; Mr. Howard—Patrick Shea; Mr. Shea—Ron Martin.

Directed by Joseph Hardy; scenery and lighting, Jo Mielziner; costumes, Sara Brook; sound, Gary Harris; associate producer, Samuel Liff; production stage manager, Mitchell Erickson; stage manager, John Handy; press, Harvey B. Sabinson, Lee Solters, Sandra Manley.

Time: The present. Place: St. Charles' School in mid-winter. The play was presented without intermission.

A mysterious, evil violence pervades a boys' school.

A Best Play; see page 148.

Norman, Is That You? (12). By Ron Clark and Sam Bobrick. Produced by Harold D. Cohen at the Lyceum Theater. Opened February 19, 1970. (Closed February 28, 1970)

Norman Chambers ....Martin Huston	Mary ....Dorothy Emmerson
Garson Hobart ....Walter Willison	Beatrice Chambers ......Maureen Stapleton
Ben Chambers ....Lou Jacobi	

Understudies: Misses Emmerson, Stapleton—Janice Mars; Messrs. Huston, Willison—Sean Simpson.

Directed by George Abbott; scenery, William and Jean Eckart; costumes, Florence Klotz; lighting, Fred Allison; production stage manager, Bernard Pollock; press, Lee Solters, Harvey B. Sabinson, Jay Russell.

Time: The present, early October. Place: A New York apartment. Act I, Scene 1: Early morning. Scene 2: Later that afternoon. Scene 3: Later that evening. Act II, Scene 1: Later that night. Scene 2: Several days later.

Comedy, an Ohio father visits his son in New York, only to discover that the son is living openly as a homosexual.

Harvey (79). Revival of the play by Mary Chase. Produced by The American National Theater and Academy, Alfred de Liagre Jr. executive producer, Jean Dalrymple executive director, in the Phoenix Theater production, T. Edward Hambleton managing director, at the ANTA theater. Opened February 24, 1970. (Closed May 2, 1970)

Myrtle Mae Simmons	Marian Hailey	Lyman Sanderson	Joe Ponazecki
Veta Louise Simmons	Helen Hayes	William Chumley	Henderson Forsythe
Elwood P. Dowd	James Stewart	Betty Chumley	Peggy Pope
Ethel Chauvinet	Dorothy Blackburn	Judge Gaffney	John C. Becher
Ruth Kelly	Mariclare Costello	E.J. Lofgren	Dort Clark
Duane Wilson	Jesse White		

Understudies: Miss Hayes—Dorothy Blackburn; Misses Costello, Blackburn, Hailey, Pope—Zoe Kamitses; Messrs. White, Ponazecki, Clark—Don Lamb; Messrs. Forsythe, Becher—Alexander Clark.

Directed by Stephen Porter; scenery and lighting, James Tilton; costumes, Nancy Potts; production stage manager, Bruce Hoover; stage manager, Don Lamb; press, Sol Jacobson, Lewis Harmon.

Time: The present. Place: The library of the old Dowd family mansion and the reception room of Chumley's Rest in a city in the Far West.

Harvey was first produced 11/1/44 at the 48th Street Theater for 1,775 performances, the 4th longest-running play in Broadway history. It won the Pulitzer Prize and was named a Best Play of its season. This is its first New York revival of record.

Georgy (4). Musical based on a novel by Margaret Forster and a screen play by Margaret Forster and Peter Nichols; book by Tom Mankiewicz; music by George Fischoff; lyrics by Carole Bayer. Produced by Fred Coe in association with Joseph P. Harris and Ira Bernstein at the Winter Garden. Opened February 26, 1970. (Closed February 28, 1970)

Georgy	Dilys Watling	Peg	Helena Carroll
James Leamington	Stephen Elliott	Jos	John Castle
Ted	Louis Beachner	Peter	Richard Quarry
Meredith	Melissa Hart	Health Officer	Cynthia Latham

Party Guests, Londoners, etc.: Kathryn Doby, Sherry Durham, Patricia Garland, Margot Head, Mary Jane Houdina, Jane Karel, Barbara Monte-Britton, Michon Peacock, Mary Zahn, Rick Atwell, Pi Douglass, Arthur Faria, Charlie Goeddertz, Neil Jones, Sal Pernice, Richard Quarry, Allan Sobek, Tony Stevens. Children: Kelley Boa, Mona Daleo, Jackie Paris, Donna Sands, Jill Streisant, Dewey Golkin, Jeffrey Golkin, Anthony Marciona, Roger Morgan, Johnny Welch. Singers: Susan Goeppinger, Del Horstmann, Don Jay, Geoff Leon, Regina Lynn.

Understudies: Miss Watling—Carol Prandis; Miss Hart—Barbara Monte-Britton; Messrs. Elliott, Beachner—John O'Leary; Misses Carroll, Latham—Myra Carter; Mr. Quarry—Allan Sobek.

Directed by Peter Hunt; choreography, Howard Jeffrey; musical direction and vocal arrangements, Elliot Lawrence; scenery and lighting, Jo Mielziner; costumes, Patricia Zipprodt; orchestrations, Eddie Sauter; dance music arrangements, Marvin Laird; production manager, Porter Van Zandt; stage manager, Philip Mandelker; press, Karl Bernstein, Dan Langan.

Time: The present. Place: London. Act I, Scene 1: A playground. Scene 2: Georgy and Meredith's flat. Scene 3: A street. Scene 4: The flat. Scene 5: James Leamington's house. Scene 6: The flat. Scene 7: London streets. Scene 8: James Leamington's house. Scene 9: The flat. Scene 10: A street. Scene 11: Apollo Cinema, Piccadilly Circus. Act II, Scene 1: The flat. Scene 2: A street. Scene 3: James Leamington's house. Scene 4: The flat. Scene 5: A playground.

Story based on the novel *Georgy Girl* (and the movie of the same title) about the romantic adventures of a plain but appealing young girl in modern London.

ACT I

"Howdjadoo"	Georgy, Children
"Make It Happen Now"	Georgy
"Ol' Pease Puddin'"	Jos, Georgy
"Just for the Ride"	Meredith, Men
"So What?"	Georgy
"Georgy"	James

"A Baby" and "Howdjadoo" (Reprise) ....Georgy, Jos, Meredith
"That's How It Is" ....Georgy, James
"There's a Comin' Together" ....Jos, Georgy, Chorus

ACT II

"Something Special" ....Georgy, Jos
"Half of Me" ....Georgy
"Gettin' Back to Me" ....Meredith
"Sweet Memory" ....Ted, James, Chorus
"Georgy" (Reprise) ....James
"Life's a Holiday" ....Jos, Georgy
"Make It Happen Now" (Reprise) ....Georgy
Finale: "There's a Comin' Together" (Reprise) ....Company

The Chinese and Dr. Fish (15). Program of two one-act plays by Murray Schisgal. Produced by Gilbert Cates at the Ethel Barrymore Theater. Opened March 10, 1970. (Closed March 21, 1970)

DR. FISH

Charlotte Mendelsohn ....Charlotte Rae   Dr. Fish ....Marvin Lichterman
Mrs. Fish ....Paula Trueman   Marty Mendelsohn ....Vincent Gardenia

THE CHINESE

Mr. Lee ....Joseph Bova   Gladys Hoffman ....Louise Lasser
Mrs. Lee ....Alice Drummond   Pu Ping Chow ....Marcia Jean Kurtz
Chester Lee ....William Devane

Standbys: Misses Drummond, Rae, Trueman—Vera Lockwood; Messrs. Bova, Gardenia—William Callan; Miss Lasser—Marcia Jean Kurtz; Miss Kurtz—Louise Lasser.

Directed by Arthur Storch; scenery, William Pitkin; lighting, Martin Aronstein; costumes, Sara Brook; production stage manager, Martin Gold; stage manager, William Callan; press, Harvey B. Sabinson, Lee Solters, Marilynn LeVine.

DR. FISH—Time: The present, 1 p.m. Place: At Dr. Fish's. Comedy, a wife's sex problems are multiplied when she consults an expert about them.

THE CHINESE—Time: The present, late afternoon. Place: At the Lees. Comedy, young man with Chinese parents is pretending to be Jewish, to his family's dismay.

* **Purlie** (89). Musical based on the play *Purlie Victorious* by Ossie Davis; book by Ossie Davis, Philip Rose and Peter Udell; music by Gary Geld; lyrics by Peter Udell. Produced by Philip Rose at the Broadway Theater. Opened March 15, 1970.

Purlie ....Cleavon Little   Gitlow ....Sherman Hemsley
Church Soloist ....Linda Hopkins   Charlie ....C. David Colson
Lutiebelle ....Melba Moore   Idella ....Helen Martin
Missy ....Novella Nelson   Ol' Cap'n ....John Heffernan

Dancers: Loretta Abbott, Hope Clark, Judy Gibson, Lavinia Hamilton, Arlene Rowlant, Ella Thompson, Myrna White, Morris Donaldson, George Faison, Al Perryman, Harold Pierson, William Taylor, Larry Vickers.

Singers: Carolyn Bird, Barbara Christopher, Denise Elliott, Synthia Jackson, Mildred Lane, Alyce Webb, Mildred Pratcher, Peter Colly, Milt Grayson, Tony Middleton, Ray Pollard.

Understudies: Mr. Little—Robert Jackson; Miss Moore—Synthia Jackson; Mr. Hemsley—Ted Ross; Messrs. Heffernan, Colson—Curt Williams; Miss Martin—Alyce Webb; Miss Hopkins—Mildred Lane; Swing Dancer—Ted Goodridge.

Directed by Philip Rose; choreography, Louis Johnson; scenery, Ben Edwards; costumes, Ann Roth; lighting, Thomas Skelton; orchestrations and choral arrangements, Garry Sherman and Luther Henderson; musical supervisor, Garry Sherman; musical conductor, Joyce Brown; dance music arrangements, Luther Henderson; production stage manager, Leonard Auerbach; stage manager, Mortimer Halpern; press, Merle Debuskey, Faith Geer.

Time: Not too long ago (Acts I & II action takes place before that of the Prologue and Epilogue). Place: South Georgia.

The last gasp of condescending paternalism on a Georgia plantation, in the story of a young preacher, Purlie, who comes home and stirs things up, as per Ossie Davis's play.

ACT I

Prologue: Big Bethel, a country church
"Walk Him up the Stairs" ....Entire Company
Scene 1: A shack on the plantation
"New Fangled Preacher Man" ....Purlie
"Skinnin' a Cat" ....Gitlow, Field Hands
"Purlie" ....Lutiebelle
"The Harder They Fall" ....Purlie, Lutiebelle
Scene 2: Outside Ol' Cap'n Commissary
"Charlie's Songs" ....Charlie
"Big Fish, Little Fish" ....Ol' Cap'n, Charlie
Scene 3: Outside Ol' Cap'n Commissary
"I Got Love" ....Lutiebelle
"Great White Father" ....Cotton Pickers
"Skinnin' a Cat" (Reprise) ....Gitlow, Charlie
Scene 4: The shack
"Down Home" ....Purlie, Missy

ACT II

Scene 1: On the plantation, 4 a.m.
"First Thing Monday Mornin' " ....Cotton Pickers
Scene 2: The shack, just before dawn
"He Can Do It" ....Missy, Lutiebelle
"The Harder They Fall" (Reprise) ....Gitlow, Lutiebelle, Missy
"The World is Comin' to a Start" ....Charlie, Company
Epilogue: Time and place as in Prologue
"Walk Him up the Stairs" (Reprise) ....Entire Company

Grin and Bare It! adapted by Ken McGuire from a play by Tom Cushing and **Postcards** by James Prideaux (16). Program of two one-act plays. Produced by Barnett Wolfe Plaxen at the Belasco Theater. Opened March 16, 1970. (Closed March 28, 1970)

POSTCARDS

Margaret ....Kate Wilkinson   Leonard ....Ray Stewart

GRIN AND BARE IT!

Diana Smith ....Joleen Fodor   Heinrich Braun ....Tom Fuccello
Derek Leet ....David Christmas   Professor
Agamemnon Smith ....James Burge   Persius Smith ....William Le Massena
Katinka ....Blanche Dee   Mrs. Smith ....Barbara Lester
Mitzi Braun ....Jeanne Pasle-Green   Aunt Minna ....Avril Gentles

Understudies: Messrs. Burge, Fuccello—Philip Larson.
Directed by Ronny Graham; scenery, David Mitchell; costumes, Dominic Poleo; lighting, Martin Aronstein; associate producers, Judith Robin, Sandra Yanowitz; production stage manager, D.W. Koehler; stage manager, Charles Kindl; press, Mary Bryant, Meg Gordean, David Rothenberg.
GRIN AND BEAR IT!—Time: Summer 1929. Place: Outside of Los Angeles. Subtitled "The Unplayable Play," this comedy is about the daughter of a nudist family who brings her fiance home to meet the folks, all of whom are stark naked.
POSTCARDS—Curtain-raiser about a man and woman competing in phrasing post cards to be sent to famous persons.

Blood Red Roses (1). Musical with book and lyrics by John Lewin; music by Michael Valenti. Produced by Seymour Vall and Louis S. Goldman in association with Rick Mandell and Bjorn I. Swanstrom at the John Golden Theater. Opened and closed at the evening performance March 22, 1970.

Guard; Evans	William Tost	Pvt. William Cockroft	Jess Richards
Guard	Bill Gibbens	Pvt. John Smalls	Philip Bruns
Queen Victoria; Bessie Bellwood; Florence		W.H. Russell	Jay Gregory
Nightingale; Alice Crabbe	Jeanie Carson	Russian Soldier	Charles Abbott
Prince Albert	Ronald Drake	Cornet Edwin May	Lowell Harris
Lord Raglan	Sydney Walker		

Directed by Alan Schneider; musical numbers staged by Larry Fuller; musical direction, Milton Setzer; scenery, Ed Wittstein; costumes, Deirdre Cartier; lighting, Tharon Musser; orchestrations, Julian Stein, Abba Bogin; production stage manager, Rick Thayer; press, Abby Hirsch.

Time: 1854-55. Place: Britain, the Crimean Peninsula during the Crimean War.

An anti-war play with songs using the Crimean War as its adverse example, with several historical characters.

ACT I

Scene 1: Buckingham Palace and environs
"The Cream of English Youth" ....British Army
"A Garden in the Sun" ....Victoria, Albert, Raglan
"In the Country Where I Come From" ....Cockroft
"The Cream of English Youth" (continued) ....Smalls, Cockroft
Scene 2: The hills of Crimea
"Black Dog Rum" ....Fusiliers
Scene 3: Another part of the terrain
"How Fucked up Things Are" ....Smalls, Cockroft
Scene 4: Stinks—detail
"The English Rose" ....Smalls, Cockroft
Scene 5: Balmoral Castle
"O Rock Eternal" ....Victoria, Albert
"Soldiers Anthem" ....Fusiliers

ACT II

Scene 1: The Crimean plateau
"Prelude" ....Fusiliers
"Blood Red Roses" ....Cockroft
"The Fourth Light Dragoons" ....Cornet May
"The English Rose" (continued) ....Smalls
Scene 2: The Cave of Harmony
"The English Rose" (continued) ....Civilians
"Song of Greater Britain" ....Bessie Bellwood
Scene 3: The hospital at Scutari
Scene 4: England again
"Song of the Fair Dissenter Lass" ....Alice Crabbe
Finale ....Entire Company

Minnie's Boys (76). Musical with book by Arthur Marx and Robert Fisher; music by Larry Grossman; lyrics by Hal Hackady. Produced by Arthur Whitelaw, Max J. Brown and Byron Goldman at the Imperial Theater. Opened March 26, 1970. (Closed May 30, 1970)

Julie Marx (Groucho)	Lewis J. Stadlen	Minnie Marx	Shelley Winters
Leonard Marx (Chico)	Irwin Pearl	Sam (Frenchie) Marx	Arny Freeman
Adolph Marx (Harpo)	Daniel Fortus	Hochmeister	Merwin Goldsmith
Herbie Marx (Zeppo)	Alvin Kupperman	Al Shean	Mort Marshall
Milton Marx (Gummo)	Gary Raucher	Cop	Doug Spingler
Mrs. Flanagan; Harpist	Jean Bruno	Sidebark	Ronn Hansen
Mrs. Krupnik;		Aerobats	Evelyn Taylor, David Vaughan,
Murdock	Jacqueline Britt		George Bunt

Cindy; Miss White House ....Marjory Edson
Maxie; Sandow ....Richard B. Shull
Telegraph Boy ....Stephen Reinhardt
Robwell ....Casper Roos
Theater Manager ....Gene Ross

E.F. Albee ....Roland Winters
Mrs. McNish ....Julie Kurnitz
Miss Taj Mahal ....Lynne Gannaway
Miss Eiffel Tower ....Vicki Frederick

Ensemble: Jacqueline Britt, Jean Bruno, Bjarne Buchtrup, George Bunt, Dennis Cole, Deede Darnell, Joan B. Duffin, Marjory Edson, Vicki Frederick, Marcelo Gamboa, Lynne Gannaway, Ronn Hansen, Elaine Manzel, Stephen Reinhardt, Casper Roos, Gene Ross, Carole Schweid, William W. Sean, Doug Spingler, Evelyn Taylor, David Vaughan, Toodie Witmer, Mary Zahn.

Understudies: Miss Winters—Thelma Lee; Messrs. Freeman, Marshall—Merwin Goldsmith; Miss Kurnitz—Jacqueline Britt; Messrs. Stadlen, Pearl—Gary Raucher; Mr. Kupperman—Stephen Reinhardt; Mr. Fortus—George Bunt; Mr. Raucher—William Sean; Messrs. Winters, Shull—Casper Roos; Messrs. Goldsmith, Hansen, Roos—Ci Herzog.

Directed by Stanley Prager; original musical numbers staged by Marc Breaux; production consultant, Groucho Marx; musical direction and vocal arrangements, John Berkman; scenery, Peter Wexler; costumes, Donald Brooks; lighting, Jules Fisher; orchestrations, Ralph Burns; dance arrangements and incidental music, Marvin Hamlisch, Peter Howard; associate producer, Peter N. Grad; production stage manager, Frank Hamilton; stage manager, John Andrews; press, Max Eisen, Warren Pincus.

The musical is based on the early years of the Marx Brothers' career, when their mother Minnie was encouraging them in their effort to make a place for themselves in show business.

ACT I

Scene 1: The street
"Five Growing Boys" ....Minnie, Neighbors
Scene 2: The Marx apartment
"Rich Is" ....Al, Marx Family
"More Precious Far" ....Julie, Herbie, Adolph, Minnie
Scene 3: Backstage Nagadoches
"Four Nightingales" ....Julie, Herbie, Adolph
"Underneath It All" ....Maxie, Girls
Scene 4: Nagadoches Hotel
"Mama, a Rainbow" ....Adolph, Minnie
"You Don't have to Do It for Me" ....Minnie, Julie, Leonard, Adolph, Herbie
Scene 5: School act
Scene 6: Onstage
"If You Wind Me Up" ....Minnie, Julie, Herbie, Adolph, Leonard
Scene 7: Backstage Chicago
"Where Was I When They Passed Out Luck?" ....Julie, Herbie, Adolph, Leonard

ACT II

Scene 1: Mrs. McNish's boarding house
"The Smell of Christmas" ....Julie, Adolph, Herbie, Leonard
"You Remind Me of You" ....Julie, Mrs. McNish
Scene 2: Outside Palace Theater
"Minnie's Boys" ....Minnie, Company
Scene 3: Albee's office
Scene 4: Minnie's Long Island home
"Be Happy" ....Minnie, Adolph, Leonard, Herbie, Miltie
Scene 5: Walnut Street Theater
"The Act" ....Julie, Herbie, Adolph, Leonard, Minnie
Finale ....Company

Look to the Lilies (25). Musical based on William E. Barrett's novel *Lilies of the Field;* book by Leonard Spigelgass; music by Jule Styne; lyrics by Sammy Cahn. Produced by Edgar Lansbury, Max J. Brown, Richard Lewine and Ralph Nelson at the Lunt-Fontanne Theater. Opened March 29, 1970. (Closed April 19, 1970 matinee)

Homer Smith ....Al Freeman Jr.
Sister Gertrude ....Maggie Task

Sister Elizabeth ....Virginia Craig
Sister Agnes ....Linda Andrews

Mother Maria ....Shirley Booth	Senora Perez ....Shirley Potter
Sister Albertine ....Taina Elg	Senora Gonzalez ....Ravah Malmuth
Lady Guitarist ....Anita Sheer	Senora Chavales ....Maggie Worth
Juanita ....Patti Carr	Guard; Poker Player ....Paul Eichel
Rosita ....Carmen Alvarez	Guard; Poker Player ....Michael Davis
Juan Archuleta ....Titos Vandis	District Atty.;
1st Policeman;	Poker Player ....Don Prieur
Msgr. O'Hara ....Richard Graham	Defense Atty. ....Ben Laney
2d Policeman; Judge ....Joe Benjamin	

Singers: Marian Haraldson (Tourist), Sherri Huff (Bus Girl), Suzanne Horn (Local), Maggie Worth (Jewelry Vendor), Marc Allen III (Indian Barkeep), Michael Davis (Trucker), Paul Eichel (Mexican Bummer), Tony Falco (Farmer), Ben Laney (Souvenir Salesman), Don Prieur (Tourist).

Dancers: Lisa Bellaran (Child), Carol Conte (Teeny Bopper), Maria DiDia (Indian Waitress), Tina Faye (Mexican Wife), Ravah Malmuth (Mexican Girl Friend), Glenn Brooks (Mexican Hippie), Harry Endicott (College Student), Gary Gendell (White Suit), Steven Ross (Ranch Hand).

Children: Lori Bellaran, Ray Bellaran.

Understudies: Miss Booth—Maggie Task; Mr. Freeman—Clifton Davis; Mr. Vandis—Ted Beniades; Miss Elg—Shirley Potter; Miss Alvarez—Carol Conte; Miss Carr—Tina Faye; Misses Task, Craig, Andrews—Marian Haraldson.

Directed by Joshua Logan; choreography, Joyce Trisler; musical direction, Milton Rosenstock; scenery and lighting, Jo Mielziner; costumes, Carrie F. Robbins; vocal arrangements and direction, Buster Davis; orchestrations, Larry Wilcox; dance arrangements, John Morris; production associate, Joseph Beruh; production stage manager, Wade Miller; stage manager, Gigi Cascio; press, Max Eisen, Warren Pincus.

Musical tells a story similar to that of the screen play *Lilies of the Field* by James Poe, based on the Barrett novel: a black vagrant handyman takes refuge with a group of nuns and is gradually coaxed to build them a chapel.

ACT I

Scene 1: The farm
"Gott Is Gut" ....Mother Maria, Sisters Albertine, Elizabeth, Agnes, Gertrude
"First Class Number One Bum" ....Homer
Scene 2: The farmhouse
"Himmlisher Vater" ....Maria, Sisters
"Follow the Lamb" ....Homer, Maria, Sisters
"Don't Talk About God" ....Homer
"When I Was Young" ....Maria
Scene 3: Juan's cafe
"Meet My Seester" ....Juanita, Rosita, Truckers
Scene 4: The farm
"One Little Brick at a Time" ....Maria, Sisters
Scene 5: Exterior Juan's cafe
"To Do a Little Good" ....Juan, Employees
Scene 6: The farm
"There Comes a Time" ....Homer
"Why Can't He See" ....Maria
Scene 7: Juan's cafe
"I'd Sure Like to Give It a Shot" ....Homer, Juanita, Rosita, Juan, Customers

ACT II

Scene 1: Farmhouse kitchen
"Them and They" ....Maria, Sisters
Scene 2: Courtroom
"Does It Really Matter" ....Homer
Scene 3: A bus stop
"Look to the Lilies" ....Maria, Sisters
Scene 4: The farm
"I Admire You Very Much Mr. Schmidt" ....Albertine
"Some Kind of Man" ....Homer

Scene 5: Juan's cafe
"Chant" ....Homer's Followers
Scene 6: The farm
"Casamagordo, New Mexico" ....Sisters
"Follow the Lamb" (Reprise)
"One Little Brick at a Time" (Reprise) ....Homer, Townspeople
Scene 7: A bus stop
"I, Yes Me, That's Who" ....Maria
Scene 8: Chapel exterior
Scene 9: Chapel interior
"I, Yes Me, That's Who" (Reprise) ....Homer

* **Applause** (72). Musical based on the film *All About Eve* and the original story by Mary Orr; book by Betty Comden and Adolph Green; music by Charles Strouse; lyrics by Lee Adams. Produced by Joseph Kipness and Lawrence Kasha in association with Nederlander Productions and George M. Steinbrenner III at the Palace Theater. Opened March 30, 1970.

Tony Announcer; Peter ....John Anania	Bob ....Howard Kahl
Tony Host ....Alan King	Piano Player;
Margo Channing ....Lauren Bacall	TV Director ....Orrin Reiley
Eve Harrington ....Penny Fuller	Stan Harding ....Ray Becker
Howard Benedict ....Robert Mandan	Danny ....Bill Allsbrook
Bert ....Tom Urich	Bonnie ....Bonnie Franklin
Buzz Richards ....Brandon Maggart	Carol; Autograph Seeker ....Carol Petri
Bill Sampson ....Len Cariou	Joey ....Mike Misita
Duane Fox ....Lee Roy Reams	Musicians ....Gene Kelton, Nat Horne,
Karen Richards ....Ann Williams	David Anderson
Bartender ....Jerry Wyatt	

Singers: Laurie Franks, Ernestine Jackson, Sheilah Rae, Jeannette Seibert, Henrietta Valor, Howard Kahl, Orrin Reiley, Jerry Wyatt.

Dancers: Renee Baughman, Joan Bell, Debi Carpenter, Patti D'Beck, Marilyn D'Honau, Marybeth Kurdock, Carol Petri, Bill Allsbrook, David Anderson, John Cashman, Jon Daenen, Nikolas Dante, Gene Foote, Gene Kelton, Nat Horne, Mike Misita, Ed Nolfi, Sammy Williams.

Understudies: Miss Fuller—Sheilah Rae; Mr. Cariou—Tom Urich; Mr. Mandan—John Anania; Mr. Maggart—Ray Becker; Miss Williams—Laurie Franks; Mr. Reams—Gene Foote; Miss Franklin—Carol Petri; Messrs. Urich, Becker—Jerry Wyatt.

Directed and choreographed by Ron Field; musical direction and vocal arrangements, Donald Pippin; scenery, Robert Randolph; costumes, Ray Aghayan; lighting, Tharon Musser; orchestrations, Philip J. Lang; dance and incidental music arrangements, Mel Marvin; production associate, Phyllis Dukore; directorial assistant, Otto Pirchner; choreographic assistant, Tom Rolla; production stage manager, Terence Little; stage manager, Donald Christy; press, Bill Doll & Company, Dick Williams, Midori Lederer, Virginia Holden, Susan Schulman.

Time: The present. Place: In and around New York.

Musical tells the *All About Eve* story in which an aspiring actress feigns hero worship for a middle-aged star in order to flatter and insinuate her way into the theater.

A Best Play; see page 178.

ACT I

Scene 1: The Tony Awards
Scene 2: Margo's dressing room
"Backstage Babble" ....First Nighters
"Think How It's Gonna Be" ....Bill
Scene 3: The Village Bar
"But Alive" ....Margo, Boys
Scene 4: Margo's living room
"The Best Night of My Life" ....Eve
"Who's That Girl?" ....Margo
Scene 5: Margo's dressing room
Scene 6: Joe Allen's
"Applause" ....Bonnie, Gypsies
Scene 7: Margo's bedroom

"Hurry Back" ....Margo
Scene 8: Margo's living room
"Fasten Your Seat Belts" ....Buzz, Karen, Howard, Duane, Bill, Guests
Scene 9: Backstage
"Welcome to the Theater" ....Margo

ACT II

Scene 1: Buzz and Karen's Connecticut home
"Inner Thoughts" ....Karen, Buzz, Margo
"Good Friends" ....Margo, Karen, Buzz
Scene 2: Margo's dressing room
"The Best Night of My Life" (Reprise) ....Eve
Scene 3: Joe Allen's
"She's No Longer a Gypsy" ....Bonnie, Duane, Gypsies
Scene 4: Margo's living room
"One of a Kind" ....Bill, Margo
Scene 5: Backstage
"One Hallowe'en ....Eve
Scene 6: Margo's dressing room
"Something Greater" ....Margo
Scene 7: Backstage
Finale ....Margo, Company

* **Borstal Boy** (71). By Brendan Behan; adapted for the stage by Frank McMahon.
Produced by Michael McAloney and Burton C. Kaiser in association with the
Abbey Theater of Dublin at the Lyceum Theater. Opened March 31, 1970.

Brendan Behan	Niall Toibin	Library Warder; Voice of Judge;	
Young Behan	Frank Grimes	Emigration Official	Brendan Fay
Sheila	Patricia McAneny	Brownie	Terry Lomax
Mrs. Gildea	Mairin D. O'Sullivan	Dale	James Woods
Liverpool Landlady	Phyllis Craig	James	Drout Miller
Inspector;		Chaplain	Don Perkins
Prison Governor	John MacKay	Warder's Wife	Amy Burke
Detective Vereker	Dean Santoro	The Borstal Boys:	
Sargeant;		Harty	Norman Allen
Warder O'Shea	Joseph Warren	Joe	Drout Miller
Charlie Millwall	Bruce Heighley	Jock	Don Billett
Mr. Whitbread	Francis Bethencourt	Rivers	Liam Gannon
Mr. Holmes;		Shaggy	Terry Lomax
Welsh Warder	Arthur Roberts	Cragg	Dean Santoro
Callan	Liam Gannon	Chewlips	Michael Cahill
Tubby; Cook	Kenneth McMillan	Tom Meadows	James Woods
Prison Chaplain;		Ken Jones	George Connolly
Gov. of Borstal	Stephen Scott		

I.R.A. Men: Brendan Fay, Liam Gannon, Don Billett, Michael Cahill. Crowd, Officials, etc.:
Tom Signorelli, Richard Yesso, Marilyn Crawley, Richard Yanko, Roslyn Dickens, Peter Hock.
Directed and designed by Tomas MacAnna; associate producer, Joyce Sloane; set super-
vision and lighting, Neil Peter Jampolis; costume supervision, Robert Fletcher; production
stage manager, William Ross; stage managers, Bernard Pollock, William G. Johnson; press, Lee
Solters, Harvey B. Sabinson, Stanley F. Kaminsky.
Time: 1939 and thereafter. Place: Ireland and England. Part I: A Liverpool Street, Dublin,
Liverpool, Walton Jail, Liverpool court. Part II: A boys' Borstal on the eastern coast of England called Hollesley Bay, aboard a ship for Ireland and the Dublin quayside.
Series of scenes dramatized from Brendan Behan's autobiography, in which Behan is caught
in England with a suitcase full of dynamite during I.R.A. troubles, is tried and sentenced
and serves a term in a Borstal (a boys' reformatory). A foreign play previously produced in
Dublin.

Candida (8). Revival of the play by George Bernard Shaw. Produced by Virginia
Snow, John Carter and Cash Baxter at the Longacre Theater. Opened April 6,
1970. (Closed April 11, 1970)

Proserpine Garnett ...... Cavada Humphrey
Rev. James Mavor Morell ..... Wesley Addy
Rev. Alexander Mill ..... Paxton Whitehead

Mr. Burgess .... Keith Mackey
Candida .... Celeste Holm
Eugene Marchbanks ...... Robert Browning

Standbys: Misses Holm, Humphrey—Paddy Croft; Mr. Addy—Paxton Whitehead; Messrs. Browning, Whitehead—William McLuckey.

Directed by Lawrence Carra; scenery, John Braden; costumes, Miles White; lighting, John Gleason; production stage manager, Mary Porter Hall; stage manager, William McLuckey; press, Frank Goodman, Les Schecter.

Time: October 1905. Place: St. Dominic's Parsonage, Victoria Park, London.

The time of the play has been changed for this production from 1895, when it was first staged. *Candida's* recent New York productions were last season by off off Broadway's Roundabout Theater, 12/7/63 by Equity Library Theater for 8 performances, 4/22/52 with Olivia de Havilland for 31 Broadway performances, and by Katharine Cornell 4/17/46 for 31 performances and 4/27/42 for 27 performances.

Marcel Marceau (23). One-man program of pantomime by Marcel Marceau. Produced by Ronald A. Wilford Associates Inc. in association with City Center of Music and Drama, Inc. at New York City Center. Opened April 7, 1970. (Closed April 26, 1970)

Presentation of cards, Don Diego Cristian; stage manager, Antoine Casanova; press, Herbert H. Breslin, Richard O'Harra.

Marcel Marceau's last New York theater appearance was 11/17/65 at the City Center for 24 performances. In this season's engagement each program consisted of selections from the following repertory: Style Pantomimes—The Kite, The Man and His Boat, The Magician, The Cage, Circus Performer, The Hands, The Painter, Revolt of the Automat, Creation of the World, The Circus, Remembrances, The Trial, The Bureaucrats, Walking Against the Wind, The Staircase, The Tight Rope Walker, The Sculptor, The Public Garden, The Mask Maker, Youth, Maturity, Old Age and Death, The Park, The Bill Poster, Contrasts, The Seven Deadly Sins; BIP Pantomimes—BIP as a Concert Performer, BIP as a Matador, BIP Dreams He Is Don Juan, BIP Goes Travelling, BIP in the Subway, BIP as a Baby Sitter, BIP as a Violin Virtuoso, BIP at a Society Party, BIP Commits Suicide, BIP as a Lion Tamer, BIP as a Skater, BIP at a Ballroom, BIP as a Soldier, BIP Travels by Sea, BIP Hunts Butterflies, BIP Plays David and Goliath, BIP the Street Musician, BIP as a Fireman, BIP Looks for a Job, BIP in Modern and Future Life.

Cry for Us All (9). Musical based on William Alfred's play *Hogan's Goat;* book by William Alfred and Albert Marre; music by Mitch Leigh; lyrics by William Alfred and Phyllis Robinson. Produced by Mitch Leigh in association with C. Gerald Goldsmith at the Broadhurst Theater. Opened April 8, 1970. (Closed April 15, 1970)

Miggsy .... Scott Jacoby
Flylegs .... Darel Glaser
Cabbage .... Todd Jones
Matt Stanton .... Steve Arlen
Kathleen Stanton .... Joan Diener
Edward Quinn .... Robert Weede
Petey Boyle .... Tommy Rall
Bessie Legg .... Helen Gallagher
Maria Haggerty .... Dolores Wilson
John "Black Jack" Haggerty .... Paul Ukena
James "Palsy" Murphy .... Edwin Steffe
Father Stanislaus Coyne ..... William Griffis

State Sen. Thomas Walsh .... Jay Stuart
Mortyeen O'Brien .... Charles Rule
Peter Mulligan .... John Ferrante
Father Maloney .... Elliott Savage
The Cruelty Man .... Taylor Reed
Mrs. Teresa Tuohy .... Fran Stevens
Fiona Quigley .... Elaine Cancilla
Jack O'Banion .... Jack Trussel
Mrs. Mortyeen O'Brien ..... Dora Rinehart
Aloysius "Wishy" Doyle .... Bill Dance
Mutton Egan .... Ronnie Douglas

Standbys: Miss Diener—Willi Burke; Messrs. Rall, Griffis, Ukena, Savage—Ted Forlow. Principal Understudies: Mr. Arlen—Jay Stuart; Mr. Weede—Edwin Steffe; Miss Gallagher—Elaine Cancilla; Messrs. Reed, Dance—Jim Stevenson.

Directed by Albert Marre; choreography, Todd Bolender; musical direction, Herbert Grossman; scenery and lighting, Howard Bay; costumes, Robert Fletcher; music supervision, Sam Pottle; orchestrations, Carlyle Hall; production stage manager, James S. Gelb; stage manager, Bob Burland; press, Harvey B. Sabinson, Lee Solters, Ted Goldsmith.

Time: A five-day period around the first of May, 1890. Place: Matt Stanton's Cafe on the corner of Court Street and Fifth Place, Brooklyn; the street outside the bar and back room; and the Haggerty parlor which adjoins it. The action also moves to the street outside Ag Hogan's flat and to the Printers' Church in lower Fulton Street. The action is played without intermission.

The tale of how a rising young Irish politician's career and marriage are ruined when the details of a previous love affair are made public, as in the play *Hogan's Goat* which was produced by the American Place Theater at St. Clements Church off Broadway 11/11/65 for 607 performances and was named a Best Play of its season.

MUSICAL NUMBERS

"See No Evil" ....Miggsy, Flylegs, Cabbage (Street Rats)
"The End of My Race" ....Matt Stanton
"How Are Ya Since?" ....Kathleen, Matt, Constituents
"The Mayor's Chair" ....Mayor Quinn
"The Cruelty Man" ....Street Rats
"The Verandah Waltz" ....Kathleen, Matt
"Home Free All" ....Matt, Street Rats, Constituents
"The Broken Heart, or The Wages of Sin" ....Street Rats
"The Confessional" ....Matt, Father Maloney
"Who to Love if Not a Stranger?" ....Kathleen
"Cry for Us All" ....Petey Boyle, Mourners
"Swing Your Bag" ....Bessie Legg
"Call in to Her" ....Kathleen, Matt
"That Slavery Is Love" ....Kathleen
"I Lost It" ....Street Rats
"Aggie, Oh Aggie" ....Quinn
"The Leg of the Duck" ....Petey
"This Cornucopian Land" ....Matt, Constituents
"How Are Ya Since?" (Reprise) ....Kathleen, Quinn
"The Broken Heart, or The Wages of Sin" (Reprise) ....Street Rats
"Cry for Us All" (Reprise) ....Constituents

* The Boy Friend (55). Musical revival with book, music and lyrics by Sandy Wilson. Produced by John Yorke, Don Saxon and Michael Hellerman at the Ambassador Theater. Opened April 14, 1970.

Hortense ....Barbara Andres
Nancy ....Lesley Secombe
Maisie ....Sandy Duncan
Fay; Lolita ....Mary Zahn
Dulcie ....Simon McQueen
Polly ....Judy Carne
Marcel; Pepe ....Marcelo Gamboa
Alphonse ....Ken Mitchell
Pierre ....Arthur Faria

Mme. Dubonnet ....Jeanne Beauvais
Bobby Van Husen ....Harvey Evans
Percival Browne ....Leon Shaw
Tony ....Ronald Young
Phillipe; Waiter ....Tony Stevens
Monica ....Carol Culver
Lord Brockhurst ....David Vaughan
Lady Brockhurst ....Marie Paxton
Gendarme ....Jeff Richards

Principal understudies: Miss Carne—Carol Culver; Mr. Young—Jeff Richards; Mr. Shaw—Paul Tracey; Miss Beauvais—Barbara Andres; Mr. Evans—Arthur Faria; Miss Paxton—Eleonore Treiber; Miss Duncan—Mimi B. Wallace.

Directed by Gus Schirmer; dances and musical numbers staged by Buddy Schwab; musical direction, Jerry Goldberg; scenery and costumes, Andrew and Margaret Brownfoot; lighting, Tharon Musser; costume supervision, Stanley Simmons; associate producer, Robert Saxon; production assistant, Ronald Snyder; production stage manager, Phil Friedman; stage manager, Larry Ziegler; press, Saul Richman, Sy Sandler.

Time: 1926. Place: Nice, France.

The Boy Friend was first produced at the Royale Theater 9/30/54 for 495 performances and was named a Best Play of its season. It was revived off off Broadway 2/4/66 for 17 performances by Equity Theater, and off Broadway in the 1957-58 season for 763 performances.

List of scenes and musical numbers appear on pages 363-4 of the 1954-55 *Best Plays* volume.

A Place for Polly (1). By Lonnie Coleman. Produced by Ken Gaston and Leonard Goldberg with David G. Meyers at the Ethel Barrymore Theater. Opened and closed at the evening performance April 18, 1970.

Tony	Alan Manson	Angela	Cathryn Damon
Joyce	Evelyn Russell	Mr. Bigelow	Daniel Keyes
Polly	Marian Mercer	Mrs. Bigelow	Dortha Duckworth
George	William Mooney	Dan Da Vinci	Robert Moberly
Otis	Konrad Matthaei		

Directed by Ronny Graham; scenery and lighting, Clarke Dunham; costumes, Frank Thompson; associate producer, Henry Stern; incidental music, William Fisher; production stage manager, D.W. Koehler; press, David Lipsky, Lisa Lipsky.

Time: The present, early autumn. Place: An apartment in Greenwich Village. Act I, Scene 1: Late Friday afternoon. Scene 2: Saturday about noon. Act II, Scene 1: Early Saturday evening. Scene 2: Later Saturday evening.

An ambitious young publisher's moral problems with a stolen manuscript.

Park (5). Musical with book and lyrics by Paul Cherry; music by Lance Mulcahy. Produced by Edward Padula, a division of Eddie Bracken Ventures, Inc., at the John Golden Theater. Opened April 22, 1970. (Closed April 25, 1970)

Young Man	Don Scardino	Man	David Brooks
Young Woman	Joan Hackett	Woman	Julie Wilson

Park Band: Oscar Kosarin (bandleader and electric piano), Richard Cooper (flute), Bernie Karl (percussion), Rick Loewus (guitar), Bruce Scott (bass), Gregory Squires (French horn).

Directed by John Stix; musical staging, Lee Theodore; arrangements and musical direction, Oscar Kosarin; scenery and costumes, Peter Harvey; lighting, Martin Aronstein; production stage manager, Henry Garrard; press, Marc Olden.

Time: The present, spring. Place: A park.

Four members of a family come together as strangers in a park and discover in each other their common human and emotional needs. Previously produced at the Center Stage, Baltimore.

ACT I

"All the Little Things in the World Are Waiting" ....Young Man
"Hello Is the Way Things Begin" ....Young Woman
"Bein' a Kid" ....Young Man, Young Woman
"Elizabeth" ....Man
"He Talks to Me" ....Woman, Man
"Tomorrow Will Be the Same" ....Quartet
"One Man" ....Woman
"Park" ....Young Man

ACT II

"I Want It Just to Happen" ....Young Woman
"I Can See" ....Woman
"Compromise" ....Young Man
"Jamie" ....Young Man, Man
"Tomorrow Will Be the Same" (Reprise) ....Ensemble
"I'd Marry You Again" ....Woman, Man
"Bein' a Kid" (Reprise) ....Quartet
"Park" (Reprise) ....Quartet

Inquest (28). By Donald Freed; based on the book *Invitation to an Inquest* by Walter and Miriam Schneir. Produced by Lee Guber and Shelly Gross at the Music Box. Opened April 23, 1970. (Closed May 16, 1970)

Ethel Rosenberg	Anne Jackson	Clerk	Ed Bordo
Julius Rosenberg	George Grizzard	Bailiff; Doctor	Abe Vigoda
Emanuel Bloch	James Whitmore	Irving Saypol	Mason Adams

Roy Cohn	Mike Bursten	Ann Sidorovich	Sylvia Gassel
Judge Kaufman	Michael Lipton	Harry Gold	Phil Leeds
David Greenglass	Jack Hollander	Ruth Greenglass	Hildy Brooks
Tessie Greenglass	Sylvie Straus		

Reporters: Charles Kindl, David Clarke, Allen Garfield; Men in the Street: Ed Bordo, Charles Kindl, Sylvia Gassel, David Clarke, Allen Garfield, Abe Vigoda; FBI Agents: Ed Bordo, Abe Vigoda, Allen Garfield, David Clarke.

Understudies: Mr. Whitmore—David Clarke; Messrs. Hollander, Leeds—Allen Garfield; Mr. Adams—Abe Vigoda; Messrs. Lipton, Grizzard—Ed Bordo; Misses Jackson, Brooks, Straus— Sylvia Gassel; Mr. Bursten—Charles Kindl.

Directed by Alan Schneider; scenery, Karl Eigsti; costumes, Sara Brook; lighting and projection consultant, Jules Fisher; projections, Ken Isaacs; sound, Gary Harris; associate producer, Bernard King; stage manager, Bill Callan; press, Mike Merrick, Nancy Love.

Time and Place: The courtroom, the world, the past. The play is divided into two acts.

The case of the executed atomic spies, Ethel and Julius Rosenberg, is re-enacted by means of courtroom data, letters, tapes, memos, etc., to argue that the defendants were innocent. Previously produced at the Cleveland Play House under the title *The U.S. vs. Julius and Ethel Rosenberg*.

* **Company** (41). Musical with book by George Furth; music and lyrics by Stephen Sondheim. Produced by Harold Prince in association with Ruth Mitchell at the Alvin Theater. Opened April 26, 1970.

Robert	Dean Jones	Joanne	Elaine Stritch
Sarah	Barbara Barrie	Larry	Charles Braswell
Harry	Charles Kimbrough	Marta	Pamela Myers
Susan	Merle Louise	Kathy	Donna McKechnie
Peter	John Cunningham	April	Susan Browning
Jenny	Teri Ralston	The Vocal Minority	Cathy Corkill,
David	George Coe		Carol Gelfand, Marilyn Saunders,
Amy	Beth Howland		Dona D. Vaughn
Paul	Steve Elmore		

Standbys: Mr. Jones—Larry Kert; Miss Stritch—Jessica James. Understudies: Messrs. Cunningham, Elmore, Coe—James O'Sullivan; Messrs. Braswell, Kimbrough—Bob Roman; Misses McKechnie, Browning—Virginia Sandifur; Misses Louise, Ralston, Myers—Alice Cannon; Misses Howland, Barrie—Audre Johnson.

Directed by Harold Prince; musical numbers staged by Michael Bennett; musical direction, Harold Hastings; scenery and projections, Boris Aronson; costumes, D.D. Ryan; lighting, Robert Ornbo; orchestrations, Jonathan Tunick; dance music arrangements, Wally Harper; production stage manager, James Bronson; stage manager, Fritz Holt; press, Mary Bryant, Meg Gordean.

Time: Now. Place: New York City.

A New York bachelor studies his married friends and reflects on the advantages and disadvantages of marriage in our modern free-swinging society.

Larry Kert replaced Dean Jones (who left the cast owing to illness) 5/29/70.

A Best Play; see page 181.

ACT I

"Company"	Robert, Company
"The Little Things You Do Together"	Joanne, Company
"Sorry-Grateful"	Harry, David, Larry
"You Could Drive a Person Crazy"	Kathy, April, Marta
"Have I Got a Girl for You"	Larry, Peter, Paul, David, Harry
"Someone Is Waiting"	Robert
"Another Hundred People"	Marta
"Getting Married Today"	Amy, Paul, Jenny, Company

ACT II

"Side by Side by Side"	Robert, Company
"What Would We Do Without You"	Robert, Company

"Poor Baby" ....Sarah, Jenny, Susan, Amy, Joanne
Tick Tock ....Kathy
   (Dance music arranged by David Shire)
"Barcelona" ....Robert, April
"The Ladies Who Lunch" ....Joanne
"Being Alive" ....Robert

The Cherry Orchard (5). Revival of the play by Anton Chekhov; translated by J.P. Davis. Produced by The American National Theater and Academy, Alfred de Liagre Jr. executive producer, Jean Dalrymple executive director, in the John Fernald Company of the Meadow Brook Theater, Oakland University, Rochester, Mich., production, John Fernald artistic director, Donald R. Britton managing director, at the ANTA Theater. Opened May 6, 1970. (Closed May 9, 1970)

Dunyasha	Rhonda Rose	Charlotta	Janet McIntire
Lopahin	Toby Tompkins	Simeonof-Pischic	William Needles
Yepihodof	K.C. Wilson	Yasha	Michael Tolaydo
Feerce	Richard Curnock	Trofimof	Jeremy Rowe
Lyoubof Ranyevskaya	Jenny Laird	Tramp; Post Office Official	Pat Freni
Varya	Bonnie Hurren	Station Master	James Sutorius
Anya	Andrea Stonorov	Guest	David Richmond
Gayef	Marshall Borden		

Directed by John Fernald; scenery, Richard Davis; costumes, Ross B. Young; lighting, Pat Simmons; stage managers, Leon Leake, Bruce L. Blakemore, John Page Blakemore; press, Howard Atlee, David Roggensack.

The Cherry Orchard was last revived in New York by APA-Phoenix 3/19/68 for 38 performances.

Rabelais (16). Play in the French language by Jean-Louis Barrault. Produced by the City Center of Music and Drama, Inc., Norman Singer general administrator, in association with Melvin Kaplan, Inc. in La Compagnie production at New York City Center. Opened May 16, 1970. (Closed May 31, 1970)

Dancer, Lantern	Maddly Bamy	Young Gargantua	Gérard Boucaron
Marguerite;		Dancing Actor	Richard Caron
Lanternland Queen	Vélérie Camille	Monk; Singer	Claude del Vitto
Lady-in-Waiting	Marie-Hélène Dasté	Dancer; Sailor	Michael Devay
Dancer; Lantern;		Shepherd Frogier; Carpalim	Louis Frémont
Lady of Abbey	Huguette Dathané	Dunghill; Xenomanes	Pierre Gallon
Dancer; Lantern	Sharon O'Connell	Farmer; Sailor;	
Dancer; Lantern	E. Pareze-Belda	Triboulet	Jean-Renaud Garcia
Dancer; Lantern	Michèle Rimbold	Play-Leader; Picrocole	Jean-Pierre Granval
Dancer;		Touchfaucet; Aeditus	Hubert de Lapparent
Lady-in-Waiting	Céline Salles	Thubal Holofernes;	
Gargamelle; Hostess of Thelema;		Putherbeus	Régis Outin
Princess Bacbuc	Jacqueline Staup	Early Pear;	
Grandgousier; Grimalkin	Jacques Alric	Ding-dong	Dominique Santarelli
Friar John	Georges Audoubert	Friar John; Wrestler	Frank Valois
Humanist; Ponorates	Jean-Louis Barrault	Trepelu; Wrestler	Bernard Vignal
Pillot; Orator; Beggar	Victor Béniard	Panurge	Henri Virlojeux
Pantagruel	Jean-Pierre Bernard		

Directed by Jean-Louis Barrault; costumes, Matias; music, Michel Polnareff; orchestrations, Jean Claudric; choreography, Vélérie Camille; transistor translation and running commentary, Faubion Bowers; production stage manager, Jean-Pierre Mathis; press, Seymour Krawitz.

Collage of Rabelais' ideas and life, with rock music and other avant-garde production elements, presented in two acts and 21 scenes.

The Engagement Baby (4). By Stanley Shapiro. Produced by Edgar Lansbury and J.I. Rodale in association with Nan Pearlman at the Helen Hayes Theater. Opened May 21, 1970. (Closed May 23, 1970)

Roger Porter	Clifton Davis	Dr. Brien	Angus Cairns
Walter Whitney	Barry Nelson	Rev. Henning	James Karen
Victor Bard	Tom Aldredge	Neusom	Norman Matlock
Vivian Whitney	Constance Towers	Miss Stone	Candy Azzara
Constanzia	Antonia Rey	Wino	Gigi Cascio
Mary Ann	Holly Peters	Other Man	Lenard Norris
Nelson Longhurst	Henderson Forsythe	Job Dispenser	James Karen
Receptionist	Marie Puma	Voice From Cave	Angus Cairns

Understudies: Messrs. Nelson, Aldredge—James Karen; Messrs. Davis, Matlock—Lenard Norris; Messrs. Forsythe, Karen—Angus Cairns; Misses Towers, Azzara, Peters, Rey—Marie Puma.

Directed by Gene Frankel; scenery, Robin Wagner; lighting, Jules Fisher; costumes, Ann Roth; music, Charles Gross; sound, Gigi Cascio; production associate, Joseph Beruh; stage manager, William Dodds; press, Max Eisen, Warren Pincus.

Time: Today. Place: New York City. The play is divided into two acts.

Successful Jewish advertising man, whose marriage is shaky, discovers that he has fathered a son by his childhood sweetheart, a black girl.

Wilson in the Promise Land (7). By Roland van Zandt. Produced by The American National Theater and Academy, Alfred de Liagre Jr. executive producer, Jean Dalrymple executive director, and the Trinity Square Repertory Company at the ANTA Theater. Opened May 26, 1970. (Closed May 30, 1970)

Woodrow Wilson	William Cain	Hippie #3	
Edith Bolling Wilson	Marguerite H. Lenert	(Woman Singer)	Barbara Meek
Rev. Dr. Joseph Wilson	Donald Somers	Hippie #4 (Young Wilson,	
Dr. Cary T. Grayson	William Damkoehler	age 16)	James Eichelberger
George Washington	Martin Molson	Hippie #5 (Facts)	Ed Hall
Thomas Jefferson	David C. Jones	Hippie #6 (Musician)	Robert Black
Andrew Jackson	Dan Plucinski	Hippie #7	
Abraham Lincoln	James Gallery	(Man With Gun)	Richard Steele
Theodore Roosevelt	George Martin	Hippie #8	
Franklin D. Roosevelt	Ronald Frazier	(Young Wilson, age 6)	Ann Sachs
The Hippies:		Hippie #9	
The Youth	Richard Kavanaugh	(Klu Kluxer)	William Damkoehler
Hippie #1		Hippie #10	
(The Scribe)	Robert J. Colonna	(Nurse)	Marguerite H. Lenert
Hippie #2			
(Gen. Sherman)	David Kennett		

Directed by Adrian Hall; scenery, Eugene Lee; costumes, John Lehmeyer; lighting, Roger Morgan; original music, Richard Cumming; stage manager, Franklin Keysar; press, Betty Lee Hunt Associates, Henry Luhrman.

Flaws in the American ideal dramatized through the character of President Wilson as a link in a historical chain of command committed to power and force, beginning and ending in the White House during 1919-20, the last two years of the Wilson Administration. Previously produced by the Trinity Square Repertory Company, Providence, R.I. and presented in New York in their production.

PLAYS PRODUCED OFF BROADWAY

Figures in parentheses following a play's title indicate number of performances. Plays marked with an asterisk (*) were still running on June 1, 1970, and their number of performances is figured from opening night through May 31, 1970, not including extra non-profit performances. In a listing of a show's numbers—dances, sketches, musical scenes, etc.—the titles of songs are identified by their appearance in quotation marks ("). Most entries of off-Broadway productions that ran fewer than 20 performances are somewhat abbreviated.

HOLDOVERS FROM PREVIOUS SEASONS

Plays which were running on June 1, 1969 are listed below. More detailed information about them appears in previous Best Plays volumes of appropriate years. Important cast changes are recorded in a section of this volume.

* **The Fantasticks** (4,220; longest continuous run of record in the American theater). Musical suggested by the play *Les Romantiques* by Edmond Rostand; book and lyrics by Tom Jones; music by Harvey Schmidt. Opened May 3, 1960.

* **You're a Good Man Charlie Brown** (1,355). Musical based on the comic strip "Peanuts" by Charles M. Schulz; book, music and lyrics by Clark Gesner. Opened March 7, 1967.

Scuba Duba (692). By Bruce Jay Friedman. Opened October 10, 1967. (Closed June 8, 1969)

Curley McDimple (931). Musical with book by Mary Boylan and Robert Dahdah; music and lyrics by Robert Dahdah. Opened November 22, 1967. (Closed January 25, 1970)

Your Own Thing (933). Musical with book by Donald Driver; suggested by William Shakespeare's *Twelfth Night;* music and lyrics by Hal Hester and Danny Apolinar. Opened January 13, 1968. (Closed April 5, 1970)

* **Jacques Brel Is Alive and Well and Living in Paris** (975). Cabaret revue with music by Jacques Brel; production conception, English lyrics, additional material by Eric Blau and Mort Shuman; based on lyrics and commentary by Jacques Brel. Opened January 22, 1968.

* **The Boys in the Band** (890). By Mart Crowley. Opened April 15, 1968.

New York Shakespeare Festival Public Theater. 1968-69 indoor schedule of four programs concluded with **No Place To Be Somebody** (250). By Charles Gordone.

Opened May 4, 1969. (Closed December 7, 1969; played 16 additional performances on Broadway and was re-produced off Broadway; see its entries in this volume)

The Repertory Theater of Lincoln Center. 1968-69 schedule of four Forum Theater programs concluded with **The Year Boston Won the Pennant** (36). By John Ford Noonan. Opened May 22, 1969. (Closed June 21, 1969)

Dames at Sea (575). Musical with book and lyrics by George Haimsohn and Robin Miller; music by Jim Wise. Opened December 20, 1968. (Closed May 10, 1970)

To Be Young, Gifted and Black (380). Excerpts from the work of Lorraine Hansberry; adapted by Robert Nemiroff. Opened January 2, 1969. (Closed December 7, 1969)

Little Murders (400). Revival of the play by Jules Feiffer. Opened January 5, 1969. (Closed November 30, 1969)

Geese (336). Program of two one-act plays by Gus Weill: *Parents and Children* and *Geese*. Opened January 12, 1969. (Closed November 2, 1969)

Peace (192). Musical based on a play by Aristophanes; book and lyrics by Tim Reynolds; music by Al Carmines. Opened January 27, 1969. (Closed July 13, 1969)

* **Adaptation** by Elaine May and **Next** by Terrence McNally (546). Opened February 10, 1969.

An Evening With Max Morath at the Turn of the Century (140). One-man musical revue arranged, compiled and performed by Max Morath. Opened February 17, 1969. (Closed June 14, 1969)

The Man With the Flower in His Mouth (80). Program of three one-act plays by Luigi Pirandello: *The License, The Jar* and the title play; American translation by William Murray. Opened April 22, 1969. (Closed June 29, 1969)

Ceremonies in Dark Old Men (320). Second 1968-69 production of the play by Lonne Elder III (see 1968-69 *Best Plays* volume for entry on first production). Opened April 28, 1969. (Closed February 15, 1970)

In the Bar of a Tokyo Hotel (25). By Tennessee Williams. Opened May 11, 1969. (Closed June 1, 1969)

De Sade Illustrated (120). By Josef Bush, from an original idea by Bill Haislip; translated and adapted from *Philosophy in the Boudoir* by the Marquis de Sade. Opened May 12, 1969. (Closed August 24, 1969)

Spiro Who? (41). By William Meyers; music composed and recorded by Phil Ochs. Opened May 18, 1969. (Closed June 22, 1969)

Philosophy in the Boudoir (39). By Eric Kahane; adapted from the play by the Marquis de Sade; English translation by Alex Szogyi. Opened May 21, 1969. (Closed June 22, 1969)

PLAYS PRODUCED JUNE 1, 1969—MAY 31, 1970

The World of Mrs. Solomon (8). Program of two one-act plays by Fannie Fertik: *Another Chance* and *The Second Mrs. Aarons*. Produced by Barry Hoffman at the Fortune Theater. Opened June 3, 1969. (Closed June 8, 1969)

Directed by Demitrius Ambandos; scenery, Mischa Petrow; lighting, Michael Davidson; production stage manager, Clifford Ammon; press, Max Gendel. With Helen Blay, Henrietta Jacobson, Robin Lane, Rashel Novikoff, Martin Shakar, Morris Strassberg, Leonard Yorr.

In *Another Chance*, a Jewish widow woos a boarder. In *The Second Mrs. Aarons* a self-made Jewish business man visits his unhappy daughter.

Promenade (259). Musical with book and lyrics by Maria Irene Fornes; music by Al Carmines. Produced by Edgar Lansbury and Joseph Beruh at the Promenade Theater. Opened June 4, 1969. (Closed January 18, 1970)

105	Ty McConnell	Mr. S	Glenn Kezer
106	Gilbert Price	Mr. T	Michael Davis
Jailer	Pierre Epstein	Waiter	Edmund Gaynes
Servant	Madeline Kahn	Rosita	Florence Tarlow
Miss I	Margot Albert	Dishwasher	Art Ostrin
Miss O	Carrie Wilson	Mayor	George S. Irving
Miss U	Alice Playten	Mother	Shannon Bolin
Mr. R	Marc Allen III		

Directed by Lawrence Kornfeld; scenery, Rouben Ter-Arutunian; costumes, Willa Kim; lighting, Jules Fisher; orchestrations, Eddie Sauter; musical director, Al Carmines; musical conductor, Susan Romann; production stage manager, Larry Whiteley; press, Max Eisen, Cheryl Sue Dolby.

Satire on the world seen through the eyes and values of a pair of convicts.

Tony Falco replaced Gilbert Price 7/7/69. Kenneth Carr replaced Ty McConnell 9/15/69. Mary Jo Catlett replaced Shannon Bolin 9/23/69.

ACT I

Scene 1: The cell
"Promenade Theme" ....Orchestra
"Dig, Dig, Dig" 105, 106
Scene 2: The banquet room
"Unrequited Love" ....Misses I, O, U, Messrs. R, S, T, Servant, Waiter, 105, 106
"Isn't That Clear?" ....Mr. S, Ensemble
"Don't Eat It" ....Ensemble
"Four" ....Misses I, O, U, Messrs. R, S, T, Servant, Waiter, 105, 106, Dishwasher
"Chicken Is He" ....Rosita
"A Flower" ....Miss I
"Rosita Rodriguez; Serenade" ....Mayor
"Apres Vous I" ....105, 106, Jailer
"Bliss" ....Servant, 105, 106, Ensemble
"The Moment Has Passed" ....Miss O
Scene 3: The street
"Thank You" ....Dishwasher
"The Clothes Make the Man" ....Servant, 105, 106
Scene 4: The park
"The Cigarette Song" ....Servant, 105, 106
"Two Little Angels" ....Mother, 105, 106
"The Passing of Time" 105, 106
"Capricious and Fickle" ....Miss U
"Crown Me" ....Servant, 105, 106

ACT II

Scene 1: The battlefield
"Mr. Phelps" ....Waiter
"Madeline" ....Waiter
"Spring Beauties" ....Ensemble
"Apres Vous I" (Reprise) ....Ensemble
"A Poor Man" 105, 106
"Why Not" ....Dishwasher, Servant, Mother, Waiter, 105, 106
Scene 2: The drawing room
"The Finger Song" ....Mr. R, Ensemble
"Little Fool" ....Mr. T, Ensemble
"Czardas" ....Servant, Miss I (Viola)
"The Laughing Song" ....Ensemble
"A Mother's Love" ....Mother
Scene 3: The cell
"Listen, I Feel" ....Servant
"I Saw a Man" ....Mother
"All Is Well in the City" ....105, 106, Ensemble

Tonight in Living Color (24). Program of two one-act plays by A.R. Gurney Jr.: *The Golden Fleece* and *The David Show*. Produced by Harlan P. Kleiman, Jeffrey C. Reiss and Orin Lehman at the Actors Playhouse. Opened June 10, 1969. (Closed June 29, 1969)

THE GOLDEN FLEECE

Betty ....Rue McClanahan   Bill ....Tim O'Connor

THE DAVID SHOW

Samuel ....Jerome Raphel   Jonathan ....F. Murray Abraham
David ....Anthony Call   Ham ....George Patterson
Saul ....Barney Martin   Bathsheba ....Holland Taylor

Directed by Jered Barclay; scenery, Merrill Sindler; lighting, Andie Wilson Kingwill; costumes, Yvonne Bronowicz; original music, Orville Stoeber; production stage manager, Sean S. Cunningham; press, Robert Ganshaw & John Prescott, Ted Goldsmith.

The Golden Fleece was previously produced by the Center Theater Group in Los Angeles and makes a Jason-Medea story of a modern marriage.

The David Show was first produced off Broadway 10/31/68 for 1 performance.

Fireworks (7). Program of three one-act plays by Jon Swan: *The Report, Football* and *Fireworks for a Hot Fourth*. Produced by Jacqueline Donnet and Joan Shigekawa in association with Guthrie Productions at the Village South Theater. Opened June 11, 1969. (Closed June 15, 1969)

Directed by Kent Paul; scenery and lighting, Stephen Hendrickson; costumes, Michael Arceneaux; special sequences, Patricia Birch; production stage manager, James Greek; press, Dorothy Ross, Fred Weterick. With Laurinda Barrett, Kristina Callahan, Haig Chobanian, Stephen Joyce, Monica Moran, Colgate Salsbury, John Wardwell, Arnold Wilkerson.

Three views of American life: the press (*The Report*), war (*Football*) and the final despairing cocktail party (*Fireworks for a Hot Fourth*).

Time for Bed—Take Me to Bed (13). Program of two one-act plays by Charles Love. Produced by Philip Bell in association with Alexander Maissel at the Provincetown Playhouse. Opened June 13, 1969. (Closed June 22, 1969)

Directed by Paul Weidner; scenery and costumes, David Loveless; lighting, William Mintzer; production stage manager, Robert Stevenson; press, Seymour Krawitz, Ellen Levene. With Victor Arnold, Alive Spivak.

Two plays about couples in love.

Whores, Wars & Tin Pan Alley (72). An evening of songs by Kurt Weill. Produced by Allen Swift at the Bitter End. Opened June 16, 1969. (Closed August 17, 1969)

Martha Schlamme   Alvin Epstein

Piano accompaniment, Ronald Clairmont; stage manager, Michael Roy Denbo; press, Robert Ganshaw & John Prescott, Ted Goldsmith.

A compilation of Kurt Weill's German and American theater music.

PART I: "Alabama Song" (lyrics by Bertolt Brecht), "Moritat" ("Ballad of Mack the Knife"; lyrics by Bertolt Brecht), "Barbara-Song," "Havanna—Lied and Duet," "Instead—of Song" (English version by Marc Blitzstein), "Ballad of Sexual Slavery" (English version by George Tabori), "Zuhalterballade" (English version by Marc Blitzstein), "Seerauber-Jenny" (English version by Marc Blitzstein), "Kanonensong" (English version by Marc Blitzstein), "Ballade vom Soldaten Weib," "Essen" (English version by Arnold Weinstein, "Wie Man Sich Bettet" (English version by Will Holt).

PART II: "Le Roi d'Aquitaine" (lyrics by Jacques Deval), Medley from *Johnny Johnson* (lyrics by Paul Green), "That's Him," "Speak Low" (lyrics by Ogden Nash), "Susan's Dream" (lyrics by Alan Jay Lerner), "September Song" (lyrics by Maxwell Anderson), "The Saga of Jenny" (lyrics by Ira Gershwin), "Lost in the Stars" (lyrics by Maxwell Anderson), Songs from *Happy End* (lyrics by Bertolt Brecht), "The Mandalay Song," "The Sailor's Tango" (English version by Will Holt), "Surabaya Johnny," "Bilbao—Song," "The Survival Song" (English version by Marc Blitzstein).

* **Oh, Calcutta!** (397). Musical revue devised by Kenneth Tynan; with contributions by Samuel Beckett, Jules Feiffer, Dan Greenburg, John Lennon, Jacques Levy, Leonard Melfi, David Newman and Robert Benton, Sam Shepard, Clovis Trouille, Kenneth Tynan and Sherman Yellen; music and lyrics by The Open Window. Produced by Hillard Elkins in association with Michael White and Gordon Crowe at the Eden Theater. Opened June 17, 1969.

Raina Barrett   Margo Sappington
Mark Dempsey   Nancy Tribush
Katie Drew-Wilkinson   George Welbes
Boni Enten   The Open Window:
Bill Macy   Robert Dennis
Alan Rachins   Peter Schickele
Leon Russom   Stanley Walden

Production conceived and directed by Jacques Levy; choreography, Margo Sappington; scenery, James Tilton; costumes, Fred Voelpel; lighting, David Segal; projected media designed by Gardner Compton and Emile Ardolino; still photography, Michael Childers; audio design, Robert Liftin; production supervisor, Michael Thoma; associate producer, George Platt; stage managers, John Actman, Harry Chittenden, Greg Taylor; press, Samuel J. Friedman.

An evening of erotica in skit, song and dance, with the cast often performing naked.

Among the numerous cast replacements have been Maureen Byrnes for Margo Sappington, Michael Riordan for George Welbes, Michael Callahan for Michael Riordan, Gene GeBauer for Michael Riordan, Martin Speer for Mark Dempsey, Lynn Oliver for Katie Drew-Wilkinson, Patricia Hawkins for Lynn Oliver, Kathrin King for Boni Enten, Eddie Phillips Jr. for Bill Macy, Mitchell McGuire for Leon Russom.

PART I: Prologue; "Taking off the Robe" and "Oh! Calcutta!"—Company; Dick and Jane —Alan Rachins, Nancy Tribush; Suite for Five Letters ("Dear Editor")—Mark Dempsey, Katie Drew-Wilkinson, Boni Enten, Miss Tribush, George Welbes; Will Answer All Sincere Replies—Bill Macy, Leon Russom, Margo Sappington, Miss Tribush; Paintings of Clovis Trouille —The Open Window; Jack and Jill—Miss Enten, Welbes; Delicious Indignities—Dempsey, Miss Drew-Wilkinson; Was It Good for You Too?—Raina Barrett, Dempsey, Macy, Rachins, Misses Enten, Tribush.

PART II: "Much Too Soon"—Company; One on One—Miss Sappington, Welbes; Rock Garden—Russom, Macy; Who: Whom—Dempsey, Misses Drew-Wilkinson, Tribush; Four in Hand—Welbes, Russom, Rachins, Macy; "Coming Together, Going Together"—Company.

Pequod (1). By Roy S. Richardson. Produced by William W. Rippner in association with Sumac Productions Corporation at the Mercury Theater. Opened and closed at the evening performance June 29, 1969.

Directed by Burt Brinckerhoff; scenery and lighting, David F. Segal; costumes, Joseph G. Aulisi; special electronic score and lyrics, Mildred Kayden; production stage manager, David Semonin; press, Robert Ganshaw & John Prescott, Ted Goldsmith. With Jeff David, Robert Eckles, Lloyd Hollar, Bella Jarrett, John Randolph Jones, Richard Kronold, Don Lochner, Dorothy Lyman, John Mahon, Jason Miller, Gary Sandy, John Tillinger, Kelly Wood.

A play-within-a-play version of Herman Melville's *Moby Dick* story.

The Glorious Ruler (8). By Michael Ackerman. Produced by Jan Maher at the Jan Hus Theater. Opened July 1, 1969. (Closed July 6, 1969)

Directed by Paul John Austin; production designed by Lorenzo Nasca; music and musical effects, Rudolph Crosswell; stage manager, Tony Giordano; press, Dorothy Ross. With John Branon, Mary Carter, Jordan Charney, Mary Hara, James La Ferla, Valerie Lee, P. Raymond Marunas, Eileen Mitchell, Don Silber, Tom Tarpey.

A re-working of the Oedipus legend.

The Negro Ensemble Company. Fourth and final program of 1969 schedule (see entry on 1970 schedule elsewhere in this listing). **Man Better Man** (23). Musical play by Errol Hill; music for this production by Coleridge-Taylor Perkinson. Produced by The Negro Ensemble Company, Douglas Turner Ward artistic director, Robert Hooks executive director, Gerald S. Krone administrative director, at St. Marks Playhouse. Opened July 2, 1969. (Closed July 20, 1969)

Tim Briscoe	David Downing	Dagger Da Silva	Aston Young
Portagee Joe	Graham Brown	Alice Sugar	Esther Rolle
Swifty	Allie Woods	Coolie	Norman Bush
Inez Briscoe	Rosalind Cash	Peloo	Afolabi Ajayi
Hannibal	Tony McKay	Pogo	William Jay
Tiny Satin	Samual Blue Jr.	Diable Papa	Damon W. Brazwell
Crackerjack	Arthur French	Minee Woopsa	Mari Toussaint
Petite Belle Lily	Hattie Winston	1st Village Woman	Frances Foster
Cutaway Rimbeau	Julius W. Harris	2nd Village Woman	Clarice Taylor

Other Villagers: Louise Heath, Marilyn McConnie, Richard Roundtree, Lennal Wainwright and Anita Wilson.

Directed by Douglas Turner Ward; choreography, Percival Borde; scenery, Edward Burbridge; costumes, Bernard Johnson; lighting, Buddy Butler; press, Howard Atlee, David Roggensack.

Time: At the turn of the century. Place: A small village on the island of Trinidad, West Indies. Act I, Scene 1: "El Toro," a general store and rum shop owned and operated by Portagee Joe, early afternoon. Scene 2: A room in the dwelling house of Diable Papa, obeahman, the following day, early morning. Act II, Scene 1: "El Toro" store, the same day, late afternoon. Scene 2: The stick-playing area, the following day, noon. Act III, Scene 1: "El Toro" store and nearby woods, the same day, several hours later. Scene 2: Diable Papa's house and nearby woods, the same day, evening. Scene 3: "El Toro" store, the same day, evening.

Village boy tries to become a champ at the game of sticks to impress the girl he loves. A foreign play.

ACT I

"Procession" ....Company
"Tiny, the Champion" ....Hannibal, Tiny, Company
"I Love Petite Belle" ....Briscoe, Company
"One Day, One Day, Congotay" ....Diable Papa, Minee

ACT II

"One, Two Three" ....Hannibal, Male Villagers
"Man Better Man" ....Minee, Male Villagers
"Petite Belle Lily" ....Hannibal, Lily, Company
"Thousand, Thousand" ....Lily, Company
"Me Alone" ....Inez, Company
"Girl in the Coffe ....Company
"Petite Belle Lily" (Reprise) ....Lily, Company

ACT III

"Coolie Gone" ....Inez, Company
"War and Rebellion" ....Lily, Company
"Beautiful Heaven" ....Diable Papa, Minee, Coolie, Peloo
"Briscoe, the Hero" (Reprise of "Tiny, the Champion" ....Hannibal, Company

New York Shakespeare Festival. Summer season of two revivals. **Peer Gynt** (19). By Henrik Ibsen; translated by Michael Meyer. Opened July 8, 1969. (Closed August 2, 1969) **Twelfth Night** (20). By William Shakespeare. Opened August 6, 1969. (Closed August 30, 1969). Produced by New York Shakespeare Festival, Joseph Papp producer, Gerald Freedman artistic director, Bernard Gersten associate producer, in cooperation with the City of New York, John V. Lindsay mayor, August Heckscher commissioner of parks, at the Delacorte Theater.

PEER GYNT

Peer Gynt ....Stacy Keach	Bridegroom; General-at-Sea;
Aase ....Estelle Parsons	Pen; Thin Person ....Robert Stattel
Kari ....Janet Dowd	Bridegroom's Father; Troll Prime
Aslak; Admiral-at-Sea;	Minister; Industrialist-at-Sea;
Asylum Keeper ....Michael Baseleon	Strange Passenger ....Albert Stratton
Solveig's Father; Priest;	Bridegroom's Mother ....Mary Nall
Button Moulder ....John Heffernan	Ingrid's Father; Troll King;
Solveig ....Judy Collins	Diplomat-at-Sea ....James Cahill
Helga ....Lisa Griffin	Three Saeter Girls ....Marilyn Meyers,
Solveig's Mother ....Paulita Sedgwick	Esther Koslow, Maria Di Dia
Ingrid; Greenclad Lady;	Boy who is Peer Gynt ....Stacy Keach
Anitra ....Olympia Dukakis	Troll Brat ....Francis Patrelle

Acting Ensemble: Bruce Cobb, Tom Crawley, James De Marse, Kevin Gardiner, Phil C. Harris, Robert Keesler, Esther Koslow, Marilyn Meyers, Mary Nall, Michael Rives, Joseph Rose, Paulita Sedgwick, Patrick Shea, Sam Tsoutsouvas.

Dance Ensemble: Loretta Abbott, Eileen Barbaris, Rodney Griffin, Edward Henkel, Sharron Miller, Francis Patrelle, David Radner, Clay Taliaferro, Nina Trasoff, Margo Travers.

Principal understudies: Miss Parsons—Jane Dowd; Mr. Baseleon—Sam Tsoutsouvas; Mr. Heffernan—Tom Crawley; Miss Collins—Esther Koslow.

Directed and adapted by Gerald Freedman; scenery, Ming Cho Lee; lighting, Martin Aronstein; costumes, Theoni V. Aldredge; songs and music, John Morris; lyrics, Gerald Freedman and John Morris; choreography Joyce Trisler; production stage manager, Michael Chambers; stage managers, Dean Compton, Gage Andretta; press, Merle Debuskey.

Peer Gynt's last professional New York staging was by Theater Incorporated at the Phoenix Theater 1/12/60 for 32 performances.

TWELFTH NIGHT

Orsino ....Ralph Waite	Feste ....Charles Durning
Curio ....Philip C. Harris	Olivia ....Sasha von Scherler
Valentine ....Stephen Collins	Malvolio ....Robert Ronan
Viola ....Barbara Barrie	Antonio ....Albert Stratton
Sea Captain ....Albert Quinton	Sebastian ....Peter Simon
Sir Tony Belch ....Stephen Elliott	First Officer ....Sam Tsoutsouvas
Maria ....Jennifer Darling	Second Officer ....Paul McHenry
Sir Andrew Aguecheek ......Tom Aldredge	Priest ....Albert Quinton

Servants: Bruce Cobb, Kevin Gardiner. Honor Guard: Thomas Crawley, James De Marse, Patrick Shea. Musicians: Leonard Handler, John McLeod, Stephen Wilensky.

Directed by Joseph Papp; scenery, Douglas W. Schmidt; lighting, Martin Aronstein; costumes, Theoni V. Aldredge; songs and music, Galt MacDermot; swordplay, Albert Quinton; production stage manager, Michael Chambers; stage manager, Dean Compton.

Twelfth Night's last professional New York production was by Joseph Papp at the Heckscher Theater 10/7/63 for 73 performances.

The Hoofers (88). Revue by Leticia Jay. Produced by the Mercury Theater in association with Leticia Jay at the Mercury Theater. Opened July 29, 1969. (Closed October 12, 1969)

Jerry Ames	Rhythm Red
Lon Chaney	Sandman Sims
Sandra Gibson	Jimmy Slyde
Chuck Green	Eva Turner
Leticia Jay	Tony White
Raymond Kaalund	Derby Wilson
Mabel Lee	

Directed by Derby Wilson; musical direction, Tiny Grimes; costumes, Angel Cheremeteff; lighting, Barbara Nollman; production stage manager, Peter Williams; press, Max Eisen.

An evening of tap-dancing, singing, comedy and mime.

ACT I: Overture—Tiny Grimes; "You Gotta Go Tap Dancing Tonight"—Company; Riffs and Introductions—Jimmy, Red, Sandra, Jerry, Tony, Chuck, Eva, Raymond, Mabel Lee, Sandman, Derby; Jimmy Slyde; Mabel Lee; Duet—Lon Chaney, Tony White; Sandman Sims; Chuck Green; Trio—Chuck, Jerry, Red; Raymond Kaalund; Sandra Gibson; Jerry Ames; Finale.

ACT II: Derby Wilson; Tiny Grimes and Band; Eva Turner; Challenge.

A Black Quartet (111). Program of four one-act plays: *Prayer Meeting or The First Militant Minister* by Ben Caldwell; *The Warning—A Theme for Linda* by Ronald Milner; *The Gentleman Caller* by Ed Bullins; *Great Goodness of Life* by LeRoi Jones. Produced by Woodie King Associates, Inc. in cooperation with Chelsea Theater Center at Tambellini's Gate Theater. Opened July 30, 1969. (Closed November 2, 1969)

PRAYER MEETING OR THE FIRST MILITANT MINISTER

Burglar .... Dennis Tate   Minister .... L. Errol Jaye

THE WARNING—A THEME FOR LINDA

Linda .... Vikki Summers	Nasty Old Man .... Jimmy Hayeson
Nora .... Louise Heath	Donald .... Paul Rodger-Reid
Joan .... Loretta Greene	Grandmother .... Minnie Gentry
Paula .... Jo-Ann Robinson	Mother .... Joan Pryor
Grandfather .... L. Errol Jaye	

THE GENTLEMAN CALLER

The Maid .... Minnie Gentry	Madame .... Sylvia Soares
The Gentleman .... Dennis Tate	Mr. Mann .... Frank Carey

GREAT GOODNESS OF LIFE

Voice of the White Judge ...... Frank Carey	Hood 1 and 3 .... Jimmy Hayeson
Court Royal .... L. Errol Jaye	Hood 2 and 4 .... Paul Rodger-Reid
Attorney Breck .... Jimmy Hayeson	Young Woman .... Anna Maria Horsford
Young Man .... Sam Singleton	Leader .... Dennis Tate

Prayer Meeting and *Great Goodness of Life* directed by Irving Vincent; *The Warning* directed by Woodie King; *The Gentleman Caller* directed by Allie Woods; scenery, John Jacobson; lighting, Marshall Williams; costumes, Gloria Gresham; sound, Helmuth Lesold; associate producer, Ed Pitt; productions stage manager, David Semonin; press, Bill Cherry.

In *Prayer Meeting* the prayers of an Uncle Tom preacher are answered by a burglar aping the voice of God. In *The Warning*, a young girl dreams of love in a household whose older women had earlier grown to hate their men. *The Gentleman Caller* dramatizes the black servant's hate for the decadent white mistress. In *Great Goodness of Life* a middle-class black man is accused of sheltering a murderer who turns out to be his own son.

Sourball (1). By Robert Shure. Produced by J & S Productions at the Province-town Playhouse. Opened and closed at the evening performance August 5, 1969.

Directed by James Kerans; scenery, Jerry N. Rojo; lighting, Edmund Seagrave; costumes, Deborah Foster; general manager, William E. Hunt; press, Saul Richman, Stan Brody. With Kate Hawley, Atherton Knight, Patrick McVey, Jeremiah Morris, Richard Niles, Bernie Passel-tiner, Enid Rodgers, Scott Robinson.

Confrontation of young idealists with practical politicians.

Arena Conta Zumbi (16). Play in the Portuguese language by Gianfrancesco Guarnieri and Augusto Boal. Produced by the Theater of Latin America at St. Clement's Church. Opened August 18, 1969. (Closed September 4, 1969)

Directed by Mr. Boal; music, Edu Lobo; musical direction, Theo do Barros; press, Sol Jacob-son. With members of the Arena Theater of Sao Paulo: Anunciacao, Germano Batista, Renato Consorte, Theo do Barros, Zezinha Duboc, Lima Duarte, Nene, Antonio Pedro, Vera Regina, Rodrigo Santiago, Cecilia Thumim.

Dramatization of a 17th-century slave uprising in northeast Brazil, led by Zumbi and his family. A foreign play previously produced in Sao Paulo and elsewhere.

NOTE: One performance of *Arena Conta Zumbi* was given in March during a special en-gagement at the Public Theater of the Arena Theater of Sao Paulo, which also offered several performances of a musical in the Portuguese, Spanish and English languages entitled *Arena Conte Bolivar* (Arena Tells About Bolivar), by Augusto Boal, with music by Theo do Barros.

The Reckoning (94). By Douglas Turner Ward. Produced by Hooks Productions, Inc. at St. Marks Playhouse. Opened September 4, 1969. (Closed November 23, 1969)

Scar	Douglas Turner	Son	Conard Fowkes
Baby	Jeannette DuBois	Missy	Louise Stubbs
Offstage News Announcer	Richard Pyatt	Josh	Joseph Attles
Governor	Lester Rawlins		

Directed by Michael A. Schultz; presented in cooperation with The Negro Ensemble Com-pany; scenery, Edward Burbridge; lighting, Martin Aronstein; costumes, Gertha Brock; special sound, James Reichert; associate producers, Clarence Avant, Al Bell Jr., Sam Engler; produc-tion stage manager, Charles Roden; press, Howard Atlee, David Roggensack.

Time: Past, present or possibly the future. Place: State capitol of a deep Southern state. The play is presented without intermission.

Drama of racism subtitled "A Surreal Southern Fable," in which a black pimp confronts a white governor on behalf of a black agitator.

Silhouettes (8). By Ted Harris. Produced by Darius V. Phillips at the Actors Play-house. Opened September 8, 1969. (Closed September 14, 1969)

Directed by John Camilla; scenery and costumes, Joseph C. Davies; lighting, Barbara Noll-man; stage manager, Charles J. Golden; press, Howard Atlee, David Roggensack. With Fred Forrest, Bill Haislip, Maude Higgins, James Racioppi, Ann Stafford.

Excessively maternal 42-year-old waitress is made pregnant by a 20-year-old man.

The End of All Things Natural (6). By G. Zoffer. Produced by Joel M. Reed at the Village South Theater. Opened September 11, 1969. (Closed September 14, 1969)

Directed by Gail Bell; scenery and lighting, Barry Arnold; costumes, Mike Masse; produc-tion stage manager, Michael J. Frank; press, Max Eisen, Jeanne Gibson Merrick. With Mar-garet Brewster, Rudy Carigi, David Ellin, Franc Geraci, Thomas Kubiak, Michael Levin, Joyce Marcella, Alexander Orfaly, Nicholas Saunders, Muni Seroff.

Subtitled "A Drama of Contemporary Russia," the story of a poet in conflict with his society.

The Ofay Watcher (40). By Frank Cucci. Produced by Harlan P. Kleiman at Stage 73. Opened September 15, 1969. (Closed October 19, 1969)

Rufus ....Cleavon Little   Daisy ....Billie Allen
Bruce Jennings ....Terry Kiser

Directed by Jerry Adler; scenery and lighting, Dahl Delu; costumes, Yvonne Bronowicz; associate producers, Jeffrey C. Reiss, Patrick McNamara; production stage manager, Martha Knight; press, Robert Ganshaw & John Prescott.

Time: The present. Place: The East Village. Scene 1: A park bench in a public square in the East Village, 5:30 a.m. in October. Scene 2: Bruce's apartment, immediately following. Scene 3: Bruce's apartment, ten days later.

Young man with a chemical formula for turning blacks into whites tries it on a black drifter, with tragic results.

The American Hamburger League (1). Revue by Norman Kline. Produced by Leonard Sillman and Orin Lehman at the New Theater. Opened and closed at the evening performance September 16, 1969.

Directed by George Luscombe; scenery, Nancy Jowsey; lighting, Paul Sullivan; costume consultant, Joseph Aulisi; production stage manager, Bud Coffey; press, Howard Atlee, David Roggensack, Stanley F. Kaminsky. With Jack Fletcher, Bill Hinnant, Jane Hoffman, Dorothy Lyman, Liz Sheridan, Richard B. Shull.

Series of comedy skits about contemporary neuroses.

Hello and Goodbye (45). By Athol Fugard. Produced by Kermit Bloomgarden in association with Commonwealth United Entertainment and Jonathan Burrows at the Sheridan Square Playhouse. Opened September 18, 1969. (Closed October 26, 1969)

Johnny ....Martin Sheen   Hester ....Colleen Dewhurst

Directed by Barney Simon; production designed by William Ritman; production stage manager, Patrick J. Latronica; press, Max Eisen, Cheryl Sue Dolby.

Time: Summer of 1965. Place: Port Elizabeth, South Africa. Act I: Evening. Act II: Two hours later.

Brother and sister meet after 15 years to rummage through family effects and their own emotional lives. A foreign play previously produced in Johannesburg, South Africa.

Salvation (239). Musical with book, music and lyrics by Peter Link and C.C. Courtney. Produced by David Black at the Jan Hus Theater. Opened September 24, 1969. (Closed April 19, 1970)

Ranee ....Yolande Bavan   Boo ....Boni Enten
Farley ....Peter Link   Dierdre ....Annie Rachel
Monday ..................C.C. Courtney   Betty Lou ....Marta Heflin
Mark ....Joe Morton   LeRoy ....Chapman Roberts

Directed by Paul Aaron; dance movement, Kathryn Posin; production designed by Joan Larkey; music arranged and conducted by Kirk Nurock; music played by Nobody Else (rock group); production stage manager, Curt Dempster; press Gifford-Wallace Inc., Tom Trenkle.

Rock musical, succession of skits and song numbers satirizing various religious and moral attitudes, played without intermission.

Numerous cast changes during the run of *Salvation* included Northern J. Calloway and then George Turner in the role of Mark, Barry Bostwick and then Jim Hall in the role of Monday, Clifford Lipson in the role of Farley, and Betty Midler in the role of Betty Lou.

MUSICAL NUMBERS

"Salvation" ....Monday, Ranee, Dierdre, LeRoy, Mark, Betty Lou
"In Between" ....Betty Lou, Dierdre, Ranee, LeRoy
"1001" ....LeRoy
"Honest Confession Is Good for the Soul" ....Monday, Boo, Farley, Company
"Ballin' " ....Company
"Let the Moment Slip By" ....Dierdre
"Gina" ....Mark, Farley, Company

"Stockhausen Potpourri" ....Company
"If You Let Me Make Love to You Then Why Can't I Touch You" ....Company
"There Ain't No Flies on Jesus" ....Cast, improvisations by LeRoy, Farley, Mark
"Deadalus" ....Ranee
"Deuteronomy XVII Verse 2" ....Mark, Betty Lou, Girls
"For Ever" ....LeRoy, Mark, Girls
"Footloose Youth and Fancy Free" ....Boo, LeRoy
"Schwartz" ....Company
"Let's Get Lost in Now" ....Mark, Company
"Back to Genesis" ....Company
"Tomorrow Is the Frst Day of the Rest of My Life" ....Farley, Company

Calling in Crazy (16). By Henry Bloomstein. Produced by Linda Otto at the Fortune Theater. Opened October 6, 1969. (Closed October 19, 1969)

Directed by Robert Greenwald; scenery, Kert Lundell; lighting, F. Mitchell Dana; production stage manager, Mary Porter Hall; press, Robert Ganshaw & John Prescott. With Kay Carney, Jill Clayburgh, Rick Lenz, Ed Preble, Marcia Wallace.

Comedy, young couple thinks up wild excuses for staying home from work and spending the time together.

A Whistle in the Dark (100). By Thomas Murphy. Produced by Josh Productions in association with Moe Weise at the Mercury Theater. Opened October 8, 1969. (Closed January 4, 1970)

Harry Carney	Charles Cioffi	Iggy Carney	Don Plumley
Hugo Carney	Anthony Palmer	Michael Carney	Michael McGuire
Betty Carney	Roberta Maxwell	Michael Carney, Senior	Stephen Elliott
Mush O'Reilly	Dermot McNamara	Des Carney	Tom Atkins

Directed by Arvin Brown; scenery, Kert Lundell; lighting, Ron Wallace; costumes, Vanessa James; production stage manager, James O'Connell; press, Max Eisen, Lenny Traube, Cheryl Sue Dolby.

Time: The present. Place: The living room of Michael Carney's house in Coventry. Act I: Late afternoon. Act II: The following night. Act III: A few hours later.

Son in conflict with his Irish family which has emigrated to England after World War II. A foreign play previously produced in London and in an American premiere at the Long Wharf Theater, New Haven, Conn.

Richard Mackenzie replaced Stephen Elliott and Barbara Hayes replaced Roberta Maxwell 12/69.

The American Place Theater. Schedule of four programs. **Mercy Street** (46). By Anne Sexton. Opened October 11, 1969; see note. (Closed November 21, 1969) **Five on the Black Hand Side** (62). By Charlie L. Russell. Opened December 10, 1969; see note. (Closed January 31, 1970) **Two Times One** (35). Program of two one-act plays: *The Last Straw* by Charles Dizenzo and *Duet for Solo Voice* by David Scott Milton. Opened March 9, 1970; see note. (Closed April 11, 1970) *****The Pig Pen** (37). By Ed Bullins. Opened April 29, 1970; see note. Produced by The American Place Theater, Wynn Handman director, at St. Clements Church.

MERCY STREET

Dr. Alex	Jerome Raphel	Arthur	William Prince
Daisy	Marian Seldes	Acolytes	Robert Bass, Chris Kalfayan,
Judith	Virginia Downing		Paul Leavin, Fritz Stokes
Amelia	M'el Dowd		

Directed by Charles Maryan; scenery and costumes, Douglas Higgins; lighting, Roger Morgan; music selected and arranged by McNeil Robinson; production stage manager, George Blanchard; press, Howard Atlee, David Roggensack.

Time: Now with the exception of time recalled, time relived and time to come. The play is presented without intermission.

Woman is driven by memories of seduction by her drunken father when she was a girl to madness and despair.

FIVE ON THE BLACK HAND SIDE

Brooks ....L. Errol Jaye	Sweetmeat ....Gerry Black
Mrs. Brooks ....Clarice Taylor	Slim ....Ed Bernard
Gail ....Jonelle Allen	Fun Loving ....Tchaka Almoravids
Booker T. .....Matthew Bernard Johnson Jr.	Black Militant ....Eugene Reynolds
Gideon ....William Adell Stevenson III	Evangelist ....Marilyn B. Coleman
Stephanie ....Patricia A. Edomy	Rolls Royce ....Kirk Kirksey
Sampson ....Thabo Quinland R. Gordon	First Junkie ....Demond Wilson
Nia ....Nia Anderson	Second Junkie ....Eugene Reynolds
Ruby ....Theresa Merritt	Marvin ....Lisle Wilson
Stormy Monday ....Judyann Elder	

Directed by Barbara Ann Teer; scenery, Edward Burbridge; costumes, Gertha Brock; lighting, Shirley Prendergast; special sound, James Reichert; production stage manager, George Blanchard.

Time: The present. Place: Harlem. The play is divided into two acts.

Middle class Harlem family comedy about a wife demanding her rights from her stuffy, overbearing husband.

THE LAST STRAW

Dr. Frank ....Edward Kovens   Anthony ....Oliver Clark

DUET FOR SOLO VOICE

Leonard Pelican ....Herb Edelman   Vassily Chort ....Vassily Chort

BOTH PLAYS: Scenery and costumes, Kert Lundell; lighting, Roger Morgan; special sound, James Reichert; production stage manager, George Blanchard.

THE LAST STRAW—Direction by Gregory C. Meland. Time: The present. Place: An office somewhere in Manhattan. Depressed young man answers a medical quack's ad promising a happier life.

DUET FOR SOLO VOICE—Directed by Martin Fried. Time: Now, 4:30 a.m. Place: The 43rd Street Hotel. Paranoid hotel clerk believes he is being stalked by a sinister figure.

THE PIG PEN

Ray Crawford ....Basil A. Wallace	Henry Carroll ....Elbert Bernard Pair
Len Stover ....Tony Thomas	Mackman ....Edward Clinton
Sharon Stover ....Laura Esterman	Ernie Butler ....Michael Coleman
Margie ....Avis McCarther	Carlos ....J. Herbert Kerr Jr.
Bobo Carroll ....Lou Courtney	Pig Pen ....Robert Patterson
John Carroll ....Milton Earl Forrest	

Directed by Dick Williams; scenery, Douglas Higgins; costumes, Gertha Brock; lighting, Ernest Baxter; music, Gene McDaniels; production stage manager, George Blanchard; stage manager, Errol Selsby.

Time: February 1965, early morning. Place: A cabin up in the hills bounding Glendale, Calif., and a bit south of Pasadena, though near enough to the city for the dwellers on that narrow road to leave their front doors and ramble to the rim, to peer at the easternmost edges of Hollywood, if the day is smog-free.

Symbolical drama of black-white relations, as an interracial party, loud and raucous, is twice interrupted by a comically bullying policeman on the night that Malcolm X was killed.

NOTE: In this volume, the off-Broadway subscription companies like The American Place are exceptions to our rule of counting the number of performances from the date of press coverage, because usually the press opening night takes place late in the play's run of public performances (after previews) for the subscription audience. In these cases, therefore, we count the first subscription performance, not the press review date, as opening night. Press dates were *Mercy Street* 10/27/69, *Five on the Black Hand Side* 1/2/70, *Two Times One* 4/5/70, *The Pig Pen* 5/15/70.

From the Second City (31). Revue written and improvised by the cast. Produced by Bernard Sahlins in an Arts and Leisure Corp. Production at the Eastside Playhouse. Opened October 14, 1969. (Closed November 9, 1969)

J.J. Barry	Pamela Hoffman
Murphy Dunne	Ira Miller
Martin Harvey Friedberg	Carol Robinson
Burt Heyman	

Directed by David Lynn; composer and musical director, Fred Kaz; "Flower Song" lyric by Sandy Holt; scenery, Steven Holmes; lighting and sound, Gary Harris; production stage manager, Harvey M. Schaps; press, Merle Debuskey, M.J. Boyer.

Satiric revue, most of it created by previous improvisation among the performers in this Chicago-based company.

Polish Laboratory Theater (Institute of Actor's Research Laboratory Theater of Wroclaw, Poland). Schedule of three programs in the Polish language. **The Constant Prince** (24). By Calderon de la Barca; adapted by Julius Slowacki; scenario by Jerzy Grotowski. Opened October 16, 1969; see note. (Closed November 2, 1969) **Acropolis** (12). Based on the text of Stanislaw Wyspianski; scenario by Jerzy Grotowski. Opened November 4, 1969. (Closed November 16, 1969) **Apocalypsis Cum Figuris** (15). Based on works of T.S. Eliot, Feodor Dostoevsky, Simone Weil and on parts of the Bible; scenario by Jerzy Grotowski. Opened November 18, 1969; see note. (Closed December 15, 1969). Produced by the Brooklyn Academy of Music in association with Ninon Tallon Karlweis and the Committee to Welcome the Polish Lab Theater, Ellen Stewart co-chairman, at the Washington Square Methodist Church.

PERFORMER	"THE CONSTANT PRINCE"	"ACROPOLIS"	"APOCALYPSIS CUM FIGURIS"
Elizabeth Albahaca			Mary Magdalene
Ryszard Cieslak	Constant Prince	Esau-Hector	Simpleton
Zbigniew Cynkutis	Mooley	Angel-Paris	Lazarus
Antoni Jahalkowski	King	Isaac-Troyan	Simon Peter
		Guardian	
Rene Mirecka	Fenixana	Rebecca-Cassandra	
Zygmunt Molik	Tarudant	Jacob-Priam	Judas
Andrezej Paluchiewicz		(supporting role)	
Stanislaw Scierski	Henri	Leah-Helen	John

ALL PLAYS—Directed by Jerzy Grotowski; literary adviser, Ludwig Flaszen; architecture, Jerzy Gurawski; press, Walter Price.

THE CONSTANT PRINCE—Costumes, Waldemar Krygier. A society gone mad torments its gentle, non-violent Prince to death.

ACROPOLIS—Corealization, properties, costumes, Josef Szajna; cooperating with director, Ryszard Cieslak. Biblical and Homeric myths applied to the doomed inmates of a concentration camp.

APOCALYPSIS CUM FIGURIS—Costumes, Waldemar Krygier; cooperating with director, Ryszard Cieslak. A symposium of dramatic attitudes toward the Second Coming.

NOTE: The run of *Apocalypsis Cum Figuris* was interrupted for special added performances of *The Constant Prince* 11/29/69 through 12/7/69. Following a three-day absence 12/8-12/10 the company presented the 5 final performances of *Apocalypsis.*

And Puppy Dog Tails (141). By David Gaard. Produced by Michael Devereaux and Swen Swenson at the Bouwerie Lane Theater. Opened October 19, 1969. (Closed January 11, 1970)

John Hendrix	George Reeder	Bud Kelcorn	Ken Kliban
Tommy Spencer	Edward Dunn	Carey-Lee Dunbar	Horton Willis

Directed by Michael Devereaux; production designed by John B. Haber; production stage manager, James Greek; press, Max Eisen, Cheryl Sue Dolby.

Time: The present. Place: John and Carey-Lee's apartment on the Upper East Side, New York City. Act I, Scene 1: An evening in early summer. Scene 2: Four hours later. Scene 3: Three weeks later, 6 p.m. on a Sunday. Scene 4: The next week, 7:30 p.m. Act II, Scene 1: Immediately following. Scene 2: A month later, 7 p.m.

A homosexual love triangle.

Go Fly a Kite (8). One-man show conceived and performed by Fredd Wayne. Produced by Bacherway Productions in association with Jay Fiondella at Tambellini's Gate Theater. Opened October 19, 1969. (Closed October 26, 1969)

Additional dialogue by Sidney Dorfman; lighting, Marshall Spiller; production stage manager, Steven Holmes; press, Bill Doll & Associates.

Impersonation of Benjamin Franklin.

A Scent of Flowers (72). By James Saunders. Produced by Lawrence Goossen and Susan Richardson at the Martinique Theater. Opened October 20, 1969. (Closed December 21, 1969)

Zoe	Katharine Houghton	Grandmother	Donna Barry
Fred	Jeremiah Sullivan	Edgar	Sydney Walker
Sid	John Colenback	Agnes	Carolyn Coates
Godfrey	John Glover	David	James Noble
Scrivens	Roderick Cook		

Directed by Brian Murray; scenery, Ed Wittstein; lighting, David F. Segal; costumes, Diedre Cartier; stage manager, Barbara Tuttle; press, Max Eisen, Warren Pincus, Cheryl Sue Dolby.

After committing suicide, a young girl reviews the events of her life leading up to its tragic end. The play is presented in three acts

Fortune and Men's Eyes (231). Revival of the play by John Herbert. Produced by Kenneth Waissman and Maxine Fox at Stage 73. Opened October 22, 1969. (Closed May 10, 1970)

Rocky	Bartholomew Miro, Jr.	Guard	Joe Dorsey
Mona	Jeremy Stockwell	Smitty	Mark Shannon
Queenie	Michael Greer	Catsolino	George Ryland

Directed by Sal Mineo; scenery and costumes, Alan Kimmel; lighting, Ken Billington; production stage manager, Gigi Cascio; press, Betty Lee Hunt.

Time: The present. Place: A boy's prison. Act I: A mid-October evening. Act II: Three weeks later. Act III: Christmas Eve.

Fortune and Men's Eyes was previously produced off Broadway 2/23/67 for 382 performances.

Robert Redding replaced Michael Greer 3/70.

Crimes of Passion (9). Program of two one-act plays by Joe Orton: *The Ruffian on the Stair* and *The Erpingham Camp*. Produced by Henry Fownes, Frank Bessell, Bruce Hoover with Leonard Mulhern and George Thorn at the Astor Place Theater. Opened October 26, 1969. (Closed November 2, 1969)

Directed by Michael Kahn; scenery, William Ritman; lighting, Richard Nelson, costumes, Jane Greenwood; production stage manager, Stephen Sobel; musical director, Conrad Susa; press, Howard Atlee, David Roggensack, Stanley F. Kaminsky. With David Birney, James Cahill, Richard A. Dysart, Bette Henritze, Zoe Kamitses, Tom Lacy, Lynn Milgrim, Tom Tarpey, Sasha von Scherler, Josef Warik, John Tillinger.

In *The Ruffian on the Stair* a vicious middle-aged couple murders a young homosexual visitor. *The Erpingham Camp* is an allegory of British society in which moronic celebrants wreck their holiday camp. Foreign plays previously produced in England.

The Haunted Host (8). By Robert Patrick. Produced by Gallery Productions at the Castle Theater. Opened October 27, 1969. (Closed November 2, 1969)

Directed by Eric Concklin; scenery, Martin L. H. Reymert; lighting, David Adams; music and lyrics by Mr. Patrick; music and lyrics arranged by Jon Bauman and Brad Burg; production stage manager, Judith Kayser; press, Reginald Denenholz, Anne Woll. With Neil Flanagan, Joseph Pichette.
Homosexual meets a young man who resembles his dead lover.

Rose (8). By Emanuel Fried. Produced by JanMar Productions, Ltd. at the Provincetown Playhouse. Opened October 28, 1969. (Closed November 2, 1969)

Directed by Charles Olsen; scenery and costumes, Misha Petrow; lighting, Michael C. Davidson; sound, Gary Harris; production stage manager, Stephen Jarrett; press, Dorothy Ross. With David Clarke, Judy Jordan, Gil Rogers, Raymond Thorne, Nadyne Turney.
Woman is involved in and beaten down by the changing American social climate from 1938 to the present.

The Local Stigmatic (8). Seven playlets by Harold Pinter: *Applicant, Interview, Last to Go, Request Stop, That's All, That's Your Trouble* and *Trouble in the Works,* and the title play by Heathcote Williams. Produced by Len Gochman, Jon Peterson and James Stevenson at the Actors Playhouse. Opened November 3, 1969. (Closed November 9, 1969)

Directed by Arthur Storch; scenery, Milton Duke; lighting, Molly Friedel; costumes, Elaine Yokoyama; music composed by Conrad Susa; production stage manager, Lawrence Spiegel; press, Max Eisen, Jeanne Gibson Merrick, Warren Pincus. With Paul Benedict, Sudie Bond, Michael Hadge, Joseph Maher, Al Pacino.
In *The Local Stigmatic* a pair of bullies who get their kicks from brutal violence beat up a film star. A foreign play previously produced in England. Some of the Pinter sketches were previously produced on American television.

Rondelay (11). Musical based on Arthur Schnitzler's *La Ronde;* book and lyrics by Jerry Douglas; music by Hal Jordan. Produced by Rick Hobard at the Hudson West Theater. Opened November 5, 1969. (Closed November 14, 1969)

Directed by William Francisco; musical numbers staged by Jacques d'Amboise; musical direction and vocal arrangements, Karen Gustafson; scenery, Raoul Pene du Bois; lighting, Neil Peter Jampolis; orchestrations, Philip J. Lang; associate producers, Martin Hodas, James Jennings; stage manager, Frank Hamilton; press, Max Eisen, Cheryl Sue Dolby. With Louise Clay, Carole Demas, Gwyda Donhowe, Shawn Elliott, Dillon Evans, Barbara Lang, Barbara Minkus, Terence Monk, Paxton Whitehead, Peter York.
Musical version of Schnitzler's *La Ronde* (Der Reige) about a series of interconnected love affairs.

* New York Shakespeare Festival Public Theater. Indoor schedule of three programs. **Stomp** (161). Multimedia protest rock musical environment entertainment created by The Combine. Opened November 16, 1969; see note. (Closed April 19, 1970). **Sambo** (37). Musical with words by Ron Steward; music by Ron Steward and Neal Tate. Opened December 12, 1969 (press date was 12/21/70). (Closed January 11, 1970) * **Mod Donna** (48). Musical with book and lyrics by Myrna Lamb; music by Susan Hulsman Bingham. Opened April 24, 1970 (press date was 5/3/70). Produced by the New York Shakespeare Festival, Joseph Papp producer, Gerald Freedman artistic director, Bernard Gersten associate producer, at the Public Theater.

STOMP was created and performed by The Combine, a group of former University of Texas students led by Doug Dyer. There are no individual credits for writing, acting, direction, design, etc. The show is a series of song numbers, skits, movies and other happenings blended into a topical satirical, multimedia protest entertainment.
NOTE: *Stomp* recessed 2/1/70 and resumed its run at the Public Theater 2/17/70.

SAMBO

Sambo	Ron Steward	Miss Sally	
Tigers	Camille Yarbrough, Rob Barnes,	Muffat	Janice Lynne Montgomery
	Jenny O'Hara, Robert La Tourneaux,	Little Boy Blue	Kenneth Carr
	Sid Marshall, Henry Baker	Jack Horney	George Turner
Untogether Cinderella	Gerri Dean	Bo Peep	Hattie Wilson

Musicians: Neal Tate, conductor, electric piano; Lew Tabackin, reeds; Virgil Jones, trumpet, flugelhorn; Bob Mann, guitar; Hal Gaylor, bass; Richard Allen, drums.

Directed by Gerald Freedman; scenery, Ming Cho Lee, Marjorie Kellogg; costumes, Milo Morrow; lighting, Martin Aronstein; musical direction, Neal Tate; musical supervision, John Morris; production manager, Andrew Mihok; stage manager, Adam G. Perl; press, Merle Debuskey.

Time: Now. Place: Here. "A black opera with white spots" with symbolic episodes depicting the black man's sense of alienation.

ACT I

"Sing a Song of Sambo" ....Sambo
"Hey Boy" ....Tigers
"I Am Child" ....Sambo, Friends
"Young Enough to Dream" ....Sambo, Company
"Mama Always Said" ....Tigers, Bo Peep, Little Boy Blue, Miss Sally Muffat,
Jack Horney, Untogether Cinderella
"Baddest Mammyjammy" ....Sambo, Company
"Sambo Was a Bad Boy" ....Company
"Pretty Flower" ....Company
"I Could Dig You" ....Sambo, Untogether Cinderella
"Do You Care Too Much" ....Company
"Be Black" ....Company
Tiger Priest ....Henry Baker
Tiger Priestess ....Camille Yarborough
"Let's Go Down" ....Little Boy Blue, Miss Sally Muffat, Bo Peep, Jack Horney

ACT II

"Astrology" ....Company
"The Eternal Virgin" ....Bo Peep
"Boy Blue" ....Little Boy Blue
"The Piscean" ....Miss Sally Muffat
"Aries" ....Jack Horney
"Untogether Cinderella" ....Untogether Cinderella
"Peace Love and Good Damn" ....Sambo
"Come on Home" ....Jack Horney, Company
"Black Man" ....Company
"Get an Education" ....Tiger (Camille Yarborough)
"Ask and You Shall Receive" ....Tigers (Jenny O'Hara, Robert La Tourneaux)
"Son of Africa" ....Sambo, Company
"I Am a Child" (Reprise) ....Sambo, Company

MOD DONNA

Donna	April Shawhan	Jeff	Larry Bryggman
Chris	Sharon Laughlin	Charlie	Peter Haig

Chorus of Women: Ellen Barber, Jani Brenn, Katharine Dunfee, June Gable, Deloris Gaskins, Liz Gorrill, Zora Margolis, Maureen Mooney, Madge Sinclair. Musicians: Dorothea Freitag conductor and piano, Carol Rowe viola, Edith Wint cello, Marsha Heller oboe, Nancy Buckingham clarinet, Karolyn Stonefelt drums.

Directed by Joseph Papp; costumes, Milo Morrow; lighting, Martin Aronstein; choreography, Ze-eva Cohen; musical direction and orchestrations, Liza Redfield; stage manager, Jane Neufeld.

Subtitled "A space age musical soap," *Mod Donna* is about a bored married couple's sexual adventures with another couple—principally in order to stimulate chorus comments on Women's Liberation and the sexual victimization of the fair sex.

ACT I

Overture: "Trapped"
"Earthworms" ....Chorus of Women
"The Incorporation" ....Chris, Jeff
"Invitation" ....Donna, Chorus
"All the Way Down" ....Chorus
"The Deal" ....Chris, Jeff, Donna, Chorus
"Liberia" ....Chorus
"The Morning After" ....Chris, Jeff, Donna
"Charlie's Plaint" ....Charlie, Chorus
"Creon" ....Frankie, Johnny, Antigone, Chorus
"The Worker and the Shirker" ....Donna, Charlie
"Food Is Love" ....Chorus
"First Act Crisis" ....Chris, Donna

ACT II

Overture: "Astrociggy"
"Second Act Beginning" ....Donna, Chris, Jeff, Chorus
"Hollow" ....Chris, Donna, Chorus
"Seduction Second Degree" ....Chris, Jeff
"Panassociative" ....Chris, Chorus
"Earth Dance" ....Chorus
"Trinity" ....Donna, Chris, Chorus
"Trapped" (Reprise) ....Donna, Chorus
"Astrociggy" (Reprise) ....Donna, Chorus
"Special Bulletin" ....Donna, Chris
"Take a Knife" ....Chris
"The Second Honeymoon" ....Donna, Jeff
"Jeff's Plaints" ....Jeff, Chorus
"Incantation" ....Chorus
"Beautiful Man" ....Chorus
"Sacrifice" ....Donna, Chris, Jeff, Charlie
"Now!" ....Chorus
"Beautiful Man" (Reprise) ....Chorus
"We Are the Whores" (Liberation Song) ....Chorus

Who's Happy Now? (32). By Oliver Hailey. Produced by Michael Ellis and Samuel Bronstein at the Village South Theater. Opened November 17, 1969. (Closed December 14, 1969)

Richard Hallen ....Ken Kercheval Horse Hallen ....Robert Darnell
Pop ....Stuart Germain Faye Precious ....Rue McLanahan
Mary Hallen ....Teresa Wright

Directed by Stanley Prager; scenery, Howard Barker; costumes, Gertha Brock; lighting, Shirley Prendergast; music by Michael Barr; lyrics by Dion McGregor; production stage manager, Otis Bigelow; press, Michael Alpert.

Time: 1941-1955. Place: Texas. Act I: 1941. Act II: 1951. Act III: 1955.

Young man competes with his father for his mother's attention and affections. Previously produced at the Mark Taper Forum, Los Angeles.

Die Schauspiel Truppe Zurich. Schedule of three programs in the German language. **Die Ehe des Herrn Mississippi** (The Marriage of Mr. Mississippi) (6). By Friedrich Duerrenmatt. Opened November 19, 1969. (Closed November 23, 1969). **Die Grosse Wut des Philipp Hots** (Philipp Hotz) and **Biedermann und die Brandstifter** (The Firebugs) (6). Program of two one-act plays by Max Frisch. Opened November 26, 1969. (Closed November 30, 1969 matinee). **Iphigenie auf Tauris** (1). By Johann Wolfgang von Goethe. Opened and closed at the evening performance November 30, 1969. Produced by The Gert von Gontard Foundation under the auspices of the Swiss ambassadors to the United States and Canada at the Barbizon-Plaza Theater.

PERFORMER	"DIE EHE DES HERRN MISSISSIPPI"	"DIE GROSSE WUT DES PHILIPP HOTZ"	"BIEDERMANN UND DIE BRANDSTIFTER"
Susi Aeberhard	Maid	Girl	Anna
Maria Becker	Anastasia	Clarissa	Mrs. Knechtling
Otto Freitag	Ueberhuber	Custom Agent	Policeman
Robert Freitag	Mississippi	Hotz	Schmitz
Fred Haltiner	Saint-Claude		Eisenring
Franz Matter	Zabernsee	Wilfrid	Biedermann
Maria Sebaldt		Dorli	Babette
Guido von Salis		Young Porter	A Ph.D.
Georg Weiss	Diege	Old Porter	

IPHIGENIE AUF TAURIS—Cast for special single performance included Maria Becker (in the title role), Robert Freitag, Fred Haltiner, Guido von Salis, Georg Weiss.

ALL PLAYS—Scenery and costumes, Theo Schweitzer; lighting, Rolf Attenhofer; stage manager, Jane Clegg; press, Nat and Irvin Dorfman.

DIE EHE DES HERRN MISSISSIPPI—Directed by Robert Freitag; technical director, Edwin Schaedlich; masks, Gertrud Krull. The play was presented in two acts. Comedy, a district attorney who has murdered his wife marries a woman he knows to be a murderess, first produced in Munich in 1952.

DIE GROSSE WUT DES PHILIPP HOTZ—Directed by Fred Haltiner. Comedy, much ado about a writer and his wife and their planned divorce.

BIEDERMANN UND DIE BRANDSTIFTER—Directed by Maria Becker; technical director, Edwin Schaedlich; masks, Gertrud Schlaeger. Object lesson in the futility of complacency and appeasement.

Little Boxes (15). Program of two one-act plays by John Bowen: *The Coffee Lace* and *Trevor*. Produced by Leonard S. Field and N. Lawrence Golden with Sullivan Productions, Inc. at the New Theater. Opened December 3, 1969. (Closed December 14, 1969)

Directed by Perry Bruskin; scenery, Helen Pond, Herbert Senn; costumes, Pamela Scofield; lighting, Molly Friedel; press, Seymour Krawitz, Ruth D. Smuckler. With Tony Tanner, Norman Barrs, Jon Beam, Dillon Evans, Beulah Garrick, Jo Henderson, Lucie Lancaster, Leona Maricle, Rosalind Ross, Jennifer Tilston, Frederic Tozere.

The Coffee Lace concerns a music hall troupe on its last legs, selling its cherished possessions. *Trevor* is about two girls pretending to their families that the same man is the fiance of each. Foreign comedies previously produced in London.

* The Repertory Theater of Lincoln Center. Schedule of four programs. **The Increased Difficulty of Concentration** (28). By Vaclav Havel; translated from the Czech by Vera Blackwell. Opened December 4, 1969. (Closed December 27, 1969) **The Disintegration of James Cherry** (28). By Jeff Wanshel. Opened January 29, 1970. (Closed February 21, 1970) **Landscape** and **Silence** (53). Program of one-act plays by Harold Pinter. Opened April 2, 1970. (Closed May 17, 1970 matinee) *** Amphitryon** (6). By Peter Hacks; translated from the German by Ralph Manheim. Opened May 28, 1970. Produced by The Repertory Theater of Lincoln Center at the Forum Theater.

THE INCREASED DIFFICULTY OF CONCENTRATION

Dr. Eduard Huml ....Harold Gould
Vlasta Huml ....Jane Hoffman
Renata ....Jacqueline Brookes
Blanka ....Alix Elias

Dr. Anna Balcar ....Leora Dana
Karel Kriebl ....Sam Schacht
Emil Machal ....Sam Umani
Mr. Beck ....George Bartenieff

Directed by Mel Shapiro; scenery and costumes, David I. Mitchell; lighting, John Gleason; sound, Pril Smiley Delson; production stage manager, Jane Ward; press, Susan Bloch.
Time: The present. Place: Dr. Huml's flat. The play is divided into two acts.
Scientist's life is disorganized by family strife and a whimsical computer. A foreign play previously produced in Czechoslovakia.

THE DISINTEGRATION OF JAMES CHERRY

James Cherry	Stephen Strimpell	Tunbunny	Jacque Lynn Colton
Elizabeth Cherry	Priscilla Pointer	Charley Johnson	James Cahill
William Cherry	James Ray	The Man	Jay Garner
Betsy Cherry	Catherine Burns	Woman	Carolyn Coates
Grandmother Cherry	Margaret Linn	Gus	Raymond Singer
Mendacious Porpentine	Robert Symonds	Bill	John Merensky

Directed by Glenn Jordan; scenery, Douglas W. Schmidt; costumes, James Hart Stearns; lighting, John Gleason; production stage manager, Frank Bayer.
Nightmarish fantasies of an angry young man.

LANDSCAPE

Duff	Robert Symonds	Beth	Mildred Natwick

SILENCE

Ellen	Barbara Tarbuck	Bates	James Patterson
Rumsey	Robert Symonds		

Directed by Peter Gill; scenery, Douglas W. Schmidt, based on designs by John Gunter; lighting, John Gleason; costumes, Douglas W. Schmidt, based on designs by Deirdre Clancy; stage managers, Tim Ward, Jane Ward.
Both plays are prose poems, with various emotions recollected in motionless tranquility—the actors remain seated and communicate aloud, though not directly to each other, in verbal images. Foreign plays previously produced (in 1969) by the Royal Shakespeare Company in London.

AMPHITRYON

Jupiter	Philip Bosco	Amphitryon	James Patterson
Mercury	James Ray	Alcmene	Priscilla Pointer
Sosias	Harold Gould	Night	Dan Sullivan

Directed by Robert Symonds; scenery, costumes and masks, James Hart Stearns; lighting, John Gleason; production stage manager, Jane Ward.
German playwright's version of the legend of Jupiter's love affair with a mortal's wife, Alcmene. A foreign play previously produced in Germany and other European countries.

Passing Through From Exotic Places (25). Program of three one-act plays by Ronald Ribman: *The Son Who Hunted Tigers in Jakarta*, *Sunstroke* and *The Burial of Esposito*. Produced by Capricorn Company, Kleiman-Reis Productions and Studley-Traub at the Sheridan Square Playhouse. Opened December 7, 1969. (Closed December 28, 1969)

THE SON WHO HUNTED TIGERS IN JAKARTA

Charles Ferris	Vincent Gardenia	Mr. Sweeney	Robert Loggia
His Wife, Edna	Tresa Hughes		

SUNSTROKE

Tomqualatruratu	Peter DeAnda	Aldous Shawcross	Robert Loggia
Arthur Goldblatt	Oliver Clark	Mrs. Virginia Shawcross	Tresa Hughes

THE BURIAL OF ESPOSITO

Nick Esposito	Vincent Gardenia	His Brother-in-law	Robert Loggia
His Wife	Tresa Hughes	His Son	Jay Hammer

Directed by Eugene Lesser; scenery, C. Murawski; lighting, William Mintzer; costumes, Joseph G. Aulisi; production stage manager, Martha Knight; press, Robert Ganshaw, John Prescott.

The Son Who Hunted Tigers in Jakarta is about a 3 a.m. intruder in a suburban household. *Sunstroke* is a parable of slavery told in terms of a modern Peace Corps assignment. *The Burial of Esposito* is the frenzy of a father who has lost his son in Vietnam.

The Moon Dreamers (24). By Julie Bovasso. Produced by Peter Moreau, Herschel Waxman and Maury Kanbar at the Ellen Stewart Theater. Opened December 8, 1969. (Closed December 28, 1969)

Bride; Tourist; Squaw ...Vincenza DiMaggio, Constantine Poutous	Salvation Army Singer ....Reigh Hagen
	Mick ....Alex Beall
Indian; Gold Star Mother; Zen Buddhist;	Mack ....LaMar Alford
Geisha ....Laura Simms, Ching Yeh, Evan Ritter	Chief of Police ....Herve Villechaize
	Bubu ....Elayne Barat
Rene Utray ....Tom Rosica	Apple Boy ....Douglas Stone
Sandra ....Jane Sanford	Strange Fruit Dancer ......Raymond Bussey
Mimi ....Zina Jasper	Groom ....Fred Muselli
Mother ....Jean David	Father ....Alan Harvey
Lawyer ....Ted Henning	Ira ....Daffi
Doctor ....Leonard Hicks	The Man at the End ....Louis Ramos

Soldiers: Louis Ramos, Alan Wynroth, Alan Harvey. Stockbrokers: Chris Christianson, Carl Wilson, Wes Williams. Doublemint Opera Trio: LaMar Alford, Maria D'Elia, Ella Luzembourg. Two Dancing Swells: John Bacher, Lanny Harrison. Ziegfeld Nurses, Hula Girls: Maria D'Elia, Roberta Hammer, Diedre Simone. Flappers, Vamps & Dance Hall Girls: Janda Lee, Mossa Ossa, Ella Luxembourg. Dancehall Boys, Dappers: John Bacher, Chris Christianson, Reigh Hagen. Sheiks, Space Boys: William Pierce, Carl Wilson, Lawrence Sellars. Chorus of Constantly Present People: Elayne Barat, Lanny Harrison, Constantine Poutous, Douglas Stone, Robert Ullman, Steven Verakus, Dennis Sokal.

Directed by Julie Bovasso; scenery, Bernard X. Bovasso; costumes, Randy Barcelo; lighting, John P. Dodd; associate director and choreographer, Raymond Bussey; musical direction, LaMar Alford; production stage manager, Wes Jensby; press, Seymour Krawitz, Ruth D. Smuckler.

Social commentary in the camp style about civilization reaching the moon while flaws persist in earthly society. Previously produced at the Cafe La Mama.

Summertree (184). Revival of the play by Ron Cowen. Produced by Sanford Farber and Eddie White at the Players Theater. Opened December 9, 1969. (Closed May 17, 1970)

Young Man ....Lenny Baker	Father ....Hy Anzel
Little Boy ....Scott Jacoby	Girl ....Elizabeth Walker
Mother ....Janet Ward	Soldier ....Hector Troy

Directed by Stephen Glassman; scenery, Janet Murray; lighting, David F. Segal; production stage manager, Iris Merlis; press, David Rothenberg.

Summertree was originally produced at the Forum Theater by The Repertory Theater of Lincoln Center 3/3/68 for 127 performances.

Linda DeCoff replaced Elizabeth Walker and Maurey Cooper replaced Hy Anzel 3/70.

Gertrude Stein's First Reader (40). Musical revue with words by Gertrude Stein; music and musical adaptation by Ann Sternberg. Produced by John Bernard Myers in association with Bob Cato at the Astor Place Theater. Opened December 15, 1969. (Closed January 18, 1970)

Michael Anthony	Sandra Thornton
Joy Garrett	Ann Sternberg (piano)
Frank Giordano	

Conceived and directed by Herbert Machiz; scenery, Kendall Shaw; lighting, Patrika Brown; production stage manager, Douglas Wallace; press, Betty Lee Hunt Associates, Henry Luhrman, Harriett Trachtenberg.

Four performers playing children are led in games, recitations and songs by a pianist.
ACT I: "Sunshine"—Entire Company; "Wildflowers"—Entire Company; "A Dog"—Entire Company; "Writing Lesson"—Joy Garrett, Sandra Thornton; Johnny and Jimmy—Frank Giordano, Michael Anthony; "The Blackberry Vine" (A Play)—Anthony (Boy), Miss Thornton (Girl), Giordano (Blackberry Vine), Miss Garrett (Narrator); "Big Bird"—Ann Sternberg; "The Three Sisters Who Are Not Sisters" (A Murder Mystery)—Entire Company; "Be Very Careful"—Entire Company.
ACT II: "New Word"—Entire Company; "Jenny"—Miss Thornton; "How They Do, Do"—Miss Garrett; Soldier—Anthony; Baby Benjamin—Giordano; "Wildflowers" (Reprise)—Entire Company; "In a Garden" (A Mini Opera)—Anthony (Philip Hall), Miss Garrett (Lucy Willow), Giordano (Kit Raccoon); "Be Very Careful" (Reprise)—Entire Company.

Seven Days of Mourning (56). By Seymour Simckes. Produced by Circle in the Square, Theodore Mann artistic director, Paul Libin managing director, Gillian Walker associate director, at Circle in the Square. Opened December 16, 1969. (Closed February 1, 1970)

Barish Shimansky	Tony Schwab		Timmy Michael
Mrs. Charpolsky	Carol Teitel	Vossen Gleich	Shimen Ruskin
Varda Shimansky (Ma)	Paula Laurence	Blindde	C.D. Creasap
Zelo Shimansky (Pa)	Stefan Gierasch	Trupke	Michael Talcott
Yanina Leishik	Nancy Franklin	Shtummer	Michael Thompson
Feivel Leishik	David Margulies	Datya	Camilla Ritchey
(Pildesh Leishik)	Jonny Allen,		

(Parentheses indicate role in which the actors alternated)

Directed by Theodore Mann; scenery, Marsha Eck; costumes, Joseph G. Aulisi; lighting, David F. Segal; stage manager, Owen Ryan; press, Merle Debuskey, Faith Geer.
Time: The 1930s. Place: The Shimansky apartment on the Lower East Side, New York City. The play is divided into two acts.
Jewish family refuses to mourn a suicide daughter.

The Brownstone Urge (7). By Gladys S. Foster and Allan Reiser. Produced by Roy Franklyn at the Actors Playhouse. Opened December 17, 1969. (Closed December 21, 1969)

Directed by Tom Hinton; scenery and costumes, Ken Lewis; lighting, Tony Quintavalla; press, Sol Jacobson, Lewis Harmon. With Reggie Baff, Ron Burrus, Martin Starkand, Donna Wandrey, Donn Whyte.
Comedy about a couple's problems with a deteriorating house in the Chelsea section of New York City.

The Whistling Wizard and the Sultan of Tuffet (167). Bil Baird's Marionettes production with book by Alan Stern; songs by Bil Baird and Alan Stern. Also **Winnie the Pooh** (23; see note). Produced by The American Puppet Arts Council, Arthur Cantor executive producer, at the Bil Baird Theater. Opened December 20, 1969. (Closed May 31, 1970)

J.P.	Fania Sullivan	Pasha	Robert Gerstein
Heathcliff	Byron Whiting	Sasha; Akimbo;	
Dooley (Wizard); Casbah	Bil Baird	Dragon	Christopher Kemble
Turtle; Ali Booby (Sultan)	Frank Sullivan	Princess Peekaboo	Olga Felgemacher

General understudy—Michael Douglas.
Directed by Gordon Hunt; musical direction and arrangements, Alvy West; production manager, Carl Harms; press, Joel Wyman.
Place: The Country of Tuffet and Land of Beyond. The play is divided into two acts.
Marionette play, a fairy tale in which the Whistling Wizard saves the Sultan's throne from an evil servant, Casbah.
NOTE: *A Pageant of Puppet Variety,* a demonstration of the art of the marionette theater, was also presented on this program, as it has been in many of the Bil Baird productions. The

Baird repertory production of *Winnie the Pooh* was presented at various times during the season.
Christopher Kemble and Bil Baird alternated in the role of the Wizard staring 2/1/70. David Canaan and Alan Gelassen replaced Robert Gerstein and alternated in the Kemble roles 2/1/70.

Love Your Crooked Neighbor (8). By Harold J. Chapler. Produced by Sarah Beldner and Lois Wahl at the Cherry Lane Theater. Opened December 29, 1969. (Closed January 4, 1970)

Faith Detweiler .....Cara Duff-MacCormick	Margaret Nelson ....Dale Berg
Ralph Nelson ....Don Warfield	Tony Nelson ....David Kerman
Frank ....Robert Weil	

Directed by Sidney Walters; scenery, Fred Sammut; costumes, Robert Anderson; lighting, Chuck Vincent; music, John Brancati; press, Max Eisen.
Part-dark, part-zany comedy about an American family coping with crime.

* The Negro Ensemble Company. Schedule of three programs. **The Harangues** (56). Program of four episodes by Joseph A. Walker; music by Dorothy A. Dinroe. Opened December 30, 1969; see note. (Closed February 15, 1970) **Brotherhood** and **Day of Absence** (64). Program of one new play and one revival by Douglas Turner Ward. Opened March 10, 1970; see note. (Closed May 3, 1970). *** Akokawe** (Initiation) (16). Program of African writings selected by Afolabi Ajayi. Opened May 19, 1970; see note. Produced by The Negro Ensemble Company, Douglas Turner Ward artistic director, Robert Hooks executive director, Gerald S. Krone administrative director, at the St. Marks Playhouse.

TRIBAL HARANGUE ONE

Ayo ....Rosalind Cash	Obataiye ....Damon W. Brazwell Jr.

TRIBAL HARANGUE TWO

Zoe Walton ....Irene Bunde	Walton ....Robert G. Murch
Cal ....Robert Hooks	Doctor ....William Jay
Jake ....David Downing	Black Men ..Julius W. Harris, Douglas Turner

TRIBAL HARANGUE THREE

Ayo ....Rosalind Cash	Obataiye ....Damon W. Brazwell Jr.

HARANGUE

Gorilla ....Julius W. Harris	Billy Boy ....Linda Carlson
Lee ....William Jay	Asura ....Douglas Turner
Cooper ....Elliot Cuker	

Musicians: Margaret Harris, piano; Jack Gregg, bass; Omar Clay, percussion; Harold Vick, reeds.
Directed by Israel Hicks; musical direction, Margaret Harris; choreography, Percival Borde; scenery, Chuck Vincent; costumes, Gertha Brock; lighting, Buddy Butler; stage manager, James S. Lucas Jr.; press, Howard Atlee, David Roggensack.
TRIBAL HARANGUE ONE—Time: The 14th or 15th century. Place: An African slave dungeon off the coast of West Africa. Ayo and Obataiye, prisoners, kill their infant son to prevent his growing up in slavery.
TRIBAL HARANGUE TWO—Time: The present. Place: A fairly expensive apartment somewhere near Dupont Circle, Washington D.C. Farce about a young black's plans to murder his white fiancee's rich Texas father.
TRIBAL HARANGUE THREE—Time: The future. After the black revolution, the characters in *Tribal Harangue One* decide to let their child grow up in possible freedom, even though his father is to be executed for rebellion.
HARANGUE—Time: The present. Place: A bar on Avenue B of New York City's Lower East Side. Man with a gun strips blacks and whites of their flimsy liberal poses.

BROTHERHOOD

Tom Jason	Tom Rosqui	James Johnson	William Jay
Ruth Jason	Tiffany Hendry	Luann Johnson	Frances Foster

DAY OF ABSENCE

Clem; 2d Man; Businessman	Allie Woods	Supervisor; Clubwoman	Clarice Taylor
Luke; 3d Man; Clan	Norman Bush	Jackson	William Jay
John; Courier; Pious	David Downing	Mayor	Arthur French
Mary	Rosalind Cash	1st Man; Industrialist;	
1st Operator; Aide	Esther Rolle	Rastus	Bill Duke
2d Operator	Frances Foster	Announcer	Tom Rosqui
3d Operator	Anita Wilson		

Directed by Douglas Turner Ward; scenery, Chuck Vincent; lighting, Ernest Baxter; costumes, Gertha Brock; special sound, James Reichert; stage manager, James Lucas Jr.

BROTHERHOOD—Time: The present. Place: The living room of a typical suburban home. A white couple asks a black couple into their home for a party, but racism gradually begins to show itself.

DAY OF ABSENCE—Time: Now. Place: An unnamed Southern town. This play was previously produced off Broadway by Robert Hooks 11/15/65 for 504 performances.

AKOKAWE

Mbari-Mbayo Players as follows: Afolabi Ajayi (Nigeria), Amandina Lihamba (Tanzania), Paul Makgoba (South Africa), Ifatumbo Oyebola (New York), Babafemi Akinlana (New York), Louis Espinosa (New York).

Negro Ensemble Compauy members as follows: Norman Bush, Frances Foster, Esther Rolle, Clarice Taylor, Allie Woods.

Guest performer: Andre Womble.

Directed by Afolabi Ajayi; scenery, Chuck Vincent; lighting, Ernest Baxter; special dance movement, Percival Borde; stage manager, James S. Lucas Jr.

A dramatized presentation of traditional and modern African writings, in an evening of music, dance, poetry and stories.

ACT I

Traditional Times
  Opening Call of Drums ....Babafemi, Oyebola
  Poem of Greetings ....Company
  Song of Ojo ....Ajayi, Bush, Makgoba, Womble
  Song of Wisdom ....Misses Lihamba, Taylor
  The Storyteller ....Ajayi, Company
The First Contact
  The European ....Misses Foster, Lihamba, Rolle
  The Prayer That Got Away ....Ajayi, Bush
  Song of War ....Makgoba, Company

ACT II

Poets in Exile
  Invocation (Wole Soyinka) ....Miss Rolle
  New York ....Miss Taylor, Womble
  First Impressions (Lafiaji) ....Miss Lihamba
  Vending Machine (J.P. Clark) ....Bush
American Impressions (Ifeanyi Menkiti)
  Harlem Blonde Bombshell ....Miss Lihamba
  Manhattan ....Makgoba
  Selma ....Misses Foster, Rolle, Taylor
  Integration ....Makgoba
New York Skyscrapers (J. Mbiti) ....Miss Taylor
Telephone Conversation ....Ajayi
Paris in the Snow (Senghor) ....Miss Foster
Negritude Poets

Prayer to Masks (Senghor) ....Makgoba, Company
Africa (Birago Diop) ....Miss Rolle
Nights of Sine (Senghor) ....Makgoba, Company
Dawn in the Heart of Africa ....Ajayi, Bush
Defiance Against Force ....Ajayi, Bush, Company
New Songs
    Merinda Love Song ....Bush, Miss Foster
    Popular Love Song ....Miss Lihamba, Makgoba
    Song of Proverbs ....Company
    Drum Finale ....Oyebola, Babafemi
NOTE: In this volume, off-Broadway subscription companies like The Negro Ensemble Company are exceptions to our rule of counting the number of performances from the date of the press coverage, because usually the press opening night takes place late in the play's run of public performances (after previews) for the subscription audience. In these cases, therefore, we count the first subscription performance, not the press review date, as opening night. Press date for *The Harangues* was 1/13/70, for *Brotherhood* and *Day of Absence* 3/17/70 for *Akokawe* 6/5/70.

Love and Maple Syrup (Amour et Sucre D'Erable) (15). Musical revue in the French and English languages devised and compiled by Lous Negin from Canadian writers and composers. Produced by Ruth Kalkstein and Edward Specter Productions by arrangement with Dorian Productions, Ltd., Louis Negin and The National Arts Center of Canada at the Mercer-Hansberry Theater. Opened January 7, 1970. (Closed January 18, 1970)

Production designed by Charles L. Dunlop; lighting, Barry Arnold; associate producers, Art and Burt D'Lugoff; song "Love and Maple Syrup" written by Gordon Lightfoot; press, David Lipsky, Marian Graham, Lisa Lipsky. With Sandra Caron, Gabriel Gascon, Judy Lander, Ann Mortifee, Louis Negin, Margaret Robertson, Bill Schustik.

Revue variations on the theme of love in Canada. A foreign play previously produced in Washington, D.C.

The Memory Bank (25). Program of two one-act plays by Martin Duberman: *The Recorder, A History* and *The Electric Map, a Melodrama*. Produced by Davis Weinstock, Michael Pantaleoni and Lewis E. Lehrman in association with First Circle Associates, Ltd. at Tambellini's Gate Theater. Opened January 11, 1970. (Closed February 1, 1970)

THE RECORDER, A HISTORY

Smyth (Interviewer) ....Jeff David   Andrews ....Fred Stewart

THE ELECTRIC MAP, A MELODRAMA

Ted ....Laurence Luckinbill   Jim ....Gil Rogers

Directed by Harold Stone; scenery and costumes, Fred Voelpel; lighting, Paul Sullivan; sound, Gary Harris; production stage manager, Steven Zweigbaum; press, Howard Atlee, David Roggensack.

In *The Recorder,* the relationship between a young historian and a great man become confused, even interchanged, during an interview. *The Electric Map* is a quarrel between brothers, one of whom has charge of an electrified tourists' map showing how the Battle of Gettysburg progressed.

Slave Ship (4). By LeRoi Jones. Produced by Oliver Rea and Chelsea Theater Center, Robert Kalfin artistic director, Michael David executive director, in association with Woodie King, at Theater-in-the-Church. Opened January 13, 1970; see note. (Closed January 20, 1970; see note)

Atowoda; Auctioneer ....Frank Adu   Modern Day Preacher ....Preston Bradley
Tawa ....Gwen D. Anderson   Iyalosa (Tsia) ....Lee Chamberlin
Akoowa;   Akano ....Bill Duke

Segilola	Jackie Earley	Salako; Rev. Turner	Tim Pelt
Adufe	Phyllis Espinosa	Sailor	C. Robert Scott
Olala	Ralph Espinosa	Noliwe	Seret Scott
Dademi	Maxine Griffith	Imani	Marilyn Thomas
Lalu; Plantation Tom	Garrett Morris	Oyo	Reeta White

Musicians: Leopoldo Fleming, congas; Charles David, soprano sax; Richard Fells, bass; Johnny Griggs, drums; Bob Ralston, saxophone; Michael Ridley, trumpet.

Directed by Gilbert Moses; designed by Eugene Lee; music, Archie Shepp, Gilbert Moses; choreography, Oliver Jones (Ali Abdou); production coodinator, Burl Hash; Yoruba teacher, Mr. Ogundipe; musical director, Leopoldo Fleming; stage manager, Peter Turner; press, Saul Richman.

Drama of Negro history from the African slave trade through Southern slavery to rebellion and an exhortation to revolt, with the action played continuously without inermission. NOTE: This production of *Slave Ship* was performed off off Broadway at the Brooklyn Academy of Music for 56 performances 11/18/69-1/4/70 before moving to Theater-in-the-Church, where it was interrupted by a strike 1/16/70 then reopened 1/20/70 for one performance, only to be closed after a fire partly damaged the theater.

Hedda Gabler (81). Revival of the play by Henrik Ibsen. Produced by J. Carduner and The Opposites Company, Eli Siegel general esthetic adviser, Ted van Griethuysen artistic director, at the Actors Playhouse. Opened January 16, 1970. (Closed April 5, 1970)

Juliana Tesman	Cindy Ames	Thea Elvsted	Anne Fielding
Berthe	Norma Novak	Judge Brack	Aldo Bonura
Jorgen Tesman	Peter Brett-Hansen	(Ejlert Lovborg)	Dov Newman, Ted van
Hedda Tesman			Griethuysen
(nee Gabler)	Rebecca Thompson		

(Parentheses indicate role in which the actors alternated)

Directed by Ted van Griethuysen; scenery, Linda Wukovich; costumes, Sandra LeMonds; lighting, Robert A. Freedman; production stage manager, David Sage; stage manager and assistant director, Roy Harris; press, Howard Atlee.

Hedda Gabler was last revived in New York in David Ross's off-Broadway production 11/9/60 for 340 performances.

* No Place To Be Somebody (152). By Charles Gordone. Produced by Jeanne Warner and Ashton Springer, by special arrangement with New York Shakespeare Festival Public Theater, at the Promenade Theater. Opened January 20, 1970.

Gabe Gabriel	Nick Smith	Mary Lou Bolton	Margaret Pine
Shanty Mulligan	Ronnie Thompson	Sweets Crane	Walter Jones
Johnny Williams	Nathan George	Mike Maffucci	Nick Lewis
Dee Jacobson	Susan G. Pearson	Louie	Michael Landrum
Evie Ames	Lynda Westcott	Judge Bolton	Ed VanNuys
Cora Beasely	Marge Eliot	Sergeant Cappaletti	Charles Seals
Melvin Smeltz	Henry Baker	Harry	Malcolm Hurd

Directed by Ted Cornell; scenery and lighting, Michael Davidson; production stage manager, Dennis Stafford; press, Robert Ganshaw, John Prescott.

Time: The past 15 years. Place: Johnny's Bar in the West Village.

This production of *No Place To Be Somebody* was much the same as the original, with the same director and many of the same actors, which opened 5/4/69 at the New York Shakespeare Festival Public Theater, played 250 performances and was named a Best Play of its season, and was produced on Broadway 12/30/69 for a special limited engagement of 16 performances (see entry in the "Plays Produced on Broadway" section of this volume). The character of Machine Dog was dropped from the play in this production.

Charles Gordone replaced Walter Jones for several performances beginning 1/24/70 and W. Benson Terry took over the role 2/3/70. Julius W. Harris replaced W. Benson Terry 3/23/70. Christopher St. John replaced Nathan George; Wally Taylor replaced Christopher St. John 4/70, and Nathan George replaced Wally Taylor 5/13/70.

Transfers (38). Program of three one-act plays by Conrad Bromberg: *The Rooming House, Dr. Galley* and the title play. Produced by Herman and Diana Shumlin and Robert L. Livingston at the Village South Theater. Opened January 22, 1970. (Closed February 22, 1970)

TRANSFERS

Stan	Ron Leibman	Ralph	Gilbert Lewis
Mack	Garrett Morris		

THE ROOMING HOUSE

Elie	Patricia Roe	Bill	Don Billett
Bob	Ron Leibman		

DR. GALLEY

Dr. Galley .... Ron Leibman

Directed by Herman Shumlin; scenery and costumes, Peter Harvey; lighting, Roger Morgan; production stage manager, Larry Zeigler; press, Seymour Krawitz.

In *Transfers* a radio reporter is mugged by the man he is interviewing while covering a Harlem riot. In *The Rooming House*, a lonely woman is degraded, deliberately, by the man who has dated her. *Dr. Galley* is a monologue by a neurotic professor who exposes the unhappy story of his life while supposedly delivering a lecture to his class.

Unfair to Goliath (73). Musical revue written by Ephraim Kishon; adaptation and lyrics by Herbert Appleman; music by Menachem Zur. Produced by Edward Schreiber in association with Alexander Beck at the Cherry Lane Theater. Opened January 25, 1970. (Closed March 29, 1970)

Hugh Alexander
Jim Brochu
Jay Devlin

Corinne Kason
Laura May Lewis

Directed by Ephraim Kishon and Herbert Appleman; musical direction, Menachem Zur; scenery and lighting, C. Murawski; costumes, Pamela Scofield; stage manager, Rick Rotante; press, Samuel J. Friedman, Ruth Cage.

Revue on Israeli themes, based on the writings of Ephraim Kishon, who is a newspaper columnist on a Tel Aviv daily.

ACT I: Overture—Menachem Zur; "The Danger of Peace Is Over"—Company; The Israeli Wonder Plate—Jim Brochu; "In the Reign of Chaim"—Company; In the Reign of Chaim, the Bus Driver—Company; Salesman With a Suitcase—Jay Devlin, Brochu, Hugh Alexander, Corinne Kason; "What Kind of Baby"—Company; The Patter of Little Feet—Laura May Lewis, Devlin, Miss Kason; An Easy Language—Devlin; "A Parking Meter Like Me"—Alexander; The Hardest Currency—Company; Unfair to Goliath—Alexander, Misses Kason, Lewis; Hello —Devlin, Miss Kason; The Generation Gap—Brochu, Miss Lewis; "The Sabra"—Brochu; Incognito—Alexander, Brochu, Misses Kason, Lewis; "The Famous Rabbi"—Company; A Brief Romance—Alexander, Miss Lewis; Back to Back—Devlin, Brochu; 2 x 2 = Schultz— Brochu, Devlin, Alexander.

ACT II: Overture—Zur; "When Moses Spake to Goldstein"—Company; "The Rooster and the Hen"—Miss Kason; Polygamy—Alexander, Miss Kason; The Brilliant Career of Professor Schapiro—Devlin, Brochu, Miss Kason; The Teacher's Lament—Devlin; Waiting—Alexander, Devlin; "What Abraham Lincoln Once Said"—Company; High Number Wins—Alexander, Devlin; We're Together—Brochu, Devlin, Misses Kason, Lewis; A Short History of Tel Aviv— Devlin, Miss Lewis, Alexander; We Are the Pioneers—Devlin, Miss Lewis, Alexander; Oldtimer—Alexander, Miss Lewis; Sallah and the Social Worker—Brochu, Alexander, Miss Lewis; "The Song of Sallah Shabeti"—Company; It's a Country—Company; The Danger of Peace Is Over (skit reprise)—Company.

* The Last Sweet Days of Isaac (144). Musical with book and lyrics by Gretchen Cryer, music by Nancy Ford. Produced by Haila Stoddard, Mark Wright and Duane Wilder at the East Side Playhouse. Opened January 26, 1970.

Isaac	Austin Pendleton	Policeman	John Long
Ingrid; Alice	Fredricka Weber		

The Zeitgeist: vocals, Charles Collins, Louise Heath, John Long; electric harpsichord, Clay Fullum; pianist, George Broderick; bass, Aaron Bell; guitar, Art Betker.

Directed by Word Baker; scenery, Ed Wittstein; costumes, Caley Summers; lighting, David F. Segal; musical direction and arrangements, Clay Fullum; production stage manager, T. L. Boston; stage manager, Charles Collins; press, Michael Alpert.

Time: The present. Place: An elevator and a jail. Part I: The elevator. Part II: I want to walk to San Francisco.

Mystic-symbolic rock musical in two parts, the first with a boy and girl trapped in the limbo of a stalled elevator, the second with them in jail, as protesters, learning about the boy's accidental death as reported on TV.

Alice Playten replaced Fredricka Weber 5/26/70.

PART I

Opening ....The Zeitgeist
"The Last Sweet Days of Isaac" ....Isaac
"A Transparent Crystal Moment" ....Isaac
"My Most Important Moments Go By" ....Ingrid
"Love You Came to Me" ....Ingrid, Isaac

PART II

"I Want to Walk to San Francisco" ....The Zeitgeist
"Touching Your Hand Is Like Touching Your Mind" ....The Zeitgeist
"Yes, I Know That I'm Alive" ....Alice, Isaac, The Zeitgeist
"I Want to Walk to San Francisco" (Reprise) ....Isaac, Alice, The Zeitgeist

* **Joy** (142). Musical revue by Oscar Brown Jr. Produced by Sunbar Productions in the High-John Production at the New Theater. Opened January 27, 1970.

        Oscar Brown Jr.   Sivuca
        Jean Pace

Lighting, F. Mitchell Dana; musicians, Norman Shobey, James Benjamin, Everaldo Ferrerra; stage manager, Robert Koch; press, Gifford/Wallace, Inc., Tom Trenkle.

A collection of songs in the Brazilian style written by Oscar Brown Jr. with occasional collaborators as noted below.

ACT I: "Time," "Under the Sun," "Wimmen's Ways," "Funny Feelin'" (with Luis Henrique), "If I Only Had" (with Charles Aznavour), "What Is a Friend" (with Luis Henrique), "Much as I Love You" (with Luis Henrique), "Sky and Sea," "Afro Blues" (with Mongo Santamaria), "Mother Africa's Day" (with Sivuca).

ACT II: "A New Generation" (with Luis Henrique), "Brown Baby," "Funky World," "Nothing But a Fool" (with Luis Henrique), "Flowing to the Sea," "Brother, Where Are You?"

Exchange (1). Musical revue with music and lyrics by Mike Brandt, Michael Knight and Robert J. Lowery; spoken material by Eric Levy. Produced by Stephanie Sills and Parallel Productions, Ltd. at the Mercer-O'Casey Theater. Opened and closed at the evening performance February 8, 1970.

Directed by Sondra Lee; musical direction and instrumental arrangements, Tom Janusz; scenery, Peter Harvey; costumes, Stanley Simmons; lighting, William Mintzer; press, Bob Ullman. With Penelope Bodry, Mike Brandt, Igors Gavon, Megan Kay, Michael Knight, Pamela Talus.

Topical cabaret-style revue with a dissent motif.

The Jumping Fool (24). By Shirl Hendryx. Produced by Qualis Productions, David Hocker and Chandler Warren at the Fortune Theater. Opened February 9, 1970. (Closed February 22, 1970)

Maria Benoy	Elizabeth Shepherd	Claude Benoy	Richard Raiford
Susan Calish	Ann Whiteside	Suphkin	Michael Pataki
George S. Benoy	Alan Bergmann	Hafry	Brendan Hanlon
Carl Cartwright	Jay Gerber	Psychiatrist	Grant Sheehan
Augie Benoy	Roger Raiford	Ticket Seller	William Poore

Directed by Allen Savage; scenery, Bill Mikulewicz; costumes, John David Ridge; lighting, Dennis Parichy; production stage manager, Michael D. Moore; press, Nat Dorfman.

A journalist is possessed by the nemesis of an acrobat whom he once disparaged.

This Was Burlesque (106). Revue based on Ann Corio's recollections. Produced by Michael P. Iannucci at the Hudson West Theater. Opened February 11, 1970. (Closed May 3, 1970)

Beautiful Marlene	Steve Mills
Harry Conley	Frank O'Brien
Ann Corio	Pepper Powell
Count Gregory	Tami Roché
Tom Dillon	Harry Ryan
Claude Mathis	

The Burley Cuties: Helen Levit, Marilyn Simon, Jinny Jasper, Vickie Daigle, Susan Stewart, Tricia Sandburg, Jennie Chandler, B.J. Hanford.

Directed and choreographed by Richard Barstow; musical conductor, Nick Francis; costumes, Rex Huntington; lighting, Steve Zweigbaum; production supervised by Ann Corio; stage manager, Thom Kirby; press, Saul Richman.

1970 edition of Ann Corio's burlesque revue previously produced in New York (in 1962) and on tour, now in its 9th year.

ACT I: Overture; The Queen of Burlesque—Ann Corio; "Hello Everybody"—The Burley Cuties; Flirtation Scene—Steve Mills, Miss Corio, Tom Dillon; Dance L'Oriental—The Burley Cuties; Music Teacher—Claude Mathis, Marry Ryan, Count Gregory, Marilyn Simon; The Pussy Cat Girl—Pepper Powell; The Minnie Scene—Harry Conley, Miss Simon; Special Attraction—Beautiful Marlene; Packing the Trunk—Mills, Ryan, Misses Corio, Jasper; "Minstrel Days"—Dillon, Cuties; Pantomime—Gregory, Ryan, Mathis, Miss Corio; Mills and Dillon (song medley); School Days—Mathis, Ryan, Misses Corio, Levit, Simon; Feature Attraction—Tami Roché; First Act Finale—Miss Corio, Dillon, Company.

ACT II: "Powder My Back"—Miss Levit, Cuties; Transformer Scene—Mathis (Dummy), Frank O'Brien (Scientist), Miss Powell (Receptionist) and Ryan, Misses Levit, Simon (Patients); Dance—Then and Now—Miss Roché, Cuties; White Cargo—Mills, Dillon, Gregory, Miss Corio; Hall of Fame—Hiss Corio; Crazy House—Mills, Company; Memories—Miss Corio; Grand Finale—Entire Company.

I Dreamt I Dwelt in Bloomingdale's (6). Musical with book by Jack Ramer; music by Ernest McCarty; lyrics by Jack Ramer and Ernest McCarty. Produced by Sam Levine at the Provincetown Playhouse. Opened February 12, 1970. (Closed February 15, 1970)

Directed by David Dunham; choreography, Bick Goss; scenery, Ed Wittstein; lighting and projection designs, Jim Hardy; production stage manager, Barbara Wood; press, Sol Jacobson, Lewis Harmon. With Lucy Saroyan, Michael Del Medico, Liz Otto, The Wet Clam (rock group).

Rock fable about a girl imagining that she lives in Bloomingdale's department store.

The White House Murder Case (119). By Jules Feiffer. Produced by Theodore Mann, Paul Libin, Harold Leventhal and Orin Lehman at Circle in the Square. Opened February 18, 1970. (Closed May 31, 1970)

Col. Dawn	Richard Libertini	Stiles	Paul Benedict
Lt. Cutler	Edward J. Moore	Cole	Paul Dooley
General Pratt	J.J. Barry	Parson	Andrew Duncan
Sweeney	Anthony Holland	President Hale	Peter Bonerz
Mrs. Hale	Cynthia Harris	Weems	Bob Balaban

Directed by Alan Arkin; scenery, Marsha Louis Eck; costumes, Albert Wolsky; lighting, David F. Segal; production stage manager, Jan Moerel; press, Merle Debuskey, M.J. Boyer.

Time: Several Presidential elections hence. Place: The White House and a battleground. The play is divided into two acts.

A game of Who Killed the First Lady? with the cabinet members as prime suspects, in the biting Feiffer style of humor.
A Best Play; see page 201.

The Criminals (15). By Jose Triana; adapted by Adrian Mitchell. Produced by the Phoenix Theater, T. Edward Hambleton managing director, John Houseman producing director, at the Sheridan Square Playhouse. Opened February 25, 1970. (Closed March 8, 1970)

Directed by David Wheeler; scenery and lighting, James Tilton; costumes, Nancy Potts; press, Reginald Denenholz, Ann Woll. With Barry Primus, Penelope Allen, Linda Selman.

Three children in an attic playing vicious games of predator and prey, accuser and accused, killer and victim. A foreign (Cuban) play previously produced in Havana, London, Ann Arbor, Mich. and elsewhere.

Billy Noname (48). Musical with book by William Wellington Mackey; music and lyrics by Johnny Brandon. Produced by Robert E. Richardson and Joe Davis at the Truck and Warehouse Theater. Opened March 2, 1970. (Closed April 12, 1970)

Billy Noname ....Donny Burks	Rev. Fisher ....Eugene Edwards	
Louisa ....Andrea Saunders	Dolores ....Hattie Winston	
Li'l Nick ....Andy Torres	Tiny Shannon ....Alan Weeks	
Big Nick ....Charles Moore	Mr. Milton ....Eugene Edwards	
Young Billy ....Roger Lawson	Barbara ....Glory Van Scott	
Young Tiny ....Thommie Bush	Harriet Van Witherspoon ..Urylee Leonardos	

People of Bay Alley, U.S.A., Friends, Students, etc.: Thommie Bush, Doris DeMendez, Eugene Edwards, J.L. Harris, Marilyn Johnson, Roger Lawson, Urylee Leonardos, Charles Moore, Joni Palmer, Andrea Saunders, Andy Torres, Glory Van Scott, Alan Weeks, Hattie Winston.

Directed by Lucia Victor; choreography, Talley Beatty; musical direction and dance music arrangements, Sammy Benskin; scenery, Jack Brown; costumes, Pearl Somner; lighting, David F. Segal; orchestrations, Clark McClellan; vocal arrangements, Sammy Benskin, Clark McClellan; associate producer, William H. Ferguson Jr.; production stage manager, Smith Lawrence; press, Merle Debuskey, Faith Geer.

Time: 1937 to the present. Place: Bay Alley, U.S.A.

A fatherless Negro child grows up and out of an American city slum.

ACT I: 1937 to 1954

Scene 1: The Champ
"King Joe" ....People of Bay Alley
Scene 2: A Child Is Born
"Seduction" ....Louisa, Li'l Nick, Big Nick, Woman in Labor (Glory Van Scott)
"Billy Noname" ....Billy
Scene 3: Boychild
"Boychild" ....Billy, Young Billy, People
Scene 4: V-J Day
"A Different Drummer" ....People, G.I. (Charles Moore)
Scene 5: Talkin' Feelings
"Look Through the Window" ....Dolores
Scene 6: . . . And the Boychild Grows
"It's Our Time Now" ....Billy, Tiny, Friends
Scene 7: Hello World
"Hello World" ....Billy, Dolores
Scene 8: Eulogy for Mama
"At the End of the Day" ....Neighbor (Urylee Leonardos)
"I Want to Live" ....Billy

ACT II: 1954 until the present

Scene 1: Bay Alley
"Manchild" ....Billy, Soul Sisters (Doris DeMendez, Marilyn Johnson, Joni Palmer)
Scene 2: A Southern University

"Color Me White" ....Billy, Tiny, Dolores, Dean (Charles Moore), Students
"We're Gonna Turn on Freedom" ....Tiny, Company
"Mother Earth" ....Barbara, Billy
Scene 3: The Movement
"Sit In—Wade In" ....Tiny, Company
Scene 4: Civil Rights H.Q., Boogaloosa
"Movin' " ....Billy, Company
Scene 5: March on Washington
"The Dream" ....Gospel Singer (Marilyn Johnson), Company
Scene 6: Harriet Van Witherspoon's Office in New York City
"Black Boy" ....Billy
Scene 7: Finale (The Company)
"Burn, Baby Burn" ....Tiny, Barbara, Militants
"We Make a Promise" ....Preacher (Eugene Edwards), Integrationists
"Get Your Slice of Cake" ....Harriet
"I Want to Live" (Reprise) ....Billy

Show Me Where the Good Times Are (29). Musical based on Molière's *The Imaginary Invalid;* book by Lee Thuna; music by Kenneth Jacobson; lyrics by Rhoda Roberts. Produced by Lorin E. Price in association with Barbara Lee Horn. Opened March 5, 1970. (Closed March 29, 1970)

Aaron	Arnold Soboloff	Kolinsky	Christopher Hewett
Rachel	Gloria LeRoy	Rothstein	Edward Earle
Annette	Neva Small	Dr. Perlman	Mitchell Jason
Bella	Cathryn Damon	Thomas Perlman	Michael Berkson
Maurice	John Bennett Perry	Madame Schwartz	Renee Orin

Men and Women of the Lower East Side: Austin Colyer, Kevin Daly, Denny Martin Flinn, Lydia Gonzalez, Maria Hero, Peggy Hewett, Sara Louise, Donna Monroe, James E. Rogers, Peter Sansone.

Directed by Morton Da Costa; choreography, Bob Herget; musical direction and vocal arrangements, Karen Gustafson; scenery, Tom John; costumes, Gloria Gresham; lighting, Neil Peter Jampolis; orchestrations, Philip J. Lang; production stage manager, Burry Fredrik; stage manager, Schorling Schneider; press, David Lipsky.

Time: Spring, 1913. Place: The bedroom of Aaron's house on Henry Street in New York City and various places on the Lower East Side.

The Molière play about a hypochondriac adapted for Jewish characters in a New York locale.

ACT I

"How Do I Feel?" ....Aaron, Rachel, Annette, Bella
"He's Wonderful" ....Annette, Rachel
"Look Up" ....Annette, Rachel, Bella, Maurice, Company
"Show Me Where the Good Times Are" ....Bella, Company
"You're My Happiness" ....Aaron, Bella
"Cafe Royale Rag Time" ....Company
"Staying Alive" ....Kolinsky, Rachel, Company
"One Big Happy Family" ....Aaron, Maurice, Bella, Annette, Rachel, Kolinsky,
                                                                Dr. Perlman, Thomas

ACT II

"Follow Your Heart" ....Bella, Ladies
"Look Who's Throwing a Party" ....Aaron, Guests
"When Tomorrow Comes" ....Maurice
"One Big Happy Family" (Reprise) ....Dr. Perlman
"The Test" ....Aaron, Rachel, Kolinsky
"I'm Not Getting Any Younger" ....Bella, Her Fellas
"Who'd Believe?" ....Aaron
Finale: Processional ....Aaron, Bella, Company
    "Staying Alive" (Reprise)
    "Show Me Where the Good Times Are" (Reprise)

Contributions (16). Program of three one-act plays by Ted Shine: *Shoes, Plantation* and *Contribution*. Produced by Jonathan Burrows in association with Ruthe Feldman and Ken Gaston Productions at Tambellini's Gate Theater. Opened March 9, 1970. (Closed March 22, 1970)

SHOES

Travis	Donald Griffith	Mr. Mack	Joe Attles
Ronald	Charles Grant	Mr. Wisely	Stanley Greene
Marshall	Jim Jones		

PLANTATION

Roscoe	Stanley Greene	Papa Joe Vesquelle	Jay Garner
Martha	Claudia McNeil	Mrs. Vesquelle	Yvonne Sherwell
Bishop	Leonard Elliott		

CONTRIBUTION

Mrs. Grace Love	Claudia McNeil	Katy Jones	Louise Stubbs
Eugene Love	Donald Griffith		

Directed by Moses Gunn; scenery and lighting, Clarke Dunham; costumes, Judith Haugan; production stage manager, Lindsay Law; press, David Lipsky, Lisa Lipsky.

In *Shoes* a lad works hard to save some money, not for a worthwhile purpose, but to buy a flashy outfit. In *Plantation*, a cracker plantation owner comes home to find that his wife has born him a black son. In *Contributions*, the militant son of a sheriff's cook comes South to take part in the sit-ins (the latter play previously produced by the Negro Ensemble Company).

The House of Leather (1). Rock musical with book by Frederick Gaines; music by Dale F. Menten; lyrics by Dale F. Menten and Frederick Gaines. Produced by William H. Semans and Richard Shapiro in association with Marshall Naify at the Ellen Stewart Theater. Opened and closed at the evening performance, March 18, 1970.

Directed by H. Wesley Balk; musical direction, Dale F. Menten; scenery and lighting, David F. Segal; costumes, Judith Cooper and James K. Shearon; press, Gifford/Wallace. With Peter DeAnda, Norma Jean Wood, Jonelle Allen, Barry Bostwick.

A New Orleans house of prostitution and its characters, in the Civil War era.

Nobody Hears a Broken Drum (6). By Jason Miller. Produced by Stuart Goodman, Peter Skolnik and Bert Steinberg at the Fortune Theater. Opened March 19, 1970. (Closed March 22, 1970)

Directed by Peter Skolnik; scenery and lighting, James F. Gohl; costumes, Joseph Aulisi; production stage manager, Howard Crampton-Smith; press, Ruth Cage, Robert Ullman. With Conrad Bain, Marilyn Chris, John Coe, Dan Morgan, John P. Ryan, Martin Shakar.

Activities of the Molly Maguires in Pennsylvania during the Civil War era.

Lyle (3). Musical based on books by Bernard Waber; book by Chuck Horner; music by Janet Gari; lyrics by Toby Garson. Produced by Marilyn Cantor Baker at the McAlpin Rooftop Theater. Opened March 20, 1970. (Closed March 21, 1970)

Directed by Marvin Gordon; musical direction and arrangements, Robert Esty; scenery and lighting, Jack Blackman; costumes, Winn Morton; production stage manager, Martha Knight; press, Ruth Cage, Robert Ullman. With Richard Bonelle, Jack Fletcher, Stanley Grover, Steve Harmon, Matthew Tobin, Ann Vivian.

Musical fable about a crocodile, based on a series of children's books.

The Madwoman of Chaillot (7). Revival of the play by Jean Giraudoux; adapted by Maurice Valency. Produced by Leonard Sillman at the Sokol Theater. Opened March 22, 1970. (Closed March 29, 1970)

Directed by Robert Henderson; scenery, Robert Fletcher; costumes, Charles Tomlinson; production stage manager, Leslie Robinson; press, Dorothy Ross. With Staats Cotsworth, Frederick O'Neal, Leonard Sillman, Jacqueline Susann, Manu Tupou, Lois Wilson, Peggy Wood, Blanche Yurka.

The Madwoman of Chaillot was last produced in New York in a musical version entitled *Dear World* 2/6/69 for 132 performances.

Nature of the Crime (24). By Larry Cohen. Produced by George H. Webb at the Bouwerie Lane Theater. Opened March 23, 1970. (Closed April 12, 1970)

Daniel Aronoff	Tony Lo Bianco	Theodore Benjiman	Gerald Gordon
James Garrett	James Antonio	Ruth Aronoff	Barbara Babcock
Samuel Ullman	Robert F. Simon	The Judge	John Benson
Kirsch	Adam Keefe		

Directed by Lonny Chapman; scenery, William Ritman; lighting, Paul Sullivan; costumes, Sara Brook; sound, Gary Harris; stage manager, Charles Hayman; press, Howard Atlee.

Scientist in conflict with the government over ownership and use of his work.

Lulu (1). Revival of the play by Frank Wedekind; translated by Mari Saville and Morton Siegel. Produced by Mari Saville in the Metropolitan Repertory Theater production at the Sheridan Square Playhouse. Opened and closed at the evening performance March 27, 1970.

Directed by Morton Siegel; scenery and lighting, David Chapman; costumes, Deidre Cartier; production stage manager, Eastern Hale; press, Seymour Krawitz. With Ronald Gilbert, Danny Hedaya, Lara Parker, Geoffrey Scott, William Severs, Harry Van Ore.

This material is translated from *Earth Spirit,* the first play in Wedekind's Lulu trilogy, about a prostitute.

The Unseen Hand and **Forensic and the Navigators** (21). Program of two one-act plays by Sam Shepard. Produced by Albert Poland in association with June Stevens at the Astor Place Theater. Opened April 1, 1970. (Closed April 18, 1970)

THE UNSEEN HAND

Blue Morphan	Beeson Carroll	The Kid	David Clennon
Willie	Lee Kissman	Sycamore Morphan	Tom Rosica
Cisco Morphan	David Selby		

FORENSIC AND THE NAVIGATORS

Forensic	Peter Maloney	1st Exterminator	Tom Rosica
Emmet	David Clennon	2d Exterminator	Ron Abbott
Oolan	O-lan Johnson-Shepard		

Directed by Jeff Bleckner; scenery, Santo Loquasto; costumes, Linda Fisher; lighting, Roger Morgan; production stage manager, Elissa Lane; press, Ganshaw/Prescott.

Images of modern civilization without narrative organization; *The Unseen Hand* takes place in an abandoned car near a California freeway; *Forensic and the Navigators* is about a group of exterminators bent on destroying anything people hold dear.

* Dark of the Moon (70). Revival of the play by Howard Richardson and William Berney. Produced by Herbert Nitke and Dyot Productions, Inc. at the Mercer-Shaw Arena Theater. Opened April 3, 1970.

Barbara Allen	Margaret Howell	Uncle Smelicue	Carlo Grasso
John	Chandler Hill	Hank Gudger	Charles Beard
Dark Witch	Christine Cooper	Floyd Allen	Patrick Cook
Fair Witch	Carole Lockwood	Mrs. Bergen	Jean David
Fair Witch Boy	George Wargo	Burt Bergen	Robert Brown
Dark Witch Boy	Bill Hall	Edna Summey	Susan Slavin
Red Witch	Lisa Tracy	Miss Metcalf	Marcia Wallace
Mr. Bergen	Thomas Craft	Mrs. Summey	Elizabeth Brown

Mr. Summey	Robert Baines	Mr. Allen	Peter De Maio
Marvin Hudgins	Earl Hindman	Preacher Haggler	Joseph Daly
Mrs. Allen	Rue McClanahan		

Directed and designed by Kent Broadhurst; lighting, Molly Friedel; additional music, Didi Favreau; sound, Gary Harris; script supervision, Howard Richardson; production stage manager, Charles Roden; press, Sol Jacobson, Lewis Harmon.

Tragic romance between mortal girl and witch boy, first produced on Broadway 3/14/45 for 320 performances.

Claudia Jennings replaced Margaret Howell 5/19/70.

Dear Janet Rosenberg, Dear Mr. Kooning (49). Program of two one-act plays by Stanley Eveling: the title play and *Jakey Fat Boy*. Produced by John Flaxman and Ralph Rosenblum in association with Richard Pilbrow at the Gramercy Arts Theater. Opened April 5, 1970. (Closed May 17, 1970)

DEAR JANET ROSENBERG, DEAR MR. KOONING

Janet Rosenberg	Catherine Burns	Alec Kooning	Kevin O'Connor

JAKEY FAT BOY

Alice	Penelope Allen	Jake	Kevin O'Connor

Directed by Max Stafford-Clark; music for *Jakey Fat Boy* by John Flaxman, lyrics by Stanley Eveling; scenery and costumes, Ben Shecter; lighting, Jules Fisher; production stage manager, Lewis Rosen; press, Mary Bryant, Meg Gordean.

Dear Janet Rosenberg, Dear Mr. Kooning is an exchange of correspondence between a middle-aged novelist and a young girl eager to worship at his feet. *Jakey Fat Boy* is about dreams of sexual glory epitomized (in the mind's eye of the leading character) by Kenneth Tynan. Foreign plays, the first previously produced in London and the second having its world premiere in this engagement.

* The Effect of Gamma Rays on Man-in-the-Moon Marigolds (64). By Paul Zindel. Produced by Orin Lehman at the Mercer-O'Casey Theater. Opened April 7, 1970.

Tillie	Pamela Payton-Wright	Nanny	Judith Lowry
Beatrice	Sada Thompson	Janice Vickery	Swoosie Kurtz
Ruth	Amy Levitt		

Directed by Melvin Bernhardt; music and sound, James Reichert; scenery, Fred Voelpel; costumes, Sara Brook; lighting, Martin Aronstein; associate producer, Julie Hughes; production stage manager, Bud Coffey; press, Alan Eichler, David Powers.

The nagging, penurious hopelessness of a widow's life is brightened momentarily by her younger daughter's fascination with the atom, which leads to a successful science-class experiment with the effect of radiation on seeds. Previously produced at the Alley Theater, Houston (1964), on New York Television Theater (1966) and the Cleveland Play House (1969).

A Best Play; see page 165.

Le Tréteau de Paris. Schedule of four programs in the French language. **Le Grand Vizir** and **Le Cosmonaute Agricole** (9). Program of two one-act plays by Rene de Obaldia. Opened April 7, 1970. (Closed April 14, 1970) **Lettre Morte** and **Architruc** (10). By Robert Pinguet. Opened April 15, 1970 matinee. (Closed April 23, 1970) **Oh! Les Beaux Jours** (Happy Days) (10). By Samuel Beckett. Opened April 24, 1970. (Closed May 3, 1970 matinee) **La Lacune, La Jeune Fille à Marier** and **Les Chaises** (8). By Eugene Ionesco. Opened May 5, 1970. (Closed May 10, 1970 matinee) Produced by Le Tréteau de Paris, Jean de Rigault executive producer, under the sponsorship of L'Association Française d'Action Artistique of the French Foreign Ministry and under the patronage of Alliance Française de New York, by special arrangement with Seff Associates Ltd., Jacques Courtines managing director, at the Barbizon-Plaza Theater.

LE GRAND VIZIR

Arthur ....Roland Bertin   Hortense ....Maia Simon
Ernest ....Gilles Guillot

LE COSMONAUTE AGRICOLE

Eulalie ....Josine Comellas   Zéphyrin ....Pierre Baton
Le Cosmonaute ....Roland Bertin

Directed by Jorge Lavelli; decor, Roland Deville; technical director, Louis Fremont.
Le Grand Vizir—Time: The present. Place: An attic. A husband uncovers his wife's infidelity with a friend while they are all three improvising a mock drama about a king, queen and
counselor.
Le Cosmonaute Agricole—Time: The present. Place: A farm courtyard in the Plain of
Beaune. Cosmonaut and farmers in a parable arguing for the exploration of man's inner spirit
instead of space.

LETTRE MORTE

M. Levert ....Olivier Hussenot   Fred ....Francis Lax
Barman; Postman ....Michel Robbe   Lili ....Anne-Marie Coffinet

ARCHITRUC

Architruc ....Michel de Ré   Le Cuisinier ....Georges Richar
Baga ....Olivier Hussenot

Lettre Morte directed by Michel de Ré; *Architruc* directed by Olivier Hussenot; scenery and
costumes, Georges Richar; sound effects, Jean Jus Forgues; technical director, Erik Retsin
d'Ambroise.
In *Lettre Morte*, protracted chit-chat first with a barman and then with a postman eases the
pain of a father whose son has left home. *Architruc* presents the pretensions of a Godot-like
make-believe king and his prime minister, dreaming dreams of glory while waiting for death.

OH! LES BEAUX JOURS

Winnie ....Madeleine Renaud   Willie ....Olivier Hussenot

Directed by Roger Blin; decor, Matias; technical director, Erik Retsin d'Ambroise.
Beckett's *Happy Days*, in which a middle-aged woman is slowly sinking in a mound of earth,
was last produced in New York by Theater 1969 Playwrights Repertory 10/12/68 for 3 performances.

LA LACUNE

L'Academicien ....Jacques Mauclair   L'Ami ....Jean-Paul Cisiphe
L'Academicien's Wife ....Claude Genia   La Bonne ....Monique Saintey

LA JEUNE FILLE À MARIER

La Dame ....Claude Genia   Le Monsieur-Fille ....Michel Degand
Le Monsieur ....Marc Duducourt

LES CHAISES

La Vieille ....Tsilla Chelton   L'Orateur ....Jean-Paul Cisiphe
Le Vieux ....Jacques Mauclair

Directed by Jacques Mauclair; scenery and costumes, Jacques Noël.
The Chairs, with an elderly couple setting up seats for an audience coming to hear a speech,
was produced by the Phoenix Theater 1/9/58 for 22 performances in English.
ALL PLAYS: Stage manager, Harry Abbott; press, Arthur Cantor.

The Nest (1). By Tina Howe. Produced by Ann McIntosh, Honor Moore and
Thayer Burch at the Mercury Theater. Opened and closed at the evening performance April 9, 1970.

Directed by Larry Arrick; scenery, Robert U. Taylor; costumes, Lizbeth Fullemann; lighting, Roger Morgan; stage manager, Robert Stevenson; press, Alan Eichler, David Powers. With Lois Markle, Sharon Gans, Jill Clayburgh, Lane Smith, Jack Aaron.

Three girls and two boy friends share a duplex.

And I Met a Man (3). By Lawrence Weinberg. Produced by Michael Todd Jr. at Lincoln Square Cabaret Theater. Opened April 10, 1970. (Closed April 11, 1970)

Directed by Timmy Everett; designed by Mischa Petrow; lighting, The Joshua Light Show, Thomas Shoesmith. With Sam Waterston, Sam Schacht, Francesa de Sapio.

Marriage in trouble when wife becomes involved with a guru.

The Drunkard (48). Musical version of the play by W.H.S. Smith; adapted by Bro Herrod; original musical numbers composed and arranged by Barry Manilow. Produced by Bro Herrod in association with Peter Perry at the 13th Street Theater. Opened April 13, 1970. (Closed May 24, 1970)

Song Leader; Barmaid;	Salvation Worker ....Donna Sanders
Julia ....Susan Rush	Lawyer Cribbs ....Christopher Cable
Song Leader; Preacher;	Edward Middleton ....Clay Johns
Barkeep ....Lou Vitacco	William Dowton ....Drew Murphy
Mary ....Marie Santell	Agnes; Carry Nation; Old Man's
Mrs. Wilson; Barmaid;	Darling ....Joy Garrett

Directed by Bro Herrod; choreography and musical numbers staged by Carveth Wells; olio curtain, Danny Michaelson; costumes, Carol Luiken; lighting, Bill Hall; stage manager, David Moyer; press, Reginald Denenholz, Anne Woll.

Scene 1: Interior of a humble cottage. Scene 2: A sylvan glade. Scene 3: A wooded grove. Scene 4: A rose-covered arbor. Scene 5: A village tavern. Scene 6: A sylvan glade in a wooded grove. Scene 7: The humble cottage. Scene 8: Broadway. Scene 9: A miserable garret. Scene 10: New York City. The play was presented in three acts.

Mid-19th century temperence drama, once produced by P.T. Barnum, revived in 1933 in Los Angeles for a very long run, now in musical version with a combination of old songs—not necessarily of the period—and new ones written for this show.

MUSICAL NUMBERS

"Something Good Will Happen Soon" ....Mary, Mrs. Wilson
"Whispering Hope" ....Mary, Mrs. Wilson
    Public domain, arrangement by Barry Manilow
"Don't Swat Your Mother, Boys" ....Cribbs
    Public domain, arrangement by Barry Manilow
"Strolling Through the Park" ....Mary, Edward
    Public domain, arrangement by Barry Manilow
"Good Is Good" ....William, Cribbs, Agnes
"Mrs. Mary Middleton" ....Preacher, William, Edward, Mrs. Wilson, Mary, Cribbs
"Have Another Drink" ....Barkeep, Edward, Carry Nation, Cribbs, Barmaids
"The Curse of an Aching Heart" ....Edward
    Public domain, arrangement by Barry Manilow
"For When You're Dead" ....Cribbs
"A Cup of Coffee" ....Edward, Cribbs
"Something Good Will Happen Soon" (Reprise) ....Julia, William, Mary, Cribbs,
                  Edward, Mrs. Wilson
"Garbage Can Blues" ....Edward
"Shall I Be an Old Man's Darling" ....Old Man's Darling
    By Will E. Haines and Jimmy Harper
"Julia's Song" ....Julia
"I'm Ready to Go" ....Edward
    Lyrics by Marty Panzer
"Do You Wanna Be Saved?" ....Mrs. Wilson, Edward, Mary, Julia, Carry Nation,
                 William, Cribbs, Barkeep

The Persians (21). By John Lewin; adapted from Aeschylus' *Persae*. Produced by the Phoenix Theater, T. Edward Hambleton managing director, Gordon Duffey artistic director for the New Phoenix, in cooperation with St. George's Church, at St. George's Church. Opened April 15, 1970. (Closed May 2, 1970)

Chorus Leader ....Robert Stattel	Messenger ....Robert Jackson
Persian Elders .....Tom Crawley, Raul Julia	Ghost of Darius ....David Spielberg
Young Woman of Chorus ....Patricia Elliott	Xerxes ....Stephen McHattie
Atossa ....Jacqueline Brookes	

Directed by Gordon Duffey; scenery and lighting, Jack Brown; costumes and masks, Nancy Potts; music, Nasser Rastegar-Nejad; production stage manager, Daniel Freudenberger; press, Sol Jacobson, Lewis Harmon.

Time: 480 B.C. Place: Susa, in front of the royal palace. At a little distance, the tomb of Darius.

Adaptation of Aeschylus' play about the defeat of the Persians by the Greeks at Salamis, pointing up parallels with our own times and situation.

How Much, How Much? (32). By Peter Keveson. Produced by Ashley Feinstein and George Gilbert at the Provincetown Playhouse. Opened April 20, 1970. (Closed May 17, 1970)

Peggy Monash ....Nancy Andrews	Joe Raidy ....Al Nesor
Carl Monash ....Hy Anzell	Sara ....Donna Pearson
Joycie Monash ....Neva Small	Max ....Maurice Brenner
Charley Gordon ....Kristoffer Tabori	Paul Gordon ....Hugh Franklin

Directed by Richard Altman; scenery and lighting, William Ritman; costumes, Whitney Blausen; stage manager, Jane Clegg; press, Michael Alpert, Dennis Helfend.

Time: The present. Place: The Manhattan apartment of the Monash family, Columbus Ave. and 85th St. Act I: Early evening, June. Act II, Scene 1: One month later. Scene 2: Later that evening.

Morality play, son of Mafia lawyer tries to go into semi-legitimate business with the impoverished family of his girl friend.

Mahagonny (8). Musical from the opera *The Rise and Fall of the City of Mahagonny* with libretto by Bertolt Brecht and music by Kurt Weill; English adaptation by Arnold Weinstein. Produced by Carmen Capalbo and Abe Margolies at the Anderson Theater. Opened April 28, 1970. (Closed May 3, 1970)

Commentator ....Evan Thompson	Alaska Wolf Joe ....Bill Copeland
Trinity Moses ....Val Pringle	Billy Bankbook ....Don Crabtree
Fatty ....Jack De Lon	Jimmy Mallory ....Frank Porretta
Leocadia Begbick ....Estelle Parsons	Pianist ....Louis St. Louis
Jenny ....Barbara Harris	Camera Men ....Ray Camp, Clint Elliot
John Hancock Schmidt ....Alan Crofoot	Toby Higgins ....Richard Miller

Bellhops: Kenneth Frett, James Hobson, Gordon Minard, Tracy Moore. Girls of Mahagonny: Holly Hamilton, Sayrah Hummel, Anne Kaye, Lani Miller, Jacqueline Penn, Veronica Redd, Lou Rodgers, Adrienne Whitney. Men of Mahagonny: Rudy Challenger, Jack Fletcher, Jimmy Justice, Keith Kaldenberg, Richard Miller, Alexander Orfaly.

Conceived and directed by Carmen Capalbo; musical direction, Samuel Matlovsky; scenery, Robin Wagner; costumes, Ruth Morley; lighting, Thomas Skelton; color projections, Larry Rivers; associate producer, Charles Rome Smith; associate conductor, Theodore Saidenberg; production stage manager, Nicholas Russiyan; stage manager, Bob Troy; press, Seymour Krawitz.

Time: The 1930s. Place: America. Act I, Scene 1: A desert waste. Scene 2: Outskirts of Mahagonny. Scene 3: A metropolis. Scene 4: On the way to Mahagonny. Scene 5: Mahogonny. Scene 6: Jenny's room. Scene 7: The tavern. Scene 8: The pier. Scene 9: Outside the tavern. Scene 10: Mahagonny. Scene 11: The wall. Act II, Scene 1: The wall. Scene 2: Eating. Scene 3: Loving. Scene 4: Fighting. Scene 5: Drinking. Scene 6: In Mahagonny. Act III, Scene 1: A cell. Scene 2: A courtroom. Scene 3: A room in Mahagonny. Scene 4: The same. Scene 5: Outside Mahagonny.

American premiere of a famous Brecht-Weill collaboration (originally in German) attacking materialism in a story about an imaginary American city founded by criminals in flight from the police. Individual musical numbers are not identified by title.

The Republic (3). By Ed Wode; based on Aristophanes' *Ecclesiazusae.* Produced by Ed Wode at the Free Store Theater. Opened April 27, 1970. (Closed April 30, 1970)

Directed by Ed Wode; music composed, arranged and performed by Malcolm; musical direction, Malcolm; scenery and lighting, Larry Opitz; costumes, Kusama; production stage manager and technical director, Ivan Spiegel; press, Ganshaw/Prescott. With Marcia Loring, Barbara Oakley, Doris Gramovot, Martha Reynolds, Richard E. Fink.

The ladies of Athens take over the government, in a classic accented to the modern notion of Women's Liberation.

* What the Butler Saw (32). By Joe Orton. Produced by Charles Woodward and Michael Kasdan by arrangement with Lewenstein-Delfont Productions Ltd. and H.M. Tennent Ltd. at the McAlpin Rooftop Theater. Opened May 4, 1970.

Dr. Prentice	Laurence Luckinbill	Nicholas Beckett	Charles Murphy
Geraldine Barclay	Diana Davila	Dr. Rance	Lucian Scott
Mrs. Prentice	Jan Farrand	Sergeant Match	Tom Rosqui

Directed by Joseph Hardy; designed by William Ritman; costumes, Ann Roth; production stage manager, Murray Gitlin; press, Betty Lee Hunt, Henry Luhrman, Ellen Levene.

Time: The present, a spring day. Place: The consulting room of an exclusive, private psychiatric clinic. The play is presented in two acts.

Black farce-comedy treatment of sex foibles in clinical surroundings. A foreign play previously produced in London.

A Best Play; see page 217.

* Colette (31). By Elinor Jones; adapted from *Earthly Paradise,* the Robert Phelps collection of Colette's autobiographical writings; original music by Harvey Schmidt; lyrics by Tom Jones. Produced by Cheryl Crawford in association with Mary W. John at the Ellen Stewart Theater. Opened May 6, 1970.

Colette	Zoe Caldwell	Daniele; Polaire; Ida; Amalia;	
Sido	Mildred Dunnock	Marguerite; Reporter	Holland Taylor
Willy	Charles Siebert	Leo; Jacques; Pierre; Jean;	
Captain; Max; Wague;		de Jouvenel; Goudeket	Barry Bostwick
Reporter	Keene Curtis	Pianist	Harvey Schmidt

Directed by Gerald Freedman; scenery, David Mitchell; costumes, Theoni V. Aldredge; lighting, Roger Morgan; production stage manager, Gage Andretta; press, David Powers, Alan Eichler.

Time: Act I—1873-1913; Act II—1925-1954. Place: France.

The life, loves and literary achievements of the noted French authoress Colette.

The Moths (1). By Ralph Arzoomanian. Produced by George Martin in association with K-R Productions at the Mercury Theater. Opened and closed at the evening performance May 11, 1970.

Directed by Ralph Arzoomanian; scenery, Jason B. Fishbein; costumes, Whitney Blausen; lighting, William Mintzer; press, Ruth Cage, Robert Ullman. With Philip Bruns, Michael Vale, Joy Claussen, Magda Harout, Dimo Condos, Miriam Lehmann-Haupt, Charles Ganimian, James Howard Laurence.

Armenian patriarch, on his deathbed, relishes his heirs' anxieties and attentions. Previously produced by the Mark Taper Forum, Los Angeles and the Washington Theater Club.

* Room Service (24). Revival of the play by John Murray and Allen Boretz. Produced by Jay H. Fuchs and Jerry Schlossberg in association with Jerry Cutler Enterprises and John Murray at the Edison Theater. Opened May 12, 1970.

Gordon Miller	Ron Leibman	Harry Binion	Frank Savino
Sasha Smirnoff	Michael Lombard	Faker Englund	George Bartenieff
Joseph Gribble	Paul B. Price	Christine Marlowe	Lucy Saroyan

Leo Davis	Tom Brannum	Dr. Glass	Alek Primrose
Hilda Manney	Barbara Dana	Bank Messenger	Christopher Guest
Gregory Wagner	Jerome Dempsey	House Detectives	Edmund Williams,
Simon Jenkins	Darrell Zwerling		Smith Lawrence
Timothy Hogarth	Joel Wolfe	Senator Blake	Fred Stewart

Directed by Harold Stone; scenery and lighting, D. Atwood Jenkins; costumes, Leigh Rand; production stage manager, Steven Sweigbaum; press, Marvin Kohn.

Room Service was first produced on Broadway by George Abbott 5/19/37 for 500 performances. Its last professional New York revival of record was produced by Bernard Hart 4/6/53 for 16 performances.

* Slow Dance on the Killing Ground (22). Revival of the play by William Hanley. Produced by Ruth Kalkstein and Center Stage Associates at the Sheridan Square Playhouse. Opened May 13, 1970.

Glas	George Voskovec	Rosie	Madeline Miller
Randall	Billy Dee Williams		

Directed by John Stix; scenery, Jason Phillips; costumes, Ritchie Spencer; lighting, C. Mitch Rogers; associate producer, Zvi Kolitz; production stage manager, James Haire; press, David Lipsky.

Slow Dance on the Killing Ground was first produced on Broadway 11/30/64 for 88 performances and was named a Best Play of its season.

The Shepherd of Avenue B by Lawrence Holofcener and **Steal the Old Man's Bundle** by Kenneth Pressman (5). Program of two one-act plays. Produced by Mark Durand and Ken Kaiserman at the Fortune Theater. Opened May 15, 1970. (Closed May 17, 1970)

Directed by Peter Galambos; scenery, Edward Burbridge; costumes, Andrew Greenhut; lighting, Dennis Parichi; press, Seymour Krawitz, Fred Weterick. With Maria Tucci, Lee Wallace, Roger De Koven, Ted Leplat.

Two studies of loneliness, guilt and evil, the first about a rag merchant living in dreams, the second a cat-and-mouse game played by a young man on an elderly neighbor.

Lemon Sky (17). By Lanford Wilson. Produced by Haila Stoddard, Mark Wright, Duane Wilder and Neal Dubrock in The Buffalo Studio Arena production at the Playhouse Theater. Opened May 17, 1970. (Closed May 31, 1970)

Alan	Christopher Walken	Carol	Lee McCain
Douglas	Charles Durning	Jerry	Steven Paul
Ronnie	Bonnie Bartlett	Jack	Willie Rook
Penny	Kathryn Baumann		

Directed by Warren Enters; scenery and costumes, Stephen Hendrickson; lighting, David Zierk; stage manager, Louis Pulvino; press, Michael Alpert, Dennis Helfend.

Time: Tonight. Place: The Playhouse Theater, New York City. The play is divided into three acts with a single intermission between Acts I and II.

A 17-year-old boy's memories of his unsuccessful efforts to establish a close relationship with his father. Previously produced by the Buffalo, N.Y., Studio Arena Theater.

* The Me Nobody Knows (16). Musical with book by Stephen M. Joseph; edited from the book *The Me Nobody Knows;* music by Gary William Friedman; lyrics by Will Holt; original idea by Herb Schapiro. Produced by Jeff Britton in association with Sagittarius Productions, Inc. at the Orpheum Theater. Opened May 18, 1970.

Rhoda	Melanie Henderson	Benjamin	Douglas Grant
Lillian	Laura Michaels	Catherine	Beverly Ann Bremers
Carlos	Jose Fernandez	Melba	Gerri Dean
Lillie Mae	Irene Cara	Donald	Paul Mace

Lloyd ....Northern J. Calloway   William ....Kevin Lindsay
Clorox ....Carl Thoma   Nell ....Hattie Winston

Directed by Robert H. Livingston; musical numbers staged by Patricia Birch; musical direction, Edward Strauss; scenery and lighting, Clarke Dunham; costumes, Patricia Quinn Stuart; media design and photography, Stan Goldberg and Mopsy; additional lyrics, Herb Schapiro; arrangemets and orchestrations, Gary William Friedman; assistant to producer, Erlinda Zetlin; production stage manager, Martha Knight; press, Samuel J. Friedman, Jane Friedman.

Musical study of underprivileged New York City children whose spoken text is taken entirely from the book *The Me Nobody Knows*, a group of writings by children between the ages of 7 and 18 attending public schools in Bedford-Stuyvesant, Harlem, Jamaica, Manhattan and Youth House in the Bronx. Lyrics to "Fugue for Four Girls," "Rejoice," "The Horse" and "War Babies" are poems exactly as the children wrote them.

ACT I

"Dream Babies" ....Melba
"Light Sings" ....William, Company
"This World" ....Company
"Numbers" ....Company
"What Happens to Life" ....Lillian, Lloyd
"Take Hold the Crutch" ....Nell, Company
"Flying Milk and Runaway Plates" ....Benjamin, Company
"I Love What the Girls Have" ....Donald
"How I Feel" ....Catherine, Carlos
"If I Had a Million Dollars" ....Company

ACT II

"Fugue for Four Girls" ....Lillie Mae, Catherine, Lillian, Nell
"Rejoice" ....Clorox
"Sounds" ....Nell, Catherine
"The Tree" ....Carlos
"Robert, Alvin, Wendell and Jo Jo" ....Rhoda, Lillian, Lillie Mae, William
"Jail-Life Walk" ....Donald, Lloyd, Clorox, Carlos
"Something Beautiful" ....Rhoda
"Black" ....Benjamin, Clorox, Lillie Mae, Lloyd, Melba, Nell, Rhoda, William
"The Horse" ....Lloyd
"Let Me Come In" ....Company
"War Babies" ....Lloyd

* **Chicago 70** (8). Play improvised by the Toronto Workshop Company; based on transcripts of the conspiracy trial of the Chicago 8 and *Alice's Adventures in Wonderland* by Lewis Carroll; Imperialist Units (interpolations) by Brent Larson. Produced by Circle in the Square, Theodore Mann artistic director, Paul Libin managing director, at the Martinique Theater. Opened May 25, 1970.

Bobby Seale ....Calvin Butler   Allen Ginsberg ....George Meteskey
Mark Lane ....Jim Lawrence   Abbie Hoffman ......Francois Regis Klanfer
Arlo Guthrie ....Ray Whelan   Linda Morse ....Diane Grant
Mayor Daley; Country Joe ......Neil Walsh   Dee Jay ....Murray Blanc

Directed by George Luscombe; scenery, Nancy Jowsey; lighting and stage manager, John Faulkner; press, Merle Debuskey, M.J. Boyer, Faith Geer.

Topical satire using Carroll's mock trial in *Alice's Adventures in Wonderland* as counterpoint for the Chicago trial in Judge Hoffman's courtroom, with added comments on America's use of power and violence through history. A foreign play previously produced in Toronto.

* **The Open Theater.** Repertory of two new plays and one revival. * **Terminal** (3). Collective work created by The Open Theater Ensemble; text by Susan Yankowitz. Opened May 26, 1970. * **The Serpent: A Ceremony** (1). Created by The Open Theater Ensemble; words and structure by Jean-Claude van Itallie. Opened May

29, 1970. * **Endgame** (2). Revival of the play by Samuel Beckett. Opened May 30, 1970. Produced by The Open Theater, Inc., Joseph Chaikin director, at the Washington Square Methodist Church.

THE ENSEMBLE

James Barbosa	Peter Maloney
Raymond Barry	Mark Samuels
Shami Chaikin	Ellen Schindler
Brenda Dixon	Tina Shepard
Ron Faber	Barbara Vann
Jayne Haynes	Lee Worley
Ralph Lee	Paul Zimet

ENDGAME

Clov	Peter Maloney	Nagg	James Barbosa
Hamm	Joseph Chaikin	Nell	Jayne Haynes

ALL PLAYS—Production supervisor, Dale Whitt; lighting, Will Mott; administrative director, Marianne de Pury; press, Howard Atlee.

TERMINAL—Co-directed by Joseph Chaikin and Roberta Sklar; costumes, Gwen Fabricant; development, Dick Peaslee, Stanley Walden (composers), Mark Kaminski, Nancy Martin, Sam Shepard (writers), Joyce Aaron, Sharon Gans, Muriel Miguel (actors), Joseph Campbell, Mossa Bildner, Kesang-tonma, Ronald Laing, Muir Weisinger. With The Ensemble.

Part I—The Dance on the Graves of the Dead: The Procession, The Calling, The Dance. Part II—The Pregnant Dying: The Private Case, Motion, Taking In and Eliminating, Breathing, The Last Biological Rites. Part III—The State of the Dying: The Embalming as Required by Law, The Interview, The Dying Resist, The Runner Who Never Gets Started, The Dying Are Drugged, The Dead Come Through—Marie Laveau and The Soldier, Cosmetics, The Witness, The Dead Come Through—The One Who Was Hit, The Dying Pray, The Dead Come Through —The Responsible One, The Initiation, The Embalming as Required by Law (Repeat), The Dead Come Through—The Executed Man and the Song, The Dying Imagine Their Judgment, Presence and Absence.

Comments upon various aspects and forms of death in skits, music, dance and mime.

THE SERPENT: A CEREMONY—Directed by Joseph Chaikin; associate director, Roberta Sklar; bruitage, Richard Peaslee, Stanley Walden, associate, Patricia Cooper. With The Ensemble.

Study of human nature in its violent aspect, in a succession of scenes composed of mime, narrated comment, music and sound, with major sequences representing events in the Garden of Eden.

A Best Play; see page 232.

ENDGAME—Directed by Roberta Sklar; costumes, Gwen Fabricant; scenic advisor, Bil Mikulevicz.

Beckett's *Endgame*'s first New York production of record took place off Broadway in the season of 1957-58. It was revived off Broadway in February 1962 by Richard Barr and Clinton Wilder.

* **Awake and Sing!** (7). Revival of the play by Clifford Odets. Produced by Willard W. Goodman, Catalyst Company, Robert J. Gibson, in association with Jane Cohen Productions at the Bijou Theater. Opened May 27, 1970.

Ralph Berger	Robert Salvio	Schlosser	Peter Bosche
Myron Berger	Salem Ludwig	Moe Axelrod	Roger Serbagi
Hennie Berger	Phoebe Dorin	Uncle Morty	Bill Macy
Jacob	Morris Strassberg	Sam Feinschreiber	Irwin Rosen
Bessie Berger	Joan Lorring		

Directed by Arthur A. Seidelman; scenery, Ethel Green; lighting, Molly Friedel; costumes, Pamela Scofield; associate producer, Marvin Pletzke; production stage manager, Clint Jakeman; press, Leslie Coven.

Odets' play about the Berger family in the Bronx was first produced on Broadway by the Group Theater 2/19/35 for 209 performances and was named a Best Play of its season. It was revived on Broadway by the Group Theater 3/7/39 for 45 performances.

Candaules, Commissioner (6). By Daniel C. Gerould. Produced by the People's Company (Studley-Traub Associates, Inc., Melanie Herman) in association with A. & B. D'Lugoff, producer Julien J. Studley, associate producer Melanie Herman, at the Mercer-Hansberry Theater. Opened May 28, 1970. (Closed May 31, 1970)

Directed by Roy Levine; scenery, Lester Polakov; costumes, Donna Tomas; lighting, William Mintzer; music and sound, James Reichert; production stage manager, Ken Glickfield; press, Ruth Cage, Bob Ullman. With Seth Allen, Robert Stocking, Marilyn Roberts.

Political satire of inept American diplomacy in a small war-torn country. Previously produced in Stanford, Calif., Repertory and Chelsea Arts Center.

Some Additional Productions

This selected listing of off-off-Broadway and other experimental productions was compiled by Robert Schroeder (see his report on the 1969-70 off-off-Broadway scene in "The Season in New York" section of this volume). Leading producing groups are identified in alphabetical order in **bold face type** and examples of their outstanding 1969-70 programs are listed. Number of performances (in parentheses), opening dates and other details are given when available, but in most cases there was no premiere or engagement of record.

Afro-American Studio. In a top-story loft of a fraternal-organization building, seating 50 and using minimal equipment, this troupe plays new and recent plays of interest to the black community. Actors are mostly non-Equity and shows run several weekends. Performances are not advertised, but a mailing list is circulated. Admission is charged.

ROOTS by Gilbert Moses, TAKE CARE OF BUSINESS by Marvin X and CLARA'S OLD MAN by Ed Bullins. Directed by Ernie McClintock. With Tim Battle, Norman Butler, Woodie Carter, Gardenia Cole, Curtis Green, Joanne Reddick, Carole Williams.

The American Theater Club. In an end-stage loft, this troupe specializes in the early American theatrical literature. Playing three weekends before 40 viewers, mostly Equity actors perform most professionally, despite minimal facilities. Performances are advertised and admission is charged.

THE TRUTH by Clyde Fitch. Directed by Richard Kuss. With Albert Amateau, Cyprienne Gabel, Joe Jamrog, Carol Moran, Ellis Santone, Richard Scribner, Susan Tabor, Kay Tornborgh.

THE FAITH HEALER by William Vaughn Moody. Directed by Ellis Santone. With Ann Dunbar, Walter Gorney, Judith Piatt, Alice Scudder, Robert Wilde.

PONTEACH by Major Robert Rogers and THE CANDIDATES by Colonel Robert Munford. Directed by Richard Kuss. With John Carpenter as Ponteach, Thomas Connolly as Candidate Wou'dbe.

ANTA Matinee Theater Series. Lucille Lortel is impresario of this series, nominally sponsored by The American National Theater and Academy, and presented on the set of whatever off-Broadway production is the current tenant of Miss Lortel's proscenium Theater de Lys. Productions are advertised and the series' mailing list is kept advised. Admission is charged. This season's schedule was:

A ROUND WITH RING (2). Entertainment based on the works of Ring Lardner; adapted by Nathan R. Teitel and Haila Stoddard; music arranged and played by Harrison Fisher. October 27, 1969. Directed by Darwin Knight and Haila Stoddard. Music by Vincent Youmans, G. Harris White, Jerome Kern, Nora Bayes, Lee Roberts, Ring Lardner. With Orson Bean, Melinda Dillon, George Hall, Ann Hodapp, Bob Lydiard, James Pritchett.

OH, PIONEERS (2). Written and directed by Douglas Taylor. November 10, 1969. With Barbara Baxley, Keith Charles, Sarah Cunningham, Patrick McVey.

DREAM OF A BLACKLISTED ACTOR (2). By Conrad Bromberg. December 15, 1969. Directed by Arthur Sherman; songs by John Duffy. With Catherine Burns, Judith Kercheval, Christopher Tabori, Rip Torn, Janet Ward.

CRUISING SPEED 600 M.P.H. by Anna Marie Barlow and MRS. SNOW by Kenneth Pressman (2). January 5, 1970. *Cruising Speed 600 M.P.H.* directed by the author; with Donald Gentry, Janet Ward. *Mrs. Snow* directed by Robert Moss; with Dennis Keith, Janet League, Patricia O'Connell.

The Blackfriars' Guild. The oldest of Manhattan's off-off-Broadway groups presents old-line Catholic moralities. The theater itself is quite interesting—very like the balconied but very small theaters in London, but nothing is happening that couldn't have happened 25 years ago. Typical of this season's offerings was:

FIVE STAR SAINT by the Rev. Edward A. Molloy. Directed by Walter Cool. The play, as usual, was double-cast, the actors alternating during run. With Leonard Frederick, Robb McIntire, Ott Selby, Burt Grosselfinger, David O'Sullivan, Richard Scribner.

Chelsea Theater Center. Now in its second year in the Brooklyn Academy of Music's "Third Stage" auditorium, this group has become the most consistent of the New York area new theater experimenters in terms of production values. Lighting and sound equipment is first-rate, and sets, acting and directing were uniformly at professional levels throughout the season. The playing area can be proscenium, end-stage or arena, and there is fly and wing space in the proscenium configuration. Productions usually run Thursday through Sunday for two weekends. Performances are advertised and admission is free. Actors are usually Equity, appearing under showcase rules. The house seats 125 to 300, depending on arrangement.

SLAVE SHIP by LeRoi Jones. Directed by Gilbert Moses; with music by Archie Shepp and Gilbert Moses; choreography by Oliver Jones (Ali Abdou); additional music by Leopoldo Fleming, Richard Fells, Johnny Griggs, Bob Ralston, Michael Ridley, Charles Davis. With Frank Adu, Preston Bradley, Garrett Morris, Tim Pelt.

THE BRASS BUTTERFLY by William Golding. Directed by Allan Leicht; musical director, Robert Barlow. With Robert Barry, Arlene Nadel, Gastone Rossilli, Sam Waterston, Paxton Whitehead, Jerrold Ziman.

THE UNIVERSAL NIGGER by Gordon Porterfield. Directed by Robert Kalfin. With Kay Carney, Dennis Helfend, Ronnie Newman, Brad Sullivan, Arthur Burghardt.

THE UNICORN FROM THE STARS by W. B. Yeats. Directed by Josephine Nichols. With John Carpenter, Jerome Collamore, Tom McDermott, Gastone Rossilli, Ed Seamon.

CANDAULES, COMMISSIONER by Daniel C. Gerould. Directed by Robert Andrew Bonnard; composer, Bill Brohn. With Martin Brennan, Katie Drew-Wilkinson, John Newton.

Circle Theater Company. This new group, composed of many of the writers, directors and actors who first made off-off-Broadway come alive, has begun operations in a loft on upper Broadway. The theater space can be used open-end or arena style, and at present equipment is rudimentary. Performances are advertised and admission is charged. Although outside actors may occasionally be used, the activity is primarily intended to develop its own membership.

A PRACTICAL RITUAL TO EXORCISE FRUSTRATION AFTER FIVE DAYS OF RAIN by David Starkweather. Directed by Rob Thirkield and the author; music by Allan Landon; scenery, Lanford Wilson. With Rod Nash, Alice Tweedie, Spalding Gray, Robert Frink, Allan Landon.

CSC (Classic Stage Company) Repertory. Playing arena style in a 75-seat storefront theater, this troupe presents season-long repertory performances of established plays, or adaptations of well known literary works. CSC is, in essence, a director-actor co-op. Equipment and sets are rudimentary, but spirit and devotion are transcendent. Performances are advertised and a sponsor-member list is circulated. Moderate admission is charged.

MAN AND SUPERMAN by George Bernard Shaw. Directed by Christopher Martin. Performed with the *Don Juan in Hell* sequence.

THE REVENGER'S TRAGEDY by Cyril Tourneur. Directed by Christopher Martin.

MOBY DICK based on the novel by Herman Melville; adapted and directed by Christopher Martin.

POOR BITOS by Jean Anouilh; translated by Lucienne Hill. Directed by Christopher Martin. With Marianne Creamer, Harris Laskawy, Christopher Martin, Ronn Mullen, Kathryn Wyman.

The Cubiculo. An experimental theater associated with the travelling Equity company known as The National Shakespeare Company, The Cubiculo seats about 50 in a well equipped end-stage theater. Performances are advertised and admission is charged. The actors, mostly Equity, perform under showcase rules. Productions run one or two weekends.

ALL FOR LOVE by John Dryden. Directed by Maurice Edwards. With Mark Curran, David Tress, Marguerite Davis, Arlene Nadel.

#*%!&#! MOTHER! by Robert Peters, directed by Philip Meister, and DADA by Jacob Zilber, directed by Al Lewis.

Dramatis Personae. Just a few doors from the former New York headquarters of The Living Theater, Dramatis Personae is in its second year of a non-Equity, weekends-only commercial run of one of the first and longest-running nude sex-simulation shows:

THE SOUND OF A DIFFERENT DRUM, "live, naked drama" by A. R. Bell.

East River Players. Playing in various auditoriums, and picking up frequent travel dates at colleges or community theater centers, this troupe specializes in drama of interest to the black community.

EENIE, MEENIE, MINIE, MOE by Robert Schroeder; with music by Bobby Banks. Choreographed by Tom Hawkins; directed by Mical Whitaker. Played at St. Peters Church by Bobby Banks, Tom Hawkins, Chuck Lulinski, Judie Messier, Trish Perry, Ila Vann.

Equity Library Theater. To showcase its members, Actors Equity Association sponsors an annual series at the Master Theater, a 300-seat house with proscenium stage, and professional-level equipment. Admission is on a donation basis. Performances are not advertised, but a mailing list is circulated.

LEND AN EAR (19). Musical revue with sketches, lyrics, and music by Charles Gaynor. October 16, 1969. Directed by Sue Lawless; dances and musical numbers staged by Judith Haskell; musical direction, James Kay. With William J. Coppola, Donna Curtis, James Harder, Charles Leipert, Joan Porter, Ted Pugh.

THE LOWER DEPTHS (12). By Maxim Gorki; adapted by Maurice Noel. November 13, 1969. Directed by Robert Moss; music by Michael Valenti. With George Addis, Al Cohen, Geraldine Court, Jeanne Kaplan, Susan Kaslow, Dan Mason.

ROMEO AND JEANNETTE (12). By Jean Anouilh; translated by Miriam John. Decem-

ber 11, 1969. Directed by Peter Galambos. With Lynn Archer, Richard Graham, Peter Haig, Arlene Nadel, Marie Puma, Robert Shea.

GETTING MARRIED (12). By George Bernard Shaw. January 15, 1970. Directed by Clinton Atkinson. With Kathleen Coyne, Michael Hawkins, John High, Deborah Jowitt, Enid Rodgers, Edward Stevlingson.

LITTLE MARY SUNSHINE (19). Musical with book, music, and lyrics by Rick Besoyan. February 12, 1970. Directed by Larry Whiteley; musical direction, Marjorie J. Brewster; choreography, Joel Conrad. With Fran Brill, Roger Ochs, Jon Peck, Eleanor Rogers, Nancy Zala.

BAREFOOT IN THE PARK (12). By Neil Simon. March 12, 1970. Directed by Christian Grey. With Anita Bayless, Lloyd Hubbard, Wendy Lesniak, Gonzalo Madurga, Bill McIntyre, Michael Saposnick.

HATFUL OF RAIN (12). By Michael V. Gazzo (in a partially rewritten version). April 9, 1970. Directed by Kent Paul. With Crickett Cannon Coan, Alex Colon, John Costopoulos, Elizabeth Harryman, Joe Kottler.

ME AND JULIET (19). Musical with book and lyrics by Oscar Hammerstein II; music by Richard Rodgers. May 7, 1970. Directed by Charles Willard; choreography, George Bunt; musical direction, Tom Janusz. With Robert Berdeen, Susan Blanchard, John Johann, Patti Mariano, Susan Schevers, John Swearingen.

Equity Theater Informals. In addition to its series at the Master Theater, Equity presents "informals" at the auditorium of the Library and Museum of the Performing Arts at Lincoln Center. Admission is free. The Equity Library Theater mailing list receives notice, and the presentations are publicized in New York City library bulletins.

THE CAINE MUTINY COURT-MARTIAL (3). By Herman Wouk. December 8, 1969. Directed by John Harkins. With Victor Argo, Kent Broadhurst, Leonard De Martino, Murray Moston, Nick Padula, Patrick Sullivan.

MARJORIE DAW (3). One-act musical by Sally Dixon Wiener; based on a short story by Thomas Bailey Aldrich. February 2, 1970.

Directed by Miriam Fond; musical direction, Theo Carus; choreography, Osa Danam. With Richard Balin, George Cavey, James Donahue, Merrill E. Joels, Gail Johnston.

LOU GEHRIG DID NOT DIE OF CANCER (3). By Jason Miller. March 2, 1970. Directed by Chet Carlin. With Miriam Carlin, Charles Faranda, Page Miller.

The Extension. Playing in a small church chapel, arena style, before up to 75 spectators, this group performs mostly new work, with an emphasis upon directorial style. Performances are advertised, and admission is charged. Casting is mostly non-Equity, and shows play several weekends.

THE FULLY-GUARANTEED FUCK-ME DOLL by Tom Eyen. Directed by Ron Link. With William Griffin Duffy, Bill Haislip, Helen Hanft, Mary Mitchell, Elsa Tresko, Marybeth Ward.

RAIN adapted and directed by Ron Link from the W. Somerset Maugham play. Music by Mark Shangold. With Roz Kelly, Michael Traven, Dennis Geisel, Megan Hunt, Sylvester Stallone, Douglas Stone.

Free Store Theater. Lower East Side store front utilized as an arena theater where the controversial *Che!* achieved notoriety. Shows are advertised expensively and Broadway-level admission is charged the 75 to 100 attendees. Shows run as long as is profitable, as many times a week, or even a night, as the producer can fill the house. This year's extravaganza:

THE REPUBLIC, musical adapted, directed, and produced by Ed Wode; from Aristophanes' *Ecclesiazusae*. Music by Carman Moore.

With Marcia Loring, Barbara Oakley, Doris Gramvoto, Martha Reynolds, Richard E. Fink.

Greenwich Mews Spanish Theater. Productions in the Spanish language, performed in the main by persons associated with the Greenwich Mews Theater. When the home stage is occupied by an off-Broadway show, performances in Spanish are produced at other houses. Shows generally play weekends for a month to six weeks.

DOÑA ROSITA LA SOLTERA by Federico García Lorca. Directed by Rene Buch, at the Village South Theater.

LA DIFUNTA by Miguel de Unamuno and CRUCE DE VIAS by Carlos Solorzano, both directed by Luz Castaños, and LAS PERICAS, directed by Rene Buch, at Theater East.

The Judson Poets Theater. The beautiful Stanford White auditorium, and its choir-loft, where the Judson group has staged seminal off-off-Broadway plays in the past, were virtually devoid of drama this season. Dance had taken over, or, if you will, dance-oratoria, or dance-opera. You name it, but it wasn't the *Home Movies* or *Promenade* sort of theater that made Judson famous. Typical of this season's presentations was:

CHRISTMAS RAPPINGS, new oratorio by Al Carmines. Presented with a chorus of 80, and dancers; choreographed by John Jones, David Vaughan and Dan Wagoner.

La Mama Experimental Theater Club. This enterprise operates two theaters, one above the other, in its new Lower East Side headquarters. The virtually identical theaters seat about 150 each and are of end-stage configuration. Sound and lighting equipment is first rate, but there is no fly or wing space. When casting is done by La Mama personnel, actors receive a specially-arranged showcase pay level, if they are Equity members. But more often than not, packages are booked in, as assembled by college groups, visiting directors, or others not normally associated with La Mama. Because of sound transmission interference, shows cannot be run simultaneously in the two theaters, so the one goes up early, the other after the conclusion of the first performance. Shows normally play Wednesday through Sunday, for two weeks. Notices of performances appear in the *Village Voice*, and while admission is nominally restricted to "members," anyone with the admission price in hand is admitted.

HEAVEN GRAND IN AMBER ORBIT by Jackie Curtis. This production packaged by John Vaccaro, who refers to his unit as The Playhouse of the Ridiculous. The unit has been in existence for several seasons, but was for the first time, this season, booked into La Mama for a series of repertory performances.

SHANGO by Susan Sherman; adapted from a Cuban play of the same title by Pepe Carril. Directed by Joseph Bush; developed at La Mama in association with a fund-supported dance theater activity; Yoruba chants compiled by Rogelio Marinez Fure; additional chants by John Amira and Betty Barney; original music by Walter Burns; lyrics by Susan Sherman.

THE UNSEEN HAND by Sam Shepard. Package assembled by director Jeff Bleckner. With Beeson Carroll, Lee Kissman, Bernie Workentin, Sticks Carleton, Victor Eschbach.

SECOND DOOR LEFT by Alexander Popovic. Directed by the author; music by Thomas Wagner. Guest-author show assembled by the La Mama staff.

CAPTAIN JACK'S REVENGE by Michael Smith. Directed by the author, who also assembled the package. With Ondine, Lucy Silvay, Jeffrey Herman, Peter Murphy, Wally Androchuck, John Vaccaro.

THE DIRTIEST SHOW IN TOWN by Tom Eyen. Directed by "Jerome" Eyen; package assembled by Tom Eyen and The Theater of the Eye Repertory Company.

A RAT'S MASS by Adrienne Kennedy. Directed by Seth Allen; music by Lamar Alford; package assembled by Seth Allen. With Mary Alice, Marilyn Roberts, Roger Robinson.

ARDEN OF FAVERSHAM, anonymously-derived Elizabethan tragedy, and UBU by Alfred Jarry. Directed by Andrei Sherban, visiting Rumanian director, preparatory to a European tour; music by Lamar Alford. With William Griffin Duffy, Michele Collison, Bill Crystal, Lou Zeldis, Sabin Epstein, Lamar Alford.

THE ONLY JEALOUSY OF EMER, play with music by William Butler Yeats and RENARD, a "grotesque" by Igor Stravinsky; music by Barbara Benary. Directed by John Braswell and Wilford Leach; package grew out of work conducted at Sarah Lawrence College; after La Mama booking was moved, billed as a La Mama Company, into a non-Equity commercial run at the Performing Garage.

The Mannhardt Theater Center. In an end-stage loft seating 50, with good technical facilities, this school-associated group stages several productions each year. Performances are advertised and admission is charged. Casts include students and some Equity actors. Shows run for approximately 10 performances, spread over a month or so.

BATHTUB by Nick Boretz. Directed by Renata Mannhardt; music, Art O'Reilly. With Frank Coppola, Marlene Fisher, Spencer Holden.

The New Theater Workshop. On the stage of the New Theater, on or around the set of whatever off-Broadway show may be playing there, the Workshop presents plays by new authors, staged by experienced actors and directors, or "directors' projects," utilizing scripts by experienced writers, played by experienced actors. As a rule, three performances are given of each play or project, at times when the off-Broadway show using the same stage is not scheduled. The theater seats about 275. Plays are cast under Equity showcase rules, usually using only Equity players. No admission is charged, and no one is paid. The end-stage configuration features professional-level sound and lighting. There is fly and wing space. Performances are not publicly advertised, but members of the public are placed on the mail-invitation list by request.

RIP TORN'S RICHARD, adaptation of Shakespeare's *Richard III* created in a director's workshop by Rip Torn and associates, including Geraldine Page.

THE MOONLIGHT FILE by Mick Daugherty. Directed by Dino Narizzano. With Marge Eliot, Charles Siebert, Mel Winkler.

FAME and THE REASON WHY, program of two one-act plays by Arthur Miller. Directed by Gino Giglio. With Kim Chan, Marilyn Chris, Gene Gross, Rose Roffman, Eli Wallach, Richard Kiley.

THE HERMIT'S COCK, by Allen Boretz. Directed by Bert Convy. With Bruce Kornbluth, Joey Faye, Anne Anderson, Avril Gentles. (At The Eastside Playhouse, owing to temporary unavailability of the New Theater).

The Open Theater. One of the most publicized of the organic-acting exponents, in the Grotowski tradition, this troupe travels frequently and gives only a relatively few public performances each season at its own rehearsal loft. Some performances are advertised publicly, some are not, and admission is sometimes charged, sometimes not. The troupe is a closed membership organization, for the most part made up of actors who eschew professional ambitions. The membership alternates in roles, so that any one "characterization" is likely to be the result of contributions by several members who have either rehearsed or enacted the role. Therefore, listings of players for each production are not applicable to this situation. The major productions this season were:

TERMINAL created by the Open Theater Ensemble under the direction of Joseph Chaikin and Roberta Sklar, texts by Susan Yankowitz, with the participation of Mark Kaminski, Nancy Martin and Sam Shepard, writers, and Dick Peaslee and Stanley Walden, composers.

ENDGAME by Samuel Beckett, directed by Roberta Sklar.

The Other Stage. The experimental wing of the enterprise that began as the New York Shakespeare Festival and then expanded into the Public Theater, The Other Stage utilizes whatever space is not occupied by one of the Public Theater's admission-charging productions. Other Stage presentations are free and are advertised. Actors are usually Equity. Since the playing area varies room by room, any one of a wide variety of configurations may be employed. Technical facilities are excellent. Other Stage presentations are usually offered Wednesday through Sunday for two weeks and play before sizes of audiences that vary as the rooms and set-ups vary.

THE HAPPINESS CAGE by Dennis J. Reardon. Directed by Tom Aldredge. With Charles Durning, Bette Henritze, Martin Sheen, Harris Yulin.

X HAS NO VALUE by Cherrilyn Miles. Directed by Walter Jones; choreography, Carole Johnson. With Frank Caltabiano, Baci, Joetta Cherry, Rosalyn Gibson, Emmett Jackson, Gwen Mitchell, Betty Williams, Aston Young.

TRELAWNY OF THE WELLS by Arthur Wing Pinero. Directed by Robert Ronan. With Robert Ronan, Sasha von Scherler, Nancy Dussault, Konrad Matthaei, George Bartenieff, Janet Dowd, Mary Hamill.

The Performance Group. This group was formed by Richard Schechner as an outgrowth of Jerzy Grotowski's N.Y.U. acting seminar and built a long run last season with its *Dionysus in 69*, performed in a remodeled garage downtown. This season's program closed after a very short run.

MAKBETH, a collage derived from William Shakespeare's *Macbeth*. Devised by Richard

Schechner.

Roundabout Theater. Along with the CSC Repertory, the Roundabout is off-off-Broadway's answer to the APA and Lincoln Center. CSC plays in true repertory fashion, while Roundabout takes them one at a time, like Lincoln Center, but the repertory is much the same—classics and recent near-classics. Playing arena-style in a supermarket basement before some 80 attendees, with minimal sets and equipment, the troupe manages several-month runs, five or six shows a week. No other off-off-Broadway group has built a theater-party business so expertly. Shows are advertised and admission is charged. The actors are some Equity, some not.

MACBETH, by William Shakespeare. Directed by Bill Accles; electronic score by John Kraus.

TRUMPETS AND DRUMS, by Bertholt Brecht; translated by Rose and Martin Kastner; music by Erich Bulling. Directed by Gene Feist.

OEDIPUS, an adaptation of Sophocles' play

by Anthony Sloan. Directed by Gene Feist. With Gordon Heath.

LADY FROM MAXIM'S, a new version of the Georges Feydeau play by Jon Carlson and Gene Feist. Directed by Gene Feist. Repertory troupe includes Sterling Jensen, Elizabeth Owens, Marc Devon, Jack Axelrod, Bill Roulet.

Stage Directors and Choreographers Workshop. Undertaken for the same purpose as Equity's Library Theater—to showcase the services of its members—the directors' and choreographers' union has been staging two-to-three-performance productions at the auditorium of the Library and Museum of the Performing Arts at Lincoln Center. In the spring of 1970 the group acquired its own building, where showcase productions will be staged when remodeling has been completed.

YOU NEVER KNOW, musical with music and lyrics by Cole Porter; book adapted by Rowland Leigh from the European original by Siegfried Geyer and Karl Farkas. Directed and choreographed by William E. Hunt and

Zoya Leporska; musical direction, Don Bettisworth. With James Harwood, William Shust, Ann Wedgeworth, Kelly Wood, Maxton Latham, Merle Albertson.

Theater-at-noon. Playing two lunch time performances each weekday in a nicely refurbished arena stage theater midtown (at St. Peter's Gate, Lexington Ave. and 54th St.) a group of Equity actors whose art is in the right place specialize in classics and adaptations of classics. Performances are not advertised, except by banners to attract passers-by. Admission is on a donation basis. Coffee is served, and the cabaret arrangement encourages lunch-carrying.

MADNESS AT NOON, a musical revue adapted by cast members from Lewis Carroll. Directed by MacIntyre Dixon. With Roy

Clary, Lois de Banzie, MacIntyre Dixon, Saundra MacDonald, Richard Novello, Ronald Willoughby.

Theater Genesis. Formerly one of the most active of the off-off-Broadway arenas, this end-stage loft seating some 100, and reasonably well equipped technically, has been seldom used this season. When it has been, it has housed packages assembled outside and booked in. An exception was a house-originated production, scheduled for the customary three weekends, utilizing an unpaid, partially Equity cast, and playing on a donation basis in the auditorium of St. Mark's Church in the Bowery —the church housing the theater-loft. This production was:

THE DEER KILL by Murray Mednick. Directed by Ralph Cook. With Beeson Carroll, Walter Hadler, Judith Kercheval, Ralph Lee, Jacqueline Segal.

Thresholds. One of New York's most successful exponents of organic acting techniques. The membership troupe works together closely the year round and mounts three or four public performances a season, each of which runs weekends for five or six weeks. Performances are advertised and admission is charged. Presentations are arena-style in a well equipped room seating about 30.

PINION, adapted by Donna Carlson from *The Countess Cathleen* by William Butler Yeats. Directed by the author.

THE VENTURI, conceived and directed by John Parkinson.

TODAY WE SAW A TURTLE by David Kerry Heefner. Directed by the author.

A SEASON IN HELL, adapted from the works of Arthur Rimbaud by David Kerry Heefner. Directed by the author.

Workshop of the Players' Art. Outgrowth of the old Die Grüne Kakadu, this is one of the most prolific of the off-off-Broadway troupes. Performances are staged virtually year-round, Thursdays through Sundays, with each production running four or five weekends. The arena stage house seats about 50, shows are advertised and admission is charged. The acting company, partially Equity, is in the main a membership group operating substantially in repertory fashion. Equipment is moderate, but effective in the small theater.

BAAL by Bertolt Brecht; English version by Eric Bentley and Martin Esslin. Directed by Martin L. H. Reymert.

THE END OF THE WORLD by Keith Neilson. Directed by Dick Gaffield.

SUMMERTIME by Ugo Betti. Directed by Harry Orzello. Acting troupe includes David Gale, Harry Orzello, Ken Hill, Helen Adam, Patricia Hawkins, Eve Packer, Nicki Kaplan, Robert Hazelton.

CAST REPLACEMENTS AND TOURING COMPANIES

Compiled by Stanley Green, author of The World of Musical Comedy

The following is a list of the more important cast replacements in productions which opened in previous years, but which were still playing in New York during a substantial part of the 1969-70 season; or were still on a first class tour; or opened in 1969-70 and sent out a first-class touring company in that same season. The name of the character is listed in *italics* beneath the title of the play in the first column. In the second column directly opposite appears the name of the actor who created the role (and the original New York opening date appears in *italics* at the top of this column). Immediately beneath the actor's name are the names of subsequent replacements, together with the date of replacement when available. The third column gives information about first-class touring companies, including

London companies (produced under the auspices of their original Broadway managements). Where there is more than one roadshow company, #1, #2, #3, etc. appear before the name of the performer who created the role in each company (and the city and date of each company's first performance appears in *italics* at the top of the column). Their subsequent replacements are also listed beneath their names, with dates when available.

A note on bus-truck touring companies appears at the end of this section.

ADAPTATION/NEXT

	N.Y. Opening: 2/10/69	*#1 Boston Opening: 9/17/69* *#2 Los Angeles Opening:* *10/23/69* *#3 Chicago Opening: 2/27/70*
ADAPTATION		
Games Master	Graham Jarvis Dick Yarmy 9/22/69 Phillip R. Allen 4/27/70	#1 Bill Story #2 Graham Jarvis #3 William Wise
Players (male)	Paul Dooley Marvin Lichterman 8/25/69 Richard Ramos 10/26/69	#1 Don Billett #2 Bob Barend #3 Joe Greco
Players (female)	Carol Morley Stockard Channing 3/21/70	#1 Stockard Channing #2 Rose Arrick #3 Fawne Harriman
Contestant	Gabriel Dell R.G. Brown 7/7/69 Mark Gordon 11/1/69 Dick Yarmy 4/27/70	#1 Phillip R. Allen #2 Gabriel Dell #3 Spencer Milligan
NEXT		
Marion Cheever	James Coco Dick Van Patten 9/22/69 William Hickey 11/1/69	#1 William Young #2 James Coco #3 Mike Nussbaum
Sgt. Thech	Elaine Shore Patricia Fay 4/20/70	#1 Joan Tolentino #2 Elaine Shore #3 Karen Woodward

THE BOYS IN THE BAND

	N.Y. Opening: 4/15/68	*#1 London Opening: 2/11/69* *#2 Los Angeles Opening:* *3/10/69* *#3 Boston Opening: 5/3/69*

Michael	Kenneth Nelson
	Eric James 1/25/69
	David Daniels 3/4/69
	Carleton Carpenter 11/11/69
	George Pentacost 2/10/70
		#1 Kenneth Nelson
		  Douglas Lambert
		#2 Dennis Cooney
		  Eric James
		#3 George Pentacost

Donald	Frederick Combs Leon Russom 1/25/69 Don Briscoe 5/69 Curt Dawson 11/11/69 Paul Rudd 4/7/70	#1 Frederick Combs Graham James #2 Brian Taggert #3 Christopher Carroll

Emory	Cliff Gorman Tom Aldredge 10/22/68 Matthew Tobin 1/25/69 Jere Admire 11/11/69 Page Johnson 4/14/70	#1 Tom Aldredge Terry Scully #2 Cliff Gorman Joe Ross Page Johnson #3 Jere Admire
Larry	Keith Prentice Christopher Berneu 1/25/69	#1 Keith Prentice Tony Anholt # Peter Ratray Richard Krisher #3 Alan Castner
Hank	Laurence Luckinbill Konrad Matthaei 1/25/69 Wayne Tippit 3/11/69 John Devlin 11/11/69 Rex Robbins 4/14/70	#1 Laurence Luckinbill William Gaunt #2 Konrad Matthaei George Robertson #3 Rex Robbins
Bernard	Reuben Greene Harold Scott 1/25/69 Robert Christian 4/21/70	#1 Reuben Greene Neville Aurelius #2 Guy Edwards #3 Robert Christian
Cowboy	Robert La Tourneaux Ted LePlat 1/25/69 Donald Clement 2/17/70	#1 Robert La Tourneaux John Hamill #2 Roger Herren #3 Paul Rudd
Alan	Peter White David O'Brien 1/25/69 Nicolas Coster 9/9/69 Nicholas Pryor 11/11/69 Jered Mickey 4/21/70	# Peter White Donald Douglas #2 Richard Roat #3 Nicholas Pryor
Harold	Leonard Frey Michael Lipton 1/25/69 Edward Zang 3/11/69	#1 Leonard Frey John Carlisle #2 Michael Lipton #3 Bill Moor

BUTTERFLIES ARE FREE

	N.Y. Opening: 10/21/69	*Los Angeles Opening: 5/19/70*
Don Baker	Keir Dullea	Wendell Burton
Mrs. Baker	Eileen Heckart	Eve Arden
Jill Tanner	Blythe Danner	Ellen Endicott-Jones

CABARET

		#1 New Haven Opening: *12/26/67*
	N.Y. Opening: 11/20/66	*#2 London Opening: 2/28/68*
Master of Ceremonies	Joel Grey Danny Meehan 9/11/67 Joel Grey 9/25/67 Martin Ross 1/1/68	#1 Robert Salvio Charles Abbott #2 Barry Dennen

Clifford Bradshaw	Bert Convy	#1 Gene Rupert
	John Cunningham 7/30/68	#2 Kevin Colson
	Ken Kercheval 8/26/68	
	Larry Kert 12/9/68	
	Alfred Toigo 6/3/69	

Sally Bowles	Jill Haworth	#1 Melissa Hart
	Penny Fuller	#2 Judi Dench
	Jill Haworth	
	Anita Gillette 11/4/68	
	Tandy Cronyn 6/30/69	
	Melissa Hart 7/28/69	

Fraulein Schneider	Lotte Lenya	#1 Signe Hasso
	Peg Murray 2/12/68	#2 Lila Kedrova
	Lotte Lenya 2/26/68	Thelma Ruby 8/28/68
	Despo 6/10/68	
	Lotte Lenya 10/7/68	
	Susan Willis 6/3/69	

| *Herr Schultz* | Jack Gilford | #1 Leo Fuchs |
| | George Voskovec 6/10/68 | #2 Peter Sallis |

CEREMONIES IN DARK OLD MEN

#1 N.Y. Opening: 2/4/69
#2 N.Y. Opening: 4/28/69

Mr. Russell B. Parker #1 Douglas Turner
#2 Richard Ward

Adele Eloise Parker #1 Rosalind Cash
#2 Bette Howard

Theopolis Parker #1 William Jay
#2 Billy Dee Williams
Antonio Fargas 7/1/69
Ron Mack

Bobby Parker #1 David Downing
#2 Richard Mason
Freeman Roberts
Lenard Norris

CURLEY MCDIMPLE

N.Y. Opening: 11/22/67

Jimmy Paul Cahill
Ray Becker 5/7/68
Don Emmons 5/24/68

Sarah Helon Blount
Nell Evans 9/24/68
Mary Boylan 10/29/68

Alice Joyce Nolen
Ronni Richards 1/7/69
Gwen Hillyer
Joyce Orlando

Curley McDimple   Bayn Johnson
                       Robbi Morgan 1/7/69
                       Janina Mathews
                       Robbi Morgan (alt.)

Miss Hamilton   Norma Bigtree
                       Jane Stuart 8/20/68
                       Norma Bigtree 6/11/69
                       Helen Honkamp

Mr. Gillingwater   Gene Galvin
                       Hansford Rowe
                       Gene Galvin
                       Hansford Rowe
                       Richard Durham

DAMES AT SEA

		#1 San Francisco Opening:
		6/25/69
		#2 London Opening: 8/27/69
	N.Y. Opening: 12/20/68	*#3 Hollywood Opening: 3/10/70*
Ruby	Bernadette Peters	#1 Marti Rolph
	Pia Zadora 6/17/69	#2 Sheila White
	Bonnie Franklin 7/69	#3 Barbara Sharma
	Barbara Sharma 12/5/69	
	Loni Zoe Ackerman 2/24/70	
Dick	David Christmas	#1 Jess Richards
	Kurt Peterson 3/70	#2 Blayne Barrington
		#3 Ron Husmann
Joan	Sally Stark	#1 Amandah Peppar
	Judy Knaiz	#2 Rita Burton
		#3 Amandah Peppar
Mona Kent	Tamara Long	#1 Barbara Lacey
	Janie Sell 10/28/69	#2 Joyce Blair
		#3 Laara Lacey
Hennessey	Steve Elmore	#1 Byron Palmer
	Raymond Thorne 2/70	#2 Kevin Scott
		#3 Tom Hatten
Lucky	Joseph R. Sicari	#1 Anthony Teague
		#2 William Ellis
		#3 Anthony Teague

THE FANTASTICKS

	N.Y. Opening: 5/3/60	*London Opening: 9/7/61*
El Gallo	Jerry Orbach	Terence Cooper
	Gene Rupert	
	Bert Convy	
	John Cunningham	
	Don Stewart 1/63	
	David Cryer	

Keith Charles 10/63
John Boni 1/13/65
Jack Mette 9/14/65
George Ogee
Keith Charles
Tom Urich 8/30/66
John Boni 10/5/66
Jack Crowder 6/13/67
Nils Hedrick 9/19/67
Keith Charles 10/9/67
Robert Goss 11/7/67
Joe Bellomo 3/11/68
Michael Tartel 7/8/69

Luisa

Rita Gardner   Stephanie Voss
 Carla Huston
 Liza Stuart 12/61
 Eileen Fulton
 Alice Cannon 9/62
 Royce Lenelle
 B.J. Ward 12/1/64
 Leta Anderson 7/13/65
 Carole Demas 11/22/66
 Leta Anderson 8/7/67
 Carole Demas 9/4/67
 Anne Kaye 1/23/68
 Carole Demas 2/13/68
 Anne Kaye 5/28/68
 Carolyn Mignini 7/29/69

Matt

Kenneth Nelson   Peter Gilmore
 Gino Conforti
 Jack Blackton 10/63
 Paul Giovanni
 Ty McConnell
 Richard Rothbard
 Gary Krawford
 Bob Spencer 9/5/64
 Erik Howell 6/28/66
 Gary Krawford 12/12/67
 Steve Skiles 2/6/68
 Craig Carnelia 1/69
 Erik Howell 7/18/69
 Samuel D. Ratcliffe 8/5/69
 Michael Glenn-Smith 5/26/70

FIDDLER ON THE ROOF

#1 San Diego Opening: 4/11/66
N.Y. Opening: 9/22/64 *#2 London Opening: 2/16/67*

Tevye

Zero Mostel   #1 Luther Adler
 Luther Adler 8/15/65   Paul Lipson (mats.)
 Herschel Bernardi 11/8/65   9/20/67
 Harry Goz 8/14/67   Paul Lipson 10/9/67
 Herschel Bernardi 9/18/67 Theodore Bikel 12/28/67
 Harry Goz 11/6/67   Paul Lipson 7/2/68
 Jerry Jarrett 5/12/69   Harry Goz 3/70
 Harry Goz 9/8/69   #2 Topol
 Jerry Jarrett 1/5/70   Alfie Bass 2/68
 Paul Lipson 1/19/70   Lex Goudsmit 8/69
       Alfie Bass 2/70

Golde	Maria Karnilova	#1 Dolores Wilson
	Martha Schlamme 4/9/68	Mimi Randolph 4/2/68
	Dolores Wilson 7/1/68	#2 Miriam Karlin
	Rae Allen 7/15/68	Avis Bunnage 2/68
	Peg Murray 6/30/69	Hy Hazell 8/69
		Avis Bunnage 5/11/70
Yente	Beatrice Arthur	#1 Ruth Jaroslow
	Florence Stanley 6/65	Lois Zetter
		Jennie Ventriss 7/68
		Marise Counsell
		#2 Cynthia Grenville
Tzeitel	Joanna Merlin	#1 Felice Camargo
	Ann Marisse 5/65	Kathleen Noser
	Joanna Merlin 10/66	Leona Evans 7/68
	Bette Midler 2/67	Susan Lehman
	Rosalind Harris 2/70	Gretchen Evans
	Judith Smiley 5/5/70	#2 Rosemary Nichols
		Norma Dunbar 2/68
Motel	Austin Pendleton	#1 David Garfield
	Leonard Frey	Stanley Soble 3/67
	David Garfield 3/67	Peter Marklin 7/68
	Peter Marklin 6/2/70	#2 Jonathan Lynn
		Geoff L'Cise 5/68
Perchik	Bert Convy	#1 Joseph Masiell
	Leonard Frey	Virgil Curry
	Gordon Gray	Keith Baker
	Richard Morse	#2 Sandor Eles
		Harvey Sokolov 5/68
Hodel	Julia Migenes	#1 Royce Lenelle
	Mimi Turque 4/67	Barbara Coggin 7/68
	Adrienne Barbeau 10/68	Chris Callan
		#2 Linda Gardner
		Dilys Watling 8/67

FORTY CARATS

	N.Y. Opening: 12/26/68	*Cincinnati Opening: 9/29/69*
Ann Stanley	Julie Harris	Barbara Rush
	June Allyson 1/5/70	
Billy Boylan	Murray Hamilton	Scott McKay
	Tom Poston 12/22/69	
Maude Hayes	Glenda Farrell	Audrey Christie
	Violet Dunn 2/24/69	
Mrs. Margolin	Polly Rowles	Imogene Bliss
	Sudie Bond 5/4/70	
Peter Latham	Marco St. John	Stephen Collins
	Peter Galman 1/5/70	
Mrs. Latham	Nancy Marchand	Eileen Letchworth
	Mary K. Wells 3/2/70	

GEORGE M!

	N.Y. Opening: 4/10/68	San Francisco Opening: 5/8/69
George M. Cohan	Joel Grey Jerry Dodge 12/16/68 Joel Grey 12/23/68	Joel Grey Darryl Hickman 10/21/69
Nellie Cohan	Betty Ann Grove	Betty Ann Grove
Jerry Cohan	Jerry Dodge	Jerry Dodge
Agnes Nolan	Jill O'Hara Sheila Sullivan 8/26/68 Deborah Deeble 12/30/68	Pamela Peadon
Josie Cohan	Bernadette Peters Patti Mariano 8/26/68	Jennifer Williams

THE GREAT WHITE HOPE

	N.Y. Opening: 10/3/68	Cleveland Opening: 9/15/69
Jack Jefferson	James Earl Jones Yaphet Kotto 9/8/69	Brock Peters
Eleanor Bachman	Jane Alexander Maria Tucci 9/8/69	Claudette Nevins
Goldie	Lou Gilbert Martin Wolfson 9/8/69	Marty Greene
Clara	Marlene Warfield Norma Donaldson 9/8/69	Gloria Edwards

HADRIAN VII

	N.Y. Opening: 1/8/69	Stratford, Ont. Opening: 8/4/69
Fr. William Rolfe	Alec McCowen Roderick Cook 6/30/69 Alec McCowen 7/14/69 Barry Morse 9/8/69	Hume Cronyn

HAIR

		#1 London Opening: 9/27/68
		#2 Los Angeles Opening:
		   11/22/68
		#3 San Francisco Opening:
		   8/15/69
		#4 Chicago Opening: 10/13/69
		#5 Las Vegas Opening: 12/3/69
		#6 Toronto Opening: 1/12/70
		#7 Boston Opening: 2/23/70
		#8 Seattle Opening: 4/18/70

	#1 N.Y. off-Bway Opening:
	   10/29/67
	#2 N.Y. Bway Opening:
	   4/29/68	

Berger	#1 Gerome Ragni Steve Curry 12/22/67	#1 Oliver Tobias #2 Gerome Ragni

	#2 Gerome Ragni 　　Steve Curry 11/22/68 　　Barry McGuire 1/69 　　Peter Link 　　Oatis Stephens 　　Allan Nicholls 　　Oatis Stephens 2/70	#3 Bruce Hyde 　　Roger Cruz #4 Michael DeLano #5 James Benton #6 Kid Carson #7 Richard Spiegel #8 Eric
Claude	#1 Walker Daniels #2 James Rado 　　Barry McGuire 11/22/68 　　Joseph Campbell 　　Butler 1/69 　　Kim Milford 　　Eric Robinson 　　Robin McNamara 8/69 　　Keith Carradine 10/69 　　Allan Nicholls 2/70	#1 Paul Nicholas #2 James Rado #3 Eron Tabor 　　Bruce Paine #4 Ken Griffin #5 Lyle Kang #6 Clint Ryan #7 Paul Fitzgerald #8 Skip Bowe
Sheila	#1 Jill O'Hara #2 Lynn Kellogg 　　Diane Keaton 7/68 　　Heather MacRae 1/69 　　Melba Moore 10/69 　　Victoria Medlin 12/69	#1 Annabel Leventon #2 Jennifer Warren #3 Maria Cordero 　　Nancy Blossom #4 Rosemary Llanes #5 Sheri Nojima #6 Gale Garnett #7 Karen Benson #8 Janis Gotti

HAMLET

	N.Y. Opening: 5/1/69	*Boston Opening: 6/16/69*
Hamlet	Nicol Williamson	Nicol Williamson
Gertrude	Constance Cummings	Constance Cummings Nan Martin 7/9/69
1st Player	Roger Livesey	Roger Livesey Malcolm Terris 6/30/69
Gravedigger	Roger Livesey	Roger Livesey Mark Dignam 6/30/69
Polonius	Mark Dignam	Mark Dignam
Claudius	Patrick Wymark	Patrick Wymark

HELLO, DOLLY!

		#1 Minneapolis Opening: 4/9/65 　*London Opening: 12/2/65* *#2 San Diego Opening: 9/7/65* *#3 Louisville Opening: 11/15/65* *#4 Denver Opening: 4/19/67* *#5 Washington Opening:* 　*10/11/67* 　*Boston Opening: 1/13/70*
	N.Y. Opening: 1/16/64	
Dolly Gallagher 　*Levi*	Carol Channing 　Ginger Rogers 8/9/65	#1 Mary Martin 　Dora Bryan 5/14/66

Martha Raye 2/27/67
Betty Grable 6/12/67
Bibi Osterwald 11/6/67
Pearl Bailey 11/12/67
Thelma Carpenter 1/10/69
Pearl Bailey 1/23/69
Thelma Carpenter 1/29/69
(Wed. mats only to 3/5/69)
Thelma Carpenter 7/19/69
Pearl Bailey 7/28/69
Thelma Carpenter 9/6/69
Pearl Bailey 10/9/69
Thelma Carpenter 10/11/69
(all mats. to 12/13/69)
Phyllis Diller 12/26/69
Ethel Merman 3/28/70

#2 Carol Channing
    Eve Arden 6/13/66
    Carol Channing 10/66
#3 Betty Grable
#4 Ginger Rogers
    Dorothy Lamour 8/23/67
    (alternating to 10/18/67)
#5 Pearl Bailey

Horace Vandergelder

David Burns
Max Showalter 3/13/67
Cab Calloway 11/12/67
Richard Deacon 12/26/69
Jack Goode 3/28/70

#1 Loring Smith
    Bernard Spear 5/14/66
#2 Horace MacMahon
    Milo Boulton 11/65
#3 Max Showalter
#4 David Burns
    Max Showalter 8/23/67
    Coley Worth
#5 Cab Calloway

Cornelius Hackl

Charles Nelson Reilly
Lawrence Holofcener
Carleton Carpenter
Will Mackenzie 8/9/65
Jack Crowder 11/12/67
Bill Mullikin 12/26/69
Russell Nype 3/28/70

#1 Carleton Carpenter
    Garrett Lewis 12/2/65
    Gordon Clyde 10/66
#2 Garrett Lewis
    Carleton Carpenter
    Rex Robbins 6/13/66
    Peter Walker 3/67
#3 Arthur Bartow
    Peter Walker
#4 Bill Mullikin
#5 Jack Crowder
    Chapman Roberts 1/13/70
    Nate Barnett 3/70

Irene Malloy

Eileen Brennan
Patte Finley 8/9/65
June Helmers 4/67
Emily Yancy 11/12/67
Ernestine Jackson 12/6/69
June Helmers 12/26/69

#1 Marilynn Lovell
    Jill Martin 5/66
#2 Joanne Horne
#3 June Helmers
#4 Patte Finley
    Mary Nettum 3/68
#5 Emily Yancy
    Mary Louise 1/13/70

Barnaby Tucker

Jerry Dodge
John Mineo 8/66
Harvey Evans 7/67
Winston DeWitt Hemsley
11/12/67
Danny Lockin 12/26/69

#1 Johnny Beecher
#2 Harvey Evans
    Danny Lockin
    Don Slaton 1/67
#3 Danny Lockin
#4 Danny Lockin
    Don Slaton 3/68
#5 Winston DeWitt Hemsley

Minnie Fay

Sondra Lee
Alix Elias 4/67

#1 Coco Ramirez
    Sylvia Tysick 10/66

Leland Palmer 7/67	#2 Barbara Dougherty
Chris Calloway 11/12/67	Isabelle Farrell 1/67
Sherri Peaches Brewer	#3 Billie Hayes
3/68	Harriet Lynn
Georgia Engel 12/26/69	#4 Sondra Lee
	Isabelle Farrell 3/68
	#5 Chris Calloway

JACQUES BREL IS ALIVE AND WELL AND LIVING IN PARIS

(Alternate casts at almost every N.Y. performance; dates following names refer to when performers first joined the company)

#1 London Opening: 6/3/68
#2 Chicago Opening: 9/12/68
#3 Toronto Opening: 11/26/68
#4 Los Angeles Opening: 6/10/69
#5 Washington Opening: 6/17/69
#6 San Francisco Opening:
9/17/69
#7 Boston Opening: 4/30/70

N.Y. Opening: 1/22/68

Original cast	Elly Stone	#1 Elly Stone
	Mort Shuman	Mort Shuman
	Shawn Elliott	Shawn Elliott
	Alice Whitfield	Alice Whitfield
		#2 Alice Whitfield
N.Y. replacements	Robert Guillaume 1/22/68	Robert Guillaume
	June Gable 1/22/68	Joe Masiell
& alternates	Betty Rhodes 5/28/68	Aileen Fitzpatrick
	Chevi Colton 6/22/68	#3 Arlene Meadows
	Joe Masiell 6/22/68	Stan Porter
	Juanita Franklin 7/68	Robert Jeffrey
	Adam Stevens 7/68	Judy Lander
	Wayne Sherwood 7/16/68	#4 Elly Stone
	Fleury Dantonakis 7/24/68	Robert Guillaume
	Amelia Haas 7/30/68	George Ball
	Stan Porter 8/1/68	June Gable
	John C. Attle 8/13/68	#5 Fleury Dantonakis
	George Ball 8/20/68	Stan Porter
	Denise LeBrun 8/20/68	John C. Attle
	Aileen Fitzpatrick 8/20/68	Sally Cooke
	Jack Eddleman 9/17/68	#6 Betty Rhodes
	Jack Blackton 10/8/68	Robert Guillaume
	Elinor Ellsworth 1/25/69	George Ball
	Rita Gardner 4/1/69	Teri Ralston
	Sally Cooke 5/11/69	#7 Elly Stone
	J.T. Cromwell 5/20/69	Stan Porter
	Dominic Chianese 5/27/69	Robert Jeffrey
	Michael Johnson 5/27/69	Arlene Meadows
	Teri Ralston 5/27/69	
	Joe Silver 6/3/69	
	Norman Atkins 3/3/70	
	Margery Cohen 3/10/70	

MAME

N.Y. Opening: 5/24/66

#1 Baltimore Opening: 8/28/67
#2 San Francisco Opening:
4/29/68

#3 *Las Vegas Opening: 12/30/68*
#4 *London Opening: 2/20/69*

Mame Dennis   Angela Lansbury
   Sheila Smith 2/13/67
   Angela Lansbury 2/27/67
   Celeste Holm 8/15/67
   Angela Lansbury 8/29/67
   Janis Paige 4/1/68
   Jane Morgan 12/2/68
   Ann Miller 5/26/69

#1 Celeste Holm
#2 Angela Lansbury
#3 Susan Hayward
   Celeste Holm 3/10/69
#4 Ginger Rogers
   Juliet Prowse 8/69
   Ginger Rogers 9/15/69

Vera Charles   Beatrice Arthur
   Sheila Smith 3/27/67
   Beatrice Arthur 4/10/67
   Anne Francine 7/10/67
   Audrey Christie 4/1/68
   Anne Francine 9/23/68

#1 Vicki Cummings
#2 Anne Francine
#3 Delphi Lawrence
#4 Margaret Courtenay

Agnes Gooch   Jane Connell
   Helen Gallagher 4/29/68
   Marilyn Cooper 12/15/69

#1 Loretta Swit
#2 Jane Connell
#3 Loretta Swit
#4 Ann Beach

MAN OF LA MANCHA

#1 *New Haven Opening: 9/24/66*
#2 *London Opening: 4/25/68*
#3 *2nd London Opening: 6/10/69*

N.Y. Opening: 11/22/65

Don Quixote   Richard Kiley
(Cervantes)   José Ferrer 5/28/66
   John Cullum 2/24/67
   José Ferrer 4/11/67
   David Atkinson 7/14/67
   Laurence Guittard 5/22/68
   (matinees only)
   Hal Holbrook 7/1/68
   Bob Wright 9/23/68
   David Holliday 10/12/68
   (matinees only)
   David Atkinson 9/8/69
   Claudio Brook 9/22/69
   Jack Dabdoub 10/20/69
   (matinees only)
   Keith Michell 12/22/69
   Somegoro Ichikawa 3/2/70
   Charles West 5/11/70

#1 José Ferrer
   Richard Kiley 4/11/67
   José Ferrer 7/17/67
   Richard Kiley 8/7/67
   Keith Andes 9/19/67
   José Ferrer 9/23/68
   Bob Wright 9/15/69
#2 Keith Michell
#3 Richard Kiley

Aldonza   Joan Diener
   Marion Marlowe 1/17/67
   Maura K. Wedge 4/11/67
   Bernice Massi 7/25/67
   Patricia Marand 2/68
   (matinees only)
   Carolyn Maye 3/20/68
   (matinees only)
   Barbara Williams 11/11/68
   (matinees only)
   Gaylea Byrne 5/5/69
   Marilyn Child 5/28/69
   (matinees only)

#1 Maura K. Wedge
   Joan Diener 4/11/67
   Marion Marlowe 7/31/67
   Carolyn Maye 11/7/67
   Natalie Costa 3/18/68
   Maura K. Wedge 10/15/68
#2 Joan Diener
   Ruth Silvestre 9/68
#3 Ruth Silvestre

Emily Yancy 12/3/69
(matinees only)

Sancho Panza	Irving Jacobson Pierre Olaf 7/5/66 Irving Jacobson 7/19/66 Joey Faye 11/1/68 Tony Martinez 10/69 Sammy Smith 4/13/70 Titos Vandis 5/11/70	#1 Harvey Lembeck Tony Martinez 9/19/67 Sammy Smith 10/69 #2 Bernard Spear #3 Bernard Spear
Innkeeper	Ray Middleton Wilbur Evans 4/11/67 Ray Middleton 9/19/67	#1 Wilbur Evans Ray Middleton 4/11/67 Wilbur Evans 9/11/67 Earle MacVeigh 10/16/67 George Wallace 10/16/68 Marvin Brody 10/14/69 #2 David King #3 Charles West
Padre	Robert Rounseville	#1 Dale Malone Norman Kelley 7/1/68 Dale Malone 6/30/69 #2 Alan Crofoot #3 Gordon Wilcock

PLAY IT AGAIN, SAM

	N.Y. Opening: 2/12/69	*London Opening: 9/9/69*
Allan Felix	Woody Allen Bob Denver 1/12/70	Dudley Moore
Dick Christie *	Anthony Roberts Lawrence Pressman 8/69	Terence Edmond
Linda Christie *	Diane Keaton Sheila Sullivan 1/12/70	Lorna Heilbron

* In London, characters were known as Brian and Sally Morris

PLAZA SUITE

		#1 San Francisco Opening: 9/16/68 *#2 Chicago Opening: 10/14/68*
	N.Y. Opening: 2/14/68	*#3 London Opening: 2/18/69*
Sam, Jesse, Roy	George C. Scott Alfred Sandor Nicol Williamson 5/27/68 George C. Scott 6/17/68 E. G. Marshall 9/9/68 Dan Dailey 3/3/69 Lawrence Weber 5/19/69 Don Porter 5/26/69	#1 Dan Dailey #2 Forrest Tucker Howard Keel 8/4/69 Forrest Tucker 10/13/69 #3 Paul Rogers
Karen, Muriel Norma	Maureen Stapleton Barbara Baxley 2/13/69 Maureen Stapleton 6/10/69	#1 Lee Grant #2 Betty Garrett #3 Rosemary Harris

Peggy Cass 1/5/70
Maureen Stapleton 5/25/70
Peggy Cass 6/8/70

THE PRICE

	N.Y. Opening: 2/7/68	#1 London Opening: 3/4/69 #2 New Haven Opening: 9/24/69
Victor Franz	Pat Hingle Albert Salmi 10/14/68	#1 Albert Salmi #2 Michael Strong
Esther Franz	Kate Reid	#1 Kate Reid #2 Betty Field
Gregory Solomon	Harold Gary David Burns 6/10/68 Harold Gary 2/10/69	#1 Harold Gary #2 Harold Gary
Walter Franz	Arthur Kennedy Shepperd Strudwick 10/14/68	#1 Shepperd Strudwick #2 Shepperd Strudwick

PROMISES, PROMISES

	N.Y. Opening: 12/1/68	#1 London Opening: 10/2/69 #2 San Diego Opening: 5/11/70
Chuck Baxter	Jerry Orbach	#1 Anthony Roberts Bob Sherman 4/70 #2 Anthony Roberts
Fran Kubelik	Jill O'Hara	#1 Betty Buckley #2 Melissa Hart
J.D. Sheldrake	Edward Winter	#1 James Congdon #2 Bob Holiday
Dr. Dreyfuss	A. Larry Haines Norman Shelly 11/69	#1 Jack Kruschen Bernard Spear 4/70 #2 Jack Kruschen
Marge MacDougall	Marian Mercer Pam Zarit 12/1/69	#1 Kelly Britt Julia McKenzie 4/70 #2 Kelly Britt

1776

	N.Y. Opening: 3/16/69	San Francisco Opening: 4/23/70
John Adams	William Daniels	Patrick Bedford
Benjamin Franklin	Howard Da Silva	Rex Everhart
John Dickinson	Paul Hecht	George Hearn
Edward Rutledge	Clifford David David Cryer 5/30/69 John Cullum 5/19/70	Jack Blackton

| *Stephen Hopkins* | Roy Poole | Truman Gaige |

| *Thomas Jefferson* | Ken Howard
John Fink 5/30/69
Jon Cypher 9/16/69
Peter Lombard 11/24/69 | Jon Cypher |

| *Abigail Adams* | Virginia Vestoff
Ellen Hanley 12/69
Virginia Vestoff 2/16/70 | Barbara Lang |

| *Richard Henry Lee* | Ronald Holgate | Gary Oakes |

| *Martha Jefferson* | Betty Buckley
Mary Bracken Phillips
8/28/69 | Pamela Hall |

SHEEP ON THE RUNWAY

N.Y. Opening: 1/31/70   *Washington Opening: 5/5/70*

| *Joseph Mayflower* | Martin Gabel | Martin Gabel |

| *Ambassador Wilkins* | David Burns | David Burns |

| *Martha Wilkins* | Elizabeth Wilson | Helen Stenborg |

YOU'RE A GOOD MAN CHARLIE BROWN

#1 *San Francisco Opening:*
   6/1/67
#2 *Toronto Opening: 10/18/67*
#3 *Boston Opening: 12/18/67*
#4 *London Opening: 2/1/68*
#5 *Los Angeles Opening: 3/12/68*

N.Y. Opening: 3/7/67   #6 *Cleveland Opening: 1/28/69*

| *Charlie Brown* | Gary Burghoff
Sean Simpson 3/4/68
Bob Lydiard 8/68
Alfred Mazza 2/69 | #1 Wendell Burton
#2 David-Rhys Anderson
    Alan Lofft 12/67
#3 Jim Ricketts
    Ken Kube 6/68
#4 David-Rhys Anderson
#5 Gary Burghoff
#6 Bob Lydiard |

| *Lucy* | Reva Rose
Boni Enten 6/11/68
Ann Gibbs 12/69 | #1 Jenell Pulis
#2 Boni Enten
    Minnie Gaster 1/68
    Cathy Wallace 3/69
#3 Ann Gibbs
    Minnie Gaster
#4 Boni Enten
#5 Judy Kaye
#6 Ann Hodapp |

| *Snoopy* | Bill Hinnant
Don Potter 12/69 | #1 Austin O'Toole
#2 Don Potter
    Grant Cowan 1/68
#3 Bob Becker
    Pat McKenna 5/68 |

T.D. Johnston 12/21/68
#4 Don Potter
#5 Robert Towers
#6 Alfred Roberge

YOUR OWN THING

		#1 Toronto Opening: 6/13/68
		#2 San Francisco Opening:
		7/10/68
		#3 Los Angeles Opening: 7/29/68
		#4 Boston Opening: 12/21/68
		#5 London Opening: 2/6/69
	N.Y. Opening: 1/13/68	*#6 Wilmington Opening: 4/21/69*

Sebastian	Rusty Thacker	#1 Bruce Scott
	Bruce Scott 7/29/68	#2 Gerry Glasier
	Rusty Thacker 4/69	#3 Rusty Thacker
	Frank Andre	#4 Gerry Glasier
	Richard Kim Milford	#5 Gerry Glasier
	Gerry Glasier	#6 Gerry Glasier
	Randy Herron	

Viola	Leland Palmer	#1 Sandy Duncan
	Sandy Duncan 7/29/68	#2 Bonnie Franklin
	Priscilla Lopez 3/69	#3 Leland Palmer
	Jill Choder 4/69	#4 Jill Choder
		#5 Leland Palmer
		#6 Priscilla Lopez

Orson	Tom Ligon	#1 Les Carlson
	Les Carlson 7/29/68	#2 Peter Jason
	Raul Julia	#3 Tom Ligon
	Dan Hamilton	#4 Carleton Carpenter
	Bruce Jacobs	#5 Les Carlson
		#6 Tom Ligon
		Allan Hunt 9/69

Olivia	Marian Mercer	#1 Sally Stark
	Marcia Rodd 2/68	#2 Renata Vaselle
	June Compton	#3 Marcia Rodd
	Sally Stark 7/29/68	#4 June Compton
	Donna Christie	#5 Marcia Rodd
	June Compton 3/69	#6 Paula Kelly
	Lee Chamberlin 6/69	Sheree North 8/69
	Luba Lisa 1/27/70	Gretchen Wyler 9/69

ZORBÁ

	N.Y. Opening: 11/17/68	*Philadelphia Opening: 12/26/69*
Zorba	Herschel Bernardi	John Raitt
Hortense	Maria Karnilova	Barbara Baxley
Leader	Lorraine Serabian	Chita Rivera
Nikos	John Cunningham	Gary Krawford

BUS-TRUCK TOURS

These are touring productions designed for maximum mobility and ease of handling in one-night and split-week stands (with occasional engagements of a week or more). Among Broadway shows on tour in the season of 1969-70 were the following bus-truck troupes:

Rosencrantz and Guildenstern Are Dead (and *Hamlet*) with Robert Burr, 86 cities, 9/4/69-4/11/70

Cabaret with Tandy Cronyn and Jay Fox, 112 cities, 8/19/69-5/9/70

Spofford with Hans Conried, 63 cities, 9/8/69-3/21/70

The Price with Douglas Watson, Joseph Buloff, Betty Miller and Carle Bensen, 42 cities, 2/2/70-3/26/70

Your Own Thing, 99 cities, 10/2/69-4/15/70

Fiddler on the Roof with Bob Carroll/Harry Goz, 52 cities, 12/27/69-6/1/70 (continuing)

I Do! I Do! with Phil Ford and Mimi Hines, 115 cities, 9/11/69-6/1/70 (continuing)

Man of La Mancha with David Atkinson and Natalie Costa, 60 cities, 9/27/69-2/28/70

Canterbury Tales with Constance Carpenter, Ray Walston and Martyn Green, 15 full-week stands, 12/29/69-4/11/70

Mame with Sheila Smith/Patrice Munsel, 103 cities, 9/25/69-6/1/70 (continuing)

FACTS AND
FIGURES

LONG RUNS ON BROADWAY

The following shows have run 500 or more continuous performances in a single production, usually the first, not including previews or extra non-profit performances, allowing for vacation layoffs and special one-booking engagements, but not including return engagements after a show has gone on tour. Where there are title similarities, the production is identified as follows: (p) straight play version, (m) musical version, (r) revival.

THROUGH MAY 31, 1970

(PLAYS MARKED WITH ASTERISK WERE STILL PLAYING JUNE 1, 1970)

Plays	Number Performances	Plays	Number Performances
Life With Father	3,224	Hellzapoppin	1,404
Tobacco Road	3,182	The Music Man	1,375
My Fair Lady	2,717	Funny Girl	1,348
*Hello, Dolly! †	2,603	Angel Street	1,295
*Fiddler on the Roof	2,370	Lightnin'	1,291
Abie's Irish Rose	2,327	The King and I	1,246
Oklahoma!	2,212	Cactus Flower	1,234
South Pacific †	1,925	Guys and Dolls	1,200
*Man of La Mancha	1,910	Cabaret	1,165
Harvey ††	1,775	Mister Roberts	1,157
Born Yesterday	1,642	Annie Get Your Gun	1,147
Mary, Mary	1,572	The Seven Year Itch	1,141
The Voice of the Turtle	1,557	Pins and Needles	1,108
Barefoot in the Park	1,530	Kiss Me, Kate	1,070
Mame (m)	1,508	The Pajama Game	1,063
Arsenic and Old Lace	1,444	The Teahouse of the August	
The Sound of Music	1,443	Moon	1,027
How To Succeed in Business		Damn Yankees	1,019
Without Really Trying	1,417	Never Too Late	1,007

† Both *South Pacific* and *Hello, Dolly!*—and probably many other shows over the years—interrupted their runs for special one-booking engagements outside New York City. *South Pacific's* run was originally recorded as 1,925 performances but was cut back starting with the 1960-61 *Best Plays* volume to the 1,694 performances it played prior to just such a special booking. In the opinion of the present editor *South Pacific's* record should show the full 1,925 performances, which are restored in this volume's long-run list.

†† The figure of 1,694 performances given for *Harvey* in this section of last year's volume, *The Best Plays of 1968-69*, was an error which we regret and wish to correct.

Plays	Number Performances	Plays	Number Performances
Any Wednesday	982	The Diary of Anne Frank	717
A Funny Thing Happened on the Way to the Forum	964	I Remember Mama	714
		Tea and Sympathy	712
The Odd Couple	964	Junior Miss	710
Anna Lucasta	957	Seventh Heaven	704
Kiss and Tell	956	Gypsy (m)	702
*Plaza Suite	953	The Miracle Worker	700
The Moon Is Blue	924	Cat on a Hot Tin Roof	694
Bells Are Ringing	924	Li'l Abner	693
Luv	901	Peg o' My Heart	692
Can-Can	892	The Children's Hour	691
Carousel	890	Dead End	687
Hats Off to Ice	889	The Lion and the Mouse	686
Fanny	888	White Cargo	686
Follow the Girls	882	Dear Ruth	683
Camelot	873	East Is West	680
*Hair	869	Come Blow Your Horn	677
The Bat	867	The Most Happy Fella	676
My Sister Eileen	864	The Doughgirls	671
Song of Norway	860	The Impossible Years	670
A Streetcar Named Desire	855	Irene	670
Comedy in Music	849	Boy Meets Girl	669
You Can't Take It With You	837	Beyond the Fringe	667
La Plume de Ma Tante	835	Who's Afraid of Virginia Woolf?	664
Three Men on a Horse	835	Blithe Spirit	657
The Subject Was Roses	832	A Trip to Chinatown	657
Inherit the Wind	806	The Women	657
No Time for Sergeants	796	Bloomer Girl	654
Fiorello!	795	The Fifth Season	654
Where's Charley?	792	Rain	648
The Ladder	789	Witness for the Prosecution	645
Oliver	774	Call Me Madam	644
State of the Union	765	Janie	642
The First Year	760	The Green Pastures	640
You Know I Can't Hear You When the Water's Running	755	Auntie Mame (p)	639
		A Man for All Seasons	637
Two for the Seesaw	750	The Fourposter	632
Death of a Salesman	742	*Promises, Promises	625
Sons o' Fun	742	The Tenth Man	623
Gentlemen Prefer Blondes	740	Is Zat So?	618
The Man Who Came to Dinner	739	Anniversary Waltz	615
Call Me Mister	734	The Happy Time (p)	614
West Side Story	732	Separate Rooms	613
High Button Shoes	727	Affairs of State	610
Finian's Rainbow	725	Star and Garter	609
Claudia	722	The Student Prince	608
The Gold Diggers	720	Sweet Charity	608
Carnival	719	Bye Bye Birdie	607

Plays	Number Performances	Plays	Number Performances
Broadway	603	Dial "M" for Murder	552
Adonis	603	Good News	551
Street Scene (p)	601	Let's Face It	547
Kiki	600	Milk and Honey	543
Flower Drum Song	600	Within the Law	541
Don't Drink the Water	598	The Music Master	540
Wish You Were Here	598	Pal Joey (r)	540
*Forty Carats	597	What Makes Sammy Run?	540
A Society Circus	596	What a Life	538
Blossom Time	592	The Unsinkable Molly Brown	532
The Two Mrs. Carrolls	585	The Red Mill (r)	531
Kismet	583	A Raisin in the Sun	530
Detective Story	581	The Solid Gold Cadillac	526
Brigadoon	581	Irma La Douce	524
No Strings	580	The Boomerang	522
Brother Rat	577	Rosalinda	521
Show Boat	572	The Best Man	520
The Show-Off	571	Chauve-Souris	520
Sally	570	Blackbirds of 1928	518
Golden Boy (m)	568	Sunny	517
One Touch of Venus	567	Victoria Regina	517
Happy Birthday	564	Half a Sixpence	511
Look Homeward, Angel	564	The Vagabond King	511
The Glass Menagerie	561	The New Moon	509
I Do! I Do!	560	The World of Suzie Wong	508
Wonderful Town	559	*1776	506
Rose Marie	557	Shuffle Along	504
Strictly Dishonorable	557	Up in Central Park	504
A Majority of One	556	Carmen Jones	503
The Great White Hope	556	The Member of the Wedding	501
Toys in the Attic	556	Panama Hattie	501
Sunrise at Campobello	556	Personal Appearance	501
Jamaica	555	Bird in Hand	500
Stop the World—I Want to Get Off	555	Room Service	500
Floradora	553	Sailor, Beware!	500
Ziegfeld Follies (1943)	553	Tomorrow the World	500

LONG RUNS OFF BROADWAY

Plays	Number Performances	Plays	Number Performances
*The Fantasticks	4,220	Charlie Brown	1,355
The Threepenny Opera	2,611	Little Mary Sunshine	1,143
The Blacks	1,408	*Jacques Brel Is Alive and Well and Living in Paris	975
*You're a Good Man			

Plays	Number Performances	Plays	Number Performances
Your Own Thing	933	Krapp's Last Tape and	
Curley McDimple	931	The Zoo Story	582
Leave It to Jane (r)	928	The Dumwaiter and	
*The Boys in the Band	890	The Collection	578
The Mad Show	871	Dames at Sea	575
A View From the Bridge (r)	780	The Crucible (r)	571
The Boy Friend (r)	763	The Iceman Cometh (r)	565
The Pocket Watch	725	*Adaptation and Next	546
The Connection	722	The Hostage (r)	545
Scuba Duba	692	Six Characters in Search of an	
The Knack	685	Author (r)	529
The Balcony	672	Happy Ending and Day of	
America Hurrah	634	Absence	504
Hogan's Goat	607	The Boys From Syracuse (r)	500
The Trojan Women (r)	600		

DRAMA CRITICS CIRCLE VOTING 1969-70

The New York Drama Critics Circle voted *Borstal Boy* the best play of the season on the second ballot by a plurality of 26 points in weighted voting after no play achieved a majority of first choices on the first ballot. After *Borstal Boy* was named best play, the 21 members of the Circle present and voting (see summary) decided that it should be considered a foreign play although its adapter, Frank McMahon, is an American citizen living in Dublin, where this stage version of Brendan Behan's autobiography was first produced by the Abbey Theater. Other best-play points on this ballot (counting 3 for each critic's first choice, 2 for his second and 1 for his third) were distributed as follows: *The Effect of Gamma Rays on Man-in-the-Moon Marigolds* 22, *Indians* 19, *Child's Play* 16, *Last of the Red Hot Lovers* 15, *Approaching Simone* 6, *The Constant Prince* 6, *The White House Murder Case* 6, *A Scent of Flowers* 2, *Butterflies Are Free* 2, *Operation Sidewinder* 2, *Terminal* 2, *A Whistle in the Dark* 1, *Who's Happy Now?* 1.

Having named *Borstal Boy* a foreign play, the critics decided to vote on a best American play. *The Effect of Gamma Rays on Man-in-the-Moon Marigolds* and *Indians* tied on the second ballot with 30 points each by the same scoring method as above. The tie was broken in favor of *Marigolds* by a runoff show of hands. Other points in the category of best American play were distributed as follows: *Child's Play* 21, *Last of the Red Hot Lovers* 12, *The White House Murder Case* 12, *Approaching Simone* 7, *Operation Sidewinder* 4, *Who's Happy Now?* 4, *Terminal* 3, *Butterflies Are Free* 2, *The Unseen Hand* 1.

The critics voted *Company* the best musical of the season on the first ballot by a simple majority of 13 first-choice votes (Harold Clurman, Ethel Colby, Jack Gaver, Brendan Gill, Martin Gottfried, Henry Hewes, Ted Kalem, Jack Kroll, Emory Lewis, Leo Mishkin, John O'Connor, William Raidy, Marilyn Stasio) against 7 for *Applause* (Clive Barnes, William H. Glover, Edward S. Hipp, Walter

Kerr, Hobe Morrison, George Oppenheimer, Richard Watts Jr.) and 1 for *Sambo* (John Lahr). John Chapman of the *Daily News,* the Circle's 22d member, was not present and did not vote by proxy.

Here's the way the Circle's members' votes went on the second ballots for best play and best American play (first-ballot votes are indicated by first choices):

SECOND BALLOT FOR BEST PLAY

Critic	1st Choice (3 pts.)	2d Choice (2 pts.)	3d Choice (1 pt.)
Clive Barnes *Times*	The Effect of Gamma Rays on Man-in-the-Moon Marigolds	Indians	Approaching Simone
Harold Clurman *The Nation*	Borstal Boy	Indians	Marigolds
Ethel Colby *Journal of Commerce*	Borstal Boy	Last of the Red Hot Lovers	Marigolds
Jack Gaver *UPI*	Child's Play	Borstal Boy	Indians
Brendan Gill *New Yorker*	Borstal Boy	Child's Play	Indians
William H. Glover *AP*	Marigolds	Borstal Boy	Indians
Martin Gottfried *Women's Wear Daily*	The Constant Prince	Approaching Simone	Who's Happy Now?
Henry Hewes *Saturday Review*	The White House Murder Case	A Scent of Flowers	Terminal
Edward S. Hipp *Newark News*	Child's Play	Marigolds	Borstal Boy
Ted Kalem *Time*	Marigolds	Borstal Boy	A Whistle in the Dark
Walter Kerr *Times*	Marigolds	Butterflies Are Free	White House
Jack Kroll *Newsweek*	Approaching Simone	Marigolds	Borstal Boy
John Lahr *Village Voice*	Indians	Operation Sidewinder	Terminal
Emory Lewis *Bergen Record*	Indians	White House	Borstal Boy
Leo Mishkin *Morning Telegraph*	Red Hot Lovers	Indians	Marigolds
Hobe Morrison *Variety*	Red Hot Lovers	Child's Play	Borstal Boy
John O'Connor *Wall St. Journal*	The Constant Prince	Borstal Boy	Marigolds
George Oppenheimer *Newsday*	Child's Play	Red Hot Lovers	Marigolds
William Raidy *Newhouse Papers*	Borstal Boy	Red Hot Lovers	Indians
Marilyn Stasio *Cue*	Indians	Borstal Boy	Child's Play
Richard Watts Jr. *Post*	Red Hot Lovers	Child's Play	Marigolds

SECOND BALLOT FOR BEST AMERICAN PLAY

Critic	1st Choice (3 pts.)	2d Choice (2 pts.)	3d Choice (1 pt.)
Clive Barnes	The Effect of Gamma Rays on Man-in-the-Moon Marigolds	Indians	Approaching Simone
Harold Clurman	Indians	Marigolds	Operation Sidewinder

Ethel Colby	Marigolds	Last of the Red Hot Lovers	Child's Play
Jack Gaver	Child's Play	Indians	Red Hot Lovers
Brendan Gill	Indians	Child's Play	Operation Sidewinder
William H. Glover	Marigolds	The White House Murder Case	Indians
Martin Gottfried	Approaching Simone	Who's Happy Now?	Marigolds
Henry Hewes	White House	Terminal	Indians
Edward S. Hipp	Child's Play	Marigolds	Indians
Ted Kalem	Marigolds	Who's Happy Now?	Child's Play
Walter Kerr	Marigolds	Butterflies Are Free	White House
Jack Kroll	Approaching Simone	Marigolds	White House
John Lahr	Indians	Operation Sidewinder	Terminal
Emory Lewis	Indians	White House	The Unseen Hand
Leo Mishkin	Indians	Marigolds	Red Hot Lovers
Hobe Morrison	Red Hot Lovers	Child's Play	Indians
John O'Connor	Marigolds	White House	Indians
George Oppenheimer	Child's Play	Marigolds	Indians
William Raidy	Red Hot Lovers	Indians	Child's Play
Marilyn Stasio	Indians	Child's Play	White House
Richard Watts Jr.	Child's Play	Red Hot Lovers	Marigolds

Choices of some other critics:

Critic	Best Play	Best Musical
Judith Crist "Today"	Borstal Boy	Company
Edwin Newman WNBC-TV	Marigolds	(Abstain)
Theodore Hoffman Westinghouse Broadcasting	A Patriot for Me	Company
Norman Nadel Scripps-Howard	Marigolds	Company
Tom Prideaux Life	No Place To Be Somebody	Company
Leonard Harris WCBS-TV	Borstal Boy	Company
John Chapman Daily News	Child's Play	Applause

NEW YORK DRAMA CRITICS CIRCLE AWARDS

Listed below are the New York Drama Critics Circle Awards, classified as follows:
(1) Best American Play, (2) Best Foreign Play, (3) Best Musical, (4) Best, regardless of category.

1935-36—(1) Winterset
1936-37—(1) High Tor
1937-38—(1) Of Mice and Men, (2) Shadow and Substance
1938-39—(1) No award, (2) The White Steed
1939-40—(1) The Time of Your Life
1940-41—(1) Watch on the Rhine, (2) The Corn Is Green
1941-42—(1) No award, (2) Blithe Spirit
1942-43—(1) The Patriots
1943-44—(2) Jacobowsky and the Colonel
1944-45—(1) The Glass Menagerie
1945-46—(3) Carousel

1946-47—(1) All My Sons, (2) No Exit, (3) Brigadoon
1947-48—(1) A Streetcar Named Desire, (2) The Winslow Boy
1948-49—(1) Death of a Salesman, (2) The Madwoman of Chaillot, (3) South Pacific
1949-50—(1) The Member of the Wedding, (2) The Cocktail Party, (3) The Consul
1950-51—(1) Darkness at Noon, (2) The Lady's Not for Burning, (3) Guys and Dolls

1951-52—(1) I Am a Camera, (2) Venus Observed, (3) Pal Joey (Special citation to Don Juan in Hell)

1952-53—(1) Picnic, (2) The Love of Four Colonels, (3) Wonderful Town

1953-54—(1) Teahouse of the August Moon, (2) Ondine, (3) The Golden Apple

1954-55—(1) Cat on a Hot Tin Roof, (2) Witness for the Prosecution, (3) The Saint of Bleecker Street

1955-56—(1) The Diary of Anne Frank, (2) Tiger at the Gates, (3) My Fair Lady

1956-57—(1) Long Day's Journey Into Night, (2) The Waltz of the Toreadors, (3) The Most Happy Fella

1957-58—(1) Look Homeward, Angel, (2) Look Back in Anger, (3) The Music Man

1958-59—(1) A Raisin in the Sun, (2) The Visit, (3) La Plume de Ma Tante

1959-60—(1) Toys in the Attic, (2) Five Finger Exercise, (3) Fiorello!

1960-61—(1) All the Way Home, (2) A Taste of Honey, (3) Carnival

1961-62—(1) The Night of the Iguana, (2) A Man for All Seasons, (3) How To Succeed in Business Without Really Trying

1962-63—(4) Who's Afraid of Virginia Woolf? (Special citation to Beyond the Fringe)

1963-64—(4) Luther, (3) Hello, Dolly! (Special citation to The Trojan Women)

1964-65—(4) The Subject Was Roses, (3) Fiddler on the Roof

1965-66—(4) The Persecution and Assassination of Marat as Performed by the Inmates of the Asylum of Charenton Under the Direction of the Marquis de Sade, (3) Man of La Mancha

1966-67—(4) The Homecoming, (3) Cabaret

1967-68—(4) Rosencrantz and Guildenstern Are Dead, (3) Your Own Thing

1968-69—(4) The Great White Hope, (3) 1776

1969-70—(4) Borstal Boy, (1) The Effect of Gamma Rays on Man-in-the-Moon Marigolds, (3) Company

PULITZER PRIZE WINNERS

1917-18—Why Marry?, by Jesse Lynch Williams

1918-19—No award

1919-20—Beyond the Horizon, by Eugene O'Neill

1920-21—Miss Lulu Bett, by Zona Gale

1921-22—Anna Christie, by Eugene O'Neill

1922-23—Icebound, by Owen Davis

1923-24—Hell-Bent fer Heaven, by Hatcher Hughes

1924-25—They Knew What They Wanted, by Sidney Howard

1925-26—Craig's Wife, by George Kelly

1926-27—In Abraham's Bosom, by Paul Green

1927-28—Strange Interlude, by Eugene O'Neill

1928-29—Street Scene, by Elmer Rice

1929-30—The Green Pastures, by Marc Connelly

1930-31—Alison's House, by Susan Glaspell

1931-32—Of Thee I Sing, by George S. Kaufman, Morrie Ryskind, Ira and George Gershwin

1932-33—Both Your Houses, by Maxwell Anderson

1933-34—Men in White, by Sidney Kingsley

1934-35—The Old Maid, by Zoe Akins

1935-36—Idiot's Delight, by Robert E. Sherwood

1936-37—You Can't Take It With You, by Moss Hart and George S. Kaufman

1937-38—Our Town, by Thornton Wilder

1938-39—Abe Lincoln in Illinois, by Robert E. Sherwood

1939-40—The Time of Your Life, by William Saroyan

1940-41—There Shall Be No Night, by Robert E. Sherwood

1941-42—No award

1942-43—The Skin of Our Teeth, by Thornton Wilder

1943-44—No award

1944-45—Harvey, by Mary Chase

1945-46—State of the Union, by Howard Lindsay and Russel Crouse

1946-47—No award.

1947-48—A Streetcar Named Desire, by Tennessee Williams

1948-49—Death of a Salesman, by Arthur Miller

1949-50—South Pacific, by Richard Rodgers, Oscar Hammerstein II and Joshua Logan

1950-51—No award

1951-52—The Shrike, by Joseph Kramm

1952-53—Picnic, by William Inge

1953-54—The Teahouse of the August Moon, by John Patrick

1954-55—Cat on a Hot Tin Roof, by Tennessee Williams

1955-56—The Diary of Anne Frank, by Frances Goodrich and Albert Hackett

1956-57—Long Day's Journey Into Night, by Eugene O'Neill

1957-58—Look Homeward, Angel, by Ketti Frings

1958-59—J. B., by Archibald MacLeish

1959-60—Fiorello!, by Jerome Weidman, George Abbott, Sheldon Harnick and Jerry Bock

1960-61—All the Way Home, by Tad Mosel

1961-62—How to Succeed in Business Without Really Trying, by Abe Burrows, Willie Gilbert, Jack Weinstock and Frank Loesser

1962-63—No award

1963-64—No award

1964-65—The Subject Was Roses, by Frank D. Gilroy

1965-66—No award

1966-67—A Delicate Balance, by Edward Albee

1967-68—No award

1968-69—The Great White Hope, by Howard Sackler

1969-70—No Place To Be Somebody, by Charles Gordone

ADDITIONAL PRIZES AND AWARDS, 1969-70

The following is a list of major prizes and awards for theatrical achievement. In all cases the names of winners—persons, productions or organizations—appear in **bold face type.**

1969 NOBEL PRIZE IN LITERATURE to **Samuel Beckett.**

MARGO JONES AWARDS (for encouraging production of new playwrights). **The Trinity Square Company** of Providence, R.I., **Adrian Hall** (Margo Jones medallion winner) director, "for encouraging new playwrights by giving professional productions of their plays." Los Angeles Center Theater Group's **New Theater for Now** program, **Gordon Davidson** and **Edward Parone** directors, for workshop productions.

JOSEPH MAHARAM FOUNDATION AWARDS (for design by Americans). Straight play scene design, **Jo Mielziner** for *Child's Play.* Musical scene design, **Boris Aronson** for *Company.* Costume design, **Theoni V. Aldredge** for *Peer Gynt.*

NATIONAL ACADEMY OF THE LIVING THEATER FOUNDATION (On Stage Hall of Fame Award). **Barbra Streisand.**

BRANDEIS UNIVERSITY CREATIVE ARTS AWARDS (medal and citation in the theater arts). Medal to **Arthur Miller** for "eloquent and stirring statements" in his plays. Citation to **The Open Theater,** off-off-Broadway group, for "bold experimentation

without self-indulgence" and, with its production of *The Serpent,* creating "the single most effective example of a new and original theater style thus far seen in this country."

GEORGE JEAN NATHAN AWARD (for criticism). **John Lahr.**

CLARENCE DERWENT AWARDS (for best non-featured performances). **Pamela Payton-Wright** in *The Effect of Gamma Rays on Man-in-the Moon Marigolds.* **Jeremiah Sullivan** in *A Scent of Flowers.*

VILLAGE VOICE OFF-BROADWAY (OBIE) AWARDS (for off-Broadway excellence, selected by a committee of judges whose members were Jack Kroll, John Lahr and John Simon). Best play, **The Effect of Gamma Rays on Man-in-the-Moon Marigolds** and **Approaching Simone** (tie). Best foreign play, **What the Butler Saw.** Best musical, **The Last Sweet Days of Isaac** and **The Me Nobody Knows** (tie). Best performance, **Sada Thompson** in *The Effect of Gamma Rays on Man-in-the-Moon Marigolds.* Distinguished playwriting, **Murry Mednick** for *The Deer Kill,* **Vaclav Havel** for *The Increased Difficulty of Concentration.* Distinguished performances, **Beeson Carroll** in *The Unseen Hand,* **Vincent Gardenia** in *Passing*

Through From Exotic Places, **Harold Gould** in The Increased Difficulty of Concentration, **Anthony Holland** in The White House Murder Case, **Lee Kissman** in The Unseen Hand, **Ron Leibman** in Transfers, **Rue McClanahan** in Who's Happy Now?, **Roberta Maxwell** in A Whistle in the Dark, **Austin Pendleton** and **Fredricka Weber** in The Last Sweet Days of Isaac, **Pamela Payton-Wright** in The Effect of Gamma Rays in Man-in-the-Moon Marigolds. Distinguished direction, **Alan Arkin** for The White House Murder Case, **Melvin Bernhardt** for The Effect of Gamma Rays on Man-in-the-Moon Marigolds, **Maxine Klein** for Approaching Simone, **Gilbert Moses** for Slave Ship. Distinguished special effects, **Gardner Compton** and **Emile Ardolino** for Oh! Calcutta! Special citations to **Charles Ludlam**, **John Vaccaro**, **Roger Foreman** and **Stanley Silverman**, the **Chelsea Theater Center** and **Andre Gregory**.

THEATER WORLD AWARDS (for promising new acting talent). **Susan Browning** in Company, **Donny Burks** in Billy Noname, **Catherine Burns** in Dear Janet Rosenberg, Dear Mr. Kooning, **Len Cariou** in Henry V and Applause, **Bonnie Franklin** in Applause, **David Holliday** in Coco, **Katharine Houghton** in A Scent of Flowers, **Melba Moore** in Purlie, **David Rounds** in Child's Play, **Lewis J. Stadlen** in Minnie's Boys, **Kristoffer Tabori** in How Much, How Much?, **Fredricka Weber** in The Last Sweet Days of Isaac.

OUTER CIRCLE AWARDS (voted by critics of out-of-town periodicals, for distinctive achievement in the New York theater). Best play, **Child's Play**. Best musical, **Company**. Best off-Broadway play, **The White House Murder Case**. Best off-Broadway musical, **The Last Sweet Days of Isaac**. Outstanding performances, **Sandy Duncan** in The Boy Friend, **Bonnie Franklin** in Applause, **Lewis J. Stadlen** in Minnie's Boys, **Brian Bedford** in Private Lives, **Frank Grimes** and **Niall Toibin** in Borstal Boy.

ANNUAL VARIETY POLL OF LONDON CRITICS—Bests of the 1968-69 season. New British play, **Hotel in Amsterdam**. New British musical, **Close the Coalhouse Door**. New foreign play, **The Price**. New foreign musical, **Hair**. Male lead performance, straight play, **John Gielgud** in 40 Years On. Female lead performance, straight play, **Joan Plowright** in The Advertisement. Male lead performance, musical, **Edward Woodward** in Two Cities. Female lead performance, musical, **Polly James** in Anne of Green Gables. Male supporting performance, straight play, **Harold Gary** and **Albert Salmi** (tie) in The Price. Female supporting performance, straight play, **Elizabeth Spriggs** in A Delicate Balance. Male supporting performance, musical, **Hiram Sherman** in Anne of Green Gables. Female supporting performance, musical, **Barbara Hamilton** in Anne of Green Gables. Promising new actor, no choice. Promising new actress, **Angela Pleasence** in The Ha-Ha and The Spoils. Decor, **Carl Toms** for Love's Labours Lost. Director, **Patrick Garland** for 40 Years On and Brief Lives. Promising playwright, **Peter Barnes** for The Ruling Class.

STRAW HAT AWARDS (for excellence in American summer theater, sponsored by the Council of Stock Theaters). Best new play, **Butterflies Are Free** by Leonard Gershe. Best starring performance by an actress, **Betsy Palmer** as Miss Brodie in The Prime of Miss Jean Brodie. Best starring performance by an actor, **Barry Nelson** as the dentist in Cactus Flower. Most promising new acting talent, **Susan Bracken** in You Know I Can't Hear You When the Water's Running. Achievement award (for a career which began in summer stock), **Bette Davis**.

THEATER LaSALLE AWARD (for distinguished service to the American theater outside New York City). **Peggy Wood**, for her work with The American National Theater and Academy.

THE DRAMA DESK AWARDS

The Drama Desk Awards are voted by the editors, critics and reporters who are members of Drama Desk, a New York organization of theater journalists. Selections are made from a long list of nominees. Voters are asked to check only those candidates whose work they actually saw, and awards are won on the basis, not of number of votes alone, but of percentage of votes by those who saw the show. Recipients of the Drama Desk Awards for 1969-70 were as follows, in alphabetical order in each category:

OUTSTANDING PERFORMANCES. Lauren Bacall in *Applause*, Brian Bedford in *Private Lives*, Zoe Caldwell in *Colette* (highest percentage of any nominee, 82 per cent), Ryszard Cieslak in *The Constant Prince*, Colleen Dewhurst in *Hello and Goodbye*, Sandy Duncan in *The Boy Friend*, Stephen Elliott in *A Whistle in the Dark*, Frank Grimes in *Borstal Boy*, Tammy Grimes in *Private Lives*, Stacy Keach in *Indians* and *Peer Gynt*, Ron Leibman in *Transfers* and *Room Service*, Cleavon Little in *Purlie* and *The Ofay Watcher*, Ethel Merman in *Hello, Dolly!*, Melba Moore in *Purlie*, Austin Pendleton in *The Last Sweet Days of Isaac*, Lewis J. Stadlen in *Minnie's Boys*, James Stewart in *Harvey*, Sada Thompson in *The Effect of Gamma Rays on Man-in-the-Moon Marigolds*, Niall Toibin in *Borstal Boy*, Christopher Walken in *Lemon Sky*, Fritz Weaver in *Child's Play*.

OUTSTANDING DIRECTOR. Alan Arkin for *The White House Murder Case*, Ron Field for *Applause*, Jerzy Groowski for *The Constant Prince*, *The Acropolis* and *Apocalypsis Cum Figuris*, Joseph Hardy for *Child's Play*, Hal Prince for *Company* (highest percentage of any nominee, 60 per cent).

OUTSTANDING SCENE DESIGN. Boris Aronson for *Company* (highest percentage of any nominee, 77 per cent), Jo Mielziner for *Child's Play*, Fred Voelpel for *The Memory Bank*.

OUTSTANDING COSTUME DESIGN. Theoni V. Aldredge for *Peer Gynt*, *Electra* and *Colette*, Willa Kim for *Promenade* and *Operation Sidewinder*, Freddy Wittop for *A Patriot for Me* (highest percentage of any nominee, 52.7 per cent).

OUTSTANDING CHOREOGRAPHER. Ron Field for *Applause* (67.5 per cent).

OUTSTANDING COMPOSER. Stephen Sondheim for *Company* (74.1 per cent), Kurt Weill for *Mahagonny*.

OUTSTANDING LYRICIST. Stephen Sondheim for *Company* (80 per cent), Bertolt Brecht for *Mahagonny*.

OUTSTANDING BOOK WRITER FOR A MUSICAL. George Furth for *Company* (55 per cent).

MOST PROMISING PLAYWRIGHTS. Stanley Eveling for *Dear Janet Rosenberg, Dear Mr. Kooning*, Susan Yankowitz for *Terminal*, Paul Zindel for *The Effect of Gamma Rays on Man-in-the-Moon Marigolds* (86.9 per cent).

MOST PROMISING MUSICAL WRITERS. C.C. Courtney and Peter Link for *Salvation*, Nancy Ford and Gretchen Cryer for *The Last Sweet Days of Isaac*.

THE TONY AWARDS

The Antoinette Perry (Tony) Awards are voted by members of The League of New York Theaters, by the governing bodies of the Dramatists Guild, Actors Equity, the Society of Stage Choreographers and the United Scenic Artists, and by members of the first and second night press lists, from a list of three or four nominees in each category. Nominations are made by a committee serving by invitation of The League of New York Theaters, which is in charge of the Tony Awards procedure. The 1969-70 nominating committee was composed of Hobe Morrison, Martha Deane, Brendan Gill, Marilyn Stasio, Leo Mishkin and Al Hirschfeld. 453 ballots were sent out for voting on the following list of nominees (winners are listed in **bold face type**):

BEST PLAY. *Borstal Boy* adapted by Frank McMahon from Brendan Behan's autobiography, produced by Michael McAloney and Burton C. Kaiser in association with the Abbey Theater of Dublin; *Child's Play* by Robert Marasco, produced by David Merrick; *Indians* by Arthur Kopit, produced by Lyn Austin, Oliver Smith, Joel Schenker and Roger L. Stevens; *Last of the Red Hot Lovers* by Neil Simon, produced by Saint-Subber.

BEST MUSICAL. *Applause* based on the film *All About Eve* and the original story by Mary Orr, book by Betty Comden and Adolph Green, music by Charles Strouse, lyrics by Lee Adams, produced by Joseph Kipness and Lawrence Kasha in association with Nederlander Productions and George M. Steinbrenner III; *Coco* with book and lyrics by Alan Jay Lerner, music by Andre Previn, produced by Frederick Brisson; *Purlie* based on the play *Purlie Victorious* by Ossie Davis, book by Ossie Davis, Philip Rose and Peter Udell, music by Gary Geld, lyrics by Peter Udell, produced by Philip Rose.

ACTOR—Dramatic star. James Coco in *Last of the Red Hot Lovers*, Frank Grimes in *Borstal Boy*, Stacy Keach in *Indians*, **Fritz Weaver** in *Child's Play*.

ACTRESS—Dramatic Star. Geraldine Brooks in *Brightower*, **Tammy Grimes** in *Private Lives*, Helen Hayes in *Harvey*.

ACTOR—Musical star. Len Cariou in *Applause*, **Cleavon Little** in *Purlie*, Robert Weede in *Cry for Us All*.

ACTRESS—Musical star. **Lauren Bacall** in *Applause*, Katharine Hepburn in *Coco*, Dilys Watling in *Georgy*.

ACTOR—Dramatic featured or supporting. Joseph Bova in *The Chinese and Dr. Fish*, **Ken Howard** in *Child's Play*, Dennis King in *A Patriot for Me*.

ACTRESS—Dramatic featured or supporting. **Blythe Danner** and Eileen Heckart in *Butterflies Are Free*, Alice Drummond in *The Chinese and Dr. Fish*, Linda Lavin in *Last of the Red Hot Lovers*.

ACTOR—Musical featured or supporting. **Rene Auberjonois** in *Coco*, Brandon Maggart in *Applause*, George Rose in *Coco*.

ACTRESS—Musical featured or supporting. Bonnie Franklin and Penny Fuller in *Applause*,

Melissa Hart in *Georgy*, **Melba Moore** in *Purlie*.

DIRECTOR—Play. **Joseph Hardy** for *Child's Play*, Milton Katselas for *Butterflies Are Free*, Tomas MacAnna for *Borstal Boy*, Robert Moore for *Last of the Red Hot Lovers*.

DIRECTOR—Musical. Michael Benthall for *Coco*, **Ron Field** for *Applause*, Philip Rose for Purlie.

SCENE DESIGNER. Howard Bay for *Cry for Us All*, Ming Cho Lee for *Billy*, **Jo Mielziner** for *Child's Play*, Robert Randolph for *Applause*.

COSTUME DESIGNER. Ray Aghayan for *Applause*, **Cecil Beaton** for *Coco*, W. Robert Lavine for *Jimmy*, Freddy Wittop for *A Patriot for Me*.

LIGHTING DESIGNER. **Jo Mielziner** for *Child's Play*, Tharon Musser for *Applause*, Thomas Skelton for *Indians*.

CHOREOGRAPHER. Mischael Bennett for *Coco*, Grover Dale for *Billy*, **Ron Field** for *Applause*, Louis Johnson for *Purlie*.

SPECIAL AWARDS. **Alfred Lunt, Lynn Fontanne, Noel Coward, Joseph Papp.**

VARIETY'S POLL OF NEW YORK DRAMA CRITICS
1968-69 BROADWAY SEASON

Each year, representative New York drama critics are polled by *Variety* to learn their choices for Broadway's bests other than best play or musical. Results of the balloting in the 1968-69 season were published in midsummer 1969, much too late to be included in the 1968-69 *Best Plays* volume, but for the record we list them here. Nineteen critics participated: Clive Barnes, John Chapman, Harold Clurman, Ethel Colby, Richard Cooke, Jack Gaver, William Glover, David Goldman, Martin Gottfried, Leonard Harris, Henry Hewes, Ted Kalem, Walter Kerr, Alvin Klein, Sandy Lesberg, Edwin Newman, John Simon, Marilyn Stasio, Peggy Stockton. Names of those cited in the various categories appear below, together with the number of critics' votes received. Winners in the various categories are listed in **bold face type.**

MALE LEAD—Straight play. **James Earl Jones** in *The Great White Hope* (14), Alec McCowen in *Hadrian VII* (3), Donald Pleasence in *The Man in the Glass Booth* (1), Nicol Williamson in *Hamlet* (1).

FEMALE LEAD—Straight play. **Jane Alexander** in *The Great Whtie Hope* (10), Julie Harris in *Forty Carats* (3), Linda Lavin in *Cop-Out* (2), Christine Pickles in *The Misanthrope* (1), No Choice (3).

MALE LEAD—Musical. **Jerry Orbach** in *Promises, Promises* (9), Jack Cassidy in *Maggie Flynn* (4), William Daniels in *1776* (4), Herschel Bernardi in *Zorbá* (1), Jay Garner in *Red, White and Maddox* (1).

FEMALE LEAD—Musical. **Maria Karnilova** in *Zorbá* (6), **Angela Lansbury** in *Dear World* (6), Dorothy Loudon in *The Fig Leaves Are Falling* (4), Jill O'Hara in *Promises, Promises* (1), No Choice (2).

ACTOR—Supporting role. **Al Pacino** in *Does a Tiger Wear a Necktie?* (8), Ron Leibman in *We Bombed in New Haven* (2), Herbert Berghof in *In the Matter of J. Robert Oppenheimer* (1), Philip Bosco in *King Lear* (1), Howard Da Silva in *1776* (1), A. Larry Haines in *Promises, Promises* (1), Ken Howard in *1776* (1), John McGiver in *The Front Page* (1), Marco St. John in *Forty Carats* (1), Charles White in *The Front Page* (1), No Choice (1).

ACTRESS—Supporting role. **Marian Mercer** in *Promises, Promises* (4), Sandy Duncan in *Canterbury Tales* (3), Jane Alexander in *The Great White Hope* (2), Lauren Jones in *Does a Tiger Wear a Necktie?* (2), Blythe Danner in *The Miser* (1), Karen Grassle in *The Gingham Dog* (1), Maria Karnilova in *Zorbá* (1), Audra K. Lindley in *Fire* (1), Lorraine Serabian in *Zorbá* (1), Brenda Vaccaro in *The Goodbye People* (1), Marlene Warfield in *The Great White Hope* (1), No Choice (1).

MOST PROMISING NEW BROADWAY ACTOR. **Al Pacino** in *Does a Tiger Wear a Necktie?* (6½), Rene Auberjonois in *Fire* (2), Keith Charles in *Celebration* (2), William Devane in *The Watering Place* (1), Richard Dreyfuss in *But Seriously* (1), Ken Howard in *1776* (1), Ron Leibman in *We Bombed in New Haven* (1), Robert Salvio in *Billy* (1), Dustin Hoffman in *Jimmy Shine* (½), No Choice (3).

MOST PROMISING NEW BROADWAY ACTRESS. **Lauren Jones** in *Does a Tiger Wear a Necktie?* (4), Jane Alexander in *The Great White Hope* (3), Francesca Annis in *Hamlet* (2), Sandy Duncan in *Canterbury Tales* (2), Betty Buckley in *1776* (1), Blythe Danner in *The Miser* (1), Fionnuala Flan-

agan in *Lovers* (1), Marian Mercer in *Promises, Promises* (1), Ann Miller in *Mame* (1), No Choice (3).

BEST DIRECTOR. **Edwin Sherin** for *The Great White Hope* (11), Gordon Davidson for *In the Matter of J. Robert Oppenheimer* (1), Peter Hunt for *1776* (1), Harold J. Kennedy for *The Front Page* (1), Robert Moore for *Promises, Promises* (1), Harold Pinter for *The Man in the Glass Booth* (1) Harold Prince for *Zorbá* (1), Michael A. Schultz for *Does a Tiger Wear a Necktie?* (1), No Choice (1).

BEST SET DESIGNER. **Ming Cho Lee** for *Billy* (5), Boris Aronson for *Zorbá* (4), Derek Cousins for *Canterbury Tales* (2), Oliver Smith for *Dear World* and *Come Summer* (2), Ed Wittstein for *Celebration* and *The Man in the Glass Booth* (2), Will Steven Armstrong for *Forty Carats* (1), Jo Mielziner for *1776* (1), No Choice (2).

BEST COSTUME DESIGNER. **Patricia Zipprodt** for *1776* (5), Patricia Zipprodt for *Zorbá* (3), Tanya Moiseiwitsch for *The House of Atreus* (3), Ed Wittstein for *Celebration* (2), Robert Fletcher for *Hadrian VII* (1), Loudon Sainthill for *Canterbury Tales* (1), Freddy Wittop for *Dear World* (1), No Choice (3).

BEST COMPOSER. **Burt Bacharach** for *Promises, Promises* (7), Sherman Edwards for *1776* (3), John Kander for *Zorbá* (1), Harvey Schmidt for *Celebration* (1), John Sebastian for *Jimmy Shine* (1), No Choice (4), Invalid Votes (2).

BEST LYRICIST. **Hal David** for *Promises, Promises* (5), Sherman Edwards for *1776* (4), Fred Ebb for *Zorbá* (2), Tom Jones for *Celebration* (1), John Sebastian for *Jimmy Shine* (1), No Choice (4), Invalid Votes (2).

MOST PROMISING PLAYWRIGHT. **John Guare** for *Cop-Out* (8), Howard Sackler for *The Great White Hope* (6), Israel Horovitz for *Morning* (1), Terrence McNally for *Noon* (1), Don Petersen for *Does a Tiger Wear a Necktie?* (1), Lanford Wilson for *The Gingham Dog* (1), No Choice (1).

1969-70 BROADWAY SEASON

Twenty critics participated in *Variety's* 1969-70 poll of New York drama critics: Clive Barnes, Harold Clurman, Ethel Colby, Jack Gaver, William Glover, Martin Gottfried, Leonard Harris, Henry Hewes, Ted Kalem, Walter Kerr, Alvin Klein, Stuart Klein, John Lahr, Leo Mishkin, Norman Nadel, Edwin Newman, John O'Connor, George Oppenheimer, Marilyn Stasio, Peggy Stockton. Names of those cited in the various categories appear below, together with the number of critics' votes received. Winners in the various categories are listed in **bold face type.**

MALE LEAD—Straight play. **Fritz Weaver** in *Child's Play* (7), Stacy Keach in *Indians* (4), Niall Toibin in *Borstal Boy* (2), Brian Bedford in *Private Lives* (1), Keir Dullea in *Butterflies Are Free* (1), Frank Grimes in *Borstal Boy* (1), Pat Hingle in *Child's Play* (1), Lou Jacobi in *Norman, Is That You?* (1), Paul Shenar in *Three Sisters* (1), James Stewart in *Harvey* (1).

FEMALE LEAD—Straight play. **Tammy Grimes** in *Private Lives*. (8½), Helen Hayes in *Harvey* (3), Geraldine Brooks in *Brightower* (1), Joan Hackett in *Park* (1), Eileen Heckart in *Butterflies Are Free* (1), Linda Lavin (1) and Marcia Rodd (1) in *Last of the Red Hot Lovers*, Jessica Tandy in *Camino Real* (1), Blythe Danner in *Butterflies Are Free* (½), No Choice (2).

MALE LEAD—Musical. **Cleavon Little** in *Purlie* (13). Robert Shaw in *Gantry* (2), Len Cariou in *Applause* (1), John Castle in *Georgy* (1), Robert Weede in *Cry for Us All* (1), No Choice (2).

FEMALE LEAD—Musical. **Lauren Bacall** in *Applause* (13), Melba Moore in *Purlie* (5), Katharine Hepburn in *Coco* (1), No Choice (1).

ACTOR—Supporting role. **Ken Howard** in *Child's Play* (4), Lewis J. Stadlen in *Minnie's Boys* (3), Len Cariou in *Applause* (2), Dennis King in *A Patriot for Me* (2), Rene Auberjonois in *Coco* (1), Joseph Bova in *The Chinese and Dr. Fish* (1), Tom Brannum in *Room Service* (1), David Burns in *Sheep on the Runway* (1), Frank Grimes in *Borstal Boy* (1), Terry Kiser in *Paris Is Out!* (1), Paul Shenar in *Three Sisters* (1), Manu Tupou (1) and Sam Waterston (1) in *Indians*.

ACTRESS—Supporting role. **Melba Moore** in *Purlie* (6), Novella Nelson in *Purlie* (3), Sandy Duncan in *The Boy Friend* (2), Alice Drummond in *The Chinese and Dr. Fish* (2), Bonnie Franklin in *Applause* (2), Linda Lavin in *Last of the Red Hot Lovers* (2), Elaine Stritch in *Company* (2), Susan Browning in *Company* (1).

MOST PROMISING NEW BROADWAY ACTOR. **Frank Grimes** in *Borstal Boy* (5), Kristoffer Tabori in *The Penny Wars* (4), Lewis J. Stadlen in *Minnie's Boys* (3), Ken

Howard in *Child's Play* (2), William Cain in *Wilson in the Promise Land* (1), Ron O'Neal in *No Place To Be Somebody* (1), Manu Tupou in *Indians* (1), No Choice (3).

MOST PROMISING NEW BROADWAY ACTRESS. **Catherine Bacon** in *The Penny Wars* (3), **Blythe Danner** in *Butterflies Are Free* (3), Marcia Jean Kurtz in *The Chinese and Dr. Fish* (2), Melba Moore in *Purlie* (2), Pamela Myers in *Company* (2), Susan Browning in *Company* (1), Martha Galphin in *Brightower* (1), Joan Hackett in *Park* (1), No Choice (5).

BEST DIRECTOR. **Harold Prince** for *Company* (7), Joseph Hardy for *Child's Play* (6), Ron Field for *Applause* (2), Tomas Mac-Anna for *Borstal Boy* (2), Stephen Porter for *Private Lives* (2), William Ball for *Three Sisters* (1).

BEST SET DESIGNER. **Boris Aronson** for *Company* (15), Jo Mielziner for *Child's Play* (4), Douglas Schmidt for *The Time of Your Life* (1).

BEST COSTUME DESIGNER. **Cecil Beaton** for *Coco* (6), Freddy Wittop for *A Patriot for Me* (5), Marjorie Slaiman for *Indians* (2), Ray Aghayan for *Applause* (1), Matias for *Rabelais* (1), No Choice (5).

BEST COMPOSER. **Stephen Sondheim** for *Company* (14), Gary Geld for *Purlie* (1), Richard Peaslee for *Indians* (1), Charles Strouse for *Applause* (1), No Choice (3).

BEST LYRICIST. **Stephen Sondheim** for *Company* (19), Betty Comden and Adolph Green for *Applause* (1).

MOST PROMISING PLAYWRIGHT. **Robert Marasco** for *Child's Play* (10), George Furth for *Company* (2), Charles Gordone for *No Place To Be Somebody* (2), Art Buchwald for *Sheep on the Runway* (1), Leonard Gershe for *Butterflies Are Free* (1) Sam Shepard for *Operation Sidewinder* (1), No Choice (3).

OUTSTANDING BROADWAY PRODUCER. **Harold Prince** (13), David Merrick (3), American National Theater and Academy (ANTA) (1), No Choice (3).

1969-70 PUBLICATION
OF RECENTLY-PRODUCED PLAYS

Anna-Luse and Other Plays. David Mowat. Calder & Boyars.
Che! Lennox Raphael. Contact
Close the Coalhouse Door. Alan Plater. Methuen.
Cop Out, Muzeeka and *Home Fires* by John Guare. Grove.
Crystal and Fox and *The Mundy Scheme* by Brian Friel. Farrar, Straus and Giroux.
Dionysus in 69. Richard Schechner (editor). Farrar, Straus and Giroux.
Forty Carats. Jay Allen. Random House.
Forty Years On. Alan Bennett. Faber and Faber.
Four Black Revolutionary Plays: *Experimental Death Unit 1, A Black Mass, Great Goodness Of Life, Madheart.* LeRoi Jones. Bobbs-Merrill.
The Gingham Dog. Lanford Wilson. Hill and Wang.
Hair. Gerome Ragni and James Rado. Pocket Books.
Honour and Offer. Henry Livings. Methuen.
The Hunter. Murray Mednick. Bobbs-Merrill.
Indians. Arthur Kopit. Hill and Wang.
Landscape and *Silence.* Harold Pinter. Methuen.
The Marowitz Hamlet and *The Tragical History of Dr. Faustus.* Charles Marowitz (adaptor). Penguin.
Morning, Noon and Night. Israel Horovitz, Terrence McNally and Leonard Melfi. Random House.
Naked Hamlet. Joseph Papp and Ted Cornell (adaptors). Macmillan.
No Place To Be Somebody. Charles Gordone. Bobbs-Merrill.
Oh! Calcutta! Kenneth Tynan and others. Grove.
Play It Again, Sam. Woody Allen. Random House.
Promises, Promises. Neil Simon. Random House.
The Real Inspector Hound. Tom Stoppard. Grove.
The Ruling Class. Peter Barnes. Heinemann.
A Scent of Flowers. James Saunders. Heinemann.
1776. Peter Stone. Viking.
Stop, You're Killing Me. James Leo Herlihy. Simon and Schuster.
Sweet Eros, Next and Other Plays. Terrence McNally. Random House.
To Be Young, Gifted and Black. Lorraine Hansberry. Prentice Hall.
Three Short Plays: *The Swamp Dwellers, The Trials of Brother Jero* and *The Strong Breed.* Wole Soyinka. Oxford.
The Travails of Sancho Panza. James Saunders (adaptor). Heinemann.
Two Plays: *Song of the Lusitanian Bogey* and *Discourse on Vietnam.* Peter Weiss. Atheneum.
The Watering Place. Lyle Kessler. Random House.
What the Butler Saw. Joe Orton. Methuen.
The White House Murder Case. Jules Feiffer. Grove.
The Wind in the Branches of the Sassafras (Rockefeller and the Red Indians). Rene de Obaldia. Methuen.
Who's Happy Now? Oliver Hailey. Random House.
The Year Boston Won the Pennant. John Ford Noonan. Grove.
Your Own Thing. Donald Driver. Dell.
Zorbá. Joseph Stein. Random House.

A SELECTED LIST OF OTHER PLAYS PUBLISHED IN 1969-70

Best Short Plays of 1969. Stanley Richards, editor. Chilton.
Christopher Fry Plays: *A Phoenix Too Frequent; Thor, With Angels;* and *The Lady's Not for Burning.* Oxford.
The Collected Plays of John Whiting. Two volumes. Theater Arts.
The Comedies of Terence: *The Woman of Andros; The Brothers; The Self-Tormentor; Phormio; The Mother-in-Law; The Eunuch.* Translated by Frank O. Copley. Bobbs-Merrill.

Dingo. Charles Wood. Grove.
The Disorderly Women. John Bowen. Methuen.
The Escape. William Wells Brown. Prologue Press.
50 Best Plays of the American Theater. Clive Barnes. Four volumes. Crown.
Five Plays: *In the Wine Time; Goin' a Buffalo; A Son, Come Home; The Electronic Nigger; Clara's Ole Man.* Ed Bullins. Bobbs-Merrill.
Five Plays of Alexander Ostrovsky: *It's a Family Affair; The Poor Bride; The Storm; The Scoundrel; The Forest.* Translated by Eugene K. Bristow. Pegasus.
Flight. Mikhail Bulgakov. Grove.
Four Plays: *The Chalk Garden; The Last Joke; The Chinese Prime Minister* and *Call Me Jack.* Enid Bagnold. Heinemann.
The Heretic. Morris L. West. Morrow.
The Investigation and *Hot Buttered Roll.* Rosalyn Drexler. Methuen.
Kaspar and Other Plays. Peter Handke. Farrar Straus.
A Limb of Snow and *The Meeting.* Anna Marie Barlow. Dramatists Play Service.
The Little Mrs. Poster Show. Henry Livings. Methuen.
Modern Drama From Communist China: *Snow in Midsummer, Dragon Beard Ditch, The Women's Representative, Magic Aster, The Red Lantern, The Passer-By, The White-Haired Girl, Yesterday, Letters From the South.* Walter J. and Ruth I. Meserve (editors). New York University Press.
Modern Short Comedies From Broadway and London: *Black Comedy* by Peter Shaffer; *Losers* by Brian Friel; *The Shock of Recognition* by Robert Anderson; *The Sponge Room* by Keith Waterhouse and Willis Hall; *George's Room* by Alun Owen; *Bea, Frank, Richie and Joan* by Renee Taylor and Joseph Bologna; *Visitor From Mamaroneck* by Neil Simon; *Trevor* by John Bowen; *Shadows of the Evening* by Noel Coward; *The Diary of Adam and Eve* by Sheldon Harnick and Jerry Bock; *Noon* by Terrence McNally; *Madly in Love* by Paul Ableman. Stanley Richards, Editor. Random House.
New Black Playwrights: *Happy Ending* by Douglas Turner Ward; *Day of Absence* by Douglas Turner Ward; *A Rat's Mass* by Adrienne Kennedy; *Family Meeting* by William Wellington Mackey; *Tabernacle* by Paul Carter Harrison; *Goin'a Buffalo* by Ed Bullins. Edited by William Couch. Louisiana State University Press.
Ornifle. Jean Anouilh. Hill and Wang.
A Season in the Congo. Aime Cesaire. Grove.
Tambourines to Glory. Langston Hughes. Hill and Wang.
Three New Dramatic Works and 19 Other Short Plays. William Saroyan. Phaedra.
Three Plays: *Christopher Columbus, Melissa* and *Kouros.* Nikos Kazantzakis. Simon and Schuster.
Three Plays: *Don't Destroy Me; Yes and After; The World's Baby.* Michael Hastings. W. H. Allen.
Three Plays: *The Widowing of Mrs. Holroyd; A Collier's Friday Night; The Daughter-in-Law.* D.H. Lawrence. Penguin.
Time and the Conways and Other Plays. J. B. Priestley. Penguin.
When We Are Married and Other Plays. J. B. Priestley. Penguin.
Woyzeck. Georg Buchner. New Translation by Henry J. Schmidt. Avon.
A Yard of Sun. Christopher Fry. Oxford.

MUSICAL AND DRAMATIC RECORDINGS OF NEW YORK SHOWS

Title and publishing company are listed below. Each record is an original New York cast album unless otherwise indicated.

Applause. ABC.
The Boy Friend (revival). Decca.
The Boys in the Band. A & M.
Canterbury Tales. Capitol.

Celebration. Capitol.
Coco. Paramount.
Company. Columbia.
Dames at Sea. Columbia.
Fiddler on the Roof (original London cast). CBS.
Hello, Dolly! (movie sound track). RCA Victor.
Hello, Dolly! (original Israeli cast). CBS International.
In the Matter of J. Robert Oppenheimer. Caedmon.
Jimmy. RCA Victor.
Joy. RCA Victor.
The King and I (original Israeli cast). CBS International.
The Last Sweet Days of Isaac. RCA Victor.
Man of La Mancha (original Israeli cast). CBS International.
Max Morath at the Turn of the Century. RCA Victor.
Minnie's Boys. RCA Victor.
The Miser (Lincoln Center Repertory revival). Caedmon.
Oh! Calcutta! United Artists.
Oliver (original Israeli cast). CBS International.
Paint Your Wagon (movie sound track). Paramount.
Peace. Metromedia.
Promenade. RCA Victor.
Purlie. Ampex.
Salvation. Capitol.
Sweet Charity (original London cast). CBS.
Zorbá. Capitol.

THE BEST PLAYS, 1894-1969

Listed in alphabetical order below are all those works selected as Best Plays in previous volumes in the *Best Plays* series. Opposite each title is given the volume in which the play appears, its opening date and its total number of performances. Those plays marked with an asterisk (*) were still playing on June 1, 1970 and their number of performances was figured through May 31, 1970. Adaptors and translators are indicated by (ad) and (tr), and the symbols (b), (m) and (1) stand for the author of the book, music and lyrics in the case of musicals.

PLAY	VOLUME	OPENED	PERFS.
ABE LINCOLN IN ILLINOIS—Robert E. Sherwood	38-39	Oct. 15, 1938	472
ABRAHAM LINCOLN—John Drinkwater	19-20	Dec. 15, 1919	193
ACCENT ON YOUTH—Samson Raphaelson	34-35	Dec. 25, 1934	229
ADAM AND EVA—Guy Bolton, George Middleton	19-20	Sept. 13, 1919	312
*ADAPTATION—Elaine May; and NEXT—Terrence McNally	68-69	Feb. 10, 1969	546
AFFAIRS OF STATE—Louis Verneuil	50-51	Sept. 25, 1950	610
AFTER THE FALL—Arthur Miller	63-64	Jan. 23, 1964	208
AFTER THE RAIN—John Bowen	67-68	Oct. 9, 1967	64
AH, WILDERNESS!—Eugene O'Neill	33-34	Oct. 2, 1933	289
ALIEN CORN—Sidney Howard	32-33	Feb. 20, 1933	98
ALISON'S HOUSE—Susan Glaspell	30-31	Dec. 1, 1930	41
ALL MY SONS—Arthur Miller	46-47	Jan. 29, 1947	328
ALL THE WAY HOME—Tad Mosel, based on James Agee's novel *A Death in the Family*	60-61	Nov. 30, 1960	333
ALLEGRO—(b, 1) Oscar Hammerstein II, (m) Richard Rodgers	47-48	Oct. 10, 1947	315
AMBUSH—Arthur Richman	21-22	Oct. 10, 1921	98
AMERICA HURRAH—Jean-Claude van Itallie	66-67	Nov. 6, 1966	634
AMERICAN WAY, THE—George S. Kaufman, Moss Hart	38-39	Jan. 21, 1939	164
AMPHITRYON 38—Jean Giraudoux, (ad) S. N. Behrman	37-38	Nov. 1, 1937	153
ANDERSONVILLE TRIAL, THE—Saul Levitt	59-60	Dec. 29, 1959	179

NECROLOGY

MAY 1969—JUNE 1970

PERFORMERS

Adams, Frances Sale (77)—August 6, 1969
Alexander, Ben (58)—July 5, 1969
Alvarez, Julio (63)—September 30, 1969
Ames, Harry (76)—August 11, 1969
Anderson, James—September 14, 1969
Andrews, Stanley (77)—June 23, 1969
Bacon, Max (65)—December 3, 1969
Bancroft, Charles (58)—May 17, 1969
Bandel, Emma Frederick (3)—July 30, 1969
Barrat, Robert (78)—January 7, 1970
Barrett, Jane—July 20, 1969
Baum, Mrs. H. William (88)—March 9, 1970
Begley, Ed (69)—April 29, 1970
Belgado, Mario (63)—June 24, 1969
Bender, Russell (59)—August 16, 1969
Bennett, Enid (71)—May 14, 1969
Bernes, Mark (57)—August 18, 1969
Betton, George—June 4, 1969
Blanchard, Mari—May 10, 1970
Bodel, Burman (58)—July 17, 1969
Bolger, Robert (32)—August 23, 1969
Boydston, Hazel Allen—August 12, 1969
    Sister of Gracie Allen
Bozyk, Max (71)—April 5, 1970
Bradley, Lovyss (63)—June 21, 1969
Briant, August W. (82)—February 27, 1970
Burke, Billie (84)—May 14, 1970
Byles, Bobby (38)—August 26, 1969
Campbell, Violet (77)—January, 1970
Carman, Allan (72)—October 11, 1969
Carr, Philip (38)—September 7, 1969
Carron, George (40)—April 23, 1970
Ciannelli, Eduardo (80)—October 8, 1969
Clark, Sylvia—March 31, 1970
Clunes, Alec (57)—March 13, 1970
Collyer, Bud (61)—September 8, 1969
Corelli, Kathryn (70)—April 24, 1970
Corrigan, Lloyd (69)—November 7, 1969
Crawford, Howard M. (55)—November 24, 1969
Cummings, Vicki (50)—November 30, 1969
Dalziel, May (68)—September 30, 1969
D'Arcy, Roy (75)—November 15, 1969
Dare, Ernest (87)—September 17, 1969
Davis, Mildred (68)—August 19, 1969
    Wife of Harold Lloyd
De Aubry, Diane (79)—May 23, 1969
de Castrejon, Blanca (53)—December 26, 1969

Delima, Margaret Linley (67)—May 24, 1969
Dixon, Harland (83)—June 27, 1969
Doble, Frances—December, 1969
Dot, Doreen (70)—July, 1969
Dowling, Constance (49)—October 28, 1969
Downe, Alan S. (57)—January 20, 1970
Eastman, Joan (32)—August 24, 1969
Edwards, James (58)—January 4, 1970
Ellis, Patricia (49)—March 26, 1970
Farebrother, Violet (81)—September 27, 1969
Feussner, Alfred (33)—August 25, 1969
Fletcher, Lawrence M. (70)—February 11, 1970
Fogarty, Jan (65)—September 8, 1969
Foran, Anna E. (77)—May 12, 1969
    Dancing team of Foran Sisters
Ford, Corey (67)—July 27, 1969
Ford, Edward H. (82)—January 27, 1970
Foster, Donald (80)—December 22, 1969
Foulger, Byron (70)—April 4, 1970
Fredericks, Charles (50)—May 14, 1970
Garland, Judy (47)—June 22, 1969
Gerstle, Frank (53)—February 23, 1970
Gillespie, Marie—August 24, 1969
Glynne, Howell (64)—November 24, 1969
Gorcey, Leo (54)—June 2, 1969
Graves, Elsie Elizabeth (78)—October, 1969
Gray, Duncan (76)—June 18, 1969
Gray, Edward Earl (71)—September 15, 1969
    "Monsewer" Eddie Gray
Gray, Elaine—August, 1969
Gray, Lawrence (71)—February 2, 1970
Griffiths, Doris (68)—April 11, 1970
Gurie, Sigrid (58)—August 14, 1969
Gwynne, Jack (74)—December 7, 1969
Hamilton, Karen Sue (23)—September 3, 1969
Hamilton, Roy (40)—July 20, 1969
Hanley, Jimmy (51)—January 13, 1970
Hanlon, William A.—September 8, 1969
Hare, Rene Vivian (72)—August 4, 1969
Harven, Jane (50)—September 12, 1969
Hayes, Paul (86)—July 30, 1969
Hayworth, Vinton (64)—May 21, 1970
Hazell, Hy (47)—May 10, 1970
Healy, Dan (90)—September 1, 1969
Hecht, Ted (61)—June 24, 1969
Henie, Sonja (57)—October 12, 1969
Hennecke, Clarence R. (74)—August 28, 1969
    Member of original Keystone Cops
Hindle, Winifred—December 18, 1969
Hoffman, Howard R. (76)—June 26, 1969

Hopper, William (55)—March 6, 1970
Horne, David (71)—March 15, 1970
Householder, Cyril (73)—October 1, 1969
Holliday, Marjorie (49)—June 16, 1969
Hull, Maryann (39)—April 20, 1970
Hunt, Martita (69)—June 13, 1969
Hunter, Jeffrey (42)—May 27, 1969
Huntington, Nathaniel (87)—April 10, 1970
Hutchinson, Leslie (69)—August 18, 1969
Ingram, Rex (73)—September 19, 1969
Irving, Frederick R. (75)—August, 1969
James, Skip (67)—October 3, 1969
Jenks, Si (93)—January 6, 1970
Karns, Roscoe (77)—February 6, 1970
Keane, Claire Whitney (79)—August 27, 1969
Keen, Malcolm (82)—January 30, 1970
Kelly, Dorothy H. (51)—November 28, 1969
Kendrick, Brian (40)—March 11, 1970
Kennedy, Joe (80)—December 13, 1969
King, Bob Brown (33)—May 12, 1970
Koerber, Hilde (63)—June 1, 1969
Kress, Gladys (67)—October 29, 1969
Lancaster, John (67)—January 11, 1970
Landreth, Gertrude Griffith (72)—November 25, 1969
Langley, Stuart (60)—April 2, 1970
La Rocque, Rod (70)—October 15, 1969
Lawton, Frank (64)—June 10, 1969
Lee, Gypsy Rose (56)—April 26, 1970
Le Fre, Albert (99)—March, 1970
Lewis, Martin (81)—April, 1970
Lewis, Ripple (45)—July 10, 1969
Lincoln, Alpheus (78)—May 22, 1970
Linden, Tommy—November 19, 1969
Little, James F. (62)—October 12, 1969
Lloyd, Mildred Davis (68)—August 18, 1969
Long, W. Bethell Jr. (53)—November 2, 1969
Lorne, Constable (55)—December 21, 1969
Louis, Anita (53)—April 25, 1970
Lynch, Brid (55)—October 27, 1969
McEntee, Mrs. Millicent Evison (93)—January 29, 1970
McGrail, Walter B. (81)—March 19, 1970
McNaughton, Gus (86)—December, 1969
Malcolm, John (63)—October 21, 1969
Mann, Erika (63)—August 27, 1969
    Daughter of Thomas Mann
March, Hal (49)—January 19, 1970
Marle, Arnold (82)—February 21, 1970
Marsh, Howard—August 7, 1969
Martin, Harry (67)—January 15, 1970
Mason, Richard (24)—April 30, 1970
Masters, Ruth (75)—September 22, 1969
Mears, Marion (71)—January 26, 1970
Membrives, Lola (86)—November, 1969
Millard, Harry W. (41)—September 2, 1969
Miller, Martin (70)—August 26, 1969
Milton, Betty Rea—September 9, 1969
Minner, Kathryn (77)—May 26, 1969
Mitchell, Ian Priestley (77)—September 19, 1969
Mitchell, James I. (78)—August 3, 1969

Morris, Johnny (83)—October 7, 1969
Morris, Mary (74)—January 16, 1970
Munshin, Jules (54)—February 19, 1970
Murray, Kathleen (41)—August 24, 1969
Nagel, Conrad (72)—February 24, 1970
Neill, Richard R. (94)—April 8, 1970
Netcher, Roszika (Rosie) Dolly (71)—
    February 1, 1970. Last of Dolly Sisters
Newburg, Frank (83)—November 11, 1969
Norman, Maurice (82)—November, 1969
O'Donnell, Cathy (45)—April 11, 1970
O'Hagan, Mrs. John D. (78)—December 27, 1969
O'Leary, Bryan (36)—May 16, 1970
Oliphant, Julie (60)—September 11, 1969
Oscar, Henry (78)—December 28, 1969
Osterman, Rolfe A. (78)—June 18, 1969
Ostroska, George (32)—December 8, 1969
Paulsen, Arno (69)—September 17, 1969
Payne, Leon (52)—September 11, 1969
Pepper, Barbara (57)—July 18, 1969
Perry, Charles—October 22, 1969
Portman, Eric (66)—December 7, 1969
Powers, Leona (73)—January 7, 1970
Price, Nancy (91)—March 31, 1970
Ramos, Carlos (62)—November 6, 1969
Robb, Lotus—September 28, 1969
Robbins, Richard (50)—October 23, 1969
Rognan, Lorraine (57)—August 22, 1969
Romer, Tomi (45)—July 21, 1969
Ross, Chris (24)—May 5, 1970
Roth, Albert A. (71)—November 24, 1969
Russell, David Forbes (77)—November 7, 1969
Ryan, Dick (72)—August 12, 1969
Sage, Edward (41)—December, 1969
Sidney, Mabel (85)—October 18, 1969
St. Clair, Lydia—January 1, 1970
St. Clair, Maurice (67)—May 9, 1970
Savile, Geoffrey (87)—October 7, 1969
Schweid, Mark (78)—December 2, 1969
Scott, Hal (73)—October 31, 1969
Scott, Leslie (48)—August 20, 1969
Seton, Bruce (60)—September 27, 1969
Shaw, Jack (88)—April 7, 1970
Shayne, Al (82)—June 20, 1969
Shields, Arthur (74)—April 27, 1970
Shriner, Herb (51)—April 24, 1970
Singleton, Catherine (65)—September 9, 1969
Sorokin, Rachel (84)—June 28, 1969
Steppat, Ilse (52)—December 22, 1969
Stevens, Inger (35)—April 30, 1970
Sudlow, Joan (78)—February 1, 1970
Sully, William—November 6, 1969
Sutherland, William A. (52)—October 20, 1969
Sutton, Paul (58)—January 31, 1970
Sverdlin, Lev (57)—August 31, 1969
Sylvie (88)—January, 1970
Talmadge, Natalie (70)—June 19, 1969
Tara, Sheila (81)—October 21, 1969
Tate, Sharon (26)—August 9, 1969

Taylor, Robert (57)—June 8, 1969
Teege, Joachim (44)—November 23, 1969
Thomas, Ruth (59)—March 23, 1970
Travers, Roland (88)—May 1, 1970
Van Eyck, Peter (56)—July 15, 1969
Vanne, Marda—April 27, 1970
Vasquez, Manuel (19)—April 25, 1970!
Vernon, Wally (64)—March 7, 1970
Vivian, George (85)—May 10, 1970
Voltaire, Jeanne (70)—March 13, 1970
Walburn, Raymond (81)—July 26, 1969
Waldron, Jack (76)—November 21, 1969
Warren, Suzanne Le Mesurier (75)—
    September 3, 1969
Watson, Fanny (84)—May 17, 1970
    Vaud. team Watson Sisters
Watt, Hannah—November, 1969
Wentworth, Clayton (62)—July 16, 1969
Western, George (74)—August 16, 1969
White, Ruth (55)—December 3, 1969
Whiteley, Leonora C. (93)—July 21, 1969
Widdecombe, Wallace (100)—July 12, 1969
    Oldest member of Equity
Wieman, Mathias (67)—December 3, 1969
Williams, Hugh (65)—December 7, 1969
Williams, Spence (76)—December 13, 1969
    Andy of TV "Amos 'n' Andy"
Wilson, Lillian Brown (83)—June 8, 1969
Wilson, Wayne (71)—January 4, 1970
Winchell, Mrs. Walter (64)—February 5,
    1970. Former June Magee
Wing, Dan (46)—June 14, 1969
Winrow, Samuel (89)—June 14, 1969

PLAYWRIGHTS

Adamov, Arthur (61)—March 16, 1970
Armstrong, Charlotte (64)—July 18, 1969
Arno, Owen G. (35)—July 24, 1969
Bardoly, Dr. Louis S. (75)—May 22, 1969
Besoyan, Rick (45)—March 13, 1970
Black, Jean Ferguson (68)—September 13,
    1969
Bodley, Ellen—November 20, 1969
Crommelynck, Fernand (84)—March, 1970
Dell, Floyd (82)—July 23, 1969
Endore, Guy (69)—February 12, 1970
Godfrey, Peter (70)—March 4, 1970
Hawkes, Kirby (67)—March 30, 1970
Inge, Benson (61)—April 23, 1970
Johnson, Hall (82)—April 30, 1970
Kaye, Benjamin (86)—March 25, 1970
Knittel, John (79)—April 26, 1970
Lytton, Bart (56)—June 29, 1969
Mandelstam, Abraham (86)—October 15,
    1969
Maschwitz, Eric (68)—October 27, 1969
O'Hara, John (65)—April 11, 1970
Panetta, George (59)—October 16, 1969
Reach, James (60)—March 5, 1970
Seff, Manuel (74)—September 22, 1969
Tackaberry, John (55)—June 24, 1969
Treadwell, Sophie (79)—February 20, 1970

Unger, Mrs. Stella (65)—February 15, 1970
Watkins, Maurine (68)—August 10, 1969

COMPOSERS AND LYRICISTS

Bestor, Don (80)—January, 1970
Brenders, Stan (65)—May 31, 1969
Burke, Kevin (25)—September 1, 1969
Durham, Richard (80)—September 1, 1969
Edwards, Tommy (47)—October 23, 1969
Fina, Jack—May 13, 1970
Flanagan, William, Jr. (46)—September 1,
    1969
Hargreaves, Anthony—July 5, 1969
Henderson, Thomas—August 9, 1969
Jason, Will (69)—February 10, 1970
Johnstone, Thomas (81)—January 1, 1970
Kosma, Joseph (63)—August 7, 1969
Lewis, Curtis R. (50)—May 22, 1969
Loeb, John Jacob (60)—March 2, 1970
Loesser, Frank (59)—July 26, 1969
Miller, Sonny (64)—September 13, 1969
Moore, Douglas (75)—July 25, 1969
Munro, Billy (76)—October 16, 1969
Newman, Alfred (68)—February 17, 1970
Reynolds, Alfred (85)—October 18, 1969
Rich, Max (72)—April 22, 1970
Shaw, Sidney (45)—May 29, 1969
Souris, Andre (70)—February 12, 1970
Stutz, Dick (60)—October 9, 1969
Vintner, Gilbert (60)—October 10, 1969
Woods, Harry M. (73)—January 13, 1970

PRODUCERS, DIRECTORS, CHOREOGRAPHERS

Alperson, Edward L. (73)—July 3, 1969
Andoga, Victor (91)—September 23, 1969
Arnold, Doris (61)—October 4, 1969
Blair, George (64)—April 20, 1970
Brown, Dennis (55)—November 29, 1969
Bryan, John (58)—June 10, 1969
Davis, Eugene C.—August 16, 1969
De Bear, Archie (81)—March 15, 1970
Deppe, Hans (71)—September 23, 1969
Drucker, Frances (69)—March 6, 1970
Edwards, Harry D. (82)—July 5, 1969
Farrell, Anthony Brady (69)—January 3,
    1970
Feldstein, Robert D. (42)—September 19,
    1969
Freedley, Vinton (77)—June 5, 1969
Harari, Ezra (76)—April 12, 1970
Kohlmar, Fred (64)—October 13, 1969
McCarey, Leo (71)—July 5, 1969
Meyer, Rudy (67)—October, 1969
O'Neil, Standish (75)—October 31, 1969
Parker, Joseph S. (57)—April 28, 1970
Sharp, Oliver (38)—August 14, 1969
Sinclair, Robert B. (65)—January 2, 1970
Summerton, Peter (40)—June 14, 1969
Thompson, Palmer (51)—December 15, 1969
Viehman, Theodore (81)—February 16, 1970

von Sternberg, Josef (75)—December 22, 1969
Ward, Richard H. (59)—January, 1970

CONDUCTOR

Bailey, Rector (57)—April 4, 1970

DESIGNERS

Abrahams, Joseph B. (84)—July 1, 1969
Armstrong, Will Steven (39)—August 12, 1969
Chaney, Stewart (59)—November 9, 1969
Gorno, Jimmy (65)—July 26, 1969
Lawler, Richard H., Sr. (67)—September 25, 1969
Sainthill, Loudon (50)—June 9, 1969

CRITICS

Bolton, Whitney (69)—November 4, 1969
Burslem, Ashworth (55)—September 20, 1969
Cohen, Harold (63)—November 7, 1969
Coton, A. V. (63)—July 7, 1969
Crawford, Charles (44)—May 31, 1969
Davis, John B. (76)—April 15, 1970
Disher, Maurice Wilson (76)—November 24, 1969
Ehrenreich, Herman (69)—March 31, 1970
Griffith, Richard (57)—October 17, 1969
Hicklin, Ralph (48)—March 31, 1970
Houk, Norman C. (73)—May 5, 1970
Irvin, Bill (64)—March 21, 1970
Jarman, Peter—November, 1969
Krutch, Joseph Wood (76)—May 22, 1970
McKenzie, Joseph (62)—September, 1969
Mitchell, Grover E. (60)—May 18, 1969
Potter, Stephen (69)—December 2, 1969
Reed, Peter Hugh (77)—September 25, 1969
Sweetland, Reynolds (79)—March 9, 1970

MUSICIANS

Ali, Ismail (46)—January 5, 1970
Ayres, Mitchell (58)—September 5, 1969
Barnes, Emile (78)—March 5, 1970
Barocco, Dominick J. (76)—January 29, 1970
Brown, Allen (55)—August 19, 1969
Chase, Tommy (62)—September 2, 1969
Connell, James W. (56)—May 16, 1969
Cooley, Spade (59)—November 23, 1969
Foster, George (Pops) (77)—October 30, 1969
Golden, Hugh (60)—May 18, 1969
Gordon, Jack—August 6, 1969
Heath, Ted (69)—November 18, 1969
Henderson, Robert (59)—December 9, 1969
Hodges, Johnny (63)—May 11, 1970
Jacob, William (40)—May 24, 1969
Jackson, Clifton Luther (67)—May 24, 1970
Johnson, Edward Thomas (68)—September 18, 1969
Jones, Brian (26)—July 3, 1969

Jones, Eugene W. (33)—June 11, 1969
Kazebierg, Nathan (57)—October 22, 1969
Kenyon, George Hancock (64)—October 23, 1969
Kimic, Robert C. (63)—March 11, 1970
Krinsky, Herman (59)—July 30, 1969
McIntyre, Mark (53)—May 13, 1970
Manetta, Manuel (80)—October 10, 1969
Mayhew, Jack (61)—May 24, 1969
Mondello, Victor—August 14, 1969
Morgan, Russ (65)—August 7, 1969
Myles, Lee (57)—December 1, 1969
O'Hara, Raymond E. (66)—November 7, 1969
O'Hare, Husk (75)—April 22, 1970
Orben, Walter (55)—May 29, 1969
Pastor, Tony (62)—October 31, 1969
Pena, Ralph (42)—May 20, 1969
Reichman, Joe (72)—April 7, 1970
Rosenkrantz, Baron Timme (58)—August 11, 1969
Sargent, Kenny (63)—December 20, 1969
Spargo, Tony (72)—October 30, 1969
Walker, Joseph (69)—September 16, 1969
Watkins, Sammy (65)—July 26, 1969
Watson, Ivory (60)—November 4, 1969
  Orig. member of The Ink Spots
White, Josh (61)—September 5, 1969

OTHERS

Abrahams, Barney (62)—July 25, 1969
  Philadelphia Shubert Theater manager
Aaronoff, Alma S. (53)—August 17, 1969
  Public relations
Bestry, Harry (80)—July 15, 1969
  Theatrical agent
Bradley, J. Kenneth (66)—June 24, 1969
  Trustee of American Shakespeare Festival
Brotherton, Thomas J. R. (77)—July 31, 1969
  Theater treasurer
Brown, Henry C. (44)—January 19, 1970
  Talent agent
Burke, William (74)—January 23, 1970
  Director of Madison Square Garden
Caldwell, Bryan (54)—July 14, 1969
  Public relations
Carroll, Clifford A. (69)—January 26, 1970
  Theater page editor, N.Y. *Journal-American*
Cass, H. Marie (77)—June 22, 1969
  With MacDowell Colony
Clow, William E. II (40)—April 2, 1970
  Broadway production assistant
Connolly, Charles (90)—August 12, 1969
  Manager of The Players
Cooper, Jack (81)—January 12, 1970
  First black radio personality
Dale, Al (48)—May 28, 1969
  Talent agent
Davis, Mrs. Hallie Flanagan (78)—July 23, 1969. Theater and education
East, Patrick (48)—June 30, 1969
  Agent and publicist

Eastman, Carl (61)—January 16, 1970
Actors' agent
Edelstein, Rose—July 28, 1969
Production manager for producers
Ellison, Ada—July 28, 1969
Production manager for producers
Epstein, Howard (51)—December 11, 1969
Attorney
Evans, E. Walter (80)—March 10, 1970
Pres. of Billboard Publishing
Foster, Harry (78)—March 24, 1970
Head of Foster's Agency, London
Fox, Harry (67)—October 18, 1969
Music publishers' agency
Gallo, Fortune (91)—March 28, 1970
Italian-born showman
George, Sam J.—July 26, 1969
Theater manager
Glaser, Joseph G. (72)—June 6, 1969
Booking agent
Gould, Dave (70)—June 3, 1969
Dance director
Greene, William (43)—March 12, 1970
Exec. director Cleve. Play House
Gregory, Susan (25)—March 12, 1970
Asst. stage manager
Gross, Seymour (56)—February 10, 1970
Writer, stage manager, actor
Harding, Alfred (77)—June 28, 1969
Editor of Equity Magazine
Harper, David H. (41)—December 4, 1969
Teacher, negotiator for Equity
Heck, Howard (73)—June 8, 1969
Box-office treasurer, Carnegie Hall
Herzog, Howard C. (64)—February 5, 1970
Gossip column, Milwaukee *Sentinel*
Holizman, Abram (63)—March 11, 1970
Managing director of Roseland
Hope, George (58)—June 21, 1969
Hope, Ivor (78)—June 15, 1969
Brothers of Bob Hope.
Jacobs, Steven (32)—August 13, 1969
Talent scout
Jennings, Dean S. (64)—October 1, 1969
Writer
Johnson, Oscar (71)—March 27, 1970
Shipstad's & Johnson's *Ice Follies*
Joyce, Billy (73)—February 15, 1970
Agent
Kaplan, Harriet I. (52)—July 9, 1969
Theatrical agent
Kornzweig, Ben (59)—October 10, 1969
Public relations
LaMarr, Richard (66)—January 7, 1970
Theatrical agent
Lehman, Robert (77)—August 9, 1969
Banker to entertainment firms
Liebling, William (75)—December 29, 1969
Theatrical agent
Light, Norman (70)—March 1, 1970
General manager, Shubert Theaters
Lincoln, Jean (34)—August 16, 1969
Agent
Linley, Margaret (65)—May 24, 1969
Casting director

McCance, Larry (52)—January 3, 1970
Canadian rep. of Equity
McLaughlin, Leonard (77)—January 31, 1970
Manager of Ford's Theater
Mann, Frances (68)—June 23, 1969
Dancer and play doctor
Manson, Edward (77)—July 21, 1969
Public relations
Merrick, Mahlon (69)—August 7, 1969
Musical director for Jack Benny
Moody, Michaux (78)—May 12, 1970
Mgr. Richmond Va. Arts Assn.
Muir, Florabel (81)—April 27, 1970
Columnist, N.Y. *Daily News*
North, Rex (52)—June 15, 1969
Newspaper columnist
O'Connell, Jerry (64)—July 14, 1969
House and road co. mgr.
Pegler, Westbrook (74)—June 24, 1969
Newspaper columnist
Perelman, Mrs. Laura (58)—April 10, 1970
Playwright; wife of S. J. Perelman
Pigue, William W. (62)—March 16, 1970
Newspaperman and publicist
Prager, Bernard (71)—June 4, 1969
Executive
Rauh, Ida (92)—February 28, 1970
Founder of Provincetown Players
Reid, Ian (51)—October 7, 1969
Toronto talent agent
Roberts, Joseph L. (61)—March 16, 1970
Public relations
Ruben, Neal (38)—May 27, 1969
Writer; producer; film critic
Sardi, Vincent Sr. (83)—November 19, 1969
Founder of Sardi's restaurant
Scarborough, Earl of (72)—June 29, 1969
Former Lord Chamberlain
Schmidt, Art (68)—June 7, 1969
Public relations
Schonceit, Louis (74)—May 17, 1970
Owner of Mackey's Ticket Agency
Seligman, Selig (51)—June 20, 1969
Producer; vice pres. of ABC
Shubert, Mrs. J. J.—March 27, 1970
Widow of Jacob J. Shubert
Small, William (84)—September 22, 1969
Exec. sec. of Independent Theater Owners
Stebbins, Walter C. (70)—August 30, 1969
Show biz executive and writer
Sullivan, Rev. Edward S. (72)—January 11, 1970. "Circus Priest"
Timin, Carl L. (63)—January 9, 1970
Executive director, Friars Club
Wagner, Rev. C. Everett (73)—September 8, 1969. Pastor of "The Actors' Church"
Ward, Henry (63)—November 15, 1969
Night club editor, Pittsburgh *Press*
Weber, Sid (57)—May 30, 1969
Public relations
Wright, Cobina—April 9, 1970
Writer of Hollywood scene
Yates, Irving (75)—July 26, 1969
Vaudeville booker

INDEX

Play titles are in **bold face** and ***bold face italic*** page numbers refer to pages where cast and credit listings may be found.